HEALTH ECONOMICS & POLICY

Fourth Edition

HEALTH
ECONOMICS & POLICY

Fourth Edition

James W. Henderson
Baylor University

SOUTH-WESTERN
CENGAGE Learning™

Australia • Brazil • Japan • Korea • Mexico • Singapore • Spain • United Kingdom • United States

SOUTH-WESTERN
CENGAGE Learning™

**Health Economics and Policy,
Fourth Edition**
James W. Henderson

Vice President of Editorial, Business:
 Jack W. Calhoun

Editor-in-Chief: Alex von Rosenberg

Senior Acquisitions Editor: Steve Scoble

Senior Developmental Editor: Susanna C.
 Smart

Marketing Manager: Betty Jung

Content Project Manager: Cliff Kallemeyn

Senior First Print Buyer, Manufacturing:
 Sandee Milewski

Production Service: Pre-Press PMG

Compositor: Pre-Press PMG

Senior Art Director: Michelle Kunkler

Internal Designer: Juli Cook

Cover Designer: Joseph Pagliaro Graphic
 Design

Cover Images: © Lauren Nicole/Digital
 Vision

For product information and technology assistance, contact us at
Cengage Learning Customer & Sales Support, 1–800–354–9706

For permission to use material from this text or product,
submit all requests online at **www.cengage.com/permissions**
Further permissions questions can be emailed to
permissionrequest@cengage.com

ISBN-13: 978-0-324-64518-7

ISBN-10: 0-324-64518-X

South-Western Cengage Learning
5191 Natorp Boulevard
Mason, OH 45040
USA

Cengage Learning products are represented in Canada by
Nelson Education, Ltd.

For your course and learning solutions, visit **academic.cengage.com**

Purchase any of our products at your local college store or at our
preferred online store **www.ichapters.com**

Printed in the United States of America
1 2 3 4 5 6 7 12 11 10 09 08

BRIEF CONTENTS

CONTENTS

With spending topping $2 trillion in 2006, health care costs more in the United States than any of its developed country counterparts. The presidential elections of 2008 serve as a watershed in the health care reform debate. For years important domestic issues have been postponed because of foreign policy considerations. Spending growth continues to outpace that of gross domestic product. Medicare seems unsustainable. The numbers of the uninsured swell as firms drop coverage due to rising premiums. With no solution in sight, the debate heats up. The expanding role of government in the provision of care is evident at both ends of the age spectrum. As post-War baby boomers become Medicare eligible, the pressure on spending is unlikely to subside. Nine million uninsured children is a focal issue for those advocating further expansion of the State Children's Health Insurance Program. Health Economics and Policy provides important background information, not only on these two important programs affecting the young and the elderly, but addresses the entire spectrum of economic and policy issues that affect the rest of the population.

This text's primary goals are to enable readers to

- Recognize the relevance of economics to health and medical care and to apply economic reasoning to better understand health-related issues.

- Understand the mechanisms of health care delivery in the United States within broad social, political, and economic contexts.

- Explore the changing nature of health and medical care and its implications for medical practice, medical education and research, and health policy.

- Analyze public policy in health and medical care from an economic perspective.

To accomplish these goals, the book's 16 chapters are organized into four parts.

PART ONE—THE RELEVANCE OF ECONOMICS IN HEALTH AND MEDICAL CARE

The text begins with a basic overview of the health care industry with emphasis on the economic issues that affect medical care delivery and finance. Chapter 1 examines the nature of the economic problem as it pertains to health care. Chapter 2 demonstrates the usefulness of economics in understanding medical care issues—including matters of life, death, disability, and suffering. Chapter 3 examines problems encountered in applying standard economic models to the study of health care markets. Chapter 4 introduces the readers to the tools of economic evaluation as they are applied to medical care with special emphasis on cost-effectiveness analysis, the preferred technique among most health economists.

Technical appendices appear at the end of each of the first three chapters. They are intended for use by more advanced students. Appendix 1A provides an overview of the challenges of measuring medical price inflation using the medical care price index. Appendix 2A serves as a primer on graphing while 2B introduces important statistical tools used in empirical studies. The two appendices at the end of Chapter 3 present the neoclassical models of consumer choice and production.

PART TWO—DEMAND-SIDE CONSIDERATIONS

Part 2 examines the demand side of the market. Chapter 5 identifies and describes various factors that influence the demands for health and health care. It explores and explains observed patterns in the quality and price of medical care. Chapter 6 discusses the market for health insurance, comparing and contrasting the private and social insurance models. Chapter 7 evaluates the efficiency of alternative health care delivery systems, primarily HMOs and PPOs, in containing medical care costs.

PART THREE— SUPPLY-SIDE CONSIDERATIONS

The supply side of the health care market is discussed in Part 3. Chapter 8 looks at the market for health care practitioners and how their behavior is influenced by recent changes in the health care sector, namely managed care. Other sub-sectors are examined through discussion of the markets for nurses and for dentists. Chapter 9 summarizes major theories of hospital behavior and describes the role of not-for-profit hospitals in the U.S. health care industry. The U.S. pharmaceutical industry and the challenges facing drug and device innovators and their target markets are discussed in Chapter 10.

PART FOUR—PUBLIC POLICY IN MEDICAL CARE DELIVERY

Part 4 begins with a reality check discussing the factors that contribute to high U.S. spending on medical care. Why do Americans spend so much of medical care? Is it because we have more money? Are we less efficient in the production of health services? Or do we simply have more health problems than anyone else? Chapter 11 addresses the factors that challenge the delivery of health care services in the United States. The text's final four chapters squarely address health policy and its economic implications. Chapter 12 analyzes the roles of government, the family, and religion in improving access to health care. Medicare, Medicaid, and other government programs are introduced and their economic impact examined. The appendix to that chapter addresses some issues of making projections of economic data. Chapter 13 covers recent changes in reimbursement schemes (diagnosis related groups and resource based relative value scales) and their effects on quantity, quality, and accessibility of medical care. Chapter 14 summarizes important characteristics of medical care delivery systems in six major developed nations—Canada, France, Germany, Japan, Switzerland, and the United Kingdom. Chapter 15 describes health care reform initiatives in the United States and summarizes major U.S. policy alternatives. Finally, Chapter 16 restates the major lessons to be learned from the economic approach to public policy.

PEDAGOGICAL FEATURES

This text's ultimate focus is on public policy. The technical tools of economics are important, but they are not treated as ends to themselves. Instead, theory is employed as a way of preparing students to address policy questions.

Each chapter includes a number of special features called "Issues in Medical Care Delivery." They summarize important studies in medical research, epidemiology, public health, and other fields as they relate to the economics of health care delivery. Another feature found in most chapters is the "Profile" of individuals who have made significant contributions to health economics. Many profiled individuals are economists; some are physicians; all have had a profound impact on how we view health, health economics, and health policy.

The "Back of the Envelope" features show the economic way of thinking, using graphs. These and similar graphical presentations are frequently used by economists in informal settings. They might represent scribbles on the back of an old envelope that are used to make a point during lunch with colleagues. Topics include: the valuation of a life, how to calculate a rate of return, the notion of elasticity, the welfare implications of subsidies, the impact of employer mandates, cost-benefit calculations, and the cost effectiveness of disease prevention, among many others. Developing the ability to use models in this way is an important goal of this book.

Chapter 1 introduces 10 key economic concepts that serve as unifying themes throughout the book. As you read you will notice the key icon in the margin reminding you that the adjacent material is related to that key concept. Other marginal notations include definitions of key words and phrases, recommended Web sites where you can go for additional information, and policy issues related to the reading.

NEW IN THE FOURTH EDITION

The most obvious change in the fourth edition is the new approach to the confounding issues discussion. Instead of separate chapters, the issue is presented in one. Chapter 11 compares and contrasts U.S. lifestyle, cultural, and economic characteristics with those of six developed countries. The argument is made and supported that the use of traditional medical outcomes data to rank health care systems is flawed and should be used carefully.

The discussion on the pharmaceutical industry from the previous edition has been extended from a section of a chapter to its own chapter. Much of this material has been extensively rewritten with new sections on the role of patents in the innovation process and issues in pharmaceutical pricing.

A section on the Swiss health care system has been added to Chapter 14. This addition serves as an introduction to the role of market-driven responses to health care reform that are discussed in Chapter 15. New sections on consumer-directed health plans and the new Massachusetts health care plan highlight the discussion on market alternatives.

LEVEL

Health Economics and Policy is written with the non-economics major in mind, but contains enough economic content to challenge economics majors. My class at Baylor University is composed of both economics majors and pre-medical students, most of whom have little or no economics background. There are usually a number of other business majors, many of whom are interested in studying health care administration in the future. I also use this text in a required graduate course for MBA students who are concentrating in health care administration. All these students are good thinkers and most have done well despite having had no previous economics coursework.

The text is appropriate for an introductory health economics course offered in an economics department, in a health care administration graduate program, or in a school of public health, college of medicine, or school of nursing or pharmacy.

SUPPLEMENTARY ITEMS

An Instructor's Manual provides support to instructors who adopt Health Economics and Policy, 4th edition. The manual includes suggested answers to the end-of-chapter questions, lecture suggestions, and test questions. In my teachings of Health Economics I have improved student engagement and comprehension of concepts by providing television and movie clips to introduce discussion topics in my class. I've had great success with this and have included a chapter break out of what I use from both TV and Movie clips in my classroom. These are only suggestions and we are NOT offering any video or movie clips to accompany the text. If you are interested in possibly implementing these in your class, I have provided clear instructions on using these clips.

The text's Web site contains resources for both students and instructors. You can access the Web site using http://academic.cengage.com/economics/henderson. The site also provides access to Economic Applications, a feature that includes EconNews articles, EconData links, and EconDebates.

ACKNOWLEDGMENTS

As the sole author of this book, I take full responsibility for its contents. But a single individual could not complete a project of this magnitude. I owe a great deal to my Baylor University colleagues who during our Friday morning coffee hour discussions sharpened my focus and challenged my inconsistencies. A number of capable research assistants have contributed to the revision of this issue. Most notably, I'd like to thank Rae Snider whose help was invaluable in preparing my health policy video clips.

Instructors from across the country have reviewed the manuscript as it was being revised for this and previous editions. Their comments and suggestions have been important to me, and the book is better because of their efforts. Thanks go to:

Monica Cain, Winston-Salem State University

Greg Delemeester, Marietta College

Anoshua Chaudhuri, San Francisco State University

Susanne Rassouli-Currier, University of Colorado

Abigail C. Tilton, Texas Woman's University

I am also grateful to the hundreds of Baylor University students who used this book in its first three editions and even earlier in manuscript form. Their comments have proven invaluable in developing an integrated framework for discussing health care issues.

Of course, I could never have completed the project without the support of my family. Thank you, Betsy, Luke, and Jesse for your understanding, love, and patience. And Lisa as the newest member of the family, your role is as important as the rest. Thanks to you all.

James W. Henderson

U.S. Medical Care: Crisis or Conundrum

The concern over the future of health care revolves around three broad issues: quality, access, and affordability. As private health insurance coverage gradually declines, and the number of uninsured steadily rises, emerging public consensus indicates a system in need of reform. Gaps in coverage, combined with the upward trend in medical care spending over the past several decades, add to the commonly held belief that the United States has a health care crisis. What exactly is the nature of this health care crisis? Is it a crisis in spending? Or is it the way we pay for medical care? Many are concerned over access to care for the uninsured and the prospects for continued access for those who currently have insurance. An additional concern is whether quality may deteriorate as medical care is increasingly provided in a **managed care** environment.

Recent polls indicate that most insured Americans are satisfied with the quality of their own health insurance plan. In fact, over 80 percent of Americans said that the medical care that they or their family received during the past year was good to excellent. Access, on the other hand, is a real concern. About half are concerned that if they become seriously ill, they will not be able to afford the medical care they need (Donelan et al., 1999).

Those without insurance coverage who lack the resources to pay out-of-pocket must rely on public assistance and private charity for the care they receive. Even those with health insurance lack the assurance of continued coverage. Because most workers receive their health insurance as an employee benefit, losing a job can mean losing access to medical care. Thus, it is not a contradiction for a survey respondent to be satisfied with the health care received personally, and at the same time believe that the system is flawed and needs to be rebuilt.

The "experts" have a completely different perspective of the health care crisis, including the problem, its cause, and preferred solutions (Blendon et al., 1993). They see the health care crisis as one of rising aggregate spending and the government's inability to sustain the expansion of its two major programs, **Medicare** and **Medicaid**. Experts themselves are sharply divided on the cause of the crisis. Some think the problem is the unrestrained use of medical technology. Others believe the culprits are the increased use of health insurance and tax subsidies that encourage individuals to overinsure. Proposed solutions address the perceived causes. If technology is being overused, restrict patient access to expensive procedures. If subsidized insurance is the problem, limit the subsidy.

Although the uninsured receive fewer services and less coordinated care, they do have access to high-quality medical care through public clinics and hospital

---

POLICY ISSUE

How can we best deal with the trade-off between quality and access on the one hand and affordability on the other?

managed care
A delivery system that originally integrated the financing and provision of medical care in one organization. Now the term encompasses different arrangements designed to coordinate services and control costs.

POLICY ISSUE

Most privately insured Americans receive health insurance coverage through their employer, while those without insurance rely on public assistance and charity care.

Medicare
Health insurance for the elderly provided under an amendment to the Social Security Act, divided into two parts: mandatory hospital insurance and voluntary physicians insurance.

Medicaid
Health insurance for the poor financed jointly by the federal government and the states.

emergency departments.[1] Traditionally, indigent care has been financed directly by taxpayers and private charities and indirectly by shifting costs to those with insurance coverage. In 2001, for example, estimates of this **cost shifting** were as high as $34.5 billion, amounting to approximately $1,000 for every uninsured person (Hadley and Holahan, 2003). This kind of availability may be undesirable and inefficient, but it is access. When surveyed, 25 percent of the uninsured stated that they delayed care in the past year due to cost, but only half that number stated that they had an unmet medical need because of the cost of care (Kaiser, 2007). Is it accurate to refer to the circumstances surrounding the delivery and financing of health care in the United States as a crisis, or is it merely a conundrum—a problem that the wealthiest country in the world ought to address?

cost shifting
The practice of charging higher prices to one group of patients, usually those with health insurance, in order to provide free care to the uninsured or discounted care to those served by Medicare and Medicaid.

HISTORICAL DEVELOPMENTS IN THE DELIVERY OF MEDICAL CARE

No matter where a health care discussion begins, the topic of conversation soon turns to the issue of affordability. Employees and employers complain about high **premiums**, patients and providers note high treatment costs, and policymakers lament high and rising spending. Each perspective presents a different aspect of the same problem. In 2007, the average cost of a health insurance policy was $12,106 for a family and $4,479 for an individual (Kaiser, 2007). The average cost per hospital stay was over $8,000, and Americans spent almost $2 trillion on health care—16 percent of the **gross domestic product (GDP)**.

premium
A periodic payment required to purchase an insurance policy.

gross domestic product (GDP)
The monetary value of the goods and services produced in a country during a given time period, usually a year.

From 1971 to 2006, the annual growth in nominal health care spending ranged between 4.4 percent and 15.6 percent, increasing at an annual compound rate of almost 10 percent for that 35-year period. Over that same period, the Consumer Price Index (CPI), a popular measure of the rate of inflation, increased an average of 4.7 percent per year. With nominal health care spending increasing at twice the overall rate of inflation, real spending (adjusted for inflation) grew approximately 5 percent per year. Figure 1.1 depicts the relative growth rates in nominal and real spending from 1971 to 2006.

Many commentators are encouraged by the dramatic slowing of the real rate of growth in health care spending during the 1990s, falling from 6.1 percent in

POLICY ISSUE

How many years does it take to constitute a trend?

Figure 1.1: Growth in Nominal and Real Health Expenditures, 1971–2006

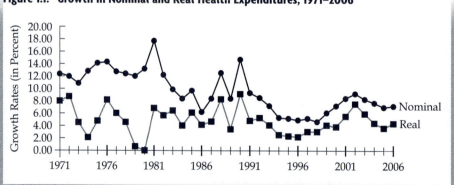

---

[1] Since 1985, the Emergency Medical Treatment and Active Labor Act (EMTALA) has made it illegal for hospital emergency departments to deny care to anyone requesting care. Turning away patients because of lack of health insurance is not an option.

1990 to 2.1 percent in 1996. History, however, warns against using such short trends as tools for policymaking. The 1972 to 1974 time period saw real growth rates fall from 8.2 percent to 2.1 percent, only to rise again to 8.6 percent by 1976. Beginning in that year, real growth rates started falling again, to less than 2 percent by 1980. This was followed by a steady upward march until 1990. By 2002, growth in real spending had reached 7.3 percent. Since then, real rates have fallen back to around 3 percent.

The major concern over health care spending is not that it is high; the concern is that the steady upward spiral does not seem to have an end to it. Government projections predict that medical care spending will rise to $3.4 trillion by 2016, almost 20 percent of GDP (Center for Medicare and Medicaid Services, CMS, 2007). Although economic theory has yet to determine what the optimal percentage ought to be, the United States spends more on medical care by virtually every measure than any other country in the world. If the optimal percentage is not known, what does it mean to spend 8 percent or 10 percent or 16 percent of a country's GDP on medical care? And, more importantly, should the amount spent on medical care be a concern to policy makers?

> **POLICY ISSUE**
>
> What is the optimal percentage of GDP that a country should spend on health care? Is a continuously growing percentage affordable?

Postwar Experience

Medical care spending in the United States over the post-World War II period is summarized in Table 1.1. The four summary measures provide evidence that medical care spending is high and growing. During the decade of the 1950s, total spending increased at a rate of 8 percent per year. Total spending at the beginning

Table 1.1: United States Health Care Spending Summary Measures, Various Years

Year	Total Spending (in billions)	Percent Change[1]	Percent of GDP	Per Capita Spending
1950	$ 12.7	—	4.5	$ 82
1960	27.5	8.0	5.2	148
1970	74.9	10.5	7.2	356
1975	133.1	12.2	8.1	605
1980	253.9	13.7	9.1	1,102
1985	439.9	11.6	10.4	1,820
1990	714.0	10.2	12.3	2,813
1995	1,016.5	7.3	13.6	3,783
2000	1,353.6	5.9	13.8	4,790
2001	1,469.6	8.6	14.5	5,148
2002	1,603.4	9.1	15.3	5,559
2003	1,732.4	8.0	15.8	5,952
2004	1,852.3	6.9	15.9	6,301
2005	1,973.3	6.5	15.9	6,649
2006	2,105.5	6.7	16.0	7,026

Source: Centers for Medicare and Medicaid Services (CMS) website, *http://www.cms.hhs.gov/NationalHealthExpendData/02_NationalHealthAccountsHistorical. asp#TopOfPage* (Accessed January 8, 2008).

[1] Annual rate of change from the previous year listed.

The National Institutes of Health provides an overview of its programs and activities at

http://www.nih.gov/

Employee Retirement Income Security Act (ERISA)
Federal legislation passed in 1974 that sets minimum standards on employee benefit plans, such as pension, health insurance, and disability. The statute protects the interests of employees in matters concerning eligibility for benefits. The law also protects employers from certain state regulations. For example, states are not allowed to regulate self-insured plans and cannot mandate that employers provide health insurance to their employees.

self-insurance
A group practice of not buying health insurance, but setting aside funds in the amount of the combined premiums to cover any losses incurred by members of the group.

entitlement program
Government assistance programs where eligibility is determined by a specified criteria, such as age, health status, and level of income. These programs include Social Security, Medicare, Medicaid, TANF, and many more.

of the decade was $12.7 billion, doubling by its end. Medical care spending as a percent of GDP increased from 4.5 to 5.2 percent, and per capita medical care spending increased from $82 in 1950 to $148 ten years later.

The 1960s was the first of three decades characterized by rapid growth in medical care spending. The annual compound rate of growth in medical care spending was 11.5 percent between 1960 and 1990. At the beginning of that 30-year period, medical care spending was $27.5 billion, 5.2 percent of GDP, and $148 per capita. By 1990, it stood at $714.0 billion, 12.3 percent of GDP, and $2,738 per capita. Contributing factors included increased federal government involvement in the payment for medical care services for specific groups—Medicare for the elderly and Medicaid for the indigent—and cost shifting by providers to subsidize care for those without insurance.

Rapid advancement in medical technology and the subsequent cost-containment strategies that emphasized regulation and planning characterized the 1970s. The federal government became a major force in biomedical research and development with the expansion of the National Institutes of Health. Technological advances that included open-heart surgery, organ transplantation, various types of imaging, and the ability to preserve and prolong life in the intensive care unit increased public awareness of medicine and served as a major cost driver. While it all seemed justifiable, this emphasis on advanced technologies precipitated a growing concern over cost issues.

Federal legislation, specifically the National Health Planning Act of 1974, created a network of government planning agencies to control medical care costs. In addition, states passed certificate-of-need (CON) laws to limit the growth in hospital investment in capital improvements and technology. Even a brief national experiment with wage and price controls during the Nixon presidency did little to curb the growth in medical care costs and spending.

Possibly the most significant piece of legislation affecting health care was not viewed as particularly significant at the time. The **Employee Retirement Income Security Act (ERISA)** of 1974 was passed to regulate the corporate use of pension funds. One provision of the act exempted self-insured health plans from state-level health insurance regulations. The passage of ERISA provided an incentive for employers to switch to **self-insurance**. Today, more than half of all workers who participate in group health insurance plans are employed by companies who self-insure.

The 1980s ushered in a change in direction in health care policy, resulting in a shift away from regulation and planning and toward a greater reliance on market forces. A president who wanted to lower taxes and a Congress that refused to cut spending characterized the era. Federal budget deficits grew dramatically. By the end of the decade, those areas of the budget in which spending was mandated—the **entitlement programs** including Medicare and Medicaid—grew seemingly without limit and came under intense pressure to reduce their rate of growth. During this period, the introduction of alternative payment schemes and delivery systems was significant. **Prospective payment**, **capitation**, the use of **diagnosis-related groups** to pay hospitals, and the introduction of a **relative-value scale** to pay physicians are all examples of these changes. Health maintenance organizations, preferred provider organizations, and other systems of managed care became more common.

The 1990s saw a moderation in the growth in spending. Most experts attribute at least part of the slowdown to the movement of patients into managed care. The annual percentage increase in nominal spending fell from 15.9 percent in 1981 to around 5 percent in the mid 1990s. A steady increase in growth rates resulted in an annual change of 9.1 percent in 2002, settling to 6.7 percent in 2006. The expansion of medical care spending as a percentage of GDP remained between 13.0 and 14.0 percent until 2001, when it nudged above 14 percent for the first time.

The federal government has taken more of an activist role in health care policy in the past decade. Although an attempt to completely restructure the health care system failed in 1994, important legislation has been enacted that is expected to improve access to care.[2]

The Question of High and Rising Spending

Why do Americans spend so much on medical care? Various researchers have explored this issue, and several explanations have been offered. The reason cited most often for the rise in spending include the expansion of the third-party payment system, an aging population, the rise in medical malpractice litigation, and the increased use of medical technology (Aaron, 1991).

Insurance use has increased dramatically over the past four decades. Out-of-pocket spending has fallen from about half of total spending to 12.5 percent. At the same time, per capita spending on health care has increased more than 45 times. Common sense tells us that the demand for medical care increases as the cost to the individual declines. In all societies, the elderly demand more medical care than the nonelderly. As the U.S. population ages, more medical care is demanded. This trend will likely continue as the baby-boom generation reaches retirement age beginning in 2010.

Medical malpractice premiums represent costs that are passed on to patients in the form of higher fees. Those costs alone reached $29.4 billion in 2005 (Tillinghast-Towers Perrin, 2006). Additionally, fear of malpractice litigation changes the way physicians carry out the practice of medicine, resulting in the increased use of **defensive medicine**, practices and procedures whose primary purpose is to reduce the risk of a lawsuit. Estimates of the cost of this practice range from $60 billion to $100 billion per year (American College of Obstetricians and Gynecologists, 2003). The use of expensive technology has become an imperative in most medical practices. If withheld, even in situations where the probability of success is extremely low, the physician will be accused of negligence and likely sued for malpractice.

Many other factors contribute to the increased spending. The imbalance of information between provider and patient is seen by some as a major factor contributing to the increase in spending. The patient is typically uninformed and finds it difficult to get informed. Because the medical practitioner serves as both adviser and provider of care, he has the potential to recommend procedures and services with little expected benefit to the patient—a practice known as **physician-induced demand**.

Others have focused on certain aspects of the U.S. institutional setting as a major reason for the rise in expenditures. In particular, some see the restrictions on competition due to licensing requirements as important. The 125 medical schools in the United States enroll approximately 67,000 students. Not one new school has been accredited since 1985. In contrast, the original 15 countries that comprise the European Union have a combined population that is approximately

---

prospective payment
Payment determined prior to the provision of services. A feature of many managed care organizations that base payment on capitation.

capitation
A payment method providing a fixed, per capita payment to providers for a specified medical benefits package. Providers are required to treat a well-defined population for a fixed sum of money, paid in advance, without regard to the number or nature of the services provided to each person. This payment method is a characteristic of health maintenance organizations and many preferred provider organizations.

diagnosis-related group
A patient classification scheme based on certain demographic, diagnostic, and therapeutic characteristics developed by Medicare and used to compensate hospitals.

relative-value scale
An index that assigns weights to various medical services used to determine the relative fees assigned to them.

defensive medicine
Medical services that have little or no medical benefit; their provision is simply to reduce the risk of being sued.

---

[2] At the federal level, Congress established the Health Insurance Portability and Accountability Act (HIPPA) of 1996 providing insurance portability to individuals with health insurance. In 1997, Congress passed the Children's Health Insurance Program (CHIP), the largest expansion of a federal medical program since its original enactment. In late 2003, Congress voted to expand the coverage for outpatient prescription drugs within the Medicare program.

1.5 times that of the United States.[3] Their 220 medical schools enroll almost 40,000 new students each year, or 2.3 times the 17,000 new students enrolled in U.S. medical schools annually (Curtoni and Sutnick, 1995). Furthermore, supply constraints are exacerbated by the increased specialization of U.S. physicians. The ratio of specialists to generalists is 70:30, roughly the reverse of that in most other developed countries.

ISSUES IN MEDICAL CARE DELIVERY

Spending Somebody Else's Money

A *Wall Street Journal* article provides an interesting example of how spending someone else's money distorts the decision-making process.

A 70-year-old man suffering from a ruptured abdominal aortic aneurysm was brought to the hospital. After several weeks in the intensive care unit — with all the modern technology that goes with it — and a three-month stay in the hospital, the bill approached $275,000, none of which would be paid out-of-pocket by the patient. The man's physician determined that his poor eating habits, caused by poorly fitting dentures, were contributing to his slow recovery. He requested that the hospital dentist perform the necessary adjustments. Later, the doctor discovered that the man had not allowed the dentist to adjust the dentures. When asked the reason, the man replied, "$75 is a lot of money." It seems that Medicare would not pay for the adjustment, so it would have been an out-of-pocket expenditure for the patient.

When you're spending somebody else's money, $275,000 does not seem like a lot. But when you are spending your own money, $75 is a lot. Our reliance on a third-party payment system is the major institutional feature that contributes to rising costs and increased spending. Cost-conscious consumers have little or no role in a system dominated by **third-party payers**.

Source: James P. Weaver, "The Best Care Other People's Money Can Buy," *Wall Street Journal*, November 19, 1992, A14.

third-party payers
A health insurance arrangement where the individual, or an agent of the individual, pays a set premium to a third party (an insurance company, managed care organization, or the government) which in turn pays for health care services.

Economic theory suggests that an increase in the number of physicians would decrease the prices they charge for their services. For many years, economists believed that the American Medical Association (AMA), through its control over medical schools via the accreditation process, controlled the number of licensed physicians and thus kept prices high (Friedman and Kuznets, 1945). The evidence presented in Table 1.2 makes it difficult to present a strong case that restrictions in supply have caused prices to increase. Over the past 20 years, the number of active physicians has increased by two-thirds, but the population has increased less than 20 percent. As a result, the physician–population ratio has actually increased by over 38 percent, from 18.3 physicians per 10,000 population in 1980 to 26.9 physicians per 10,000 population in 2005. Comparable numbers in the European Union place the number of practicing physicians at 1.3 million, or 33.3 per 10,000 population.

[3] The 15 countries in the European Union include Austria, Belgium, Denmark, Finland, France, Germany, Greece, Ireland, Italy, Luxembourg, The Netherlands, Portugal, Spain, Sweden, and the United Kingdom.

Table 1.2: Physicians and Physician–Population Ratio United States, Various Years

Year	Number of active physicians	Active physicians per 10,000 population
1975	340,280	—
1980	414,916	18.3
1985	497,140	20.1
1990	547,310	22.0
1995	625,443	23.8
2000	692,368	25.2
2001	713,375	25.0
2002	719,431	25.0
2003	736,211	25.3
2004	744,143	25.3
2005	762,438	26.9

Source: *Health, United States,* 2007.

The predominance of **not-for-profit** providers has also been cited as a major factor in the spending increase (Goodman and Musgrave, 1992). Physicians are trained in not-for-profit medical schools, they work in predominantly not-for-profit hospitals, and the majority of their fees are paid by not-for-profit insurance companies (e.g., Blue Cross and Blue Shield) or the government. This reliance on not-for-profit institutions creates a dynamic environment in which innovation in general is encouraged, but where cost-saving innovations are seldom encountered.

not-for-profit
A business classification that is exempt from paying most taxes. In return for this tax-exempt status, the firm is restricted in how any operating surplus may be distributed among its stakeholders.

Changes in Medical Care Delivery

The last 30 years have witnessed major changes that have affected medical care delivery and costs. The shift from private to public sector financing, the shift from out-of-pocket spending to third-party payment, the changes in hospital usage and pricing, deregulation, and the growth in managed care have all had profound effects on medical care delivery and pricing.

Shift From Private to Public Financing Quite possibly, the single most important change affecting medical care delivery has been the shift from private to public sector financing. Referring to Table 1.3, the private sector was responsible for $3 of every $4 spent in the industry in 1960. The government role in financing was modest, standing at less than 25 cents out of every medical care dollar. The introduction of Medicare and Medicaid in the mid-1960s resulted in an increase in the government's share of spending, to almost 40 percent by the end of the decade. Even though the government's total share has remained at about half of total spending, the federal share has nearly tripled, from 10.6 percent in 1960 to 33.5 percent in 2006. This translates into a federal budgetary obligation that has grown from $2.9 billion to $704.9 billion in four and a half decades. Even as the federal share has exploded, the share of state and local governments has remained relatively stable at around 13 percent.

Shift to Third-Party Payment Even as the private share of total spending has fallen, the role of private insurance has expanded. Private insurance paid a little more than 20 percent of the total cost of medical care in 1960, with that share rising

Table 1.3: Financing of Health Care Expenditures, Various Years In Billions of Dollars and Percentage of Total Personal Spending

Category	1960 $	1960 %	1970 $	1970 %	1980 $	1980 %	1990 $	1990 %	1995 $	1995 %	2000 $	2000 %	2005 $	2005 %	2006 $	2006 %
Private Funds	20.7	75.3	46.8	62.5	147.6	58.1	427.3	59.9	551.7	54.3	757.1	55.9	1,076.5	54.6	1,135.2	53.9
Out-of-Pocket Payments	12.9	46.9	24.9	33.2	58.6	23.1	136.1	19.1	146.3	14.4	192.9	14.3	247.1	12.6	256.5	12.2
Private Health Insurance	5.9	21.5	15.5	20.7	68.9	27.1	233.7	32.7	325.2	32.0	455.2	33.6	685.5	34.7	723.4	34.3
Other Private	2.0	7.3	6.4	8.5	20.1	7.9	57.5	8.0	80.2	7.9	109.0	8.0	143.9	7.3	155.3	7.4
Public Funds	6.8	24.7	28.1	37.5	106.3	41.9	286.7	40.1	464.8	45.7	596.1	44.1	896.8	45.4	970.3	46.1
Federal	2.9	10.6	17.7	23.6	71.6	28.2	193.9	27.2	327.3	32.2	417.5	30.9	639.1	32.4	704.9	33.5
State and Local	3.9	14.2	10.4	13.9	34.8	13.7	92.8	13.0	137.5	13.5	178.6	13.2	257.7	13.0	265.4	12.6
Medicare[1]	—	—	7.7	10.3	37.2	14.7	109.5	15.3	184.4	18.1	224.3	16.6	338.0	17.1	401.3	19.1
Medicaid and SCHIP[2]	—	—	2.8	3.7	26.0	10.2	73.7	10.3	144.9	14.3	203.5	15.0	325.2	16.5	323.7	15.4
Total Health Care Spending[3]	27.5	100.0	74.9	100.0	253.9	100.0	714	100.0	1,016.5	100.0	1,353.6	100.0	1,973.3	100.0	2,105.5	100.0

Source: Centers for Medicare and Medicaid Services (CMS) website, accessed January 8, 2008.
http://www.cms.hhs.gov/NationalHealthExpendData/02_NationalHealthAccountsHistorical.asp#TopOfPage

[1] Included in federal spending.
[2] Included in federal, state, and local spending.
[3] Columns do not add to total due to double-counting for Medicare, Medicaid, and SCHIP.

to about one-third by 1990, where it has remained since that time. The major change in private spending has been the dramatic decline in private, out-of-pocket spending. Approximately half of total health care expenditures were classified as out-of-pocket spending in 1960. By 2006, that total had fallen to 12.2 percent. With the increased importance of third-party payers such as government and private insurers, the insured patient has relatively little out-of-pocket spending at the point of purchase.

Payment by third parties provides little incentive on the part of provider or patient to control spending. As long as insurance companies are willing to pay the bills, physicians will continue to provide all the care that patients request. Patients have no incentive to limit their utilization. Even when the expected benefit of a procedure is small, in most cases it will be demanded, because the patient's share of the cost is small.

It should come as no surprise that the cost of services covered by insurance—public and private—has risen at a faster rate than the cost of services that are not covered. Why? When consumers purchase goods and services at discount prices, they tend to purchase more than if they paid the full price. What other reasonable explanation would explain the crowds that flock to clearance sales, and enthusiastic consumer acceptance of discount malls? Health economists refer to this phenomenon as **moral hazard**. Between 1970 and 2006, hospital spending for services usually covered by insurance increased 20 times over, whereas spending on eyeglasses—something typically not covered by insurance—increased only 10 times over. Insulating patients from the full cost of medical care has had the effect of making patients insensitive to the prices that are being charged, and at the same time has encouraged greater utilization.

moral hazard
Insurance coverage increases both the likelihood of making a claim and the actual size of the claim. Insurance reduces the net out-of-pocket price of medical services and thus increases the quantity demanded.

Change in Hospital Usage and Pricing   Hospital usage has also changed dramatically. As seen in Table 1.4, almost every measure of inpatient hospital usage has fallen in the past 30 years, in some cases quite dramatically. The number of hospital beds is down, admissions are down, the average length of stay is down, and occupancy rates have fallen significantly. Some would go so far as to say that hospitals have gone from overcrowded to underused. Another important trend is the shift from inpatient to outpatient care. The number of per capita outpatient visits has tripled since 1970, and outpatient visits per hospital admission are also three times higher.

Table 1.4: Short-Stay Community Hospital Characteristics, United States

Category	1970	1980	1990	1995	2000	2003	2005
Beds (per 1,000 population)	4.17	4.38	3.73	3.32	2.92	2.79	2.71
Admissions (per 1,000 population)	144.0	159.6	125.4	117.9	117.1	119.4	118.9
Average length of stay (days)	7.7	7.6	7.2	6.5	5.8	5.7	5.6
Outpatient visits (per 1,000 population)	657.2	893.2	1,211.6	1,578.5	1,845.7	1,934.0	1,971.7
Outpatient visits per admission	4.6	5.6	9.7	13.4	15.8	16.2	16.6
Percent occupancy	78.0	75.6	66.8	62.8	63.9	66.2	67.3

Source: *Health United States*, various years.

Cost Plus was the standard approach for hospital pricing from the inception of Medicare until 1983, when pricing shifted to prospective payment using diagnosis-related groups (DRGs). Under DRG pricing, payment is fixed in advance and based on the principal diagnosis at the time of hospital admission. In contrast, private insurance pays hospitals negotiated prices based on discounts from billed charges. As a result, the financial risk of treating patients has shifted from the payer to the provider, creating an incentive for providers to limit access to care. Many providers are affiliated with networks of providers that offer discounts to group members. Because all must abide by the fee limits placed on them by Medicare and Medicaid, actual transaction prices are deeply discounted from the invoice prices that show up on their bills.

Deregulation and the Growth in Managed Care   Deregulation has resulted in an explosion of facilities and practices previously considered unthinkable. The use of ambulatory surgery centers has risen, as has the construction of physician-owned clinics and hospitals. More physicians are advertising, more practices offer evening and weekend hours, and some physicians are even making house calls.

The managed care approach is the prevailing form of insurance in the U.S. market. By 1999, nine out of ten employees covered by employer-based **group insurance** were enrolled in a managed care plan (a health maintenance organization, a preferred provider organization, or a point-of-service plan). The rest were still in a traditional **indemnity insurance** plan. The increased popularity of managed care has begun to change the incentive structure within the industry, forcing providers to consider costs more carefully. No longer are physicians' fees constrained by a pricing model that limits fees to usual, customary, and reasonable (UCR) levels.

In 1986, the federal government established a pricing model for Medicare based on a relative-value scale (RVS). The Medicare RVS is an index of resource use for every medical procedure across all specialty areas. It translates into a fee schedule by adjusting resource use by a monetary conversion factor. Most fees charged by physicians are in some way tied to this index.

Many physicians participate in at least one risk-sharing contract with a health plan, in which they receive payment under a capitation arrangement. *Capitation* is defined as a fixed fee, paid in advance, for all necessary care provided to a well-defined group. Providing care for a fixed fee changes the nature of the physician–patient relationship. With cost increasingly an issue, the provider has a stake in eliminating all unnecessary care, which increases the risk that potentially beneficial care will be denied in the name of cost savings.

group insurance
A plan whereby an entire group receives insurance under a single policy. The insurance is actually issued to the plan holder, usually an employer or association.

indemnity insurance
Insurance based on the principle that someone suffering an economic loss receives a payment approximately equal to the size of the loss. An insured person who suffers a loss merely makes a claim and receives compensation equal to the loss.

THE NATURE OF MEDICAL CARE AS A COMMODITY

Before undertaking the study of medical care using economics, it is important to understand the differences between medical care and other commodities. If medical care were just like any other commodity, the use of economics to explain pricing and allocation decisions would not be questioned. But if it is substantially different, strict reliance on economic models may lead to inaccurate predictions and, ultimately, to serious policy mistakes.

Just how different is medical care from other commodities? Using the pioneering work of Kenneth Arrow (1963) as a guide, we can identify a number of distinguishing characteristics that contribute to the uniqueness of medical care as a commodity. First, unlike other commodities, the demand for medical care is irregular. Except for the small percentage of care that may be defined as preventive,

POLICY ISSUE

Can medical care be treated like any other commodity for policy purposes, or is it sufficiently different that it must be treated as a special case?

medical care demand follows an accidental injury or the onset of an illness. As a result, medical care is commonly associated with discomfort, pain, and suffering. It may even be an issue of life or death, depending on the nature of the accident or illness. Thus, access to medical care often has implications on the patient's ability to return to a state of normal functioning.

Second, the medical care transaction is characterized by information problems that disproportionately affect patients. All consumers are frequently confronted with difficulties in collecting information about a product, but the problem is particularly acute for medical care consumers due to the complexity of medical knowledge. The typical consumer of medical care is poorly informed and finds it difficult to become well informed. Because of this information imbalance, patients rely on their physicians to diagnose their illnesses and prescribe treatments, and they expect the physician to proceed without consideration for his or her own personal gain. Thus, the medical transaction carries with it ethical overtones unlike any other transaction. To protect the interests of the uninformed public, government has established licensing requirements and educational standards to ensure a minimum level of quality among providers, and provider organizations have adopted codes of conduct to guard against unethical behavior.

In addition to the information problem, the medical transaction is characterized by widespread **uncertainty**. An individual can rarely predict the onset of an illness and usually cannot predict his or her demand for medical care.[4] Physicians are confronted with uncertainty in diagnosis and treatment. Any given medical condition can be taken care of using a number of different treatment alternatives. One physician may recommend surgery; another may take a wait-and-see attitude. Both decisions are based on the interpretation of diagnostic tests and the physician's best judgment. And treatment is not always clearly linked to the outcome. Thus, medicine is an art as much as it is a science.

Another interesting feature of the market for medical care is the widespread reliance on not-for-profit providers, especially in the provision of hospital services. Because trust plays such a big role in the patient–provider relationship, restraining the profit motive may be desirable. The conventional wisdom would have us believe that the absence of the profit motive will mean decision making without the influence of **self-interest** on the part of providers. Even with over 85 percent of the nation's hospitals either government owned or otherwise not-for-profit, the profit motive has not been totally eliminated from the medical care sector. Most physicians' practices are for profit, as are virtually all pharmaceutical companies, retail drug stores, and long-term care facilities.

Although it is difficult to predict the onset of illness for any one individual, it is possible to predict the number of people who will suffer from a particular medical condition within a large group of individuals. In order to spread the risk of financial loss due to an illness, the individual is willing to purchase insurance. Because the probability of a loss is predictable for large groups, insurance companies emerge to underwrite that risk and sell insurance policies. As a result, insurance has become the primary means of payment for medical care. With third parties financing most of the costs of medical care, individuals are insulated from the full cost of the care they receive. Those with insurance will demand more medical care than equally healthy individuals who are uninsured. Providers will adjust treatment recommendations

uncertainty
A state in which multiple outcomes are possible, but the likelihood of any one outcome is not known.

self-interest
A behavioral assumption of neoclassical economics that individuals are motivated to promote their own interests.

Dr. Mike Magee's "Health Commentary" offers weekly discussions on important health issues. Popular topics on his blog include Men's and Women's health, aging, and health care reform. Check it out at

http://healthcommentary.org

---

[4] Notable exceptions to this observation include the treatment of certain chronic conditions that may be postponed with little risk and the provision of elective procedures, such as cosmetic surgery, pregnancy, and corrective orthopedics.

depending on the insurance status of their patients and the willingness of third-party payers to cover certain procedures.

Do these characteristics mean that economic principles are not applicable to medical care markets? A "yes" answer to this question would do away with any reason to proceed further. Medical care is a unique commodity in many ways, but its uniqueness does not preclude the use of economic theory to help us understand resource allocation and pricing decisions in this critical industry. The challenge we face is not whether the theory is applicable but how to apply it.

HEALTH ECONOMICS DEFINED

Health economics emerged as a subdiscipline of economics in the 1960s with the publication of two important papers by Kenneth J. Arrow (1963) and Mark V. Pauly (1968), both published in the *American Economic Review*. Arrow's paper is considered by many to be the seminal contribution to the field of health economics and health policy. Recognizing its importance, the *Journal of Health Politics, Policy, and Law* (Peterson, 2001) devoted a special issue to the paper's important contributions, including a forward written by Pauly.

Health economists examine a wide range of issues, extending from the nature and production of health to the market for health and medical care to the microeconomic evaluation of health care interventions and strategies. Figure 1.2 provides a diagrammatic overview of the structure of health economics. Beginning with the box labeled "Nature of Health," we can ask ourselves a number of questions: What does it mean to be healthy? How do we measure health? What is the best possible way to measure quality of life? Because of the nature of the questions being asked, research on this topic is interdisciplinary. Even though economists are not the only ones studying these questions, their contributions have been significant. The development of the quality of life measure, called the *quality-adjusted life year* (QALY), was in part a result of the participation of economists.

Grossman (1972) developed an economic framework for the study of medical care demand in which medical care is simply one of many factors used to produce good health. In this framework, "Production of Health" looks at the determinants of health, including income, wealth, education, genetics, and public health. Our ability to maintain a desired level of health depends to a great extent on the lifestyle choices we make. The topic "Confounding Factors" develops the influence of, for example, tobacco, alcohol, drugs, obesity, and sexually transmitted diseases on our ability to produce good health for a given level of medical care spending. The aging population and the introduction of new technology affect the ability of the market to allocate resources in such a way as to effectively satisfy consumer demand.

The principle activity of health economists outside the United States is *microeconomic evaluation*, or the evaluation of alternative ways to treat a specific medical condition. Policy makers within fixed-budget systems find it necessary to conduct studies comparing the costs and consequences of diagnosis and treatment options in order to make informed decisions on the optimal allocation of scarce resources. Cost-benefit analysis, with its welfare economics framework, provides the foundation for most of the research in economic evaluation, and health economists have adapted that framework in developing cost-effectiveness analysis, the evaluation method of choice in medical care decision making.

Figure 1.2:   The Structure of Health Economics

Source: Adapted from Alan Maynard and Panos Kanavos, "Health Economics: An Evolving Paradigm,"*Health Economics* 9, 2000, 183–190.

The primary focus of U.S. health economists is the market for health care. The boxes in Figure 1.2 numbered 5 through 7, and the topics covered in them, summarize this emphasis. The "Demand for Health Care" is affected by the elements discussed in boxes 1 and 2, the nature and production of health. The early contribution of economics to the study of health care demand considered improving health to be one way to increase future productivity (Mushkin, 1962). Thus, the demand for health care is not only influenced by a desire to feel better when ill, it is also viewed as investment in human capital. Factors affecting the demand for medical care include the socioeconomic characteristics of the population, patient demographics, access barriers (including cost-sharing arrangements), and the role of providers in determining the type and level of care prescribed.

The "Supply of Health Care" encompasses a broad spectrum of economics on such topics as production theory, input markets, and industrial organization. Specific issues examined include the cost of production, input substitution, and the nature and role of incentives. Demand and supply interact with one another to establish "Market Equilibrium." Markets are able to effectively allocate scarce resources where they are most productive by establishing a price for everything.

Analysis of the overall goals and objectives of the health care system is the subject of "Macroeconomic Evaluation." How well is the system performing? Is it accessible? Is it affordable? Is quality at the desired level? It is here where national and international comparisons are made. How does our system compare to those of our neighbors? Finally, "Health Policy and Planning" involves the interaction of private sector, government, and nongovernmental organizations (NGOs) in setting national goals, determining the strategies for reaching those goals, and establishing the rules of the game that regulate how medical care markets work.

Health care systems are constantly changing. Policymakers and planners are always looking for better ways to produce, deliver, and pay for a growing menu of medical care services demanded by an insatiable public. The goal of this book is to provide you with the tools to better understand the role of economics in this important task.

TEN KEY ECONOMIC CONCEPTS

Given the complexity of economic theory, it may come as a surprise that economic thought is guided by a relatively small number of key concepts. These concepts will serve as unifying themes throughout the book.

1. *Scarcity and choice* address the problem of limited resources and the need to economize. Not enough resources are available to meet all the desires of all the people, making rationing in some form unavoidable. We are forced to make choices among competing objectives—an inescapable result of **scarcity**.

2. *Opportunity cost* recognizes that everything and everyone has alternatives. Time and resources used to satisfy one set of desires cannot be used to satisfy another set. The cost of any decision or action is measured in terms of the value placed on the opportunity foregone.

3. *Marginal analysis* is the economic way of thinking about the optimal allocation of resources. Choices are seldom made on an all-or-nothing basis—they are made at "the margin." Decision makers weigh the trade-offs, a little more of one thing and a little less of another. In this environment, consideration is given to the incremental benefits and incremental costs of a decision.

4. *Self-interest* is the primary motivator of economic decision makers. Driven by the power of self-interest, people are motivated to pursue efficiency in the production and consumption decisions they make. According to the well-known eighteenth-century economist Adam Smith, this pursuit of self-interest, moderated by market competition, causes each individual to pursue a course of action that promotes the general goals of society.

5. *Markets and pricing* serve as the most efficient way to allocate scarce resources. The market accomplishes its tasks through a system of prices, what Adam Smith called the "invisible hand." The invisible hand can allocate resources because everyone and everything has a price. Prices increase if more is desired and decrease if less is desired. Firms base their production decisions on relative prices and relative price movements. The price mechanism becomes a way to bring a firm's output decisions into balance with consumer desires—something that we refer to as **equilibrium**.

6. *Supply and demand* serve as the foundation for all economic analysis. Pricing and output decisions are based on the forces underlying these two economic concepts. Goods and services are allocated among competing uses by striking

scarcity
A situation that exists when the amount of a good or service demanded in the aggregate exceeds the amount available at a zero price.

opportunity cost
The cost of a decision based on the value of the foregone opportunity.

equilibrium
The market-clearing price at which every consumer wanting to purchase the good finds a willing seller.

a balance, or attaining an equilibrium, between consumers' willingness to pay and suppliers' willingness to provide. This is rationing via prices.

7. *Competition forces* resource owners to use their resources to promote the highest possible satisfaction of society, including consumers, producers, and investors. If resource owners do this well, they are rewarded. If they are inept or inefficient, they are penalized. Competition takes production out of the hands of the less competent and places it into the hands of the more efficient to constantly promote more efficient methods of production.

8. *Efficiency* in economics measures how well resources are being used to promote social welfare. Inefficient outcomes waste resources, but the efficient use of scarce resources enhances social welfare. The fascinating aspect of competitive markets is how the more-or-less independent behavior on the part of thousands of decision makers serves to promote social welfare. Consumers attempt to make themselves better off by allocating limited budgets. Producers seek maximum profits by using cost-minimizing methods.

9. *Market failure* arises when the free market fails to promote the efficient use of resources by either producing more or less than the optimal level of output. Sources of market failure include natural monopoly, externalities in production and consumption, and **public goods**. Other market imperfections, such as incomplete information and immobile resources, also contribute to this problem.

10. *Comparative advantage* explains how people benefit from voluntary exchange when production decisions are based on opportunity cost. The individual or entity that has the lowest opportunity cost of production is said to have a comparative advantage.

http://

"Health Economics—Places to Go" provides links to sites related to health economics, health policy, managed care, and more.

http://www.medecon.de/HEC.HTM

public good
A good that is nonrival in distribution and nonexclusive in consumption.

SUMMARY AND CONCLUSIONS

The medical care industry in the United States is large and growing in relative size. Medical care is one of the largest industries in the vast U.S. economy. At more than $2.1 trillion, it was five times larger than the domestic auto industry and four times larger than the total defense budget in 2005. In addition, medical care employed more people and exported more goods and services than either defense or automobiles. It may be difficult to imagine, but the economic output of the U.S. medical care industry was almost 20 percent larger than the entire French economy.

As shown in Figure 1.3, a potpourri of public and private sources finances U.S. medical care. The public sector directly finances 46.1 percent of total spending. Private health insurance and private philanthropy finance 41.7 percent, leaving 12.2 percent to come from direct, out-of-pocket payments from individuals.

Most of the money Americans spend on medical care covers either hospital or physicians' services (see Figure 1.4).

The percentage of total spending in these two areas has remained at around 50 to 55 percent. Other professional services, pharmaceuticals, and nursing home care combine for approximately one-fourth of the total spending. The other five percent comprises home health care and other medical products and services. Even though it represents only 10.3 percent of total spending, pharmaceutical spending is the fastest growing portion of expenditures with an 80 percent increase since 2000.

The U.S. system of medical care delivery is far from perfect. Its weaknesses are easily identified. Critics claim there are too few primary care physicians and too many specialists, leading to greater reliance on acute and specialty care and underutilization of **primary and preventive care**. The gaps in health insurance coverage limit reliable access for many low-skilled workers and their families. Only recently has federal legislation introduced a modest measure of **portability** in the market for group health

Figure 1.3: Where the Money Comes From . . .

- Other Private Sources 7.4%
- State & Local Government 12.6%
- Federal Government 33.5%
- Out-of-Pocket 12.2%
- Private Health Insurance 34.3%

Figure 1.4: How the Money's Spent

- Public Health 2.8%
- Research and Construction 6.6%
- Administration 6.9%
- Hospital Care 30.8%
- Nursing Home Care 5.9%
- Other Medical Products 2.8%
- Prescription Drugs 10.3%
- Home Health Care 2.5%
- Physicians' Services 21.3%
- Other Professional 10.1%

insurance. Even with changes in the law, many people are still considered uninsurable because of preexisting conditions.

The system also has its strengths, and its defenders argue that quality is unquestionably high. Citing evidence from polls, they note that around 85 percent of Americans are happy with the quality of their own medical care arrangements. It should be noted that the same polls show that one-third feel the system has so much wrong with it that it needs to be completely rebuilt (Donelon et al., 1999). The U.S. system has progressed much faster than its European counterparts in developing quality assessment and output measures. The United States is still the world leader in innovation, research, and the development of state-of-the-art technology.

The growth in medical care spending has moderated somewhat since 1990. It could be that the aggressive action by employers and state governments to reverse the escalation in spending is finally paying off, or possibly that the threat of government intervention at the federal level has served to intimidate providers, who now fear public backlash and political reprisals. Whatever the reason, spending growth has moderated without significant legislative action.

In general, spending growth in the public sector has outpaced spending growth in the private sector. Since

1990, private medical spending has grown at an annual rate of 6.41 percent, while public medical spending has risen at an annual rate of 7.95 percent. Over that time, Medicare spending has increased 7.89 percent per year, and

Medicaid 10.25 percent. Regardless of the measures used, health care expenditures continue their upward trend, and policy makers continue to debate ways to address the crisis. Or should we say *conundrum*?

QUESTIONS AND PROBLEMS

1. Thomas Sowell, a senior fellow at the Hoover Institution, has stated that we "have difficulty understanding the strange way words are used by politicians and the media." We often think of a crisis in terms of an emergency, a situation of utmost urgency, maybe even life or death. According to Sowell, politicians use the term differently. They define a crisis as any situation they want to change. How do you define the term *crisis*? Does the United States have a health care crisis?

2. Discuss the magnitude of the financing problem in medical care. What are the major reasons that medical spending is absorbing an increasing share of national output?

3. How important is cost containment in establishing a national health care policy? In addition to controlling costs, what are the alternative goals for a national medical care system?

4. What do economists mean by *scarcity*? Why is the concept so important in economic analysis?

REFERENCES

American College of Obstetricians and Gynecologists, "Who Will Deliver My Baby? Ob-Gyns, Patients Push U.S. Senate for Tort Reform," ACOG News Release, April 28, 2003.

Henry J. Aaron, *Serious and Unstable Condition: Financing America's Health Care*, Washington, DC: The Brookings Institution, 1991.

Kenneth J. Arrow, "Uncertainty and the Welfare Economics of Medical Care," *American Economic Review* 53(5), December 1963, 941–973.

Robert J. Blendon, Tracey Stelzer Hyams, and John M. Benson, "Bridging the Gap Between Expert and Public Views on Health Care Reform," *Journal of the American Medical Association* 269(19), May 19, 1993, 2573–2578.

Centers for Medicare and Medicaid Services, National Health Expenditure Data available at http://www.cms.hhs.gov/ NationalHealthExpendData/, 2007.

Sergio Curtoni and Alton I. Sutnick, "Numbers of Physicians and Medical Students in Europe and the United States," *Academic Medicine* 70(8), August 1995, 688–691.

Karen Donelan, Robert J. Blendon, Craig A. Hill, Catherine Hoffman, Diane Rowland, Martin Frankel, and Drew Altman, "Whatever Happened to the Health Insurance Crisis in the United States? Voices From a National Survey," *Journal of the American Medical Association* 276(16), October 23/30, 1996, 1346–1350.

Karen Donelan, Robert J. Blendon, Cathy Schoen, Karen Davis, and Katherine Binns, "The Cost of Health System

Change: Public Discontent in Five Nations," *Health Affairs* 18(3), May/June 1999, 206–216.

Milton Friedman and Simon Kuznets, *Income from Independent Professional Practice*, New York: National Bureau of Economic Research, 1945.

John C. Goodman and Gerald L. Musgrave, *Patient Power: Solving America's Health Care Crisis*, Washington, DC: Cato Institute, 1992.

Michael Grossman, "On the Concept of Health Capital and the Demand for Health," *Journal of Political Economy* 80(2), March/April 1972, 223–255.

Jack Hadley and John Holahan, "Covering the Uninsured: How Much Would It Cost?" *Health Affairs—Web Exclusive* (W3), June 4, 2003, 250–265.

Stephen Heffler, Sheila Smith, Sean Keehan, et al., "Health Spending Projections through 2013," *Health Affairs—Web Exclusive* (W4), February 11, 2004, 79–93.

Kaiser Family Foundation and Health Research and Educational Trust, "Employer Health Benefits: 2007 Annual Survey," 2007 available at http://www.kff.org/insurance/7672/upload, EHBS-2007-Full-Report-PDF.pdf (Accessed September 17, 2007.)

Katharine Levit, Cynthia Smith, Cathy Cowan, Art Sensenig, Aaron Catlin, and the Health Accounts Team, "Health Spending Rebound Continues in 2002," *Health Affairs* 23(1), January/February 2004, 147–159.

Jessica H. May and Peter J. Cunningham, "Tough Trade-Offs: Medical Bills, Family Finances and Access to Care," Center for Studying Health System Change, Issue Brief No. 85, June 2004.

Selma J. Mushkin, "Health as an Investment," *Journal of Political Economy* 70(5, part 2), October 1962, 129–157.

OASDI and Medicare Boards of Trustees, 1999 *Annual Reports of the OASDI and Medicare Boards of Trustees to Congress*, based on data from the Office of the Actuary, Health Care Financing Administration, 1999.

Mark V. Pauly, "The Economics of Moral Hazard: Comment," *American Economic Review* 58(2), June 1968, 531–538.

_____, "U.S. Health Care Costs: The Untold True Story," *Health Affairs* 15(1), Fall 1993, 152–159.

Mark A. Peterson, ed., "Kenneth Arrow and the Changing Economics of Health Care," *Journal of Health Politics, Policy and Law* 26(5), October 2001.

Tillinghast-Towers Perrin, "2006 Update on U.S. Tort Cost Trends" available at http://www.towersperrin.com/tp/getwebcachedoc?webc=TILL/USA/2006/200611/Tort_2006_FINAL.pdf (Accessed September 17, 2007.)

The Medical Care Price Index

The conventional wisdom in many policy circles embraces the notion that medical care inflation is out of control. How much of the increase in medical spending is due to inflation, and how much is due to improved services and changing demographic patterns? The way we answer this question will ultimately determine the type of medical care reform we will get. It is important, therefore, to understand how price indexes are used to measure medical care price inflation.

MEASURING PRICE CHANGES WITH INDEX NUMBERS

The principal measure of inflation used by business and government policy makers is the year-to-year change in the consumer price index (CPI). The index plays an important role in determining cost of living adjustments (COLAs) for everything from union wages to social security and pension benefits to federal income tax brackets. The CPI is a fixed-weight or Laspeyres index that measures price changes for a market basket of items defined for a base time period. In other indexes, such as the GDP price deflator, the composition of the market basket changes every year to reflect different spending patterns.

A fixed-weight index has become the index of choice used to measure inflation. Because the weights do not change, movements in a fixed-weight index are due solely to changes in the prices of the goods included in the market basket. In contrast, a movement in a deflator reflects changes in prices of goods and the composition of the market basket. In reality, consumers adjust their spending away from goods whose prices increase, making it necessary to change the composition of the fixed-weight market basket periodically to better reflect consumer spending patterns. The weights for the CPI are based on a survey of consumer spending patterns and are changed approximately every ten years. The current CPI weighting scheme was revised in 1987 based on results from the 1982–1984 Consumer Expenditure Survey.

Table A1.1 presents data for the consumer price index from 1970 through 2007. Overall, the index is broken down into seven major spending categories: food (18 percent), housing (42 percent), apparel (6 percent), transportation (18 percent), medical care (6 percent), entertainment (4 percent), and other (6 percent). The index in each case equals 100 for the 1982 to 1984 time period. When interpreting these indexes, note that the inflation rate from one time period to the next can be calculated by dividing the change in the index by its previous value. For example, the CPI changed from 144.5 to 148.2 between 1993 and 1994. This change of 3.7 percentage points divided by 144.5 results in an estimated annual inflation rate of 2.56 percent. Over the time period shown, the medical care component increased at a faster rate than any other component of the CPI—over 700 percent from 1970 to 2002.

MEDICAL CARE PRICE INDEX

The major index of medical care prices, the Medical Care Price Index (MCPI), is shown in Table A1.2. Medical care is divided into commodities and services. Medical commodities are subdivided into seven categories: prescription drugs, nonprescription drugs, first aid and dressings, general medical equipment, convalescent equipment, hearing aids, and unpriced items. Medical services are divided into nine categories: physician, dental, optometry, other professional, hospital room, other inpatient, outpatient, nursing home, and unpriced. Health insurance is priced using a separate category.

Typically cited as the measure of medical care inflation, the MCPI has steadily increased since 1950. Interpreting the index as a measure of inflation suggests that medical care prices have risen at a compounded rate of over 6.35 percent since 1980, over two-thirds faster than prices in general. If this is true, we have a real problem on our hands. But can we believe what the statistics seem to tell us? Is the MCPI a good measure of medical care price inflation?

Table A1.1: Consumer Price Indexes for Major Expenditure Classes
Select Years, 1960 to 2007 (1982 to 1984 = 100)

Year	All Items (CPI-U)	All Services	Food	Housing	Apparel	Energy	Medical Care	All Items Excluding Medical Care
1960	29.6	24.1	30.0	—	45.7	22.4	22.3	30.2
1970	38.8	35.0	39.2	36.4	59.2	25.5	34.0	39.2
1980	82.4	77.9	86.8	81.1	90.9	86.0	74.9	82.8
1990	130.7	139.2	132.4	128.5	124.1	102.1	162.8	128.8
1995	152.4	168.7	148.4	148.5	132.0	105.2	220.5	148.6
2000	172.2	195.3	167.8	169.6	129.6	124.6	260.8	167.3
2001	177.1	203.4	173.1	176.4	127.3	129.3	272.8	171.9
2002	179.9	209.8	176.2	180.3	124.0	121.7	285.6	174.3
2003	184.0	216.5	180.0	184.8	120.9	136.5	297.1	178.1
2004	188.9	222.8	186.2	189.5	120.4	151.4	310.1	182.7
2005	195.3	230.1	190.7	195.7	119.5	177.1	323.2	188.7
2006	201.6	238.9	195.2	203.2	119.5	196.9	336.2	194.7
2007	207.3	246.8	202.9	209.6	119.0	207.7	351.1	200.1

Source: *Health United States,* various years

Table A1.2: The Medical Care Price Index and Its Major Components
Select Years 1950 to 2005 (1982 to 1984 = 100)

Year	Total Medical Care	Compound Rate of Change from Previous Year Listed	Medical Care Commodities	Medical Care Services
1950	15.1	—	39.7	12.8
1960	22.3	4.0	46.9	19.5
1970	34.0	4.3	46.5	32.3
1980	74.9	8.2	75.4	74.8
1990	162.8	7.4	163.4	162.7
1995	220.5	6.3	204.5	224.2
2000	260.8	3.4	238.1	266.0
2001	272.8	4.6	247.6	278.8
2002	285.6	4.7	256.4	292.9
2003	297.1	4.0	262.8	306.0
2004	310.1	4.4	269.3	321.3
2005	323.2	4.2	276.0	336.7
2006	336.2	4.0	285.9	350.6
2007	351.1	4.4	290.0	369.3

Source: *Health United States,* various years.

PROBLEMS WITH USING A FIXED-WEIGHT INDEX AS A MEASURE OF INFLATION

In reality, changes in a fixed-weight index do not accurately reflect changes in the cost of living. Using a fixed-weight index, such as the MCPI, to measure medical care price inflation introduces a substantial upward bias to the estimate. It is important that we understand the problems associated with using indexes to measure inflation and take appropriate steps when interpreting indexes to minimize the bias.

Measuring Inputs Instead of Outcomes

The MCPI measures the wrong thing. The price index measures the cost of inputs: an office visit, a day in the hospital, a surgical procedure, or a prescription drug. Patients who are ill do not desire the inputs; they are interested in the restoration of their health. But, as we will see in Chapter 5, health is difficult to define, let alone measure.

Given the difficulty in measuring health, one possible solution would be to measure the cost of curing a particular illness. For example, the average length of stay in the hospital has steadily fallen over the course of the past several decades. Reduced stays have dampened the hospital-cost escalation measured in terms of average cost per day (what the CPI measures). Even more dramatic has been the increased use of outpatient procedures to treat illnesses that formerly required extensive hospital stays. Repair of an inguinal hernia, one of the most common surgical procedures, formerly required several days in the hospital and several months of limited activity. Today the procedure is performed on an outpatient basis and requires only a few hours in the surgicenter and minimal rehabilitation time. In fact, most patients are encouraged to resume their normal daily activities as soon as possible.

The shift to outpatient surgery has greatly reduced the cost of treating many common problems, but the cost savings has largely been lost on the MCPI. As outpatient procedures grow in popularity, two things happen: First, patients who continue to be treated in the hospital are, on average, sicker than before. They require more resources on average and thus drive up the average cost of their hospital stays. Second, when an outpatient procedure actually replaces a conventional hospital procedure, as is the case with cataract surgery and lens replacement and many orthopedic surgeries, it drops out of the hospital component of the price index and is picked up later in the outpatient component. The end result of both of these factors is an increase in the MCPI, even though the cost of treating the illness has decreased.

Measuring Quality Changes

Technological progress typically results in improvements in the products and services available to consumers. Price increases due to quality improvements are mistakenly identified as inflation in a fixed-weight index. This is not a severe problem in industries in which innovation takes place slowly, but technological progress takes place at different rates in different industries. This is especially true in the medical industry, in which quality of care has improved dramatically over the past 50 years. Treatments for once untreatable diseases offer new hope. Inexpensive prevention of diseases such as polio and smallpox has led to near eradication of these once-costly illnesses, and improved surgical techniques allow patients to leave the hospital sooner and recuperate faster.

If price indexes are to be an accurate measure of changes in the cost of living, price changes due to quality improvements must have no impact on the value of the index. The Bureau of Labor Statistics (BLS) attempts to factor in quality improvements, but once again, infrequent changes in the composition of the index fail to keep up with the rapid advance of technology. As a result, quality improvements are mistakenly interpreted as pure price movements.

Accounting for New Products

The CPI, as a fixed-weight index, relies on the assumption that the product and service mix of the market basket remains unchanged. The use of this assumption makes it difficult to incorporate new products into the calculation. In some industries, this poses only minor problems. For gasoline and other components of the energy price index, this assumption works reasonably well. The same cannot be said for the medical care industry. The rapid introduction of new medicines and new technologies over the past several decades poses problems for the fixed-weight MCPI.

Infrequent revisions in the index mean that the price index fails to account for significant reductions in the price of newly discovered products. Penicillin, for example, did not enter into the index until its price had fallen to about 1 percent of its original level. A more common problem deals with the introduction of generic drugs. Generics are chemically identical to their name-brand alternatives and usually much cheaper. They do not enter into the calculation of the index until weights are periodically revised, and only then as an entirely new product. By that time, they may have captured a significant portion of the market and lowered costs to users substantially. Their addition to the index, however, does not reflect the price decline.

The introduction of the laparoscope has revolutionized many forms of surgery, from knee reconstruction for damaged ligaments to the removal of the gall bladder. In most cases, the new surgical method costs considerably less than the traditional alternative because of shorter hospital stays. Gall bladder removal using laparoscopic techniques requires a 1- to 2-day hospital stay compared with 3 to 7 days using traditional surgical techniques. Repairing a damaged anterior cruciate ligament using the new technique costs 75 percent less for the same medical result.

The BLS incorporates new products and procedures into the index by price linking, replacing the old product with a new one at some arbitrary point in time. This adjustment is made in such a way that the price index remains unchanged; price increases are considered an improvement in quality, but price decreases are simply lost to the index.

Other Problems

In addition to the problems already addressed, several other factors play an important role in creating biased indexes. These include statistical sampling problems, a substitution bias, and the use of list prices instead of transaction prices.

Use of List Prices All published indexes from the BLS use list prices in their calculations rather than transaction prices. The list price is the price paid by a full-paying patient. Information on list prices is easier to collect but may bear little resemblance to the payments that providers actually receive. As more and more providers, physicians, and hospitals enter into agreements with managed care networks and other insurers, actual transaction prices represent discounts from normal list prices. In practice, very few patients actually pay list prices for services.

Suppose a hospital that normally charges $2,500 for a hospital stay agrees to accept $2,000 from a private insurer as payment in full. In this case, $2,000 should be the price that enters into the price index. But more often than not, the discounted price differs across payers and is more difficult to determine, so the list price of $2,500 is used.

If list prices and transaction prices change at roughly the same rate, the use of list prices is not

particularly glaring. Medical discounting, however, has become an increasingly important phenomenon in recent years, so the use of list prices produces an upward bias on the medical care price index. In fact, the Centers for Medicare and Medicaid Services (CMS) have developed a transaction price index for hospital services. Since 1978, the transaction price index has increased about 70 percent as fast as the hospital index based on list prices (Tregarthen, 1993).

Sampling The high cost of collecting price data dictates that only a limited number of transactions are included in the price index. Sampling can introduce several types of biases into the price index. Because of routine discounts, list prices on the day the data are collected may not be totally representative of the prices that consumers actually pay. Prices paid in the sampled locales may not represent prices paid by most consumers. Discounts for bulk purchases and the increased popularity of generic and store brands are also lost in the sampling procedure used.

Substitution Bias Economists have observed that when the price of a good increases relative to other goods, consumers tend to buy less of it. So as the prices of goods change relative to one another, spending patterns change. Consumers substitute lower-priced items for higher-priced items. This changing pattern of spending, called the *substitution effect*, is missed completely by fixed-weight indexes like the CPI. As long as the prices of all items in the index rise at roughly the same rate, this phenomenon causes few measurement problems. Over time, however, small differences can add up and result in the statistical phenomenon called *substitution bias*. This bias does not pose a problem with a deflator, because the market basket changes annually to reflect changing spending patterns. In a fixed-weight index, the weights are changed infrequently (every ten years or so with the CPI), placing too much emphasis on goods whose prices rise the fastest.

ALTERNATIVE METHODS TO MEASURE MEDICAL CARE INFLATION

Researchers have suggested alternative measures that might better reflect changes in the price of medical care. Wilensky and Rossiter (1986) advance the case that a change in the measure of medical output would result in more accurate estimates of price changes in medical care. The most commonly used measure of output is the procedure (e.g., one dose of chemotherapy for the treatment of cancer). Alternatively, output could be defined by the case, such as treatment of cancer from diagnosis to final outcome; the episode, using a particular phase of the illness; or on a per capita basis, measuring the total cost per patient for all medical care.

Another suggested method involves defining a good by a set of characteristics demanded by consumers. This so-called hedonic approach prices those individual characteristics and recombines them to determine the quality-constant price of the good. Trajtenberg (1990) used the hedonic approach to estimate the change in the cost of computerized tomographic X-rays, or CT scans. Defining a CT scan as a set of characteristics, the hedonic index actually declined from 100 to 27.3 from 1973 to 1982. In contrast, the standard index with no quality adjustment showed an increase from 100 to 259.4.

The use of these alternative approaches, though promising in some cases, is not appropriate in others. Even when appropriate, the cost of data collection rises dramatically. Unfortunately, data collection does not seem to be very high on the list of government priorities.

SUMMARY AND CONCLUSIONS

Measuring price changes with the indexes we have available is somewhat problematic. Outputs are difficult to measure, new products are included arbitrarily, and the methods for dealing with quality improvements are inadequate at best.

Depending on how we interpret the evidence, medical care may be the fastest-rising component of the consumer price index or, using a quality-adjusted notion, medical care prices may be actually falling.

REFERENCES

Robert F. Graboyes, "Medical Care Price Indexes," *Federal Reserve Bank of Richmond Economic Quarterly* 80(4), Fall 1994, 69–89.

Joseph P. Newhouse, "Measuring Medical Prices and Understanding Their Effects," *The Journal of Health Administration Education* 7(1), Winter 1989, 19–26.

M. Trajtenberg, "Economic Analysis of Product Innovation: The Case of the CT Scanners," *Harvard Economic Studies* 160, Cambridge, MA: Harvard University Press, 1990.

Suzanne Tregarthen, "Statistics Overstate Health Care Costs," *Wall Street Journal*, August 18, 1993, A10.

Gail R. Wilensky and Louis F. Rossiter, "Alternative Units of Payment for Physician Services: An Overview of the Issues," *Medical Care Review* 43, Spring 1986, 133–156.

2

Using Economics to Study Health Issues

Understanding what economics can and cannot do is the first and possibly most important step in using economics as a tool of public policy. Economics can offer a framework to study the implications of individual decision making, and it can help define the alternative mechanisms available to improve resource allocation. It cannot provide solutions to all the problems of medical care access and delivery. When using economics to study medical care, it is important to avoid extremes. Arguing that economics does not matter, or at least should not matter, when it comes to medical care issues is as ill advised as arguing that economics is all that matters. We cannot avoid the economic implications of our actions any more than we can avoid their moral implications.

POLICY ISSUE

Does sound policy making require an understanding of economic principles?

Sound policy making is based on sound economic principles applied in a compassionate and consistent manner. The premise of this book is that policy making based on sound economics is better than policy making in an economic vacuum. Basic economics teaches us many lessons: about human behavior and the way individuals make decisions and respond to incentives, about the way people interact with each other, and about the efficient allocation of scarce resources. Economists do not claim to have the final word about how to organize and run a health care system, but they do have something relevant to add to the discussion.

The goals of this chapter are somewhat ambitious. Those of you who have been exposed to an economics course may be tempted to skip this chapter completely: Avoid that temptation. At a minimum, use the chapter to refresh your memory of the important concepts that will come into play in analyzing medical markets and the policies that affect them. Those of you who have never had the privilege of taking a course in economics will find this chapter useful in setting the tone for the rest of the book. The principal focus here will be the examination of the basic principles of supply and demand.

ISSUES IN MEDICAL CARE DELIVERY

Rhetoric in Economics

An important element of economics is conversation, so economists must be persuasive communicators. Economics has its own rhetoric, and those unfamiliar with it have a difficult time understanding it. Economists use mathematical and statistical tests to make arguments, but when you listen closely to their conversations, you hear many literary

continued

devices familiar to most freshman English students. They include figures of speech such as metaphors, analogies, and appeals to authority (e.g., Adam Smith's "invisible hand," Milton Friedman and the Chicago School, and John Kenneth Galbraith).

The rhetoric of economics comprises hundreds of special words, though you may like the term *jargon* better. Words like *inflation, expenditures, costs, prices, revenues, profits, labor, capital,* and *risk* are just a few examples of economic terminology. The rhetoric also includes dozens of graphs, a few mathematical expressions, and another favorite, diagrams and equations — the use of diagrams to model a situation, and mathematical equations to depict relationships among variables. Diagrams and mathematical expressions are efficient means of representing reality.

Some examples of economic rhetoric include the following:

- The organization of work is represented by a "production function." The economist depicting the delivery of medical care in a hospital environment by a production function is similar to the poet saying, "My love is like a red, red rose."

- Attending medical school is an investment in "human capital." Students who forgo income during medical training expect to reap high returns in the form of pay and prestige in the future.

- Prices serve as an "invisible hand" to guide decision makers in a market economy. High prices direct consumers away from certain products and toward those with relatively lower prices.

THE RELEVANCE OF ECONOMICS IN HEALTH CARE

Economics is a way of organizing our thinking about problems that confront us in our daily lives. To think like an economist requires a disciplined approach to problem solving, and sound reasoning within a systematic framework is essential. The value of economics stems from its usefulness in making sense out of complex economic and social issues, including issues in medical care delivery. Future health care decision makers will need training and knowledge in many areas: not only biology and chemistry but also statistics, epidemiology, behavioral science, ethics, decision analysis, and, of course, economics.

Economics is one of several social sciences that attempt to explain and predict human behavior. It is unique among the social sciences in establishing a context of scarcity and uncertainty. More specifically, economics is concerned with the way scarce resources are allocated among alternative uses to satisfy unlimited human wants.

The quest for **economic efficiency** stems from the fact that there are never enough resources to provide all the goods and services desired by a society. Economists call this concept *scarcity*. Using resources in one activity precludes the use of those same resources in a different activity. When resources are used in medical care delivery, those same resources are not available for use in other beneficial activities; for example, food distribution, education, housing, and national defense.

The economic concept of cost stems from the notion that resources have alternative uses. The term *opportunity cost* is defined as the potential benefit that could have been received if the resources had been used in their next-best alternative. Tax dollars used to purchase medical care for the elderly cannot be used to buy education for the young. Money spent in a rehabilitation program for drug addicts is not available to spend on prenatal care for indigent women. Adopting the

economic efficiency
Producing at a point at which average product is maximized and average variable cost is minimized.

concept of economic efficiency implies that choices should be made in a way that maximizes the total benefit from the available resources. In the practice of medical care delivery, this involves the evaluation of health care alternatives by calculating the benefits and costs of each and allocating resources in a way that maximizes the net benefits to the community.

Critical Assumptions in Economics

All scientific models start with assumptions. Economic models start by assuming **rational behavior** on the part of decision makers, meaning everyone involved in a decision behaves in a purposeful manner.[1] Economics is different from other social sciences in its emphasis on rational decision making under conditions of scarcity.

In **microeconomics**, the assumption of rational behavior establishes a consistent framework for individual decision making. We assume that individuals, in an attempt to reach certain objectives, must choose among competing alternatives. The problem becomes one of allocating scarce resources among these competing ends. In other words, we cannot satisfy every desire we have; we must make choices.

Decision makers, motivated by self-interest, respond to incentives. In fact, decision making is dominated by the pursuit of self-interest. Individuals use their resources to advance their own economic well-being. When confronted with alternative actions, they choose the one that makes them better off.[2]

People look for the best way to achieve their goals. This does not rule out impulsive behavior or mistakes. In fact, because information is costly to gather and process, decision makers often practice **rational ignorance**: They decide between alternative actions with incomplete information. From the decision maker's perspective, the information left to be gathered costs more to gather than it is worth.

Scarcity is the reason we study economics. In a world of superabundance, there would be no compelling reason to make choices. All people could have all that they wanted without concern for alternative uses. Or, if all individuals had the divine nature of saints, then our attitude would be one of relative indifference toward material goals, and scarcity would not be an issue. But we do not live in a world of superabundance, and the world is not populated by saints, so decision making must take into consideration forgone opportunities.

The Scientific Method

The challenge at hand is to understand economic relationships without the luxury of controlled experiments. Economic inquiry utilizes the scientific method in much the same way that physics and chemistry do. There are five basic steps in the scientific method:

1. Every scientist starts with a premise, or *postulate*, that serves as a foundation for the inquiry. Some may call it an *ideology* or even a *vision*. Either way it represents the scientist's understanding of the way the world works. The culture around us, the way our parents raised us, and years of scientific training and inquiry all affect the way we view the world around us. Even the

---

rational behavior
A key behavioral assumption in neoclassical economics that decision makers act in a purposeful manner. In other words, their actions are directed toward achieving an objective.

microeconomics
The study of individual decision making, pricing behavior, and market organization.

rational ignorance
A state in which consumers stop seeking information on a prospective purchase because the expected cost of the additional search exceeds the expected benefits.

---

[1] Note that it is possible to study human behavior without assuming rationality, but that would not be economics.

[2] Altruistic behavior is not ruled out; it is merely interpreted as self-interested behavior.

most unbiased among us are affected by some bias; at minimum, our biases affect the nature of our inquiry.

2. The world arouses our curiosity. Scientists are careful observers of real-world phenomena and events. These observations concerning the real world are organized and catalogued.

3. A theory is developed to explain the observed behavior or predict future behavior. Model building captures the essential features of the observed behavior. It is a meaningful abstraction, decomposing the problem into its elemental parts.

4. The scientist then formulates a hypothesis to test the predictions of the theory. This requires gathering of facts and data.

5. In the final step, hypothesis testing, we use quantitative techniques to improve our understanding of the issue and promote more accurate predictions.

In practice, an economist might approach a problem using the scientific method as follows: One vision of the way the world works might be that people who are truly motivated by self-interest will respond in measurable ways to changes in incentives. From this vision, a theory is developed that people will respond to higher out-of-pocket payments for health care by demanding fewer elective procedures. The RAND insurance experiment conducted controlled trials that randomly placed individuals into different types of health plans (Manning et al., 1987). By varying the out-of-pocket payments required of individuals, their demand for medical care was analyzed. Empirical results supported the hypothesis that higher out-of-pocket payments would lead to lower utilization, measured as fewer physician visits. The RAND experiment has spawned many studies, testing numerous different hypotheses. The way we think about health insurance pricing and payment policies has been significantly affected by this important research.

These are the steps involved in the scientific method: an ideological base; observation of events; development of a theory; hypothesis testing; and, finally, rethinking. Empirical results that run counter to expectations may cause the scientist to rethink the theory or develop a different hypothesis.

Model Building

One of the main goals of economics is to understand, explain, and predict the behavior of decision makers. To this end, economists find it necessary to simplify that behavior; this simplification is accomplished through generalization, often through the construction of models.

A model is nothing more than a way of organizing knowledge on a particular issue so that it becomes more than a set of random observations. An economic model explains how the economy, or part of the economy, works. The terms *model* and *theory* are often used interchangeably. By their very nature, models are simplifications of the real-world phenomena they attempt to explain, and model building is an exercise in abstract thinking.

Microeconomic models examine the behavior of individual decision makers—individuals, households, firms, and government agents—and the behavior of specific markets. We use microeconomic models to study how a patient's demand for a particular diagnostic test varies, depending on the out-of-pocket cost of the test. We can examine how a shortage of qualified nurses affects nurses' salaries, or how the relative income of specialists affects the demand for residency-training positions in all specialties.

economizing behavior
When individuals choose to limit their demand for goods and services voluntarily to save money.

neoclassical economics
A branch of economic thought that uses microeconomic principles to defend the efficacy of perfectly competitive markets in resource allocation.

optimizing behavior, or optimization
A technique used to determine the best or most favorable outcome in a particular situation.

positive analysis
A factually based statement whose validity can be tested empirically.

normative analysis
An economic statement based on opinion or ideology.

Problem Solving

Economics emerged as a science in the late eighteenth century with the publication of Adam Smith's *The Wealth of Nations*. Since that time, a wealth of theory has accumulated to help us understand and describe **economizing behavior**. Most microeconomic theory can be classified under the framework of **neoclassical economics**. Relying heavily on the rationality assumption, the neoclassical framework classifies all decision makers as optimizers—those who attempt to maximize their well-being. **Optimizing behavior**, or optimization, is nothing more than a decision maker seeking to accomplish certain objectives: maximize sales or profit, minimize cost, or maximize income. Economists often talk of decision-making calculus, which refers to the notion that individuals make mental calculations before arriving upon a decision. Optimization fits the calculus model well in that it evaluates a mathematical function for its maximum or minimum value.

ISSUES IN MEDICAL CARE DELIVERY

Positive and Normative Analysis

To a great extent, we will mix positive and normative analysis in our discussions. **Positive analysis** is the testing of hypotheses against facts; it examines the way things are. **Normative analysis** prescribes policies and actions to achieve certain goals; it purports to examine the way things ought to be.

The differences between positive and normative statements are easy to spot: "The United States spends more money per capita on medical care than any other country in the world" is an example of a positive statement. "Congress should guarantee universal insurance coverage by requiring all employers to provide health insurance to their workers" is a normative statement.

Positive statements are either true or false. It is the task of science to determine which they are. Normative statements are matters of opinion, so science is of little help in determining their legitimacy. Fuchs (1996), in a survey of 90 economists concerning issues in health economics and health policy, found that over 90 percent disagreed with the positive statement, "In the long run, employers bear the primary burden of their contributions to employees' health insurance." In contrast, opinion was divided almost equally on the normative statement: "National standardized health insurance benefit packages should be established." Disputes over factual information can be settled through careful observation and analysis. Settling disputes over differences of opinion, on the other hand, is almost never easy. In fact, disagreements among economists are typically disputes over normative issues, and these disagreements represent differences of opinion based on differences in ideology.

Example

ECONOMIC OPTIMIZATION

When more than one alternative is available, the optimal choice produces an outcome that is most consistent with the decision maker's stated objectives. Optimization is nothing more than discovering the best course of action given the decision maker's goals and objectives. Constrained optimization takes into consideration the cost and availability of resources. Would it be better for the hospital to enter into a contract for housekeeping services with an outside firm, or should this activity be performed in-house? Following an increase in patient volume, should physicians in a small group practice hire an office manager, an additional nurse, or both?

Choices in health care delivery must be made at two levels: individual physicians must decide on a particular course of treatment for a particular patient, and policy makers must decide on a course of action in planning the availability of health services for an entire community. The delivery of health care in any form must cover the following areas: whom to treat, when to begin treatment, where to treat, and how much treatment to offer. Of the many ways to go about choosing the best alternatives, economic efficiency will be the criterion examined in this section.

In a sense this decision making is nothing more than the classic "economic problem." Resource allocation demands that we answer three basic questions: 1) What do we produce? 2) How do we produce it? 3) Who gets it? Regardless of our perspective, whether we are examining economic systems, health care systems, business firms, individuals, or decision makers of any kind, something must drive the system to produce and distribute what people want. Just remember: what, how, and for whom? This is the economic problem that must be solved to promote growth and welfare in any modern society.

To resolve the problem, firms attempt to maximize profit, given production technology and the cost of available resources; consumers attempt to maximize satisfaction, subject to limited money income and the prices of goods consumed; and workers supply labor services in an attempt to maximize satisfaction derived from goods and services consumed and leisure time available subject to current wages. Together, this more or less independent behavior results in markets that tend toward equilibrium as represented by the familiar, or soon to be familiar, supply and demand framework.

Within this framework, what does *optimal* mean? Using the rhetoric of economics, it means that individuals will continue to purchase a good or service as long as the **marginal benefits** from consumption (*MB*) exceed the **marginal costs** (*MC*). Given that marginal benefits are declining and marginal costs are increasing as more of the good is consumed, eventually the two will be equal. As soon as *MB* = *MC*, equilibrium is reached, and the individual will consume no more. In Figure 2.1, the total benefits (*TB*) received from a medical procedure increase as more care is provided, but at a decreasing rate. For reasons both ethical and practical, medical practitioners tend to provide additional care as long as the treatment results in positive benefits. Beyond point *A*, additional medical care is considered equivocal or wasteful—the marginal benefits are not worth the medical risk.

From the perspective of economics, exhausting all possible medical benefits wastes scarce resources. In fact, any care provided beyond point *B* is wasteful, because the marginal benefits received from the additional care fall short of the marginal costs.[3] The resources used in providing the excess care could be put to better use somewhere else. Money wasted in the provision of unnecessary care cannot be used to further other important goals, such as improving education, repairing the interstate highway system, or cleaning up the environment.

When consumption is being subsidized, the cost to the consumer is less than the total resource cost, as in the case of medical care purchased with insurance.

Key Concept 1
Scarcity and Choice

Key Concept 8
Efficiency

Key Concept 3
Marginal Analysis

marginal benefit
The change in total benefits resulting from a one-unit change in the level of output.

marginal cost
The change in total cost resulting from a one-unit change in the level of output.

Key Concept 2
Opportunity Cost

---

[3] In this discussion cost is measured in terms of total resource cost, the actual opportunity cost of the resources consumed in the production of medical care, not merely the out-of-pocket cost to the consumer.

Figure 2.1: Economic Optimization

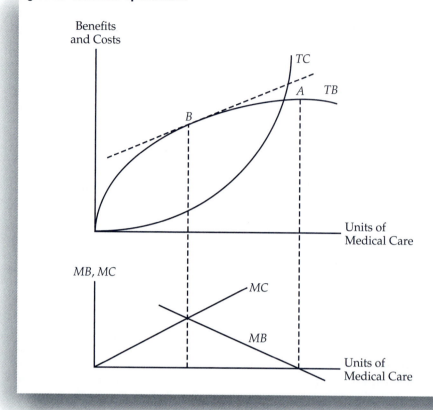

In the case of the insurance subsidy for medical care, the cost of an extra unit of care to the individual is close to zero, providing an incentive to consume medical care with low marginal benefits. When the marginal cost to the consumer is artificially low, resources are treated as if they had little or no value—a prescription for overconsumption. This tendency to overconsume means that medical care consumption is likely to be closer to point A, where the marginal benefit is close to zero, than point B, where the marginal benefit is equal to marginal cost. This phenomenon is called *flat-of-the-curve medicine*.[4]

Key Concept 9
Market Failure

SUPPLY AND DEMAND

Many consider supply and demand the two most useful concepts in economics. Regardless of the issue being studied, the analysis often hinges on some aspect of supply and demand. The theory of supply and demand is also a powerful tool in predicting future behavior. How does a change in price affect the consumer's willingness or ability to purchase a commodity? How does a change in the price of a key input affect the producer's decision about the optimal input combination to use in the production process?

Key Concept 6
Supply and Demand

In modeling behavior, economists attempt to simplify relationships. The amount of a particular commodity that a consumer plans to purchase depends on several factors. Instead of looking at the large number of variables that would affect

---

[4] The phrase "flat of the curve" is attributed to Alain Enthoven (1980).

demand, we focus on the most important ones: the price of the commodity; the price of related commodities; the number of people desiring the commodity; and consumer income, preferences, and expectations.

THE LAW OF DEMAND

The theory of demand occupies such an important place in economic analysis that it has been given the status of a law. The law of demand states:

There is an inverse relationship between the amount of a commodity that a person will purchase and the sacrifice that must be made to obtain it.

The higher the price of an item, the less it is purchased, and the lower the price, the more it is purchased. It is important to understand that this inverse, or negative, relationship holds as long as the circumstances of the consumer do not change materially. Remember, other things affect the demand relationship: prices of related items, the consumer's income, and preferences. As long as there are no changes in these other factors, the inverse relationship holds. When prices rise, less is desired. When prices fall, more is desired.

Changes in price affect the demand relationship in two very important ways: First, consumers have alternative ways to spend their money. If the price of a name-brand drug goes up, an alternative drug or even a generic can be substituted for the name brand. Or if money is tight and no insurance coverage is available, the patient can choose to skip the treatment and let the disease run its course. In any case, when price rises, the quantity demanded goes down. Economists refer to this phenomenon as the *substitution effect*.

A change in price affects the consumer in another important way. Paying higher prices for a desired commodity reduces the consumer's overall level of satisfaction. Spending more for one item leaves less to spend on everything else. With less money to spend, the consumer is unable to buy as much of everything else as before and thus feels worse off. This aspect of a price change on quantity demanded is called the *income effect*.

Part (a) of Figure 2.2 illustrates how an increase in price affects demand. Suppose that the demand for a particular commodity is represented by the demand

Figure 2.2: A Change in Quantity Demanded and a Change in the Level of Demand

(a) Decrease in Quantity Demanded

(b) Increase in the Level of Demand

curve D_1. Assuming no other changes, an increase in the price from P_0 to P_1 will reduce the amount demanded from Q_0 to Q_1. This is depicted by a movement along the stationary demand curve from point A to point B. A change in price, holding everything else constant, changes the quantity demanded.

There are many factors other than price that influence our purchasing decisions. These other factors are sometimes referred to as *ceteris paribus* conditions (remember, economics has a language of its own). These conditions are factors that are held constant when examining the relationship between price and quantity demanded. They include:

- The price of related commodities
- The number and type of people desiring the commodity
- Consumer income
- Consumer preferences
- Consumer expectations about future prices and product availability

A change in the price of a related commodity changes the demand for the commodity in question. Related commodities are either substitutes or complements. An increase in the price of a substitute increases the demand for a commodity. Coronary artery bypass graft surgery (CABGS) and cardiac angioplasty are two procedures used to accomplish the same outcome. If the price of CABGS increases, heart patients—or rather whomever is paying for the procedure—will view cardiac angioplasty as a more viable alternative. The demand for cardiac angioplasty will increase.

When the price of a complement goes down, demand goes up, because complementary goods are consumed together. Dentists often recommend that full-mouth X-rays accompany the annual dental exam; X-rays complement the annual exam. If the price of the X-ray goes down, more patients will make appointments for dental exams.

An increase in the size of the population or its composition affects demand. More people means a higher demand for all goods and services, including medical care. The addition of an infant to a family increases the demand for visits to the pediatrician. An increase in the birth rate raises the demand for disposable diapers, even if the average baby still uses the same number of diapers per day. An older population has a higher demand for treatments for chronic illnesses, such as arthritis and emphysema.[5]

A change in income affects the consumer's ability to purchase goods and services. In situations where higher income leads to increased demand, the good in question is referred to as a *normal good*. In some cases, an increase in income leads to a decrease in demand. In those situations, the good is called an *inferior good*. Medical care is usually considered a normal good. For individuals with comparable levels of health, higher income means a higher demand for medical care. Good health improves a person's ability to earn income. Higher income in turn increases the return to good health and increases the demand for medical care.

Consumer preferences play a key role in determining an individual's demand for goods and services. Some flu sufferers will consider a visit to the physician

---

[5] The examples point out the importance of distinguishing between the individual demand and market demand. Clearly, the market demand curve is determined by combining the demand curves of all the individuals actively participating in the market.

only as a last resort. They prefer to treat their ailment with over-the-counter medications. Some people hold religious beliefs (e.g., Christian Scientists) that strongly discourage the use of medical care. Others are convinced of the efficacy of chiropractors, herbalists, acupuncturists, midwives, and other alternative providers. They prefer these alternatives to the more traditional health care providers, and this shift in preferences can have a powerful impact on demand.

Consumer expectations play a key role in determining the level of demand. If consumers expect prices to change steeply and suddenly, or if they are afraid the product will be difficult to obtain in the near future, demand will rise sharply.

Finally, it is important to note that the demand for resources is a derived demand. Whenever a resource is used to produce a final product, the demand for that resource is ultimately determined by the demand for the final product. If medical care is considered an essential element in promoting the health of an individual or a group of people, an increase in the demand for health will increase the demand for medical care.

A change in one of these other factors changes the level of demand and causes a shift in the demand curve. Refer once again to Figure 2.2. Part (b) depicts a change that increases the level of demand caused by an increase in the price of a substitute commodity, a decrease in the price of a complement, an increase in consumer income, a positive shift in preferences, the expectation of a price increase, or a decline in availability in the future. Suppose the level of demand is originally D_1 in part (b). At the price P_0, the quantity demanded is Q_0. With the price held constant, an increase in consumer income will cause a rightward shift in the demand curve to D_2. This shift in the demand curve depicts an increased demand for the commodity. The consumer will now desire Q_1 at the price P_0.

To summarize, a change in the price of a commodity or service, holding everything else constant, will result in a change in quantity demanded, shown as a movement along a stationary demand curve. A change in any of the factors that affect the level of demand results in a shift in the demand curve—more or less of the commodity or service is demanded at every price level.

ISSUES IN MEDICAL CARE DELIVERY

How to Survive Supply and Demand

Succeeding in any economics course, especially a course in medical economics, depends on your mastery of the twin concepts of supply and demand. Listen carefully to economic commentators when they are queried on a complex issue in economic theory or policy, and their answer is frequently preceded by "It's all because of supply and demand." The introduction of supply and demand into the economics vocabulary is soon followed by adding supply and demand curves to the lexicon. In this hostile environment, survival depends on your ability to keep your wits about you while others around you fail. To ensure your success, follow these simple rules of survival:

- *Use common sense*. Most students already know a great deal about supply and demand. The key is to use what you know. Remember, economics is a way of thinking. For the most part, it is intuitive.

continued

Think about the market for oatmeal. Scientific evidence has suggested that consuming large quantities of oat products every day reduces the level of cholesterol in the bloodstream and thus the risk of heart attack.* What do you suppose happened to the demand for oatmeal, and its price, immediately after this information was made public? If you said that demand for oatmeal increased and its price also went up, then you already have some intuitive notion of the workings of supply and demand.

- *Learn the language.* After a few weeks in Econ 101, many students feel they are taking a foreign language. Mastery of economics requires that you learn the language of economists. When it comes to supply and demand, economists speak in graphs. Understand graphs and you understand supply and demand. If freshman literature were taught in Greek, it would be extremely difficult for the typical student. Not that the subject matter is so hard, it's the language. Introductory economics is taught in graphs. Learning to use graphs makes learning economics much easier.

- *Practice, practice, practice.* The rules of graphing are simple. Unlike a foreign language, there are no irregular verbs. But like a foreign language, it takes practice to master the subject matter. Practice whenever you can; economics is not a spectator sport. Watching your professor manipulate graphs is not enough: You have to do it yourself. Remember, demand curves are downward sloping, and supply curves are upward sloping. Economists place price on the vertical axis and quantity on the horizontal axis. Equilibrium price and quantity are determined by the intersection of the supply and demand curves.

- *Shift the appropriate curve.* The discovery that oat products have health benefits affected the market for oats. Did it affect supply or demand or both? Remember what causes shifts in the two curves. For the supply curve to shift, a change in the cost or profitability of making a product available to the market is needed. A shift in the demand curve is precipitated by anything that changes the willingness or ability of consumers to buy something. The discovery that oatmeal works like Roto-Rooter to clean out your arteries affected consumers' willingness to buy the product. So the demand curve shifted. Did it shift to the right or to the left? If in doubt at this point, go back to rule number one: An increase in demand will increase price. The only way to get this result is to shift the demand curve to the right. Shifting the demand curve to the left, or shifting the supply curve, is counterintuitive.

It is now time to test your mastery of supply and demand. Consider the market for hospital services. Use a graph similar to the one in Figure 2.5 and label the vertical axis "Price of Hospital Services" and the horizontal axis "Quantity of Hospital Services." Draw the supply and demand curves and identify the equilibrium price and the quantity of hospital services. Now suppose that due to a nursing shortage, the average salary paid to nurses increases 10 percent. What affect will this increased cost have on the market for hospital services?

*See Cynthia M. Ripsin, Joseph M. Keenan, David R. Jacobs et al., "Oat Products and Lipid Lowering: A Meta-Analysis," *Journal of the American Medical Association* 267(24), June 24, 1992, 3317–3325.

Price Elasticity of Demand

An important corollary to the law of demand is the concept of price elasticity of demand. The law of demand is used to answer the question, when price changes, what is the effect on the quantity demanded? Taking this notion one step further, price elasticity of demand is a technical concept used to answer the question, when price changes, how much does quantity demanded change? The inverse relationship between price and quantity is relatively easy to comprehend. In most cases, it is important to include not only the direction of the change but the magnitude of the change.

Price elasticity of demand measures consumer responsiveness to a change in price, holding the other variables that affect demand constant. Slope also measures the relationship between quantity demanded and price, but slope is not elasticity; slope measures the change in quantity demanded that results from a price change in absolute terms. Elasticity measures the change in relative terms.

Price elasticity of demand is defined as the percentage change in quantity demanded divided by the percentage change in price. Formally, price elasticity (ε_p) is calculated as

$$\varepsilon_p = \frac{\textit{percentage change in } Q}{\textit{percentage change in } P}$$

where Q is quantity demanded, and P is the unit price.

If consumer demand increases 10 percent because of a 5 percent price decrease, price elasticity of demand is 10 percent divided by 5 percent, or 2.0.[6] Values for the elasticity coefficient range from zero (0) to infinity (∞).

A summary of all possible values for the price elasticity coefficient is provided in Table 2.1. In the case in which price elasticity equals zero, consumers are completely unresponsive to changes in price. Their consumption patterns are fixed, and a higher price does not affect quantity demanded. Under these circumstances, demand is said to be *perfectly inelastic*, or *totally unresponsive*. The demand for addictive substances may come about as close to perfectly inelastic demand as anything. The demand for life-saving procedures, such as kidney dialysis and organ transplants, may also fall into this category.

Table 2.1: Price Elasticity of Demand

Coefficient Value	Nature of Demand	Impact of a 10 Percent Price Increase on Quantity Demanded	Impact of a 10 Percent Price Increase on Total Expenditures
$\lvert\varepsilon\rvert = \infty$	Perfectly elastic	Falls to 0	Falls to 0
$1 < \lvert\varepsilon\rvert < \infty$	Elastic	Decreases by more than 10 percent	Decreases
$\lvert\varepsilon\rvert = 1$	Unit elastic	Decreases exactly 10 percent	No change
$0 < \lvert\varepsilon\rvert < 1$	Inelastic	Decreases by less than 10 percent	Increases by less than 10 percent
$\lvert\varepsilon\rvert = 0$	Perfectly inelastic	No change	Increases by 10 percent

---

[6] The actual calculation is $[(+0.10)/(-0.05) = -2.0]$. While the price elasticity coefficient is always negative, for simplicity we usually ignore the negative sign, or more precisely, we consider its absolute value.

A more likely scenario would be the case in which a price change has an impact on quantity demanded, but the consumer response is less than proportional. In other words, we consider consumer demand somewhat unresponsive when the percentage change in quantity demanded is less than the percentage change in price. In this case, the elasticity coefficient is less than one, and demand is inelastic. Even addicts and terminally ill patients have their limits on how much they are willing or able to pay for a desired commodity.

An elasticity that is greater than one represents a change in quantity demanded that is proportionately greater than the change in price. Consumers are said to be *relatively responsive*, and in this case demand is elastic. In the rare case where the elasticity coefficient is equal to infinity, demand is *perfectly elastic*; consumers are intolerant of even small changes in price and refuse to buy the item if its price goes up at all.

An important use of the concept of price elasticity is illustrated in the right-hand column of Table 2.1. When price changes, it is important to know how much quantity demanded changes. It is also important to realize that this same information enables us to predict what will happen to consumer expenditures. With perfectly elastic demand, any price increase causes quantity demanded to fall to zero. In this case, it may be obvious that consumer expenditures also fall to zero. The case of unit elasticity may not be so obvious. When price elasticity equals one, a 10 percent price increase causes quantity demanded to fall by 10 percent, and consumer expenditures do not change. Likewise, price increases cause consumer expenditures to fall when demand is elastic and to increase when demand is inelastic.

What determines the price elasticity of demand? Why are consumers more tolerant of price changes for some items but not others? Price elasticity depends primarily on the consumer's ability to find suitable substitutes for a good or service. The easier it is to substitute, the more elastic the consumer's demand. If the consumer perceives a number of good alternatives to the item, demand is likely to be more responsive to changes in price. Patients with no established preference for a general practitioner (GP) might view a 20 percent increase in the price of an office visit as intolerable in light of the number of suitable alternative GPs in practice. However, those individuals who have an established relationship with a GP may be willing to remain a loyal patient in spite of the price increase. In this case, the GP will lose some business but not all of it.

ISSUES IN MEDICAL CARE DELIVERY

Is "Safe" Sex Really Safe?

One of the costs of risky sexual practices is an increased likelihood of contracting a sexually transmitted disease (STD) such as syphilis and gonorrhea or even AIDS. As with any activity involving human choice, the higher the perceived cost of engaging in risky sex, the less the demand for it. This suggests that by making sex "safer" through free condom distribution — in effect lowering the cost of risky behavior — public health officials may be increasing the incidence of that behavior and actually increasing the incidence of STDs.

The logic of this possibility is based on the fact that there is a demand curve for sex. It is difficult to know its exact shape, but most economists

continued

Key Concept 6
Supply and Demand

would agree that it is downward sloping. As the perceived cost of a sexual encounter (the risk of contracting an STD) falls, the number of sexual encounters will increase. The size of the increase is determined by the "risk elasticity of demand for sex."

The risk elasticity of demand for sex is defined as the percentage change in the number of sexual encounters divided by the percentage change in the risk of each encounter. If the risk elasticity is less than one, then free condom distribution will reduce the incidence of disease. If it is greater than one, the incidence of disease will increase.

Consider a closed community, where condoms must be purchased and no one uses them. According to research (Rosenberg et al., 1992), the risk of contracting three common STDs, gonorrhea, trichomoniasis, and chlamydia, during unprotected sexual activity is 23.4 in 100. If the number of risky sexual encounters is 250 per week, there will be 58 new infections every week. Assume that condoms are now distributed free of charge, and their use is widely encouraged through a sex education program. The use of condoms will result in a reduction in the incidence of STD to 18.8 per 100 risky sexual encounters — a 20 percent reduction.

If the demand for sex is inelastic, and the risk elasticity of demand is −0.50, the incidence of sexual intercourse will increase from 250 per week to 275, a 10 percent increase. In that case, there will be only 52 new cases of STD every week, a 10 percent decrease. On the other hand, if the demand for sex is elastic, and the risk elasticity of demand for sex is −1.5, sexual intercourse increases from 250 incidents per week to 325 — a 30 percent increase. In that case, there will be 61 new cases of STD reported every week, a 5 percent increase.

Does the policy of making condoms available increase or decrease the number of cases of STD? While the value of risk elasticity of demand for sex is an empirical matter, there is some evidence that sexual activity is higher in those situations in which condoms are widely available. According to Planned Parenthood, in schools with formal sex education programs and free condom distribution, the percentage of males engaging in sex increased from 60 to 84 percent, and the use of condoms actually decreased (Family Planning Perspectives, 1994). Kasun's review (1994) of seven sex education programs with easy access to condoms revealed that six resulted in an increase in sexual activity.

Any attempt by policy makers to make sex safer could actually exacerbate the problem by encouraging sexual activity. The risk elasticity of demand for sex determines whether the incidence of STD infection increases or decreases.

Sources: Dwight Lee, "Will Condoms Mean Less AIDS? It's a Question of Elasticity," *The Margin*, September/October 1989, 28; "As Adolescent Males Age, Risky Behavior Rises but Condom Use Decreases," *Family Planning Perspectives*, January/February 1994, 45–46; Jacqueline R. Kasun, "Condom Nation: Government Sex Education Programs Promote Teen Pregnancy," *Policy Review*, Spring 1994, 79; and Michael J. Rosenberg, Arthur Davidson, Jian-Hua Chen, Franklyn Judson, and John Douglas, "Barrier Contraceptives and Sexually Transmitted Diseases in Women: A Comparison of Female-Dependent Methods and Condoms," *American Journal of Public Health* 82(5), May 1992, 669–674.

Other factors that influence the degree of consumer responsiveness are the proportion of a person's income spent on the item and the urgency of the purchase. If the cost of the item comprises a substantial portion of a consumer's total income, demand will likely be elastic. Consumers are more sensitive to a price change on the purchase of big-ticket items. Insulin-dependent diabetics are more sensitive to a change in the price of syringes than the typical nondiabetic patient. The diabetic patient buys a lot more syringes per year than the nondiabetic. Finally, demand for nonurgent procedures will be more elastic than demand for emergency procedures. The more time a patient has to make a decision, the more price sensitive he or she will likely be. A patient entering the emergency room with a compound fracture does not have much time to shop around for an orthopedic surgeon. Patients desiring elective rhinoplasty, however, have the opportunity and the luxury to shop around for the best plastic surgeon, the best price, the best financing, or whatever else they consider important. A patient who shops around is more likely to find suitable alternatives.

Demand curves are typically drawn as straight lines for the sake of simplicity. There are three possibilities, as shown in Figure 2.3. Perfectly inelastic demand curves are drawn as vertical lines indicating zero response, and perfectly elastic demand curves are depicted by horizontal lines. The typical downward-sloping demand curve is shown at the right. Although slope is the same at every point, elasticity is not. The relationship between slope and elasticity at any point on the demand curve can be shown to be

$$\varepsilon = \frac{\Delta Q/Q}{\Delta P/P} = \frac{P\Delta Q}{Q\Delta P} = \frac{P/Q}{slope}$$

where Q is the quantity demanded, P is the unit price, and Δ is used to represent a change in the variable.

A demand curve with a given slope has a constantly declining elasticity. Moving from the upper left to the lower right on a downward-sloping demand curve, the P/Q ratio is declining: as price falls, quantity demanded increases. It follows that the demand curve goes from elastic to inelastic as you move down a straight-line demand curve.[7]

The Law of Supply

The theory of supply assumes that decision makers, producers in this case, are faced with scarce resources and must choose among alternative uses. Supply

Figure 2.3: Elasticity of Demand along Straight-Line Demand Curves

decisions involve the valuation of resources among competing uses. The law of supply states:

> *There is a direct relationship between the amount of a commodity that a producer will make available and the reward that is received.*

The higher the price of an item, the greater its availability. At lower prices, less will be available. Suppliers practice economizing behavior much as consumers do. The market rewards efficiency and punishes wastefulness.

Producers are concerned with cost. This concern is more than an accounting of the value of inputs; it involves establishing the opportunity cost of those inputs. In economics, cost reflects the value of resources in their next-best alternative use. In other words, forgone opportunities are an important element in determining value. Resources used in the production of one commodity are not available to produce another. Economizing behavior guarantees that resources will be used where they have the highest value. Therefore cost is determined by the value of what is being given up to produce any item.

Part (a) of Figure 2.4 illustrates how a change in the price of a commodity affects quantity supplied. Suppose that supply is depicted by the curve S_1. Assuming no other changes, an increase in price from P_0 to P_1 will increase the quantity supplied from Q_0 to Q_1. At higher prices, suppliers will transfer resources to the production of the higher-priced commodity, making more of it available to the market. A change in price, holding everything else constant, results in a change in quantity supplied and is depicted by a movement along the stationary supply curve.

Many other factors affect the availability of goods and services in a market. A change in any one of these factors, the *ceteris paribus* conditions, will change the level of supply. These other factors that affect the level of supply include:

- The prices of resources used to produce the commodity

- The number of firms supplying the commodity

- The state of technology

- Producer expectations about future prices and availability

Figure 2.4:   A Change in Quantity Supplied and a Change in the Level of Supply

(a) Increase in Quantity Supplied   (b) Increase in the Level of Supply

In general, anything that changes the costs of producing a commodity will affect the level of supply. Resources have alternative uses. In order to use resources to produce a particular commodity, producers must bid them away from their next-best alternative use. An increase in the price of a resource decreases the supply of the commodity that uses the resource as an input in the production process, and it raises its price. Technicians trained to operate the new magnetic resonance imaging (MRI) machines are in short supply. As competition bids up their wages, the cost of providing MRI services increases, shifting the supply curve for MRIs to the left and raising the price of the service in the market.

An increase in the number of suppliers increases access to a product or service. More suppliers means that consumers have more choices. The construction of a new 250-bed hospital in a community will increase the availability of inpatient hospital services to local residents. At any given price per day, there are now more beds available to serve the patient population.

New technology that reduces the cost of producing a commodity or service increases the level of supply. In the case of medical technology, certain analytical problems make it difficult to evaluate the different supply responses of cost-reducing and quality-enhancing technology. Arthroscopic surgery provides a clear example of a technological advance that represents both a cost-reducing and quality-enhancing change. The repair of a damaged anterior cruciate ligament was once a major ordeal for both surgeon and patient. Before the introduction of the laparoscope, an athlete who suffered this knee injury was faced with a four-hour surgery requiring a six-inch incision, several days in the hospital, and six weeks on crutches. Today, the same procedure can be performed as outpatient surgery. It requires three small incisions and a much shorter rehabilitation.

If suppliers expect the price of a commodity or service to fall in the future, they have an incentive to make it immediately available. If for some reason suppliers expect an increase in future availability, current supply will increase. As the medical marketplace moves systematically toward the managed care model, physicians scramble to join provider networks. Expectations create powerful incentives. As more physicians join networks, fueling expectations, others feel an urgency to join them, too.

An increase in the level of supply is illustrated graphically in part (b) of Figure 2.4. Anything that enhances a producer's ability to bring a product to the market increases the level of supply and results in a rightward shift in the supply curve. A decrease in resource costs, an increase in the number of providers, a technological advance that increases production efficiency, and the expectation of downward-price movements all increase the level of supply and cause the supply curve to shift to the right. Suppose that the supply curve shifts from S_1 to S_2. At any given price level, say P_0, providers will be willing to increase the amount supplied from Q_0 to Q_1.

To summarize, a change in the price of a commodity or service, holding everything else constant, will result in a change in the quantity supplied. This change is shown as a movement along a stationary supply curve. A change in any of the factors that affect the level of supply results in a shift in the supply curve and a change in the availability of the commodity or service at any given price.

Equilibrium

Price changes affect buyers and sellers differently. An increase in price reduces the consumer's willingness to buy and at the same time increases the producer's willingness to provide. The most fascinating aspect of the marketplace is how the more or less independent behavior of buyers and sellers results in an allocation of resources that guarantees that all consumers willing to pay the market price will find willing sellers, and all sellers willing to accept the price will find buyers.

Figure 2.5: Equilibrium

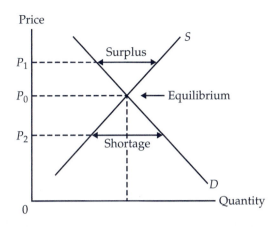

Adam Smith observed that it is as if an "invisible hand" were responsible for the price adjustments that promote the best use of resources.

We define the equilibrium price as the market price that exists when the quantity demanded equals the quantity supplied. Suppose that the price of the commodity depicted in Figure 2.5 is P_1. At that price, producers would like to sell more than consumers are willing to buy. There is a surplus, because the quantity supplied is greater than the quantity demanded. When prices are too high in the medical marketplace, hospitals, for example, will have unused capacity. This excess capacity takes the form of idle resources, empty beds, and unused operating rooms. Physicians find their appointment books unfilled and their waiting rooms empty. A surplus serves to increase competition among providers. The competition may manifest itself in many ways, but one sure way to eliminate the surplus and increase quantity demanded is to lower prices.

At the price P_2, quantity demanded exceeds quantity supplied, resulting in a shortage. Patients experience significant delays in getting appointments. When they do get an appointment, the waiting room is crowded and delays are frequent. Nonemergency surgeries have to be scheduled far in advance. Access to diagnostic imaging equipment is limited. Under these conditions, prices have a tendency to adjust upwards. Competition among consumers bids prices up and reduces quantity demanded. Coupled with an increase in quantity supplied, the shortage is eliminated.

Only one price does not result in either a surplus or a shortage. That price, P_0, the equilibrium price, clears the market. At P_0 the behavior of buyers and sellers coincides. Buyers are willing to pay the price that providers are willing to accept. Everyone who wants to buy at P_0 is able to buy, and everyone who wants to sell at that price is able to sell. In a market economy, people are free to make transactions: they are free to bid for goods and services at any price and free to offer those same goods and services at any price. When buyers seek the lowest price that producers are willing to accept, and sellers seek the highest price that consumers are willing to pay, the transaction price that clears the market is the equilibrium price.

THE COMPETITIVE MODEL

Free markets play a crucial role in the free enterprise system. The market system is grounded in the concept of consumer sovereignty: what is produced is determined by what people want and are able to buy. No one individual or group dictates what must be produced or purchased. No one limits the range of choice.

The market accomplishes its task of resource allocation through a system of prices, what Adam Smith called the "invisible hand." In a market system, resources can be allocated by this invisible hand because everyone and everything has a price. There is a tendency for prices to increase if more is desired and to decrease if less is desired.

Key Concept 5
Markets and Pricing

Firms base their production decisions on relative prices and relative price movements. The price mechanism becomes a way of bringing a firm's output decisions into balance with consumer desires, something that we refer to as *equilibrium*.

Prices serve not only as a signal to producers but as a means of rewarding popular decisions. Producers who invest in appropriate technology are able to produce goods and services desired by consumers. Their rewards come in the form of profits. Poor decisions are in turn punished by the market, and the producer suffers losses. This market discipline, accompanied by the freedom to compete within a system that allows private property ownership, is largely responsible for the efficient use of resources.

Key Concept 7
Competition

The Theory of Firm Behavior

One desirable outcome of a perfectly competitive marketplace is the efficient use of resources. The characteristics of the model of perfect competition are many buyers and sellers, a standardized product, mobile resources, and perfect information. These four characteristics guarantee that risk-adjusted rates of return will be equal to the normal rate of return for the economy, that prices are equal to minimum average cost of production, and that all transactions beneficial to both buyer and seller will take place.

Every firm must decide how much to produce and what price to charge. The choice of an output level and a pricing strategy are ultimately determined by the firm's costs. In a perfectly competitive market, the pricing decision is easy, because the product is standardized and firms must follow the dictates of the market. Firms that charge more than the market price lose customers. At the other extreme, firms have no incentive to charge a lower price, because they find willing customers at the market price. Firms are called *price takers*.

Figure 2.6 provides an illustration of the perfectly competitive market. Market price is determined by the interaction of supply and demand in part (a). At the price P_0, the representative firm can sell all it can produce. A profit maximizer will

Figure 2.6: Perfect Competition

(a) Market   (b) Representative Firm

produce every unit of output when the selling price is greater than the marginal cost of production—as long as P_0 is greater than MC. Because the competitive firm is a price taker, its demand curve is perfectly elastic at the market-determined price. In the case of a horizontal demand curve, the firm's marginal revenue (MR) curve is equal to price. Profit is maximized where $MR = MC$, or at q_0 units of output.

Competitive forces will lead to prices equilibrating at minimum average costs. At a price above P_0, price is greater than the average cost of production. Firms enjoy excess profits, or higher than normal rates of return, which encourages the entry of new firms into the market. As these new entrants establish their presence, supply increases and prices fall, until all excess profits are eliminated.

Key Concept 8
Efficiency

Price Ceilings and Price Floors

In their zeal to control rising prices, policy makers are sometimes tempted to pursue a price-fixing strategy. If prices are currently too high, why not roll them back to lower levels? Simply legislate a price that is below the current equilibrium price and make the product more affordable. In Figure 2.7, suppose the legislature sets a maximum price of P_c below the equilibrium price P_e. This **price ceiling** does two things: it reduces the availability of medical care from Q_e to Q_s, and it increases the amount requested to Q_d. The difference between Q_d and Q_s represents a shortage in the medical market. The shortage manifests itself in terms of longer delays in getting appointments, longer waits at physicians' offices, reduced access to high-tech surgical and diagnostic equipment, and lower quality of care.

Suppose the market for unskilled labor is depicted in Figure 2.8. Without government intervention, firms pay workers W_e and employ Q_e. If the government raises the cost of hiring workers by mandating that all firms provide health insurance for their employees, the cost of this new benefit raises the effective wage to W_f. This **price floor** reduces quantity demanded and increases quantity supplied. The job losers, when added to the new entrants, add to the number of unemployed workers in the labor market. Workers who keep their jobs are better off, but those who lose their jobs because of the mandate are noticeably worse off.

Policy makers are desperate to control medical care spending. Many feel that desperate times call for desperate measures. Some even think that their ability to

Figure 2.7: Price Ceiling

Figure 2.8: Price Floor

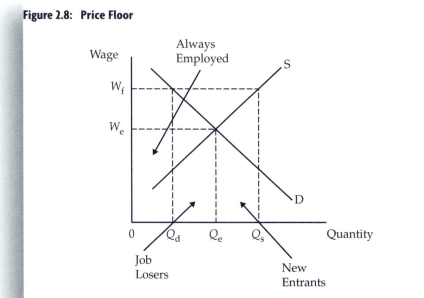

write laws also applies to the laws of supply and demand. Governments have been trying for centuries to rewrite those laws, and have all failed miserably.[8]

The Impact of an Excise Tax

The excise tax is becoming an increasingly popular way of imposing user fees on the consumption of specific items, such as gasoline, tobacco, and alcohol. Excise taxes may be set at a fixed dollar amount or at a percentage of selling price, called either a *specific tax* or an *ad valorem tax*.

In a competitive market, depicted in Figure 2.9, price and output are determined by the interaction of supply and demand. The commodity will sell for the price P_e, and Q_e will be purchased. An excise tax of a fixed amount will raise the cost of providing the commodity to the market and shift the supply curve leftward to the curve labeled $S + tax$. The dollar magnitude of the shift, measured by the vertical distance between the two supply curves, will be exactly equal to the specific tax.

The new equilibrium price will be P_c. Because producers are legally responsible for paying the tax, they only net P_s from the transaction. The difference between the price consumers pay and the price producers receive is the amount of the excise tax. At the higher price, consumers buy less of the commodity, or Q_t instead of Q_e. The excise tax generates revenues for the government of P_sP_cBC. The higher price and lower output causes a loss in surplus value—a deadweight loss from the tax of ABC.

The impact of this loss is minimized when the lost output is small; that is, when the demand curve is inelastic. It should come as no surprise that excise taxes on cigarettes, alcohol, health insurance, and hospital stays have been proposed as financing alternatives for the various health care reform options. Whenever taxes on alcohol and cigarettes are discussed, the tax is often called a *sin tax*.

---

[8] For a history of government price controls, see Robert L. Schuettinger and Eamonn F. Butler, *Forty Centuries of Wage and Price Controls: How Not to Fight Inflation*, Washington, DC: Heritage Foundation, 1978.

Figure 2.9: Excise Taxes

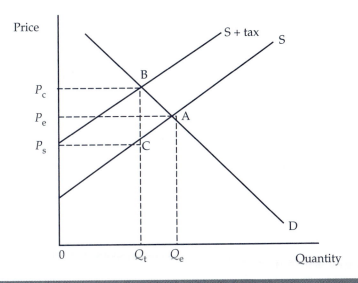

Using Game Theory to Study Economic Behavior

Game theory is a branch of applied mathematics used by economists to study strategic behavior. As individuals we interact with parents, children, siblings, spouses, friends, rivals, and colleagues, and we often find it useful to behave strategically. Strategic behavior is practiced in business, policy making, international diplomacy, and anywhere else interactive decision making takes place. The study of game theory attempts to build on strategic ability to develop a systematic approach to strategic behavior and improve strategic skills. Game theory is not a game. It involves more important issues in economics, adding another dimension to the foundational assumption of rational behavior — the interaction of two or more rational decision makers.

When considering strategic games, we frequently think of head-to-head interaction between two rivals. The prevalent view in economics is that competition improves all outcomes. Competitive markets are more efficient, prices are lower, and everyone is better off. Game theory goes beyond the simple interaction of supply and demand in the standard competitive model. No longer are we dealing with the impersonal market but with interpersonal strategic interaction between two decision makers.

Interaction can be either sequential or simultaneous. Players can take turns, each waiting to see what the other does before responding, or they can choose without prior knowledge of the other's decisions. Gambling is a zero-sum game; one person's winnings are the other person's losses. International trade is not zero-sum, because both nations generally benefit from increased economic activity. Some games are played one time, some are repeated. Sometimes information is equally available to all players,

continued

often it is asymmetrically distributed. Game theory is used to explain past events, predict future events, and advise players on the appropriate strategies under different circumstances.

The classic case of the simultaneous game is the prisoner's dilemma. The payoff structure of the prisoner's dilemma is important, because it arises in many strategic situations and thus has a wide range of applicability. The payoff matrix below depicts the predicament that two bank robbers, Bonnie and Clyde, find themselves in once captured. They are placed in separate interrogation rooms and given an opportunity to provide evidence against the other for a reduced prison sentence.

		BONNIE	
		Confess	Deny
CLYDE	Confess	20, 20	1, 30
	Deny	30, 1	5, 5

First, examine the situation from Bonnie's perspective. The payoff matrix represents the length of her prison sentence if both confess (20 years), if Clyde confesses and she does not (30 years), if she confesses and Clyde does not (1 year), and if they both choose not to confess (5 years). Even if they agreed prior to their arrest to never confess their crimes, what should she do now that they are both confronted with the opportunity to limit their sentences by confessing? Does she really trust Clyde not to confess when confronted with the same payoffs?

The prudent strategy in this situation, and Bonnie's best response, is to base her decision on what is best for her regardless of Clyde's choice. If Clyde confesses, Bonnie will spend 20 years in prison if she confesses, 30 if she does not. It is better to confess. If Clyde does not confess, Bonnie will spend 1 year in prison if she confesses and 5 if she does not. It's better to confess. Bonnie is said to have a dominant strategy; regardless of Clyde's decision, she spends less time in prison if she confesses. With this payoff structure, Clyde is faced with the same situation, so his dominant strategy is to confess. When both follow their dominant strategy, we reach a Nash equilibrium in which both confess and go to prison for 20 years.*

Regardless of the circumstances, the pursuit of the dominant strategy in a prisoner's dilemma results in lower payoff. Even though cooperative behavior would result in a higher payoff, the consequences of the other's defection are too great to take the risk. How do you avoid the consequences of opportunistic behavior? What can you do to guarantee a better outcome?

*John Nash won a Nobel Prize in Economics in 1994 for his contribution to economics in game theory.

Welfare Implications

Consider another way to look at demand and supply curves. Instead of viewing the demand curve as the amount demanded at various prices, it can be interpreted as the maximum price that consumers are willing to pay for each unit of a product. Likewise, the supply curve can be interpreted as the minimum price that providers are willing to accept for each unit of a product. From this perspective, demand curves may be viewed as "willingness-to-pay" curves and supply curves as "willingness-to-provide" curves.

Consumer Surplus Value depends on the consumer's willingness to pay. Items are valued for the utility they provide when purchased and consumed. In free markets, consumers do not pay more for a good than the subjective value they place on it. In fact, much of the time the value placed on an item exceeds its price. In those instances in which value exceeds price, consumers enjoy surplus value, or what is called *consumer surplus*.

In Figure 2.10, the demand curve DD' represents the maximum price that consumers are willing to pay to obtain a good, which is its subjective value. At the equilibrium price P_0, consumer surplus is depicted as the difference between the value consumers place on the good, shown by the demand curve itself, and the price they must pay (P_0). All Q_0 units of output sold have surplus value. The triangular area between the demand curve and the price, P_0AD, shows total consumer surplus.

Producer Surplus In the case of voluntary exchange, surplus value is created for both consumers and producers. A producer's willingness to provide goods and services is determined to a great extent by the opportunity cost of the resources used in production. Supply curves reflect these forgone opportunities. Producer surplus is defined as the difference between the price that is received and the minimum price that producers are willing to accept. Graphically, producer surplus is the area below the equilibrium price (P_0) and above the supply curve (SS').[9] Total producer surplus is the triangular area P_0AS.

Any output level other than P_0 results in a loss of surplus value and represents lost social welfare. In other words, given the demand and supply curves, DD' and SS', any price other than the perfectly competitive equilibrium price P_0 represents an inefficient outcome.

Imperfect Competition

In the case of the medical marketplace, violations of the assumptions of perfect competition are common. Although the incidence of monopoly is rare, the number of providers often falls far short of the perfectly competitive ideal. For example, many communities around the United States are served by a single hospital. Many factors determine the strength of this monopoly status; among them are the relative ease of access to other hospitals and the urgency of the services provided. Monopoly power

Figure 2.10: Consumer and Producer Surplus

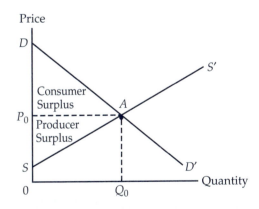

---

[9] Remember, the supply curve represents the subjective value providers place on the resources used to produce the good or service—its opportunity cost.

leads to monopoly returns, or excess payments. In the hospital industry, these extra payments are used to cross-subsidize care for the indigent population.

Other violations of the assumptions of the perfectly competitive model include entry restrictions that limit the number of providers that can practice in a particular area. These restrictions come in the form of certification requirements, such as compulsory licensure for physicians, and by limiting hospital privileges to certain providers. Information costs—in particular, unequal distribution of information between patient and provider—also present impediments to the market.

Key Concept 9
Market Failure

Supply-Side Imperfections Imperfections on the supply side of the market allow providers to enjoy monopoly returns. These imperfections usually deal with the nature of the rivalry, or the lack of rivalry, among firms. Too few firms, a nonstandardized product, barriers to entry, and information problems manifest themselves in the medical marketplace.

The presence of a single firm in a market is referred to as *monopoly*. As the sole provider in a market, monopolists have market power—the ability to set a price. This market power is inversely related to the elasticity of demand for whatever the monopolist is selling. The more inelastic the demand, the greater the market power.

Monopolists enjoy their special position in the market because, for various reasons, rivals are prevented from competing effectively. Barriers to entry may be the result of cost advantages due to size, something economists call *economies of scale*. Barriers may exist because of the sole ownership of an essential input in the production process or the franchise rights to a particular geographic region. These barriers can arise naturally or can result from legal restrictions on competitors. Whatever the source of the monopoly power, the result is a single provider serving a given market.

Monopoly is really quite rare in the U.S. economy, even in the medical marketplace. A more likely scenario is oligopoly, or the presence of a few firms in a market. The most important aspect of oligopolistic markets is the nature of the rivalry among firms. The pricing and output decisions of one firm depend on those of its rivals. The recent wave of consolidations in the managed care industry is bringing this form of market organization into the spotlight.

A single firm, or even a small number of firms, does not dominate many local markets, especially those that deal in services. Often many small firms attempt to differentiate themselves from their competitors by serving these markets by various means. Successful differentiation leads to market power. The degree of market power depends on how different the product is from its alternatives. A market with a large number of suppliers selling a variety of similar products is classified as monopolistic competition.

In all cases of imperfect competition, the firms share a common characteristic: they face downward-sloping demand curves. Firms in perfectly competitive markets, facing horizontal demand curves, have no market power: they are price takers. Whenever a demand curve is downward sloping, the pricing strategy changes. Market power allows firms to set a higher price, one that increases profit. Firms that find themselves in this situation are called *price searchers*.

Figure 2.11 illustrates the pricing and output strategy of a price searcher.[10] Faced with a downward-sloping demand curve, the firm must choose the profit-maximizing price and quantity. The price searcher is confronted with a marginal revenue curve that is situated below the downward-sloping demand curve. When the demand curve is downward sloping, the firm must lower the price to sell more

---

[10] The model discussed here is that of the single-price monopolist, one that sells to each customer at the same price. Other pricing strategies include price discrimination, in which different consumers are charged different prices depending on their price elasticity of demand.

Figure 2.11: Pricing and Output under Imperfect Competition

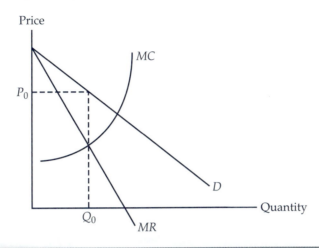

of the product. As a result, the extra revenue from the sale of one more unit of output is less than its price. To sell the extra unit of output, the provider must lower the price on all the output that could have been sold at a higher price. In other words, the marginal revenue curve is below the demand curve. It has the same intercept on the price axis and twice the slope.[11] Although the rule of thumb for profit maximization is the same, $MR = MC$, the intersection takes place below the demand curve. So the profit-maximizing output is lower than in the case of perfect competition, and the resulting price is higher.

Whether the price searcher makes a profit depends a great deal on the nature of the entry barriers. A monopolist can expect to maintain profits as long as the level of demand is maintained. In contrast, firms in monopolistic competition will see profits eliminated, because profits attract competitors, and competition for market share results in lower prices, higher costs, and lower profits.

Demand-Side Imperfections On the demand side of the market, imperfections manifest themselves in a number of ways; a limited number of buyers and imperfect information are two possibilities. The classic case of demand-side imperfections is called *monopsony*, or a single buyer. This situation emerges in medical care when consumers form into groups to consolidate their purchasing power and get lower prices from insurers and providers. The Canadian single-payer system is an example of a monopsony.

As sole purchaser in the market, the monopsonist faces an upward-sloping supply curve and a marginal cost curve that is above the supply curve. Figure 2.12 illustrates the operation of a market with a single buyer. Faced with an upward-sloping supply curve, the monopsonist must pay increasingly higher prices to obtain more output, even on those items that could have been purchased at lower prices if less had been bought. The relevant purchasing decision takes into consideration the marginal cost of purchasing one more unit of output, not the opportunity cost of that last unit of output. Instead of equilibrium occurring where supply and demand are equal, the monopsonist equates marginal cost with demand.

---

[11] A mathematical proof of this proposition follows:

Demand curve: $P = a + bQ$

Total revenue: $TR = P \times Q = (a + bQ) \times Q = aQ + bQ^2$

Marginal revenue: $MR = \dfrac{dTR}{dQ} = a + 2bQ$

Figure 2.12: Monopsony

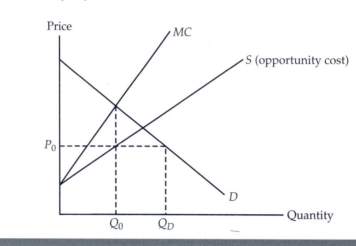

Monopsony equilibrium occurs at a lower level of output and a lower price than in the case of perfect competition. Society is worse off because fewer services are provided. At the lower price, quantity demanded (Q_D) exceeds quantity supplied (Q_0). The monopsonist exercises market power and creates a shortage that is not eliminated by competition with other purchasers, because none exists.

SUMMARY AND CONCLUSIONS

Economists seldom hesitate in applying economic tools in a variety of circumstances to evaluate individual choice and behavior. This tendency should not be misinterpreted. Few members of the economics profession believe that economics provides all the answers. As you progress through the book, it will become obvious that the health care marketplace fails to achieve its theoretical optimum in many cases, making the strict application of the neoclassical model inappropriate. The goal of this book, however, is to show that economics can provide insights into the study of human decision making that few other disciplines offer.

The central message of economics presented in this chapter can be stated briefly:

- Resources are scarce relative to unlimited human wants. Inevitably, we must face the fact that resources used in the delivery of medical care have alternative beneficial uses. To strike a balance between scarce resources and unlimited wants involves making choices. We cannot have everything we want. In the world in which most of us live, trade-offs are inevitable.
- Medical care decisions involve costs as well as benefits. For many clinicians, allowing cost considerations into treatment decisions is morally repugnant. To counter this feeling, it is essential that practitioners have a knowledge of the fundamentals of economics to provide a foundation for understanding the issues that affect medical care delivery and policy.

- It is important to strike a balance between incremental benefits and incremental costs. Most choices in medical care involve determining the level of an activity, not its very existence. The issue is not whether it is beneficial to perform widespread screenings for colon cancer, but whether it is cost effective to perform a sixth test, when five have already been done (Neuhauser and Lewicki, 1975). Decision making is seldom based on an all-or-nothing proposition. It usually involves a trade-off. If we are to spend a little more on one thing, we must be willing to spend a little less on something else.

- Human behavior is responsive to incentives and constraints. If you want people to practice economizing behavior, they must benefit individually from their own economizing. People spending other people's money show little concern for how it is spent. People spending their own money spend it more wisely.

As concern over escalating costs grows, economics takes on an increasingly important role in the study of medical issues. Future clinicians must be well-grounded in economic theory. Only then can they help shape the debate on the future direction of medical care delivery.

QUESTIONS AND PROBLEMS

1. What are the likely consequences on the U.S. market for tobacco products for each of the events listed below? Would the supply curve or the demand curve shift? In which direction? State whether the equilibrium price and quantity would increase, decrease, or stay the same. Show the changes using a standard diagram with an upward-sloping supply curve and a downward-sloping demand curve.
   a. The Food and Drug Administration classifies tobacco an "addictive substance."
   b. The Congress votes to raise the excise tax on all tobacco products.
   c. Hurricane Fran dumps 15 inches of rain on North Carolina and destroys 80 percent of that state's tobacco crop.
   d. Sixteen states sue the major tobacco companies for billions of dollars because of tobacco-related costs in their Medicaid programs.
   e. Medical evidence that more than two cups of coffee a day, considered by many to be a substitute for smoking, greatly increases the risk of stomach cancer.

2. What is the proper role of economics in the study of health and medical care? What does economics have to offer? What are its limitations?

3. "The laws of supply and demand are immutable. No one, including government, can affect a commodity's demand curve or supply curve." True or false. Comment.

4. Indicate whether the following statements are positive or normative.
   a. Smokers should pay higher health insurance premiums than nonsmokers.

   b. The United States should enact a comprehensive health care plan that provides universal coverage for all Americans regardless of their ability to pay.
   c. The primary reason for the escalation in health care spending over the past 30 years has been the rapid development of expensive medical technology.
   d. The high cost of providing health care for employees is a major reason U.S. firms are not competitive with their foreign counterparts.
   e. Individuals born with certain genetic defects that predispose them to higher medical care spending over their lifetimes should be charged higher health insurance premiums than people without those defects.

5. [This problem is based on material discussed in Appendix 2B]. The relationship between health care spending (E) and per capita national income (Y) was estimated using cross-section data from 24 developed countries. The resulting equation $E = 200 + 0.09\,Y$ relates spending and income in U.S. dollars.
   a. Interpret the coefficient on the national income variable.
   b. Complete the table.

Income in $	Health Care Spending
5,000	
10,000	
15,000	
20,000	
25,000	

   c. Graph the relationship

has had as much impact on economic thinking as any single paper written in the modern era. Members of the International Health Economics Association considered his contribution so important that they named their annual award for the outstanding published paper in health economics after him.

Born of immigrant parents in 1921, Arrow spent his early childhood in relatively comfortable surroundings. His father's business, however, fared poorly during the Great Depression, forcing Arrow to attend City College, which was free at that time to residents of New York. After graduating at the age of 19, and unable to get a job, he decided to pursue graduate studies in statistics at Columbia. Even though his interests were in mathematical statistics, he switched to economics to receive financial aid. He soon discovered his interest in economics surpassed his love for statistics.

Arrow's early work completely revolutionized the way economists think about general equilibrium and social choice. Winner of the 1972 Nobel Prize in Economics at the age of 51, he is widely considered one of the most important figures in general economic equilibrium theory and welfare theory.

In his own words, he describes his contribution to health economics as "not so much a specific and well-defined technical accomplishment as a point of view that has served to reorient economic theory" (Breit and Spencer, 1995). Arrow's work to integrate uncertainty into economic models led to his 1963 paper on the economics of medical care. In it he was able to show that the key element in insurance markets was the difference in information between the buyers and sellers of insurance. The very existence of health insurance causes individuals to spend more on medical care than they would otherwise. His emphasis on moral hazard and adverse selection served to focus research in health economics on these important issues.

Arrow joined the U.S. Air Force during the Second World War and served as a weather officer. His wartime contribution included important work on long-distance flight planning. At the time, the important theoretical work was all based on the assumption of a flat earth. Arrow's reformulation took into consideration the true nature of flight in a spherical world and helped determine optimal flight paths. After almost five years in the military, and still in his mid-twenties, he returned to Columbia University to finish his graduate studies. Before receiving his Ph.D., Arrow joined the Cowles Commission at the University of Chicago but soon moved to Stanford University, where he became a full professor at age 32. By the end of his first decade in academics, he was named president of the Econometric Society and winner of the John Bates Clark medal, given by the American Economic Association for the most distinguished work by an economist under the age of 40.

Most of his academic career has been spent at Stanford, except for 11 years at Harvard. He returned to Stanford in 1979, where he is currently emeritus Professor of Economics. In 1981, Arrow was named Senior Fellow at the Hoover Institution. In addition to his many honors and affiliations, he has been President of the American Economic Association, the Institute of Management Sciences, the Western Economic Association, the American Association for the Advancement of Science, and the International Economic Association. Often quoted and frequently criticized, his work has been so far reaching that we may never fully appreciate the extent of his contribution to economic and political thought.

Source: "Kenneth J. Arrow," in *Lives of the Laureates*, 3rd ed., edited by William Breit and Roger W. Spencer, Cambridge, MA: The MIT Press, 1995, 43–58; and "Interview with Kenneth Arrow," *The Region, Review of the Federal Reserve Bank of Minneapolis*, December 1995.

REFERENCES

Michael Drummond, Greg Stoddart, Roberta LaBelle, and Robert Cushman, "Health Economics: An Introduction for Clinicians," *Annals of Internal Medicine* 107(1), July 1987, 88–92.

Alain Enthoven, *Consumer Choice Health Plan*: *The Only Practical Solution to the Soaring Cost of Medical Care*, Reading, MA: Addison-Wesley, 1980.

Victor R. Fuchs, "Economics, Values, and Health Care Reform," *American Economic Review* 86(1), March 1996, 1–24.

_____, "The Cost Effectiveness of Prenatal Care," *Health Care Financing Review* 15(4), Summer 1994, 21–32.

Michael L. Ile, "When Health Care Payers Have Market Power," *Journal of the American Medical Association* 263(14), April 11, 1990, 1981–1982, 1986.

Willard G. Manning, Joseph P. Newhouse, Naihua Duan, Emmett B. Keeler, Arleen Leibowitz, and M. Susan Marquis, "Health Insurance and the Demand for Medical Care: Evidence from a Randomized Experiment," *American Economic Review* 77(3), June 1987, 251–277.

Duncan Neuhauser and Ann M. Lewicki, "What Do We Gain from the Sixth Stool Guaiac?" *New England Journal of Medicine* 293(5), July 31, 1975, 226–228.

Dorothy P. Rice, Sandler Kelman, Leonard S. Miller, and Sarah Dunmeyer, *The Economic Costs of Alcohol and Drug Abuse and Mental Illness*: 1985, San Francisco, CA: Institute for Health and Aging, University of California at San Francisco, 1990.

Anne A. Scitovsky and Dorothy P. Rice, "Estimates of the Direct and Indirect Costs of Acquired Immunodeficiency Syndrome in the United States, 1985, 1986, and 1991," *Public Health Reports* 102, 1987, 5–17.

Lester C. Thurow, "Medicine Versus Economics," *New England Journal of Medicine* 313(10), September 5, 1985, 611–614.

Graphing Data

Someone once said that a picture is worth a thousand words. Economists must take this axiom to heart. Seldom will an economist get far into a discussion without reaching for a pencil and paper. The picture often takes the form of a **graph**, one of several ways that economists use to convey ideas.

SOME BASICS OF GRAPHING

Most graphs that we use in economics are two-variable graphs. The relationship between the two variables is illustrated by drawing two axes perpendicular to each other. The dependent variable is usually plotted on the vertical, or y axis; the independent variable on the horizontal, or x axis. Point a in Figure 2A.1 represents a combination of the variables x and y equal to x_0 and y_0, respectively. The x-y values for point a are called the **coordinates** of point a.

Graphs are used to describe relationships between variables. Scatter diagrams are often used for this purpose. The scatter diagram in Figure 2A.1 suggests that variable x and variable y are associated

Figure 2A.1: Graphing Two Variables Using a Scatter Diagram

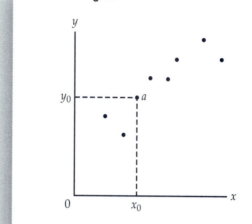

with one another; as the value of x increases, the corresponding values of y are also larger. Economists use scatter diagrams to get a feel for the relationship between two variables, looking for linkages, a correlation, or simply a random pattern.

When a relationship between variables is hypothesized, it is often depicted by a linear function or curve. Straight-line relationships can be expressed by the familiar equation $y = mx + b$, where m is the slope of the line and b is its y intercept. Graphically,

Figure 2A.2: Slope and Intercept

(a) Straight Line

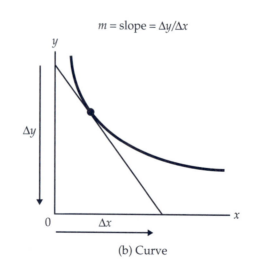

(b) Curve

this relationship is shown in part (a) of Figure 2A.2. The slope of a straight line is calculated by dividing the change in the variable on the *y* axis (Δy) by the change in the variable on the *x* axis (Δx). The slope of the curve in part (b) below is determined by the slope of its tangent, a straight line that touches the curve at only one point.

The slope of a function or curve is a convenient way to describe the relationship between two variables. A slope of $+3.0$ indicates that for every one unit increase in the variable measured on the *x* axis, the variable on the *y* axis increases by 3. The intercept represents the value of the variable measured on the axis *y* when the variable on the *x* axis has a value of zero.

FUNCTIONAL RELATIONSHIPS

Graphs are an efficient means of expressing relationships between variables. Often the relationship between two variables is functional in nature, implying dependence or causation. A causal relationship has a **dependent** and an **independent** variable. The value of the dependent variable is determined by the value of the independent variable. Suppose that we want to examine the relationship between the amount of money spent on medical care and the health of a person or a group of people. Instead of spending one or two pages of valuable paper describing this relationship, I can simply use a graph to convey the main idea.

Figure 2A.3 indicates that there is a direct (positive) relationship between the level of health and the amount spent on medical care. The higher the level of spending, the healthier the person or population. The shape of the line indicates that there is a limit to how much health you can buy with increased medical care spending. Additional medical spending buys progressively smaller increments of health. There are

other variables that affect the relationship between health and medical spending, such as genetics and lifestyle choices. Smokers as a group experience more respiratory and circulatory problems than nonsmokers. Figure 2A.4 depicts the relationship between the level of health and medical spending for smokers and nonsmokers. The graph indicates that at any given level of spending, nonsmokers are healthier than smokers on average.

Sometimes two variables are indirectly (negatively) related to one another. The relationship between infant mortality rates and birth weights is a good example of this phenomenon. Empirical data suggest that as birth weight increases, mortality rates decline. Figure 2A.5 illustrates the negative relationship between infant mortality and birth-weight category. Some hypotheses question whether high mortality rates are due to low birth weights or some other factor, such as prematurity (Behrman, 1995). Those issues will be discussed later.

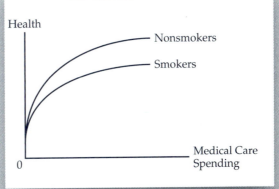

Figure 2A.4: The Functional Relationship of More than Two Variables

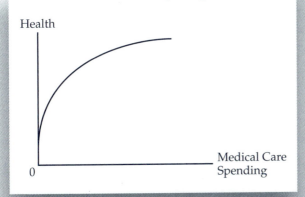

Figure 2A.3: The Functional Relationship Between Health and Medical Care Spending

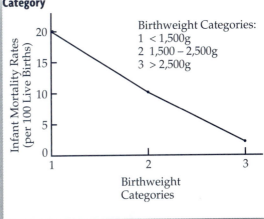

Figure 2A.5: Infant Mortality by Birth Weight Category

For now, focus your attention on the nature of the relationship and how to depict it graphically.

As we discussed earlier, one of the important concepts in economics is optimization. Efficient production techniques promote the goals of average cost minimization. Optimal pricing strategies enable firms to maximize profits. Graphs showing a minimum or a maximum are illustrated in Figure 2A.6.

Part (a) illustrates the hypothetical relationship between the average cost of services and the number of beds in a typical community hospital. This U-shaped relationship is typical of average costs in producing a product or service. As the size of the operation increases, average costs decrease. If the operation expands beyond a certain level, average costs begin to increase. The most efficient level of operation for the hospital, the optimal level, is B_0.

A functional relationship with a maximum is shown in part (b). Here the relationship between the total revenues of a physician's practice and the number of patient visits is illustrated. To generate more patient visits, a physician must offer discount prices to some groups—a practice that is typical for physicians who participate in managed care networks. What is the optimal pricing policy? A physician trying to maximize total revenue will charge a price that will result in a volume of business equal to V_0.

Time-Series Graphs

On occasion it is important to examine how variables change over time. The use of longitudinal, or time-series, graphs often illustrates trends in a data series. Time-series graphs typically use daily, weekly, monthly, quarterly, or annual data to track changes

Figure 2A.6: Minimum and Maximum Values

(a) Minimum Value

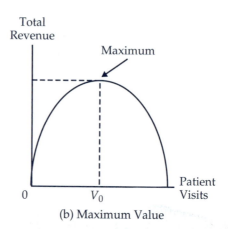

(b) Maximum Value

Figure 2A.7: U.S. Health Care Spending 1970–2001

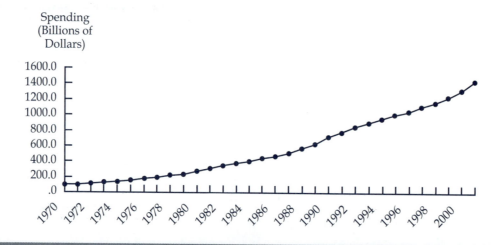

in an economic variable. Figure 2A.7 graphs the changes in U.S. health care spending over three decades. Health care spending has shown a long-term upward trend since 1970. Starting at less than $100 billion, it has risen dramatically to almost 20 times that amount in just over three decades.

If we were interested in examining the relationship between health care spending and income, we could collect data on spending and income in a single country over a number of years. While a time series on two variables provides insight into the relationship, so many other factors change over time that we may not be sure of our results. Figure 2A.8 illustrates a time-series relationship between per capita health care spending and per capita gross domestic product (GDP) in the United States between 1970 and 2001.

Cross-Section Graphs

Another approach to graphing the same relationship is the use of cross-section data. A cross-section graph provides a number of observations on two variables at a given point in time across different entities: individuals, firms, states, or countries. Figure 2A.9 illustrates the same relationship for the year 2000 using data from the Organization for Economic Cooperation and Development (OECD). The two graphs depict the relationship between income and spending. Each point on the time-series graph shows U.S. spending compared to income over a number of years. The cross-section graph shows the same two variables for 28 different countries during a single year. Each point represents income and spending (in U.S. dollars) for a given country.

Figure 2A.8:   Per Capita Health Care Spending and Per Capita GDP (United States, 1970–2001)

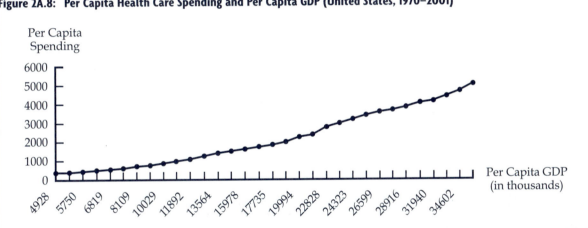

Figure 2A.9:   Relationship between Health Care Spending and Income in OECD Countries (Per Capita Amounts, 2000)

Source: Richard E. Behrman, ed., *The Future of Children: Low Birth Weight* 5(1), Spring 1995.

Statistical Tools

DESCRIPTIVE STATISTICS

Whenever we are confronted with a body of data, the challenge is how to summarize the relevant information to make it useful to the reader. Economic researchers are often confronted with large amounts of data, hundreds and sometimes thousands of observations on a number of variables. A useful way of summarizing large amounts of data is by way of a graph, sometimes called a **histogram**.

Figure 2B.1 shows the distribution of maternity patients by age at Hillcrest Baptist Memorial Hospital in Waco, Texas, for 1991. A simple viewing of the histogram tells us much about the ages of the 2,476 mothers who delivered that year. The youngest was 12 years old, the oldest 44—a spread of 32 years. The most frequent age was 25 years, the approximate center of the distribution.

Histograms can be summarized by statistical measures. These statistical measures help define the center of the distribution and the spread around the center. These concepts are formally called *central tendency* and *dispersion*.

Measures of Central Tendency

Measures of central tendency are often used to describe the typical value in a data set. The most commonly used measure of central tendency is the **mean**. Often referred to as the *average*, the mean of a distribution is the sum of the individual values divided by the total number of cases. Summing the ages for the maternity patients comes to 64,137 years. Dividing by the total number of patients (2,476) gives a mean value of 25.9 years.

Reporting the mean value as the typical value can be misleading, because it may place too much

Figure 2B.1: Histrogram Showing the Distribution of Obstetrics Patients by Age, Hillcrest Baptist Memorial Hospital, Waco, Texas, 1991

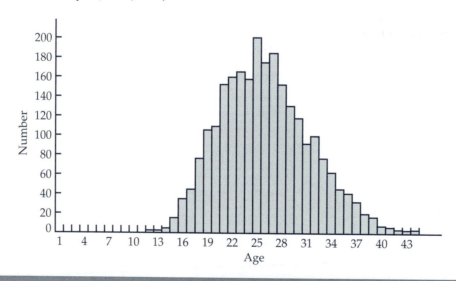

weight on extreme values. Suppose five infants were born on a given day, and their mothers were 42, 27, 25, 23, and 22 years old. The average age of these five women is

$$\frac{42 + 27 + 25 + 23 + 23}{5} = 28 \; years$$

By weighting the observations equally, the 42-year-old causes the measure of central tendency, or mean in this case, to be inflated and not very typical of the rest of the data.

When dealing with data that has a relatively small number of unusually large or small numbers, many researchers use an alternative measure of central tendency known as the **median**. The median is a popular summary statistic for demographic data with extreme values or outliers. To calculate the median, the values of a group of numbers are ranked from largest to smallest. In the case of an odd number of observations, the median is the middle number. In the case of an even number of observations, the median is the average of the middle two values. Its position at the fiftieth percentile implies that exactly half of the distribution falls above the median and half falls below it. The median age of the five new mothers listed above is 25 years, a much better indication of the typical age of that sample of patients. The median for all 2,476 maternity patients is 26 years.

Another measure of central tendency is the **mode**. The mode is the value occurring most frequently in the distribution. The most common age of the five maternity patients listed above is 23. For the entire group it is 25. The mode is used primarily on those occasions where the distribution has more than one mode. Under these circumstances, care should be taken to understand what is truly typical of the data values. Confounding factors may cause measures of central tendency to convey quite different results concerning the overall data set. Without controlling for these confounding factors, reliance on a single measure of central tendency may produce spurious results.

Measures of Dispersion

Focusing on the central tendency can obscure other interesting features of a collection of numbers. Concentrating on averages would lead us to conclude that a person standing with one foot in a bucket of scalding hot water and the other foot in a bucket of ice water is, on average, comfortable. Instead of simply looking at the central tendency of the data, it is useful to examine the way the numbers spread out around the center or average. Deviations around the average are typically indexed by statistical measures termed the *variance* and the *standard deviation*.

The **variance** is a measure of the dispersion of the data around the mean (average) value. It is one way of describing how closely individual observations in a data set cluster around the mean. The sample variance, denoted s^2, is calculated as follows:

$$s^2 = \frac{\sum_{i=1}^{n}(x_i - \overline{X})^2}{N}$$

where X_i is the "*i*th" observation of the variable X, $\overline{X}$ is the sample mean, and N is the number of observations in the sample. The deviations from the mean, $X_i - \overline{X}$, are squared to take into consideration all values above or below the mean. Otherwise, deviations for values below the mean would enter the numerator as negative numbers and result in an artificially low measure of dispersion. Whenever the values of a variable are similar, the variance will be small. Variance, or the variability in the observed values, is a key concept in statistics and plays an important role in the calculation of many statistical tests and procedures. In fact, one of the goals in empirical research is to explain as much of the variance as is practicable.

A related measure of dispersion around the mean is the **standard deviation**. Even though the variance is computed in terms of squared values of the deviations, the standard deviation measures the average deviation; it is an estimate of how far on average the values are from the mean value. Mathematically, the standard deviation is the square root of the variance. This measure of deviation has more intuitive appeal, because it is measured in the same units as the original variable. If the variable being considered is years, variance is measured in square years and standard deviation in years. For our sample of maternity patients, the variance is 28.6 square years, and the standard deviation is 5.3 years.

Another common issue concerning a distribution is its shape. A distributions that is symmetrical is often called a **normal distribution**. A distribution that has a long tail is called a **skewed distribution** (see Figure 2B.2 above). A normal distribution is bell shaped and can be reconstructed rather well from its summary statistics, mean and standard deviation. For a normal distribution, roughly 70 percent of the

Figure 2B.2: Skewed and Normal Distributions

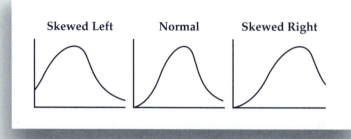

observations fall within plus-or-minus one standard deviation of the mean, and about 95 percent fall within two. For our maternity patients, over 72 percent fall within one standard deviation (±5.3 years) of the mean, 25.9 years. In other words, 1,787 of the 2,476 patients are between the ages of 20 and 31 years. Additionally, over 96 percent (2,386 out of 2,476) are between the ages of 15 and 36 years, or two standard deviations from the mean.

CORRELATION

Descriptive statistics are useful when dealing with one variable at a time. However, a study of the relationship between two or more variables is more interesting and requires other techniques. The scatter diagram described in Appendix 2A is one way of examining the relationship between two variables (see Figure 2A.1). Consider the points on a scatter diagram: A tight clustering around a straight line indicates a strong linear association between the two variables. A loose clustering indicates a weak linear association.

The strength of the association can be measured by a summary statistic commonly called the **correlation coefficient**. The correlation coefficient may be visualized as an expression of how two variables are "co-related." It is calculated using the respective standard deviations and means of the variables. Practically speaking, a perfect correlation between two variables indicates that all the observations lie on a straight line that is either positively sloped or negatively sloped. In these two cases, the correlation coefficient will have the value of either +1 or −1. If the two variables show no tendency to increase or decrease together, the points on a scatter diagram will show no clustering. In such cases, the correlation coefficient will have the value of zero.

It is important to understand that a correlation coefficient indicates an association between two variables. Association, however, does not imply causation. Suppose researchers found a strong negative correlation between the number of cases of influenza and the amount of ice cream consumed. Could we say that eating ice cream reduces the incidence of influenza? As popular as this would be with the children of the world, we cannot honestly make the statement. If it were true, physicians would encourage the consumption of ice cream to reduce the chances of contracting an influenza virus.

Correlation may be telling us that there is a third factor at work in the influenza–ice cream connection: namely, the season of the year. Coincidentally, the flu is most prevalent during the winter months, when ice cream sales are low, and least prevalent during the summer months, when ice cream sales are high. Correlation says nothing about these confounding factors. If it were possible to control for all of these confounding factors, correlation would provide a much stronger argument for causation. What is needed is a way of controlling for these other factors.

REGRESSION — Progression

Simple measures of central tendency and dispersion reveal little about the way two or more variables are "co-related." An empirical technique used to determine the nature of the **statistical relationship** among a dependent variable and one or more independent variables is called *regression analysis*. Regression analysis not only allows us to identify systematic relationships among variables, it provides estimates of the relative magnitude of the various relationships. The relationships may be discussed in terms of independent and dependent variables, stimuli and response, explanatory and explained variables, or cause and effect. Because it is one of the most frequently used empirical techniques in economic research, it is important to have a clear understanding of this powerful tool.

Least Squares Methodology

Regression analysis is used to identify a dependent relation of one variable or a set of variables to another. Most regression models use the least squares method for estimating parameters. The least squares method provides a means of fitting a curve to a set of data points. This technique is not without its methodological problems. Moving the line closer to some points moves it farther away from other points. Solving the problem is simple. First, find the average distance from the line to all points. Second, minimize the average distance. The least squares method uses this approach with one difference: instead of using the average distance, it uses the average of the squared distance. This approach avoids the problem of positive and negative differences canceling each other out, hence the name *ordinary least squares*.

Suppose we are interested in examining the causes of increased health care spending. The first step in our analysis is to specify the variables to include in the model. The variables that influence health care spending are numerous and may include income, age, and gender among other things. To simplify our discussion, we will specify a simple regression model with one dependent variable and one independent variable. The dependent variable is health care spending and the independent variable is income.

Step two in the analysis involves collecting reliable estimates for the two variables. Two approaches are possible: time series and cross section. A time-series approach would require the collection of data over time, locating data from a published source that looks at spending and income over time for a single entity, such as a state, region, or country. A cross-section approach requires data from a number of entities during a single time period.

Data for a cross-section analysis of the effect of income on spending is provided in Table 2B.1. The data come from the Organization of Economic Cooperation and Development for 28 developed nations. Income is defined as per capita GDP, and spending is defined in per capita terms. All values are translated into U.S. dollars using purchasing power parity exchange rates.

After collecting the data, the third step is to decide on the functional form of the relationship, or the regression equation. The two standard choices are linear and multiplicative. The linear form can be written as $E = a + bY$, where E is per capita health care expenditures and is per capita GDP. The multiplicative form can be written $E = aY^b$. Although the linear model is simpler, the multiplicative form has its advantages. One advantage is the coefficient b in a log transformation of the equation ($\log E = \log a + b \log y$) has a simple economic interpretation—it is an estimate of "income elasticity."

Table 2B.1: Per Capita GDP and Per Capita Health Care Spending in OECD Countries, 2000 (Purchasing Power Parity U.S. Dollars)

Country	Per Capita GDP	Per Capita Spending	Country	Per Capita GDP	Per Capita Spending
Mexico	8,845	491	Sweden	26,146	2,195
Slovak Republic	11,279	641	Belgium	26,239	2,293
Hungary	12,204	817	Germany	26,269	2,780
Czech Republic	13,802	987	Australia	26,473	2,350
Korea	15,186	893	Netherlands	27,183	2,348
Greece	16,481	1,556	Austria	28,046	2,233
Portugal	16,857	1,519	Iceland	28,139	2,562
Spain	20,080	1,497	Canada	28,187	2,580
New Zealand	20,214	1,611	Ireland	28,200	1,793
United Kingdom	24,933	1,813	Denmark	28,734	2,398
Italy	25,245	2,060	Switzerland	29,553	3,160
Finland	25,414	1,699	United States	34,602	4,540
France	25,594	2,387	Norway	36,248	2,787
Japan	26,003	1,984	Luxembourg	48,537	2,719

Source: *OECD Health Data 2003: Comparative Analysis of 30 Countries*, Organization for Economic Cooperation and Development, Paris, 2003.

Choosing the simple linear model, the simple regression model that relates per capita health care spending to per capita gross domestic product for these 28 OECD countries is written

$$E_1 = a + bY_i + u_i$$

where i represents the subscript of each observation (countries numbered 1 through 28) and u_i represents the random elements in the relationship.

Figure 2B.3 plots the actual data on spending and income provided in Table 2B.1. The constant term represents the intersection of the regression line with the axis, and the coefficient on income represents its slope. Using the least squares technique, the regression estimate predicts that, on average, for every one-dollar increase in income health care, expenditures increase ten cents.

In social science and demographic research, often more than one causal variable is identified. The technique used in this situation is called *multiple regression analysis*. Researchers use multiple regression to control for confounding variables; that is, other variables associated with changes in the dependent variable. For example, health care spending may also

depend on other factors, such as the percentage of population covered by insurance or the number of active physicians per capita. A multiple regression equation adding these two regressors would be written in linear form as

$$E = a + bY + cI + dP$$

where I is the percentage of the population with health insurance coverage, and is the number of active physicians per 100 population.[12] The coefficient on the income variable would now show the independent effect of income on expenditures, free from the influence of insurance coverage and the availability of providers.

Measures of Significance

Foremost on the minds of researchers is the reliability of the estimated coefficients. The accuracy of a regression equation can be determined by a number of significance tests. The *standard error of the estimate* (*SEE*) is the standard deviation of the dependent variable after controlling for the influence of the all the independent variables. When data points are widely dispersed about the estimated regression line,

$$E = -17.29 + 0.084\ Y$$

Predictor	Coefficient	St. Dev.	t-ratio
Constant	−17.29		
Y	0.084	0.0117	7.15

$$F = 51.2 \qquad\qquad R^2 = 66.3\%$$

Figure 2B.3: Least-Squares Relation between Health Care Spending and Income in OECD Countries (Per Capita Amounts, 2000)

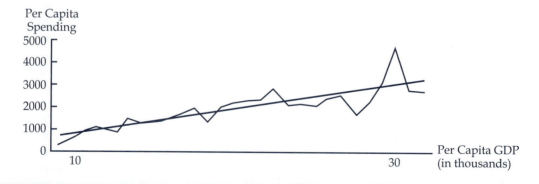

standard error is large. If all the data points were to fall on the regression line, the standard error would be zero.

One of the objectives of regression analysis is prediction. Standard error provides an estimate of the accuracy of a prediction based on a particular regression equation. Based on statistical probabilities, when there are roughly 30 or more observations, there is a 95 percent probability that the dependent variable will lie within two standard errors of its estimated value. The smaller the standard error, the greater the confidence in the accuracy of the estimate.

Often the standard error of the estimate is used to estimate confidence intervals around a given estimated equation. The 95 percent confidence interval has a range of roughly ±2 standard errors around the estimate.

A second measure of accuracy is the *coefficient of determination*, or R^2. The coefficient of determination is an estimate of the percentage of variation in the dependent variable explained by the independent variables, sometimes called *goodness* of fit. R^2 ranges between zero and one. The higher its value, the greater the overall explanatory power of the regression equation.

Standard error and R^2 are both important significance measures, but neither addresses the question of whether the independent variables as a whole explain a significant proportion of the variation of the dependent variable. The *F statistic* fills this void. Values of range from zero upward. At the extreme, when R^2 equals zero, equals zero.

Whether a particular value of the statistic indicates a significant set of regressors depends not only on its value, but also on the number of regressors and the number of observations on which the estimated equation is based. In general, the larger F is, the greater the likelihood that the set of independent variables explains a significant proportion of the variance in the dependent variable.

Critical values of F are provided in statistical tables that are readily available in almost all introductory statistics textbooks. Roughly speaking, with five or fewer independent variables and 25 or more observations, values of that are greater than 3 or 4 indicate a statistically significant proportion of the variance explained by the set of independent variables. Smaller sample sizes and a larger number of independent variables require larger values of for significance.

In addition to the significance of the overall equation, often the researcher is interested in the significance of each independent variable. The standard deviation, or standard error, of the coefficient for each independent variable provides a means of creating a test statistic expressly for this purpose. The most commonly used *t statistic* in regression analysis is calculated to determine if an individual coefficient is statistically different from zero. The *t* value is calculated by dividing the coefficient estimate by its standard error. Values of *t* greater than 2 are usually associated with coefficients that are statistically different from zero. The critical values of the statistic are found in tables in most introductory statistics textbooks.

SUMMARY AND CONCLUSIONS

With the development of the microcomputer, data analysis is no longer the exclusive purview of statisticians. A standard personal computer equipped with a statistical software package gives the user a powerful set of tools for analyzing information.

The analytical techniques discussed in this appendix are among the most commonly used in the social sciences. Many of the referenced articles use them extensively. A thorough understanding of these tools will go a long way in making the study of health economics more enjoyable and easier.

3

Analyzing Medical Care Markets

market failure
A situation in which a market fails to produce the socially optimal level of output.

A compelling argument can be made that medical care delivery is far more complex and dynamic than is typically the case in the standard treatment of the market process. The trade-off between equity and efficiency is quite acute, calling for active government involvement to ensure that the process works. Critics of government involvement offer an equally compelling argument. Even well-meaning government policy has its unintended consequences. Oversight is costly and serves to impede growth and productivity in the private sector.

In this chapter, we will examine the competitive market model and its applicability to the medical market. After considering the breakdown in the traditional market model, we will then examine how governments intervene to address the problems that arise. A general discussion of the causes and consequences of **market failure** will be followed by a more specific examination of market failure in medical markets. Government intervention in the form of regulation, public provision, and licensing will then be discussed. Finally, the question of how to deal with government failure is addressed.

THE MEDICAL CARE MARKETPLACE

As costs have escalated, and the number of uninsured individuals has increased, calls for government intervention have mounted. Proponents of more government involvement in medical care claim that medical care is far too complicated to be left to market forces. Because medicine is difficult to understand, patients must rely on their physicians' recommendations. Others add that medical care is a social good and too important to leave to the workings of the impersonal marketplace. Some argue that the externalities involved in medicine, particularly in the area of infectious diseases, require collective action to maximize the benefits to society. Many base their support for government intervention on ethical grounds, claiming that the provision of medical care based on the ability to pay is morally repugnant. Together these arguments are responsible, in varying degrees, for the development of government-financed medical care in most developed countries throughout the world.

Those who oppose more government involvement argue that the U.S. system has remained, for the most part, market based, which is in part evidence of the deep American distrust of federal government involvement in health care matters.[1]

---

[1] Blendon and colleagues (1995) note that only 7 percent of Americans express a "great deal of confidence" in federal health care agencies, compared with 19 percent of Canadians and 41 percent of Germans.

Experience has taught that government-run programs are costly. For example, when originally proposed in the mid-1960s, Medicaid spending was projected to reach $9 billion in 1990; the actual cost in 1990 was $109 billion. The preamble to the original Medicare bill actually prohibited any federal "supervision or control over the practice of medicine or the manner in which medical services are provided." Anyone familiar with medical care delivery is well aware of how the federal government has violated the original intent of this legislation.

Health Care Spending

One of the major factors driving the health care reform debate is spending, including total spending, spending per person, and spending as a share of total economic output. Referring to Table 3.1, national health expenditures rose to $2,105.5 billion in 2006, 16.0 percent of GDP. Of this amount, 83.7 percent, or $1,762.0 billion, was for personal health care expenditures. This category of spending includes the purchase of all goods and services associated with individual health care, such as hospital care, the services of physicians and dentists, prescription drugs, vision care, home health care, and nursing home care.

Hospital Care Spending on hospital services increased to $648.2 billion in 2006. Hospital costs, valued as actual revenues received, experienced five years of accelerated growth between 1987 and 1991. For much of the decade of the 1990s, the growth in hospital spending moderated due primarily to aggressive cost-control efforts on the part of private payers. From 2000 to 2005, hospital spending grew at a compound rate of 7.62 percent, increasing concerns that spending would continue to accelerate. Hospital care accounted for 36.8 percent of personal health care spending, and patients paid for approximately 3 percent of hospital care out-of-pocket.

Physicians' Services Spending on physicians' services amounted to 25.4 percent of the total spent on personal health care in 2006. The total of $447.6 billion tends to mask the importance of physicians in the health care sector. Even though only 25 cents of every medical care dollar flows directly to physicians, they are indirectly responsible for most of the rest. Physicians admit patients to hospitals, recommend surgeries, prescribe drugs and eyeglasses, and in general oversee the entire health care delivery system. Roughly 10 percent of physicians' services are financed by patient out-of-pocket payments.

Prescription Drugs and Other Medical Products Consumers spent $216.7 billion on pharmaceuticals and another $59.3 billion on other medical products in 2006. This category accounts for 15.7 percent of personal health care spending and is one of the fastest growing categories of spending. Patients pay only 22 percent of all prescription drugs out-of-pocket.

Other Personal Health Care Spending Other spending includes payments for dentists' services and other professional services, nursing home care, and home health services. When combined, these categories of care accounted for approximately 18.6 percent of all personal health care spending. Nursing home care amounted to $124.9 billion and 7.3 percent of total personal health care spending in 2006, making it the fourth largest spending category. Dental services accounted for $91.5 billion, and other professional services, $58.9 billion. Home health spending at $52.7 billion has increased four times since 1990.

Prospects for the Future The average American consumed $7,026 in medical care in 2006. At this level, United States per capita spending on medical care is anywhere

National Center for Health Statistics (NCHS) is the principal health statistics agency in the United States. Its goal is to provide accurate, relevant, and timely statistical information that will guide actions and policies to improve the health of the American people.

http://www.cdc.gov/nchs/

Table 3.1: National Health Expenditures, Select Years in billions of dollars (unless otherwise stated)

Category	1960	1970	1980	1990	1995	2000	2003	2004	2005	2006
Hospital Care	$ 9.2	$27.6	$101.0	$251.6	$ 340.7	$ 417.1	$ 525.4	$ 564.4	$ 605.5	648.2
Physician and Clinical Services	5.4	14.0	47.1	157.5	220.5	288.6	366.7	393.6	422.6	447.6
Dental Services	2.0	4.7	13.3	31.5	44.5	62.0	76.9	81.5	86.6	91.5
Other Professional Services	0.4	0.7	3.6	18.2	28.5	39.1	49.0	52.4	56.2	58.9
Home Health Care	0.1	0.2	2.4	12.6	30.5	30.5	38.0	42.7	47.9	52.7
Nursing Home Care	0.8	4.0	19.0	52.6	74.1	95.3	110.5	115.2	120.7	124.9
Prescription Drugs	2.7	5.5	12.0	40.3	60.9	120.6	174.2	188.8	199.7	216.7
Other Medical Products	2.3	5.0	13.6	33.7	40.9	49.5	54.8	55.9	57.6	59.3
Other Personal Health Care	0.6	1.2	3.3	9.6	23.0	37.0	50.3	53.2	56.8	62.2
Personal Health Care	**$23.3**	**$62.9**	**$215.3**	**$607.5**	**$ 863.7**	**$1,139.6**	**$1,445.9**	**$1,547.7**	**$1,653.7**	**$1,762.0**
Government Administration and Net Cost of Private Health Insurance	1.2	2.8	12.2	39.2	58.1	81.8	121.0	129.0	133.6	145.4
Public Health Activities	0.4	1.4	6.4	20.0	31.0	43.4	53.8	53.9	56.3	58.7
Noncommercial Biomedical Research	0.7	2.0	5.4	12.7	18.3	25.6	35.5	38.8	40.6	41.8
New Construction	1.9	5.8	14.5	34.7	45.4	63.2	76.3	83.0	89.1	97.6
National Health Expenditures	**$27.5**	**$74.9**	**$253.9**	**$714.0**	**$1,016.5**	**$1,353.6**	**$1,732.4**	**$1,852.3**	**$1,973.3**	**$2,105.5**
Per Capita Personal Spending (dollars)	$ 126	$ 301	$931	$2,397	$ 3,214	$ 4,033	$ 4,967	$ 5,264	$ 5,572	$ 5,879
Per Capita National Spending (dollars)	$ 148	$ 356	$1,102	$2,813	$ 3,783	$ 4,790	$ 5,952	$ 6,301	$ 6,649	$ 7,026
National Spending as a Percent of GDP	5.2	7.2	9.1	12.3	13.7	13.8	15.8	15.9	15.9	16.0

Source: Centers for Medicare and Medicaid Services (CMS) Web site (accessed September 13, 2007). http://www.cms.hhs.gov/NationalHealthExpendData/02_NationalHealthAccountsHistorical.asp#TopOfPage from 40 to 300 percent higher than in other developed countries. Much of the difference is predictable: countries with higher living standards, measured by per capita income, spend more on promoting health.

Although high per capita spending paints a dramatic picture of spending disparities, the share of output devoted to medical care is more reflective of shifts in priorities. The percentage of GDP devoted to medical care spending has risen dramatically in the United States since the late 1960s, from less than 6 percent to 16 percent. In comparison, in most developed countries worldwide, the percentage ranges from 9 to 11 percent. Increasing health care expenditures as a percent of GDP may reflect a conscious choice on the part of the consuming public to spend more for health care. Or it may reflect an inefficient approach to health care financing and a piecemeal attempt at reform that to date has been concentrated on community hospital inpatient services, virtually ignoring every other aspect of medical care delivery.

Clearly, the United States spends more on medical care, and devotes a larger percentage of economic output to medical care, than any other country in the world. Although interesting, these facts ignore three important questions: What is a reasonable percentage of output to devote to medical care spending? How much can we afford? Are we getting our money's worth?

First of all, no one knows the ideal percentage of GDP that medical care spending should consume. We do know, however, that as income increases, spending on services, including health care, tends to increase. Wealthy countries spend proportionately more on medical care than poor countries. Since the United States is among the leaders in per capita income in the industrialized world, it should come as no surprise that U.S. medical care spending is the highest.

Second, a growing economy allows more resources to be devoted to those areas of the service sector where productivity may lag, including medical care, education, police protection, and the performing arts. In an economy where productivity is growing in most sectors and declining in none, consumers can have more of everything. It is merely a matter of devoting a different proportion of income to the production of the various sectors (Baumol, 1993). This reapportionment is accomplished by transferring resources from those sectors where productivity is increasing to those where it is stagnant.

Baumol refers to the phenomenon of lagging productivity in the service sector as the "cost disease of personal services." Applying his reasoning to medical care, the lag in productivity may be traced to two main factors: First, medical services are hard to standardize, making it difficult to automate. Before you can cure someone, it is necessary to diagnose the problem. Diagnosis and cure are done on a case-by-case basis. Thus, efficiency and productivity tend to lag behind the rest of the economy. Second, most people perceive that quality of care is positively correlated with the amount of time the physician spends with the patient. Thus, it is difficult to reduce the labor content of medical services. Physicians who speed up the examination process are often accused of shortchanging their patients. This same reasoning may also be applied to education, the performing arts, legal services, and insurance.

Finally, empirical evidence indicates that the increase in health care spending witnessed over the past 40 years provides substantial benefits to society that far outweigh the associated costs. Lichtenberg's (2002) analysis strongly supports the hypothesis that medical innovation in the form of new drugs and overall health care spending contributed positively to increased longevity between 1960 and 1997. In fact, he concluded that the most cost-effective way to increase life expectancy is through increased spending on new drug development. Cutler and McClellan

POLICY ISSUE

The U.S. spends significantly more on health care than any other country in the world. Are we getting our money's worth?

(2001) examine the benefits of technological change in five common conditions: heart attacks, low-birth weight infants, depression, breast cancer, and cataracts. They conclude that health care spending on these conditions is worth the cost of care.

Access to Care

According to recent census estimates, approximately 47 million Americans were without health insurance in 2005, creating mounting pressure on policy makers to come up with a plan to ensure access to medical care for all Americans (DiNavas, Proctor, and Smith, 2007). It is interesting to note that over 40 percent of the uninsured are between the ages of 18 and 34, age categories that use relatively less medical care.

Having no health insurance is not the same thing as having no access to medical care. In fact, the uninsured in this country receive about 60 percent of the medical care per capita of those with insurance. Nonelderly Americans who were privately insured spent $2,484 per capita on medical care in 2001, compared to $1,587 for the uninsured. In contrast, per capita spending in Canada was $1,173, approximately three-fourths of U.S. spending on the uninsured. While uninsured Americans are not going without care, they do receive less care than insured Americans (Hadley and Holahan, 2003).

The ideological struggle surrounding medical care reform has focused on two competing visions of universality. One vision argues for **universal coverage** in a system that requires mandatory participation, and the other supports **universal access** in a voluntary system in which everyone can buy health insurance if they desire to do so. The debate has not progressed far beyond an argument over the percentage of the population that would have health insurance under the various alternatives. To truly advance the debate, we must address the critical issue of individual rights versus social responsibility. Is access to medical care an individual right, or is it a social responsibility to provide access to those who cannot afford to pay for it? How we choose to answer this question will go a long way toward determining the future of medical care delivery and finance.

universal coverage
A guarantee that all citizens will have health insurance coverage regardless of income or health status. Coverage usually includes a well-defined benefits package and mandatory participation.

universal access
A guarantee that all citizens who desire health insurance will have access to health insurance regardless of income or health status. Those who cannot afford insurance are usually subsidized, and participation is voluntary.

Medical Outcomes

The third area of concern is the health of the population. Those critical of the U.S. delivery system cite the relatively poor health outcomes experienced in this country. The typical indicators used for comparisons are presented in Table 3.2. Male life expectancy at birth is the lowest among the six countries listed, at 75.2 years. Female life expectancy, also last among the six countries listed, is 80.4 years. Infant mortality rates are the highest in the United States, over two times the Japanese rate. Spending, both as a percentage of GDP and on a per capita basis, is much higher in the United States. In fact, per capita spending in Switzerland, ranked second behind the United States, is less than 65 percent of U.S. spending. Using these indicators, it appears that we may not be getting enough value for the money being spent. Is the U.S. system delivering an inferior product, or is there another way to look at the evidence?

The use of health indicators to praise or fault a delivery system ignores the contribution of the underlying demographic and social factors entirely. Health indicators reflect more than health care delivery. Life expectancy and infant mortality say a lot about environment, lifestyle choices, and social problems. The U.S. system must deal with a higher incidence of most of these problems than other industrialized countries—drug abuse, violence, reckless behavior, sexual promiscuity, and illegitimacy. These problems complicate the delivery of medical care and are, in part, responsible for the poor health indicators.

Table 3.2: Commonly Cited Health Indicators, 2005

Country	Life Expectancy at Birth[1] Males	Life Expectancy at Birth[1] Females	Infant Mortality Rate[2]	Health Care Spending (% of GDP)	Per Capita Health Care Spending[3]
Canada	77.8[4]	82.6[4]	5.3[4]	9.8	$3,326
France	76.7	83.8	3.6	11.1	3,374
Germany	76.2	81.8	3.9	10.7	3,287
Japan	78.5	85.5	2.8	8.0[4]	2,358[4]
Switzerland	78.7	83.9	4.2	11.6	4,177
United Kingdom	76.9	81.1	5.1	8.3	2,724
United States	75.2[4]	80.4[4]	6.8[4]	15.3	6,401

Source: *OECD Health Data 2007*, Paris: Organization for Economic Cooperation and Development, 2007.

[1] In years.
[2] Perinatal deaths per 1,000 live births.
[3] In PPP dollars.
[4] 2004.

Others argue that other indicators more accurately reflect the effectiveness of a health care system. In particular, how does the system treat people who are critically ill? The story is much different when disease-specific death rates are examined. Data from the OECD in Table 3.3 provide details for death rates per 100,000 for the top ten causes of death in the United States in 2002. Overall, the U.S. had the highest death rate that year. In the ten specific categories listed, the United States ranked in the top three in four of them. In the top two categories, the United States ranked high: third in heart disease and stroke and fifth in cancer. In fact, for almost every type of cancer, five-year survival rates in the United States are among the highest in the world.

In Table 3.4, Verdecchia and colleagues (2007) provide international comparisons of age-adjusted five-year survival rates for different types of cancer. Using data from European and U.S. cancer registries, they find that the United States has the highest survival rates for most types of cancer. For all malignancies, men in the United States have a 66.3 percent survival rate five years after diagnosis, and women have a survival rate of 62.9 percent. Whether Americans with cancer actually live longer is another issue. The higher five-year survival rates may be the result of earlier screening. No doubt when cancer is diagnosed earlier, there is a better chance that it can be controlled. So earlier screening is likely to lead to longer life expectancies.

As presented in Table 3.5, U.S. life expectancy at age 80 ranks second among males in the seven countries listed, behind only Japan, and third among females, behind Canada and Japan. The other three indicators shown in the table provide a measure of the efficiency of the system in delivering medical care. The U.S. has the lowest average acute inpatient length of stay at 5.6 days. Most government-run systems pay a fixed rate per hospital day, resulting in comparatively long average stays in the hospital. Over the course of the typical hospital stay, the later days are usually less costly than the earlier days. Keeping patients in the hospital longer provides the opportunity for hospitals to recover the higher costs of the first

Table 3.3: Crude Death Rate per 100,000 population, 2002
Top Ten Causes of Death, United States

Cause of Death	Canada[1]	France	Germany	Japan	Switzerland	UK	USA
All Causes	558.1	565.0	623.0	449.3	514.9	647.2	666.7
Diseases of the Circulatory System	175.5	149.7	268.1	129.8	175.6	240.1	235.0
Malignant Neoplasms	173.2	172.7	166.7	146.5	144.1	182.1	166.3
Accidents and Adverse Effects	38.3	51.5	32.7	42.5	37.9	27.5	52.3
Cerebrovascular Diseases	35.3	34.6	52.2	55.2	31.7	63.4	39.9
Diseases of the Nervous System	24.2	22.8	13.6	5.3	20.7	18.1	25.0
Diabetes Mellitus	19.6	11.4	16.6	5.9	12.9	7.5	20.9
Infectious and Parasitic Diseases including AIDS	8.2	11.0	8.2	9.4	5.8	5.7	18.0
Pneumonia and Influenza	10.2	10.0	12.7	34.5	11.5	31.4	15.3
Mental Disorders	14.1	16.7	6.7	1.7	20.3	15.8	12.5
Chronic Liver Disease and Cirrhosis	6.9	11.7	15.4	7.1	NA	10.1	9.5

Source: *OECD Health Data 2007*, Paris: Organization for Economic Cooperation and Development, 2007.

[1] 1997.

Table 3.4: Age-Adjusted 5-year Survival Rates
2000–2002 (In percentages)

Country	Colorectal	Breast Cancer	Prostate Cancer	All types (Men)	All types (Women)
France	59.9	NA	NA	NA	NA
Germany	61.2	78.2	85.3	50.0	58.8
Italy	59.4	83.7	85.0	49.8	59.7
Sweden	59.8	86.3	82.5	60.3	61.7
Switzerland	63.8	84.5	87.3	54.6	61.1
United Kingdom[1]	51.8	77.8	NA	44.8	52.7
Europe average	56.2	79.0	77.5	47.3	55.8
United States	65.5	90.1	99.3	66.3	62.9

Source: Verdecchia et al., 2007.

[1] England only.

Table 3.5:   Other Important Health Indicators, 2004

Country	Life Expectancy at Age 80[1]		Acute Care Inpatient Length of Hospital Stay	Hospital Beds per 1,000 Population	Physicians per 1,000 Population
	Males	Females			
Canada	8.1	10.0	7.3	2.9	2.1
France	7.8[3]	9.7[3]	5.5	3.8	3.4
Germany	7.2[2]	8.5[2]	8.7	6.4	3.4
Japan	8.4	11.2	20.2	8.4	2.0
Switzerland	7.5[2]	9.3[2]	8.8	3.9	3.8
United Kingdom	7.1[3]	8.6[3]	6.6	3.2	2.3
United States	8.2	9.8	5.6	2.8	2.4

Source: *OECD Health Data 2007,* Paris: Organization of Economic Cooperation and Development, 2007.

[1] In years.
[2] 2003.
[3] 2002.

few days. Longer stays translate into a need for more hospital beds per capita, representing a waste of hospital resources. Predictably, the United States has the fewest number of hospital beds per 1,000 population.

The United States ranks third in terms of the number of physicians per 1,000 population. When physician payments are based on established fee schedules, physicians are able to compensate for low fees by requiring extensive follow-up visits. In France, with the second highest physician-to-population ratio, patients saw their physician an average of 6.6 times in 2004. In Japan, with the fewest physicians per capita, the average was 13.8. The typical American had 3.8 physician's visits that year. In general, patients find it easier to schedule appointments in the United States, and they spend more time with their physicians during each appointment.

THE COMPETITIVE MARKET MODEL

Adam Smith asserted in his famous treatise, *The Wealth of Nations,* that individual decision making is motivated by self-interest. Guided by the "invisible hand" of the market, this self-serving behavior, in turn, serves to promote the interests of others. In other words, when markets exhibit certain ideal conditions, or perfectly competitive conditions, optimizing behavior on the part of individuals and firms leads to efficient outcomes.

Following the traditions established by Smith and the classical school of economics, modern-day economists evaluate markets according to the twin criteria of efficiency and equity. There are two aspects of efficiency—**allocative efficiency** and **technical efficiency**. Allocative efficiency may be viewed as efficiency in the final distribution of consumption. Consumers buy a good until the benefits received from the last unit purchased equals the price.[2] Thus, everyone purchasing a good

Key Concept 4
Self-Interest

allocative efficiency
The situation in which producers make the goods and services that consumers desire. For every item, the marginal cost of production is less than or equal to the marginal benefit received by consumers.

technical efficiency
Efficiency in production, or cost efficiency.

---

[2] Downward-sloping demand curves are implied from the law of diminishing returns, indicating that the last unit of a good purchased has a marginal value equal to its market price.

places a marginal value on the good at least equal to its market price. When everyone pays the same price for the good, there is no way to reallocate consumption from consumers to nonconsumers without lowering overall consumer welfare.

Technical efficiency may be thought of as efficiency in production, or cost efficiency. In perfectly competitive markets, producers must minimize costs to maximize profits. When all producers pay the same input prices, goods and services that are produced will have marginal valuations that are higher than goods and services that could have been produced with the same resources. In summary, perfect competition guarantees both allocative and technical efficiency.

Key Concept 8
Efficiency

Equity considerations are also important when evaluating economic systems. Even though the issue of equity is based on some standard of fairness, ideological differences dictate whether that standard is defined either in terms of outcomes or in terms of opportunities. For example, one economist might define equity in terms of final outcomes. In this case, any differences in infant mortality rates between, say, whites and African Americans would be viewed as inequitable and obviously the result of unequal access to the medical care system. How else could you possibly explain the large gulf between the 5.7 deaths per 1,000 live births among white Americans and 13.6 among African Americans (Matthews and MacDorman, 2007)?

POLICY ISSUE

How important is equity in determining the effectiveness of a health care delivery system?

Another economist might have a unique perspective on the same issue. Defining equity in terms of opportunities rather than outcomes, the same disparities in mortality rates would be interpreted another way. From this perspective, even in a world of equal opportunities, there will be varied outcomes. Blaming the differences on unequal access ignores demographic differences such as age, education, and marital status between the two population cohorts. Additionally, differences in lifestyle choices are also important, including the decision to smoke cigarettes, drink alcohol, or take drugs during pregnancy. Whether defined in terms of outcomes or opportunities, equity has become an important component in the evaluation of markets, especially medical markets.

Few people will argue against the importance of an equitable distribution of health care availability. But health care is like any other desirable commodity: It is subject to an equity–efficiency trade-off. Access to medical care differs according to individual circumstances, such as age, gender, income, geographic location, and insurance coverage. No matter how much we may desire equity, it comes at a price; mandating equity may be desirable, but it is costly.

The formal argument for competitive markets is based on the notions of economic efficiency and social equity, but some favor competition simply because it guards against the concentration of market power and promotes consumer sovereignty. Competition among providers and their desire to satisfy consumer preferences ensures against consumer exploitation. Consumers always have alternative sources of supply in competitive markets. Cost-conscious behavior on the part of consumers increases their sensitivity to price changes. Individual providers face perfectly elastic demand curves when cost-conscious consumers have alternative sources of supply. Consequently, prices of goods and services equal the marginal cost of production.

Key Concept 7
Competition

When markets work, prices reflect the valuation of forgone opportunities. As equilibrium is reached, marginal values and prices converge, and the value of the goods and services that are produced is greater than the value of the goods and services that could have been produced with the same resources. In other words, if individuals in society placed a higher value on the last dollar spent on medical care than on the last dollar spent on, say, education, then they would demand that more be spent on medical care and less on education, until the marginal valuations were equal.

MARKET FAILURE

According to Murphy's Law, if anything can go wrong, it will. Various imperfections in medical markets make the task of delivering a product equitably and efficiently more difficult. When the underlying assumptions of competitive markets are not met, markets fail to deliver the **optimal output levels** (Rice, 1998). Markets fail to allocate resources optimally when firms have market power, when there are externalities in consumption and production, and when the good produced is a public good.

Market Power

Any departure from perfect competition—whether it be monopoly, oligopoly, cartel, monopolistic competition, monopsony, or any other market structure imperfection—violates the optimality considerations discussed earlier. A profit-maximizing firm with market power sets prices at levels that exceed marginal costs. To maintain those prices, the firm must restrict output to levels that are less than optimum. Prices will be too high, costs will be too high, resources will be underutilized, and society will suffer an economic loss.

Market power is depicted graphically by any departure from perfectly elastic demand curves. Figure 3.1 points out the differences in pricing and output between firms in perfectly competitive markets and those with market power. When demand curves are perfectly elastic, they are drawn as horizontal lines. Profit maximizers set marginal revenue (MR) equal to marginal cost (MC). With price equal to marginal revenue, $MR = MC$ at the same output level (Q_0) where $P_0 = MC$ (the condition for allocative efficiency).

Market power gives a firm some control over its pricing decisions. Raising price reduces quantity sold without the complete loss of customers. With a downward-sloping demand curve, the firm's marginal revenue is less than the price it charges. Setting MR equal to MC now results in a lower output level (Q_1) and the ability to charge a higher price (P_1). Higher prices, lower output, and underutilization of resources result in a loss in welfare as measured by the loss in consumer and producer surplus.

In spite of these problems, monopoly may still be the most effective way to organize production in a market. When production is subject to economies of scale, the long-run average cost curve declines continuously. Competition will

Key Concept 9
Market Failure

optimal output level
A market equilibrium in which the marginal benefit received from every unit of output is greater or equal to the marginal cost of producing each unit. The social optimum is that output level at which the marginal benefit of the last unit produced is equal to its marginal cost.

Key Concept 3
Marginal Analysis

Figure 3.1: The Consequences of Market Power on Price and Output

natural monopoly
A firm becomes a natural monopoly based on its ability to provide a good or service at a lower cost than anyone else such as to satisfy consumer demand completely.

result in the exit of all but one firm. That remaining firm, the **natural monopoly**, will not set price competitively; and since $P > MC$, output is not provided at its optimal level. To correct this misallocation of resources, the most effective option may be regulation.[3]

Using Figure 3.2 to illustrate this point, suppose the firm has a long-run average cost curve that is downward-sloping as it crosses the market demand curve. Under these circumstances, a single firm can supply enough output to satisfy consumer demand and can do so at progressively lower unit costs.[4] Shielded from competition from rival firms, the monopolist has no compelling reason to be efficient. Focusing solely on profit maximization, the firm will produce less than the optimal level of output (Q_0), and prices will be higher than if the market were competitive (P_0). To correct this problem, government price controllers often try to establish a maximum price the monopolist can charge that more closely approximates the perfectly competitive solution. Setting a price at P_1, for example, enables the firm to earn a normal return on its investment and produce at higher output levels (Q_1).

Market power in an input market also causes an inefficient allocation of resources. A monopsonist, as the sole buyer of a particular resource, faces an upward-sloping supply curve instead of a perfectly elastic supply curve. As a result, the firm has some discretion over the price it pays for the resource. If more is desired, then the firm must pay a higher price. If less is desired, then prices fall accordingly. The results are shown in Figure 3.3, where the monopsonist faces a situation in which the marginal cost of the resource is greater than the price of the resource. Instead of setting demand equal to supply and paying P_0 to employ Q_0 units of the resource, the monopsonist equates demand—its assessment of the marginal value of the resource used in production—with the marginal cost of the resource, and employs

Figure 3.2: Regulating the Natural Monopoly

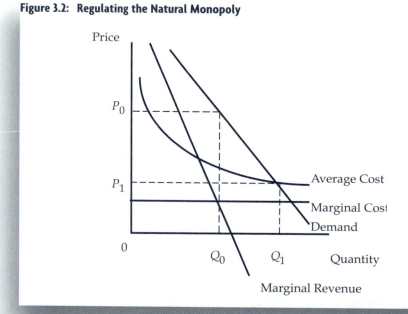

---

[3] Certain tax and subsidy schemes might actually be more efficient, but discussion of these alternatives is beyond the scope of this presentation.

[4] Because price, represented by the demand curve, is above the average cost curve at every point, the firm can increase sales by lowering price and still make an economic profit.

**Figure 3.3:   The Consequences of Market Power on Price and Output
in Resource Markets**

Q_1 units of the output. At this level of utilization, the monopsonist has only to pay
P_1 to satisfy the firm's demand for resources.

Market power in the resource market enables firms to employ fewer resources
and pay lower prices for their use than if the market were perfectly competitive.
The result of this lost output is lost income to resource owners and fewer goods
and services available to consumers. In summary, market power insulates a firm
from the competitive forces that ensure allocative and technical efficiency, resulting
in a loss to society.

BACK-OF-THE-ENVELOPE

Monopsony: When Buyers Have Market Power

Market power on the buyers' side, called *monopsony,* gives buyers more
leverage in determining the prices they pay for goods and services. If
buyers have the ability to consolidate their demand under the control of
a single collective, they may have market power. In this case, the monopsonist would function as a buyers' union. In today's language, this union
would be called an *alliance* or a *cooperative*. The larger the cooperative,
the more control the group can assert over the prices charged to its
members. As already discussed, equilibrium for the monopsonist occurs
at a price and output level that is below the level that would exist in
perfectly competitive markets, representing lost economic welfare.

Even with the lost productivity, some still argue that monopsony
provides a net benefit to society. Proponents of market power for buyers
agree that the unilateral exercise of market power should be illegal
on either side of the market. They contend, however, that providers in
medical markets already exercise a significant degree of market power
on the sellers' side of the market. The use of power on the buyers' side
represents a countervailing force that encourages competitive behavior
among sellers and promotes the efficient use of resources.

The formal explanation of this phenomenon is described in most
intermediate microeconomics textbooks under the heading "**bilateral
monopoly**." A bilateral monopoly exists in a market when there is only
one buyer seeking the output of a single seller. In other words, bilateral

continued

bilateral monopoly
When there is monopoly
on the seller's side of the
market and monopsony
on the buyer's side.

monopoly is characterized by monopsony on the demand side and monopoly on the supply side. In the following graph, *D, MR,* and *MC* are the demand, marginal revenue, and marginal cost curves confronting the monopolist seller. Profit maximizing price and output, P_2 and Q_2, are determined by $MC = MR$ at point *A*.

A monopsonist with absolute control over demand could force the monopolist to behave like a firm in a perfectly competitive market. Under these conditions, *MC* is also the firm's supply curve. Likewise, MC_B becomes the relevant marginal cost of buying an additional unit of the output. The monopsonist attempts to equate the marginal cost of buying with its own marginal valuation of the product (MV_P) at point *B*. At the optimal level of output, Q_1, the monopsonist pays the lowest price the provider is willing to accept and still cover marginal cost, P_1.

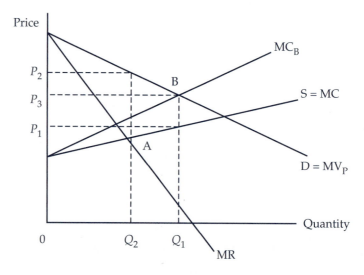

In terms of the final price, the negotiated outcome will fall somewhere between the two extremes, P_1 and P_2. The exact solution depends on the relative bargaining strengths of the two sides. The monopoly provider enters the negotiations wanting a higher price and lower output than the monopsony buyer. To avoid an impasse, the monopolist will likely offer somewhat lower prices and slightly more output. The monopsonist will agree to pay more than P_1 if the monopolist provides more than Q_2. As long as price does not fall below P_3, the final output level will fall between Q_1 and Q_2. Thus, for bilateral monopoly to benefit society, bargaining strengths of buyers and sellers must be approximately equal. If either side has a disproportionate share of the bargaining power, it will be able to tilt the balance in its favor to the detriment of society. (Technical note: Relative bargaining strengths and the final outcome will be different if the supply curve is so steeply sloped that $Q_2 > Q_1$. In this case, the monopolist wants to provide more output than the monopsonist wants to buy, weakening the monopolist's bargaining position.)

Source: Michael L. Ile, "When Health Care Payers Have Market Power," *Journal of the American Medical Association* 263(14), April 11, 1990, 1981–1982,1986.

externality
A cost or benefit that spills over to parties not directly involved in the actual transaction and is thus ignored by the buyer and seller.

Externalities

Sometimes the actions taken by individuals in the process of producing or consuming will have an effect on the welfare of others. An **externality** may be either positive or negative, depending on whether it benefits or harms other people. By maintaining her property, a homeowner generates a positive externality for all her neighbors. Not only is it pleasing to look at a freshly painted house and well-kept garden, but the market values of surrounding properties are enhanced at the same time.

Examples of negative externalities abound. Anyone smoking a cigar in a crowded room imposes costs on everyone else in the room. Everyone has less fresh air to breathe than if the smoker were forced to internalize all the costs of his smoking. A factory that dumps toxic waste into a nearby river shifts some of the cost of production (i.e., waste disposal) onto those people who live downstream from the plant. The same can be said about acid rain, traffic congestion, and the many other examples of negative externalities that could be listed.

Externalities affect economic efficiency, and normal market mechanisms have no way of accounting for them. Decision makers are not required to absorb the costs of negative externalities and have no way to capture the benefits of positive externalities. The result is a level of output that is nonoptimal.

Externalities exist as by-products of the decision to produce and consume. Because formal markets do not exist for these by-products, they are produced in nonoptimal quantities. Take, for example, the case of automobile emissions in a crowded metropolitan area. By choosing to drive your own car to work, you impose costs on others in the form of carbon monoxide emissions from the exhaust. A large percentage of the costs of commuting are internalized. You pay for the car, the gasoline, and the insurance. But your fellow commuters pay the costs that cannot be internalized, namely the costs of the by-products of your commute: traffic congestion and air pollution.

Figure 3.4 illustrates the impact of an externality in a private market, the daily commute to work or school. Externalities arise because the driver does not internalize the full cost of the commute. Graphically, the vertical distance between the marginal social cost (MSC) curve and the marginal private cost (MPC) curve represents the external costs that the driver forces others to pay. Individual decision makers determine their own commuter miles by equating marginal benefit (MB) with MPC. Given the additional costs that society at large must pay, the number of commuter miles actually driven (Q_m) is greater than the optimal number (Q^*). To incorporate these externalities into individual decision making requires some form of collective action to force commuters to pay the full costs of their actions. For

Figure 3.4: The External Costs of a Daily Commute

example, through their elected representatives, voters may decide to reduce the number of commuter miles driven by private automobiles by erecting toll booths on all major freeways or simply forcing everyone who drives into the city to pay a commuter tax. In either case, the goal is to force private decision makers to take into account the external costs of their actions. By moving the *MPC* closer to the *MSC*, the number of commuter miles driven will approach its optimal level, Q^*.

In the case of positive externalities, the competitive output rate will be too small if the decision maker cannot capture the externalities generated. The problem emerges because the marginal private benefit is less than the marginal social benefit. When marginal cost and marginal private benefit are equated, the resulting output is less than optimal.

BACK-OF-THE-ENVELOPE

Optimal Output: Private versus Public Goods

The market demand for a private good is derived by horizontally summing all the individual demands. In this case, total output is the sum of the amounts consumed by each individual in the market. When goods are rival goods, the amount consumed by one individual cannot be consumed by anyone else. In the diagram below, assume two consumers with demand curves D_1 and D_2. Equating market demand (ΣD) with supply results in a price of P_0 and an optimal output level of Q^*. Given the market price, each consumer will demand a level of output where price is equal to the marginal cost of production.

In the case of a public good, the market demand curve is determined by the group's willingness to pay for a given level of output. (In this case, the group consists of two people, 1 and 2.) Since the good is nonrival, the market demand curve is derived by summing the individual demand curves vertically, instead of horizontally, as was the case for a private (rival) good. At the optimal level of output (Q^*), the group is willing to pay P_3, the sum of P_1 and P_2. Remember that Q^* is the optimal level for the good, because

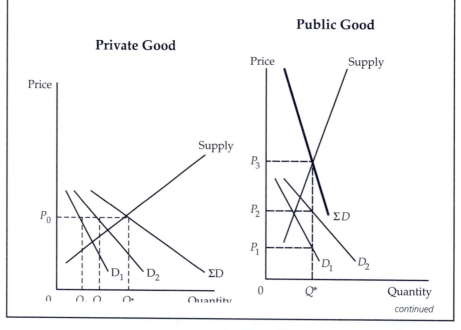

continued

at that level, the marginal social benefit is equal to the marginal social cost of production.

In the society at large, identifying the marginal social benefit curve is problematic. No one is required to reveal his or her individual marginal valuations, so determining society's willingness to pay becomes a challenge. Some individuals will find it worthwhile to become **free riders**. Because of peer pressure, the free-rider problem may not be a big issue when there are only two people in the group. But in a large society, no one person places a high enough marginal value on the good to ensure its provision. In other words, the marginal costs are substantially higher than any one person's or small group's demand (D_s in the diagram below). Under these circumstances, the market simply will not ensure the production of the good; its cost will simply be too high for anyone to absorb without collective action.

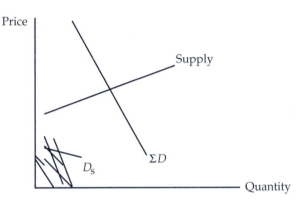

free rider
An individual who does not buy insurance, knowing that in the event of a serious illness, medical care will be provided free of charge.

Public Goods

Markets distribute goods efficiently when people spend their own money to enjoy the benefits of consumption. The market for Nike shoes works because those unwilling to pay the price for Nikes do not own Nikes. The market mechanism provides purchasers with the benefits of consumption and excludes nonpurchasers from receiving those benefits. Additionally, the benefits flow to specific individuals. Consumption of a crispy taco by one person does not satisfy the hunger of another.

In certain situations, these two characteristics do not hold. In fact, many important goods, such as national defense and air traffic control, do not exhibit them fully. Nonexcludable and **nonrival goods** are called *public goods*. Nonexcludability in the distribution of a good results when the costs of preventing nonpayers from consuming are high, making it difficult to impose prices on these individuals. Once a strategic national defense system is operational, there is no way to exclude individuals from its protective umbrella simply because they refuse to pay their share of the costs.

Nonrivalry in consumption means that more than one person can enjoy the benefits of consuming a commodity without affecting the enjoyment of the other. One person's consumption does not reduce the benefit received by someone else. In technical terms, the marginal cost of providing the good to additional consumers is zero. For example, after the Army Corps of Engineers builds a levy, any number of houses may be built in the flood plain without increasing the marginal cost of flood control. If an air traffic control system is in place, the marginal cost of monitoring the flight path of an additional aircraft is zero.

nonrival goods
A good or service which does not, when consumed by one individual, limit the amount available to anyone else.

nonexcludable goods
A good or service that is difficult to limit to a specific group of consumers. In other words, if the item is available to anyone, it becomes available to everyone.

Serious efficiency problems arise when we attempt to provide **nonexcludable goods** through private markets. To understand the problem, note the difference between the provision of excludable and nonexcludable goods. Transactions involving private (excludable) goods take place in markets as long as the individual's marginal valuation of that good exceeds its price. Individuals have no incentive to lie about the marginal value placed on a good. Because of excludability, if you understate the marginal value you place on a good, you run the risk of not getting the good and losing out on the marginal benefits of consumption. If you have ever witnessed an auction of any kind, you are familiar with this concept. Marginal valuations are reflected in the prices individuals are willing to pay for items that are being auctioned. You must make those marginal valuations known, or you run the risk of finding yourself empty-handed at the end of the auction.

In contrast, when goods are nonexcludable, there is an incentive for individuals to understate their true marginal valuations. If I can enjoy all the benefits of consumption without paying for that privilege, why pay? Those individuals who refuse to pay for a good while still enjoying the benefits of consumption are called *free riders* (some might even call them *freeloaders*). Public television provides a good example of the free-rider problem. The number of people who watch public television far exceeds the number who subscribe. Of course, some ride free, but others have to pay, or no one rides at all. And that's the point. Private markets tend to undersupply nonexcludable goods.

The case of public goods is simply a special kind of positive externality. So to ensure its availability at optimal levels, public provision of the good may be required. Governments can require individuals to participate in paying for goods through the power to tax. Clearly, all goods publicly provided are not public goods. Whether the good is provided by a government entity is not the issue. Governments often engage in the provision of private goods, for example, by staging concerts in the park and collecting garbage. In both cases, nonpayers may be excluded from consumption at very little cost, eliminating the problem of the free rider.

Even strong defenders of the market admit that private markets do not always provide goods and services at efficient levels. But those critical of market outcomes must address the issue of whether the government can do a better job. Is government provision any more efficient than private provision? Does it result in a more equitable distribution of resources? Is a more equitable distribution of resources worth the cost? We will focus on this question later in the chapter.

POLICY ISSUE

Is government provision of medical care more efficient than provision through the private market?

merit good
A good whose benefits are not fully appreciated by the average consumer and thus should be provided collectively.

ISSUES IN MEDICAL CARE DELIVERY

Medical Care as a "Merit Good"

Economic models predicting consumer behavior usually assume, among other things, that individuals know what they want and are able to rank their preferences. But often people avoid what is good for them and choose items that are actually harmful. Recognizing this fact, Musgrave (1959) classified certain goods as **merit goods** to describe commodities that ought to be provided even if private demand is lacking. Since merit goods have benefits that are not fully appreciated by the average consumer, their consumption should be encouraged through collective action.

Many would place medical care in the merit-good category. Individuals lacking the ability to fully appreciate the importance of primary and preventive care will underconsume when it comes to this valuable commodity.

continued

Whether this classification is merely a case of imposing preferences on society, or whether it is a genuine merit-good situation, is open to debate.

The usual arguments used to justify government involvement in medical care delivery and finance include market failure, information problems, third-party financing, and even merit goods. These arguments are often compelling, if not always convincing. But when using the merit-goods argument, we must be careful that we are not merely replacing a personal value judgment — that everyone is entitled to medical care — with formal terminology to justify our personal preferences (Baumol and Baumol, 1981).

Sources: Richard A. Musgrave, The Theory of Public Finance, New York: McGraw-Hill, 1959; William J. Baumol and Hilda Baumol, "Book Review," *Journal of Political Economy* 89(2), April 1981, 425–428.

MARKET FAILURE IN MEDICAL MARKETS

The obvious starting point in analyzing market failure in medical markets begins with the three causes of market failure discussed above. How prevalent are monopolies in medical markets? Are there significant externalities in consumption and production? Is medical care a public good, nonexcludable in distribution and nonrival in consumption?

BACK-OF-THE-ENVELOPE

The Economics of Subsidizing Childhood Immunizations

Public health officials recommend that children receive a full round of vaccinations — including polio, measles, mumps, and whooping cough — before the age of two. To the extent that any children are not vaccinated, the entire childhood immunization program is undermined. The children who go unvaccinated are more likely to get sick, which lowers their welfare. They are also more likely to serve as carriers of the disease and infect others, which lowers the welfare of everybody else. The situation describes the classic case of positive externalities in consumption, where the marginal private benefits (MPB) fall short of the marginal social benefits (MSB).

POLICY ISSUE

Should everyone be required to participate in an immunization program designed to protect the entire population against a communicable disease?

continued

Consumers, unable to capture the total benefit of their decision to vaccinate, respond only to private benefits. Thus, market demand is the sum of the individual marginal private benefits (MPB). The market would equilibrate at point A, where $MPB = MSC$ with price equal to P_1 and the equilibrium number of vaccinations Q_1. Due to the positive externalities associated with vaccination, the marginal social benefit curve (MSB) is above MPB. Welfare maximization would equate MSB with MSC at point C and produce Q_2 output at a price P_2. Without a built-in mechanism that enables consumers to capture these external benefits, the relevant demand curve is MPB instead of MSB. Equating demand with supply results in equilibrium at P_1 and Q_1. Output falls short of its optimal level, and a social loss depicted by the triangle ABC occurs.

One way to improve social welfare would be to subsidize consumption. A subsidy equal to P_2 would remove the gap between MPB and MSB. Graphically, this is shown by the dashed line labeled "MPB + subsidy." With the subsidy, demand is now D^*, and the equilibrium quantity is Q_2. Providers receive a price of P_2, and consumers receive the vaccinations for a net price of zero (P_2 minus the subsidy). Under these circumstances, MSB equals MSC, output is at its optimal level, and economic welfare is maximized. Economists almost always argue in favor of subsidies for the private provision of goods and services over direct government provision.

POLICY ISSUE

Are subsidies to private providers better than direct government provision when the goal is to improve economic welfare?

Traditional Sources of Market Failure

Even though absolute market power in medical markets may be hard to find, lack of competition can still be a significant problem. Most metropolitan areas are served by more than one hospital due to the simple fact that economies of scale in the hospital industry are exhausted at relatively low levels of capacity. Even in communities as small as 180,000 people, two or three hospitals providing most general services could coexist. In smaller communities, the lack of competition presents a greater challenge for market proponents. In these small markets, some inpatient services must be shared to avoid substantial inefficiencies (Kronick et al., 1993).

Even in larger communities with multiple facilities, some providers may have a degree of market power. There are some services and procedures that exhibit significant economies of scale, such as organ transplantation and various imaging technologies that include CT scans (computerized tomography) and MRIs (magnetic resonance imaging).

Although a pure monopoly may be difficult to find, firms often engage in collusive behavior to avoid competition. Recognizing that it is in their collective interest not to engage in price competition, providers differentiate their products to make direct price comparisons difficult. There is competition along the lines of quality and the number of services offered, but not price. Differentiation is often accomplished when providers agree to specialize, for example, with one hospital offering cardiac care and another obstetric care. This type of market segmentation is relatively easy, because most medical care is provided locally.

Externalities arise in medical care in a number of circumstances. The most obvious type of externality is associated with public health programs. Modern society can be a breeding ground for all sorts of communicable diseases. The ability of the Public Health Service to enforce health regulations and monitor contagious diseases serves to improve public health. Related activities include the provision of clean water, clean air, and adequate sewage disposal, which greatly reduce the incidence of diseases such as cholera and dysentery. In addition, immunization against mumps, measles, small pox, polio, and whooping cough offers protection for more than one individual. The benefits extend to the entire population by eliminating potential carriers of the diseases. In other words, the incremental value to society is greater than the value to the individual alone. In a private market, fewer vaccinations would occur than is socially optimal and may call for collective action in the form of mandates or subsidies or both.

ISSUES IN MEDICAL CARE DELIVERY

The Lessons from SARS

For those traveling to Canada, Europe, and Asia during the spring of 2003, SARS became a household word. Severe acute respiratory syndrome, or SARS for short, leaped onto the front pages of newspapers from Toronto to Singapore to Tokyo. Reminiscent of the 1995 movie *Outbreak*, in which a lethal virus spreads from an African monkey, SARS challenged the ability of the public health community to react to the real-life outbreak of a deadly disease.

How easy is it to control a new infectious disease? That depends on how it is transmitted, how hard it is to catch, whether apparently healthy individuals can spread the disease, and whether the organism can find an appropriate host in a nonhuman species. The SARS challenge was complicated by the fact that the disease originated in China, and Chinese authorities failed to report the existence of SARS for months, and then tried to hide the extent of the spread of the disease.

With no treatment yet available, efforts to control the disease have been very crude: identifying everyone infected, tracing everyone they have come into contact with, and isolating them all. Tracing everyone may be impossible, so the only option may be mass quarantines, school closures, and cancelled vacations and holidays.

All things considered, SARS was relatively mild as far as epidemics go. As of June 11, 2003, the World Health Organization (WHO) had received reports of 8,435 probable cases from 29 countries, including 70 from the United States. There were 789 deaths, translating into a mortality ratio of 9.4 percent. The world community was lucky this time. We may not be so lucky when the next deadly bug comes along. Designer facemasks may not be enough to protect us from a bug that is more contagious than SARS. In the meantime, the public health community must come up with better systems and procedures to effectively enforce large-scale quarantines to give the medical research community time to study the infectious disease agents and come up with the appropriate medical response.

The next time you hear reports of some strange illness in a remote corner of the globe, don't think it will have no impact on your life. Let us hope that the health authorities have learned valuable lessons from SARS.

Source: Daniel Haydon and Olivia Judson, "A Health Warning to the World," *Financial Times*, May 9, 2003, 13.

http://

Many philanthropic organizations are using the Internet to advance their messages. The United Way of America has an extensive network of activities funded largely through payroll deductions. It may be found at

http://www.unitedway.org

http://

Research for the prevention, detection, and treatment of cancer is the goal of the American Cancer Society at

http://www.cancer.org

http://

Raising funds to benefit children and its affiliated hospitals is the mission of the Children's Miracle Network at

http://www.cmn.org/

http://

Volunteer opportunities and fund-raising information may be found at the Web site for the Ronald McDonald Houses. Ronald McDonald House Charities may be found at

http://www.rmhc.com/

Many argue that social or philanthropic externalities are associated with the consumption of medical care. These consumption externalities arise because the healthy and economically well-to-do derive satisfaction, a type of social solidarity, from knowing that the sick and indigent also receive medical care. Individuals who share this philanthropic desire can and do join together and fund private foundations and medical organizations. The annual Jerry Lewis telethon provides individuals with the opportunity to unite in the fight against muscular dystrophy. Personal contributions to the United Way, the Ronald McDonald House, the Children's Miracle Network, the American Cancer Society, and numerous other national and local organizations advance the fight against certain diseases and provide access to medical treatments that might otherwise be prohibitively expensive.

Given the nature of the externality, even those who refuse to contribute enjoy the benefits of knowing that medical research is finding cures for certain diseases and that certain medical services are available for those who cannot afford to pay for them. If this consumption externality exists and is significant, then collective action through government can be used to provide medical care to that segment of the population that cannot afford to buy it privately. Those who would not contribute privately now share the responsibility through mandatory taxation. Collective action determines the nature of the subsidy, the level of taxation, and the method of distribution.

in-kind transfer
Welfare subsidies provided in the form of vouchers for specific goods and services, such as food stamps and Medicaid.

The medical subsidy is almost always an **in-kind transfer** rather than a cash payment. Beneficiaries prefer cash rather than services. They almost always find themselves better off with the cash. Donors generally prefer in-kind benefits because of the lack of guarantees that cash would be used for medical care. In fact, Waldo and colleagues (1989) indicate that a cash transfer to the elderly equivalent to their per capita share of Medicare would do more to improve their welfare than the current subsidy for medical services. It seems that donors—in this case, taxpayers—care about health differently than other aspects of the recipient's well-being, which includes whether the food they eat is healthy or whether the house they live in is adequately heated and cooled.

POLICY ISSUE

Should medical care subsidies take the form of direct cash payments or in-kind transfers?

Externalities may also be associated with exceptionally large medical expenditures. Frequently, those with incomplete or no health insurance coverage have medical bills that exceed their ability to pay. Faced with this event, they default on their obligation, and the community must pick up the tab. In other words, providers are forced to write off the expenses as bad debts and shift the costs of care onto privately insured patients.[5] The fact that we are unable, or at least unwilling, to exclude anyone from access to medical care for financial reasons gives rise to the problem of the free rider. For this reason, many advocate mandatory health insurance covering catastrophic (high-cost) episodes of illness. In this way, everyone would be forced to participate in the cost of providing medical care, and the free-rider problem would be moderated.

Pure medical research that has no easily captured commercial value fits the definition of a public good. This is the type of medical research that is packaged and published primarily in medical journals. Much of the information that is shared in this manner shows other medical practitioners ways of combining activities and procedures into a particular mode of treatment. Unless patentable medical devices are included in the procedures, it is difficult for those responsible for the discovery to capture the benefits of their research. Good examples include radial keratonomy and the use of lasers in ophthalmological surgery.

Many will argue that medical research should be treated as a public good and financed collectively through government. In this way, basic advances financed

---

[5] Medical care providers usually report the delinquent debtor to the appropriate credit bureau. This has become so common that many lenders, such as commercial banks and consumer credit companies, regularly ignore a default on a would-be borrower's credit history if the debt was associated with medical care (private conversation with Bart Cooper, GMAC).

by the taxpayer would belong in the public domain, freely available to potential users. The other side of the argument recognizes that academicians conduct much of our medical research. Working within the university and medical school setting, they are able to capture the benefits of their discoveries through the rules of promotion and tenure, so at least a portion of the benefits is translated into career enhancement opportunities and personal prestige. Some may choose to keep their findings out of the public domain in order to earn royalties or other payments.

To the extent that medical care has characteristics associated with market power among providers, externalities in production and consumption, and public goods, the level of services provided will fall short of the optimal level as defined by competitive markets.

POLICY ISSUE

Is medical research a public good, thus strengthening the argument in favor of government financing of basic medical research?

ISSUES IN MEDICAL CARE DELIVERY

Advertising Professional Services: The Case of Optometry

In most private markets, consumers gain access to important information through advertising. The argument against advertising professional services is based on the belief that advertising may mislead consumers, undermine quality, and ultimately raise prices. Professional associations representing medical practitioners have led the battle defending the long-standing restrictions on price advertising in medical markets.

Economic theory argues in favor of advertising in markets characterized by **asymmetric information** between buyers and sellers, where sellers have all the information and buyers have none. For example, advertising provides consumers with information on alternative sources of supply. This results in lower prices, because consumer demand for individual providers becomes more elastic. In addition, one of the goals of advertising is to increase consumer demand. To the extent that advertisers realize this benefit, they can take advantage of economies of scale in production and actually lower prices to consumers.

Although advertising may result in lower prices, its effect on product quality is less certain. In theory, high-quality providers have more to gain by advertising through repeat purchasers. In practice, however, low-quality providers advertise more. Ultimately, the effect of advertising on quality will be determined by consumer demand for quality and provider determination to produce quality, with the latter governed in large part by ethical standards established by the specific profession.

Considering all the evidence, a federal appeals court ruled in 1980 that physicians and other medical professionals could advertise prices and services. Kwoka (1984), studying the market of optometric services, was one of the first to examine the impact of advertising on prices and quality. Results indicated that advertisers' prices and quality were lower and that nonadvertisers' prices also fell. However, the quality of the services offered by nonadvertisers actually increased. Given a sufficiently large number of nonadvertisers, overall quality in the market increased. Kwoka estimated that quality-adjusted prices for optometric services fell by 20 percent as a result of advertising, so loosening restrictions on advertising in optometry actually improved economic welfare.

Source: John E. Kwoka, Jr., "Advertising and the Price and Quality of Optometric Services," *American Economic Review* 74(1), March 1984, 211–216.

asymmetric information
A situation in which information is unequally distributed between the individuals in a transaction. The person with more information will have an unfair advantage in determining the terms of any agreement.

POLICY ISSUE

Should physicians and other health care providers be allowed to advertise?

Imperfections in Medical Markets

Other imperfections contribute to the failure of medical markets to provide the socially optimal level of service (see Pauly, 1988). These imperfections include imperfect information, barriers to entry, and the prevalence of third-party payers.

Imperfect Information Lack of information presents serious problems in a market economy. In medical markets, the problems that arise may be even more serious. Most patients are poorly informed about virtually every aspect of the medical transaction. They are usually aware of their symptoms and syndromes, but seldom do they understand the underlying causes of their medical conditions. They have scarcely an opportunity to form a learned opinion about the physician's diagnosis or the prescribed treatment. In most cases, anything other than a complete recovery is not part of the expected outcome.

The overall lack of information available to patients is compounded by the difficulty in securing the information, measured in terms of time and expense. As a result, most patients rely almost exclusively on their provider to keep them informed on matters dealing with their medical condition, its diagnosis, and treatment alternatives. Patients also have little knowledge about price and quality differences among alternative providers. This imbalance of information between patient and provider, referred to as *asymmetric information*, has led to two important market defects.

First, patients are not able to judge price and quality differences among providers. As a result, providers can charge prices that are higher than the prevailing prices in the market for a given level of quality, or they may choose to offer a lower level of quality for a given price. The impact of this phenomenon can be seen in the variation in prices paid and the quantities of medical care provided to similar groups of patients. Evidence for these variations has been compiled by examining, for example, surgery rates for common procedures. In cases where alternative intervention strategies are not available—such as appendectomy, hernia repair, and hysterectomy—the variation in surgery rates is relatively low. But in cases where alternative treatments are available—such as tonsillectomy, disc surgery, and coronary artery bypass grafts—variation is high—up to four times the rate of the low-variance surgeries (Phelps, 1992).

The second problem may be described as an agency problem. The physician serves as the agent of the patient, and the patient delegates most of the decision-making authority to the physician. The expectation, in turn, is that the patient's best interests will be the top priority. The dual role of provider of services on the one hand and the agent in charge of information on the other creates a dilemma: The physician is in a position to induce the patient to purchase more medical care than is actually needed. Physicians can recommend not only medical care with little marginal value, medical care on the flat of the curve, but also medical care that may actually harm the patient. At the other extreme, enrollees in managed care organizations may find themselves denied care that offers positive net benefits, because it is not in the financial interest of the provider to offer that care.

This information problem does not mean that medical markets are hopelessly noncompetitive. Market mechanisms have arisen to minimize the impact of these information differences. The medical community has created licensing, certification, and accreditation requirements for physicians, specialists, hospitals, and medical schools to assure minimum quality standards. Professional organizations establish ethical standards. And if this is not enough, the threat of a malpractice lawsuit is always a reminder of the importance of promoting the best interests of the patient.

Keep in mind that other markets also exhibit this information problem and are relatively competitive. The market for personal computers is a good example. Except for a small segment of the market, the general public is woefully ignorant of the differences between RAM and ROM, the number of meg in a gig, and the merits of Pentium and Celeron processors. Are there good reasons to buy a Mac instead of a PC? Do I want a zip drive or a DVD? Do I need an internal fax modem? Even with all this consumer ignorance, the market for personal computers is extremely competitive. Why? Because an informed minority provided the initial market discipline. They wrote the newsletters, contributed to the magazines, and spent endless hours on the Internet participating in forums and posting on bulletin boards. The demand for information fostered by this group created awareness among all consumers.

When consumers perceive that acquiring and using information best serves their own interests, there will be a demand for information. Consumers in medical markets do not perceive that their interests are served by spending time and money to acquire information. The third-party payer—the insurance company or the government—expropriates any savings from the search. Change that aspect of the medical marketplace, and consumers will have an incentive to become informed. Virtually all types of medical care, except emergency care, would be purchased in markets with enough informed consumers to ensure economic discipline. The demand for information is evident in the managed care marketplace, where many organizations and networks are reporting to their constituencies on how well they perform in certain critical areas, including primary and preventive care, surgical outcomes, and cost (Kenkel, 1994).

Key Concept 3
Marginal Analysis

Barriers to Entry An important characteristic found in competitive markets is easy entry and easy exit of suppliers. Profits serve as a signal to prospective providers. If profits are greater than normally expected for a given level of risk, firms will enter the market and drive down prices, and profits will adjust to normal levels. Lower-than-normal profits will result in the opposite response, with marginally profitable firms leaving the market and driving up prices and profits for those who remain.

Entry barriers restrict resource movements and result in imperfect competition. Examples of barriers in medical markets are found in numerous restrictions on tasks performed and investments made. The licensing and certification of practitioners are two of the most common ways to restrict entry into the medical profession. The stated purpose of this policy is consumer protection, and its aim is to keep uninformed patients from seeking services from incompetent providers. **Certificate-of-need (CON)** laws require hospitals to secure approval from government planning agencies before adding new capacity or investing in expensive equipment. CON legislation seeks to eliminate the duplication of costly programs within a service area. Restrictions may sound good in theory, but one of the unintended consequences of any limits placed on a market is the elimination of competition. Reduced competition leads to market power, and market power leads to market failure.

certificate-of-need (CON)
Regulations that attempt to avoid the costly duplication of services in the hospital industry. Providers are required to secure a certificate of need before undertaking a major expansion of facilities or services.

Third-Party Payers In traditional markets, individuals spending their own money provide the discipline that culminates in the efficient provision of goods and services. One of the main reasons medical markets are not efficient is that consumers do not spend their own money. Only about 3 cents of every dollar spent on hospital services, and 20 cents out of every dollar spent on physicians' services, comes directly from patients' out-of-pocket spending. The rest is paid by third parties, primarily health insurance companies and the government. Therein lies the major problem in medical markets. Typically, pricing reflects the interaction of consumers' willingness to pay for goods and services and their ability to buy them. Medical markets regularly ignore the desires of those without insurance and those without the ability to pay for care out-of-pocket. The desires of those who have insurance are distorted by the subsidy provided by their insurance.

A system financed primarily through retrospective **fee-for-service** insurance reimbursement is open-ended. Providers are able to pass through all their costs, no matter how inefficient the production of services. The system can be described as a **cost-plus pricing** system (Goodman and Musgrave, 1992). In a cost-plus environment, there is no incentive for providers to search for more efficient methods of production, and patients have no incentive to search for providers who offer lower prices. In competitive markets, providers are rewarded for offering quality products at the lowest price. In cost-plus markets, providers are rewarded by offering more services at higher prices, passing on the additional costs to the third-party payers.

Several factors led to the growth and expansion of the cost-plus system from the end of the Second World War through the 1980s. The American Medical Association (AMA) controlled medical licensing. This not-for-profit institution effectively limited competition in the medical profession by requiring that anyone wishing to practice medicine must graduate from an AMA-approved medical school. Not-for-profit and government-run institutions dominated the hospital sector. Without the economic discipline provided by the profit motive, hospitals competed for physicians. Operating surpluses were directed toward investment in new services and expensive equipment by physician-dominated boards. As a result, excess capacity in beds, nursing staffs, and allied personnel were used to maximize the ability of physicians to generate income for themselves. Finally, Blue Cross and Blue Shield dominated the health insurance industry, and the addition of Medicare and Medicaid in the 1960s meant that not-for-profit payers were financing over half of all medical care provided. This dominance created an atmosphere in which cost was a secondary consideration. Without a cost constraint, the only thing that mattered was the patient's health. Whether the procedure provided a net benefit was not an issue.

Restraint was not present on the demand side either, because insurance was paying the bills. Conventional health insurance distorts the decision-making process by making it appear that medical care is cheap at the point of purchase. Medical care, of course, is not cheap. But cost-plus reimbursement by third-party payers provides an incentive for people to demand interventions that provide little benefit.

The cost-plus system began to run into problems during the 1980s. No matter how prosperous a nation is, there is a limit to how much its people are willing to spend on any single item. As health care spending approached and exceeded 10 percent of gross domestic product, showing no signs of slowing down, policy makers and planners began to address concerns about the "health care crisis." Thus began the bureaucratic struggle to slow the growth in health care spending.

In its early stages, this struggle focused on reimbursement strategies and restrictions on access to services. Medicare and Medicaid placed restrictions on providers by creating fee schedules and changing the method of reimbursement from **retrospective payment** to prospective payment. Private payers did the same, using the strategy of managed care. In both cases, the focus was not on changing buyer behavior but on limiting unnecessary procedures and services.

The move to prospective payment creates incentives on the supply side to limit care. The desires of patients becomes a secondary consideration, subordinated to the desire to control costs. The stage is set for the next phase of the cost-plus

fee-for-service
The traditional payment method for medical care in which a provider bills for each episode of care.

cost-plus pricing
A pricing scheme in which a percentage profit is added to average cost.

POLICY ISSUE

Conventional health insurance virtually eliminates any cost-conscious behavior on the part of the parties involved in the medical care transaction.

retrospective payment
Payment determined after delivery of the good or service. Traditional fee-for-service medicine determines payment retrospectively.

cycle. Either the system will evolve into one in which individuals are motivated by the economic discipline of the market or into one dominated by the bureaucratic discipline of the government.

GOVERNMENT INTERVENTION IN MEDICAL MARKETS

Government involvement in the medical marketplace is extensive. This involvement includes financing, direct provision, regulation, and subsidization. More than 45 percent of all health care spending comes directly from government sources, including Medicare, Medicaid, and the various health plans covering government employees and their dependents, both civilian and military. Government regulators are responsible for licensing, occupational health and safety, the administration of food and drugs, environmental protection, public health, and other oversight functions. Finally, the government uses features of the tax code to subsidize and encourage the provision of group insurance in employer-sponsored plans.

Regulation

The health care industry is one of the most heavily regulated industries in the United States economy. Price controls, entry restrictions covering both providers and hospitals, and regulations on the development and introduction of new drugs and medical devices are the major areas of regulatory control affecting the health care economy.

Price Controls The United States has a long history of placing restrictions on markets in the form of wage and price controls. World War II, the Korean War, and the wage-price freeze that was part of the stabilization program enacted during the Nixon Administration are a few of the instances in which government has attempted to fight inflation by freezing prices. Since the inception of Medicare and Medicaid, medical markets have been subject to price controls of one variety or another. In the beginning, physicians' fees were limited to **usual, customary, and reasonable (UCR) charges**. Under UCR, physicians could charge the minimum of the doctor's usual fee, defined by the median fee during the past year, and the customary fee, defined by the fees charged by other doctors in the area. The use of UCR resulted in a steady escalation of physicians' fees. The formula left no reason for a physician's usual fee to be lower than the customary fee charged in the area. If the usual fee was the minimum in the formula, Medicare paid the usual fee. As individual fees escalated, area fees escalated. The underlying incentive was always to make sure that your usual fee was not the minimum.

> **usual, customary, and reasonable (UCR) charges**
> A price ceiling set to limit fees to the minimum of the billed charge, the price customarily charged by the provider, and the prevailing charge in the geographic region.

Medical prices continued to rise faster than the rate of overall inflation. As prices increased, spending increased. Efforts to limit spending growth shifted to the hospital sector in the early 1980s with the introduction of prospective payment. This new approach paid hospitals for an episode of treatment instead of using the usual cost-plus method. Under prospective payment, hospitals were paid according to the expected cost of treating a particular patient based on the principal diagnosis.[6] If the actual cost of treatment was less than the payment, the hospital kept the surplus. If actual costs were greater, the hospital absorbed the loss or shifted the costs to other patients. Prospective payment changed the incentive structure completely. Hospitals were no longer rewarded for providing more services at a higher cost, and it was actually in their best interest to limit the amount and quality

---

[6] Other factors included in the reimbursement formula are the percentage of free care provided to indigents, whether the institution is a teaching hospital, and whether it is located in an urban area.

of services offered and to limit admissions and discharge patients as quickly as possible. Although hospital admissions moderated, and average length of stay fell dramatically, the use of outpatient services increased dramatically, leading some to question whether the potential for savings has been exhausted (Schwartz, 1987).

Attributing the spending restraint to the method of paying hospitals, the focus shifted back to physicians' fees. The 1990s saw the advent of the relative-value scale for determining allowable physician fees. Basing fees on resource use, the relative-value scale is an attempt by bureaucrats to mimic markets. If the value scale is set correctly, prices will be set at levels that would exist in a competitive market. The relative-value scale has redefined the payment structure, treating evaluation and patient management services to higher relative fees while lowering relative fees paid for invasive procedures.

Entry Restrictions   The government has a long history of licensing, certifying, and accrediting medical care providers. Although the stated purpose of these restrictions is consumer protection, some evidence exists that the self-interest of the providers may be the driving force behind the practice (Kessel, 1958; Moore, 1961). Licensing attempts to limit the likelihood that incompetent providers will treat uninformed patients. Originally, licensing merely placed restrictions on who was allowed to open a medical practice. As time passed, restrictions were expanded to cover a wide range of activities deemed unethical by practicing physicians. These activities included advertising, price cutting, and other conduct considered unprofessional. Clearly, licensing laws serve not only to protect patients but also to limit the number of practitioners, thus protecting physicians from would-be competitors.

Food and Drug Administration (FDA)
A public health agency charged with protecting American consumers by enforcing federal public health laws. Food, medicine, medical devices, and cosmetics are under the jurisdiction of the FDA.

Limits on New Product Development   Congress established the **Food and Drug Administration (FDA)** in 1938 to oversee the entry of new drugs and medical devices into the medical market. The FDA does not allow new drugs on the market until they have been thoroughly tested and ultimately proved safe and effective.[7] Even though the FDA has had several major successes in the past (the most notable was keeping the tranquilizer, thalidomide, off the U.S. market), the FDA approval process is the reason the time from the discovery of a promising chemical compound to drug approval averages 12 years.

The welfare effects of overly restrictive policies regarding new drug introduction are not always clear. Eliminating all risk is impractical, because using and consuming any drug carries with it some level of risk. The optimal level of risk is not zero, but the potential costs and benefits of introducing a new drug must be weighed. Regulators must consider the two types of statistical errors, referred to as Type I and Type II errors, when evaluating the safety and efficacy of a new drug. For simplicity, assume that a drug is either safe or unsafe and that the FDA either approves the drug for use or rejects it.

Type I error occurs when a safe drug is rejected; in other words, the review process results in a false negative. Type II error occurs when an unsafe drug is approved, a false positive. Regulators are much more concerned about avoiding Type II errors, approving drugs that harm patients. The consequences of approving an unsafe drug are obvious; patients suffer complications, get sicker, and die. The consequences of rejecting a safe drug are hidden; patients do not have access to a drug that might improve their health. Critics argue that the bias inherent in the regulatory process is harmful to the most vulnerable patients, those who are

---

[7] In 1971 proof of efficacy was added as a requirement for new drug approval. In other words, the drug not only had to be safe, it had to work as claimed.

critically ill and have few alternative treatments available to them. Clearly, the FDA serves an essential function in the new-drug approval process. Allowing the market to be the sole determinant in drug availability would result in market failure by subjecting poorly informed patients to undue levels of risk.

ISSUES IN MEDICAL CARE DELIVERY

FDA Regulation: The Case of the Cardiopump

How can a patient who has no pulse give informed consent? Developers of the cardiopump, a cardiopulmonary resuscitation device for heart-attack victims, must find a satisfactory answer to this question before the FDA will allow further testing. Manual CPR exerts downward pressure on the chest and must rely on the chest to reexpand naturally. The cardiopump, which looks like a modified toilet plunger, exerts pressure in both directions, pulling blood back into the heart and oxygen back into the lungs.

The product is available elsewhere around the world, including England, Germany, Sweden, Canada, Australia, Japan, and Chile. In fact, it is a standard device in ambulances in Austria and France. But the FDA considers it a "significant risk device" that requires informed consent before it can be used on anyone in a medical trial. For the developers of the device, this designation represents a catch-22. Before the device can be used in a trial, the patient must give informed consent. But how can a patient with no pulse give informed consent?

The FDA is literally protecting patients to death. Approximately one million Americans have heart attacks every year. Of the 700,000 who are given CPR, only 20,000 survive to leave the hospital. Based on a limited sample in St. Paul, Minnesota, survival rates could increase by as much as 35 percent with the use of the cardiopump. That estimate fits comfortably within the range of a 10 to 50 percent improvement in expected survival rates. Extrapolating that number nationally implies that the device could save 7,000 lives annually.

The caution of the FDA is understandable. Regulators are sensitive to the criticisms that resound in the halls of Congress when a drug or medical device harms a single person during its testing. The agency's success in keeping the tranquilizer thalidomide off the market in the 1960s is an excellent case in point. In contrast, the 7,000 people whose lives could be saved every year with the approval of the cardiopump are silent in their protest. When we are talking about life-or-death situations, would it not be wise to reconsider the requirement for informed consent?

Source: Alexander Volokh, "Feel a Heart Attack Coming On—Go to France," *Wall Street Journal,* August 2, 1994, A14.

Tax Policy

Policy makers and planners often use tax subsidies to encourage certain types of behavior. (Those who do not qualify for them call these subsidies "loopholes.") Federal and state income tax provisions subsidize the purchase of health insurance. A key ruling by the Tax Court after the Second World War exempted certain nonwage benefits from being included in an employee's taxable income. It was during this period of wage and price controls that government policy makers chose to use the power to tax—or in this case, the power not to tax—to encourage employers to offer group health insurance to their workers. Since that time, group health insurance has been a nontaxable benefit for employees and, at the same time, a tax-deductible expense for employers.

Sheils and Hogan (1999) estimate that the subsidy in terms of forgone tax revenues exceeded $100 billion in 1998. The value of the subsidy to the individual is equal to the annual insurance premium paid by the employer multiplied by the individual's marginal tax bracket. The benefits of the tax subsidy increase as a person's income increases. If the annual premium paid by the employer is $4,000, a person in the 15 percent marginal tax bracket saves $600 a year in taxes by receiving the benefit instead of the income. In contrast, a person in the 42 percent tax bracket saves $1,680 on the same policy.[8]

One of the major consequences of this tax subsidy is that individuals demand more health insurance when it is purchased by their employers than if they had received the income and bought it themselves. Most economists will agree that paying insurance premiums with before-tax dollars leads to overconsumption of medical care. Paying for expensive insurance with before-tax dollars makes more sense than paying for expensive medical care with after-tax dollars. As a result, indemnity insurance policies traditionally have had low deductible and copayment requirements.

ISSUES IN MEDICAL CARE DELIVERY

Market Forces: The Best Way to Control Prices?

Do prices in medical markets respond to competitive pressures like prices in other markets? As medical care costs continue to rise, some doubt whether competition can be relied upon to rein in medical spending. One medical market in which competition is having a major impact is the market for certain pharmaceutical drugs. The industry has seen a major trend in the past decade with the development of "look-alike" drugs. Look-alikes are drugs with different chemical properties but equivalent medical benefits. Vasotec and Capoten are the two industry leaders in the ACE inhibitor class of heart drugs, capturing as much as 80 percent of the market in 1990. The recent introduction of Lotensin, at up to half the price of the leaders, has changed the nature of that market completely.

The trend toward look-alike drugs makes sound business sense. The industry leader has already proven the efficacy of the drug, so introducing a similar drug into the class poses less risk to the developer. But with no proven therapeutical advantages, the makers of Lotensin chose a marketing strategy based on deep price discounts and a guarantee to users of a fixed price for life. The potential payoffs could be enormous. For example, in the $2 billion ACE inhibitor market, a 5 percent market share translates into $100 million in annual sales.

Other big markets have experienced this same competitive pressure from look-alikes. Paxil has undercut Prozac and Zoloft, popular antidepressants. Similar stories could be told in the markets for antibiotics, ulcer medications, and cholesterol-reducing drugs. The result has been

continued

---

[8] The self-employed did not always enjoy the same tax preference. The Tax Reform Act of 1996 allowed the self-employed to deduct only 25 percent of the cost of personal health insurance (up to a maximum of total self-employment income). The percentage increased over time and reached 100 percent in 2003.

a dramatic reduction in the rate of increase in pharmaceutical prices in the past several years. Price increases during the 1980s regularly topped two to three times the rate of inflation in general. During the 1990s, drug inflation has moderated to as low as 5.7 percent in 1992. With the annual rate of inflation stabilizing at just over 3 percent, pharmaceutical companies still have a way to go before their goal of stability in real prices is within reach.

Responsibility for this price slowdown may be attributed to the buying power of the big institutional purchasers, such as Kaiser Permanente, a large West coast **health maintenance organization (HMO)**. Using their monopsony power (see Back of the Envelope earlier in this chapter), the HMOs have been able to negotiate deep price discounts of as much as 40 to 60 percent below list prices and rebates of up to 75 percent of average wholesale prices. In return, the look-alikes are accepted on the HMO **formulary**, the list of drugs covered by the HMO.

Market forces will continue to exert downward pressure on drug prices as long as buyers have reliable alternatives to the established drugs. We may even expect that makers of the established drugs may soon begin discounting their products to discourage competition.

Source: Elyse Tanouye, "Drug Prices Get Dose of Market Pressure," *Wall Street Journal*, March 11, 1993, B1, B5.

health maintenance organization (HMO)
An insurer and provider of medical care.

formulary
A list of approved pharmaceutical drugs that will be covered under a health plan. Other drugs are typically unavailable to members of the plan.

Government Failure

Even markets that work perfectly offer no guarantee that the efficient allocation of resources will satisfy the public's desires for equity in the distribution of goods and services. On the other hand, no credible evidence supports government remedies as the answer for the perceived inequities either. It is debatable whether government solutions will always improve welfare. Markets may fail, but governments may be just as prone to failure. And correcting government failure is inherently more difficult than correcting market failure.

Few will question the intentions of government involvement in medical care. Everyone is in favor of improved access and lower costs. But careful consideration of the unintended consequences of government intervention is equally important. Choosing a health care strategy for yourself and your family is a difficult task. Choosing some other agent to make that decision for you is not only difficult, it can be dangerous. Transferring decision making from the private sector to the public sector substitutes bureaucratic discipline for economic discipline.

The notion of perfect competition in markets is just as rare as the notion of perfect democracy in political science (Becker, 1958). Criticism directed at market failure—without at least admitting the possibility of government failure—is dishonest, or at minimum naive. Voters face considerable obstacles in getting their collective voices heard. The interval between elections is long: two to six years. The viable choices are limited, usually to the two major-party candidates, and agreement with every aspect of a candidate's platform is highly unlikely. Special interest groups, through subsidized lobbying efforts, have disproportionate influence on the decision-making process. And at the same time, protecting minority desires when government is by majority rule poses a problem.

These cautions should not discourage us from using government intervention as a strategy to ensure efficient market performance and equitable outcomes. But they should stand as a warning against relying too heavily on government to solve all our problems. Frequently, solutions proposed by well-meaning government

POLICY ISSUE

Does imperfect government address the issues of equity and efficiency in health care delivery better than imperfect markets?

cost containment
Strategies used to control the total spending on health care services.

Key Concept 4
Self-Interest

Key Concept 7
Competition

Key Concept 4
Self-Interest

policy makers ignore the realities of the real world. We may not be able to create heaven on earth, but we may be able to improve the circumstances of millions of Americans with the right mix of market discipline and bureaucratic oversight.

The appropriate perspective in this debate is not whether the proposed system is efficient or fair (Pauly, 1997). No matter which alternative approach is chosen, it will be imperfect in its implementation. The appropriate perspective is whether efficiency and fairness are best addressed by imperfect government or imperfect markets.

SUMMARY AND CONCLUSIONS

Traditional microeconomics views the price mechanism as the invisible hand that leads to economic welfare maximization in a perfectly competitive market. In this chapter, we have examined the requirements necessary for competitive markets to result in equitable and efficient outcomes. Sources of market failure—including market power, externalities, and public goods—were described and discussed. Other sources of failure were applied to medical markets, including information problems, barriers to entry, and third-party payers.

The invisible hand is not able to perform its usual function in a system dominated by government decision makers. When government oversees production and consumption, it is the visible, tangible hand, or its equivalent, that determines prices. With complete knowledge of consumer preferences and producer capabilities, the efficiency problems could be solved. Following the reasoning of Lerner (1944), the planning agency must obtain the prices of all inputs and outputs, publish and distribute a list containing this information, and instruct all decision makers to act as if they were maximizers in a perfectly competitive market. In other words, substitute the superior wisdom of the planners for the collective wisdom of the masses.

Markets sometimes fail to produce the optimal level of output. The challenge facing policy makers is to intervene only in those situations in which government action can improve welfare. Substituting government failure for market failure is not welfare enhancing. We need policy makers who understand this important lesson and

intervene, not when they see market failure, but whenever government actions will actually take us closer to the social optimum.

If medical markets are to work, that is, if they are to produce acceptable levels of efficiency and equity, the following conditions must be present (Enthoven, 1988):

- Decisions must be made by well-informed, cost-conscious consumers. Motivated by self-interest, and adequately informed about treatment alternatives, cost-conscious consumers will economize because they will personally benefit from such behavior. The patient/buyer must be an active participant in the decision-making process if **cost containment** is to be achieved.

- Competition among providers is essential. Competition guards against undue concentration, because substitutes are readily available. Coupled with the first condition, consumer demand is sensitive to price changes.

- Cost-conscious decisions are possible only if consumers who desire to enter the market have money to spend. Often phrased in terms of equity, the real issue is economic self-sufficiency. As such, medical care markets require either universal insurance coverage or universal access to insurance. The choice depends on whether the majority of the populace is concerned with equal outcomes or equal opportunities. Satisfying this condition ensures that the system is morally acceptable to a majority of the people.

PROFILE

Mark V. Pauly

If one journal article can launch a career, Mark Pauly has shown us how it can be done. His 1968 article in the *American Economic Review,* entitled "The Economics of Moral Hazard," has become essential reading for anyone desiring to understand the effects of health insurance on health care utilization and cost. After receiving his Ph.D. in 1967, Pauly catapulted himself into the epicenter of health economics with his classic treatise.

After brief academic appointments at Northwestern University and his alma mater, the University of Virginia, Pauly moved to the University of Pennsylvania's Wharton School, where he became the Executive Director of the Leonard Davis Institute of Health Economics. Founded in 1967, the Leonard Davis Institute (LDI) has maintained a commitment to health services research and education in an interdisciplinary setting. Pauly was named Bendheim Professor in 1990 and is currently chairperson of the Health Care Systems Department.

One article can launch a career, but the reputation of a scholar is based on continuous research output. *Continuous* may not be the appropriate term to describe Pauly's contribution to the health economics literature — *unbelievable* is probably better. Along with numerous books, articles, and monographs, his research interests encompass medical economics and the role of markets in medical care, national health care policy, and health insurance. In addition, he is a member of the editorial boards of the *Journal of Health Economics*, the *Public Finance Quarterly*, and the *Journal of Risk and Uncertainty*. He is also an elected member of the Institutes of Medicine of the National Academy of Science.

Pauly is one of a handful of health economists worldwide who argue that competition, when appropriately defined and understood, can work effectively in medical markets. Contrast this belief with the mainstream thought that gives little consideration to market solutions for the problems of medical care delivery and finance, and you begin to understand why many of his colleagues consider him an anomaly within the profession.

His belief that the incentive structure can shape both the behavior of patients and providers has resulted in his teaming with John C. Goodman, director of the National Center for Policy Analysis, in publishing the article "Tax Credits for Insurance and Medical Savings Accounts" in the Spring 1995 issue of *Health Affairs*. This innovative approach to health care reform recommends the use of tax credits, **medical savings accounts**, and high-deductible health insurance to improve both efficiency and equity in the health care sector. A colleague who does not share Pauly's faith in market solutions referred to his belief in markets as a "disease." If Pauly's insistence on a place for markets in health care delivery and finance is a disease, he is not likely to accept the cure without a struggle, especially when the proposed cure is a government-run system.

On more than one occasion, after a previous speaker had stirred the audience into a feeding frenzy on the various evils of the U.S. medical care delivery system, Pauly has stepped to the podium only to quiet the crowd with his clear analytical approach and keen insight into the underlying issues, providing balance to a discussion in which balance is often lacking. If the essential ingredients for making enlightened choices are knowledge and academic inquiry, Mark Pauly has advanced our ability to make enlightened choices through his outstanding contribution to the field of health economics and the economics of insurance.

Source: Mark V. Pauly, *curriculum vitae* and personal communication.

medical savings account
A tax-exempt savings account used in conjunction with high-deductible health insurance. Individuals pay their own medical expenses using funds from the savings account up to the amount of the deductible. Once the deductible is met, the insurance policy pays all or most of the covered expenses.

QUESTIONS AND PROBLEMS

1. What is market failure? What are the major reasons that a free, unregulated market in medical care might not be optimal?

2. Proponents of a government-run health care system argue that the market does not work well in the medical care industry. What evidence do they use to support this claim?

3. Explain how market failure can be used to justify government intervention in medical care markets.

4. How do price controls affect the workings of a perfectly competitive market? Use a supply-demand diagram as part of your answer.

5. What assumptions of the perfectly competitive marketplace are violated in medical markets? How does each affect equilibrium price and quantity?

REFERENCES

Gerard F. Anderson and Peter S. Hussey, *Multinational Comparisons of Health Systems Data*, Commonwealth Fund, October 2000.

William J. Baumol, "Do Health Care Costs Matter?" *The New Republic* 209(21), November 22, 1993, 16–18.

Gary S. Becker, "Competition and Democracy," *Journal of Law and Economics* 1, October 1958, 105–109.

Robert J. Blendon et al., "Who Has the Best Health System? A Second Look," *Health Affairs* 14(4), Winter 1995, 220–230.

David M. Cutler and Mark McClellan, "Is Technological Change in Medicine Worth It?" Health Affairs 20(5), September/October 2001, 11–29.

Carmen DiNavas-Walt, Bernadette D. Proctor, and Jessica Smith, *Income, Poverty, and Health Insurance Coverage in the United States: 2006*, P60–233, August 2007.

Alain C. Enthoven, "Managed Competition: An Agenda for Action," *Health Affairs* 7(3), Summer 1988, 25–47.

John C. Goodman and Gerald L. Musgrave, *Patient Power: Solving America's Health Care Crisis*, Washington, DC: Cato Institute, 1992.

Jack Hadley and John Holahan, "How Much Medical Care do the Uninsured Use, and Who Pays for it?" *Health Affairs* Web Exclusive, February 12, 2003, W3, 66-81.

D. L. Hoyert, K. D. Kochanek, and S. L. Murphy, "Deaths: Final Data for 1997," *National Vital Statistics Reports* 47(19), Hyattsville, MD: National Center for Health Statistics, 1999.

Paul J. Kenkel, "Health Plans Face Pressure to Find 'Report Card' Criteria that Will Make the Grade," *Modern Healthcare*, January 10, 1994, 41.

Reuben A. Kessel, "Price Discrimination in Medicine," *Journal of Law and Economics* 1, October 1958, 20–53.

Richard Kronick, David C. Goodman, John Wennberg, and Edward Wagner, "The Marketplace in Health Care Reform: The Demographic Limitations of Managed Competition," *The New England Journal of Medicine* 328(2), January 14, 1993, 148–152.

Abba Lerner, *The Economics of Control*, New York: Macmillan, 1944.

Frank R. Lichtenberg, "Sources of U.S. Longevity Increase, 1960–1997," NBER Working Paper No. 8755, Cambridge, MA: National Bureau of Economic Research, February 2002.

T.J. Matthews and Marian F. MacDorman, "Infant Mortality Statistics from the 2004 Period Linked Birth/Infant Death Data Set," *National Vital Statistics Reports* 55(14), Centers for Disease Control, June 13, 2007.

Thomas G. Moore, "The Purpose of Licensing," *Journal of Law and Economics* 4, October 1961, 93–117.

Mark V. Pauly, "A Primer on Competition in Medical Markets," in *Health Care in America: The Political Economy of Hospitals and Health Insurance*, edited by H. E. Frech III, San Francisco: Pacific Research Institute for Public Policy, 1988, 27–71.

_____, "Who was that Straw Man Anyway? A Comment on Evans and Rice," *Journal of Health Politics, Policy, and Law*, April 1997, 467–473.

Charles E. Phelps, "Diffusion of Information in Medical Care," *Journal of Economic Perspectives* 6(3), Summer 1992, 23–42.

Thomas Rice, *The Economics of Health Reconsidered*, Chicago, IL: Health Administration Press, 1998.

William B. Schwartz, "The Inevitable Failure of Current Cost-Containment Strategies: Why They Can Provide Only Temporary Relief," *Journal of the American Medical Association* 257(2), January 9, 1987, 220–224.

John Sheils and Paul Hogan, "Cost of Tax-Exempt Health Benefits in 1998," *Health Affairs* 18(2), March/April 1999, 176–181.

Irwin M. Stelzer, "There is No Health Care Crisis," *Wall Street Journal*, January 25, 1994, A12.

Arduino Verdecchia et al., "Recent Cancer Survival in Europe: A 2000–02 Period Analysis of EUROCARE-4 Data," *Lancet Oncology* 8, September 2007, 784–796.

Daniel Waldo et al., "Health Expenditures by Age Group, 1977–1987," *Health Care Financing Review* 10(4), Summer 1989, 111–120.

The Economics of Consumer Choice

To explain consumer behavior economists use a simple model based on the concept of utility. The theory posits that individuals derive satisfaction, or utility, from consuming goods and services. The more goods and services consumed the higher the level of satisfaction achieved. A consumer's ability to satisfy his or her desire for goods is limited by the amount of money income to spend and the prices of the goods available for purchase. The three prerequisites for the development of a theory of consumer choice are: (1) there must be goods to buy, (2) consumers must have money to spend, and (3) they must be able to rank their preferences.[9]

As in all neoclassical economics, consumers are assumed to be maximizers. In the case where there are two goods available for consumption, consumers are interested in maximizing utility subject to a budget constraint, or

Maximize $U = U(X, Y)$
subject to $M = P_X X + P_Y Y$

where U is the level of utility, X and Y are the two goods in question, M is the money income available for spending on the two goods, and P_X and P_Y are their respective prices.

CONSUMER PREFERENCES: INDIFFERENCE CURVES

Economists depict consumer preferences graphically with indifference curves. An indifference curve illustrates the various combinations of goods that are equally satisfying to the consumer. In Figure 3A.1, having X_0 of good X and Y_0 of good Y places the consumer at point R on the indifference curve labeled

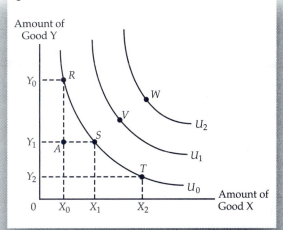

Figure 3A.1: Indifference Curves

U_0. Points S (X_1 and Y_1) and T (X_2 and Y_2) are likewise on U_0, indicating that these three combinations of X and Y provide the same level of satisfaction. The consumer is said to be indifferent as far as these three alternatives are concerned.

Higher levels of satisfaction are depicted by higher indifference curves. A combination of goods on indifference curve U_1 such as V is preferred to R, S, and T. Similarly, W on indifference curve U_2 is preferred to V. Because W is preferred to V and V is preferred to R, S, and T, the transitive nature of preferences implies that W is also preferred to R, S, and T.

When the consumer is able to rank all available alternatives, the set of indifference curves represents a preference map. Indifference curves serve the same purpose on this preference map that contour lines

---

[9] The model does not require that consumers have the ability to attach numerical values to the utility levels. The requirement is that they be able to rank their preferences in an ordinal sense; e.g., most preferred to least preferred.

serve on a topographical map. As you move along an indifference curve, the level of utility stays the same. As you move along a contour line, the elevation stays the same. Move from one indifference curve to another and the level of utility changes. Move from one contour line to another and you move to a different elevation.

Indifference curves have certain properties that are important in the development of the theory of consumer choice. They are all negatively sloped, indicating that combinations of goods that have more of one good and the same or more of the other good are preferred. This property indicates that the goods in question are desirable. The consumer prefers more to less.

Indifference curves are typically drawn convex to the origin (they bow in, as shown in Figure 3A.1). Convexity implies that consumers are more willing to give up good Y for some amount of X when Y is plentiful. If the consumer has only a small amount of Y, it will take more X in the exchange to keep the consumer at the same level of satisfaction. The marginal rate of substitution (MRS) is defined as the amount of Y that the consumer would be willing to give up for a small increase in X and maintain the same level of utility. In other words, MRS is the importance attached to an additional unit of good X in terms of the amount of Y given up.

Movement from R to S on indifference curve U_0 results in a different combination of X and Y. Point S has more X, but less Y than point R. The slope of U_0, defined as the change in the amount of Y relative to the change in the amount of X, is also the marginal rate of substitution. The movement from R to S may be broken down into two distinct moves. A move from R to A lowers the level of utility by reducing the amount of good Y. For small movements along U_0, this change in utility is equal to the marginal utility of Y (the change in utility resulting from a unit change in Y) multiplied by the total change in Y, or $(MU_Y) \times (\Delta Y)$. Similarly, a move from A to S restores utility to

its previous level due to the increase in the amount of good X. Using the same logic, that change is equal to $(MU_X) \times (\Delta X)$. These two changes offset each other and are thus equal in magnitude, so $\Delta Y/\Delta X = MU_X/MU_Y$. In other words, the slope of the indifference curve ($\Delta Y/\Delta X$), the MRS good X for good Y, equals the ratio of the marginal utilities of the two goods (MU_X/MU_Y).[10]

Indifference curves do not intersect one another. Intersecting curves would present a logical inconsistency. Points on any one indifference curve provide the consumer with the same level of utility. Points on a separate indifference curve are equally satisfying to the consumer but at a different level of utility. If two indifference curves intersect, the point of intersection would be on both curves simultaneously. The implication is that points on the two indifference curves represent the same and different levels of utility simultaneously.

CONSUMER CONSTRAINTS: THE BUDGET LINE

Consumers have a limited capacity to satisfy their preferences. Because of limited money income and positive prices for the goods and services, the ability to achieve the desired level of consumption is constrained. The consumer's money income constraint may be written $M = P_X X + P_Y Y$. By rearranging terms, the constraint may be written in the form of an equation, or budget line, as follows

$$Y = (M/P_Y) - (P_X/P_Y)X$$

M/P_Y is the value of Y when $X = 0$ and is equal to the Y intercept. The corresponding X intercept, M/P_X, is the value of X when $Y = 0$. The slope of the budget line, P_X/P_Y, is the relative prices of the two goods. The budget line represents all combinations of goods X and Y the consumer is able to buy. Any combination of X and Y that is on or below the budget line is attainable. Given the prices of the two goods, the consumer does

---

[10] **This derivation may be shown more formally using the Lagrangian multiplier method. The consumer's effort to maximize utility** $U = U(X, Y)$ **is constrained by limited money income,** $M = P_X X + P_Y Y$. **The problem becomes one of maximizing** $L = U(X,Y) + \lambda(M - P_X X - P_Y Y)$. **Setting the partial derivatives of** L **with respect to** X, Y, **and** λ **equal to zero gives**

$$\partial L/\partial X = \partial U/\partial X - \lambda P_X = 0$$
$$\partial L/\partial Y = \partial U/\partial Y - \lambda P_Y = 0$$
$$\partial L/\partial \lambda = M - P_X X - P_Y Y = 0$$

Solving the first two equations for λ **and setting them equal to each other yields**

$$\lambda = (\partial U/\partial X)/P_X = (\partial U/\partial Y)/P_Y$$

In other words,

$$\lambda = MU_X/P_X = MU_Y/P_Y$$

not have enough money to reach points above the budget line. In our model, we assume the consumer spends all budgeted money for the two goods, and thus ends up on the budget line, not below it.

Holding prices constant, changes in income will shift the budget line. Using Figure 3A.2, it can be seen that increases in income shift the curve to the right and decreases in income shift it to the left. Changes in relative prices will cause the curve to rotate. Holding P_Y constant, if P_X increases, the curve will rotate to the left. If P_X decreases, it will rotate to the right.

CONSUMER CHOICE: THE CONCEPT OF EQUILIBRIUM

Consumer preferences, graphically depicted by indifference curves, represent what the consumer is willing to buy. The money income constraint, depicted by the budget line, represents what the consumer is able to buy. Determining consumer choice is a matter of bringing together these two concepts—willingness to buy and ability to buy. The consumer's decision on how to allocate scarce money income between the two goods is an attempt to match preferences with spending power—wants with affordability, willingness to buy with ability to buy—and in the process attain maximum satisfaction.

Individuals adjust their consumption behavior to the point where they cannot increase total utility without increasing their budget. Graphically, the choice may be shown as one of finding a point of tangency between the consumer's budget line and the highest attainable indifference curve. This point is identified by superimposing the preference map over the budget line and determining the unique point of tangency. This point of tangency represents an equilibrium because it is the only point where the slope of the indifference curve equals the slope of the budget line.

The consumer maximizes utility at point B in Figure 3A.3. Points like A do not represent equilibrium since the consumer can reach a higher level of utility simply by moving down the budget line toward point B, spending the same amount of money, purchasing a different combination of X and Y, and reaching a higher level of utility. Likewise, the consumer could move down indifference curve U_1, maintain a constant level of utility, and spend less money. At point B, the slope of the indifference curve, MU_X/MU_Y, is equal to the slope of the budget line, P_X/P_Y. Thus, the equilibrium condition as already stated is satisfied. In equilibrium, $MU_X/MU_Y = P_X/P_Y$. This condition may be rewritten $MU_X/P_X = MU_Y/P_Y$. In the case where the number of goods the consumer may choose from is equal to n instead of two, this condition may be written

$$MU_X/P_X = MU_Y/P_Y = \cdots = MU_n/P_n$$

Figure 3A.3: Consumer Equilibrium

Figure 3A.2: Income and Price Changes with Budget Lines

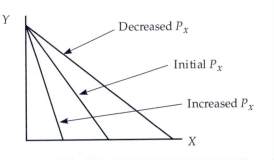

It may be said the consumer maximizes utility when the last dollar spent on each good consumed provides the same increment to utility as the last dollar spent on every other good.[11] This equilibrium condition provides one point on the individual's demand curve for each good consumed, X_0 at price P_X. Changing the price of the good and finding the new level of consumption identifies additional points on the demand curve. Connecting all these price-quantity pairs in a separate graph traces out the actual demand curve.

IMPLICATIONS OF THE MODEL

The shapes of indifference curves depend on the consumer's own assessment of the desirability of the available alternatives. Consumers with a strong preference for X will have relatively steep indifference curves. Those with strong preferences for Y will have indifference curves that are relatively flat. One possible extension of the model might be to examine the consequences of preference switching. The left-hand side of Figure 3A.4 shows the equilibrium between physicians' office visits (V) and other uses of income (Y). The healthy consumer will have a relatively flat preference map, indicating a strong desire to spend money on goods other than visits

to the physician. With equilibrium at point A, this consumer will spend Y_1 income on all other goods and visit the physician V_1 times per year, resulting in a utility level of U_1.

The onset of an illness results in a preference switch, depicted by a steeper preference map on the right. The consumer now places more importance on visits to the physician relative to other spending. The result is a new equilibrium at point B, spending Y_2 on other goods, V_2 visits to the physician, and utility on indifference curve U_1. If the consumer cannot afford to reduce spending on other goods below Y_1, the preferred equilibrium cannot be attained. Instead the consumer will remain at point A, spending Y_1 on other goods, visiting the physician V_1 times, and attaining a lower level of utility, U_0.

CONCLUSION

The model of consumer choice discussed in this appendix is used to explain and predict consumer behavior. Even though consumers may not consciously apply this decision calculus in each and every situation, this does not mean that the model serves no useful purpose. Remember the model was developed to explain and predict. If it helps us accomplish these tasks, it serves us well.

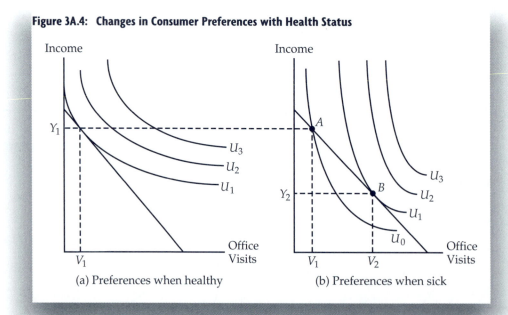

Figure 3A.4: Changes in Consumer Preferences with Health Status

(a) Preferences when healthy

(b) Preferences when sick

---

[11] The marginal utility of the last dollar spent on every good is equal to the λ in the previous footnote.

Production and Cost in the For-Profit Sector

In a world of competitive markets, firms that are successful in minimizing costs will earn a normal profit. Cost minimization is accomplished by the efficient use of resources. In this appendix, we will examine production and cost in a competitive market where firms attempt to maximize profits.

PRODUCTION WITH TWO VARIABLE INPUTS

Economists describe the production process as a functional relationship between inputs and outputs. The so-called **production function** shows the maximum output that can be produced from a given level of inputs using the available technology. Unlike utility, output is a measurable concept—bushels of grain, tons of steel, barrels of oil, or number of appendectomies performed. The inputs include land, natural resources, machinery, labor, and the entrepreneurial energies used to combine them and produce a product or service that people wish to buy. The production process with two variable inputs, labor (L) and capital (K), may be depicted in its generalized form

$$Q = Q(L, K)$$

where Q represents the amount of the good produced and $Q(\ldots)$ the mathematical relationship describing the production process. Production functions are usually presented in one of three forms: a table, an equation, or a graph.

Figure 3B.1 summarizes the output levels that may be attained when labor and capital are combined according to the production function $Q = 100\,LK$. The amount of labor used in the production process is listed across the bottom of the table, and the amount of capital is listed along the left-hand side. Interpreting the data in the table is straightforward. For example, when five units of capital are combined with six workers, the firm is able to produce 548 units of output. Different combinations of labor and capital will result in different levels of output. As long as the inputs are used efficiently, the firm will produce exactly the level of output shown in the table.

Production Isoquants

It is possible to produce the same level of output using different combinations of the two inputs. For example, the firm may produce 316 units of output using ten units of capital and one unit of labor. The same level of output can be produced using five units of capital and two units of labor, two units of capital and five units of labor, or one unit of capital and ten units of labor. A similar observation may be made about 200 units of output, or 400 units, or any one of many different levels of output. The curves drawn in the body of the table represent the different combinations of L and K that produce the same level of output. These equal quantity curves are called **isoquants**, and serve the same purpose in production theory as indifference curves in consumer theory.

Plotting the isoquants in Figure 3B.2 provides a clear picture of the production levels that are attainable using the various combinations of labor and capital. The firm may use a number of different combinations of labor and capital to produce Q_1 units of output. Although only three are shown below, an infinite number of isoquants exist, one for every possible level of output. Because isoquants farther from the origin represent higher levels of output, $Q_3 > Q_2 > Q_1$.

Isoquants are usually drawn convex to the origin. The slope of the isoquant measures the ability to substitute one input for the other while maintaining the same level of output. As the firm adjusts its input mix, the ability to substitute, called the

Figure 3B.1: Changes in Consumer Preferences with Health Status

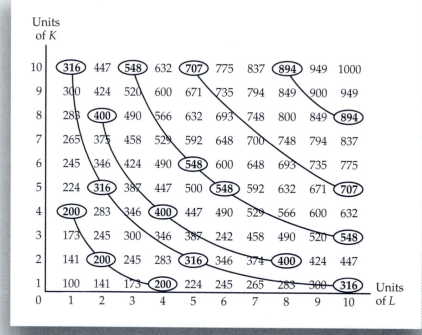

Note: Above table produced from a Cobb-Douglas production function of the form $Q = 100\sqrt{LK} = 100\ L^{0.5}\ K^{0.5}$.

Figure 3B.2: Changes in Consumer Preferences with Health Status

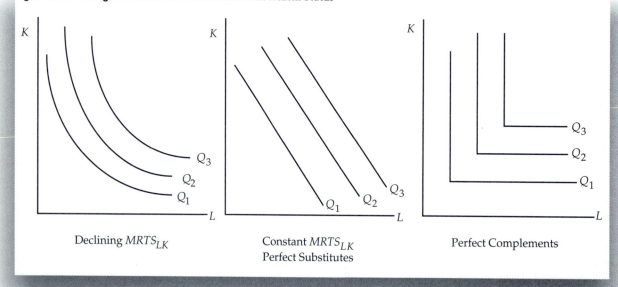

marginal rate of technical substitution (MRTS), changes. When the production process uses a large amount of capital relative to labor, the marginal productivity of labor is high relative to that of capital. One additional worker can easily make up for the reduction of capital. Substitution of labor for capital is relatively easy and the marginal rate of technical substitution labor for capital ($MRTS_{LK}$) is relatively high.

When the amount of capital employed is low relative to the number of workers, the marginal productivity of labor is low relative to that of capital. It takes many more workers to make up for a reduction in capital. In other words, substitution of labor for capital is more difficult when capital is scarce relative to the number of workers competing for its use. Thus, as we move down an isoquant, using more labor and less capital, the $MRTS_{LK}$ declines.

All along the isoquant, the marginal rate of technical substitution is the slope of the isoquant. It can be shown that $MRTS_{LK}$ is the ratio of the marginal product of labor to the marginal product of capital (MP_L/MP_K).[12] If labor and capital are perfect substitutes, $MRTS_{LK}$ will be the same regardless of the amount of labor and capital used in the production process. In this case, the isoquant will be a downward-sloping straight line. If instead labor and capital are perfect complements, always used in fixed proportions, the isoquants are L-shaped.

Production in the Short Run

When a firm uses its resources efficiently, the only way to increase output is to increase the amount of inputs used. In most cases, it is easier to increase the workforce than it is to add capital equipment. Inputs whose levels can be adjusted quickly, such as labor, are called **variable inputs**. Inputs that take more time to increase, such as machinery, are called **fixed inputs**. The time lags required for these adjustments further define the production process as either short run or long run. In the case of a two-input production function, the **long run** is defined as the time period where both inputs are variable. The **short run** is the time period where one of the inputs, usually capital, is fixed.

In the short run, the only way to change output is to change the amount of the variable input used. The amount of the fixed input cannot be changed. In other words, the size or scale of the operation is fixed in the short run. From Figure 3B.1, short-run production may be shown by fixing the capital input at, say, five units and varying the amount of labor used from one to ten units. Presented in tabular form that information is shown in Table 3B.1.

From the first two columns, production increases as the number of workers hired increases. The **average product** of labor (AP_L) and the **marginal product** of labor (MP_L) may also be derived from the data on the **total product** of labor (TP_L). The average product, a measure of technical efficiency, is calculated by dividing the total product of labor by the number of workers, or $AP_L = TP_L/L$. The marginal product is the change in total product when one additional worker is hired. It is calculated by dividing the change in the total product by the change in the

Table 3B.1   Short-Run Production with $K = 5$

Units of Labor	Total Product	Capital-Labor Ratio	Average Product	Marginal Product
0	0	∞	—	—
1	224	5.00	224	224
2	316	2.50	158	92
3	387	1.67	129	71
4	447	1.25	112	60
5	500	1.00	100	83
6	548	0.83	91	48
7	592	0.72	85	44
8	632	0.63	79	40
9	671	0.56	75	39
10	707	0.50	71	36

[12] The MRTS at any point on an isoquant may be derived by taking the total differential of the production function $Q = Q(L, K)$, and setting it equal to zero.

$$dQ = (\partial Q/\partial K)dL + (\partial Q/\partial K)dK = 0$$

As the amount of L and K change along an isoquant, the level of output does not change, or $dQ = 0$. Solving this equality for the slope of the isoquant, $dK/dL = (\partial Q/\partial L)/(\partial Q/\partial L)$. Since $(\partial Q/\partial K)$ equals MP_L and $(\partial Q/\partial K)$ equals MP_K,

$$dK/dL = MP_L/MP_K MRTS_{LK}$$

number of workers used in the production process, or $MP_L = \Delta TP_L / \Delta L$.

The production function utilized in this discussion illustrates an important empirical observation in short-run production, the **law of diminishing returns**. Holding the amount of capital constant, each added worker has less capital on average to work with, as evidenced by a constantly declining capital-labor ratio (K/L). So each additional worker contributes less to output than the previous worker. The law of diminishing returns is not based on an economic theory, it is physical law that holds true for production in general.

Although the law of diminishing returns characterizes every short-run production process, marginal product and average do not always decline from the outset. Some production processes display increasing marginal and average product initially due to the benefits derived from specialization and the division of labor. Figure 3B.3 presents a generalized short-run production function. As the number of workers increases, total product increases at an increasing rate up to point A. Beyond point A, production continues to increase as more workers are used, but at a decreasing rate. The rate of increase in output slows until a maximum output is reached at point B. Beyond point B, given the amount of capital available per worker, further increases in output are not possible. Adding workers actually decreases output.

Firms do not operate where the marginal product of an input is negative. Doing so would imply the firm could increase its output by decreasing the amount of the input used, increasing revenue and lowering cost. Thus, efficient production occurs when the marginal products of all inputs are positive.

Figure 3B.3: Generalized Production in the Short Run

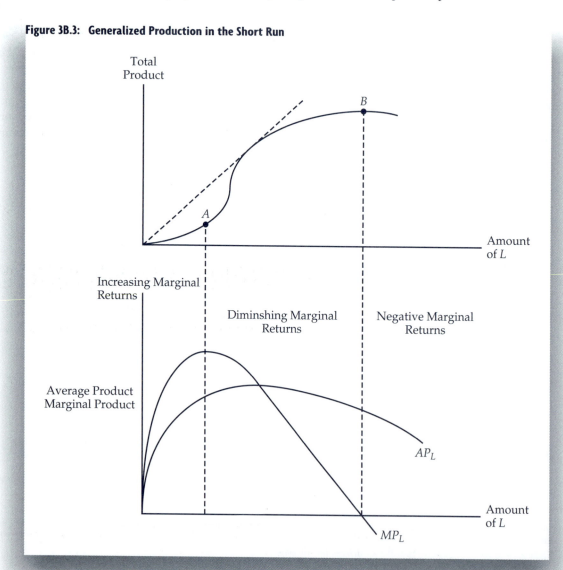

OPTIMAL INPUT USE

The profit-maximizing firm will attempt to maximize output from the resources committed to production. The firm faces a resource constraint determined by the cost of inputs and the amount of money it is willing to spend. When two inputs, labor (L) and capital (K), are used in production, the constraint may be written $C = wL + rK$, where C is the total cost, w is the wage rate paid labor, and r is the unit cost of capital. This cost constraint may be rewritten as an **isocost curve**, or $K = (C/r) - (w/r)L$. The isocost curve is shown in Figure 3B.4, and may be interpreted as all possible combinations of L and K that can be hired for a total cost equal to C_i when input prices equal w and r. The more money the firm is willing to commit to production, the farther the isocost curve is from the origin and the greater the output that can be produced.

The slope of the isocost curve is the relative price of the inputs, or $-(w/r)$. Combining the isoquant map with the relevant isocost curve allows us to determine the combination of inputs the profit-maximizing firm will choose. Maximizing output at a given level of cost requires that the firm use the optimal or least-cost combination of the inputs. This is shown in Figure 3B.5 at point E where the isocost curve is just tangent to the isoquant Q_1. At the point where the isoquant is tangent to the isocost curve, their slopes are equal. In other words, the slope of the isoquant, or the $MRTS_{LK} (= MP_L/MP_K)$, equals the slope of the isocost curve, or w/r, when the firm is using the least-cost combination of inputs L and K. Formally, this equilibrium condition may be written $MRTS_{LK} = MP_L/MP_K = w/r$.[13]

The equilibrium condition may also be written $MP_L/w = MP_K/r$. In this form it is easily seen that firms adjust the amounts of labor and capital used until the marginal product from the last dollar spent on labor is equal to the marginal product from the last dollar spent on capital.

EXTENSIONS OF THE MODEL

The optimal input mix for producing a given level of output will change as the relative prices of the inputs change. Figure 3B.6 illustrates the least-cost method

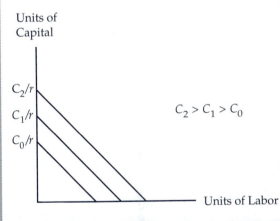

Figure 3B.4: Isocost Curves

Units of Capital

C_2/r
C_1/r
C_0/r

$C_2 > C_1 > C_0$

Units of Labor

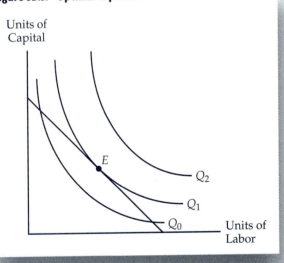

Figure 3B.5: Optimal Input Use

Units of Capital

E

Q_2
Q_1
Q_0

Units of Labor

[13] The mathematical derivation of the equilibrium condition in production mirrors that of the equilibrium condition in consumer theory. Using the Lagrangian multiplier method, it can be shown that the firm's effort to maximize output $Q = Q(L, K)$ is limited by a total cost constraint, $C = wL + rK$. The problem becomes one of maximizing $L = Q(L, K) + \lambda(C - wL - rK)$. Setting the partial derivatives of L with respect to L, K, and λ equal to zero gives

$$\partial L/\partial U = \partial U/\partial L - \lambda w = 0$$
$$\partial L/\partial K = \partial U/\partial K - \lambda r = 0$$
$$\partial L/\partial \lambda = C - wL - rK = 0$$

Solving the first two equations for λ and setting them equal to each other yields

$$\lambda = (\partial Q/\partial L)/w = (\partial Q/\partial K)/r$$

In other words,

$$\lambda = MP_L/w = MP_K/r$$

Figure 3B.6: Producing Medical Care When the Price of Physician's Services Varies

of producing Q^* medical care at two different prices for physicians' services. When the price of physicians' services is high (P_H), equilibrium will be at point H, using S_H. If physicians are paid less, holding the price of other medical inputs (P_O) constant, the same level of medical care will be provided using a different mix of physicians' services and other medical inputs. At low physicians' prices (P_L), equilibrium will be at point L, using S_L physicians' services.

The model provides several interesting implications. When the fees paid physicians are relatively high, the physician-population ratio will be relatively low and patients will visit their doctors less often. Additionally, higher physicians' prices encourage the use of other medical inputs. Thus, when physicians' prices are higher, we expect medical care to be produced using more capital per patient.

ESTIMATING PRODUCTION FUNCTIONS

The simplest and most widely used production function in empirical work is of the Cobb-Douglas variety. The Cobb-Douglas production function may be written as $Q = AL^\alpha K^\beta$ where α and β are positive

parameters estimated from the empirical data. Using this functional form, the exponents represent output elasticities, or the percentage change in output for every 1 percent change in the quantity of the input used. In the case of the labor input, a 1 percent increase in L will result in an α percent increase in Q. Likewise for capital, a 1 percent increase in K will result in a β percent increase in Q.[14] If $\alpha + \beta = 1$, the production function exhibits const'ant returns to scale. In this case a 1 percent increase in the amount of both inputs used yields a 1 percent increase in output. If $\alpha + \beta > 1$, say 1.2, then a 1 percent increase in L and K results in a 1.2 percent increase in Q and the production function exhibits increasing returns to scale.

The Cobb-Douglas production function is estimated empirically by first taking the logarithm of both sides, resulting in

$$\log Q = A + \alpha \log L + \beta \log K$$

Regressing $\log Q$ on $\log L$ and $\log K$ provides estimates of the output elasticities from the estimated coefficients (refer back to the statistical appendix to Chapter 2 for the discussion on regression analysis).

---

[14] The marginal products of labor and capital for a Cobb-Douglas production function are determined as follows:

$$MP_L = \partial Q / \partial L = \alpha A L^{\alpha-1} K^\beta = \alpha(Q/L)$$

$$MP_K = \partial Q / \partial K = \beta A L^\alpha K^{\beta-1} = \beta(Q/K)$$

The output elasticities E_K and E_L are

$$E_L = (L/\partial Q)/(Q/\partial L) = (L/Q)(\alpha Q/L) = \alpha$$

$$E_K = (K/\partial Q)/(Q/\partial K) = (K/Q)(\beta Q/K) = \beta$$

PRODUCTION TO COST

Cost may be divided into two categories: fixed and variable. Costs associated with the fixed inputs, costs that do not change as the level of production changes, are **fixed costs**. Costs associated with the variable inputs, costs that change as the level of production changes, are **variable costs**. Using the twoinput production function introduced above with capital representing the fixed input and labor the variable input, capital costs are fixed costs and labor costs are variable costs.

Total cost is the amount that must be spent on all inputs to produce a given level of output, including all applicable opportunity costs.[15] Total cost is comprised of fixed costs and variable costs, all the costs associated with the capital inputs and all the costs associated with the variable inputs. Using the same notation developed earlier, the total cost function may be written $C = rK + wL$. In other words, the production function and the prices of inputs determine the firm's total cost function. The production function determines how much capital and labor are used in the production process, and the respective input prices determine the total amount spent on each input.

In practice, the short-run total cost curve may be derived from the short-run production function. With the amount of capital available fixed in the short run, rK is constant and represents fixed costs. In order to increase the level of output, the amount of labor used must increase. The production function determines the amount of labor needed to produce any given level of output. The short-run variable cost associated with each level of output (Q) is determined by the amount of labor required (L) multiplied by the cost of labor (w). Figure 3B.7 depicts the short-run total cost function associated with the production function shown in Figure 3B.3. Note the symmetry. In the range of output where production increases at an increasing rate (up to point A in Figure 3B.3), cost increases at a decreasing rate. When production increases at a decreasing rate, cost increases at an increasing rate.

This relationship is much clearer when viewed from the perspective of the short-run average and marginal cost curves. By definition, average variable cost (AVC) is the total variable cost (TVC) divided by the level of output produced (Q), or $AVC = TVC/Q$.

Since $TVC = wL$, $AVC = wL/Q$ or $w(L/Q)$. Remembering that Q/L is the average product of labor (AP_L), we note $AVC = w/AP_L$. As the average product of labor increases, average variable cost decreases. When AP_L reaches its maximum AVC reaches its minimum. As AP_L decreases, AVC increases.

Likewise, the relationship between marginal cost (MC) and the marginal product of labor (MP_L) can be determined: $MC = \Delta TVC/\Delta Q$. Substituting wL for TVC yields $MC = \Delta wL/DQ$. In competitive labor markets, the firm is a price taker, so the only way to change wL is to change L, implying $MC = w(\Delta L/\Delta Q)$. Because $\Delta Q/\Delta L$ is the marginal product of labor, $MC = w/MP_L$. As marginal product increases, marginal cost decreases. When MP_L reaches its maximum, MC reaches its minimum. As MP_L decreases, MC increases. Thus, we expect shortrun average costs and short-run marginal costs to be U-shaped, initially decreasing, then reaching a minimum, and finally increasing.

The relationship between average costs and marginal costs is shown in Figure 3B.8. Average total cost is the sum of average fixed cost and average variable cost. As long as marginal cost is below average cost, notice that average cost decreases. When marginal cost rises above average cost, average cost

Figure 3B.7: Short-Run Total Cost Curves

---

[15] Opportunity costs include both the explicit costs associated with actual payments to resources used in production and the implicit costs associated with the owners' time and investment. Explicit costs are all those costs recorded by the firm for accounting purposes, including rent paid on buildings, salaries paid to workers, and interest paid on loans. Implicit costs are the opportunity costs of using resources owned by the firm, including forgone earnings on money invested in the business.

begins to increase. Thus, marginal cost intersects each average cost curve at its respective minimum.[16]

LONG-RUN COSTS

Long-run costs are also U-shaped, but for different reasons. In the long run the firm has the option of increasing the size of its physical plant. Doing so often means the use of more efficient equipment, specialized labor, and lower average costs. The economic principle is called economies of scale. The long-run average cost curve may be thought of as an envelope curve, depicting the least-cost option for producing each level of output. Figure 3B.9 shows the long-run average costs associated with three different plant sizes: small (AC_S), medium (AC_M), and large (AC_L). The minimum cost of producing each level of output depends on the size of the physical plant. If the desired level of output is less than Q_1, the firm will minimize cost if it uses the small plant. For output levels between Q_1 and Q_2, costs are minimized using the medium-sized plant. For output levels greater than Q_2, the large plant minimizes costs.

The envelope curve in the diagram on the righthand side depicts all possible plant sizes. Competition will force the firm to use the plant whose costs are given by AC_4, the optimal plant. Firms that do not use this sized plant will find themselves with higher costs than their competitors, and they will lose money.

CONCLUSION

The theory discussed in this appendix provides a summary of the economic theory of the firm. The material is not intended to cover the full range of topics presented in a microeconomics course, but it should be sufficient to give the reader a broad overview of the standard neoclassical theory of the firm.

Figure 3B.8: Short-Run Average and Marginal Cost Curves

Figure 3B.9: Long-Run Average Cost

---

[16] For those with a little knowledge of calculus, the intersection of average and marginal cost at minimum average cost may be shown by noting that the slope of the average cost curve is equal to zero at its minimum; that is, its first derivative is equal to zero at its minimum. For the average variable cost curve

$$\frac{dAVC}{dQ} = \frac{d(TVC/Q)}{dQ} = 0$$

$$= \frac{Q(dTVC/dQ) - TVC(dQ/DQ)}{Q2} = 0$$

Dividing both terms in the numerator and factoring out $1/Q$ results in

$$\frac{1}{Q}[MC - AVC] = 0$$

For the right side of the expression to equal zero, $MC = AVC$, or marginal cost equals average variable cost when the slope of average variable cost equals zero (when AVC has reached its minimum).

CHAPTER 4

Economic Evaluation in Health Care[1]

As we have seen, the existence of trade-offs is an inevitable fact of life that we all must come to grips with sooner or later. Eventually every physician must decide if the improvement in a patient's health is worth the additional spending for a particular intervention. Even those physicians who ignore costs will weigh the benefits in terms of medical efficacy.

In society at large, health insurers and health plans must decide whether to cover a specific intervention or treatment. The formulary committee for a health maintenance organization must decide which drugs in a particular category will be available to HMO members. The administrator of a hospital must decide where to invest the hospital's capital budget. Government agencies must determine which drugs will be eligible for reimbursement through public programs. By considering costs and benefits, these decision makers are actually applying economic analysis to their particular situations. In other words, they are looking for ways to improve how resources are used in pursuit of better health for individual patients, for groups of patients, or for society as a whole.

Key Concept 3
Marginal Analysis

Some may consider valuing life in monetary terms immoral or unethical, but the consequences of ignoring valuation are substantial. Too often, health effects are ignored when we focus on cost. But when our focus is solely on health, cost issues are ignored. With no clear guidelines, decisions are made on a case-by-case basis, and rules are applied arbitrarily.

This chapter discusses the use of economic evaluation in health care decision making. In the first two sections, we explore the importance and meaning of economic evaluation. The third section provides a detailed discussion of the types of economic evaluation, including cost-of-illness studies, cost-benefit analysis, and cost-effectiveness analysis. Because cost-effectiveness analysis is currently the preferred method for analyzing treatment options in healthcare, this technique is the focus of this chapter. Details are provided for calculating the incremental cost-effectiveness ratio, issues in measuring costs and benefits (including a discussion of the quality-adjusted life year), and the steps in performing a cost-effectiveness analysis. Section four is a discussion on the use of modeling in economic evaluation, looking specifically at decision analysis and Markov modeling. Section five looks at the trend toward standardization of economic evaluation techniques, particularly in Europe. Section six summarizes several case

[1] Much of the content and examples used in the presentation of this chapter can be traced, either directly or indirectly, to the 2003 training program "Health Economics of Pharmaceuticals and Other Medical Interventions." I would like to thank Gisela Kobelt, director of the European School of Health Economics, and all the presenters and participants for their efforts in making the program worthwhile.

studies using the techniques discussed in the chapter. The final section provides a summary and conclusions.

ISSUES IN MEDICAL CARE DELIVERY

Medicare Rationing Under the Name of "Functional Equivalence"

Without the benefit of an act of Congress, much less a congressional debate, Medicare officials have adopted policies that limit what the program will pay for new drugs and medical procedures. Using what Thomas Scully, previous director of the Centers for Medicare and Medicaid Services (CMS), called "functional equivalence," agency officials are making decisions on whether Medicare will cover certain drug treatments and what prices it will pay.

Functional equivalence is virtually identical to reference pricing, a favorite method of price controls used by many European health care systems to control the price of prescription drugs. It works something like this: the appropriate government agency negotiates the price of every new prescription drug; then, using the best scientific evidence available, it pegs the price at the same level of the low-price drug that treats the same disease or condition.

Medicare already controls the prices of every physician's visit and hospital stay for the nation's 33 million senior citizens covered by the program. Under the guise of spending tax dollars prudently, the agency is making medical decisions about the efficacy of new drug treatments without the necessary expertise. Two recent decisions illustrate the approach:

- The new biotech drug Aranesp was developed to treat anemia in cancer patients. Not only is it faster acting and longer lasting than the existing drug Procrit, Aranesp can be administered less often, making it a less invasive treatment. But CMS determined that there was not enough evidence to justify the difference in price between the two drugs, and it set reimbursement rates for Aranesp at one-third of its market price.
- Medicare patients cannot receive Nexium, a new drug developed to treat ulcers caused by acid reflux and the resulting esophagitis. Even though medical trials indicate that patients treated with Nexium had fewer physician's visits, faster healing, and fewer hospitalizations, agency officials determined that the drug was identical to Prilosec, which became available in a cheaper generic form in December 2002.

Federal efforts to hold down spending are not new. In fact, a federal advisory committee in early 2003 urged CMS to weigh costs and benefits in its drug-coverage decisions. Under Medicare law, the agency has broad powers to set payments at any level. The question to consider is not whether costs should be compared to benefits, but who should make those comparisons. Is this the task of lawyers, lobbyists, and politicians? Or should physicians, scientists (including economists), and patients make these decisions?

Source: Robert Goldberg, "Medicare Reform, French Style: Tom Scully Can't Wait to Put Price Controls on Drugs," *Washington Times*, April 30, 2003, A23.

IMPORTANCE OF ECONOMIC EVALUATION

Because we live in a world of scarce resources, we do not have the ability to satisfy the desires of all the people all of the time. Different people have different objectives. We must make choices, and often these choices are difficult, if not downright unpleasant. Beneficial projects compete for the same resources: Investing in a new mammography-screening program may preclude the local hospital from expanding its prenatal care program. Paying for the newest and most expensive drugs to treat asthma, high blood pressure, and diabetes may mean that the health plan requires physicians to perform sigmoidoscopy instead of colonoscopy for routine colon cancer screening.

Key Concept 2
Opportunity Cost

    Every day we are forced to make choices among competing alternatives. We do not have unlimited resources, so programs compete for the same funds, and some worthwhile programs go unfunded. How we make these decisions is critically important. In most cases, the way we address these issues is a matter of quality of life; but in many cases, it is a matter of life and death. In either case, it is important that we approach resource allocation decisions in health care in a clear and systematic way.

Key Concept 1
Scarcity and Choice

MEANING OF ECONOMIC EVALUATION

Before we get too far into our discussion, it may be helpful if we define what we mean by economic evaluation. Drummond and colleagues (1997) use the term to mean "the comparative analysis of alternative courses of action in terms of both their costs and consequences." Economic evaluation is a comparative analysis. There must be at least two alternatives, or interventions, under consideration to perform a comparative analysis. We typically do not compare an intervention or procedure to doing nothing, unless doing nothing is a reasonable option. "What about clinical trials?" you may ask. Human testing is often done in a clinical setting, where one, experimental group of patients is given the treatment under consideration, often a drug being tested, and a second, control group is given a placebo (a sugar pill). Remember, this is a clinical setting. It is a test, the scientific equivalent of the gold standard; and at the end of the test, no one suggests that the sugar pill, the do-nothing strategy, is a reasonable option.

    As stated above, an economic evaluation examines alternative courses of action. We do not examine a treatment option in isolation from all other treatment options. Economic evaluation compares alternative treatment options that are reasonable alternatives to treating a well-defined medical condition. Mandelblatt and colleagues (2002) studied the most effective use of resources associated with a general-population screening program for cervical cancer. The study examined the cost effectiveness of Pap testing alone, HPV testing alone, or a joint use of the two tests at two screening intervals, two and three years, beginning at age 20 and continuing until age 65 or 75 or until death. The analysis compared costs and consequences for 18 different screening strategies.

    The comparisons in an economic evaluation are made in terms of costs and consequences. The specific costs to be included in the analysis are largely determined by the perspective taken; the view differs among an individual patient, a health insurance company, a health plan, a government agency, or society as a whole. Costs include direct and indirect costs, both tangible and intangible. The consequences of an action are the benefits that accrue primarily to individuals, unless, of course, significant externalities are associated with the treatment, such as benefits that result from a vaccination program. The primary tasks required to successfully conduct an economic evaluation are to identify, measure, value, and compare all the relevant costs and consequences. All of these issues will be explored in more detail below.

TYPES OF ECONOMIC EVALUATION

Three types of economic evaluation are frequently used in health care decision making: cost-of-illness studies, cost-benefit analysis, and cost-effectiveness analysis (Garber, 2001). Each in its own unique way is really nothing more than an attempt to logically weigh the costs and consequences of alternative medical actions.

Cost-of-Illness Studies

Cost-of-illness studies merely look at the question, "What is the cost?" The quantification of the economic burden of a specific disease provides information on the cost structure related to that disease for a specific population in a well-defined geographic area. Because there is no outcome measure per se, a cost-of-illness study is not an economic evaluation in the strictest sense of the term. It does provide important information to policy makers and health economists on the burden of a disease. In that sense, a cost-of-illness study may be a first, important step in cost identification leading to an economic evaluation.

Providers can use this type of analysis to guide medical decision making when the clinical effectiveness of treatment options is equivalent. Under these circumstances, a better description might be cost-minimization analysis, a study to determine the low-cost treatment option to bring about a defined health outcome (e.g., the low-cost option to treat acute otitis media, or middle ear infection).

POLICY ISSUE

A large percentage of health care spending is attributable to life-style factors.

Druss and colleagues (2001) examined the economic burden of five chronic conditions affecting the U.S. population in 1996: mood disorders, diabetes, heart disease, asthma, and hypertension. Medical care costs to treat these five conditions amounted to $62.3 billion, with heart disease and hypertension making up over half of the total. Additionally, the cost of treating coexisting medical conditions totaled $207.7 billion. Adding to the total health costs of $270 billion, the estimated $36.2 billion in lost earnings due to missed work brings the total societal costs for those who suffer from these five conditions to over $306 billion.

Finkelstein and colleagues (2003) estimated the national medical spending attributable to overweight and obesity to be $92.6 billion (in 2002 dollars). Even though the estimate in obesity-related expenditures is less than 6 percent of total health care spending, the research indicates that over one-third of the annual increase in health care spending is associated with conditions attributable to obesity: type 2 diabetes, cardiovascular disease, musculoskeletal disorders, sleep apnea, gallbladder disease, and several types of cancer, including endometrial and post-menopausal breast, kidney, and colon cancer. Other cost-of-illness studies have examined the societal costs of AIDS (Scitovsky and Rice, 1987), alcohol, drug abuse, mental illness (Rice et al., 1990), and cocaine-exposed infants (Henderson, 1991).

Even though the results of cost-of-illness studies are interesting, they do not answer questions related to the most effective options for treating the disorders. To answer questions concerning optimal resource allocation, we must try a different approach to economic evaluation—either cost-benefit analysis or cost-effectiveness analysis.

Cost-Benefit Analysis

Managers of for-profit firms must make decisions on how to allocate their firms' scarce resources among alternative investment projects. If a firm is to maximize profits and remain competitive in the marketplace, the net gain from a project (benefits minus costs) should also be maximized. The financial analysis of alternative investment projects is known as *capital budgeting*.[2] But private sector managers are not the only decision makers who have to make these capital budgeting decisions. Public sector managers must make decisions on how to spend scarce tax dollars to maximize the public welfare. The use of capital budgeting, a technique developed for and applied to decision making in a market environment, is not applicable in a not-for-profit environment. Public sector managers make these decisions, in most cases, insulated from the full discipline of the market that directs private sector managers.

A simple extension of the capital budgeting process is cost-benefit analysis. First developed to assist government agencies in making decisions about the provision of public goods, cost-benefit analysis is an analytical technique that compares all the costs and all the benefits arising from a program or project. Thus, cost-benefit analysis is to the public, not-for-profit sector what capital budgeting is to the private, for-profit sector.

Key Concept 3
Marginal Analysis

As we saw in Chapter 2, the optimal use of resources requires that every program or project undertaken by the public sector have a marginal social benefit (MSB) that exceeds its marginal social cost (MSC). The problem for public sector decision makers is that the information required to construct MSB and MSC curves is not readily known, making it difficult to determine the social optimum. Cost-benefit analysis is a practical attempt to ensure optimal choice in the absence of markets, while remaining true to the traditional welfare economics approach (Sen, 1977).

Elements of a Cost-Benefit Analysis Given the budgetary constraints on most public policy decisions, cost-benefit analysis is often used to justify expenditures on specific public sector projects. By forcing decision makers to determine whether the benefits from the project are worth the associated costs, measuring both in monetary terms, only those projects that show a positive net benefit are warranted on economic grounds. Alternatively, the ratio of benefits to costs can be calculated, and only those projects with a benefit-cost ratio greater than or equal to one are accepted.

In practice, benefits and costs accumulate over time, so they must be adjusted for the time value of money through the use of present value discounting. The concept of time preference simply recognizes that a dollar today is worth more than a dollar in the future. The inherent uncertainty of the future and the forgone opportunities of not having the dollar today are the two biggest reasons that people place a higher value on today's dollar. Because most people have a positive time preference, future costs and benefits must be discounted to make them comparable with current costs and benefits.

Key Concept 2
Opportunity Cost

Most people are familiar with the concept of compounding, or earning interest on interest. Suppose that you could invest $1,000 in a 12-month certificate of

---

[2] Any good managerial economics textbook will have a chapter analyzing long-term investment decisions, and many will have a chapter on public sector decision making; see, for example, McGuigan, Moyer, and Harris (2002).

deposit (CD) with a guaranteed 10 percent annual return. One year from now, that initial $1,000 investment would be worth $1,100. The general formula may be stated as follows:

$$FV_1 = PV(1 + r)$$

where

$$FV_1 = \text{the future value of the initial investment in one year}$$

$$PV = \text{the present value of the initial investment}$$

$$r = \text{the annual return on the initial investment, or interest rate}$$

Compounding would require that you expand the number of time periods that you leave the money in the CD. At the end of the second year, you would have $1,210.[3] Continuing this logic through n periods, the formula for compounding is:

$$FV_n = PV(1 + r)^n$$

In other words, an investment of PV today will grow to FV_n in n years at an annual interest rate of r percent.

Discounting takes the opposite perspective. If an individual wishes to have FV_n in n years, then PV would have to be invested at an interest rate of r percent. To solve this problem, we simply solve the above equation for PV and get:

$$PV = FV_n / (1 + r)^n$$

This same fundamental relationship may be used to estimate the present value of a stream of earnings, Y_i, per year for n years. This may be written:

$$PV = \frac{Y_1}{(1 + r)^1} + \frac{Y_2}{(1 + r)^2} + \cdots + \frac{Y_n}{(1 + r)^n}$$

Assuming a constant discount rate (r) over time, this expression may be written more simply as:

$$PV = \sum_{t=1}^{n} \frac{Y_t}{(1 + r)^t}$$

This relationship may be adapted to depict the present value of a net benefits stream over time (NB) by defining the stream of earnings (Y_i) in the above equation as the difference between the annual benefits (B_i) and the annual costs (C_i) of the project:

$$NB = \sum_{t=1}^{n} \frac{B_t - C_t}{(1 + r)^t}$$

Projects are accepted only if the present value of the net benefits stream is positive. Alternatively, the relationship may be presented as a benefit-cost ratio. In this case, the ratio of benefits to costs must be greater than one before a project is accepted.

$$B/C = \sum_{t=1}^{n} \frac{B_t}{(1 + r)^t} \bigg/ \sum_{t=1}^{n} \frac{C_i}{(1 + r)^t}$$

---

[3] This calculation would be $[\$1,000 \times (1 + 0.1)] \times (1 + 0.1)$.

Valuing Benefits Cost-benefit analysis requires that all benefits and costs be valued in monetary terms. Valuing benefits is usually not a cause for concern when the project involves the construction of a dam or an interstate highway. However, when the technique is applied to medical care, the practice is equivalent to placing a monetary value on human life.

Placing a dollar value on life may be unsettling to many, but the monetization of benefits is necessary to calculate a benefit-cost ratio. The technique rests entirely on the premise that the values used in social decision making are simply the sum of all individual values. As we saw earlier, the values individuals place on things are based on the prices they are willing to pay for them. Benefits are typically valued using the willingness-to-pay approach. An individual's willingness to pay for an improvement in health depends on four factors: wealth, life expectancy, current health status, and the possibility of substituting current consumption for future consumption (Bleichrodt and Quiggin, 1999). To the extent that the results of a cost-benefit analysis applied to a medical care decision reflect the willingness and ability to pay of the individuals who stand to benefit, the subsequent allocation of medical resources based on that analysis may be viewed suspiciously, because it will likely favor certain groups: the wealthy, the young, and those with serious health problems.

It is the task of decision makers to ensure that spending and investment decisions reflect stakeholder values. Individual providers make decisions with the values of their patients as the primary consideration and those of the hospital, health plan, and community of secondary importance. On the other hand, government policy makers are more likely to take the perspective of society as a whole and be as concerned with equity and other welfare considerations as they are with economic efficiency.

POLICY ISSUE

What is the value of a human life?

ISSUES IN MEDICAL CARE DELIVERY

Intergenerational Equity and the "Fair Innings" Approach

For decades economists have considered the challenge of balancing equity against efficiency in issues related to access to life's essentials, in particular food and shelter. The reality that we face in our attempt to satisfy unlimited wants is the scarcity of resources. It is essential that we use resources wisely, but we must also be sensitive to the distribution of the benefits that flow from their use. In a world of trade-offs, we must establish priorities.

Medical care is no different. We have the technical capabilities that allow us to live longer and better. But even in the developed world, we do not have the resources required to extend unlimited access to medical care.

Alan Williams (1997) examines this issue using the concept of "fair innings." Based on egalitarian ideology, it reflects the notion that every person is entitled to a normal life span. An individual who does not live out this normal life span has been deprived in some way of his or her "fair innings." In reality we view the death of a young person differently than the death of someone older. It is not nearly so tragic for someone who is 85 to die than it is for someone who is 25. One lived beyond her "fair innings," the other's life was cut short before he could do the same.

continued

> To successfully use this approach in health resource allocation, efficiency is defined as maximizing health gain using some well-defined measure (life years or quality-adjusted life years). In addition, equity must take into consideration certain characteristics of the person receiving the medical care, such as age and lifestyle choices.
>
> If our definition of equality is relevant to population segments, it is reasonable to apply it over a lifetime and not just at one point in time. Consider a population with two distinct groups; call them Group A and Group B (these may be defined by race, sex, or socioeconomic status). Suppose that the life expectancy of Group A is 75 years and that of Group B is 80 years. To the extent that public policy can bring about a change in this outcome, it seems reasonable to call for a change in public policy to narrow this five-year difference. For the sake of equity, this outcome could be orchestrated by weighting the additional years differently, according to group membership. In other words, an additional year of life of someone in Group A would carry a higher weight than an additional year for a Group B member. The relevant question for policy purposes becomes, how many life years in population life expectancy are you willing to give up to narrow the gap in life expectancy between Group A and Group B? Even if the current distribution of resources is efficient, how much efficiency are you willing to sacrifice to improve equity?
>
> With philosophers, theologians, and ethicists weighing in on the social justice discussion, the fair innings argument provides economists with a platform to bring quantifiable, outcome-based arguments into the discussion.
>
> **Source:** Alan William, "Intergenerational Equity: An Exploration of the 'Fair Innings' Argument," *Health Economics* 6, 1997, 117–132.

Choosing a Discount Rate The choice of the discount rate is one of the most critical factors in determining the net present value of a project or program. In fact, the present value of a net-benefits stream is inversely related to the discount rate. Higher discount rates place more importance on costs and benefits realized early in the life of the program. Costs and benefits realized far into the future are discounted substantially.

In theory the appropriate discount rate used to evaluate an investment depends on the opportunity cost of funds or, to be more specific, the risk-adjusted rate of return on the next-best investment alternative. For many private investment opportunities, the appropriate discount rate is the interest rate that must be paid on funds borrowed to undertake the project.

In the final analysis, the choice of discount rate depends critically on the perspective taken in the analysis. From the perspective of society, the appropriate discount rate should be reflective of society's collective time preference, or the rate at which future consumption is collectively discounted. In practice, there are a number of interest rates that might be used, ranging from the prime lending rate charged by large money-center banks to their best customers, to the interest rate on U.S. government treasury bonds. In those countries that require an economic evaluation before a medical device or new drug is approved for reimbursement, the typical discount rate is between 1.5 and 6 percent.[4]

---

[4] Australian and Canadian guidelines require a mandatory 5 percent discount rate; the UK calls for costs to be discounted at 6 percent and benefits at 1.5 percent; and the Netherlands mandates 4 percent (Hjelmgren et al., 2001).

Applying Cost-Benefit Analysis A number of studies have used the cost-benefit approach to examine the effectiveness of medical care programs. One of the early applications of cost-benefit analysis in medical care is the classic study of poliomyelitis by Weisbrod (1971). The study compared the costs and benefits of the medical research program that led to the development of the Salk and Sabin vaccines used against polio. The analysis included only a subset of benefits, focusing on reduced treatment costs and increased productivity. Per capita benefits were estimated as the sum of the market value of work lost due to premature mortality, the market value of work lost to morbidity, and the savings from resources used to treat and rehabilitate. Work-loss estimates were defined as the present value of expected future earnings lost due to the effects of the disease. Research costs were estimated as the sum of the awards for polio research. Weisbrod used several estimates for the vaccination costs to determine rates of return on the research. Rates of return on the basic research program ranged from 4 percent for the high-cost estimate to 14 percent for the low-cost estimate with the most likely rate of return about 11 to 12 percent. Even though Weisbrod's study focused on polio research, the analysis showed that the methodology could be applied to a wide range of programs in the medical research field.

The use of cost-benefit analysis in medical care prior to 1980 was reviewed by Hellinger (1980). More recent examples include the study by Goddeeris and Bronken (1985) on gonorrheal screening in asymptomatic women and the examination of a vaccination program by Jackson and colleagues (1995). Clarke (1998) examined the costs and benefits of a mobile mammographic screening program for rural Australia. Ginsberg and Lev (1997) studied the treatment of amyotrophic lateral sclerosis.

Cost-Effectiveness Analysis

If improving the health of a given population is the primary goal of health policy, then the preferred measure of health benefits may be the health outcomes themselves and not their dollar value. Cost-effectiveness (CE) analysis, developed outside the welfare economics framework, is a way to quantify trade-offs between resources used and health outcomes achieved without having to value health outcomes in monetary terms—a prospect that appeals to many policy makers.

The intuitive appeal of cost-effectiveness analysis is based on its pragmatic approach to resource allocation, sometimes referred to as a *decision-makers' approach*. The entire framework of CE analysis sounds like an economic problem: maximize the level of health for a given population subject to budget constraints. Thus, CE analysis provides a practical guide for choosing between programs when limited budgets do not allow decision makers to implement every program that might improve the health of the population.

Key Concept No. 1
Scarcity and Choice

Elements of a Cost-Effectiveness Analysis Cost-effectiveness analysis relates the cost of two or more treatment options to a single, common consequence that differs among options (e.g., blood pressure reduction, hip fractures avoided, or increased life expectancy). The treatment options may be different treatments for the same condition, such as kidney dialysis compared with kidney transplantation, or unrelated treatments with a common effect, such as the life-saving treatment for heart disease compared to end stage renal failure.

The usefulness of CE analysis is more limited when the effectiveness of treatment options is measured differently, or when there are multiple measures of effectiveness. If one treatment option prevents premature death and the other reduces disability days, comparing the two is more problematic. One way around this dilemma, other than placing monetary values on outcomes and using cost-benefit analysis, is to use utility measures—actual measures of health preferences—for health outcomes. Cost-utility analysis, a special case of CE analysis, addresses quality of life concerns through the use of quality-adjusted life years (QALYs) determined by the presence of intangibles such as pain, suffering, and disability. More will be said about QALYs later.

Incremental Cost-Effectiveness Ratio (ICER)   When decision makers are faced with limited budgets, CE analysis provides a systematic methodology to achieve the best overall health benefit for a given population. When the most effective treatment option for a medical condition is also the least expensive, the choice is easy. The difficulty arises when the most effective treatment option is more expensive. Policy makers need an objective measure to help determine the preferred treatment option.

The measure provided by CE analysis is the incremental cost-effectiveness ratio (ICER). The incremental cost-effectiveness ratio provides a way to compare the differences in costs and effectiveness of two treatment options using the following formula:

$$ICER = \frac{C_B - C_A}{E_B - E_A}$$

where

$C_{A, B}$ = costs of treatment options A and B
$E_{A, B}$ = clinical effectiveness of treatment options A and B

When CE analysis is used in clinical decision making, the usual approach is to define the treatment option being studied (treatment B) and an alternative treatment option for comparison (treatment A). If $C_A > C_B$ and $E_A < E_B$ option A is both more costly and less effective. In this case, we say that treatment option B dominates. If $C_A < C_B$ and $E_A > E_B$, option B is both more costly and less effective. In this case, we say that treatment option A dominates. In both of these cases, further analysis is unnecessary; the most effective treatment option is also cheaper, and the choice is simple. If, however, $C_B > C_A$ and $E_B > E_A$, the choice is not as obvious, and a CE analysis is in order.

The ICER may be clearly depicted graphically as seen in Figure 4.1. The gain in effectiveness is plotted on the y axis, the net present value of the total costs, on the x axis. With each treatment option represented by a point on the graph, it is easy to see that the higher the point, the more effective the treatment; the farther to the right, the more expensive the treatment.

Using this graphical presentation, the ICER comparing the two treatment options is the inverse of the slope of the line between points A and B. A steeply sloped line indicates a low ICER, or a substantial improvement in health effects for a relatively small cost. As the slope gets flatter, the ICER increases, which is indicative of higher cost interventions relative to their effectiveness.

If a number of treatment options are being considered for the same medical problem, the graphical presentation clearly depicts the preferred strategies (Mark, 2002). Points A through G in Figure 4.2 represent the costs and effects of seven options for the screening or treatment of a disease. The options that form the solid line $ABDFG$ represent the economically rational subset of treatment options. Points that lie below the line, such as points C and E, represent treatment

Figure 4.1: Incremental Cost-Effectiveness Comparing Two Treatment Options

Figure 4.2: Incremental Cost-Effectiveness Comparing Multiple Treatment Options

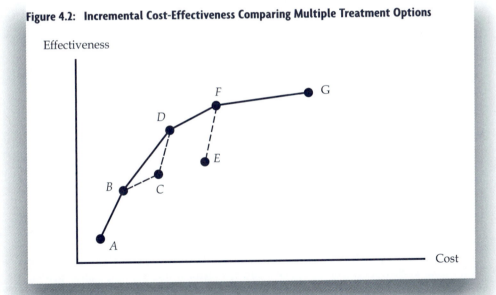

options that are dominated by those that are on the line.[5] As the slope of the line gets flatter, the ICER increases, providing a clear depiction of the theoretical construct called the *flat of the curve* (Enthoven, 1980).

---

[5] Note that the treatment option represented by point *E* is not only less effective than the one represented by point *D*, it is more expensive. Thus, treatment option *E* is strictly dominated by treatment option *D*. The treatment option represented by point *C* is dominated due to the logic of extended dominance. Because there are points on the line between *B* and *D* that represent combinations of options *B* and *D* that are more effective and cheaper, *C* is dominated by a combination of treatment options *B* and *D*.

Measuring Costs and Effects All types of economic evaluation require the measurement of costs and effects, the inputs and outputs associated with the treatment. The costs of the treatment are the opportunity cost of the resources used in providing the treatment minus the value of any resources saved due to the treatment. Costs may be classified as direct, indirect, or intangible. Direct costs are typically divided into direct medical and direct nonmedical costs. Direct medical costs include the cost associated with the use of medical resources. This includes hospitalization, outpatient visits, medical procedures, laboratory testing, pharmaceutical drugs, medical devices, and other medical services, such as home care and nursing care. Direct nonmedical costs are those costs typically borne by patients and their families. These costs include transportation expenses; home services such as cleaning, cooking, shopping, and other personal maintenance services; and other nonmedical investments, such as home remodeling to accommodate a physical handicap.

Key Concept 2
Opportunity Cost

Indirect costs are the costs related to lost productivity. This includes sick leave, reduced productivity at work, and other productivity losses due to early retirement or premature death. Intangible costs are those costs associated with a diminished quality of life. These costs include pain and suffering, grief and anxiety, and disfigurement. Because they are difficult to measure, these costs are often ignored.[6]

The effectiveness of a treatment is measured in terms of the improvement in health associated with it, which may be expressed in terms of surrogate, intermediate, or final measures. Surrogate measures examine the clinical effect of a treatment option or its clinical efficacy; these may be stated in terms of blood pressure, cholesterol level, bone-mass density (BMD), or tumor size. Intermediate measures include clinical effectiveness, or outcome, measures and may be stated in terms of events, such as heart attack, stroke, hip fracture, remission/recurrence of cancer, or death. Scores on standard evaluative exams, such as the EuroQol, SF 36, or MMSE, are also intermediate measures. Final outcomes measure economic effectiveness and may be stated in terms of events avoided, infections cured, disease-free days, life years saved, or quality-adjusted life years gained.

Generally speaking, the clinical endpoints—both the surrogate and intermediate measures—should be linked to final economic outcomes, or endpoints, in order to calculate the cost effectiveness of the various treatment options. Representing these linkages usually requires some type of modeling using epidemiological data to estimate the transition probabilities from one stage in the course of a treatment to another. It is possible to determine the probability of a hip fracture using BMD scores at various ages, and the probability of heart attack or stroke at different blood pressure and cholesterol levels by age and gender. Ideally, we are interested in avoiding the consequences of an event rather than the clinical event itself. Thus, final outcomes are preferably measured in terms of improvements in survival and quality of life.

Survival Measures Even though survival may be stated in a number of different ways, for the purpose of economic evaluation, it is typically measured in terms of the number of years of life. When comparing the effects of two treatment options, the difference in life expectancy between the two is the preferred survival measure. Evidence of differences in survival is usually determined from the results

---

[6] One line of economic research, highlighted by the work of Kip Viscusi, attempts to develop a measure of utility in monetary terms. This approach, when used to value health benefits, values an individual's or society's willingness to pay for improvements in health. See Viscusi and Aldy (2003) for an extensive literature review on the topic.

of a clinical trial. Seldom do clinical trials last long enough to provide complete information to calculate differences in life expectancy between the treatment and nontreatment groups.[7]

Using the approach in Kobelt (2002), the problem with calculating the survival benefit of a particular treatment is illustrated in Figure 4.3. The two survival functions in the graph represent the percentage of each group that survives over time. The area under the survival function is a measure of life expectancy. Thus, the area between the two survival functions represents the difference in life expectancy between the two groups. Suppose that the two groups have been chosen to test the effects of a new pharmaceutical drug for the treatment of heart disease. At the end of the 18-month trial, 90 percent of the treatment group is still alive, but only 77 percent of the control group is alive. For simplicity, assume that 20 percent of each group dies each year after the trial, implying that all are dead five years after the trial is over.[8]

The gain in life expectancy during the trial due to the treatment is the area of the triangle ABC. The calculation is $1/2 (0.90 - 0.77) \times 1.5$, or 0.0975 years.[9] Even if the treatment does not increase the overall longevity of the group receiving the drug, there is still a gain in life expectancy after the trial ends, represented in the graph by the triangle BCD. The posttrial gain in life expectancy for the treatment group is $1/2 (0.90 - 0.77) \times 5$, or 0.325 years. Thus, the total gain in life expectancy for the group receiving the new drug is 0.4225 years, with over three-fourths of that gain coming after the trial is over. At the beginning of the trial, life expectancy without the treatment was 3.25 years. As a result of the treatment, life expectancy increased to 3.6725 years, or 13 percent.

Figure 4.3: Improved Life Expectancy Due to Clinical Treatment

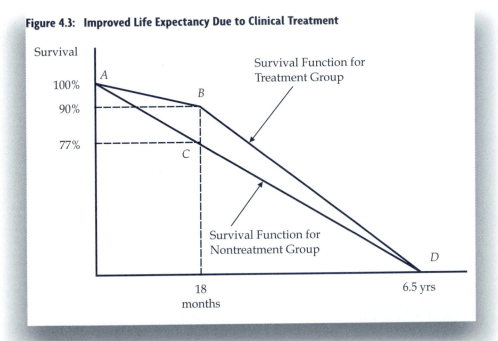

---

[7] Clinical trials usually last 1 to 3 years, much less than the life expectancy of the typical participant.

[8] The typical survival function is not linear, but is drawn convex to the origin, or decreasing at a decreasing rate. The usual function may be written $S(t) = e^{-\lambda t}$. In this functional form, life expectancy is $1/\lambda$.

[9] Remember that the area of a triangle is $\frac{1}{2}$ base $\times$ height.

Quality of Life Measures Quite often improvements in life expectancy do not fully capture the benefits of a medical intervention. Extending life can result in a decrease in the quality of life. Furthermore, an intervention may result in quality-of-life improvements without actually extending life. What is needed is a measure of effectiveness that captures improvements in the quality of life, as well as extensions in the length of life. The quality-adjusted life year, or QALY (pronounced *kwa-lee*), serves such a purpose.

The concept of the QALY was first introduced in the study of chronic renal failure (Klarman et al., 1968). The actual term was used for the first time a decade later (Weinstein and Stason, 1977) and has since become the quality of life measure of choice in CE analysis. The measure simultaneously captures the value of reduced morbidity (improved quality of life) and reduced mortality (increased quantity of life).

The QALY may be viewed as life expectancy with a preference weight or quality weight attached to each year. Life is affected by functional limitations, pain and suffering, and the daily burden of a disease; all have an impact on the utility attached to each additional year of living. Normally, an additional year of life while suffering the effects of a particular disease will have less weight associated with it than an additional year of life in a healthy state. To use the QALY concept to represent quality of life for the health states under consideration, quality weights must be attached to the various health states. These quality weights are based on individual preferences for the various health states, measured on an interval scale anchored by death (equal to zero) and perfect health (equal to one).

A QALY is a probability-weighted average of the expected quality of life estimates associated with each possible health state. A QALY converts the number of years spent in a given health state to a smaller number of years spent in perfect health, which, according to the individual's preferences, is equally satisfying.

Consider a 55-year-old male with type 2 (non-insulin-dependent) diabetes. Complications from type 2 diabetes include kidney disease, retinopathy, and damage to the nervous system that results in more than half of all lower-limb amputations in the United States. The risk of heart disease and stroke are two to four times greater for someone with diabetes. Normally, a 55-year-old male could expect to live an additional 25 years; however, diabetes shortens life expectancy by an average of 10 years. Thus, a 55-year-old male with diabetes can expect to live to age 70. Based on individual preferences, suppose our subject places a utility value of 0.4 on each of his 15 remaining years. His 15 remaining years have a QALY value of 6 (15 × 0.4). Based on individual preferences, the total utility of living an additional 15 years with type 2 diabetes is the same as the total utility of living an additional 6 years in perfect health. Thus, this man would equate living 15 years with diabetes to living 6 years in perfect health.

Using Figure 4.4, the utility of living one year with diabetes, $U(h_i)$, is 40 percent of the utility of living one year in perfect health, $U(h_1)$. The total utility over the 15 remaining years of life, $15U(h_i)$, is equal to the total utility of living 6 years in perfect health, $6U(h_1)$.

Some disagree on whose preferences should be measured in determining QALY weights—people currently with the specific disease or the general population. If people with the disease (in this case, those with type 2 diabetes) were surveyed, they would be asked to compare their current health to their ideal health. If the general population were surveyed, they would be asked to rate a described, hypothetical health state.

Figure 4.4: Using Preferences for Health States to Calculate QALY

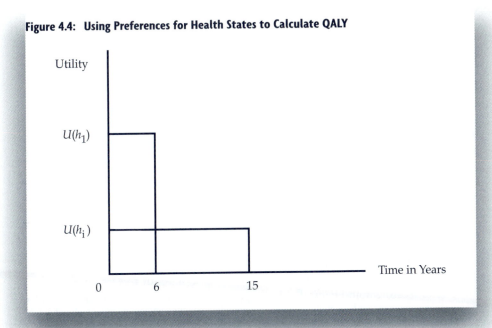

A second major issue is how to measure quality of life. The World Health Organization (WHO) defines quality of life along three dimensions of well-being: physical, mental, and social. Using a quality of well-being (QWB) approach, Kaplan and colleagues (1998) developed a classification system using four patient attributes: mobility, physical activity, social activity, and a symptom-problem complex. Dolan and colleagues (1996) used a time trade-off technique to measure preferences. This so-called EuroQol includes five health state attributes—mobility, self-care, usual activities, pain/discomfort, and anxiety/depression—to define 245 possible health states. Both approaches have been linked with the QALY to serve as a measure of the level of utility associated with the various health states.

Another option is to calculate the QALY using the standard time trade-off method, in which the individual is offered two alternatives:

- The chronic health state i for t years, followed immediately by death

- Perfect health for x years (where x is less than t), followed immediately by death

Time (x) is varied until the individual is indifferent to the two alternatives. The utility of the chronic health state is determined by the individual's preferences for perfect health. Thus, the value of one year in the chronic health state (h_i) is x/t. Consider the 55-year-old male with type 2 diabetes. He can expect to live an additional 15 years ($i = 15$) with the disease. If he would be willing to sacrifice 6 years of his life with the disease to live in perfect health, $x = 9$. Based on personal preferences, he has placed a QALY value of 0.6 on one year in the disease state ($x/t = 9/15$).

An alternative approach to calculating QALYs uses the standard gamble. Used to measure the utility that a person attaches to a particular health state, the standard gamble is a direct application of one of the fundamental axioms of classical utility theory (von Neumann and Morgenstern, 1944). Intuitively, the premise behind the standard gamble is simple:

- A treatment is available for individuals in the chronic disease state.

- When it works, the treatment provides a permanent cure. When it does not work, the result is immediate death.

- How high does the risk of dying have to be before the patient refuses treatment?

- The utility value of each year in the chronic disease state is equal to the associated probability that the treatment works.

More formally, the axiom is based on the continuity of preferences and states that if there are three outcomes (x_1, x_2, and x_3), some probability p exists whereby the individual is indifferent to the certain outcome x_1, and the risky prospect that comprises outcome x_2 with probability equal to p and outcome x_3 with probability equal to $1 - p$.

Consider a situation where an individual in the chronic disease state x_1 (preferred to death) has the choice to reject treatment and remain in x_1 for the remainder of her life (t years) or to accept a treatment that has two possible outcomes: perfect health, x_2, for t years with a probability equal to p, or sudden death, x_3, with a probability equal to $1 - p$. Based on the continuity of preferences axiom, the probability p can be adjusted until the individual is indifferent to the two alternatives: either rejecting treatment and living in the chronic disease state for t years, or accepting the risk of treatment and living t years in perfect health with a probability equal to p, or dying immediately. Under these conditions, the health preference weight for each year of living in chronic disease state x_1 is equal to p, the probability that the treatment will be fatal.

Steps in Performing a Cost-Effectiveness Analysis

The pieces involved in actually conducting a CE analysis are all in place. All that is left now is to actually set one up. The following steps summarize the process:

1. Rank the alternative treatment options by health benefit (beginning with the one with the lowest benefit).

2. Eliminate treatment alternatives that are strictly dominated.

3. Calculate the ICER between each treatment option and the next most expensive option.

4. Eliminate treatment options that display extended dominance.

5. Determine which treatment options have an ICER that is below the cut-off ICER.

Nothing in the exercise provides information on what society is willing to pay for a particular health benefit; in other words, we do not know what the optimal ICER should be. This step is somewhat problematic for those wanting to avoid valuing health benefits which is implicit in choosing a cut-off value. One approach has been to construct league tables.

The concept of the league table originated from European football rankings (soccer for Americans). In a health care application, these so-called league tables compare the ICER for various interventions. The usual practice is to compile ICERs for a number of common medical interventions from a literature search and to place the intervention under study in the mix. In this context, a case for or against a particular intervention can be made through comparison with other interventions. Garber and Phelps (1997) provide a good example of a league table listing the cost per life year gained for a number of commonly used medical interventions. The usual practice is to discard interventions with high ICERs indicative of poor value in favor of interventions with low ICERs indicative of good value. A commonly used rule of thumb places the cutoff at $50,000 per QALY, or roughly twice annual per capita income.

APPROACHES TO MODELING IN ECONOMIC EVALUATION

The biggest challenge in conducting a cost-effectiveness analysis is the availability of quality data. The proverbial gold standard for data on the costs and effectiveness of various treatment options is the randomized trial. In practice, however, randomized trial data is not always available. As we discussed earlier, trial periods are typically too short to capture all the costs and consequences of the treatment options. Additionally, randomized trials are costly to undertake and are driven by the requirements to prove safety and efficacy. Under the controlled conditions of randomized trials, many of the variables that would determine effectiveness and efficiency in the course of normal clinical practice are not present, limiting the researcher's ability to generalize from the trial results. These limitations highlight the importance of using sound modeling techniques as a framework for economic evaluation. The two modeling frameworks frequently used in economic evaluation are decision trees and Markov models (Kuntz and Weinstein, 2001).[10]

Decision Trees

Decision trees provide a logical framework for decision analysis, clearly illustrating the sequential nature of the decision-making process and capturing the uncertain nature of the environment in which decisions are made. Decision trees are designed to analyze problems that involve a series of choices that are in turn constrained by previous decisions. They provide a convenient way to show the effects of choices and the impact of the probabilities of subsequent events on final outcomes.

The elements of a decision tree flow logically from an initial decision point, or decision node. Branches from a decision node represent courses of action taken by the decision maker. Chance events, shown as chance nodes in the decision tree, are all possible outcomes that stem from each decision. Branches from chance nodes represent the events that result from each decision and their associated probabilities. Final outcomes are shown by terminal nodes and represent the stopping point in the decision analysis.

Figure 4.5 represents the elements of a simple decision tree with one decision node: whether to choose treatment A or treatment B. The decision to choose either treatment is followed by a chance node: live or die. In this simple decision tree, the only difference in the sequence of events is the probabilities associated with life or death after the choice of treatments is made. The probabilities of life and death are p and $1 - p$ if treatment A is chosen and q and $1 - q$ if treatment B is chosen. This simple model has four possible terminal nodes, each with an associated cost (C_i) and effect (E_i).

When decision trees are used in the economic evaluation of health care decisions, the model is solved using a technique called *roll back*. In other words, the tree is solved working from right to left, as if there were no uncertainty involved in the process. The expected cost of each possible action is calculated by summing the costs of each branch multiplied by the probability of reaching the terminal point of that branch. Each treatment option is ranked by expected cost, and then incremental cost-effectiveness ratios are calculated.

---

[10] TreeAge Software developed the decision analysis software used in developing the figures in this section. TreeAge has been producing decision analysis tools used in the medical care industry since 1988. In addition to cost-effectiveness analysis and Markov modeling, the software can be used for Monte Carlo simulation in clinical decision making, epidemiological modeling, and pharmaceutical outcomes research. A student version of their DATA™ software is available on their Web site http://www.treeage.com/.

Figure 4.5: Simple Decision Tree

The data required to evaluate treatment options using decision analysis are typically gathered from different sources. Because clinical trials are usually protocol driven, they seldom collect all the information required to complete an economic evaluation. The usual practice in gathering data for the analysis involves integrating information from different sources, including disease data from epidemiological studies, patient management data from clinical practice, and resource utilization data from accounting sources.

	TREATMENT A	TREATMENT B
Mortality rate	5%	10%
Life expectancy for survivors	20 years	10 years
Initial treatment cost	$50,000	$20,000
Follow-up costs, year 1	$20,000	$10,000
Annual follow-up costs, all subsequent years	$2,000	$2,000

Suppose the information above has been gathered on the costs and effectiveness of the two treatments described above.[11] Total cost for survivors receiving treatment A is $108,000; for decedents, it is $50,000. Survivors live an additional 20 years, and decedents experience sudden death. For the group receiving treatment B, the cost for survivors is $48,000; for decedents, it is $20,000. Survivors of treatment B live an additional 10 years.

At each decision node, the expected cost and consequences of each treatment option is calculated. For treatment A, the expected cost is $105,100 [0.95 ($108,000) + 0.05 ($50,000)] and the expected benefit is 19 life years saved [0.95 (20 years) + 0.05 (0 years)].[12] For treatment B, the expected cost is $45,200 [0.90 ($48,000) + 0.10 ($20,000)] and the expected benefit is 9 life years saved [0.90 (10 years) + 0.10 (0 years)].

---

[11] In this simple example, costs and consequences are not discounted.
[12] The calculation for expected cost for either treatment is the sum of the cost for survivors multiplied by the probability of surviving, and the cost for decedents multiplied by the probability of dying.

TREATMENT	EXPECTED COST	EXPECTED BENEFIT	INCREMENTAL COST	INCREMENTAL BENEFIT	ICER
B	$45,200	9 years	—	—	—
A	$105,100	19 years	$59,900	10 years	$5,990

The treatment options are then ranked by expected cost, from lowest to highest. After calculating the incremental cost and incremental benefit of the treatment options, the ICER is calculated. In this example, treatment A results in an additional 10 years of life expectancy at a cost of $59,900, or $5,990 per life year gained.

Key Concept No. 3
Marginal Analysis

Markov Models

Decision trees can be as simple or as complex as the decisions they model. But when there are numerous health states, including the possibility of transitions from one health state to another and back again, the decision tree may become far too complex to handle the problem efficiently. This problem of complex and recurring disease states is particularly challenging when modeling the progression of a chronic condition, such as loss of bone density, breast cancer, and the many forms of dementia. A Markov model is the appropriate choice for modeling such recurring health states.

Disease states and disease transitions may be modeled effectively with a Markov cycle tree, depicted in Figure 4.6.[13] This simple model shows two mutually exclusive health states, or Markov states, corresponding to all possible health states. The health states, alive or dead in this example, are shown at the Markov node. Transition subtrees, constructed at the transition node, depict the progression of the disease from one state to another. Transitions between disease states are based on probabilities that certain events occur—probabilities determined using data from epidemiological studies or clinical trials. In this example, there are only two events: live and die. The probability of living is p, and the probability of dying is $1 - p$.

The branches of the transition subtree end with a terminal node, indicating the end of a cycle, not the termination of the process. Transition subtrees are recursive and continue for a predetermined number of time periods, called *Markov cycles*, or until everyone who began the process ends up in the absorbing state; in

Figure 4.6: Simple Markov Cycle Tree

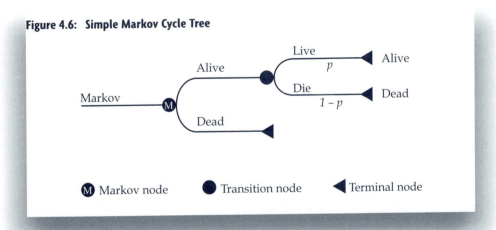

M Markov node   Transition node   Terminal node

[13] The simple Markov model described in Figure 4.6 is actually a life-expectancy model. Age memory can be programmed into the Markov process, changing the transition probabilities from cycle to cycle.

this case, dead.[14] The length of each Markov cycle is fixed and should represent an interval that has clinical meaning for the disease being studied. If cycles are too short, disease transitions are infrequent. If they are too long, individuals transition from one health state to another and back again during the same cycle, and the explanatory power of the model is diminished.

Markov Decision Models

One of the most practical ways to take advantage of the power of the decision tree and the Markov model is to combine the two, creating a Markov decision model. In this format, the model starts at the initial decision node of a decision tree, where two treatment options are available. But instead of attaching a chance node to each option, a Markov node is attached. Now the decision model has two Markov processes, each associated with a treatment option, and we have a valuable tool for economic evaluation.

Each Markov process has costs and utilities associated with it. As the Markov process proceeds and participants transition from one health state to another, costs and utilities accumulate for each treatment group. The economic evaluation must keep track of these costs and utilities, so expected costs and expected utilities (usually QALYs) can be calculated. The expected values are calculated on a per capita basis and compared across treatment options to determine incremental cost-effectiveness ratios.

Figure 4.7 provides an example of a Markov decision model that may be used to estimate the cost effectiveness of a new drug treatment for Alzheimer's disease, a form of dementia. In this example, data on the clinical effectiveness of the new drug, call it treatment A, is collected from a clinical trial in which the control group is given a placebo (no treatment). There are three health states for patients suffering from the disease—mild, moderate, and severe—and one absorbing state: death. The underlying disease progression is shown by transitions from one health state to another. For example, there are three possible transitions for someone beginning a cycle with a diagnosis of mild Alzheimer's: mild-to-mild, mild-to-moderate, or mild-to-dead. Those with severe Alzheimer's have only two transition possibilities: severe-to-severe or severe-to-dead.

The development of Alzheimer's is slow and difficult to confirm. Even though the actual diagnosis of Alzheimer's is not possible without a postmortem analysis of brain tissue, several cognitive tests are used to measure the patient's mental ability. One popular instrument is the Mini Mental State Exam (MMSE). The MMSE is scored on a 30-point scale. Mild Alzheimer's is linked to scores ranging from 21 to 26, moderate Alzheimer's to scores between 10 and 20, and severe Alzheimer's to scores below 10.

This Markov decision model was used to estimate the expected costs and expected utilities (measured in QALYs) resulting from four years of treatment with donezepil (Neumann, Hermann, and Kuntz, 1999). The data used in estimating the incremental cost effectiveness of the drug therapy came primarily from a 24-week clinical trial (Clegg et al., 2000).

It is beyond the scope of this chapter to go into much more detail on the use of Markov models in economic evaluation. For those interested in more information on the subject, there is much literature on the process. The interested reader might begin with Briggs and Sculpher (1998).

---

[14] Transition states are temporary, tunnel, or absorbing. Individuals move in and out of temporary states. The progression through a tunnel state follows a predetermined path; e.g., the progression of a pregnancy. No one escapes an absorbing state once it has been entered.

Figure 4.7:   Markov Decision Model with Two Markov Processes

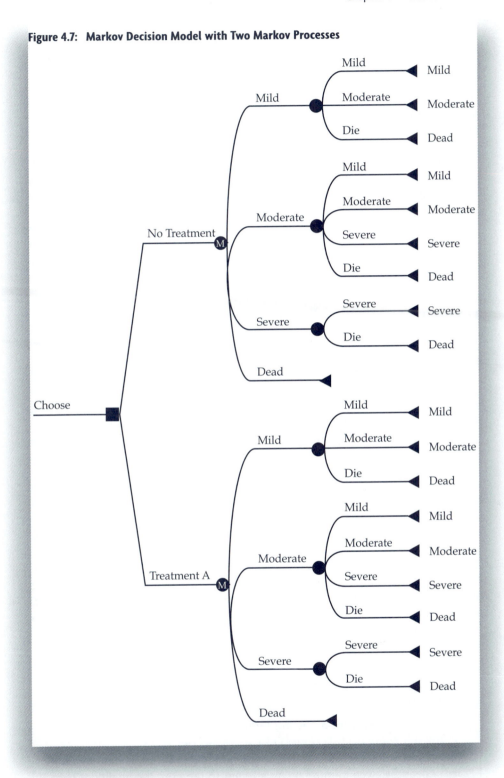

Sensitivity Analysis

The reliability of the results of any economic evaluation depends on the quality of the data used in the study. Due to uncertainty, economic evaluations may be sensitive to changes in key assumptions and parameters. One way to determine whether the results are influenced by this uncertainty is to conduct a sensitivity analysis. A sensitivity analysis is a way of systematically exploring the variability of the results due to uncertainty. A basic sensitivity analysis entails changing the model's parameters or assumptions one at a time. A one-way sensitivity analysis might test the variability of the results to a change in the transition probability from one health state to another, or the initial cost of a treatment option, or the utility associated with a particular health state. Two-way or multiway sensitivity analyses are also quite common.

The typical sensitivity analysis described above is called a *cohort analysis*. Conducted with one of the decision models described above, a hypothetical cohort of individuals is followed through every event and cycle, expected costs and utilities are estimated, and treatment options are compared using calculated ICERs. This process is repeated for every parameter/assumption change, and the impact on final results are compared. Other approaches to sensitivity analyses include Monte Carlo simulations, in which a large patient cohort is tracked through the model individually. The simulations are repeated over and over to estimate the variance in results associated with the parameters.

STANDARDIZATION OF ECONOMIC EVALUATION TECHNIQUES

Health care systems around the world are setting standards for economic evaluations, and they are making reimbursement decisions for various treatment options based on those evaluations. In 1992, Australia became the first country to issue formal guidelines for mandatory economic evaluation of all pharmaceutical products prior to reimbursement (Commonwealth, 1992). The National Institute for Health and Clinical Excellence (NICE), established as part of the National Health Service (NHS) in 1999, is making similar decisions in the United Kingdom. Its mission is to provide individual patients, health care professionals, and the British public with clear guidance on the efficacy, clinical effectiveness, and cost effectiveness of both individual health technologies—including pharmaceutical drugs, medical devices, diagnostic techniques, and other medical procedures—and the clinical management of specific health conditions (NICE, 2001).

Hjelmgren and colleagues (2001) provided a detailed study of the similarities and differences of the health economics guidelines that have been issued in Europe, North America, and Australia. Presented in table format, the authors classified the 25 guidelines into three categories: seven formal, eight informal, and ten dealing with methodological issues. Most countries in the European Union already require, or will soon require, the submission and approval of formal economic evaluations for all new and existing medical technologies before they can be reimbursed by the public sector.

BACK-OF-THE-ENVELOPE

Checklist for Assessing Economic Evaluations

As the interest in the economic evaluation of health care interventions has grown, so too has the interest in publishing the results of those studies in peer-reviewed journals. In an attempt to promote the quality of the economic evaluations published in the *British Medical Journal*, the editors established a working group to clarify the components of an acceptable article. The guidelines are grouped under three major headings: study design, data collection, and analysis and interpretation of results.

continued

I. Study design addresses seven issues:

1. Is the research question clearly stated?
2. Is the economic importance of the research question clearly stated?
3. Is the perspective of the analysis clearly stated and justified?
4. Is the rationale for the choice of comparison alternatives stated?
5. Are alternative treatment options clearly described?
6. Is the type of economic evaluation clearly stated?
7. Is the type of economic evaluation justified given the question addressed?

II. Data collection addresses 14 issues:

8. Are the sources of the effectiveness data clearly stated?
9. Is a systematic overview of the studies used as data sources provided?
10. If based on several studies, are details on the method of data synthesis provided?
11. Are the outcome (utility) measures clearly stated?
12. Are valuation methods clearly stated?
13. Are details provided identifying the individuals making the valuations?
14. Are productivity changes (indirect) reported separately?
15. Is the relevance of productivity changes discussed?
16. Are resource prices and quantities reported separately?
17. Is the methodology for estimating prices and quantities described?
18. Are all currency and pricing data clearly recorded?
19. Are all inflation adjustments and currency conversions clearly stated?
20. Is the model clearly explained?
21. Is the choice of model and key parameters justified?

III. Analysis and interpretation of results addresses 14 issues:

22. Is the time horizon for costs and benefits stated?
23. Is the discount rate used stated?
24. Is the choice of discount rate justified?
25. If costs and benefits are not discounted, is rationale stated?
26. If stochastic data are used, are confidence intervals and statistical tests discussed?
27. Is the sensitivity analysis explained?
28. Is the choice of variables for the sensitivity analysis justified?
29. Is the range over which the parameters are varied stated?
30. Are all relevant alternatives compared?
31. Is the incremental analysis reported?
32. Are all major outcomes presented in both disaggregated and aggregated forms?
33. Is the original study question answered?
34. Does the reported data support the conclusions?
35. Are conclusions accompanied by the appropriate caveats?

Even though the guidelines are not intended to stifle innovative approaches, they are meant to improve the quality of economic evaluations that are eventually published in the *BMJ*. Many of you who read these guidelines may never submit an economic evaluation to the *BMJ*, but knowing what goes into a publishable economic evaluation will help you read, understand, and critique those you read from other sources.

Source: Michael F. Drummond, T. O. Jefferson et al., "Guidelines for Authors and Peer Reviewers of Economic Submissions to the *BMJ*," *British Medical Journal* 313, August 3, 1969, 275–283.

CASE STUDIES

There are literally hundreds of studies, using the techniques discussed in this chapter, published in journals around the world each year. The following section highlights three recent studies that clearly illustrate the use of these techniques in lung cancer screening, cervical cancer screening, and the drug treatment of Alzheimer's disease.

Lung Cancer Screening

The prevalence of smoking in the United States and the deadly nature of the disease make population-based screening for lung cancer an important policy issue. Approximately 50 million adult Americans between the ages of 45 and 75 are current, quitting, or former heavy smokers. Over 170,000 Americans are diagnosed annually with lung cancer—and only 15.7 percent survive five years after diagnosis.[15] In contrast, the U.S. five-year survival rate for breast cancer is 90.1 percent, and that of prostate cancer is 99.3 percent (Verdecchia et al., 2007).

Mahadevia and colleagues (2003) examined the cost effectiveness of regular lung cancer screening using helical computed tomography (CT). The study began with three hypothetical cohorts of 100,000 adults in each of the three smoking categories. If annual screening began at age 60, the program would prevent 553 lung cancer deaths over a 20-year period for every 100,000 screened—a 13 percent reduction in the death rate from lung cancer. The program would also result in 1,186 unnecessary biopsies per 100,000 screenings. At a cost of $500 per CT scan, if one half of all adult smokers received an annual screening, the program cost, discounted over 20 years, would be over $115 billion. The risk profile of the screened population affects the cost effectiveness of the program. If only former smokers are screened, the cost per QALY is $2.3 million. If screening is limited to current smokers, the cost per QALY is $116,300. Even with the prospective life-saving consequences of CT screening, age and smoking status may not represent high enough risk factors to make population-based screening cost effective.

Cervical Cancer Screening

At one time, cervical cancer was the leading cause of death among women in the United States. With the introduction of widespread screening, the death rate has declined to less than 8 per 100,000. Even with relatively low incidence rates in both Europe and the United States, deaths from cervical cancer number in the thousands annually, a relatively large number for an otherwise preventable disease (Henderson, 2004).

Mandelblatt and colleaguse (2002) examined the social costs and quality-adjusted life expectancy of a number of different testing strategies for cervical cancer. With a model simulating the natural progression of the disease, they compared 18 different screening strategies using a combination of testing for the human papillomavirus (HPV), the traditional Papanicolaou (Pap) test, and a combination of the two at two- to three-year intervals, beginning at age 20 and continuing to 65 years, 75 years, or death. Direct costs for screening, diagnosis, and treatment were included in the analysis, along with the indirect costs of the patients' time associated with the process. Eliminating the screening options that were dominated, either strictly or via extended dominance, the six strategies listed below comprised the frontier of economically rational strategies.

---

[15] The same is true in Europe, where the five-year survival rate is 10.9 percent (Verdecchia et al., 2007).

SCREENING STRATEGY	EXPECTED COST	EXPECTED QALYs SAVED	ICER
No screening	$5,018	26.8666	
Pap every 3 years to age 75	6,833	27.0200	$11,830
Pap every 2 years to age 75	7,280	27.0350	29,781
Pap every 2 years to death	7,308	27.0355	56,440
Pap plus HPV every 2 years to age 75	7,934	27.0444	70,347
Pap plus HPV every 2 years to death	7,980	27.0450	76,183

The following QALY adjustments for each year in the various health states were used: 0.97 for healthy and diagnosed with a low-grade squamous intraepithelial lesion (LSIL); 0.93 for having a high-grade lesion; 0.9 for having local invasive cancer; 0.7 for regional invasive cancer; and 0.5 for distant invasive cancer. Of course, 1 represents perfect health and 0 is death. Maximum benefit in terms of QALYs saved results from Pap plus HPV testing every two years until death with an incremental cost of $76,183. Stopping the screening at age 75 captures approximately 98 percent of the benefits of lifetime screening at an incremental cost that is about $6,000 lower. Combining Pap plus HPV testing in a population screening program consistently saves more lives but at higher costs. Sensitivity analysis revealed that if the cost of the HPV test fell from $30 to $5, the use of the HPV test every two years until death would become the cost-effective strategy, with an ICER of $50,100.

Drug Treatment for Alzheimer's Disease

Alzheimer's disease usually strikes individuals over the age of 65. The most common type of dementia, over 15 million people worldwide suffer from this progressively degenerative disease, a number that is expected to rise to 81 million by 2040. Alzheimer's was responsible for 65,800 deaths in the United States in 2004, and was the third most costly disease behind only heart disease and cancer.

Wimo and colleagues (2003) examined the costs and consequences of donepezil treatment in patients with mild to moderate Alzheimer's disease. Patients were evaluated as part of a one-year clinical trial in which patients were randomized into a treatment group that received the therapy and a placebo control group. Mean annual health care costs were $16,438 for the treatment group, including $1,280 for the donepezil, and $16,147 for the control group. Average caregiver costs, both direct and indirect, were $8,531 for the treatment group and $9,919 for the control group. Average total costs for the treatment group were $24,969; those for the control group were $26,066. Patients receiving the treatment showed cognitive and functional benefits as evidenced by scores on two cognitive tests.

Jönsson and colleagues (2000) reviewed several studies on the effectiveness of donepezil (including Neumann, Hermann, and Kuntz, 1999) and found that patients who received the drug had better outcomes in terms of both less time spent in more severe states and improved quality of life. In three of the five studies reviewed, donepezil was the dominant strategy (better outcome with a slight cost saving), and it was only slightly more costly in the other two. Donepezil was found to be a cost-effective treatment when prescribed to patients with mild to moderate Alzheimer's disease.

SUMMARY AND CONCLUSIONS

This chapter provided an overview of economic evaluation in health care decision making. Techniques that have become standard practice in Europe over the past decade are not as well integrated in the decision-making process in the United States. Of the three types of economic evaluation discussed, cost-effectiveness analysis is by far the most widely used technique for evaluating the economic efficiency of medical treatment options. The use of modeling in economic evaluation was also emphasized, highlighting the importance of strong quantitative skills for anyone interested in using this valuable analytical tool.

Even though economic evaluation as a tool has the potential to bring cost-conscious behavior back into the decision-making process, it is not the only thing that matters when judging health care alternatives. Equity in the distribution of care and the quality of care are also important considerations. The quantitative value of an incremental cost-effectiveness ratio should never be the sole consideration in the decision to fund or not to fund a treatment program. The fact that one treatment option has a higher or a lower ICER means very little by itself. The number of patients who are affected by the program, the number and quality of treatment alternatives, and the final impact on overall spending is also critically important.

Cost-effectiveness considerations are more formally integrated into health policy making in Canada, Australia, and Europe. Health economists abroad are more familiar with the methodology and receive substantially more formal training in the concepts and techniques that define the discipline. In fact, if you use the term "health economics" in Europe, it is assumed you mean "economic evaluation."

With only a few minor exceptions, economic evaluation has yet to be used extensively in the appraisal of medical technology in the United States (Eddy, 1991). Ignoring cost-effectiveness issues may no longer be an option for U.S. policy makers. U.S. citizens want comprehensive coverage. They are concerned with issues of affordability and accessibility and are obsessed with freedom of choice. Federal officials in charge of Medicare and Medicaid, the medical programs for the elderly and indigent, are looking carefully at cost as a factor in deciding whether to pay for certain pharmaceuticals. Federal efforts to hold down drug spending will only increase if Congress expands the Medicare program to include a pharmaceutical benefit for the 33 million senior citizens eligible for the program. It may be just a matter of time before these government-run programs begin to ask for formal cost-effectiveness studies to accompany all applications for approval of new medical technologies, creating what the Europeans call "the fourth hurdle" in the medical technology approval process.

POLICY ISSUE

To what extent should economic evaluation be incorporated into medical decision making?

PROFILE

Bengt Jönsson

Bengt Jönsson is part of what could arguably be called Sweden's first family of health economics. He and his wife, Gisela Kobelt, regularly collaborate on research projects and are assisted by Bengt's son, Linus, when additional analytical brainpower is needed. Born into a family without academic traditions, Jönsson managed to challenge the Swedish academic system that rewards a pedigree to become one of the most respected health economists in all of Europe.

Jönsson was born in the port city of Helsingborg, located at the narrowest point of the Oresund (one of the world's most frequented sounds and the gateway to the North Sea). He was raised in the small industrial town of Höganäs 10 miles to the north. Jönsson received his academic training at nearby Lund University, just across the sound from Copenhagen. His undergraduate degree in economics and statistics allowed him to combine his interest in social issues with his training in math and science. His interest in health economics was driven in part by Swedish national politics. Given the significant growth in Sweden's welfare state at the time, there was surprisingly little academic interest in the subject.

continued

Jönsson's masters' thesis in 1972 was a study of the rationale for subsidized childcare. Although these services were interesting and important, the study of the childcare industry did not lend itself to his vast technical expertise. While visiting a bookstore at the University of York that summer, Jönsson came across a book on health economics coauthored by Anthony J. Culyer and Michael H. Cooper. Subsequent conversations with Culyer and Alan Williams provided the inspiration for the dissertation that followed.

While a lecturer in the economics department at Lund, Jönsson completed his Ph.D. in 1976. After a short tenure as director of the Swedish Institute for Health Economics at Lund, he became Sweden's first professor of health economics and director of the Center for Medical Technology Assessment at Linköping University. In 1991, he moved to the Stockholm School of Economics, where he is currently Professor of Health Economics. Jönsson also serves as a member of the Scientific Advisory Board of the National Board of Health and Welfare, and is a member of the board of the Swedish Institute for Health Economics. He is associate editor of the *Journal of Health Economics* and a member of the editorial boards of both *PharmacoEconomics* and the *European Journal of Health Economics*.

Being one of the pioneers of a field and living in a small country has its advantages. Jönsson has had a stimulating research agenda with interests in technological change, health care financing and organization, and health care policy. But his most important contribution to the field has been his application of the methods of economic evaluation in health care. He has served as a consultant and policy adviser, not only in Sweden but also for the World Health Organization, the World Bank, and the Organization of Economic Cooperation and Development. These opportunities have "taught [him] modesty in terms of what you can expect to achieve in the short term" and a greater appreciation for the long-term impact of economic fundamentals. Agreeing with his younger colleagues that an academician can have only limited influence in policy making, Jönsson, with the perspective of 30 years in the discipline, "is more surprised about what has been achieved than disappointed about what is left to do."

Jönsson is an excellent cook, something you would expect from a person who lives in southern France part of the year. A better gardener than golfer, one might question how he finds the time for any of his extrascholarly pursuits. But if you are around him long enough, you realize that he will not let his work get in the way of what is really important. His wife, Gisela, summarizes it best: "He is unique and best in motivating, forming, and coaching bright, young people. I never met a teacher like him: rough, challenging, provocative — yet patient, indulgent, and kind."

Source: Bengt Jönsson, *curriculum vitae* and personal correspondence.

QUESTIONS AND PROBLEMS

1. The health authorities are considering the treatment alternatives for three types of diseases: heart disease, cancer, and infectious disease. Each year there are 10,000 new cases of heart disease, 10,000 new cases of cancer, and 5,000 new cases of infectious disease. For each diagnosis, there are a number of mutually independent treatment alternatives (including no treatment) as shown in the table on the next page.

   a. Identify all dominant treatment alternatives. Explain why each is dominant.

   b. Calculate the incremental cost, incremental QALYs, and incremental cost-effectiveness ratios (ICERs) for all economically rational strategies (ICER = incremental cost/ incremental QALYs). Why are these considered economically rational?

Treatment	Cost per Treatment	QALYs Gained
Heart Disease		
A	0	0
B	100	2
C	300	8
D	400	8
E	600	12
F	800	15
Cancer		
G	0	0
H	200	8
I	400	10
J	500	12
K	600	9
L	700	14
M	800	15
Infectious Disease		
N	0	0
O	100	2
P	350	4
R	650	6

c. Using separate graphs for heart disease, cancer, and infectious disease, show the alternative treatment options, label the dominant options, and show the economically feasible alternatives. (Place QALYs on the vertical axis and cost per treatment on the horizontal axis.)

d. The local health district has asked your opinion on the "best" strategy from a public health perspective (disease covered, treatment strategy). What do you tell them? How much will it cost?

2. A recent article in *JAMA* by Mandelblatt and colleagues (2002) compared the societal costs and benefits of human papillomavirus (HPV) testing, Pap testing, and their combination to screen for cervical cancer. The paper studied 18 different population screening strategies—Pap testing alone, HPV testing alone, and Pap plus HPV testing every 2 or 3 years for women beginning at age 20 and continuing to 65 years, 75 years, and death. The table below summarizes some of the results (low cost to high cost). Costs include screening and treatment costs, discounted over the individual's expected lifetime.

a. Identify all dominant screening strategies. Explain why each is dominant.

b. Calculate the incremental cost, incremental QALYs, and incremental CE ratios for all economically rational strategies (Incremental CE = incremental cost/incremental QALYs). Why are these considered economically rational?

c. The local health district has asked your opinion on the "best" strategy from a public health perspective. What do you tell them?

3. The following information has been gathered on the costs and effectiveness of the two treatments, A and B. In this problem, costs and consequences are not discounted.

	Treatment A	Treatment B
Mortality rate	2%	5%
Life expectancy for survivors	20 years	10 years
Initial treatment cost	$10,000	$3,000
Follow-up costs, year 1	$5,000	$1,000
Annual follow-up costs, all subsequent years	$1,000	$500

a. What is the total cost for the survivors receiving treatment A? For decedents (assuming sudden death)?

b. What is the total cost for survivors receiving treatment B? For decedents?

Strategy	Cost ($)	QALYs Saved	Incremental Cost	Incremental QALY	Incremental CE ratio
0. No screening	5,000	26.87	—	—	—
1. Pap every 3 years to age 75	6,825	27.02			
2. HPV every 3 years to age 75	6,950	27.02			
3. Pap every 2 years to age 75	7,275	27.04			
4. Pap + HPV every 3 years to age 75	7,400	27.04			
5. HPV every 2 years to age 75	7,450	27.04			
6. Pap + HPV every 2 years to age 75	7,925	27.05			

c. What is the expected cost for those patients receiving treatment A? Treatment B?

d. Draw a simple decision tree showing the costs and consequences of each treatment option.

e. Calculate the incremental cost and incremental benefit of the treatment alternatives.

f. What is the ICER?

4. A new treatment is discovered that improves survival probability from 85 percent to 95 percent. Discuss the different ways a researcher might look at these results versus the way that the marketing department might discuss them. What is the difference in the way you would view a new treatment that improves survival probability by the same absolute magnitude, say, from 5 percent to 15 percent?

5. How does cost-benefit analysis differ from cost-effectiveness analysis? Why has cost-effectiveness analysis become the method of choice for health economists around the world?

6. In what sense is a cost-of-illness study a technique of economic evaluation? In what sense is it not? What is the primary motivation for doing a cost-of-illness study?

7. Calculating costs in an economic evaluation is very important. Classify the following costs as direct (D), indirect (ID), or intangible (IT).

Cost	Classification
Transportation (ambulance or personal auto)	
Sick leave	
Informal care performed by spouse	
Visit to private practitioner	
Inpatient hospital stay	
Nursing home stay	
Reduced productivity at work	
Pain and suffering	
Home health care services	
Diagnostic test	
Surgical intervention	
Grief and anxiety	

8. How would you explain the concept of a QALY? When is it appropriate to use QALYs instead of simply improved life expectancy as the outcome measure in an economic evaluation?

9. The following table represents the costs and benefits of four alternative clinical programs designed to treat a single disease. Benefits are measured in terms of the number of lives saved.

a. Finish the table. Which is the best program in terms of the number of lives saved? In terms of the ICER per life saved?

b. How does the cost-effectiveness ratio, defined as the average cost per life saved, differ from the ICER?

c. Which program would an economist favor? What would your argument be?

10. A controversial new device, the implantable cardiac defibrillator (ICD), was used in a clinical trial to determine if it improved survival for heart-attack patients over the standard drug treatment. The trial provided the following information: Two years after the first heart attack, 85 percent of the ICD patients were still alive, compared to 70 percent of the drug treatment group. No additional data were available after the 24-month trial.

Program	Cost ($)	Lives Saved	ICER
A	100,000	10	
B	100,000	12	
C	200,000	12	
D	200,000	15	

a. What is your best guess on survival probability after the trial is over?

b. Calculate the improvement in life expectancy during the trial. What is your best estimate of improved life expectancy after the trial?

c. Graph the mortality function for both the ICD group and the drug-therapy group.

d. What is the difference in life expectancy between the two groups?

11. Choices in health care delivery must be made at two levels: 1) the individual physician prescribing a course of treatment for an individual patient and 2) the policy maker determining the availability of medical care to an entire group of patients or a community. One way to choose among alternative treatment regimes and community programs is by using the criterion of economic efficiency. Briefly describe the three types of appraisal that enter into medical economics. Discuss the unique features of each, and describe their basic strengths and weaknesses.

REFERENCES

H. Bleichrodt and J. Quiggin, "Life-Cycle Preferences, Overconsumption, and Health: When Is Cost-Effectiveness Analysis Equivalent to Cost-Benefit Analysis?" *Journal of Health Economics* 18, 1999, 681–708.

Andrew Briggs and M. J. Sculpher, "An Introduction to Markov Modeling for Economic Evaluation," *PharmacoEconomics* 13(4), April 1998, 397–409.

Philip M. Clarke, "Cost-Benefit Analysis and Mammographic Screening: A Travel Cost Approach," *Journal of Health Economics* 17(6), December 1998, 767–787.

A. Clegg et al., "Clinical and Cost-Effectiveness of Donepezil, Rivastigmine, and Galantamine for Alzheimer's Disease: A Rapid and Systematic Review," *Health Technology Assessment* 5, 2000, 1–137.

Commonwealth Department of Health, Housing, and Community Services, *Guidelines for the Pharmaceutical Industry on Preparation of Submissions to the Pharmaceutical Benefits Advisory Committee*, Canberra: Australian Government Publishing Service; 1992.

Paul Dolan et al., "The Time Trade-off Method: Results from a General Population Study," *Health Economics* 5(2), March 1996, 141–154.

Michael F. Drummond et al., *Methods of Economic Evaluation of Health Care Programmes*, Second Edition, Oxford: Oxford University Press, 1997.

Benjamin G. Druss et al., "Comparing the National Economic Burden of Five Chronic Conditions," *Health Affairs* 20(6), November/December 2001, 233–241.

David M. Eddy, "Oregon Methods: Did Cost-Effectiveness Analysis Fail?" *Journal of the American Medical Association* 266(15), October 16, 1991, 2135–2141.

John M. Eisenberg, "Clinical Economics: A Guide to the Economic Analysis of Clinical Practices," *Journal of the American Medical Association* 262(20), November 24, 1989, 2879–2886.

Alain Enthoven, *Consumer Choice Health Plan: The Only Practical Solution to the Soaring Cost of Medical Care*, Reading, MA: Addison–Wesley, 1980.

Eric A. Finkelstein, Ian C. Fiebelkorn, and Guijing Wang, "National Medical Spending Attributable to Overweight and Obesity: How Much, and Who's Paying?" *Health Affairs—Web Exclusive* W3, May 14, 2003, 219–226.

Alan M. Garber, "Recent Developments in CBA/CEA," in *Handbook of Health Economics*, Volume 1A, edited by Anthony J. Culyer and Joseph Newhouse, Amsterdam: North Holland, 2001.

Alan M. Garber and Charles E. Phelps, "Economic Foundations of Cost-Effectiveness Analysis," *Journal of Health Economics* 16(1), 1997, 1–31.

Gary M. Ginsberg and Boaz Lev, "Cost-Benefit Analysis of Riluzole for the Treatment of Amyotrophic Lateral Sclerosis," *PharmacoEconomics* 12(5), November 1997, 578–584.

John H. Goddeeris and Thomas P. Bronken, "Benefit-Cost Analysis of Screening," *Medical Care* 23, 1985, 1242–1255.

James W. Henderson "Cost Effectiveness of Cervical Cancer Screening Strategies," *Expert Review of Pharmacoeconomics and Outcomes Research* 4(3), 2004, 89–100.

_____, "Economic Impact of Cocaine and Crack Abuse: Private and Social Issues," in Glen E. Lich, ed., *Doing Drugs and Dropping Out: Assessing the Costs to Society of Substance Abuse and Dropping Out of School*. A report prepared for the Subcommittee on Economic Growth, Trade, and Taxes of the Joint Economic Committee, Congress of the United States, Washington, DC: U.S. Government Printing Office, August 1991.

Fred J. Hellinger, "Cost-Benefit Analysis of Health Care: Past Applications and Future Prospects," *Inquiry* 17(3), Fall 1980, 204–215.

Jonas Hjelmgren et al., "Health Economic Guidelines: Similarities, Differences, and Some Implications," *Value in Health* 4(3), May 2001, 225–250.

Lisa A. Jackson et al., "Should College Students Be Vaccinated against Meningococcal Disease? A Cost-Benefit Analysis," *American Journal of Public Health* 85, June 1995, 843–846.

Bengt Jönsson, Linus Jönsson, and Anders Wimo, "Cost of Dementia: A Review," in *Dementia*, edited by Mario Maj and Norman Sartorius, Chichester (UK): John Wiley and Sons Ltd., 2000, 335–363.

Robert M. Kaplan et al., "The Quality of Well-Being Scale: Critical Similarities and Differences with SF-36," *International Journal for Quality in Health Care* 10(6), December 1998, 509–520.

H. Klarman, J. Francis, and G. Rosenthal, "Cost-Effectiveness Analysis Applied to the Treatment of Chronic Renal Disease," *Medical Care* 6(1), 1968, 48–54.

Gisela Kobelt, *Health Economics: An Introduction to Economic Evaluation*, London: Office of Health Economics, 2002.

Karen M. Kuntz and Milton C. Weinstein, "Modeling in Economic Evaluation," in *Economic Evaluation in Health Care: Merging Theory with Practice*, Michael Drummond and Alistair McGuire, eds., Oxford: Oxford University Press, 2001.

Parthiv J. Mahadevia et al., "Lung Cancer Screening with Helical Computed Tomography in Older Adult Smokers: A Decision and Cost-Effectiveness Analysis," *Journal of the American Medical Association* 289(3), January 15, 2003, 313–322.

Jeanne S. Mandelblatt et al., "Benefits and Costs of Using HPV Testing to Screen for Cervical Cancer," *Journal of the American Medical Association* 287(18), May 8, 2002, 2372–2381.

David H. Mark, "Visualizing Cost-Effectiveness Analysis," *Journal of the American Medical Association* 287(18), May 8, 2002, 2428–2429.

James R. McGuigan, R. Charles Moyer, and Frederick H. deB. Harris, *Managerial Economics: Applications, Strategy, and Tactics,* Ninth Edition, South-Western College Publishing, 2002.

P. J. Neumann, R. C. Hermann, and K. M. Kuntz, "Cost-Effectiveness of Donepezil in the Treatment of Mild or Moderate Alzheimer's Disease," *Neurology* 52, 1999, 1138–1145.

NICE, *Guidance for Manufacturers and Sponsors,* London: National Institute for Clinical Excellence, June 2001, available from http://www.nice.org.uk.

Dorothy P. Rice, Sandler Kelman, Leonard S. Miller, and Sarah Dunmeyer, *The Economic Costs of Alcohol and Drug Abuse and Mental Illness:* 1985, San Francisco, CA: Institute for Health and Aging, University of California at San Francisco, 1990.

Anne A. Scitovsky and Dorothy P. Rice, "Estimates of the Direct and Indirect Costs of Acquired Immunodeficiency Syndrome in the United States, 1985, 1986, and 1991," *Public Health Reports* 102, 1987, 5–17.

Amartya Sen, "Social Choice Theory: A Re-examination," *Econometrica* 45(1), January 1977, 53–89.

Arduino Verdecchia, Silvia Francisci, Hermann Brenner, Gemma Gatta et al., "Recent Cancer Survival in Europe: A 2000–02 Period Analysis of EUROCARE-4 Data," *Lancet Oncology* 8, September 2007, 784–796.

John von Neumann and Oskar Morgenstern, *Theory of Games and Economic Behavior,* Princeton University Press, 1944.

W. Kip Viscusi and Joseph E. Aldy, "The Value of a Statistical Life: A Critical Review of Market Estimates throughout the World," NBER Working Paper No. 9487, February 2003.

M. Weinstein and W. Stason, "Foundations of Cost-Effectiveness Analysis for Health and Medical Practices," *New England Journal of Medicine* 296(13), March 31, 1977, 716–721.

Burton A. Weisbrod, "Costs and Benefits of Medical Research: A Case Study of Poliomyelitis," *Journal of Political Economy* 79(3), May/June 1971, 527–544.

Anders Wimo et al., "An Economic Evaluation of Donepezil in Mild to Moderate Alzheimer's Disease: Results of a 1-Year, Double-Blind, Randomized Trial," *Dementia and Geriatric Cognitive Disorders* 15, 2003, 44–54.

Demand for Health and Medical Care

Most people place a high priority on their health and consider access to quality medical care essential to achieving their health goals. Michael Grossman (1972) first introduced economic researchers to the notion that the demand for medical care is derived from the more fundamental demand for good health. Creating the economic framework for the formal study of the demand for medical care, Grossman's work established two approaches for consideration: In the first, medical care is viewed as an input in the production function for health, and in the second, as an output produced by medical care providers.

Using the first approach, medical care is one of several factors that may be used to improve the health status of an individual or population. Other factors may be even more important in producing good health, including improvements in living standards, advances in medical research, changes in lifestyle, reductions in environmental pollution, and better nutrition.

The production of health with medical care as an input is the subject of the first section of this chapter. Alternatively, the process may be viewed as one in which various inputs are combined to produce the final product we call medical care. These inputs include the services of physicians, dentists, and hospitals, prescription drugs, medical equipment, and other medical devices. In the second section of this chapter, we see how this approach enables us to evaluate the performance of the medical services industry from the perspective of production efficiency.

THE DEMAND FOR HEALTH

Americans value health, as evidenced by the fact that the pursuit of good health is a multibillion dollar business. In addition to the money spent on medical care, countless dollars are spent on health foods, fitness videos, and weight-loss programs. As important as good health is to our overall well-being, it would be a mistake to conclude that every person considers good health the primary goal in life. Our day-to-day behavior undermines this notion. Otherwise, how do you explain our overconsumption of food, alcohol, and drugs?[1] How can you explain the popularity of such risky behavior as motocross, skydiving, and bungee jumping? Why do many people refuse to wear seat belts? Why all the fuss about motorcycle helmets?

---

[1] According to the government's technical definition of obesity, over 60 percent of American males and 50 percent of American females are either overweight or obese (Cutler et al., 2003). Almost 40 percent of Americans are classified as obese, or at least 35 pounds overweight (Wessel, 2003), and an estimated 300,000 to 582,000 deaths annually are associated with diseases related to obesity (Allison et al., 1999).

Why do so many people still smoke cigarettes? With the recent resurgence of sexually transmitted diseases, why do so many still practice risky sexual behavior?

As we begin to think about the demand for health, our starting point will be the relationship between health and the factors that contribute to it. Within this framework, medical care is but one of many inputs that contribute to improving the health of the population. Two important questions will be addressed: What is the most efficient way to produce and distribute health? And what is the incremental contribution of medical care to the production of health?

The Production of Health

In economics, production is depicted as a functional relationship that shows how inputs are combined to produce output. Specifically, the health-production function summarizes the relationship between health status and the various factors that may be used to produce good health. The relationship may be written as follows:

$$\text{Health} = H \text{ (medical care, other inputs, time)}$$

Simply stated, people use medical care in combination with other inputs and their own time to produce good health.[2] In much the same way, teachers' services, books, and an individual's own time are used to produce knowledge. Similarly, baseball, hot dogs, apple pie, and the family Chevy are used to produce an enjoyable afternoon at the ballpark.

The hypothesized relationship between health status and medical care spending is shown in Figure 5.1. Stated in terms of the health status of an individual or a population, it is expressed graphically as a positively sloped function that increases at a decreasing rate. As the amount of medical care spending increases, health status improves. The incremental change in health status declines, however, as more is spent on medical care. In other words, at low levels of overall medical spending, additional spending improves health status substantially. At higher levels of medical spending, the same increase in spending buys a smaller improvement in health status. The economic principle is the law of eventually diminishing marginal returns, or more simply, the law of diminishing returns.[3] Graphically, the law of diminishing returns may be depicted in the top half of the diagram by a total product curve flattening out as medical care spending increases.

The relationship between the change in medical care spending and the change in health status is shown in the lower diagram. The marginal product of medical spending is inversely related to overall spending, indicating that the process of improving health is subject to the law of diminishing returns. In economics, decisions are seldom made on an all-or-none basis. It is almost always an issue of adjusting priorities, a little more of this and a little less of that. The use of the marginal product graph shows how much extra health can be produced by increasing the amount spent on medical care.[4] Understanding this relationship is critical, because most issues in health care relate to changes in the level of medical care provided. The relevant issues deal with marginal changes in utilization and spending, not overall utilization and spending.

Key Concept 3
Marginal Analysis

---

[2] Formally, H(. . .) is the shorthand way of describing the process whereby inputs are combined to produce health.

[3] The production function in Figure 5.1 has the parabolic form $HS = a + bM - cM^2$, where HS denotes health status and M medical care spending. The constant term, a, represents the level of health realized with no medical care spending.

[4] The difficulty in measuring health status makes the practical application of this relationship somewhat tenuous.

Figure 5.1: The Relationship between Health Status and Medical Care Spending

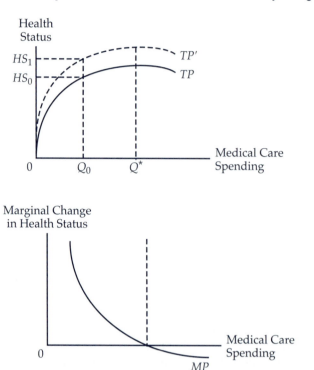

Economists and policy makers use the information provided by the marginal product curve to make decisions on the allocation of scarce resources among competing alternatives, such as education, police protection, and economic infrastructure projects. The marginal product curve makes a clear distinction between the impact of medical care on total health status and its marginal contribution to health status.

Medical care spending is not the only thing that improves health. Other factors that affect health status, such as lifestyle, environmental pollution, and technological developments, will shift the total product curve. For example, the presence and severity of respiratory problems are associated with high levels of air pollution. In many major metropolitan areas, automobile emissions are the single largest contributor to air pollution. The incidence of respiratory problems will likely fall with reductions in automotive emissions. Better eating habits and increased exercise will also improve health status. These improvements are depicted graphically by shifting the health status production function from TP to TP'. At every level of medical care spending, improving these other factors will result in better health.

Another way to look at the relationship is to view the production function as the maximum health status that can be achieved at a given level of medical care spending. If an individual is spending Q_0 on medical care, holding the other factors that affect health status constant, the maximum health status achievable is HS_0. There are two obvious ways to improve health status: spend more on medical care, and move to a higher point on a stationary health production function (TP), or make better lifestyle decisions and shift the entire curve upward (TP'). At high levels of spending, even more spending on medical care does not buy much of an improvement in health status. The curve has already flattened out. Without spending any more money on

POLICY ISSUE

medical care, however, HS_1 can be achieved with changes in lifestyle, such as losing weight, getting more exercise, and reducing stress.

One additional clarification may be in order before proceeding further: The health status production function is drawn with a negative slope at spending levels greater than Q^*. Beyond that point, more spending does not result in improvements in health. While it may be unlikely that we will ever reach that point as a society, in individual cases it may be a possibility. The graphical depiction recognizes the possibility of **iatrogenic disease**, net harm caused to a patient because of too much medical care. Prolonging death for a terminally ill patient with no chance of survival may be considered too much if the interventions are painful and the extra life gained is negligible. Quality of life is important. In another sense, as we saw in the last chapter, too much medical care may be defined as intervention with little benefit relative to cost, because money spent on patients who do not benefit is money that cannot be spent on those it can help.

Every year thousands of patients are harmed, some permanently, by unnecessary procedures and overmedication. After comparing the results of a Harvard Medical School Study of New York hospital records and a similar study from California, Brennan (1992) concluded that adverse events occurred in approximately 4 percent of all hospitalizations. In addition, more than one-fourth of the adverse events can be attributed to substandard care, often the result of overtreatment or improper treatment. A 1999 study conducted by the Institute of Medicine estimated that medical errors are responsible for the deaths of at least 44,000 Americans annually, possibly as many as 98,000 (Kohn, Corrigan, and Donaldson, 1999).

A given level of health may be achieved using different combinations of the inputs. Of interest to economists and policy analysts is the most efficient way to combine the inputs to generate the maximum output possible. In this context, efficiency refers to economic efficiency, or that combination of inputs that minimizes the cost of producing a given level of health. To determine the efficiency of resource allocation in health care, we begin by estimating the production function for health. Before we can estimate the production function for health, we must first agree on a measure of health status.

Measures of Health Status

Everyone has his or her own opinion on what constitutes good health. Health is more than the absence of disease. The preamble to the Constitution of the World Health Organization adopted in 1946 defines health as "a state of complete physical, mental, and social well-being and not merely the absence of disease or infirmity." The drawback in using such a definition is that in its broadest sense, health and well-being depend on everything. Health policy becomes all policy. If we are to give our discussion on the relationship between health status and medical spending practical importance, it is critical that we develop a quantifiable measure of health status. No single measure can capture all of the aspects relating to life and the quality of life that are considered important. Studies in the production of health have used such quantifiable measures of health as life expectancy and **mortality** rates. Disability statistics, lost days due to illness, the incidence of high blood pressure, and other measures of **morbidity** have also been used as measures of health status, including the quality-adjusted life year discussed in Chapter 4.

Mortality One of the most common aggregate measures of health status is the crude death rate for a given population, measured as the number of deaths per 100,000 population. Often this measure is adjusted for age, gender, and race to make comparisons among subgroups across geographic regions or countries more

iatrogenic disease
An injury or illness resulting from medical treatment.

Key Concept 3
Opportunity Cost

The Web site for the National Library of Medicine provides information on every significant program for the world's largest biomedical library. Access to databases, upcoming events, research programs, and publications may be found at

http://www.nlm.nih.gov/

Key Concept 8
Efficiency

mortality
The probability of death at different ages, usually expressed as the number of deaths for a given population, either 1,000 or 100,000, or the expected number of years of life remaining at a given age.

morbidity
The incidence and probability of illness or disability.

meaningful. Table 5.1 ranks the top ten causes of death in the United States in 1980 and 2004. Heart disease and cancer are responsible for over half of the deaths in this country annually and have been for the past 20 years. Add to that strokes and the number increases to roughly two-thirds. After these three, no single cause is responsible for more than 5 percent of the total deaths. In fact, after the top ten, no single cause is responsible for more than 1 percent of the total.[5] Not shown by the table is the fact that the leading causes of death vary considerably by age. Overall, unintentional injuries were the leading cause of death for all age groups from 1 to 44 years. HIV infection, once among the leading causes of death overall, was the sixth leading cause of death for Americans between the ages of 25 and 44. Cancer was the leading cause of death for those between 45 and 64 years of age, and for those over age 65, heart disease was the leading cause.

Other commonly used measures include male and female life expectancies at birth and infant mortality rates. At least two problems arise from using mortality rates to measure health status. First, when studying the health status of individuals, aggregate mortality rates have little meaning. Second, mortality rates tend to be poor indicators of the quality of life. A low crude death rate does not always indicate a healthy population.

Morbidity   An alternative way to measure health status is to consider the prevalence of certain diseases or medical conditions. Typical morbidity measures include restricted-activity days due to illness, the incidence rate of certain chronic

Table 5.1: Top Ten Causes of Death, 1980 and 2004

Cause of Death	1980 Number	Percent	Cause of Death	2004 Number	Percent
All Causes	1,989.8	100.0	All Causes	2,397.6	100.0
1. Diseases of the Heart	761.1	38.3	1. Diseases of the Heart	652.5	27.2
2. Malignant Neoplasms	416.5	20.9	2. Malignant Neoplasms	553.9	23.1
3. Cerebrovascular Diseases	170.2	8.6	3. Cerebrovascular Diseases	150.1	6.3
4. Unintended Injuries	105.7	5.3	4. Chronic Obstructive Pulmonary Diseases	122.0	5.1
5. Chronic Obstructive Pulmonary Diseases	56.1	2.8	5. Unintended Injuries	112.0	4.7
6. Pneumonia and Influenza	54.6	2.7	6. Diabetes Mellitus	73.1	3.0
7. Diabetes Mellitus	34.9	1.8	7. Alzheimer's Disease	66.0	2.8
8. Chronic Liver Disease and Cirrhosis	30.6	1.5	8. Pneumonia and Influenza	59.7	2.5
9. Atherosclerosis	29.4	1.5	9. Nephritis, Nephritic Syndromes, and Nephrosis	42.5	1.8
10. Suicide	26.9	1.4	10. Septicemia	33.4	1.4

Source: *Health, United States, 2006 with Chartbook on Trends in the Health of Americans*, Table 31.

[5] Only three of the top ten causes of death in the United States make the worldwide top ten list. In addition to diseases of the heart, cerebrovascular disease, and chronic obstructive pulmonary disease, the top ten killers worldwide include tuberculosis, malaria, measles, and lower respiratory infections and diarrhea in children under five years of age (World Health Organization, *World Health Report* 110(4), July–August 1995, 509).

conditions, and a self-assessment of health status. Table 5.2 ranks the top 15 health conditions in terms of workdays lost and restricted activity days.

Although the rank ordering differs, the number of workdays lost and the number of restricted activity days have the same causes. Arthropathies or other orthopedic impairments are responsible for the most activity impairments; and, more specifically, back problems result in the most workdays lost. Chronic conditions with the highest overall prevalence, but not necessarily the highest number of restricted-activity days, include chronic sinusitis, arthritis, asthma, chronic bronchitis, and diabetes.

Newhouse and Friedlander (1980) used six physiological measures to analyze the health status in a particular geographic region in relation to the level of medical resources available. The measures they used were diastolic blood pressure, serum cholesterol concentration, electrocardiogram abnormalities, abnormal chest X-rays, presence of varicose veins, and a periodontal index. The first three measures were chosen because of their association with cardiovascular disease, the number one cause of death. The latter three were included for the following reasons: abnormal chest X-rays are associated with cancer, the presence of varicose veins reflects the general status of the body's connective tissues, and periodontal disease reflects overall preventive-care practices.

Using morbidity measures has one serious drawback: Because the observed relationship between medical care spending and the incidence of high blood pressure, for example, is negative, more medical care reduces the incidence of hypertension. Care should be taken when graphing the relationship as we did in Figure 5.1. Because of the negative relationship, health status must be defined as the absence of the specific condition.

**Table 5.2: Selected Conditions with the Highest Number of
Work Days Lost and Activity Impairments, 1996**

Condition	Workdays Lost (Millions)	Rank	Activity Impairments (Thousands)	Rank
Acute Respiratory Infection	69.2	4	1,949.6	3
Arthropathies	67.2	5	3,070.5	1
Asthma	31.4	7	690.4	9
Back Problems	83.0	1	1,380.9	5
Cardiac Dysrythmias	7.2	12	528.7	13
Cerebrovascular Disease	8.2	13	1,084.1	6
Chronic Obstructive Pulmonary Disease	57.5	6	889.3	7
Congestive Heart Failure	1.1	15	494.6	14
Diabetes	27.5	8	1,954.0	2
Hypertension	12.0	11	544.3	12
Ischemic Heart Disease	21.8	9	638.3	10
Mood Disorders	78.2	2	1,400.9	4
Motor Vehicle Accidents	70.0	3	808.6	8
Peripheral Vascular Disorders	12.8	10	591.4	11
Respiratory Malignancies	2.5	14	121.5	15

Source: Druss et al., 2002.

Key Concept 3
Marginal Analysis

Quality of Life   Some may view measuring health status as a nice academic exercise, but it is a deadly serious proposition for health policy planners. In a world of scarce resources, some means of resource allocation is inevitable. Responsible planning requires the actual scheme to be clearly stated and easily understood, and those responsible for its implementation should be accountable for their decisions. Effective resource allocation requires establishing a measurable output. Otherwise, it is based on intuition without regard to explicit information on costs and benefits.

Recall from the previous chapter a measure of quality of life popular among European policy makers, called the quality-adjusted life year, or QALY. This measure of health status combines quality of life and survival duration into an index that is frequently used to evaluate programs and analyze clinical decisions, especially in countries with government-run systems on fixed budgets. The QALY provides a common unit of measurement that allows valid comparisons across alternative programs.

Possibly the most appropriate use of QALY analysis is the consideration of resource allocation within a single program. Setting priorities within the waiting list for kidney transplants provides a useful example. Members of the relevant population suffer from the same, end-stage renal disease (ESRD), and share the same disease-specific outcome measure. The use of the QALY approach arouses strong opinions among both supporters and critics. Those interested in more information about QALYs are directed to the vast British literature on the subject (see Broome, 1988; Culyer, 1990; Lockwood, 1988; and Loomes and McKenzie, 1990).

Determinants of Health Status

Medical care is not the only factor that contributes to the production of health. Others include income and education, environmental and lifestyle factors, and genetics. Research on the relationship between health status and medical care frequently has found that the marginal contribution of medical care to health status is rather small. Some argue that at the current level of overall medical care spending, we are at the flat of the curve (Enthoven, 1980). Referring back to Figure 5.1, the flat of the curve would correspond to a level of medical care utilization at which spending approaches the point where *TP* is maximized. As spending approaches *Q**, the marginal productivity of additional spending approaches zero, and we are on the flat of the curve. Further spending will buy only small improvements in health. Even though this generalization may be true for overall spending, it is obvious that we are not on the flat of the curve for some services, including primary, prenatal, and preventive care. In either case, any significant improvements in health status are more likely to originate from factors other than medical care. The easiest way to improve health may be to shift the production function for health.

Income and Education   The link between an individual's state of health and socioeconomic status may not be direct, but the theoretical underpinnings are obvious. Income, education, and employment represent a level of social advancement that, to a large extent, determines access to medical care. (In the U.S. system, employment determines insurance coverage to a great degree.) In turn, improved access to care improves health.[6]

---

[6] There is a glaring weakness with this line of reasoning. Countries with universal medical coverage experience the same correlation between socioeconomic status and health. For example, age-standardized mortality rates in the United Kingdom are twice as high for men in the lowest occupational classification. England's lowest socioeconomic group has infant mortality rates that are double those of the highest socioeconomic group, a difference that has persisted since the late 1940s. In Scandinavia, with its relatively homogeneous population, age-standardized mortality rates vary significantly across occupational categories. Certain low-income occupations, such as restaurant workers, have mortality rates that are twice as high as some high-income occupations, such as school teachers.

This association does not prove that low socioeconomic status causes poor health. It may be that low status is merely associated with the actual determinants of poor health. Other factors associated with socioeconomic status that may provide a more direct link include nutrition, housing, environment, and even individual time preference. Although the issue provides a wealth of data to examine, no real consensus has emerged.

Pappas and colleagues (1993) examined mortality rates for Americans at various income levels. Their research shows that the 1986 death rates for Americans with incomes less than $9,000 were significantly higher than those for Americans earning more than $25,000. More importantly, these differences have widened since 1960. They concluded that socioeconomic status is a strong indicator of health status.

Guralnik and colleagues (1993) have shown that one of the most important factors influencing good health and life expectancy is education (independent of income levels). The research still begs the relevant question: Does more schooling result in better health, or are the two variables related in some other way?

Research represented by Grossman (1972) and others assumes that individuals with more education are more efficient producers of good health. Education increases the ability to understand the importance of avoiding unhealthy behavior, the ability to communicate with health practitioners and understand instructions, and the ability to take advantage of the services available in the medical marketplace. By improving long-term opportunities, education increases the return on investing in health improvements.

Examining the relationship between income and health at the national level requires a completely different perspective. In comparisons of modern industrial nations, little correlation emerges between the level of national income and the various measures of health. When countries from the less developed world are included, however, a connection between income and health can be made. This connection is probably due to better **public health** measures as the level of development increases, including sanitary water and sewage systems and immunization programs that reduce the spread of disease.

> **POLICY ISSUE**
>
> Does additional medical care spending on the poor significantly improve their health status?

> **public health**
> Collective action undertaken by government agencies to ensure the health of the community. These efforts include the prevention of disease, identification of health problems, and the assurance of sanitary conditions, especially in the areas of water treatment and waste disposal.

ISSUES IN MEDICAL CARE DELIVERY

The Income/Health Gradient

The evidence is strong and persistent, across time and across countries, that a relationship exists between health outcomes and income. There is also a belief that health resources are more equitably distributed in those countries with a government-run system; and because access in those countries is not determined by personal financial resources, health outcomes would also be more equitably distributed. Many researchers have examined this issue, but most have not had the data required to actually estimate the health/income gradient at the individual level.

The usual results show a much steeper gradient in the United States between the averages of the health indicator when comparing those above and below median income. The greater variance in income in the United States biases the results when using above and below median income comparisons, forcing a steeper gradient on U.S. data.

continued

O'Neill and O'Neill (2007) solve this problem by using Canadian and U.S. data on individuals that incorporate a continuous income variable into the analysis. They regress two health status variables, Health Utility Index and self-reported health status, on income for the two countries separately and compare. In all of the models estimated, the income/health gradient is significantly steeper in Canada than in the United States. Regardless of the health care system, government-run or market oriented, the health/income gradient is a reality. Free access to medical care does not translate into equal health outcomes.

Source: June E. O'Neill and Dave M. O'Neill, "Health Status, Health Care and Inequality: Canada vs. the U.S." NBER Working Paper No. 13429, Cambridge, MA: National Bureau of Economic Research, September 2007.

POLICY ISSUE

Much of the illness experienced by residents of industrialized countries is due to lifestyle and environmental factors, including the food we eat and the air we breathe.

Environmental and Lifestyle Factors Our discussion on market failure due to externalities in Chapter 3 emphasized the economic costs associated with environmental problems such as air and water pollution. In addition to the high economic costs, the toll on human life and the quality of life is also significant. For example, the American Cancer Society estimates that 65 percent of all cancer in the United States can be linked to lifestyle and environmental factors, including the air we breathe and the food we eat. Exposure to environmental toxins, especially during infancy and childhood, can be linked to illness in children. Harmful chemicals, such as lead, mercury, and polychlorinated biphenyls (PCBs), are associated with poor fetal growth, poor growth during childhood, reduced intelligence (measured by IQ), small head circumference (associated with mental retardation), and decreased lung capacity (Shannon and Graef, 1992; Rogan et al., 1986; Needleman and Bellinger, 1990).

Regardless of the level of income and education, health status depends to a large degree on personal behavior. Lifestyle factors that include diet, exercise, sexual behavior, cigarette smoking, substance abuse, and brushes with violence are important determinants of health status. The observed relationship between health status and socioeconomic status is interesting. But insufficient evidence prevents a determination of whether we are actually witnessing a link between socioeconomic status and health, lifestyle behavior and health, or possibly socioeconomic status and lifestyle behavior, or all three.

ISSUES IN MEDICAL CARE DELIVERY

Genetic Discrimination

When is a person considered sick? In California, a person cannot be considered sick until he or she exhibits symptoms of an illness. This issue is not as silly as it may seem on the surface: It is a serious legal matter. We are already becoming extremely sophisticated in our ability to diagnose ailments at very early stages. In fact, hundreds of tests are currently available to identify a person's genetic predisposition to a number of inherited diseases.

From a medical perspective, the availability of genetic information can be lifesaving. Genetic testing can provide valuable information to

continued

medical providers on the probability that a person might contract a specific disease. Better predictability improves the chance of prevention. From an insurance perspective, this same information can be used to determine eligibility for health insurance coverage or even the level of premiums.

Otherwise healthy individuals may be unable to secure health insurance coverage because of information about their genetic makeup. Entire families could be denied insurance coverage, even infants before they are born, because someone in the family carries a recessive gene for a disease, such as sickle cell anemia or Tay Sachs disease. (Carriers of a disease possess a recessive gene, but will never contract the disease.)

The growing trend toward preventive medicine will increasingly use genetic analysis to forecast an individual's likelihood to contract a particular disease. Who should have access to this genetic information? How should it be used? Given the expensive nature of disease treatment, if genetic tests are performed, it is understandable that health insurance firms would want access to the information. Individuals who have information about their potential health problems are likely to desire additional health insurance coverage. Is it fair to deny this information to insurance companies who are being asked to underwrite the future costs? It is illegal to discriminate against a person on the basis of sex or race? Should it also be illegal to discriminate against someone on the basis of his or her DNA?

Source: Seth Shulman, "Preventing Genetic Discrimination: California Law Prohibits Discriminating Against People Genetically Predisposed to Rare Diseases," *Technology Review* 98(5), Massachusetts Institute of Technology Alumni Association, July 1995, 16.

POLICY ISSUE

Should the results of genetic tests be made available to all stakeholders: patients and their families, medical providers, and health insurance payers?

Genetic Factors Two factors play a critical role in determining the health of an individual: the risk of exposure to a particular disease and the ability of the individual to resist the disease and recover from its consequences once exposed. The former is the purview of public health, the latter is determined largely by genetics. Thinking about the etiology of certain inherited diseases, sickle cell anemia for example, differs from thinking about causation in infectious diseases. If a critical number of bacteria enter the system, you get sick. If the bacteria are *Salmonella typhi*, you get salmonellosis. With certain cancers, the process is different. Cells mutate and multiply, and sometimes a single cell can become cancerous through a series of events. Inherited traits may predispose individuals to certain diseases.

Our genetic makeup is determined directly by our parents. You receive 50 percent of your genes from your father and 50 percent from your mother. You share 50 percent of your genes with your siblings, or 100 percent if you happen to be an identical twin. These are all referred to as your first-degree relatives. You get 25 percent of your genes from each grandparent, and you share that same percentage with each aunt and uncle. These are called second-degree relatives. You also get 12.5 percent of your genes from each great-grandparent, so there is a chance that their genetic defects could surface in you.

Attempts to understand the hereditary factor in determining the predisposition to certain diseases have received a great deal of attention. Genetic research has focused on the mapping of the 100,000 plus genes in the human body with one of the goals being to determine the genes responsible for certain forms of inherited diseases. The inheritance of a particular gene greatly increases the risk of acquiring certain diseases. For example, women with a family history of ovarian cancer have a lifetime risk of developing the disease of about 40 percent, compared with the

The National Cancer Institute is the largest of the 17 biomedical institutes that comprise the National Institutes of Health (NIH). It serves to coordinate all research on the causes, prevention, detection, diagnosis, and treatment of cancer. Check it out at

http://www.cancer.gov

general population's risk of about 7 percent. Other genes are associated with an increased incidence of colon, breast, uterine, and prostate cancers. Genetic factors may account for as much as 10 to 15 percent of all colorectal cancers and 5 to 10 percent of breast cancers (Marra and Boland, 1995).

A hereditary component is suspected in many different disorders. A strong family predisposition is a significant factor in allergies, hypertension, obesity, cystic fibrosis, sickle cell anemia, and even snoring. Heredity may also be linked to pancreatic cancer, certain melanomas, and even kidney and lung cancer. But scientists are still trying to understand the biological basis for many diseases. A mere clustering of a common disease in certain families is not enough to prove a genetic link. The cause may be environmental, or it may be lifestyle related instead of genetic. But as the genetic components of many diseases are being discovered, a complete family medical history is becoming an important tool in the early diagnosis and treatment of certain diseases. Until more is known, choose your parents well.

The Relationship Between Social Class and Health

Most of the research on health disparities across socioeconomic groups has centered on racial differences in health. There is no question that health disparities exist across race and ethnic groups, as seen in differences in the selected mortality rates in Table 5.3. While race is important in determining health status, there is growing evidence that social class may also play an important role.

Two studies of white-collar, government workers in the United Kingdom, known as the Whitehall studies, document the existence of a social gradient in mortality and morbidity (Marmot, Shipley et al., 1984; Marmot, Bosma et al., 1997). In both studies, the lower the grade level of the employee group, the higher the mortality rate from most major causes of death. The gradient is not represented by a threshold employment grade. As we move up the grade ladder, each subsequently higher grade has better health outcomes. Two important observations emerge: First, the social gradient is relatively stable over time. Income levels and life expectancy have risen over time in the developed world, but the health disparity remains. Second, the social gradient exists in Britain and most of the rest of the developed world, where there is some form of government-run health care, and in the United States, where there is not (Marmot, 2001).

Health might determine social position to some extent. While it is plausible that unhealthy people migrate to poor neighborhoods, it is unlikely that these migratory patterns are the sole reason for the observed differences. Lifestyle may be important, but that begs the question: Why are there socioeconomic differences in alcohol and tobacco use, physical activity, hypertension, diabetes, cholesterol

Table 5.3: Mortality Rates by Sex and Race, Selected Causes, 2004
Deaths per 100,000

	White Male	Black Male	White Female	Black Female
HIV	3.8	29.2	0.9	13.0
Lower respiratory disease	51.1	40.9	38.4	20.9
Maternal mortality	—	—	7.5	32.3
Homicide	5.3	35.1	1.9	6.3
Suicide	19.6	9.6	5.0	1.8
Firearm related	15.4	34.5	2.7	3.6

levels, and obesity? This phenomenon is not simply a matter of one group, largely defined (i.e., the rich), living longer than everyone else (i.e., the poor). The social gradient indicates that everyone is affected. Whatever the causes, people in lower social classes die at younger ages and are more susceptible to whatever diseases are affecting the population.

The Role of Public Health and Nutrition

Research by Thomas McKeown (1976) has served as the basis for most of our understanding concerning the improvement in mortality. Ranked in order of importance, McKeown attributed the secular decline in mortality rates in Europe and North America to four major sources:

- Living standards, primarily better nutrition and housing, advanced dramatically.

- Intervention of public health authorities improved sanitary conditions in the growing urban centers. Water purification and the treatment and disposal of sewage vastly improved the water supplies.

- Certain diseases declined in importance because of reduced exposure and increased natural immunity.

- Advances in medical science increased the ability to treat certain conditions. Improvements in surgery enabled physicians to treat accidents and digestive disorders, especially appendicitis; obstetric and pediatric care improved treatment of pregnant women and infants; and immunizations contributed to the control of certain diseases.

The result was a decline in waterborne diseases responsible for intestinal infections, including cholera, dysentery, diphtheria, and other diarrheal diseases. Food hygiene, especially with respect to milk, improved significantly leading to a reduction in the number of infant deaths. The spread of airborne diseases resulting in upper-respiratory problems, such as bronchitis, pneumonia, influenza, and smallpox, became less of a problem because of reduced exposure due, in part, to the diligence of health officials in controlling the spread of these diseases.

Most of the reduction in mortality occurred before effective medical interventions were discovered. When considering the reasons for increased longevity, the role of public health intervention should not be overlooked. The U.S. Public Health Service was formed in 1912, emerging from the Marine Hospital Service. The purview of public health includes the control of communicable diseases, epidemics, and environmental hazards. Public health activities promote health through immunization programs, quarantines, and standards for clean air, clean water, sewage disposal, and the safe handling of food.

Although few critics argue with McKeown's list of reasons for the decline in mortality and morbidity, they do question his rankings and the relative importance he places on each. In particular, Woods and Hinde (1987) question McKeown's conclusion that up to half of the decrease in mortality was due to improved nutrition. They agree that nutrition played a significant role in determining the health of a population by increasing the resistance to disease. Obviously, the overt types of malnutrition, including rickets and beriberi, contribute to poor health. More importantly, an undernourished population lends itself to more frequent infections and more serious infections. Woods and Hinde, however, placed more weight on the importance of improvements in environmental conditions and less on nutrition. Neither attributed much of the decline in the incidence of disease to improvements in medical care.

POLICY ISSUE

Improvements in public health programs are responsible for much of the improvement in human life span experienced over the past century.

POLICY ISSUE

Improvements in public health may do as much to improve life expectancy in the less developed world than increases in medical care spending.

The relationship between nutrition, mortality, and morbidity is complicated. Better nutrition played a significant role in the reduction in mortality from infectious disease, in particular, childhood diseases related to respiratory and intestinal infections. But McKeown's (1976) research, based on national data, did not include data on infant mortality, an important cause of death until well into the twentieth century. The debate rages regarding whether environmental or nutritional improvements had the most impact on health among demographers and is likely to continue for some time. It is important to note that the increased availability of medical care is only one way to improve the health status of an individual or population. In the developed world at least, better lifestyle decisions and a cleaner environment may do more to improve health than increased availability of medical care. In the less developed world, better sanitation, potable water, and improved living conditions top the list.

ISSUES IN MEDICAL CARE DELIVERY

Fifty Years at the CDC

Centers for Disease Control (CDC)

Established in 1946, this agency of the U.S. Department of Health and Human Services is charged with promoting the public health of Americans around the world.

For years, the control of the spread of infectious diseases has been tightly linked to the **Centers for Disease Control (CDC)**. When public health officials were faced with problems of immunization or eradication, they turned to the CDC. July 1, 2006, marked the sixtieth anniversary of the establishment of the Atlanta-based operation. But the task of the CDC is much more complex than its mission statement would indicate: To promote health and quality of life by preventing and controlling disease, injury, and disability. The issues are no longer merely epidemiological. The world of public health is now more complicated than studying and stopping chains of infection. The challenge has become less scientific and more behavioral.

- How do we promote healthy lifestyles?

- Should nicotine be classified as an addictive substance and kept out of the hands of minors?

- Can we reduce the homicide rate by requiring the registration of handguns?

- What is the best way to break the chain of HIV infection, condoms or quarantine?

Much of the work of the CDC is still related to the original mission. The CDC had representatives in Zaire in 1995 to study the outbreak of the deadly Ebola virus. The world looked to the CDC for reassurance that this was an isolated occurrence and not the first of many exotic viruses to emerge from the wilderness to infect modern civilization. Similar stories can be told about Legionnaires' disease, toxic shock syndrome, severe acute respiratory syndrome (SARS), and bird flu.

Even critics of the organization view the study of infectious diseases as an important element in prevention and cure. Their concern deals with the controversial issues, such as a recommended ban on all cigarette advertising to reduce teenage smoking, the promotion of condom use to control the spread of HIV, and mandatory licensing of handguns to reduce the rate of homicides.

continued

The very nature of the operation places the CDC in contact with the unloved populations of the world and opens it up to criticism. Promiscuous gay men, drug addicts, violent teenagers, and the homeless receive a great deal of attention. Critics contend that too much money and too much effort are spent on medical issues affecting these groups. Instead, they argue, attention should be focused on keeping healthy people from getting sick. Even though AIDS accounts for less than one percent of the deaths annually, the HIV/AIDS budget is almost one-third of the total CDC budget. In comparison, cancer accounts for 25 percent of the annual deaths and cardiovascular disease over 40 percent.

The twenty-first century task of the CDC is even more complicated. With over 70 percent of the deaths in the United States the result of chronic diseases, the future of the medical care delivery system lies in disease prevention. Not only is prevention difficult to sell, prevention research is complicated and costly. It is much easier to study the effectiveness of a drug treatment, or how to cure a disease, than it is to demonstrate a pattern of disease prevention. Chronic illness lacks immediacy. Lung cancer materializes as a result of a lifetime of poor decisions about smoking. It is difficult to convince someone that their decision to smoke today will affect their quality of life 40 years from now. For many young smokers, their chance of dying violently at a young age far surpasses the perceived risk of a few cigarettes. With a combined budget of a little over $2 billion, and about 6,000 employees, the CDC has set out to find practical uses for basic medical research. It is not nearly as easy as it sounds.

Source: Anne Rochell, "Turning 50: The CDC's Midlife Crisis," *Dallas Morning News*, January 28, 1996, 12J.

THE DEMAND FOR MEDICAL CARE

As medical care spending continues to escalate, the search for alternatives to slow its growth has focused on the supply side of the market. Modifying provider behavior is seen by some as the only way to control runaway spending. By ignoring the demand side of the market, we may be forgoing one of the most powerful forces available for cost control: individual self-interest. A basic understanding of the demand side of the market is an important step toward fiscal responsibility in medical care. In this section, we will identify and examine the factors that determine the demand for medical care.

Key Concept 4
Self-Interest

Medical Care as an Investment

One demand-side approach treats medical care the same as any other investment that enhances future productivity. Stated in economic terms, medical care increases human capital (Fuchs, 1982; Mushkin, 1962). Resources used to improve health reduce current consumption, resulting in a decrease in the amount of money available to spend on items other than health care, with the expectation that future consumption will increase because of the ability to work longer and earn more money. Individual willingness to invest in health improvements is determined by several factors: the current cost of medical care, the size of the future payoff, the time span over which the payoff is realized, and individual time preference. It is irrelevant whether the human capital investment is spending on medical care or spending for a college education. Individuals who are willing to invest in a college education are the same individuals who are willing to spend time and money on improving their health. Thus, the association between health and educational attainment is significant.

POLICY ISSUE

The most powerful force for controlling medical spending is the cost-conscious consumer.

Key Concept 2
Opportunity Cost

Demand for medical care is not based solely on the desire to feel better but also on the desire to increase productivity. Within this framework, the demand for medical care has a consumption component and an investment component. People who invest in their health desire to have more healthy days available to produce income and leisure. This view incorporates the concept of the depreciation of health capital as one ages and the use of medical care to slow the process.

The model of derived demand provides the basis for our study of the determinants of medical care demand. The demand for medical care is derived from the demand for good health. Using this framework, the demand for medical care is inversely related to its price. Other relevant factors affecting the level of demand will now be examined.[7]

Factors Influencing Demand

The demand for medical care is determined to a great extent by patient need. Admittedly, need is a difficult concept to define, but one thing is certain: *need* and *demand* are not synonymous. Needs tend to be self-defined and thus represent unconstrained desires. Defining medical care demand in terms of self-defined need is a prescription for wasting medical care resources. As a society, we can never fully satisfy unconstrained desires. In economics, demand is defined in terms of the sacrifice an individual is willing to make to obtain a given amount of a particular good or service. In this context, to restrain medical care spending, we simply modify the incentive structure.

Key Concept 6
Supply and Demand

Following Intriligator (1981), an individual's demand for medical care may be depicted by the demand curves in Figure 5.2, where Q_M represents some minimum level of medical care required to maintain health. Society is unwilling to allow anyone to fall below this minimum threshold, and this minimum level will vary depending on the individual's current health status. Individuals with acute or chronic health problems will require more medical care. The demand curve D_0 represents the level of care established by the medical community as the clinical standard.

Figure 5.2: Demand Based on Need versus Willingness to Pay

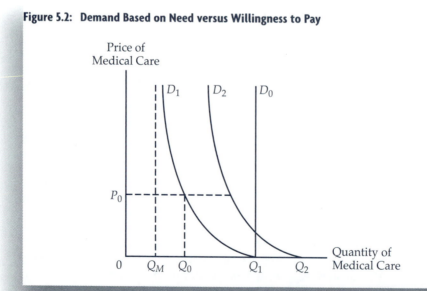

---

[7] **Further discussion of the human capital model may be found in Chapter 8.**

It is the level of care that should be provided without consideration for cost. Medical planners often use D_0 to determine future requirements for medical facilities and personnel. Planning based solely on clinical standards (medically defined need) ignores the price of medical care completely. Under these circumstances, demand is treated as if it were perfectly inelastic. Consumers desire the same level of services (Q_1) regardless of the price they pay.

Demand based on willingness to pay does not ignore need completely. Clinical need is merely considered one of several determinants of demand. In this case, demand is shown by the downward-sloping demand curve D_1. As the price of care changes, quantity demanded changes. When medical care is free to the patient ($P = 0$), the quantity demanded will be Q_1. As patients are required to pay more out-of-pocket, they demand less. When price rises to P_0, quantity demanded falls to Q_0. In this framework, health status becomes a demand shifter that changes the level of demand. If health deteriorates, the level of demand increases, and the demand curve shifts to the right to D_2. If health improves, the demand curve shifts to the left. Note that when demand shifts to D_2, clinical need also increases to Q_2.

The following discussion examines the major factors that influence medical care demand. Factors can be categorized as patient factors and physician factors. Patient factors include health status, demographic characteristics, and economic standing. Physicians affect demand through their standing as both providers of medical services and advisers to, or agents of, their patients. Because physicians also serve as agents, they are in a unique position to create demand for their own services. Medical care demand may be viewed as a functional relationship between medical care and its determinants.

$$\text{Medical Care} = M\ (HS,\ DC,\ ES,\ PF)$$

where patient factors include health status (HS), demographic characteristics (DC), and economic standing (ES). Physician factors are denoted by PF. M (. . .) is a shorthand depiction of how these factors interact to generate a demand for medical care.

Patient Factors With medical care, as with any other commodity or service, consumers must decide among the available alternatives designed to satisfy their desires. For the demand relationship to have any economic meaning, patients must have money to spend on treatment alternatives and the ability to rank them in order of preference. Otherwise, patients are merely pawns in the game of medical resource allocation.

Substitutes in medical care are the alternative methods of treatment that lead to the same outcome. Natural childbirth results in a newborn infant, but so does cesarean delivery. Balloon angioplasty, along with stainless-steel stents, is one way to treat blocked coronary arteries; bypass graft surgery is another. Tennis elbow will improve in time with RICE (rest, ice, compression, and elevation); for those less patient, cortisone injections will also do the trick. Other examples include surgery performed on an outpatient instead of an inpatient basis; the use of the laparoscope for abdominal and knee surgeries; and lithotripsy instead of abdominal surgery to treat kidney stones. In most cases, the choice of treatment alternative is not solely a physician decision. The desires of patients are also taken into consideration.

Health Status A patient seeking treatment for a medical condition typically initiates medical treatment. The patient's desire for treatment is often a response to an accident, injury, or other episode of illness. Thus, an individual's demand for medical treatment is usually triggered by the onset of an episode of illness. The desire to remain healthy will increase the demand for preventive care. For example, many people visit the local clinic annually for a flu shot to avoid the onset of an illness, women are encouraged to visit their gynecologists regularly for preventive tests, and some people see their dentists twice a year for check-ups and cleanings.

The acute care model of medical treatment follows an expected pattern: a patient develops a medical condition (illness, injury, pregnancy, etc.), seeks out a physician, receives treatment, and either recovers or dies. Increasingly, a significant minority of patients does not fit the pattern. Their medical conditions do not go away. Instead of recovering or dying, they simply live on with a chronic medical problem.

ISSUES IN MEDICAL CARE DELIVERY

Treatment Alternatives for Peptic Ulcers

What is the best way to treat duodenal ulcers? Until recently, most members of the medical profession felt that the overproduction of stomach acid due to stress, diet, or environmental factors was the major cause of this common peptic ulcer. If excess acid is the source, then the best treatment is the use of an acid blocker such as Tagamet, Zantac, Prilosec, or the "little purple pill," Nexium. Recent information made available by the National Institutes of Health indicate that a common bacterium causes most duodenal ulcers, opening up a new treatment pattern that includes acid blockers and antibiotics.

Research by Imperiale and colleagues (1995) examined the costs of three different treatments: 1) treat with acid blockers initially, and if the problem recurs, verify the presence of bacteria by endoscopy and treat with antibiotics; 2) prescribe routine endoscopy followed by acid blockers and antibiotics if bacteria are present; otherwise use acid blockers alone; and 3) use acid blockers and antibiotics, and resort to endoscopy only if the problem recurs within a year.

All three methods are proven means of treating this common form of peptic ulcer. But recurrence rates are extremely high with acid blockers alone, and endoscopy is an expensive diagnostic test, costing as much as $3,000. Because research confirms that a high percentage of ulcer patients are also infected with the bacterium, avoiding the invasive test can save money. Thus, the most cost-effective treatment may be an aggressive regimen of acid blockers and antibiotics without the expensive diagnostic testing.

Source: Thomas F. Imperiale, Theodore Speroff, Randall D. Cebul, and Arthur J. McCullough, "A Cost Analysis of Alternative Treatments of Duodenal Ulcers," *Annals of Internal Medicine* 123(9), November 1, 1995, 665–672.

Chronic illness, defined as a condition where a complete cure is not possible, has become a major factor in U.S. health care spending. In fact, chronic conditions begin to dominate medical care demand as a person ages. The incidence of Parkinson's, Alzheimer's, and other dementias increases as we age. Individuals who once died of heart attack or stroke in their sixties are living into their eighties only to experience the effects of a chronic illness. Arthritis, diabetes, hypertension, and heart disease are growing problems among the elderly. A 65-year-old suffering from a chronic illness spends on average $1,000 to $2,000 more annually on medical care than a similar person without the chronic condition. Chronic conditions are responsible for a majority of the health care spending in the United States, and the top five—heart disease, cancer, stroke, emphysema, and diabetes—are responsible for over two-thirds of all deaths (Joyce, Keeler, Shang, and Goldman, 2005). Using

Medical Expenditure Panel Survey data, Druss and colleagues (2001) estimated that treatment costs for five chronic conditions—mood disorders, diabetes, heart disease, hypertension, and asthma—and the comorbidities associated with them accounted for over half of the total cost of health care in 1996.

Chronic conditions are not solely a feature of the elderly population. An increase in the number of HIV infections and the cost of treating AIDS are a growing concern. Other sexually transmitted diseases, especially syphilis, Chlamydia, and HPV, and respiratory diseases such as tuberculosis and pneumonia, are increasingly resistant to traditional methods of treatment. These realities are all subtle reminders that we have not won the battle against infectious disease.

Demographic Characteristics Individual and population demographics are also important determinants of medical care demand. First of all, a growing population will increase the demand for medical care. Even as the population grows, the family structure is changing dramatically, increasing the demands on the medical care sector. More single parents, more women in the labor force, later marriages, fewer children per family, and greater mobility translate into fewer opportunities for direct family care and a greater reliance on medical providers.

An aging population is another factor contributing to increased demand for medical care. Using the terminology of the Grossman model (1972), as a person grows older, the stock of health capital begins to depreciate. Over the life cycle, people attempt to offset their depreciating stocks by increasing their spending on medical care. In addition to the increased frequency of chronic conditions discussed above, the elderly are more likely to suffer from cancer, heart attack, stroke, osteoporosis, poor eyesight, and hearing loss. All of these conditions are costly and contribute to the increased per capita spending for medical care.

Substantial differences are noted in medical care demand by sex (Sindelar, 1982). Early in the life cycle, men and women spend approximately the same amounts on medical care. Later in life, especially during the childbearing years, women spend approximately 50 percent more than men. Women are hospitalized more often (primarily due to 1.9 child births per fertile female), but when men are hospitalized, they remain in the hospital 50 percent longer. Men are more able to substitute home health care for hospital care, especially older men, because they typically have a wife at home to take care of them. Older women, because they live longer than their husbands, are more likely to be living alone with no one at home to take care of them. Single individuals, regardless of age, are hospitalized more often than married people.

Men suffer more frequent health losses due to lifestyle choices, such as drinking, smoking, and overeating. With more women in the labor force, patterning themselves after their male counterparts, these differences in lifestyle factors are beginning to narrow. As women continue to act more like men, with higher rates of smoking, drinking, and stress, some medical experts suggest that they may one day start dying like men.

Economic Standing In the United States, education, income, and medical care spending have always been closely associated. Historically, individuals with higher incomes have demanded more medical care. More recently, the importance of income in determining medical care demand has diminished with the increase in third-party insurance coverage.[8] The availability of insurance increases demand

Links to over 100 sites with health information for women are available at the National Institutes of Health at

http://health.nih.gov

POLICY ISSUE

When spending someone else's money, consumers have little incentive to limit their demand.

---

[8] With no adjustment for health status, individuals with less than $14,000 in income had 7.3 physicians' visits on average in 1993. Individuals with over $50,000 had 5.8 (Health United States, 1994, Table 75, p. 169). The differential narrows when health status is considered. The poor and near poor still see the doctor more often than the nonpoor, with 5.7, 5.3, and 5.1 annual visits for each group (Health United States Chartbook, 1993, Figure 26, p. 36).

for medical care by lowering direct out-of-pocket payment requirements. When someone else is paying the bills, there is no incentive to limit demand. Beginning in the early 1980s, individuals with higher incomes actually had fewer physicians' visits than those with lower incomes (reported in Somers, 1986). In spite of the importance of third-party coverage, direct out-of-pocket payments still account for about 15 percent of all personal health care expenditures, keeping income high on the list of important economic factors.

Income levels are highly correlated with educational levels. The association between income and education has fostered a huge body of economic research on the economic rewards of education, called *human capital theory*. Formal recognition of human capital research as a legitimate area of study may be attributed to the work of Nobel laureate Gary Becker (1964) and Jacob Mincer (1974).[9]

The role of education as a determinant in the demand for medical care goes beyond its association with higher incomes. It is hypothesized that higher levels of education make a person a better consumer of medical care services. Education improves a person's ability to recognize symptoms of medical problems early, when treatment is less expensive. Those with more education have healthier occupations; they eat better and are more efficient users of medical care.

financial risk
The risk associated with contractual obligations that require fixed monetary outlays.

With its complex system of private and public insurance programs, the United States has developed a system of third-party insurance to spread the **financial risk** associated with sickness and injury. Third-party payers, including private insurance and the government, cover 80 percent of all medical care spending. Patients who are not directly responsible for their spending decisions tend to demand more medical care than they would otherwise purchase with their own money. Medical care that carries no out-of-pocket cost is treated as if it had no underlying resource cost. The result is moral hazard, demanding more than the social optimum. (See Chapter 6 for a more complete discussion of moral hazard.)

deductible
The amount of money that an insured person must pay before a health plan begins paying for all or part of the covered expenses.

Recognizing that health insurance acts to increase the level of demand, health insurance providers offer policies with features that serve to reduce moral hazard. The features typically include **deductibles**, **coinsurance**, and **copayments**. The deductible is the initial amount the policyholder must pay before the insurance coverage begins paying. Coinsurance is the percentage of the total, beyond the deductible, that the policyholder pays. A copayment is a fixed dollar amount charged directly to the patient at the time of treatment.

coinsurance
A standard feature of health insurance policies that requires the insured person to pay a certain percentage of a medical bill, usually 10 to 30 percent, per physician visit or hospital stay.

The impact of health insurance on medical care demand is depicted in Figure 5.3. D_0 represents the demand for medical care for a person with no insurance (subscript indicates the percentage of medical care paid by insurance). D_{50} is that same individual's demand curve with a policy that requires a 50 percent coinsurance rate. With 50 percent coinsurance, the insurance company pays half, and the policyholder pays half, and the policyholder demands Q_1 at price P_0. Without insurance the individual would pay the full price for the medical care, P_0, and demand only Q_0. Thus, the availability of insurance, or more generally reducing the coinsurance rate, increases the demand for medical care by rotating the demand curve upward.[10] In the case of full insurance, with a coinsurance rate equal to zero, the demand curve would rotate to the vertical and become D_{100}, and quantity demanded would be equal to Q_2 at a zero price to the patient.

copayment
A standard feature of many managed care plans that requires the insured person to pay a fixed sum for each office visit, hospital stay, or prescription drug.

---

[9] See the human capital discussion in Chapter 8.

[10] More technically, the availability of insurance also makes the policyholder less sensitive to changes in the price of medical care. Demand is more inelastic when consumers spend a smaller percentage of their budgets on an item. Remember, as you move downward and to the right on a straight-line demand curve, price elasticity falls.

Figure 5.3:   The Effect of Insurance on Medical Care Demand

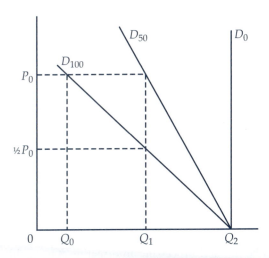

Even as insurance coverage has expanded, approximately 15 percent of the population is without medical insurance at any one point in time. This situation presents an interesting dilemma for policy makers. Those who are fully insured are probably using more medical care than they really need. At the same time, those who have no insurance are probably using less.

The presence of insurance has changed the nature of medicine over the past half century by changing the incentive structure pertinent to the purchase of medical care. Insurance, to a degree, has distorted the medical market by creating a bias toward acute care instead of preventive care, specialty care instead of primary care, and hospital care instead of home care (Weisbrod, 1991). The direction of research and development is determined by what insurance will buy. As new technology and procedures become available, pressure mounts to include them under covered services. Efforts to restrain demand by deductibles and coinsurance, managed care networks, and alternative delivery mechanisms result from a growing awareness of the distortions caused by the third-party payment mechanism.

Of all the factors that affect the demand for medical care, the economic factors are more important for policy considerations because they are more readily affected by public policy. Demographic factors change gradually. The population grows older, more couples divorce, and fewer children are born, but these factors are not easily manipulated by public policy.

In addition to the personal factors, changing attitudes and preferences of the population have a tremendous impact on demand. Over the last 50 years, the public attitude toward medicine has become increasingly positive. Once viewed with a certain amount of distrust, the medical profession today is highly respected. Part of that increased respect is due to the increased ability to actually cure patients of their ailments. With each new drug, with each new procedure, faith in medicine continues to grow.

As quickly as attitudes toward the medical profession have improved, there began a new movement toward patient autonomy. Terminally ill patients are increasingly demanding the "right to die." Patients suffering poor outcomes are questioning the quality of their care and turning to the tort system to rule on claims of malpractice.

POLICY ISSUE

The availability of health insurance has changed the incentive structure within the medical care market.

POLICY ISSUE

The movement for more patient autonomy has created added pressures to increase medical care spending.

All these economic factors have contributed to a growing demand for medical care and are at least partly responsible for increased medical spending.

Physician Factors Even though only 20 percent of all medical spending goes for physicians' services, physicians determine the vast majority of total spending. Physicians prescribe the drugs, admit patients into hospitals, and order the tests. Their influence on demand stems from the physician's dual role as adviser to the patient and provider of services.

A vast economic literature has been developed examining the **principal–agent relationship**. An agency relationship exists where an individual, the principal, gives someone else, the agent, authority to make decisions on his or her behalf. Problems arise when the interests of the principal and the agent diverge. In medicine, patients are relatively uninformed concerning alternative diagnoses and treatments. They are willing to trust physicians to make choices for them because of the difficulty in gathering and understanding medical information. But the physician's role as supplier can create a conflict of interest.

A physician's ability to induce demand is greatly enhanced when patients have a difficult time gathering and processing information. Given this unique position, physicians can serve as imperfect agents, serving their own interests over those of their patients. In other words, they have the ability to influence their patients' demand for the services they personally provide. In theory, efficacy and cost guide a physician faced with alternative treatment options for a particular disorder. If two treatments are equally effective, the physician can choose the cheaper alternative and save the patient money, or the more expensive alternative and buy a new flat screen television for the den.

principal–agent relationship
A relationship in which one person (the principal) gives another person (the agent) authority to make decisions on his or her behalf.

ISSUES IN MEDICAL CARE DELIVERY

Self-Referral: The Real Culprit in High Spending?

One of the most important ethical issues confronting the medical community is the practice of self-referral. With increasing frequency, physicians in most communities are supplementing their incomes with profits from ownership interests in medical facilities. Holding interest in a diagnostic laboratory, imaging center, physical therapy center, or mammography center is not a conflict of interest per se; however, the potential for abuse is substantial.

These facilities actually seek out physicians as investors and often refuse to offer ownership interest to nonphysicians. The reason is obvious: physicians refer patients. Information problems abound in medical markets and are particularly troublesome in the market for referral services. Patients requiring the specialized services of a diagnostic testing center are particularly vulnerable to the provision of unnecessary services. Lacking the expertise to evaluate treatment alternatives, the patient expects the physician to act as a well-meaning agent in recommending treatment. But physicians who have financial interests in these outside facilities tend to order more tests, charge higher fees for them, and have higher total bills. Hillman and colleagues (1992) found that self-referring physicians ordered two to eight times more lab tests and charged up to six times more for them. Mitchell and Scott (1992) found that physicians who owned interests in physical therapy centers referred 39 to 45 percent more patients and generated 30 to 40 percent higher net revenues.

The AMA's official position is that self-referral is an ethical practice as long as the patient is informed of the physician's interest in the outside

continued

facility. Most states have enacted legislation to force disclosure of any financial interest in a testing facility, and a few have gone so far as to prohibit
ownership. Recognizing self-referral as a potential problem, Congress has
enacted legislation to eliminate the practice when Medicare and Medicaid
patients are involved.

Self-referral is emerging as an important economic issue. When the
physician is largely responsible for both sides of a transaction, clearly the
potential for abuse exists. Developing a workable policy on ownership of
facilities, and balancing it against the rights of the individual to invest in
such facilities, will challenge reformers' intent on reigning in the escalating
costs of medical care.

Sources: Bruce J. Hillman, George T. Olson, Patricia E. Griffith, Jonathan H. Sunshine, Catherine A.
Joseph, Stephen D. Kennedy, William R. Nelson, and Lee B. Bernhardt, "Physicians' Utilization and
Charges for Outpatient Diagnostic Imaging in a Medicare Population," *Journal of the American
Medical Association* 268(15), October 21, 1992, 2050–2054; and Jean M. Mitchell and Elton
Scott, "Physician Ownership of Physical Therapy Services," *Journal of the American Medical
Association* 268(15), October 21, 1992, 2055–2059.

Standard economic analysis assumes that the demand and supply curves are
independent of one another. A given increase in supply results in a new equilibrium
reached by moving down a stationary demand curve. The equilibrium price falls,
and more output is purchased and supplied. Demand inducement posits, however,
that a given exogenous shift in supply causes a shift in demand as providers advise
their patients to buy more medical care.

Beginning with demand curve D_0 in Figure 5.4, when the supply curve is S_0,
equilibrium is at point a and price and quantity are P_0 and Q_0. An increase in supply
to S_1 should result in a new equilibrium at point b with P_2 and Q_2. If the demand
curve is inelastic, as it is expected to be, the new price/quantity equilibrium will be

Figure 5.4: Demand Inducement Associated with an Increase in Supply

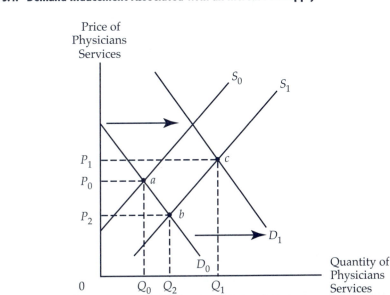

at a lower level of total spending.[11] In other words, P_2 times Q_2 will be less than P_0 times Q_0. More physicians and lower overall spending translate into lower average incomes, unless demand shifts at the same time.

The demand inducement hypothesis recognizes that physicians, rather than allow their incomes to fall, may recommend additional procedures, perform more surgeries, and schedule more follow-up visits—all increasing the demand for their services. This shift in the demand curve to D_1 results in a new equilibrium at point c with P_1 and Q_1 and an increase in total spending. Mechanisms that serve to support demand inducement include fee splitting and referral fees, which provide a means for a referring physician to share in the service charges by specialists and hospitals (Waldholz and Bogidanich, 1989). Another common practice is self-referral: physicians have patients tested and treated in facilities where they have a financial interest. Physician ownership is prevalent in ambulatory surgery centers, diagnostic imaging centers, and testing laboratories.

The potential for demand inducement is naturally limited. Patients will eventually detect a practice style that consistently overtreats and will change providers if they do not agree with the practice. The potential for inducement is greatest in those areas where the procedure is a one-time event, such as surgery.

The important issue is not whether physicians have the capability to induce demand, but whether they actually practice demand inducement. Studies examining the demand inducement hypothesis show mixed results. Early research focused on the association between the physician–population ratio and physician fees. Fuchs and Kramer (1986) concluded that the most important factor influencing the demand for physicians' services was the number of physicians. Reinhardt (1985) provided an alternative explanation for the observed positive association between the supply of physicians and the fees they charge. Physicians may simply be migrating into areas where the demand for their services is higher.

physician-induced demand
A situation in which providers take advantage of uninformed consumers to purchase services that are largely unnecessary.

The confusing body of research on the subject of **physician-induced demand** represented by these two studies has several implications. First, the phenomenon is probably not as widespread as it was once thought to be. Physicians may have the ability to induce demand, but the extent to which they use this ability is difficult to estimate empirically. In any event, recent changes in the payment structure in medical care delivery, including capitation and diagnosis-related fees, have reduced the incentive to practice demand inducement. Second, because we are dealing with a complex phenomenon in an environment of imperfect information, we may never know empirically the full extent of physicians' ability to induce demand for their services (Pauly, 1988). As patients, payers, and lawmakers become more knowledgeable about medical practices and procedures, the phenomenon of demand inducement will likely become less of a concern.

Measuring Demand

Literally hundreds of studies have attempted to measure the impact of the various factors influencing the demand for medical care. Early research focused on the differences in utilization between individuals who had health insurance and those

---

[11] **Proof of this assertion follows. Total revenue (*TR*) is calculated by multiplying the price of a good (*P*) times the quantity purchased (*Q*).**

$$TR = P \times Q$$

Taking the total differential $\quad dTR = Q\,dP + P\,dQ$

Factoring QdP $\quad dTR = Q\,dp\,[1 + (P\,dQ)/(Q\,dP)]$

or $\quad dTR = Q\,dP\,[1 + \varepsilon_p]$ **where ε_p is the price elasticity of demand**

When price falls (when *dP* is negative) and demand is inelastic ($\varepsilon_p < 1$), then total revenue falls (*dTR* is negative).

who did not.[12] Newhouse (1978) has provided an excellent review of the early research quantifying the relationship between out-of-pocket payments and the amount of medical care demanded. Even individuals with comprehensive insurance coverage have different out-of-pocket payment requirements due to differences in deductibles and copayments. Deductibles and copayments may be treated analytically as subsidies to the unit price of medical care. As the subsidy varies, the effective unit price to the individual patient varies. The research focus is on the impact of these price variations on the quantity of medical care demanded, alternatively defined in the various studies as physicians' services, hospital services, dental services, and pharmaceutical services.

In addition to price variations and differences in income and insurance coverage, time costs measured by the hourly wage also affect the demand for medical care. You should recall from our discussion of price elasticity of demand in Chapter 2 that elasticity measures the responsiveness of quantity demanded to a change in the price. Empirical studies measuring medical care demand have focused on the calculation of the various elasticities. In addition to price elasticity, the medical care studies have also estimated income elasticity, insurance elasticity, time-cost elasticity, and **cross-price elasticity** among different types of medical care.

cross-price elasticity
The sensitivity of consumer demand for good A as the price of good B changes.

Estimating Demand Functions Demand is typically estimated using regression analysis. The process is not nearly as straightforward as it may seem. The subject of the analysis can be the individual, the household, or an entire population. The unit of measurement may be the number of physicians' visits, the number of hospital admissions, the length of hospital stays, or total medical care spending; and variations in quality of services and intensity of services come into play. When studies include different countries, the way currency translations are made—either by using market exchange rates or purchasing power parity exchange rates—affects the results. It should come as no surprise then that estimates of demand elasticities vary considerably across studies.

Calculating Elasticities The literature on this subject contains considerable disagreement regarding the magnitude of the various elasticity estimates. Table 5.4 provides a summary of the elasticity estimates from a number of representative studies. Mean estimates of price elasticity usually range from a low of −0.1 to a high of −1.5, depending on study design and dependent variables. Clearly, estimates indicate that demand for medical care in most cases is inelastic with respect to price. Additionally, the higher the patient's out-of-pocket spending, the greater the price elasticity of demand. The demand for outpatient visits is more elastic than the demand for hospital care (Davis and Russell, 1972). Increase the coinsurance rate, and demand becomes more elastic (Rosett and Huang, 1973). Demand for preventive care is more price-elastic than demand for hospital services (Manning et al., 1987), because individuals pay a larger share of the cost of preventive care than hospital care.

Taking the empirical evidence as a whole, consumer demand seems to be relatively unresponsive to changes in the price of medical care. That does not mean that quantity demanded does not change when price changes, only that the percentage change in quantity demanded will be less than the percentage change in price. Based on the cited studies, a 10 percent increase in price will lead to a small decrease in quantity demanded, anywhere from 1 to 7 percent. When dealing with levels of expenditure that total in the billions of dollars, every 1 percent change in quantity demanded is $20 billion.

---

[12] See Donabedian (1976) for a comprehensive review of this literature.

Table 5.4: Price and Income Elasticities from Selected Studies

Study	Dependent Variable	Elasticity
Price Elasticities		
Davis and Russell (1972)	Outpatient Visits	−1.00
	Hospital Admissions	−0.32 to −0.46
Rosett and Huang (1973)	Hospital and Physician Spending	−0.35 to −1.50
Newhouse and Phelps (1976)	Hospital Length of Stay	−0.06 to −0.29
	Physicians' Office Visits	−0.08 to −0.10
Manning et al. (1987)	Overall Spending	−0.22
	Hospital Care	−0.14
	Preventive Care	−0.43
Wedig (1988)	Level of Care	−0.16 to −0.23
Newhouse et al. (1993)	Medical Care	−0.22
Eichner (1998)	Medical Care	−0.62 to −0.75
Income Elasticities		
Rosett and Huang (1973)	Household Medical Spending	0.25 to 0.45
Newhouse (1977)	Per Capita Medical Spending	1.15 to 1.31
Parkin, McGuire, and Yule (1987)	Per Capita Medical Spending	0.80 to 1.57
Gerdtham and Jönsson (1991)	Per Capita Medical Spending	1.24 to 1.43
Moore, Newman, and Fheili (1992)	Short-Run Per Capita Spending	0.31 to 0.86
	Long-Run Per Capita Spending	1.12 to 3.22
Murray, Govindaraj, and Musgrove (1994)	Total Health Expenditures	1.43
Manning and Marquis (1996)	Medical Expenditures	0.22
Okunade and Murthy (2002)	Per Capita Real Health Care Spending	1.29 to 1.64

income elasticity of demand
The sensitivity of demand to changes in consumer income, determined by the percentage change in quantity demanded relative to the percentage change in consumer income.

luxury or superior good
Goods are considered superior if an increase in consumer income causes the percentage of the consumer's income spent on the good to increase and vice versa.

Estimates of the **income elasticity of demand** for medical care vary considerably, depending on whether the relationship being studied is the impact of individual income on personal medical expenditures or national income on aggregate medical expenditures. Research by Newhouse (1977) represents the conventional wisdom on income elasticities using national income and expenditure data. Using data from 13 developed countries, Newhouse found income elasticities to be greater than one. If this is true, medical care is, at least on the margin, a **luxury or superior good.**[13] When income increases, demand increases, and the percentage of income spent on luxury goods also increases.[14] The policy implications are far reaching. If medical care is a luxury good, countries with higher per capita incomes will spend a greater percentage of income on medical care. Since there is no corroborating evidence that countries that spend more on medical care have healthier populations, this additional spending on medical care may not improve physiological health status much at all.

---

[13] Income elasticity, defined as $e_m = \dfrac{\textit{Percentage change in quantity demanded}}{\textit{Percentage change in income}}$, is used to classify goods as inferior or normal, depending on whether it is negative or positive. Economists often classify goods as necessities if $e_M \leq 1$ and luxuries if $e_M > 1$.

[14] Define the percentage of income (*M*) spent on good *X* as $P_X Q_X / M$. The issue being addressed is what happens to this percentage when there is a change in income (ΔM). If the percentage increases, the following ratio will be greater than one.

Work by Parkin, McGuire, and Yule (1987) casts doubt on these earlier findings; it concluded that when estimated correctly, the income elasticity of demand for medical care is less than one, making it a **necessity** rather than a luxury good. Their work does, however, support the conclusion that income elasticities are greater when estimated across countries than when they are estimated across individuals within the same country. Gerdtham and Jönsson (1991) and Moore, Newman, and Fheili (1992) responded to the criticisms of Parkin, McGuire, and Yule. Using alternative models with different functional forms, and alternative ways of converting currencies to dollars, they concluded that the income elasticity of demand for medical care is greater than one, at least in the long run. More recently, Murray, Govindaraj, and Musgrove (1994) and Okunade and Murthy (2002) have calculated income elasticities that ranged from 1.29 to 1.64, indicating that when GDP (or per capita GDP) increases by 1 percent, health expenditures increase anywhere from 1.29 to 1.64 percent, implying that medical care is a luxury good.

Nyman (1999) provides an argument for income elasticity estimates significantly greater than those coming from the original RAND study and other studies that provide income elasticity estimates less than one (Manning and Marquis, 1996). According to this argument, the availability of health insurance provides an income transfer from those who are healthy to those who are ill. Reasonable estimates of this income effect could result in income elasticity estimates many times larger than the low estimates, even on the individual level. More remains to be done on this issue.

What conclusion should we draw from this seemingly contradictory evidence? Is medical care a luxury or a necessity? The answer may be that medical care is a necessity at the individual level and a luxury at the national level. An increase in an individual's income has little effect on his or her demand for medical care. An increase in national income, on the other hand, may result in significant increases in medical care spending at the national level.

The RAND Health Insurance Study Most of the empirical research on the demand for medical care is based on nonexperimental data. Typical of most social science research, nonexperimental data may be either longitudinal or cross-sectional in nature, but it is always based on the actual historical experience of a sample of

POLICY ISSUE

Defining medical care as a necessity or a luxury may depend on whether the issue is being addressed to an individual or a nation.

necessity
A good or service with an income elasticity between zero and one.

(continued from previous page)

$$\frac{\text{Percentage after } \Delta M}{\text{Percentage before } \Delta M} = \frac{P_x(Q_x + \Delta Q_x)}{M + \Delta M} \div \frac{P_x Q_x}{M}$$

$$= \frac{P_x(Q_x + \Delta Q_x)}{P_x Q_x} \times \frac{M}{M + \Delta M} \qquad \text{multiply 2nd term by } \frac{\frac{1}{M}}{\frac{1}{M}}$$

$$= [1 + (\Delta Q_x/Q_x)] \times \left[\frac{1}{1 + (\Delta M/M)}\right]$$

$$= \frac{1 + (\Delta Q_x/Q_x)}{1 + (\Delta M/M)} \qquad \text{multiply by } \frac{\frac{M}{\Delta M}}{\frac{M}{\Delta M}}$$

$$= \frac{\frac{M}{\Delta M} + \left[\frac{\Delta Q_x}{Q_x} \times \frac{M}{\Delta M}\right]}{\frac{M}{\Delta M} + 1} \qquad e_M = \frac{\Delta Q_x}{Q_x} \times \frac{M}{\Delta M}$$

$$= \frac{\frac{M}{\Delta M} + e_M}{\frac{M}{\Delta M} + 1}$$

The value of the ratio depends on the relationship between e_M and one. If $e_M > 1$, the percentage of income spent on good X increases when income increases. If $e_M < 1$, the percentage of income spent on good X decreases when income increases.

individuals. In contrast, experimental data are used in the physical sciences, such as chemistry, biology, and physics, disciplines in which controlled experiments are possible. In a controlled experiment, individuals are randomly assigned to different groups, sometimes referred to as the *control group* and the *experimental group*. The use of data from a controlled experiment eliminates the self-selection bias inherent in nonexperimental data. When individuals are free to choose their groups, at least part of the differences in outcomes is due to differences in tastes for different programs. Those individuals who expect to have higher medical care costs will usually select more generous health insurance policies.

The RAND Corporation conducted the most extensive controlled experiment in health insurance from 1974 to 1982.[15] Over that period, approximately 7,000 individuals were randomly placed into one of 14 separate insurance plans and one health maintenance organization. Some plans had deductibles and others did not. Copayments ranged from 0 to 95 percent with a maximum out-of-pocket outlay of up to $1,000 per participant. A number of studies have used data from the RAND Health Insurance Study, most notably Manning and colleagues (1987). Overall the results indicate that individual demand responds to cost sharing. Manning's price elasticity estimate was approximately -0.17 when comparing free care with a 25 percent coinsurance requirement. Over the coinsurance range of 25 percent to 95 percent, the overall price elasticity of demand was estimated at -0.22, ranging from -0.14 for hospital care to -0.43 for preventive care. For those provided with free medical care, demand was about 50 percent higher than for those who had to pay 95 percent of the total cost. Finally, once admitted to the hospital, the type of plan had little effect on the level of spending.

From these results it may be concluded that changes in out-of-pocket spending explain a small but significant portion of the overall change in medical care spending. Changes in deductibles and coinsurance can have an effect on the overall quantity of medical services demanded. Increasing the out-of-pocket spending required of individuals will have a dampening effect on demand for medical care, with the notable exception of hospital spending once a person is admitted to the hospital.

RAND is a nonprofit institution established to improve public policy through research and publications. Interdisciplinary in nature, the organization has a health sciences program that can be accessed at

http://www.rand.org/
research_areas/health/

SUMMARY AND CONCLUSIONS

The demand for medical care is derived from the individual's desire for good health. Accessing medical care is only one of a number of ways that individuals can improve their health. In fact, when the other factors are taken into consideration, the marginal contribution of medical care is relatively small. The contribution of environmental, lifestyle, and genetic factors weighs heavily in determining overall health.

Individual patient factors play a key role in determining the demand for medical care. These patient factors include health and demographic characteristics. Seldom do individuals seek medical care unless there is at least a perceived illness.[16] Age, race, and sex are also important contributors to medical care demand. Even though these patient factors are important, policy makers are more interested in economic factors that affect demand. Individual incomes, the level of out-of-pocket spending, and the availability of medical insurance are more easily manipulated and thus studied more intensively.

The physician–patient relationship is also the subject of a great volume of literature. The dual role of the physician as adviser to the patient and provider of services

---

[15] Even though RAND did not totally eliminate self-selection in its experimental design, it reduced it by making it costly for individuals to choose alternate plans.

[16] The case of preventive care is of course the major exception to this statement. Even with preventive care, however, the patient is attempting to avoid an illness.

places physicians in a unique position to create demand for their services. Despite literally dozens of studies on the subject, it is difficult to know the extent of physician-induced demand.

Empirical research on the demand for medical care has taught us a great deal:

- Using the economic standards established by the concept of price elasticity, demand seems to be relatively insensitive to price changes, usually the result of changes in coinsurance rates. Even a modest coinsurance requirement from 0 to 20 percent will reduce demand significantly.

- While individual income elasticities are low, probably less than one, at the aggregate level they tend to be higher, or somewhat greater than one. In other words, medical care may be treated as a necessity good at the individual level and, at the same time, as a luxury good at the national level.

The most important lesson of this chapter may be that economic incentives do matter in determining the demand for medical care. Therefore we must be careful how we use incentives. In all fairness, we do not want to exclude the sick and poor from medically necessary care simply because they cannot afford to pay for it.

QUESTIONS AND PROBLEMS

1. According to studies undertaken by the U.S. Department of Agriculture, the price elasticity of demand for cigarettes is between −0.3 and −0.4 and the income elasticity is about +0.5.
   a. Suppose Congress, influenced by studies linking cigarette smoking to cancer, plans to raise the excise tax on cigarettes so the price rises by 10 percent. Estimate the effect the price increase will have on cigarette consumption and consumer spending on cigarettes (in percentage terms).
   b. Suppose a major brokerage firm advised its clients to buy cigarette stocks under the assumption that, if consumer incomes rise by 50 percent as expected over the next decade, cigarette sales will double. What is your reaction to this investment advice?

2. In what ways is medical care different from other commodities? In what ways is it the same?

3. If a wealthy person chooses to spend large sums of money to increase the probability of surviving an ordinarily fatal disease, should the rest of society object? Explain.

4. It is difficult to argue against the scientific merit of medical discoveries such as treatments for cancer or AIDS. Is scientific merit alone sufficient to determine the rational allocation of medical funds in such high-cost cases? What other kinds of information are relevant?

5. What does it mean to be on the "flat of the curve" in health care provision? Why do some argue that

the United States is on the flat of the curve? Why is this phenomenon not an issue in a developing country?

6. "Estimating a model of health care demand by the individual patient is a futile exercise, because physicians determine what their patients use."

   Comment. Does the model of a utility-maximizing consumer have any application in medicine?

7. In what sense is health care an investment? In what sense is it pure consumption?

8. Some argue that the price elasticity of demand can be used to determine whether a good or service is a luxury or a necessity. In medical care, a procedure with an elastic demand would be considered optional, or elective, and a procedure with an inelastic demand would be a medical necessity. Should planners use price elasticity of demand as a guide to defining services that are medically necessary? What are the advantages of such a classification scheme? What are the drawbacks?

9. What has been the role of public health measures in improving the health status of the population?

10. Visit the Web site of the National Center for Health Statistics. Spend some time studying the leading causes of death for different age groups at http://www.cdc.gov/nchs/data/nvsr/nvsr56/nvsr56_05.pdf. What are the three leading causes of death for each age cohort listed? What are some of the policy implications?

REFERENCES

David B. Allison, Kevin R. Fontaine, JoAnn E. Manson, June Stevens, and Theodore B. Van Itallie, "Annual Deaths Attributable to Obesity in the United States," *Journal of the American Medical Association* 282(16), October 27, 1999, 1530–1538.

Gary S. Becker, Human Capital: *A Theoretical and Empirical Analysis, with Special Reference to Education*, New York: Columbia University Press, 1964.

Troyen A. Brennan, "An Empirical Analysis of Accidents and Accident Law: The Case of Medical Malpractice Law," *St. Louis University Law Journal* 36, Summer 1992, 823–878.

John Broome, "Good, Fairness, and QALYs," in J. M. Bell and Susan Mendus, eds., *Philosophy and Medical Welfare*, New York: Cambridge University Press, 1988, 57–73.

David M. Cutler et al., "Why Have Americans Become More Obese?" NBER Working Paper No. 9446, Cambridge, MA: National Bureau of Economic Research, January 2003.

Anthony J. Culyer, "Commodities, Characteristics of Commodities, Characteristics of People, Utilities, and the Quality of Life," in S. Baldwin, C. Godfrey and C. Propper, eds., *Quality of Life: Perspectives and Policy*, London and New York: Routledge, 1990, 9–27.

Karen Davis and Louise B. Russell, "The Substitution of Hospital Outpatient Care for Inpatient Care," *Review of Economics and Statistics* 54(2), May 1972, 109–120.

J. Dixon and H. G. Welch, "Priority Setting: Lessons from Oregon," *Lancet* 337 (8, 746), April 13, 1991, 891–894.

A. Donabedian, *Benefits in Medical Care Programs*, Cambridge, MA: Harvard University Press, 1976.

Benjamin G. Druss et al., "The Most Expensive Medical Conditions in America," *Health Affairs* 21(4), July/August 2002, 105–111.

Benjamin G. Druss, Steven C. Marcus, Mark Olfson et al., "Comparing the National Economic Burden of Five Chronic Conditions," *Health Affairs* 20(6), November/December 2001, 233–241.

Matthew J. Eichner, "The Demand for Medical Care: What People Pay Does Matter," *American Economic Review Papers and Proceedings* 88(2), May 1998, 117–121.

Alain C. Enthoven, *Health Plan*, Reading, MA: Addison–Wesley, 1980.

Katherine M. Flegal, Richard P. Troiano, Elsie R. Pamuk, Robert J. Kuczmarski, and Stephen M. Campbell, "The Influence of Smoking Cessation on the Prevalence of Overweight in the United States," *New England Journal of Medicine* 333(18), November 2, 1995, 1165–1170.

Victor R. Fuchs, "Time Preference and Health: An Exploratory Study," in Victor R. Fuchs, ed., *Economics Aspects of Health*, Chicago: University of Chicago Press, 1982, 93–120.

——— and Marcia J. Kramer, "Determinants of Expenditures for Physicians' Services," in Victor R. Fuchs, ed., *The Health Economy*, Cambridge, MA: Harvard University Press, 1986, 67–107.

Ulf-G. Gerdtham and Bengt Jönsson, "Conversion Factor Instability in International Comparisons of Health Care Expenditure," *Journal of Health Economics* 10(2), July 1991, 227–234.

Michael Grossman, "On the Concept of Health Capital and the Demand for Health," *Journal of Political Economy* 80(2), March/April 1972, 223–255.

Jack M. Guralnik, Kenneth C. Land, Dan Blazer, Gerda G. Fillenbaum, and Laurence G. Branch, "Educational Status and Active Life Expectancy Among Older Blacks and Whites," *The New England Journal of Medicine* 329(2), July 8, 1993, 110–116.

Michael D. Intriligator, "Major Policy Issues in the Economics of Health Care in the United States," in J. van der Gaag and M. Perlman, eds., *Health, Economics, and Health Economics*, Amsterdam: North Holland Publishing, 1981.

Geoffrey F. Joyce, Emmett B. Keeler, Baoping Shang, and Dana P. Goldman, "The Lifetime Burden of Chronic Disease among the Elderly," *Health Affairs* – Web Exclusive, September 26, 2005, W5-R18-R29.

Linda T. Kohn, Janet M. Corrigan, and Molla S. Donaldson, *To Err Is Human: Building a Safer Health System*, Washington, DC: National Academy Press, 1999.

Katherine R. Levit, Arthur L. Sensenig, Cathy A. Cowan et al., "National Health Expenditures, 1993," *Health Care Financing Review* 16(1), Fall 1994, 247–294.

M. Lockwood, "Quality of Life and Resource Allocation," in J. M. Bell and S. Mendus, eds., *Philosophy and Medical Welfare*, New York: Cambridge University Press, 1988, 33–56.

G. Loomes and L. McKenzie, "The Scope and Limitations of QALY Measures," in S. Baldwin, C. Godfrey, and C. Propper, eds., *Quality of Life: Perspectives and Policy*, London and New York: Routledge, 1990, 84–102.

Willard G. Manning, Howard L. Bailit, Bernadette Benjamin, and Joseph P. Newhouse, "The Demand for Dental Care: Evidence from a Randomized Controlled Trial in Health Insurance," *Journal of the American Dental Association* 110(6), June 1987, 895–902.

Willard G. Manning and Melinda S. Marquis, "Health Insurance: The Trade-off between Risk Pooling and Moral Hazard," *Journal of Health Economics* 15, 1996, 609–640.

Michael Marmot, "Inequalities in Health," *New England Journal of Medicine* 345(2), July 12, 2001, 134–136.

M. G. Marmot, M. J. Shipley, and G. Rose, "Inequalities in Death: Specific Explanations of a General Pattern?" *Lancet* 1, 1984, 1003–1006.

M. G. Marmot, H. Bosma, H. Hemingway et al., "Contributions of Job Control and Other Risk Factors to Social Variations in Coronary Heart Disease Incidence," *Lancet* 350, 1997, 235–239.

Thomas McKeown, *The Rise of Modern Population*, New York: Academic Press, 1976.

John B. McKinlay, Sonja M. McKinlay, and Robert Beaglehole, "A Review of the Evidence Concerning the Impact of Medical Measures on Recent Mortality and Morbidity in the United States," *International Journal of Health Services* 19(2), 1989, 181–208.

Biancarlo Marra and C. Richard Boland, "Hereditary Nonpolyposis Colorectal Cancer: The Syndrome, the Genes, and Historical Perspectives," *Journal of the National Cancer Institute* 87(15), August 1995, 1114–1125.

Jacob Mincer, *Schooling, Experience, and Earnings*, New York: National Bureau of Economic Research, 1974.

William J. Moore, Robert J. Newman, and Mohammad Fheili, "Measuring the Relationship Between Income and NHEs," *Health Care Financing Review* 14(1), Fall 1992, 133–139.

C. J. L. Murray, R. Govindaraj, and P. Musgrove, "National Health Expenditures: A Global Analysis," *Bulletin of the World Health Organization* 72(4), 1994, 533–692.

Selma J. Mushkin, "Health as an Investment," *Journal of Political Economy* 70 (5, part 2), October 1962, 129–157.

H. L. Needleman and D. Bellinger, "Low-Level Lead Exposure and the IQ of Children: A Meta-Analysis of Modern Studies," *Journal of the American Medical Association* 263(5), February 2, 1990, 673–678.

Joseph P. Newhouse, "Insurance Benefits, Out-of-Pocket Payments, and the Demand for Medical Care: A Review of the Recent Literature," *Health and Medical Care Services Review* 1(4), July/August 1978, 1–15.

———, "Medical Care Expenditure: A Cross-National Survey," *Journal of Human Resources* 12(1), Winter 1977, 115–125.

——— and Lindy J. Friedlander, "The Relationship Between Medical Resources and Measures of Health: Some Additional Evidence," *Journal of Human Resources* 15(2), Spring 1980, 200–218.

——— and Charles E. Phelps, "New Estimates of Price and Income Elasticities of Medical Care Services," in R. N. Rosett, ed., *The Role of Health Insurance in the Health Services Sector*, New York: National Bureau of Economic Research, 1976, 261–312.

_____ and the Insurance Experiment Group, *Free for All? Lessons from the RAND Health Insurance Experiment*, Cambridge MA: Harvard University Press, 1993.

John A. Nyman, "The Economics of Moral Hazard Revisited," *Journal of Health Economics* 18, 1999, 811–824.

Albert A. Okunade and Vasudeva N. R. Murthy, "Technology as a 'Major Driver' of Health Care Costs: A Cointegration Analysis of the Newhouse Conjecture," *Journal of Health Economics* 21, 2002, 147–159.

Gregory Pappas, Susan Queen, Wilbur Hadden, and Gail Fisher, "The Increasing Disparity in Mortality Between Socioeconomic Groups in the United States, 1960 and 1986," *New England Journal of Medicine* 329(2), July 8, 1993, 103–109.

David Parkin, Alistair McGuire, and Brian Yule, "Aggregate Health Care Expenditures and National Income," *Journal of Health Economics* 6(2), June 1987, 109–127.

Mark V. Pauly, "Is Medical Care Different? Old Questions, New Answers," *Journal of Health Politics, Policy and* Law 13(2), Summer 1988, 227–237.

Uwe Reinhardt, "The Theory of Physician-Induced Demand: Reflections After a Decade," *Journal of Health Economics* 4(2), June 1985, 190–193.

W. J. Rogan, Beth C. Gladen, James D. McKinney, Nancy Carreras, Pam Hardy, James Thullen, Jon Tingelstad, and Mary Tully, "Polychlorinated Biphenyls (PCBs) and Dichlorodiphenyl Dichlorethene (DDE) in Human Milk: Effects of Maternal Factors and Previous Lactation," *American Journal of Public Health* 76(2), February 1986, 172–177.

Richard N. Rosett and Lien-fu Huang, "The Effect of Health Insurance on the Demand for Medical Care," *Journal of Political Economy* 81(2), March/April 1973, 281–305.

M. W. Shannon and J. W. Graef, "Lead Intoxication in Infancy," *Pediatrics* 89(1), January 1992, 87–90.

Jody L. Sindelar, "Differential Use of Medical Care by Sex," *Journal of Political Economy* 90(5), October 1982, 1003–1009.

Anne R. Somers, "The Changing Demand for Health Services: A Historical Perspective and Some Thoughts for the Future," *Inquiry* 23(1), Winter 1986, 395–402.

Michael Waldholz and Walt Bogidanich, "Patients for Sale," two-part series in *The Wall Street Journal*, February 28 and March 1, 1989, A1, A12.

Gerald J. Wedig, "Health Status and the Demand for Health: Results on Price Elasticities," *Journal of Health Economics* 7(2), June 1988, 151–163.

Burton A. Weisbrod, "The Health Care Quadrilemma: An Essay on Technological Change, Insurance, Quality of Care, and Cost Containment," *Journal of Economic Literature* 29(2), June 1991, 523–552.

David Wessel, "We're Not Too Fat, It's Technology's Fault," *Wall Street Journal*, February 12, 2003, A2.

Robert Woods and P. R. Andrew Hinde, "Mortality in Victorian England: Models and Patterns," *Journal of Interdisciplinary History* 18(1), Summer 1987, 27–54.

CHAPTER 6

The Market for Health Insurance

Many who argue that the United States has a medical care crisis point to the 47 million Americans who are uninsured (2006). Not only has the number of uninsured grown significantly over the last decade, the percentage of the population without insurance has grown from 13 percent in 1987 to 15.8 percent in 2006 (DiNavas, Proctor, and Smith, 2007). As the number of uninsured grows, the pressure to do something about the way we finance medical care intensifies. To address this problem rationally, we must understand the principles that govern the provision of insurance.

Because a firm appreciation of our historical roots is necessary to understand how we can effectively reform our system of medical care financing, this chapter will examine the development of employer-based insurance in the United States. A discussion of the theory of risk and insurance will serve as the basis for understanding the demand for private health insurance. We will then address the issue of market failure in the provision of medical care, focusing on the institutional features in the U.S. setting. Finally, we will examine the primary concern of reformers—the uninsured. Who are they? How are they affected by lack of insurance coverage? How do they pay for medical care?

HISTORICAL SETTING

Insurance coverage for health services in the United States was first made available in 1798 (refer to Table 6.1). Funded by mandatory payroll deductions, the U.S. Marine Hospital Services provided prepaid hospital care for eligible seamen. Although the first company to offer sickness insurance was organized in 1847, most of the early insurance policies covered loss of income due to accidents or disability rather than health services due to illness.

Plans offering medical benefits became more prevalent in the 1870s and 1880s. Many of these policies offered coverage to employees in certain industries and to individuals who suffered from certain diseases. By the beginning of the twentieth century, 47 insurance companies were actively writing policies covering accidental injury. Collectively, they had written over 463,000 individual policies. Most early plans offered protection against the loss of income due to illness or disability. In 1899, the Aetna Life Insurance Company began offering disability coverage for all diseases except tuberculosis, venereal disease, insanity, and alcohol or drug-related problems. Until the 1920s, loss of income was the largest single cost associated with an accident or illness.

Table 6.1: Important Dates in the Development of the U.S. Health Insurance Industry

Date	Event
1798	Congress established U.S. Marine Hospital Services for seamen.
1847	The first insurer to issue sickness insurance was organized: The Massachusetts Health Insurance Company of Boston.
1849	New York state passed first general insurance law.
1850	Individual accident insurance became available with the chartering of the Franklin Health Assurance Company of Massachusetts. For a 15-cent premium, the insured could receive $200 in the event of injury due to a railway or steamboat accident and payment of $400 in the event of total disability.
1870	Companies in several industries, including mining, lumber, and railroads, began developing plans to cover medical services.
1890	Policies providing benefits for disability from specified diseases were first offered.
1899	Aetna Life Insurance Company offered insurance covering disabilities caused by most diseases.
1910	Montgomery Ward and Company offered employees an insured plan regarded as the first group health insurance policy.
1920s	Individual hospitals began offering hospital expense benefits on an individual, prepaid basis.
1929	First health maintenance organization, the Ross-Loos Clinic, was established in Los Angeles.
1929	A group of Dallas teachers arranged with Baylor University Hospital to provide room and board and specified ancillary services at a predetermined monthly cost; considered the forerunner of Blue Cross insurance.
1932	First city-wide Blue Cross plan offered by a group of Sacramento hospitals.
1935	Social Security Act provided, for the first time, grant-in-aid to states for public health activities.
1937	The Blue Cross Commission was organized.
1939	The first Blue Shield plan (surgical-medical), called *California Physicians' Service*, developed.
1940s	During WW II, due to the freezing of wages, group health insurance became an important component of collective bargaining for employees.
1949	Major medical expense benefits were introduced by Liberty Mutual to supplement basic medical care expenses.
1956	Disability insurance was added to the Social Security System.
1959	Continental Casualty Company issued the first comprehensive group dental plan written by an insurance company.
1964	Prescription drug expense benefits were introduced.
1966	Medicare and Medicaid become law.
1972	Medicare extended to disabled and end-stage renal disease patients.
1973	Health Maintenance Organization Act passed by Congress.
1974	ERISA passed regulating provision of employee benefit plans, an encouragement for firms to self-insure.
1988	Medicare Catastrophic Care Act passed.
1989	Medicare Catastrophic Care Act repealed.
1996	Health Insurance Portability and Accountability Act (HIPAA) passed.
1997	State Children's Health Insurance Program (SCHIP) initiated.
2003	Medicare Modernization Act (MMA) passed.

Source: *Source Book of Health Insurance Data, 1990*, Health Insurance Association of America.

Group health insurance was first offered in 1910 to the employees of Montgomery Ward and Company. The policy, written by the London Guarantee and Accident Company in New York, provided cash benefits in the event of disability or illness. The rest of the world moved toward mandatory insurance coverage after the First World War, but the movement never gained acceptance in the United States.

During the 1920s, hospitals began offering prepaid plans to individuals that covered hospital benefits. This practice was expanded in 1929 by Baylor University Hospital in Dallas, Texas. In what is considered the forerunner of the Blue Cross plans, the hospital agreed to provide a group of Dallas teachers 21 days of hospital care and related services annually for a fixed monthly premium. In the same year, one of the first health maintenance organizations (HMOs), the Ross-Loos Clinic in Los Angeles, was formed. Another important HMO, Kaiser Permanente, can trace its origins back to the 1930s.[1]

The Great Depression challenged the hospital sector to maintain its solvency. With people unable to afford hospital care, hospital occupancy rates fell to 50 percent. In 1932, a group of Sacramento, California, hospitals combined resources to offer the first area-wide plan supported by more than one hospital. Within three years, similar plans in 13 states provided a guaranteed cash flow to financially strapped hospitals. The California Physicians Service first introduced prepayment for physicians' services in 1939. Later known as *Blue Shield*, the plan provided medical and surgical benefits for a fixed monthly fee for members of employee groups earning less than $3,000 annually.

In the aftermath of the Second World War, group health insurance became a major feature of the collective bargaining process. A wage-price freeze forced firms to offer nonwage benefits to attract and keep employees. A 1954 ruling by the Internal Revenue Service exempted employer contributions to health insurance benefits from employee taxable income. Today the tax exemption is a significant feature of the health insurance market in the United States, and it is responsible for the predominance of employment-based group insurance (Thomasson, 2000). The next two decades witnessed improvements in insurance coverage. **Major medical** benefits were introduced in 1949, and dental care, prescription drugs, and vision care were added to many plans in the 1950s.

In 1965, after repeated failures to pass a nationwide universal insurance plan, Congress passed comprehensive coverage for the elderly and indigent, Medicare and Medicaid. A new era of government involvement in medical care financing saw its beginnings. Much of the upward pressure on health care spending can be traced to this legislation. As spending increased, so did pressure to control the cost spiral. The Health Maintenance Organization Act in 1973, the Employee Retirement and Income Security Act (ERISA) in 1974, and the Medicare Catastrophic Care Act in 1988 were all attempts to curb runaway costs and improve access to those without insurance. Reform legislation that increased the role of the federal government in health care delivery and finance included the Health Insurance Portability and Accountability Act (HIPAA), State Children's Health Insurance Plan (SCHIP), and the Medicare Modernization Act (MMA). HIPAA established rules for insurance portability and patient privacy, SCHIP expanded coverage for low-income children who did not qualify for Medicaid, and MMA added outpatient prescription drug coverage to Medicare. MMA also expanded private insurance options by increasing access to health savings accounts.

major medical
Health insurance to provide coverage for major illnesses requiring large financial outlays, characterized by payment for all expenses above a specified maximum out-of-pocket amount paid by the insured (often $1,000 to $5,000).

---

[1] **Kaiser actually celebrates 1947 as its founding year, when it opened its enrollment to the public.**

Reformers and would-be reformers must understand the development of the employer-based insurance system and its place in the business culture. Anyone ignoring this rich history runs the risk of misreading public sentiments concerning health care reform.

Types of Insurance

The current policy debate over health care reform is based on two opposing views to health care financing: the indemnity, or casualty, insurance approach and the **social insurance** approach. Private insurance adopts the indemnity approach, providing reimbursement for certain medical expenditures or direct payments to those unable to work due to accident or injury. This category of insurance includes fire, theft, casualty, life, and in the United States, health insurance. It is based on the premise that the premium should reflect expected medical spending. Those individuals who have higher expected spending should pay higher premiums. Social insurance is the basis of all assistance programs associated with the welfare state: cash assistance, public education, and health care for the elderly. The social insurance model ignores expected spending when calculating premiums. Instead of high-risk individuals paying higher premiums, individuals with higher incomes pay higher premiums. Subsidies are used extensively across risk categories to ensure that high-risk, low-income individuals can afford to purchase insurance.

The United States uses a combination of the indemnity insurance approach and the social insurance approach. Everyone covered by private insurance sees his or her premiums determined by the indemnity insurance approach. Most policies are written as group policies, and premiums are relatively uniform within groups, varying by size of family. Premiums reflect expected use and vary across groups, depending on past claims experience. So policies are community rated within groups and experience rated across groups, which means that everyone within the group pays the same premium, but premiums across groups differ. Groups with higher health care spending pay higher premiums. Proponents of this approach argue that not only is it more efficient, it is more equitable. To the extent that medical costs are based on lifestyle choices, individuals should pay for the choices they make. Individuals and groups who practice a healthy lifestyle and are more cost conscious should be rewarded with lower premiums. Those who choose to indulge in unhealthy behavior should pay higher premiums.

The elderly, the disabled, the indigent, and those suffering from certain diseases, such as kidney failure, have their medical coverage provided by social insurance. Medicare and Medicaid are the two major social insurance programs in the United States. Proponents of this approach argue from the premise of individual rights and social responsibility. Some argue that justice dictates that all individuals be provided with medical care as an individual right. If indeed access to medical care is a right, its provision is the socially responsible thing to do. Because participation is mandatory, the savings in administrative costs offset any loss in efficiency caused by a departure from the indemnity approach.

In general, health insurance may be classified into two broad categories: medical expense insurance that provides reimbursement for actual expenditures and disability income insurance that provides periodic payments when the insured individual is unable to work. Although the combination of policies is virtually endless, all contain certain basic health insurance benefits that may be offered separately or in combination with other benefits.

- Hospitalization provides daily room and board, the usual hospital services, and supplies required during a normal hospital stay.

social insurance
Serves as the basis of all government redistribution programs. An insurance plan supported by tax revenues and available to everyone regardless of age, health status, and ability to pay.

POLICY ISSUE

Is access to medical care an individual right? Should it be?

- Physicians' or surgical expense policies provide set allowances for surgical procedures performed by licensed physicians and for physicians' inpatient hospital visits.

- Major medical insurance is designed to cover large medical bills with few limitations imposed on specific items. This type of insurance is often issued as a supplement to hospitalization with deductibles, coinsurance provisions, and a maximum limit on out-of-pocket spending.

- Dental insurance typically emphasizes preventive dentistry with coverage on examinations, X-rays, and cleanings. Coverage for fillings, extractions, bridgework, dentures, root canals, inlays, and orthodontics includes substantial copayments (up to 50 percent) and a relatively low annual spending limit.

- Disability income protection provides periodic payments when an insured is unable to work as a result of illness, accident, or injury. Policies are provided on both a group and an individual basis with employers providing most disability insurance coverage through group policies. In 2000, 70 percent of all full-time employees had long-term disability insurance, and 61 percent had short-term disability insurance (U.S. Chamber of Commerce, 2000).

- Long-term care insurance provides long-term nursing home care for individuals with chronic illnesses and disabilities, both physical and mental. The first policies were written in 1985; by 2001, over 8.3 million policies had been issued. Still only 10 percent of Americans over the age of 65 have long-term care coverage (HIAA, 2003).

Health Insurance Providers

Providers are generally classified as commercial insurance carriers, Blue Cross and Blue Shield associations, and managed care organizations. Almost 1,300 commercial insurance companies provide health insurance coverage to over 200 million Americans. Most operate nationally. Some offer only health insurance, but many also offer property and casualty insurance, liability coverage, and life insurance. Typically, premiums are **experience rated;** that is, based on past spending. Employers with lower spending receive better rates from commercial insurers.

The Blue Cross and Blue Shield System is actually a federation of 39 independent associations operating regionally around the United States. Blue Cross plans provided health benefits for 99.3 million Americans in 2006. Under most state laws, the "Blues" receive preferential treatment as nonprofit associations.[2] They are taxed at lower rates and typically have lower overhead expenses. Originally the Blue Cross and Blue Shield plans offered insurance at premiums based on **community rating**. This practice is all but extinct, because competition has increased pressure on all insurance providers to lower premiums.

Managed care organizations—in particular, health maintenance organizations and **preferred provider organizations (PPOs)**—offer comprehensive health care coverage where the provider is responsible for the health care services of enrollees for a fixed fee. More will be said about this arrangement in Chapter 7.

In addition, an increasing number of health insurance plans are handled directly by the sponsoring employers through self-insurance. By 1985 over half

experience rating
Basing health insurance premiums on the utilization experience of a specific insured group. Premiums may vary by age, gender, or other risk factors, which are often taken into consideration when estimating the likely use of medical services.

community rating
Basing health insurance premiums on the health care utilization experience of the entire population of a specific geographic area. Premiums are the same for all individuals regardless of age, gender, risk, or prior use of health care services.

preferred provider organization (PPO)
A group of medical providers that have contracted with an insurance company or employer to provide health care services to a well-defined group according to a well-defined fee schedule. By accepting discount fees, providers are included on the list of preferred providers.

---

[2] There are obvious exceptions to this statement in states where Blue Cross and Blue Shield have converted to for-profit entities—most notably in California.

The Blue Cross and Blue
Shield Association Web
site with links to all the
regional associations can
be found at

http://www.bluecares.com/

of company-sponsored group insurance plans were operated under Administrative Service Only (ASO) arrangements and Minimum Premium Plans (MPPs). Under ASO arrangements, third-party administrators (TPAs) process claims and handle paperwork for a set fee. MPPs offer insurance against large, unpredictable claims.

Approximately 83 percent of the civilian population under age 65 has hospital insurance, surgical health insurance, or both. Of the population over 65 covered by Medicare, approximately 60 percent carry private supplemental coverage (Medigap insurance). Thus, about 15 percent of the civilian population is without health insurance protection.

PRIVATE INSURANCE DEMAND

Individuals enter insurance contracts to spread risk. The insurance contract is sold for a premium based on the expected cost incurred if a specific event takes place. In the seventeenth century, Lloyds of London started as a coffee house where ship owners contracted with wealthy merchants to underwrite the expenses incurred if a ship was lost at sea.

The most straightforward application of the traditional indemnity insurance contract is term life insurance. A policy is purchased for a given premium and pays a predetermined amount to named beneficiaries when the insured person dies. Another application is property casualty insurance. In this case, when an insured asset is damaged, the policy pays to restore its value to the undamaged state.

ISSUES IN MEDICAL CARE DELIVERY

Important Concepts in Health Insurance

Adverse selection is a situation in which a high-risk individual is able to conceal his or her true risk level and purchase insurance for the average premium. A disproportionate number of these high-risk individuals in any risk pool will threaten the pool's solvency.

Expected value of an outcome is the weighted average of all possible outcomes, with the probabilities of those outcomes used as weights. In other words, $E(x) = \sum x_i p_i$, where $E(x)$ is the expected value, x_i is the ith outcome, and p_i is its associated probability. The expected value is summed over all possible outcomes.

Free rider refers to an individual who does not buy insurance, knowing that in the event of a serious illness, medical care will be provided free of charge.

Moral hazard arises because the fact that a person has insurance coverage increases both the likelihood of making a claim and the actual size of the claim. Insurance reduces the net out-of-pocket price of medical services and thus increases the quantity demanded.

Probability of an event is the likelihood or chance that the event will occur. Probability is measured as a ratio that ranges in value from zero to one. A probability of one means that an event is certain to happen: it happens every time. A probability of 0.25 means that the event happens one-fourth of the time.

Risk is a state in which multiple outcomes are possible, and the likelihood of each possible outcome is known or can be estimated.

Uncertainty is a state in which multiple outcomes are possible, but the likelihood of any one outcome is not known.

expected value of an outcome
The weighted average of all possible outcomes, with the probabilities of those outcomes used as weights.

probability
The likelihood or chance that an event will occur. Probability is measured as a ratio that ranges in value from zero to one.

risk
A state in which multiple outcomes are possible, and the likelihood of each possible outcome is known or can be estimated.

uncertainty
A state in which multiple outcomes are possible but the likelihood of any one outcome is not known.

Health insurance is similar to term life insurance and property casualty insurance with a few notable exceptions. When first developed, the typical health insurance policy paid a specified amount for a given medical condition, such as a broken leg or a severed limb. The major problems with this arrangement were 1) the difficulty in verifying the seriousness of the medical condition and 2) the wide variation in the cost of treating similar medical conditions. These two problems placed too much risk on the insured and led to the development of the service-benefit policy, which covers billed expenses. This form of insurance was the predominant form of health insurance through the 1980s.

The Theory of Risk and Insurance

The theory of risk and insurance is based on the pioneering work of Friedman and Savage (1948) Individuals enter into insurance contracts to share the uncertainty of financial risk with others. It is impossible to determine whether one particular individual will suffer from a medical condition, such as a heart attack or stroke. When individuals are combined into large enough groups, or risk pools, the probability that someone in the group will suffer from heart attack or stroke can be systematically estimated. The estimated probability of an event is based on its past frequency of occurrence. Larger groups improve the accuracy of the prediction.

Key Concept 3
Marginal Analysis

Tracing health care spending back to 1928, Berk and Monheit (2001) show a remarkable stability in distribution of health care expenditures over time. Using national survey data, they estimate that in 1996, 5 percent of the population was responsible for 55 percent of the aggregate health care spending. Additionally, the top 10 percent of the users accounted for 69 percent of the spending, the top 30 percent accounted for 90 percent, and the top half accounted for 97 percent of the total spending.

Some individuals are more willing to take chances than others. But even people who willingly take chances generally prefer less risky situations. Most people try to avoid risk. The dominant attitude among the population is risk aversion. Attitudes toward risk are depicted by the marginal utility of income. When evaluating two alternatives with the same expected value, a risk-averse individual will choose a certain prospect over the uncertain prospect. Risk aversion is shown by a diminishing marginal utility of income, measuring the rate of change of the total utility of income.

The more income a person has, the higher that person's level of utility. In addition, each additional increment to income increases utility by an amount smaller than the previous increment. Figure 6.1 depicts the total utility of income curve for a risk-averse person. Total utility is drawn concave from below, that is, increasing at a decreasing rate. As income increases from w_0 to w_1, total utility increases from u_0 to u_1. As the level of income increases, each increment to income increases utility by a smaller amount. In other words, as income increases from w_1 to w_2, the change in utility is less than it was when income increased from w_0 to w_1, an equal increment.

When actual outcomes are uncertain, individuals do not know where they will end up on their utility-of-income curve. Even though no one can know with certainty the actual income they will receive in a given time period, their expected income can be estimated. *Expected utility* is the average of all possible utilities weighted by their respective probabilities. When making a choice under conditions of uncertainty, individuals attempt to maximize expected utility. Assume there are two possible health states: sick and healthy. A probability of being sick equal to 5 percent means a 95 percent probability of being healthy. (The sum of

Figure 6.1: The Total Utility of Income Curve

the probabilities of all possible health states must equal 100 percent.) If the cost of treating the illness is equal to $20,000, a person with an annual income of $50,000 has an expected income of $49,000.[3]

Risk is costly, and a risk-averse person will pay to avoid the consequences of risk. To illustrate this principle, take the case of health insurance. An individual facing the uncertainty of an illness has two choices: 1) purchase insurance and voluntarily reduce wealth by the amount of the premium, or 2) self-insure, facing the small probability of a financial loss should an illness occur. It is impossible to know the actual probability that any one person will suffer from an illness. With a large population, the proportion of the population that suffered from the illness in a previous time period can be used to estimate the probability.

Risk pooling will work as long as the group purchasing insurance has the same probability of illness as the overall population. In that case, they are able to share the costs of treating the illness by collecting premiums from everyone and paying benefits to those who become ill. For this arrangement to work, the insurance company must collect enough in premiums to pay out all claims, cover all operating and administrative costs, and have a reasonable profit left over for the owners of the company.

To illustrate how this works, consider the following example: Suppose our prospective insurance customer faces a 4 percent probability of suffering from an illness that would result in a catastrophic financial loss equal to an entire year's income of $50,000. Under these circumstances, the range of uncertainty extends from a net income of zero (if ill) to $50,000 (if healthy). The expected utility of income is depicted by a straight line from the origin, where net income is zero because of illness, to the point on the actual utility-of-income curve corresponding to $50,000: the net income for a healthy person.[4] The concave utility of income depicts the level of utility associated with a guaranteed income (i.e., no uncertainty).

---

[3] Expected income is the weighted average of the two possible outcomes. The calculation is the sum of the income at each health state weighed by the probability that state will occur, or $E(Y)$ ($50,000 \times 0.95$) + ($30,000 \times 0.05$) = $47,500 + $1,500 = $49,000.

[4] Expected utility is calculated by summing the utility enjoyed at each health state adjusted (multiplied) by its respective probability. The expected utility curve is derived by varying the probability of each health state, from zero to one, and plotting the results.

The straight-line expected utility-of-income curve is utility adjusted for the different probabilities of illness. In other words, this straight line represents the expected utility of the $50,000 loss associated with the illness at all the probabilities between zero and one. The difference between the two curves represents the reduction in utility associated with the risk of illness.

Choice under conditions of uncertainty means that a person tries to maximize expected utility. Because the probability of illness is 4 percent, the probability of not being ill is 96 percent. Referring to Figure 6.2, expected wealth in this case is $48,000, and expected utility is $96U$.[5]

Given the utility-of-income curve shown in the figure, our prospective insurance customer has the same level of utility (equal to $96U$) with a guaranteed income of $45,000 or an expected income of $48,000. In other words, this person's actual level of utility is the same when he has a 100 percent probability of an income level of $45,000 or a 96 percent chance of $50,000 coupled with a 4 percent chance of zero income. The difference between $48,000 and $45,000 (or $3,000) is the price of uncertainty. In this case, if insurance can be purchased for less than $5,000, the individual will be better off; that is, the individual will be at a higher level of utility.

Obviously, many people have similar utility-of-income curves, all risk averse; otherwise insurance companies would not sell millions of insurance policies annually. If 1,000 people in a group seek insurance, an insurer can expect that 40 will make claims totaling $2 million. The insurer must charge a minimum of $2,000 per person to cover the expected payout, but it can charge up to $5,000 per person: the expected payout plus the price of uncertainty. Remember, the difference between the maximum value of the insurance and the minimum cost of the insurance is the value of the risk reduction: the price of uncertainty. As long as the administrative costs and profit of the insurance company are less than the price of uncertainty, insurance can be successfully marketed to this group. With no insurance, each

Figure 6.2: The Choice of Insurance

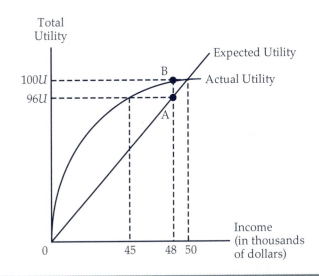

---

[5] $E(Y) = (0.96 \times \$50,000) + (0.04 \times \$0) = \$48,000. \ E(U) = (0.96 \times 100U) + (0.04 \times 0U) = 96U.$

individual in the group has an expected utility of $96U$. When insurance costs less than $5,000, utility is higher. The person is better off insured, depicted by point B than uninsured, depicted by point A.

Several factors affect the decision to buy insurance. The shape of the utility-of-income curve is important. Obviously, individuals who are risk seekers or risk neutral will not buy insurance.[6] The magnitude of the loss also plays a key role in the decision. When the range of uncertainty is large (i.e., when the potential financial loss is large relative to the actual level of income), the distance between the actual utility curve and the expected utility curve is greater than when the range of uncertainty is small. The greater the expected loss, the greater the maximum value of the insurance, and the higher the likelihood that the individual will purchase insurance. As the probability of the loss changes, the likelihood of buying insurance changes. Even those who are risk averse do not buy insurance when the probability of a loss is at one of the extremes. The perceived cost of the risk is too low to stimulate demand at low probabilities, and minimum cost of the insurance is too high as the probability of illness approaches certainty. As with the demand for any product, it goes without saying that the price of the insurance and the level of income also play important roles in determining whether or not insurance will be purchased.

Health Insurance and Market Failure

Insurance pools are designed to spread the risk of high-cost, low-probability events. Hospitalization falls into this category, and insurance pays 97 percent of all hospital expenses. Coverage for low-cost, high-probability events—such as dental care, eyeglasses, and prescription drugs—is not as generous. Insurance covers less than half of the overall spending for dental care and eyeglasses (Levit et al., 1994) and only about two-thirds for prescription drugs. The premium paid by the policyholder is equal to the insured's expected spending, a markup to cover administrative overhead, and a profit—on average, approximately 20 percent. For an individual to purchase insurance, the markup must be less than the perceived value of the risk of self-insurance.[7] In these situations, where the likelihood of use is high and the costs are relatively low, the markup exceeds the value of the risk reduction, and the customer chooses not to buy insurance.

The dominant feature in the medical marketplace is the reliance on the third-party payment mechanism. Just as insurance has shaped the market for medical care, the emergence of health insurance as an employment-based, tax-free benefit has shaped the market for health insurance. This feature has expanded coverage to medical services that normally would not be covered if insurance were purchased individually, creating a strong incentive for overconsumption (Pauly, 1986).

The aggregate value of this tax subsidy is estimated at over $100 billion. In other words, if employer-based health insurance were treated as a taxable benefit, federal income tax receipts would rise by that amount (Gruber and Levitt, 2000). The benefits of this tax subsidy flow primarily to those with generous health plans. Over 60 percent of the tax savings go to the highest-paid 20 percent of the population. The average worker with employment-based health insurance saves about $800 per year in taxes. At the extremes, the uninsured and low-income workers get no tax benefits, and those earning between $100,000 and $200,000 save $1,710 (Goodgame, 1994).

POLICY ISSUE

The health insurance tax subsidy distorts the salary package in favor of non-taxable benefits.

Key Concept 9
Market Failure

net loading costs
The difference between the actual premium and the minimum cost of the insurance based on actuarial principles.

---

[6] For the risk seeker, risk contributes to utility. The actual utility function falls below the expected utility function, implying that risk adds to the level of utility. The risk-neutral person is indifferent to uncertainty. Risk has neither benefit nor cost associated with it.

[7] This statement assumes that the insurer and the policyholder place the same value on the expected payout.

There is widespread agreement among economists that this favorable tax treatment distorts the composition of the typical employee compensation package. The theoretical argument is strong. For a person in the 28 percent tax bracket, it takes $1.39 in gross income to provide $1.00 in after-tax income. With this tax treatment, it only takes $1.00 to provide $1.00 in health benefits. This kind of subsidy provides a strong incentive to accept a compensation package disproportionately weighted in favor of nontaxable health benefits. Although it is clear that the tax subsidy matters, the empirical estimates of the impact are less precise.

As health benefits have expanded to cover routine care, the goal of insurance has expanded from spreading risk to insulating against all out-of-pocket spending. In 2006, out-of-pocket spending in the United States was 12.2 percent of total medical care spending.[8] Under these circumstances, providers have less incentive to provide care efficiently, which limits competition, raises costs, and lowers the quality of services.

POLICY ISSUE

The health insurance tax subsidy distorts the salary package in favor of non-taxable benefits.

Information Problems

Although the medical care sector in the United States has many problems, it is difficult to say how many of these problems can be traced directly to the traditional reliance on markets. The perceived failure of the medical marketplace to efficiently allocate resources and control spending has led most developed nations worldwide to adopt a system of extensive, collective involvement through social insurance. One of the most promising routes to understanding the functioning of the medical marketplace is by tracing the implications of widespread information problems in that market. Information costs are a central factor in economic decision making. The most challenging problems that arise because of costly information are due to unequal access to information. One party to an economic transaction has more and better information than all other parties. Several issues arise when access to information is not equal, or, to say it more formally, when information is asymmetrically distributed; that is, when there is imperfect consumer information on price and quality, moral hazard, and adverse selection.

Consumer Information Problems For a market to work, consumers must behave rationally, have income to spend, and know their own preferences. When consumers have trouble gathering and understanding information, the ability to make informed decisions is compromised (Rice, 1998). Health care markets are seriously deficient in this regard. The quality of information tends to be poor with most information passed from consumer to consumer by word-of-mouth with little formal advertising. Not only is medical information difficult to gather, it is also difficult to understand. A great deal of medical decision making is based on highly technical information. Physicians spend a great deal of time in medical school to learn how to interpret the technical data on which they base diagnosis and treatment. Patients are usually not equipped to make the same decisions. It is this dual role as provider and adviser that can lead to abuse. Finally, the cost of poor decision making is often quite high.

Cost-conscious decision making also requires that consumers know the prices paid for the services they buy. This requirement is important and, at the same time, controversial. Prices of goods and services should reflect the value placed on them by individual consumers or society as a whole. However, many question the ethics of placing a monetary value on improved health status. The information issue is not

[8] A similar situation exists in the rest of the developed world. Out-of-pocket spending is higher in Canada, Germany, Japan, and Switzerland, ranging from 13.1 percent in Germany to 30.5 percent in Switzerland.

what the price should be, but whether consumers should know the prices they are expected to pay. Better information on prices, often referred to as *price transparency*, would allow consumers to make price comparisons across providers and result in more efficient markets.

The Economics of Moral Hazard Information about the present and future is costly. Economic modeling no longer utilizes the assumption of perfect and costless information exclusively, but has attempted to recognize information costs as a central factor in decision making. Nobel laureate George Stigler (1961) wrote, "Information occupies the slum dwelling in the town of economics." Now it seems that all of the interesting problems in economics are due to the fact that information is costly.

Information costs present problems during economic transactions. All contracts involve expectations of future behavior. Moral hazard occurs anytime there is an opportunity to gain from acting differently from the implied principles of a contract. There is always a chance that a contract will change the risk-taking behavior of one or both parties involved. The problem arises when parties to a contract cannot monitor each other's performance. Because private actions are hidden from view, both parties have an opportunity to gain from unpredictable behavior. If people were perfectly honest, writing contracts would be easy. But people are often opportunistic. People who are moral in most ways may still take advantage of situations when their behavior cannot be monitored. By exploiting the imbalance of information existing between the two parties to the contract, a person is engaging in economic opportunism—attempting to secure more utility than would be permitted or anticipated by a particular agreement.

BACK-OF-THE-ENVELOPE

The Economics of Opportunistic Behavior

In market transactions, there is a high probability that one or both parties to a transaction has inside information — knowledge of certain traits, characteristics, or behavior not readily available to the other party — and will try to exploit this advantage. A person who purchases an insurance contract is likely to engage in opportunistic behavior, knowingly or unknowingly. Without the policyholder's knowledge, the insurance company may establish guidelines or create incentives to encourage providers to limit access to certain costly tests and procedures, a form of opportunistic behavior. One could argue that this sort of behavior is unethical or even immoral. Regardless of its origin, taking unfair advantage of private information when there is a potential for personal gain impedes the efficient workings of markets.

We can illustrate this inefficiency using a simple prisoner's dilemma game. Suppose the insurer and policy owners have two options: predictable or opportunistic. The payoffs shown represent different levels of utility or satisfaction with the outcome.

		INSURER	
		Predictable	Opportunistic
POLICY	Predictable	80, 80	30, 100
OWNER	Opportunistic	100, 30	50, 50

continued

> In the above case, both parties to the insurance contract have a dominant strategy; the best response is opportunistic behavior. If the insurer's behavior is predictable, the policy owner will be at a higher level of utility (100 instead of 80) by being opportunistic. The same is true for the insurer. When both play their dominant strategies (Opportunistic, Opportunistic), their combined utility is 100. The optimal payoff would be for them to cooperate, share private information, and practice predictable behavior.
>
> It may be possible to set up a situation in which, through penalty or reward, the cooperative outcome (Predictable, Predictable) can be achieved, and welfare can be maximized. Suppose that predictable behavior is rewarded in such a way that utility increases by 25. In this case, the dominant strategy changes for each party, and predictable behavior can be achieved all around.
>
> | | | INSURER | |
> | --- | --- | --- | --- |
> | | | **Predictable** | **Opportunistic** |
> | **POLICY** | **Predictable** | 105, 105 | 55, 100 |
> | **OWNER** | **Opportunistic** | 100, 55 | 50, 50 |
>
> The reward may be structured by providing a rebate to the policy owner, if medical care spending is below a certain threshold, or if no claims are made during the year. For the insurer, it may mean rewarding carriers that get high marks from enrollees or that satisfy certain benchmarks for preventive services.

The fact that a person has insurance coverage increases expected medical care spending. Two aspects to moral hazard affect both patient and provider. Having insurance 1) increases the likelihood of purchasing medical services and 2) induces higher spending in the event of an illness.[9]

Key Concept 4
Self-Interest

These information problems affect the structure of insurance contracts. The person with insurance recognizes that the service is "sale priced." Patients experience net prices as low as 10 to 20 cents on the dollar, especially for hospital and physicians' services. It naturally follows that people pursue the rational tendency of purchasing more services than they would under full-invoice pricing. Lowering the cost of medical care to the individual through the availability of insurance increases the amount purchased.

It is easy to understand how this happens: A person visiting a physician for a battery of diagnostic tests will behave differently if he has insurance coverage. A patient with full insurance coverage will ask about the benefits of the tests, the nature of the complications, and the amount of time required for the entire procedure. A physician with a fully insured patient will provide the tests knowing that the insurance company will pay the bill. Seldom will cost enter the discussion. On the other hand, the uninsured patient will ask about the cost of the tests, the cost of alternative tests, whether the tests are absolutely necessary, and the likely consequences if they are postponed or skipped completely. And the physician of a

---

[9] In practice, economists view moral hazard as one aspect of the law of demand. Patients respond to lower net prices by purchasing more. Providers recognize that demand for their services is price inelastic and thus charge higher prices and prescribe more services.

patient without insurance will take the patient's financial situation into consideration when choosing which tests to run.

Studies by the RAND Corporation and others have shown that individuals who receive free care use more medical services than those who are required to pay a portion of the cost. It is widely understood that health insurance, by lowering the out-of-pocket cost of medical care to the individual, may increase the amount demanded. In other words, people demand more medical care when it is covered by insurance.

From a strictly economic perspective, we can argue that the response of seeking more medical care when one has insurance than when one does not is a result of rational economic behavior, not moral turpitude. The quantity of medical care demanded by an individual is a function of 1) tastes and preferences for medical care, 2) income, 3) the extent of the illness, and 4) the price charged for medical services. The effect of insurance on medical care expenditures is that it reduces the price paid by the individual, from a positive market price to some lower price. Even if illness is a perfectly random event, the presence of medical insurance will alter the randomness of medical expenditures, unless the demand for medical care is perfectly inelastic.

Pauly (1968) presented these ideas more formally. Consider that there are three health events that can take place during a particular time period:

I_1 = a person will not be sick (with probability $p_1 = 0.5$)

I_2 = a person will be moderately ill (with probability $p_2 = 0.25$)

I_3 = a person will be seriously ill (with probability $p_3 = 0.25$)

Using Figure 6.3, the position of the individual's demand curve for medical care during any time period depends on which health event occurs. Assume perfectly inelastic demand curves D_1, D_2, and D_3 corresponding to the events. With no medical insurance, the individual faces the probability p_1, that he will incur no medical expenses; p_2, that he will need 50 units of medical care at a cost of $50 \times MC$; and p_3, that he will require 200 units of medical care at a cost of $200 \times MC$, where MC is the cost of one unit of medical care.

Figure 6.3: The Effect of Moral Hazard on Medical Care Demand

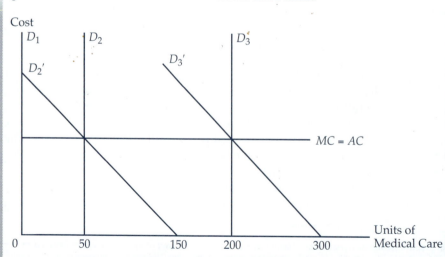

The expected value of the individual's medical care expenses equals $62.5 \times MC$. The calculation is $(0.5 \times 0) + (0.25 \times 50 \times MC) + (0.25 \times 200 \times MC)$. Arrow's (1963) welfare proposition indicates that the risk-averse individual will prefer paying a premium of $62.5 \times MC$ for medical insurance to risking the probability distribution with the mean equal to $62.5 \times MC$.

Suppose, however, that the individual's demand curves are not perfectly inelastic. If, instead, they are as D_2' and D_3'; the individual without insurance faces the probability distribution as above with mean $62.5 \times MC$. However, to indemnify against medical costs, the actuarially necessary insurance premium will be equal to $112.5 \times MC$, which is equal to $(0.5 \times 0) + (0.25 \times 150 \times MC) + (0.25 \times 300 \times MC)$. In such a case, the individual may prefer taking the risk to purchasing the insurance.

The presence of demand curves that are not perfectly inelastic implies that the individual will alter his or her desired expenditures for medical care when insurance is present. The individual who has insurance that covers all cost demands medical care as though it had a zero price. If the demand for medical care has a price elasticity greater than zero, forcing individuals to purchase insurance will create inefficiencies. For an efficient solution, some form of price rationing at the point of service may be necessary; that is, deductibles and coinsurance.

Adverse Selection Adverse selection arises because individuals have more information about expected medical expenditures than insurance companies. The ability of prospective insurance customers to conceal their true risks can result in some insurance groups having a disproportionate number of insureds who use medical care more frequently than might be expected. This leads to higher-than-average premiums for the group and creates an incentive for low-risk individuals to drop out of the group in search of lower-cost coverage elsewhere.

Adverse selection may be illustrated using the following example: Assume that there are 1,000 individuals, each with a 4 percent chance of a $50,000 loss. The insurer expects 40 claims, or $2,000,000 in losses, and requires a premium of $2,000 plus loading costs (overhead and profit). Suppose the original pool of individuals is merged with one that has 1,000 people, each with a 30 percent chance of making a $50,000 claim. There will be 300 additional claims and an additional $15,000,000 in medical spending. If the insurer cannot distinguish between the two groups, the premium must rise for everyone, because the minimum cost of insuring each of the 2,000 people is $8,500. If members of the high-risk segment were pooled separately, their premium would be $15,000, so $8,500 is a bargain for them. For members of the low-risk segment of the pool, the premium increase is staggering.

The problem is shown using Figure 6.4. Assuming that risk preferences are the same for individuals in each group, we can use the same utility function to illustrate their situations. Low-risk individuals can self-insure, ending up at point A with the 4 percent risk of a $50,000 loss; or, when pooled separately, they may purchase insurance for $2,000 plus loading costs as long as they end up no lower than point B on their (income certain) utility curve. They enjoy a utility level of at least U_2 in either case. High-risk individuals may choose to self-insure and end up at point E with a 30 percent risk of catastrophic loss; or when pooled separately, they may purchase insurance for $15,000 plus loading costs as long as they end up no lower than point F on their (income certain) utility curve. The utility level of the high-risk group can be no lower than U_0.

When the two groups are pooled together, a premium of $8,500 plus loading allows all members of the two groups to end up at point D and experience a utility level of U_1 with certainty. High-risk group members may choose to go without insurance and end up at point E with utility of U_0, or they may buy pooled insurance

Figure 6.4: The Impact of Adverse Selection on Risk Pooling

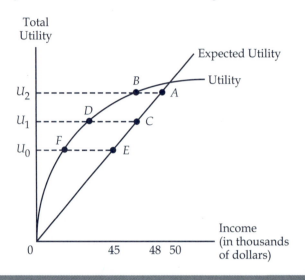

and end up at point D with utility of U_1. Low-risk users may buy pooled insurance and end up at point D with utility of U_1, or choose not buy insurance at all and end up at point A with utility level U_2. In this example, low-risk users will forgo the purchase and self-insure, leaving high-risk users in a separate pool with the higher premium of $15,000 plus loading costs. The only way to guarantee the solvency of the high-risk insurance pool is to force members of the low-risk group to remain in the pool.

Insurers' Response to Information Problems Moral hazard and adverse selection are information problems. Both arise due to the inability of insurers to monitor customer behavior and identify prospective risk. The typical insurer's response to the overspending associated with moral hazard is charging deductibles and coinsurance. Deductibles are set amounts of spending before the insurance pays any part of the claim. In the traditional fee-for-service indemnity plan, the typical deductible is anywhere from $100 to $300. Whether the deductible works to discourage spending depends on the probability that total spending will exceed the deductible. In practice, deductibles seem to have some depressing effect on spending when expected spending is below the deductible. Otherwise, they have little impact. Obviously, one way to increase the impact of the deductible is to increase its size. Deductibles of $2,500 will reduce spending more than deductibles of $250.

In most cases, the insured patient pays a fixed percentage of every claim. The typical coinsurance rate of 10 to 20 percent provides a measure of discipline to the cost-conscious patient. Higher coinsurance rates raise the marginal cost to the insured and serve to restrain spending to some degree. This cost sharing usually stops after total out-of-pocket spending reaches some predetermined limit, anywhere from $2,000 to $5,000.

The insurer's response to adverse selection is twofold: Insurance companies will only underwrite prospective risk. The insurer will try to determine the expected level of spending prior to entering into the contract. This risk rating of prospective customers is done either through the use of a questionnaire, a physical exam, or a combination of the two. In addition, insurance companies will not provide insurance for known ailments. A **preexisting condition** is associated with

preexisting condition

A medical condition caused by an injury or disease that existed prior to the application for health insurance. Policies often exclude preexisting conditions from individual coverage or, at minimum, include them only after a waiting period (usually 6 to 12 months).

an extremely high probability of use (approaching unity). Without the ability to spread risk, the insurance premium would likely exceed the expected spending. High-risk consumers experience no gain from joining a risk pool with other high-risk consumers, so they have little demand for this high-cost insurance.[10]

The failure of the market to provide opportunities for the chronically and congenitally ill to purchase insurance at average premiums should come as no surprise. The purpose of insurance is to share risk, not wealth. Policy makers, even those not interested in wealth redistribution, have used market failure to justify the provision of social insurance as a safety net. Since the private insurance market cannot provide adequate insurance for those with preexisting conditions, it seems reasonable that the government take on this responsibility by operating and subsidizing high-risk insurance pools.

Other policy makers justify the provision of social insurance because of the external costs associated with the uninsured (e.g., high-cost emergency room use, cost-shifting, social unrest). Social insurance makes a pooling solution possible. Low risks are required to support the risk pool through compulsory taxation or higher insurance premiums. This approach to insurance is used in the United States in both means-tested (Medicaid) and an age-tested (Medicare) programs. It is used less effectively in state-sponsored, high-risk pools for those with preexisting conditions.

> **POLICY ISSUE**
>
> Should the government provide insurance for high-risk individuals with pre-existing conditions?

THE OPTIMAL INSURANCE PLAN

Insurance plan design must address the information problems. The perfect insurance plan design would only pay for medical care that would be chosen by self-insured individuals. Suppose a person is faced with a 10 percent probability of incurring a $20,000 medical expense. A risk-averse individual would be willing to pay a premium of at least $2,000 rather than self-insure. (The additional amount over $2,000 that the person would be willing to pay for the insurance depends on the degree of risk aversion.) After purchasing insurance, if the person becomes ill and spends $30,000, the additional $10,000 spending is due to moral hazard.

Using standard demand theory, the implications of moral hazard are simple. The reduced net price that an insured person pays for medical care has both a substitution effect and an income effect. Moral hazard is the substitution effect, the additional spending beyond the amount that a fully-informed person would, prior to the illness, voluntarily contract to cover. The income effect is the systematic transfer of income from the pool of healthy persons to those who become ill. The transfer allows individuals who become ill to purchase medical care that would be unaffordable without insurance.

Insurers use deductibles and coinsurance in response to moral hazard. This form of risk sharing encourages patients to compare the marginal cost of medical care to its marginal benefit. Risk sharing provides incentives for providers and insurers to offer the medically appropriate amount of care. In the current environment, individuals with generous insurance coverage seek more care than those who are uninsured, and providers recommend higher levels of care.

> **POLICY ISSUE**
>
> Most Americans receive their health insurance through employer-sponsored plans.

---

[10] The Health Insurance Portability and Accountability Act passed in 1996 somewhat modified the provision of insurance to those with preexisting conditions. An individual who has insurance and subsequently becomes ill may not be denied continued coverage under any circumstances. The policy is portable across plans. Individuals without insurance coverage who are sick may still be denied coverage.

The optimally designed insurance plan balances the benefits of greater risk sharing with the costs of moral hazard (Cutler and Zeckhauser, 2000). If the goal is to control overspending, the solution is to make people responsible for more of their own care. Higher deductibles and larger copays will result in cost-conscious behavior on the part of both patients and providers.

Third-party insurance requires some method of assigning individuals to risk pools. Adverse selection arises because insurers find it difficult to identify prospective risk and charge premiums that accurately reflect the average risk of pool participants. Efficient pooling requires that individuals be grouped with others of similar risk and charged premiums to reflect that risk.

In the United States, about 68 percent of nonelderly Americans with private insurance are covered under group policies sold to employers or employee associations. Such pools are created without regard to individual risk categories: The sick are pooled with the healthy, the young with the old. The only thing they share in common is the fact that they work for the same company. The policy implications of employer-sponsored insurance are important. Unless plan premiums are based on employee income, everyone pays the same premium. Younger employees pay the same premium as older employees, even though they use less medical care. Sorting people into pools based on expected spending means that those with low risk pay lower premiums than those with high risk.

Additionally, group insurance means that individuals do not own their own insurance policies. Without individual ownership, portability among employer groups has been a chronic problem, especially if a preexisting medical condition affects the person's eligibility across plans.

When plans set premiums according to community ratings, commercial insurers are forced to look for ways to offer low-risk groups better rates. To successfully attract groups with lower-than-average risks, plans must offer insurance at lower premiums. Because high-risk individuals are attracted to more generous plans, low-risk individuals will choose less generous plans to avoid subsidizing the sick, and plans will try to attract them by offering insurance with fewer benefits. This practice is often referred to as **cream skimming**. Two studies suggest that individuals are attracted to plans with lower premiums (Buchmueller, 1998; Cutler and Reber, 1998). When individuals are willing to switch plans for small premium savings, plans become vulnerable to a death spiral resulting from adverse selection. Healthy individuals switch from comprehensive plans to less generous plans, leaving the generous plans with individuals who, on average, have higher levels of spending. Their departure results in even higher premiums for the generous plans, more dropout, and premiums rise further. Ultimately, the generous plan has problems attracting anyone because of high premiums and is cancelled.

cream skimming
A practice of pricing insurance policies so that healthy (low-risk) individuals will purchase coverage and those with a history of costly medical problems (high-risk) will not.

Risk adjustment is not the problem. Efficiency dictates that premiums reflect expected spending. In other words, those with higher risk should pay higher premiums. Pooling by age, sex, and geographic location is appropriate. Premiums could also be adjusted within pools for certain lifestyle choices, such as smoking or obesity. Several approaches to risk adjustment are being used. Medicare+Choice has adopted a diagnosis-based model (Ellis, Pope et al., 1996; Rowels, Weiner et al., 1996) and the Swiss use an *ex post* expenditure adjustment model (Beck, Spycher, Holly, and Gardiol, 2003).

Many policy makers mistakenly believe that insurance companies make money by denying coverage to those identified as high risks. If insurance companies were free to set premiums according to strict actuarial principles, then high-risk individuals would pay higher premiums, and there would be no incentive to cream skim. Cream skimming is the result of regulation in the insurance industry, not competition (Pauly, 1984). Without an efficient mechanism of risk-adjusted premium differentials, the likelihood of cream skimming exists. If those with higher risk cannot afford higher premiums, the issue is an income problem and not an insurance problem. The solution is not community-rated premiums, it is appropriate subsidies to those who cannot afford the actuarially fair premium.

Key Concept 6
Supply and Demand

ISSUES IN MEDICAL CARE DELIVERY

What Does an Arm and a Leg Cost?

Although there is little argument that industrialization has benefited society, with it came many problems that dramatically changed family and work life. Cottage industries became large manufacturing organizations, thus increasing the concerns for worker safety. In many respects, workers' rights with respect to injury and death were largely ignored until the last half of the nineteenth century. Common law liability rules made it difficult for injured workers to collect benefits from their employers.

Gradually the courts began to recognize the employer's responsibility to provide a safe workplace, and by the early 1900s, states began the slow process of drafting legislation to formally establish the responsibility. In 1911, Wisconsin passed the first **workers' compensation** law that was subsequently declared constitutional. By the end of that decade, all but six states and the District of Columbia had such legislation. It was not until 1948 that the last state, Mississippi, adopted its own workers' compensation law.

Workers' compensation establishes a **no-fault** approach to addressing worker safety and health issues in the employment setting. Workers' compensation laws cover virtually all types of injuries "arising out of and in the course of employment." The laws provide medical, disability income, death, and rehabilitation benefits. Perhaps the most controversial category of benefits compensates injured workers for permanent partial disabilities. Each state establishes a schedule of benefits for certain types of injuries. In Rhode Island, the loss of an arm at the shoulder results in a maximum payment to the injured worker of $28,080. In nearby New Hampshire, that same loss would be worth $132,930. Illinois values the arm at $196,719. A worker who loses a leg at the hip receives $28,080 in Rhode Island, $88,620 in New Hampshire, and $180,325 in Illinois. A worker losing an arm and a leg would receive $24,000 in Puerto Rico and $373,100 in Pennsylvania. That same worker, if engaged in interstate commerce working for the railroad, would receive $722,616 regardless of where the injury occurred.

In 2007, the nationwide cost of workers' compensation benefits was estimated at almost $50 billion. Given its costs, it is not surprising that state legislators are constantly under pressure to tinker with the system.

Source: State Workers' Compensation Laws, U.S. Department of Labor, Employment Standards Administration, Office of Workers' Compensation Programs, January 1992.

workers' compensation
Insurance to protect employees against financial loss caused by work-related injury or illness.

no-fault
A method of compensating for injury where no attempt is made to determine fault. The magnitude of injury becomes the basis of the compensation and is the only issue in the legal proceedings.

The Practice of Self-Insurance

As insurance premiums rise, private sector employers have increasingly looked to self-insurance as a means of reducing the cost of providing health insurance to their workers. Currently, over half of all private insurance is provided in plans where the employer of the group assumes all or a significant part of the financial risk. The growth of self-insurance is easy to understand. Most private insurance **underwriting** is based on experience rating in the first place. After experiencing a large number of medical episodes, an employer may be able to predict medical expenses from year to year. Thus, it is practical for large employers to self-insure. The predictability of expenses and the ability to spread risk over a large group makes self-insurance feasible.

Firms that self-insure do not actually contract with an insurance company to assume the financial risk. Instead, they accept this responsibility internally by simply placing funds previously paid in insurance premiums into a reserve account to pay medical claims directly. Many self-insured firms arrange for commercial insurance companies to administer their plans and handle claims processing, actuarial services, and utilization reviews. A large percentage of the plans limit risk through **reinsurance**, a cap on spending at some stop-loss threshold.

Government regulation provides a strong incentive for firms to self-insure. Most states levy a tax on premiums that insurers must pass on to their customers. This extra premium expense does not apply to self-insured plans. Firms that self-insure are also exempted from providing state-mandated benefits that apply to all private insurance plans. Specifically, the provisions of the Employee Retirement Income Security Act (ERISA) of 1974 superseded state laws and prohibited the application of state mandates to self-insured plans. Finally, states that sponsor high-risk insurance pools require commercial insurance carriers to participate in providing insurance to those individuals with preexisting conditions. Usually self-insured plans are not required to participate.

The increased popularity of self-insurance has changed the nature of risk rating. Firms that are large enough to self-insure do so. Community rating is no longer a viable way to determine premiums for groups with below-average levels of risk. Even Blue Cross-Blue Shield, traditionally a proponent of community rating, has been forced to abandon the practice in favor of experience rating for large firms that have the option of self-insuring.

→ *Uninsured Americans* *Possible project.*

MEDICAL CARE FOR THE UNINSURED

It is important to understand the nature and extent of the problems associated with being uninsured. The most recent estimates from the Census Bureau place the number of uninsured at 47 million (DiNavas, Proctor, and Smith, 2007). As the numbers grow, the pressure mounts to provide some relief for the situation. Providing coverage for the uninsured is a formidable task. Understanding who the uninsured are and the reasons they lack insurance coverage are critical in developing policy to deal with the problem.

The majority of the uninsured can be categorized as working poor. These are individuals who earn too much to qualify for cash assistance and are therefore ineligible for Medicaid. Either they work for smaller firms where health insurance is not part of the employee benefit package, or they choose not to take up the insurance offered by their employer. They do not consider the purchase of health insurance a very good buy for the money. Premiums can be as much as 10 to 40 percent higher when sold to small businesses because of additional sales and administrative expenses.

Not everyone without health insurance is poor. Over one-third of the uninsured have incomes at least three times the official poverty level. While the number of uninsured poor has remained fairly stable in recent years, the higher-income

underwriting
The insurance practice of determining whether or not an application for insurance will be accepted. In the process, premiums are also determined. Factors considered may include age, gender, health status, and prior use of health care services.

reinsurance
Stop-loss insurance purchased by a health plan to protect itself against losses that exceed a specific dollar amount per claim, per individual, or per year.

POLICY ISSUE

State regulations create incentives for firms to set up self-insured plans.

POLICY ISSUE

Over 47 million Americans do not have a health insurance.

http://

Health insurance statistics are available from the U.S. Census Bureau Web site at **http://www.census.gov/hhes/ www/hlthins/hlthins.html** uninsured have seen the most dramatic increase in numbers. In fact, households with over $50,000 in income have experienced the greatest growth in the number of uninsured of all income groups.

Individuals with preexisting health conditions represent a substantial number of the uninsured. Insurers try to avoid offering coverage at average premiums to individuals with diabetes, cancer, AIDS, heart disease, or other special health problems. If insurance is available at all, the premiums are high. The size of this group has been estimated at less than 1 percent of the population, or less than 10 percent of the uninsured.

Other reasons explain why some people fail to purchase insurance. They may have no intention of using medical care at all. Low users may be very healthy, have an extreme dislike for formal medical services, or simply not believe in medical care. Some people are not as risk averse as the typical buyer of health insurance. For them a policy that costs more than the actuarially fair premium is simply too expensive. No doubt a significant portion of the uninsured can be classified as free riders. They can afford to buy insurance but do not because they feel that if they become seriously ill, medical care will be provided, and someone else will pay for it.

How Many Americans Are Uninsured?

There is a great deal of confusion about the actual number of uninsured in the country. The most commonly cited estimates of the number of uninsured originate from the Census Bureau's Current Population Survey (CPS). Based on a nationally representative sample, the survey has been conducted annually since 1980. The CPS estimate is intended to measure the number of Americans uninsured for the entire year. Based on evidence available from other surveys, the CPS estimate more likely measures the number of Americans uninsured on a specific date during the year.

There are at least 6 national surveys that gather information on the characteristics of the uninsured. In addition to the CPS, other surveys, including the Survey of Income and Programs Participation (SIPP), the National Health Interview Survey (NHIS), and the Medical Expenditure Panel Survey (MEPS), address many of the same issues. Short (2001) tackles the methodological problems associated with estimating the number of uninsured to show how different survey techniques can result in different estimates. One of the major differences across the surveys is the frequency of data collection. CPS data comes from a survey conducted in March of each year, and it asks questions about insurance status for the previous year. CPS asks for insurance status over the previous year and calculates the uninsured as the residual. Many analysts argue that individuals underreport their insurance status, especially those covered by Medicaid. SIPP interviews every four months, asking questions about insurance status for each month since the previous interview. The MEPS survey is conducted every 3 to 5 months, so the reference period varies across participants.

A study by the Congressional Budget Office analyzed data from the four surveys to estimate the number of uninsured in 1998. In that year, CPS estimated that 43.9 million Americans were uninsured for the entire year, or 18.4 percent of the population. Using MEPS, the estimate was 31.1 million, or 13.3 percent of the population. SIPP estimates placed the number at 21.1 million, or 9.1 percent of the population. When these latter two surveys were used to estimate the number of uninsured on a certain date, SIPP estimated the number at 40.5 million and MEPS put it at 42.6—both very close to the CPS estimates for the number uninsured the entire year.

Add it later
IR Needed ✗ ↑ An even larger issue may be the trend in the number and percentage of the population who go without insurance. Between 1989 and 2001, the percentage of the population without insurance fluctuated from year to year but remained essentially unchanged. Up until 1993, a rising percentage of the population without insurance could be attributable to a decrease in the portion of the population covered by employer-based insurance. However, employment-based coverage increased from 60.5 percent of the nonelderly in 1993 to 69 percent in 2006. At the same time, the number of Americans with public insurance—notably Medicaid and CHAMPUS—and private, nongroup coverage had fallen slightly. The overall impact of these changes was a minimal increase in the percentage of uninsured, from 15.2 percent in 1994 to 15.8 percent in 2006 (Bennefield, 1995; DiNavas, Proctor, and Smith, 2007). ▷

How Long Are They Uninsured?

The most persistent finding in studies of the composition of the uninsured population is that it is constantly changing. The people who are uninsured today are not the same people who were uninsured last year. Being uninsured is a temporary phenomenon for most people. Using the 1993 SIPP panel, Bennefield (1998) estimated that half of all spells without health insurance lasted less than 5.3 months. Similarly, Copeland (1998) estimated that approximately two-thirds of America's uninsured are without coverage for less than one year.

While it may look as though being uninsured is a temporary phenomenon, it should be remembered that one-third of the uninsured are without coverage for over one year. Even this number may be overstated, because many survey respondents who identify themselves as uninsured are eligible for Medicaid coverage and either do not realize it or simply have failed to apply.

Another way to look at this problem is to count the number of people who cycle into and out of the pool of uninsured each year. Instead of 20 million, or even 45 million, Short and Graefe (2003) estimated that there were almost 85 million Americans who were without insurance coverage for at least one month from 1996 to 1999. One out of every three nonelderly Americans found themselves without coverage at some point during that four-year period. But only 4 percent, or 10 million, were without coverage the entire four years and could be considered chronically uninsured.

Who Are the Uninsured?

Many people have the mistaken impression that most people without insurance are unemployed. On the contrary, 58.8 percent of all uninsured Americans were employed in full-time or part-time jobs in 2006. Approximately one in five (21.6 percent) were nonworking adults, meaning that 18.4 percent were dependent children. If dependent children are distributed proportionately according to employment status, it is a fair approximation to say that over 75 percent of the uninsured have some labor force connection—through their own employment or that of a family member.

Table 6.2 provides information on individuals without insurance. An estimated 47 million Americans were uninsured in 2006, 15.8 percent of the total U.S. population. For those under 18 years of age, 11.7 percent were uninsured. For 18- to 24–year-olds, the percentage jumped to 29.3. The percentage without insurance steadily fell in cohorts of older people, since older individuals have a higher demand for medical care and more money to spend on items such as health insurance.

**Table 6.2: Individuals without Health Insurance
By Selected Characteristics, 2005 and 2006**

Group	2005 Uninsured (000)	2005 Percentage of Group	2005 Percentage of Total	2006 Uninsured (000)	2006 Percentage of Group	2006 Percentage of Total
All persons	44,815	15.3	100.0	46,995	15.8	100.0
Race:						
White, Non-Hispanic	20,909	10.7	46.7	21,162	10.8	45.0
Black	7,006	19.0	15.6	7,652	20.5	16.3
Asian and Pacific Islander	2,161	17.2	4.8	2,045	15.5	4.4
Hispanic origin	13,954	32.3	31.1	15,296	34.1	32.5
Age:						
Under 18 years	8,050	10.9	18.0	8,661	11.7	18.4
18 to 24 years	8,201	29.3	18.3	8,323	29.3	17.7
25 to 34 years	10,161	25.7	22.7	10,713	26.9	22.8
35 to 44 years	7,901	18.3	17.6	8,018	18.8	17.1
45 to 64 years	10,053	13.6	23.4	10,738	14.2	22.8
65 years and over	449	1.3	1.0	541	1.5	1.2
Nativity:						
Native	33,034	12.8	73.7	34,380	13.2	73.2
Naturalized citizen	2,385	17.2	5.3	2,384	16.4	5.1
Not a citizen	9,396	43.1	21.0	10,231	45.0	21.8
Income:						
Less than $25,000	14,452	24.2	32.2	13,933	24.9	29.6
$25,000 to $49,999	14,651	20.1	32.7	15,319	21.1	32.6
$50,000 to $74,999	7,826	13.3	17.5	8,459	14.4	18.0
Over $75,000	7,886	7.7	17.6	9,283	8.5	19.8

Source: United States Census Bureau, *Income, Poverty, and Health Insurance Coverage in the United States: 2006,* P60-233, August 2007.

Ref. website.

Insurance is closely associated with level of income. One-fourth of the population with incomes below $25,000 does not have coverage. Less than 10 percent of those with incomes over $75,000 go without insurance. Individuals with annual incomes between one and two times the official poverty level are more likely to be uninsured than those making less than that amount. Over 35 percent of all uninsured have household incomes that exceed $50,000.

Race is also a factor in the likelihood that a person will have insurance. Even though only 11 percent of whites are uninsured, they make up 45 percent of those who do not have coverage. One in five blacks and one in three Hispanics are uninsured. A related issue is nativity, or country of origin. Approximately 13 percent of Americans born in the United States are uninsured, and 16 percent of naturalized citizens. However, 45 percent of all noncitizens go uncovered. Almost two-thirds of illegal immigrants lack health insurance, compared with one-third of all permanent residents (Derose, Escarce, and Lurie, 2007).

Why Are They Uninsured?

The fact that over 75 percent of the uninsured have some sort of labor force attachment is both troubling and reassuring. It is troubling in the sense that most people who are uninsured have a job, and at the same time reassuring, because they are already connected to the primary mechanism used in this country to provide health insurance—private sector employment.

Why is it that so many workers lack coverage? Broadly speaking, there are three primary reasons that a worker does not have health insurance (Kronic and Gilmer, 1999; Holahan and Kim, 2000):

- The employer does not offer a health plan.

- The employer offers a health plan, but the employee is not eligible for the plan because of part-time status or some other rule.

- The employer offers a plan, and the employee is eligible for that plan, but the employee chooses not to participate because the plan is either too expensive, the employee can get a better plan elsewhere (usually through a spouse's employment), or the employee does not perceive a need for a health plan.

Many of the uninsured are employed by small firms that do not provide health benefits. Small firms are at a distinct disadvantage when buying health insurance; it simply costs too much. In setting premiums for group plans, insurers usually charge small firms more per employee than they charge large firms. The estimated administrative costs for small-group plans (those with less than five employees) are about 40 percent of claims. For large-group plans (those with more than 10,000 employees), the comparable number is about 5.5 percent of claims. General and administrative expenses are higher for small-group plans, along with selling expenses and commission costs (Helms, Gauthier, and Campion, 1992).

Insurers perceive a higher level of risk in the small-group setting. The private insurance market is fragmented in nature. Instead of the concept of community rating, in which everyone in a particular geographic area pays the same premium, different groups pay different premiums based on perceived risk. Perceived risk is higher for the smaller group. One large claim can have a catastrophic impact on the calculated premium for them, effectively pricing the group out of the market or making insurance unavailable at any price.

For the same reason, small firms are not able to take advantage of self-insuring. According to a 1992 survey by Foster Higgins, over 80 percent of all private sector companies with more than 1,000 workers self-insure. Even smaller firms see the benefits offered by this practice. Half of all self-insured companies have fewer than 100 employees (Thompson, 1993). With so many firms self-insuring, up to half of all private sector employees are now in self-insured pools. Self-insurance carries with it a substantial risk of adverse selection for small firms. Sound underwriting principles would suggest a minimum of 100 to 300 employees before self-insurance is recommended.

Taking all the relevant small-group factors into consideration, it is not surprising that many small firms do not offer health benefits to their employees. In addition, small firms usually pay comparatively low wages.

The other reasons that workers go without insurance are equally important. Many part-time workers are uninsured because they do not work enough to qualify for the health plan that is offered. Many eligible workers choose not to participate in the health plan, either because it is too expensive or they are eligible through another plan, typically through a spouse. Bundorf and Pauly (2006) present an alternative explanation. They present evidence that as many as 75 percent of the uninsured can actually afford insurance coverage by two different standard definitions of affordability, but they choose to spend their money on other things.

Does Lack of Insurance Mean Poor Health?

The connection between lack of insurance and poor health may be decomposed into two parts. First, how does the lack of health insurance affect access to medical care? Second, does poor access result in poor health outcomes? Significant differences of opinion weigh in on whether the lack of insurance contributes to poor health. Evidence from the RAND Health Insurance Experiment suggests that more generous health insurance benefits have little effect on health outcomes (Newhouse, 1993). Brook (1991) provides additional evidence that the absence of insurance does not reduce the health status of the average American. While the uninsured have only about two-thirds the number of physicians' visits per year as those with insurance, and about half the number of hospital days per year, these differences in utilization do not translate into significant differences in health status. Considering the fact that the uninsured are on average younger and healthier, this result may be at least in part due to self-selection. With the exception of those who were poor and sick, there seems to be no relationship between health status and insurance status.

These differences could be due to the fact that up to one-third of the care provided to the insured is considered inappropriate or equivocal. In other words, the medical benefit does not exceed the medical risk. Because of the questionable nature of such a large percentage of the medical care provided to the insured, differences in the amount of care may not be responsible for differences in health status.

Other research suggests that those without insurance have trouble accessing the medical care system, resulting in poorer health outcomes. The access problem manifests itself in a lower likelihood of having a regular source of care (Berk, Schur, and Cantor, 1995; Bindman et al., 1995; Zuvekas and Weinick, 1999), delays in seeking care (Burstin et al., 1998; Weissman et al., 1991), and receiving fewer services than those with health insurance (Berk and Schur, 1998; Brown, Bindman, and Lurie, 1998). Even those individuals with health problems find that a lack of insurance significantly affects their access to the system (Berk, Schur, and Cantor, 1995).

Lack of insurance may lead to lower levels of utilization, but establishing a connection between reduced access and poor health outcomes is a more difficult task. The literature supporting the connection generally fails to overcome several important empirical problems.[11] Results from the RAND Health Insurance Experiment cited above (Manning et al., 1987) show that those individuals who receive free care have better control of their blood pressure and have better vision. Other studies indicate that those without insurance delay seeking needed medical care, resulting in avoidable hospitalizations (Billings, Anderson, and Newman, 1996; Bindman et al., 1995), higher than expected mortality rates (Hadley, Steinberg, and Feder, 1991; Franks, Clancy, and Gold, 1993), and poor birth outcomes (Currie and Gruber, 1996). Even though the empirical evidence is inconclusive, the argument that individuals without insurance experience poorer health outcomes is powerful. As the number of uninsured continues to grow, policy makers will find it increasingly difficult to ignore the apparent health consequences of poor access.

POLICY ISSUE

Poor access to medical care often results in poor health, especially for the chronically ill poor.

---

[11] The most notable problem is endogenity bias, a situation in which the empirical data are unable to determine whether lack of insurance leads to poor health or whether poor health decreases the probability of being insured. Additionally, the research suffers from selection bias where omitted variables that jointly determine the availability of insurance and health status are not included in the analysis.

The Safety Net for the Uninsured

Since 1985, it has been illegal for a hospital emergency department—public or private—to deny care to anyone requesting care. Contained in the Comprehensive Omnibus Budget Reconciliation Act, the Emergency Medical Treatment and Active Labor Act (EMTALA) requires a hospital to provide medically appropriate screening to determine the nature of the medical condition and either treat the condition or stabilize and transfer the patient to a facility that can. Private hospitals have been systematically reducing their free care in nonacute cases, forcing the public hospitals to absorb the burden of the responsibility of providing care to the uninsured. Estimates indicate that fewer than 10 percent of the nation's public hospitals provide almost half of all hospital care for the uninsured. Much of this uncompensated care is provided in the hospital emergency department or as a result of a hospital admission from the emergency department.

Using MEPS data, Hadley and Holahan (2003) estimated that uninsured Americans received $34.5 billion in uncompensated care in 2001. An additional $14.9 billion in free care was provided to those with insurance, bringing the total to approximately $50 billion.

Most of this "free" care is financed from municipal budgets, Medicaid subsidies for the treatment of the indigent poor, or through cost shifting. As the number of uninsured increases, and medical costs continue to climb, government budgets at all levels are coming under closer scrutiny. Competitive pressures are making it more difficult for hospitals to pass the cost of care for the uninsured on to private patients. Private insurers, employers, and payers of all kinds are increasingly unwilling to pay for the treatment of the uninsured. Payers are refusing to accept cost shifting and are negotiating discounts in return for guaranteed patient volume.

Universal insurance coverage requires accepting the principles of subsidization of those who cannot afford coverage and offering incentives to those who can. The chronically ill cannot afford risk-rated insurance premiums. If the insurance market is to provide a solution, the high risk must receive subsidies. The solution is not as simple as mandating that all insurance premiums be based on community rating, thus forcing low-risk insureds to subsidize those who are high risk. Under community rating, the healthy may face premiums that exceed the maximum value of the insurance. If the purchase of insurance is based on voluntary choice, many of the healthy will choose not to buy unless provided with strong incentives, such as tax credits when insurance is purchased, or penalties when it is not.

It is increasingly difficult to subsidize care for the elderly, the indigent, and the uninsured. One of the main casualties of increased competition in the health insurance market is the complex system of cross-subsidies for experimental treatment, care for the elderly and indigent, and medical education and research. As market pressures mount, insurance providers, along with Medicare and Medicaid, find it increasingly difficult to remain competitive if they do not restrict payments for these services. And if no one wants to pay for medical education or research and development, the quality of care will suffer.

The search for solutions to the problem of providing medical care for the uninsured has resulted in numerous options but few tangible results. Whether the suggestion involves tax increases to pay for insurance coverage for the poor, hospital surcharges on every insurance claim, or **employer mandates,** the general approach is the same—providing a subsidy, either public or private, for those who cannot afford to buy insurance on their own. The alternative is to continue to rely on the hospital industry and private-practice physicians to provide free care.

POLICY ISSUE

Competitive pressures are jeopardizing the ability of hospitals and physicians to provide free care to the uninsured. Budget pressures are forcing state and local governments to rethink how they will pay for indigent care.

Key Concept 10
Voluntary Exchange

Key Concept 5
Competition

employer mandate
A feature of certain health care reform proposals requiring employers to provide health insurance for their employees.

BACK-OF-THE-ENVELOPE

The Welfare Loss from a Subsidy

Insured customers compare benefits of services with the out-of-pocket costs incurred directly (where true costs are the total of out-of-pocket costs plus charges covered by insurance). By ignoring total cost, the decision calculus results in overuse of resources; that is, using more than the socially desirable amount. This may be the single most important factor in the escalation of total medical care expenditures.

Key Concept 9
Market Failure

The economics of an insurance subsidy can be shown graphically. Initial demand for medical care is shown by the demand curve D_0E. Access to insurance, and the subsidy it provides, causes the demand curve to become more inelastic (D_1E). Insurance consumer surplus is P_0AD_0. Because insurance does not change the value of medical care to the individual, only its price, consumer surplus with insurance is evaluated using D_0E and will be P_2D_0C. Likewise, producer surplus increases with insurance, from P_0AS to P_1BS.

Economic Concept	Before Insurance	After Insurance
Consumer surplus	P_0AD_0	P_2CD_0
Producer surplus	P_0AS	P_1BS
Cost of insurance	—	P_1BCP_2
Net gain to society	D_0AS	$D_0AS - ABC$
Deadweight loss	—	ABC

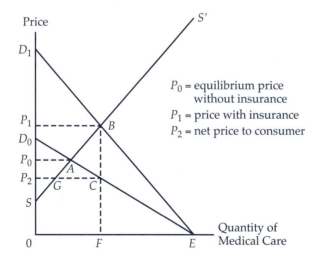

P_0 = equilibrium price without insurance
P_1 = price with insurance
P_2 = net price to consumer

Note the overlap of surpluses with insurance, the area D_0AGP_2. The cost of the insurance, P_1BCP_2, erases the overlap and part of both consumer surplus (ACG) and producer surplus (P_1BAD_0). Is society better off with the subsidy? Actually, the insurance subsidy reduces surplus by ABC. Instead of D_0AS, surplus is now $D_0AS - ABC$.

continued

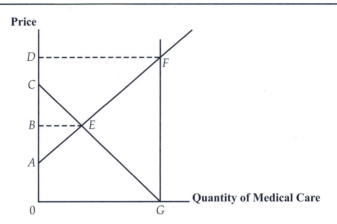

If the government provides insurance that covers 100 percent of the cost of medical care with no coinsurance requirement, the demand curve for medical care becomes perfectly inelastic. This is shown in the diagram above, where the new demand curve *FG* is instead of *CG*. The price of medical care becomes *0D*, and the quantity demanded becomes *0G*. Total cost to the taxpayers is *0DFG*, consumer surplus is *0CG*, and producer surplus is *ADF*. Expenditures exceed the combined surplus by *FEG – ACE*, representing a net welfare loss to society when *FEG* is greater than *ACE* and a net gain if the opposite is true.

In both the case of insurance with copayments and taxpayer-financed insurance with no copayments, the loss to society is caused by the consumption of medical care where the cost of care to society exceeds the net benefit to the patient.

SUMMARY AND CONCLUSIONS

Medical care in the United States, predominantly a private out-of-pocket expense as recently as 1965, is now overwhelmingly financed by third parties: government and private insurers. Government at all levels directly finances over 40 percent of all medical care. Coupled with the tax subsidy provided to purchasers of private insurance, taxpayers finance over half of all medical care spending in this country.

The private sector insures over 170 million Americans, not including the 20 million Medicare recipients who buy private supplementary insurance. Commercial insurance companies, the Blue Cross-Blue Shield plans, self-funded employer plans, and prepaid health plans provide the vast majority of this coverage. The two primary government health programs, Medicare and Medicaid, provide health care coverage to almost 70 million Americans. Medicare enrollment topped 43 million elderly and disabled in 2006, and Medicaid served more than 45 million nonelderly.

This patchwork coverage provides health insurance to approximately 84 percent of the American population but still leaves approximately 47 million more without insurance at any one point in time. Considering that over three-fourths of the uninsured have some labor-force connection, it should come as no surprise that reform proposals have focused on employment-related solutions.

Those favoring more government involvement support either the expansion of the Medicaid program or the use of employer mandates. Expanding Medicaid will require both the liberalization of eligibility criterion for specific groups and the subsidization of premiums for the working poor who would buy into the system voluntarily. Employer mandates would require that all employers provide and pay for a basic benefits package determined by the government.

Advocates of a private sector solution contend that public sector solutions are largely responsible for pricing many of the working poor out of the insurance market completely. Their response focuses on reducing the cost of private insurance to make it more affordable, either through income tax deductions or tax credits of some kind. Establishing high-risk insurance pools is one measure typically considered as a means of providing insurance for those with preexisting medical conditions. Although not a complete solution, it would offer coverage to 20 percent of the chronically uninsured and would go a long way toward providing access to this medically deserving group.

Small employers find themselves at a distinct disadvantage in the purchase of private insurance for their workers. Small size means two things: they lack the bargaining power to negotiate favorable rates with large insurers, and they have too few employees to adequately share the risk of catastrophic illness. The goal of increasing the bargaining power and spreading the risk can be accomplished by allowing firms to combine into purchasing cooperatives. Coupled with the elimination of state insurance mandates for small firms, these cooperatives would likely bring the cost of insurance down by 15 to 20 percent.

Proponents of more government involvement and proponents of the more pluralistic approach agree on very little. How big is the problem? What approach should be taken to solve it? And although little if any agreement can be found on these two issues, the two sides do share the common goal of improving access for those who are currently uninsured. Whether this is accomplished within the framework of the current private insurance system, or whether the United States will go the route of the rest of the world and allow more government involvement, is yet to be determined.

PROFILE

Uwe E. Reinhardt

Once introduced at a conference by Representative Pete Stark (D–Calif.) as an "expert on contrariness," Uwe (pronounced *oo-vuh*) Reinhardt is regarded by many as the "bad boy" of the health care reform debate. Born in 1937, Reinhardt's formative years were spent in war-torn Germany, where his family literally lived in a tool shed. During those years of abject poverty, Reinhardt grew to appreciate universal health care financed primarily through taxation. "I grew up in countries where health care was treated as a social good, where the rich paid significantly more than their health care costs to subsidize the poor," he says. "I found that a civilized environment."

Reinhardt migrated to Canada in 1956, where he attended the University of Saskatchewan. After graduation in 1964, he came to the United States to study at Yale University, where he received his Ph.D. in economics in 1970. He also holds an honorary doctorate from the Medical College of Pennsylvania. As an academic, Reinhardt is a bit unusual, in that he has taught at Princeton his entire career. His title is currently the James Madison Professor of Political Economy.

Most of his scholarly work has been in health care economics. He is on the editorial board of several journals, including *Health Affairs, New England Journal of Medicine*, and *Health Management Quarterly*. He has also served as associate editor of the *Journal of Health Economics*. This is quite a contrast for someone who was considering a Ph.D. dissertation topic on optimal tolls on the Connecticut Turnpike. Fortunately, one of Reinhardt's Yale professors suggested the economics of health care, and the rest is history.

His fascination for the topic has continued to grow over the last three decades. Over this time, Reinhardt has become a devout advocate for the uninsured. Prone to black humor about many health-related issues, Reinhardt never jokes about the plight of the uninsured. Although he does not see, nor does he want to see, health care defined as a constitutional

continued

right, he firmly believes that health care plays a social role. It is a right "implied in the social contract. . . . It's not a consumer good. It's a quasi-religious commodity. . . . It's the cement that makes a nation out of people."

Ever controversial, Reinhardt has earned the respect of individuals on both sides of the health care debate. Equally comfortable in front of a class or a congressional committee, he leaves little doubt about where he stands on the important issues surrounding health care reform.

Source: Julie Rovner, "MM Interview: Uwe Reinhardt," Modern Maturity 37(6), November–December 1994, 64–72.

QUESTIONS AND PROBLEMS

1. In what way is insuring for a medical loss different from insuring for any other loss?

2. Define the following concepts. How important are they in determining the efficient functioning of medical markets?
   a. moral hazard
   b. adverse selection
   c. asymmetric information
   d. third-party payer
   e. cream skimming

3. What are the major reasons that health insurance policies have deductibles and coinsurance features? Are they really necessary?

4. What are the four types of medical insurance? Briefly describe the coverage available with each one.

5. Should insurers be allowed to refuse health insurance policies to individuals who are genetically predisposed to certain diseases? To those whose lifestyles place them in high-risk categories for certain diseases? Support your answers.

6. One of the major issues driving the health care reform debate is the number of uninsured Americans and their limited access to medical care. Describe the typical person in the United States without insurance. Does lack of insurance mean the uninsured have no access to medical care?

7. What is asymmetric information? How does it present a problem to medical providers and health insurers?

8. Why do firms self-insure?

9. Does the availability of free health care improve health status? Explain.

10. What is the purpose of deductibles and coinsurance? To what problem are insurers responding?

REFERENCES

Kenneth J. Arrow, "Uncertainty and the Welfare Economics of Medical Care," *American Economic Review* 53(5), December 1963, 941–973.

Konstantin Beck, Stefan Spycher, Alberto Holly, and Lucien Gardiol, "Risk Adjustment in Switzerland," *Health Policy* 65, 2003, 63–74.

Robert L. Bennefield, "Dynamics of Economic Well-Being: Health Insurance 1993 to 1995, Who Loses Coverage and for How Long?" U.S. Census Bureau, *Current Population Reports*, P70-64, August 1998, 1–6.

———, "Health Insurance Coverage—1994," U.S. Census Bureau, *Current Population Reports*, P60.

Mark L. Berk and Alan C. Monheit, "The Concentration of Health Care Expenditures, Revisited," *Health Affairs* 20(2), March/April 2001, 9–18.

Mark L. Berk and Claudia L. Schur, "Access to Care: How Much Difference Does Medicaid Make?" *Health Affairs* 17(1), January/February 1998, 169–180.

Mark L. Berk, Claudia L. Schur, and Joel C. Cantor, "Ability to Obtain Health Care: Recent Estimates from the Robert Wood Johnson Foundation National Access to Care Survey," *Health Affairs* 14(3), Fall 1995, 139–146.

John Billings, Geoffrey M. Anderson, and Laurie S. Newman, "Recent Findings on Preventable Hospitalizations," *Health Affairs* 15(3), Fall 1996, 239–249.

A.B. Bindman, K. Grumbach, D. Osmond et al., "Preventable Hospitalizations and Access to Care," *Journal of the American Medical Association* 274, 1995, 305–311.

Robert H. Brook, "Health, Health Insurance, and the Uninsured," *Journal of the American Medical Association* 265(22), June 12, 1991, 2998–3002.

M. E. Brown, A. B. Bindman, and N. Lurie, "Monitoring the Consequences of Uninsurance: A Review of Methodologies," *Medical Care Research and Review* 55, 1998, 177–210.

M. Kate Bundorf and Mark V. Pauly, "Is Health Insurance Affordable for the Uninsured?" *Journal of Health Economics* 25, 2006, 650–673.

H. R. Burstin, K. Swartz, A. C. O'Neil, E. J. Orav, and T. A. Brennan, "The Effect of Change of Health Insurance on Access to Care," *Inquiry* 35(4), 1998, 389–397.

Centers for Disease Control, "Oral Health 2000: Facts and Figures," available at http://www.cdc.gov/OralHealth/factsheets/sgr2000-fs1.htm, May 2000

Craig Copeland, "Characteristics of the Nonelderly with Selected Sources of Health Insurance and Lengths of Uninsured Spells," *EBRI Issue Brief* No. 198, June 1998.

Janet Currie and Jonathan Gruber, "Saving Babies: The Efficacy and Cost of Recent Expansions of Medicaid Eligibility for Pregnant Women," *Journal of Political Economy* 104(6), December 1996, 1263–1296.

David Cutler and Sarah Reber, "Paying for Health Insurance: The Tradeoff between Competition and Adverse Selection," *Quarterly Journal of Economics* 113, 1998, 433–466.

David M. Cutler and Richard J. Zeckhauser, "The Anatomy of Health Insurance," in *Handbook of Health Economics*, Volume 1, edited by A. J. Culyer and J. P. Newhouse, Elsevier Science, 2000, 563–643.

Kathryn Pitkin Derose, Jose J. Escarce, and Nicole Lurie, "Immigrants and Health Care: Sources of Vulnerability," *Health Affairs* 26(5), September/October 2007, 1258–1268.

Randall P. Ellis et al., "Diagnosis-Based Risk Adjustment for Medicare Capitation Payments," *Health Care Financing Review* 17(3), 1996, 101–128.

P. Franks, C. M. Clancy, and M. R. Gold, "Health Insurance and Mortality: Evidence from a National Cohort," *Journal of the American Medical Association* 270, 1993, 737–741.

Milton Friedman and Leonard J. Savage, "The Utility Analysis of Choices Involving Risk," *Journal of Political Economy* 56(4), August 1948, 279–304.

Victor R. Fuchs, "National Health Insurance Revisited," *Health Affairs* 10(4), Winter 1991, 7–17.

Dan Goodgame, "This May Hurt a Bit," *Time* 143(20), May 16, 1994, 50.

Jonathan Gruber and Larry Levitt, "Tax Subsidies for Health Insurance: Costs and Benefits," *Health Affairs* 19(1), January/February 2000, 72–85.

Jack Hadley and John Holahan, "How Much Medical Care Do the Uninsured Use, and Who Pays for It?" *Health Affairs – Web Exclusive*, 12 February 2003, W3–66 to W3–81.

Jack Hadley, Earl P. Steinberg, and Judith Feder, "Comparison of Uninsured and Privately Insured Hospital Patients: Conditions on Admission, Resource Use, and Outcome," *Journal of the American Medical Association* 265(3), January 16, 1991, 374–379.

Health Insurance Association of America (HIAA), *Long-Term Care Insurance in 2000*–2001, Washington, DC: HIAA, January 2003.

_____, *Source Book of Health Insurance Data 1996*, Washington, DC: HIAA, 1997.

W. David Helms, Anne K. Gauthier, and Daniel M. Campion, "Mending the Flaws in the Small-Group Market," *Health Affairs* 11(2), Summer 1992, 7–27.

Richard Kronik and Todd Gilmer, "Explaining the Decline in Health Insurance Coverage, 1979–1995," *Health Affairs* 18(2), March/April 1999, 30–47.

Katharine Levit et al., "National Health Expenditures, 1993," *Health Care Financing Review* 16(1), Fall 1994, 247–281.

Willard G. Manning, Joseph P. Newhouse, Naihua Duan, Emmett B. Keeler, Arleen Leibowitz, and M. Susan Marquis, "Health Insurance and the Demand for Medical Care: Evidence from a Randomized Experiment," *American Economic Review* 77(3), June 1987, 251–277.

Robert J. Mills and Shailesh Shandari, "Health Insurance Coverage in the United States: 2002," *Current Population Reports*, P60National Center for Policy Analysis (NCPA), "Are the Uninsured Freeloaders?" *Brief Analysis* No. 120, August 10, 1994.

Joseph Newhouse, *Free for All? Lessons from the RAND Health Insurance Experiment*, Santa Monica, CA: RAND Corporation, 1993.

Mark V. Pauly, "Is Cream Skimming a Problem for the Competitive Medical Market?" *Journal of Health Economics* 3(1), April 1984, 87–95.

_____, "The Economics of Moral Hazard: Comment," *American Economic Review* 58(2), June 1968, 531–538.

_____, "Taxation, Health Insurance, and Market Failure in the Medical Economy," *Journal of Economic Literature* 24(2), June 1986, 629–675.

Thomas Rice, *The Economics of Health Reconsidered*, Chicago, IL: Health Administration Press, 1998.

Pamela Farley Short, "Counting and Characterizing the Uninsured," *ERIU Working Paper* 2, University of Michigan, Economic Research Institute on the Uninsured, December 2001.

_____ and Deborah R. Graefe, "Battery-Powered Health Insurance? Stability in Coverage of the Uninsured," *Health Affairs* 22(6), November/December 2003, 244–255.

George Stigler, "The Economics of Information," *Journal of Political Economy* 69(3), June 1961.

Katherine Swartz, John Marcotte, and Timothy D. McBride, "Personal Characteristics and Spells without Health Insurance, *Inquiry* 30(1), Spring 1993a, 64–76.

_____, "Spells without Health Insurance: The Distribution of Durations when Left-Censored Spells are Included," *Inquiry* 30(1), Spring 1993b, 77–83.

Melissa A. Thomasson, "The Importance of Group Coverage: How Tax Policy Shaped U.S. Health Insurance," NBER Working Paper 7543, Cambridge, MA: National Bureau of Economic Research, February 2000.

Roger Thompson, "Going, Going, . . .Gone?" *Nation's Business* 81(7), July 1993, 24.

U.S. Chamber of Commerce, *2000 Employee Benefits Study,* Washington, DC: U.S. Chamber of Commerce, 2000.

Congressional Budget Office, "How Many People Lack Health Insurance and for How Long?" A CBO Paper, Washington, DC: Congress of the United States, May 2003.

J. S. Weissman, R. Stern, S. L. Fielding, and A. M. Epstein, "Delayed Access to Health Care: Risk Factors, Reasons, and Consequences," *Annals of Internal Medicine* 114, 1991, 325–331.

S. H. Zuvekas and R. M. Weinick, "Changes in Access to Care, 1977–1996: The Role of Health Insurance," *Health Services Research* 34(1 Pt 2), 1999, 271–279.

CHAPTER 7

Managed Care

As recently as 1975, almost the entire insured population in the United States received medical care services financed under traditional indemnity insurance arrangements. With favorable legislation in place, the 1980s witnessed major growth in managed care along with other related changes in medical care financing and delivery. These changes were, in part, a response to the high and rising cost of medical care and the increase in the number of Americans receiving their health insurance coverage from self-insured group plans.

Managed care is a term used to describe any number of contractual arrangements that integrate the financing and delivery of medical care. Purchasers (usually employers) contract with a select group of providers to deliver a specific package of medical benefits at a predetermined price. The wide variety of financing and delivery arrangements in the market today makes it difficult to classify managed care organizations precisely, thus complicating attempts to evaluate the efficiency and effectiveness of managed care.

The initial popularity of managed care was due to the perception that it could provide significant cost savings over the more traditional fee-for-service delivery mechanism. Between 1984 and 1991, the average health insurance premium per employee increased 119 percent. At the same time, the overall increase in the price level, as measured by the change in the consumer price index, was 31 percent. With insurance premiums outpacing inflation by almost four to one, the pressure to control costs mounted accordingly.

The traditional managed care arrangement has been the health maintenance organization (HMO). There were only 37 HMOs nationwide in 1970 with 3 million enrollees, less than 2 percent of the population. Enrollment peaked in 2000 at 84.4 million, and by 2006 it had settled at 72.7 million, approximately one-fourth of the population. Table 7.1 provides enrollment information for the nation's HMOs from 1970 through 2006.

Numerous differences mark the way managed care is organized: how physicians are paid, how financial risk is shared, whether physicians see only managed care patients, or whether they also see fee-for-service patients. This chapter will focus on the historical development of managed care and its emergence as an important element of the health care delivery system in the United States and worldwide.

We begin our discussion with a brief history of the emergence of managed care as an alternative to traditional fee-for-service delivery, and then we turn to the basic categories of managed care. We will also look at the cost-saving features of managed care and the practical evidence that this form of delivery actually saves money. Finally, the future of managed care will be discussed.

Table 7.1: Enrollment in Health Maintenance Organizations, 1970–2006

Year	Enrollment (in millions)	Percentage of the Population
1970	3.0	1.5
1980	9.1	4.0
1985	21.0	7.9
1990	33.3	13.4
1995	50.9	19.4
2000	84.4	30.0
2005	69.4	23.4
2006	72.7	24.5

Source: *Health United States, 2007: with Chartbook on Trends in the Health of Americans,* 2007.

HISTORY OF MANAGED CARE

Although the concept of the prepaid medical plan can be traced back to the nineteenth century, the first health plans with the organizational structure of today's HMO were formed in the 1920s (Friedman, 1996). Industrialist Henry J. Kaiser organized one of the first managed care plans. Kaiser-Permanente, the largest managed care organization in the country today, was created to provide medical care in geographically isolated areas of northern California. Physicians working on a fixed salary provided medical care for employees of Kaiser's steel mill and shipyards, a group of relatively high-risk workers, in Kaiser-owned clinics and hospitals. The idea of using HMOs for cost-containment purposes was not an issue at the time and would not become one until the 1970s.

When Kaiser opened the plan to other patient groups in 1947, the HMO concept was still untested in the greater community. By 2007, Kaiser-Permanente was the nation's largest not-for-profit HMO, serving 8.7 million members in nine states and the District of Columbia. Kaiser medical facilities included 32 medical centers, 416 physicians' offices, and 13,729 physicians. The pioneering efforts of Kaiser and others on the West Coast served as a model for prepaid medical care.

Many physicians were opposed to the concept of prepaid medical care, calling it "contract medicine," and they organized to ban the practice entirely. Their efforts were successful in slowing the growth of managed care, limiting the number of HMOs nationally to less than 40 throughout the 1960s (Gruber, Shadle, and Polich, 1988). As recently as 1980, fewer than 10 million Americans were enrolled in managed care plans, 4 percent of the population.

Passage of Medicare and Medicaid in 1965 led to more direct federal involvement in the provision of medical care and a growing political concern for escalating costs. Research by InterStudy proposed a health maintenance strategy based on the HMO as an alternative to traditional fee-for-service medicine.[1] Despite strong opposition from provider groups and the American Medical Association, the Nixon administration embraced the concept of the **prepaid group practice** to control medical care costs.

Kaiser-Permanente is the largest not-for-profit health maintenance organization in the country, with 8.7 million members.

http://www.kaiserpermanente.org

Group Health Cooperative of Puget Sound, the nation's sixth largest not-for-profit HMO, serves over 700,000 members in the northwestern United States.

http://www.ghc.org

prepaid group practice
An arrangement through which a group contracts with a number of providers who agree to provide medical services to members of the group for a fixed, capitated payment.

---

[1] InterStudy is a research and policy institute headed by Paul M. Ellwood. For years, Ellwood invited a group of individuals interested in health policy to his Jackson Hole, Wyoming, retreat to discuss medical care reform. Out of this gathering, details of Alain Enthoven's proposal for managed competition emerged. Collectively, the group is referred to as the Jackson Hole group.

Working with congressional leaders, primarily from the Democrat Party, Richard Nixon was successful in passing legislation that defined the HMO, including a list of covered benefits, pricing and enrollment practices, physician organization, and requirements regarding financial risk. The Health Maintenance Organization Act of 1973 provided over $364 million in subsidies to nonprofit groups to establish HMOs. Even with this funding, the government fell far short of its goal of establishing 1,700 HMOs and enrolling 40 million participants by 1976. The episode sent a clear message to the medical industry: The federal government was concerned with the high cost of medical care and was willing to intervene through the legislative process. But the real lesson was that government action alone (short of overt coercion through mandatory participation) is not sufficient to push people into prepaid health plans. That task was not accomplished until corporate America began its move to managed care as a cost-control measure in the late 1980s. It took another decade of rising costs to emphasize the role of cost-effective behavior and spur the development and expansion of managed care arrangements through the private sector.

TYPES OF MANAGED CARE PLANS

Managed care has many of the aspects of the familiar all-you-can-eat buffet—a single price, paid in advance, good for everything on the menu. Just as the buffet must price its product based on the expected behavior of would-be diners, managed care must be sure that its pricing is sufficient to cover all the medical needs of its enrollees. One way the buffet can guarantee the "right" price is by offering plenty of the low-cost basics and limiting the availability of expensive entrees. Similarly, a successful pricing strategy in managed care must provide easy access to low-cost primary and preventive care as a way to discourage the use of expensive services, including specialty care and hospitalization.

Enlisting the services of a buffet supervisor, a "gatekeeper" to steer diners to the cheaper alternatives and limit access to expensive entrees, may not be harmful to most consumers. In the case of the buffet, a diet of soup and salad may be healthier than red meat and potatoes in the long run. But those diners accustomed to meat and potatoes will find the transition painful. And those with special dietary needs may actually end up worse off if their choices are limited.

Most diners understand the rules of the all-you-can-eat buffet. They do not pay $8.95 at the local eatery expecting steak and lobster. But expectations are much different in the U.S. medical care sector. Therein lies the challenge to managed care. Americans have developed a taste for unlimited access to expensive treatments. Traditional fee-for-service medicine financed through indemnity insurance is like dining with a group of co-workers on a business trip. Instead of ordering from the menu and paying separately, one member of the group agrees to pay the bill using her expense account. In other words, the boss is now paying for the meal and individual accountability is virtually nonexistent. In this situation, the incentive structure encourages overeating. We tend to be more extravagant when someone else pays the bill. In other words, we seldom practice economizing behavior when someone else will benefit from our prudent actions.

Typical managed care arrangements include health maintenance organizations (HMOs), preferred provider organizations (PPOs), **point-of-service (POS)** plans, and managed indemnity plans. Traditional managed care restricts patient choice and controls utilization of medical services more closely than managed indemnity plans. Some plans, including closed-panel HMOs, pay only for care received through an established network of providers. Others, including most PPOs and POS plans,

http://

The America's Health Insurance Plans (AHIP) represents more than 1,300 HMOs and other network-based plans, serving over 200 million Americans nationwide.

http://www.ahip.org

Key Concept 4
Self-Interest

Key Concept 7
Competition

Key Concept 4
Self-Interest

point-of-service plan (POS)
A hybrid managed care plan that combines the features of a prepaid plan and a fee-for-service plan. Enrollees use network physicians with minimal out-of-pocket expenses and may choose to go out of the network by paying a higher coinsurance rate.

group-model HMO
A group of physicians—often a large, multispecialty group practice—that agrees to provide medical care to a defined patient group, usually the employees of the corporation, in return for a fixed per capita fee or for discounted fees.

staff-model HMO
A managed care organization that serves as both payer and provider, owns its own facilities, and employs its own physicians.

network-model HMO
A managed care organization that contracts with several different providers, including physicians' practices and hospitals, to make a full range of medical services available to its enrollees.

Individual Practice Association (IPA)
An organized group of health care providers that offers medical services to a specified group of enrollees of a health plan.

practice guideline
A specific statement about the appropriate course of treatment that should be taken for patients with given medical conditions.

offer options for enrollees to obtain medical care outside the established network, but at a higher out-of-pocket costs to enrollees.

Although precise definitions are difficult, all managed care plans are designed to limit the high levels of utilization frequently found in traditional indemnity insurance plans. In the strictest sense of the term, *managed care* refers to any health plan that directs its enrollees to a panel of providers who have agreed to follow established guidelines to control utilization and cost. In the broadest sense of the term, it attempts to monitor and direct the use of health services, thereby reducing health care costs. In either case, the goal is to manage utilization to varying degrees by controlling both the patient and provider sides of the market.

Health Maintenance Organizations (HMOs)

The five recognized types of HMOs are: 1) group model, 2) staff model, 3) network model, 4) Independent Practice Association (IPA), and 5) direct contract.[2] In the **group-model HMO**, the health benefit intermediary, usually a private sector corporation, contracts with a large, multispecialty group practice to provide medical care to a defined patient population, usually the employees of the corporation. In the **staff-model HMO**, physicians are employees of the HMO. Their incomes are usually paid in the form of a fixed salary but may include supplemental payments based on some measure of performance. The **network-model HMO** utilizes contracts with several different providers, including physicians' practices and hospitals, to make a full range of medical services available to its enrollees.

The **Individual Practice Association (IPA)** contracts with individual physicians or small group practices to provide care to enrolled members. Among all variants of the managed care model, the IPA has been the fastest growing over the past decade. Payment for treating enrolled members is based on a negotiated fee-for-service schedule or a capitated payment, a fixed amount paid in advance. IPA plans select providers for various reasons that may include practice location, practice style, quality of care, and willingness to comply with established **practice guidelines**. Many physicians participating in IPAs contract with one or more managed care plans and, at the same time, maintain their own private practice where they treat non-HMO patients on a fee-for-service basis. Finally, the mixed-model HMO combines features of the other models.

ISSUES IN MEDICAL CARE DELIVERY

VivaHealth: Marketing HMOs to Ethnic Communities

It is a common practice for the makers of consumer products to tailor their marketing efforts to specific demographic and ethnic groups. Marketing Virginia Slims cigarettes to women and Colt 45 Malt Liquor to the African-American community are just two examples that come to mind. Now it seems that the health care industry is using the same approach to market its services directly to distinct groups in the various ethnic communities.

continued

---

[2] **Those interested in a more comprehensive discussion of the types of HMOs are directed to Kongstvedt (1997) and Glied (1999).**

The Latino community has been the target of an all-out effort by two Southern California HMOs. It took the founders of VivaHealth seven years to convince providers, investors, and regulators that the concept of medical care tailored for a particular ethnic group was viable. Beginning its marketing campaign in May 1994, VivaHealth became one of the first HMOs nationwide to exclusively target the Latino community.

VivaHealth has assembled a network of providers, many of whom are Latino and almost all are Spanish-speaking. VivaHealth is relying on its physicians' experience in treating members of the Latino community. An understanding of the culture and an ability to communicate are seen as major marketing advantages.

Another California HMO, FHP Health Care, has established a network of providers serving ethnic communities in East Los Angeles, including Vietnamese, Korean, Cambodian, and Chinese. Ethnic marketing is rapidly becoming a way to distinguish among providers in a market that is becoming increasingly competitive. Increased competition among providers is forcing everyone to consider more cost-effective ways of delivering medical care.

Ethnic patients present problems for providers who do not understand the culture or the language. Patients cannot follow instructions they do not understand, and providers tend to overtreat when they do not understand what the patient is trying to tell them.

Understanding the language is not the only advantage offered by these niche players. An appreciation for the unique culture is also important. Therefore, providers in other states with a large foreign-born population — including Colorado, New Mexico, Texas, and Florida — are getting into the act.

With almost 10 percent of the U.S. population foreign-born, these ethnic communities are becoming an important niche market in the medical industry. Many of these ethnic groups, including Latinos, Vietnamese, Cambodian, Korean, and Chinese, are good health risks. They are younger, healthier, and more stable than the general population. By setting uniform premiums according to ethnic group, HMOs will be able to charge about 10 percent less than the lowest premiums currently in the market. The lesson is simple: Specialization leads to cost savings through a more efficient allocation of resources. But success in the marketplace will depend on the continued ability to use this blended risk rating (experience rating within a defined ethnic community), which in turn will depend on what kind of health care reform emerges from Congress.

Source: Mary Chris Jaklevic, "Programs, Ad Campaigns Reach Out to Members of Ethnic Communities," *Modern Healthcare*, August 1, 1994, 32; and Tim W. Ferguson, "An Ethnic-Flavored HMO vs. Clinton's Cookie-Cutter," *Wall Street Journal*, February 8, 1994, A17.

Key Concept 7
Efficiency

Key Concept 8
Market Failure

Preferred Provider Organizations (PPOs)

The preferred provider organization (PPO) is emerging as one of the more popular types of managed care plans. The PPO is a health care organization that serves as intermediary or broker between the purchaser of medical care and the provider. The PPO establishes a network of providers (physicians, hospitals, dentists, pharmacies, rehabilitative services, home health care, etc.) who agree to provide medical services to a specific group of enrollees at discounted rates. In most cases, providers must agree to a set of utilization controls—that is, practice guidelines—in order to be included on the preferred list. Despite the lower fees and utilization controls, participating providers view the arrangement as a means of securing a steady volume of patients. Even though enrollees are free to use any provider, incentives and disincentives are used to encourage them to choose from the preferred list. Enrollees find their out-of-pocket costs to be higher, in the form of higher deductibles and copayments, when they receive care from providers who are not on the preferred list.

The typical arrangement provides 5 to 30 percent discounts from normal charges for physicians' services and 10 to 15 percent discounts on hospital services. The patient is usually required to make a modest copayment when using preferred physicians. When using nonpreferred physicians, however, the patient is subject to a deductible and a 20 to 40 percent coinsurance payment. Often a small copayment is required when using a preferred hospital and a much larger one when not.

The PPO typically lacks the strict cost-control features of the closed-panel HMO. With no risk sharing, providers have no direct incentive to control utilization in the short run. The key to controlling costs is not the discounts offered by providers, but the selection of cost-conscious providers and the threat of dropping any physician who refuses to follow the practice guidelines established by the plan.

Point-of-Service (POS) Plans

The most recent ingredient in the managed care alphabet soup is the point-of-service (POS) plan. The POS plan is a mixed-model health plan. It incorporates many of the cost-control features of HMOs along with the provider-choice features of PPOs. Enrollees are given the option of choosing among various types of plans: HMO, PPO, or managed indemnity. The choice of plan, however, does not have to be made at the time of enrollment. It is made at the point of service, each time the enrollee seeks medical treatment. POS enrollees choose a primary care "gatekeeper" to coordinate all network-based care. Offering incentives in the form of better benefits and lower copayments encourages use of the network providers.

Hybrid Varieties

closed panel
A designated network of providers that serve the recipients of a health care plan. Patients are not allowed to choose a provider outside the network.

utilization review
An evaluation of the appropriateness and efficiency of prescribed medical services and procedures, including hospital admissions, lengths of stay, and discharge procedures. A utilization review may be conducted concurrently or retrospectively.

The competitive response to the high cost of medical care has resulted in a blurring of the distinctions among the different types of medical care arrangements. Traditional indemnity insurance plans have taken on the characteristics of managed care plans, including features intended to limit physician autonomy and patient choice. Health maintenance organizations have added out-of-plan options for patients who want to consult providers who are not on the **closed panel**, or preferred list. As time passes, it is becoming more and more difficult to distinguish among the various types of arrangements. Indemnity insurance plans are incorporating utilization management methods to control costs, and HMOs are offering out-of-plan options to increase flexibility.

Network-based managed care—including HMOs, PPOs, and POS plans—is beginning to dominate health care delivery in the United States. Managed care networks are similar to group model HMOs but with one major difference: Instead of contracting with one multispecialty group practice, the network plan contracts with several. Therein lies the primary challenge to network-based care—the very success of the network depends on the ability to control costs. Without rigorous policies to control utilization, including provider risk sharing, **utilization review**, and limiting access to nonpreferred providers, such organizations will have a difficult time surviving.

Provisions included in the Medicare Modernization Act passed in 2005 have paved the way for the development of consumer-directed health plans (CDHPs). The CDHP is characterized by a higher deductible than would normally be found in a typical policy: $1,500 instead of $500. The policy is based on either a health savings account (HSA) or a health reimbursement account (HRA), in which individuals set aside pretax dollars designated to cover routine care. These plans are commonly offered by large employers to promote consumerism.

Most private sector employees who have group health insurance coverage are enrolled in some type of managed care plan. Table 7.2 provides dramatic evidence of the popularity of managed care for private sector employees. In 1979, over 98 percent of all group insurance policies were written under traditional indemnity insurance arrangements with few restrictions on choice of provider or service options. As medical care costs escalated in the 1980s, employers sought to reduce costs by moving away from traditional fee-for-service care to managed care. By 2000, less than 10 percent of the private sector was covered by traditional indemnity plans. Employees seem to be moving into the less restrictive managed care option, the PPO. Since 1993 the percentage of employees enrolled in PPOs has risen from 27 percent to 61 percent. After steady growth throughout the past decade, HMO enrollment dropped in 2007 to 23 percent of all covered employees. POS membership has fallen from a 1998 high of 19 percent to 8 percent. Only recently has the CDHP movement gained momentum, reaching 5 percent of the covered population by 2007. Just as employees moved out of traditional indemnity plans in the 1990s, many consider this move into CDHP as the first wave of consumerism in the twenty-first century.

Table 7.2:   Health Care Coverage for Private Employees with Group Insurance Percentages by Type of Plan

Type of Plan	1979	1990	1993	1995	1998	2002	2005	2007
Traditional Indemnity	98	62	48	29	13	6	3	3
Managed Care	2	38	52	71	87	94	97	97
HMO	2	20	19	27	32	31	25	23
PPO	*	13	27	29	36	49	61	61
POS	*	5	7	15	19	14	10	8
CDHP	*	*	*	*	*	*	1	5

Source: Iglehart (1992, Table 1) and Mercer Consulting (2007).

* No data available.

THE THEORY OF MANAGED CARE COST SAVING

The theoretical underpinnings of managed care suggest that medical care costs and spending may be affected by changing patient utilization, physicians' practice styles, and the introduction of new technology. Managed care arrangements are similar to traditional indemnity health insurance in many ways. A premium is charged to cover a prescribed set of medical benefits. Both use demand-side cost-sharing provisions, such as deductibles and coinsurance, to reduce moral hazard.

In addition, managed care utilizes a combination of provider-side provisions to control moral hazard and the spending associated with it. These provider-side provisions include 1) selection of providers, 2) cost-sharing arrangements, and 3) practice guidelines and utilization reviews.

Key Concept 9
Market Failure

Selection of Providers

To varying degrees, managed care limits the patient's choice of provider for a given medical service. The limits include the use of gatekeepers, closed panels, and preferred providers. A gatekeeper is a physician responsible for providing all primary medical care and coordinating access to high-cost hospital and specialty care. Patients who wish to see a specialist must first get a referral from their primary care gatekeeper. A closed panel further limits a patient's choice of physician to a list of participating providers. To be part of a panel, physicians must agree to a set of standards established by the sponsoring organization. Networks that contract with **any willing provider** ensure enrollees a wide choice of physicians, but exclusive networks result in better cost controls. The criteria for inclusion vary depending on the selectivity of the plan. At minimum, providers are usually board certified, professionally accredited, and meet medical liability standards. More selective networks consider practice styles and use only those providers who meet established goals for cost-effective use of resources. The preferred provider organization allows the patient to choose a provider who is not part of the panel. Patients who use physicians who are not part of the panel usually pay higher coinsurance rates, further discouraging off-panel utilization.

any willing provider
A situation in which a managed care organization allows any medical provider to become part of the network of providers for the covered group. Often, state law requires this practice.

Cost-Sharing Arrangements

The method of reimbursement is an important mechanism in controlling costs. Managed care utilizes various reimbursement schemes with the common goal of shifting some of the financial risk to providers. Shifting risk discourages overutilization of services, primarily the use of expensive technology, prescription drugs, referrals to specialists, and inpatient hospital procedures.

Many HMOs and some PPOs contract with primary care physicians using prospective payment or capitation—lump-sum payments per enrollee determined in advance. Prepayment shifts the financial risk to the providers. Instead of being paid on a per-service basis, primary care physicians receive a fixed payment determined in advance to provide all the medically necessary primary care for a specific group of patients. Some managed care plans withhold a percentage of the authorized payment to ensure that providers control utilization and cost.[3] Primary care physicians serve as gatekeepers and are subject to strict budgets for hospital services, specialty referrals, and prescription drugs for their covered patients. Physicians who provide care within the predetermined budgets receive bonuses. Those who do not are penalized by forfeiting part or all of their withholdings to the plan. This risk-sharing arrangement provides strong incentives to physicians to control utilization.

Key Concept 4
Self-Interest

Figure 7.1 provides a schematic depiction of the allocation of premiums for a typical capitated arrangement. In this example, the primary care physicians serve as gatekeepers to more advanced services. Enrollees, most likely employees working at the same firm, are charged a premium of $100 per member per

---

[3] In the past these withholdings have been as high as 50 percent of the capitated payment. Recently, more aggressive regulations have brought the amount of capitated payment at risk to more manageable levels.

Figure 7.1: Typical Allocation of a $100 Premium under a Capitated Contract

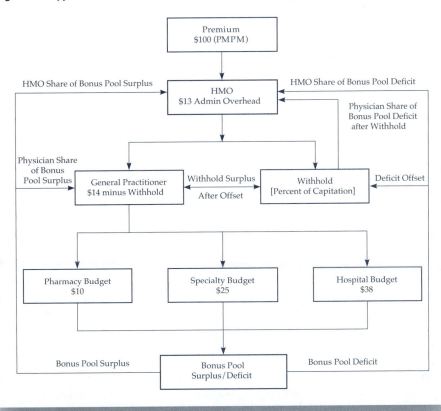

month (PMPM) for a defined package of medical benefits. The HMO uses $13 of the PMPM payment to cover operating expenses, administrative overhead, and profit. The remainder goes into four separate categories: primary care, pharmaceuticals, specialty care, and hospital care. The general practitioner serving as gatekeeper receives a capitated payment of $14 PMPM for each enrollee who designates him or her as their primary care physician. Some plans withhold a percentage of this capitated payment as insurance against expense overruns in the other three budgetary categories. The pharmacy budget receives $10 PMPM, the specialty budget receives $25 PMPM, and the hospital budget receives $38 PMPM.[4] A bonus pool is created with the surpluses or deficits in each expense category. The providers and HMO share surpluses and deficits according to a specified formula, often on a 50/50 basis. Bonus-pool deficits are covered by the physician's withholding account. Any surplus in the withholding account is paid to the physician directly. If the physician's share of the bonus pool deficit is greater than the funds in the physician's withholding account, he or she is responsible for reimbursing the HMO for the difference. Recent changes in the bonus arrangement have added positive inducements for physicians to modify their practice patterns. These inducements include a target percentage of the enrolled children receiving their inoculations in a timely manner, a target percentage of enrolled women

POLICY ISSUE

Do risk-sharing contracts affect the quality of care provided? What percentage of a physician's income should be at risk?

---

[4] The numbers used in this example are representative of the typical allocation of a $100 premium. If the premium is higher, $150 for example, the appropriate adjustment would be to multiply each number by 1.5.

POLICY ISSUE

When patients are fully insured, the therapeutic benefit of some covered services may be relatively small compared to the cost.

receiving appropriately timed cancer screenings, and specific scores on patient satisfaction surveys. Mixed bonus arrangements are much more popular than those based solely on cost considerations.

Providers paid according to the traditional fee-for-service arrangement are more likely to recommend and perform services that are reimbursed. When given an option, providers are more likely to perform services that are reimbursed more generously relative to their resource cost. Because an insured patient's share of the total cost of care is relatively small, some services are provided that have little marginal value.

In contrast, the managed care organization structures the financial arrangements to shift some of the financial risk onto physicians. Providers are given incentives to practice in a more cost-effective manner. When a cheaper care option exists, providers are rewarded for choosing it. Such an arrangement changes the incentive structure completely. Instead of encouraging the provision of too many services, as is the case with fee-for-service payment, this type of risk-sharing arrangement can, if not properly monitored, create pressures to do just the opposite and provide too few services.

Practice Guidelines and Utilization Review

Selection of providers based on conservative practice patterns and the sharing of financial risk is often insufficient to control medical care expenditures. Most medical plans encourage providers to follow practice guidelines to directly control clinical decisions. Practice guidelines are clinical rules developed to encourage providers to evaluate the marginal benefit of prescribed care more carefully. Through "evidence-based" medicine—the systematic monitoring and evaluation of treatment methods—managed care plans try to determine the relative efficacy of treatment options and their resulting cost effectiveness. Managed care is quick to adopt cost-saving innovations but slow to adopt innovations that increase costs (Baker and Phibbs, 2000).

More than 90 percent of all health plans, whether indemnity insurance or managed care, utilize some form of utilization review. The most popular technique for controlling utilization is to require some type of authorization for the use of hospital services: a preadmission review, concurrent review, or retrospective review. In addition, second surgical opinions and **case management** are used to control costs associated with surgeries.

Utilization management focuses primarily on services provided in the hospital sector. Preadmission review establishes the appropriateness of a procedure. Either the admitting physician or the patient must receive approval prior to the hospital admission. Often a maximum length of stay is specified at the same time. Concurrent review utilizes established guidelines to determine whether a hospital stay should be continued. Retrospective review examines the appropriateness of care after it has been completed. Inappropriate care is recognized, and providers who deviate from the established standards are identified.

Many managed care plans require second surgical opinions before recommended surgeries can be performed. This method of utilization control forces the physician who recommends the surgery to seek the opinion of a second physician before authorization is granted. Another commonly used utilization review technique is case management. In situations where costs and risks are high, case management is used to monitor resource use and thus lower the overall cost of treatment. A case manager, usually a member of the hospital nursing staff, often coordinates hospital care for costly conditions, such as coronary artery bypass surgery and organ transplantation.

case management
A method of coordinating the provision of medical care for patients with specific high-cost diagnoses such as cancer and heart disease.

The National Committee for Quality Assurance (NCQA) is an independent, not-for-profit organization that serves as the accrediting agency for the nation's managed care plans. NCQA maintains HEDIS, the standard report card used to rate and compare managed care plans. Links to HEDIS may be found at the NCQA Web site.

http://www.ncqa.org

Overall, managed care plans use these three mechanisms—authorization review, second opinion, and case management—to varying degrees and with different rates of success. The ability to control moral hazard depends on the combination of features utilized and how strictly they are applied. These mechanisms can also affect the choice of technology by encouraging less technology-intensive practice styles. When patients and providers are required to share in the costs of care, the use of expensive technologies is discouraged (Cutler and Sheiner, 1998).

ISSUES IN MEDICAL CARE DELIVERY

Evaluating the Effectiveness of HMOs

The use of report cards to measure performance and ensure accountability is not new. Students receive grades from their teachers, employees get performance reviews from their supervisors, and publicly held corporations are evaluated daily by the stock market. One of the most interesting trends in managed care is the movement to direct accountability through the use of a report card.

Evaluating the quality of a health plan is not simple. Not only do health experts disagree on what to measure and how to measure it, many question the usefulness of nationwide standardized reporting. A key element of President Clinton's 1994 health care reform proposal called for a federal regulatory committee to specify quality indicators that every health plan would have to measure. The demise of the Clinton plan and the emergence of a Republican majority in the Congress made the creation of a federal agency to regulate quality unlikely in the near future. But this has not stopped private organizations from developing and using their own performance measures.

Notable among efforts to develop quality scorecards is the Health Plan Employer Data Information Set (HEDIS) project developed by the National Committee for Quality Assurance (NCQA), an independent organization based in Washington, DC, that accredits health maintenance organizations. HEDIS 3.0 is a 70-item survey measuring health plan quality and performance. The instrument is an attempt to develop a standard reporting format for the nation's managed care organizations.

The elements of the typical report card include quality of service, patient access and satisfaction, membership and utilization of services, financial stability, and descriptive information on the plan's management. The quality-of-service category measures the health plan's performance in delivering specific services. This category includes: (1) preventive services, such as childhood immunizations, cholesterol screening, mammography screening, and cervical cancer screening; (2) prenatal care, including first trimester care, incidence of low–birth-weight babies, and cesarean-section rate; (3) treatment for chronic illness, such as hospital admission rate for asthma patients and diabetic patients receiving yearly eye exams; (4) mental health; and (5) substance abuse.

Membership and utilization data include length of hospital stay, outpatient visits, and enrollment turnover. Financial stability is assessed by such characteristics as performance, liquidity, efficiency, and statutory compliance. Access is measured by the ease of getting appointments.

As the scorecard movement grows, dozens of HMOs and PPOs nationwide are scrambling to develop and issue their own report cards. Employers

continued

are forming alliances to produce regional report cards (most notable among these coalitions are the North Central Texas and the New England HEDIS coalition). The HMOs serving the Federal Employees Health Benefits Program regularly survey employee satisfaction. Even national magazines such as *Newsweek* and *Consumer Reports* have contributed with surveys of their own.

Still many problems have yet to be overcome in collecting reliable data and interpreting their results. Survey techniques can be manipulated to improve a plan's scores, and the phrasing of a question can skew survey results. "How do you rate your health plan?" gets more critical responses than "How satisfied are you with your health plan?" Phone surveys yield more favorable responses than mail-in surveys. Information collected in the middle of the year tends to be more favorable than end-of-year responses.

As more groups get into the survey business, the need for standard definitions and processes becomes more critical if meaningful comparisons are to emerge. Even while HEDIS is gaining widespread acceptance because of its standardized definitions and reporting standards, many plans are balking at the thought of an independent group administering surveys to members chosen at random.

Source: Norma Harris, "Are Health Plans Making the Grade?" *Business and Health* 12(6), June 1994, 22; Paul J. Kenkel, "Health Plans Face Pressure to Find 'Report Card' Criteria that Will Make the Grade," *Modern Healthcare,* January 10, 1994, 41; and George Anders, "Polling Quirks Give HMOs Healthy Ratings," *Wall Street Journal*, August 27, 1996, B1.

EVIDENCE OF MANAGED CARE COST SAVINGS

Some evidence suggests that managed care offers employers cost savings over the traditional indemnity option. A survey by the consulting firm William M. Mercer, Inc., estimated that all forms of managed care had lower average premiums than traditional indemnity insurance in 2002. By the 2007 survey, traditional indemnity premiums were no longer reported. In 2007 POS premiums averaged $7,714, PPO premiums were $7,352, and HMO premiums were $7,120. Traditionally, HMO premiums were always the lowest, but in 2007, CDHP premiums were $5,970—almost 20 percent lower than those of HMOs (Mercer, 2007).

The story is similar when comparing single and family coverage. A survey by the Kaiser Family Foundation (2007) estimated the average annual premium across all plans for a single person to be $4,479, and for a family, $12,106. For the family, PPO premiums averaged $12,443, HMO premiums were $11,879, and POS premiums were $11,588. Family CDHP premiums were lower than other coverage, averaging $10,693. The story was essentially the same for single coverage. PPO premiums averaged $4,638, POS premiums were $4,337, HMO premiums were $4,299, and CDHP premiums were $3,869.

Empirical evidence supporting managed care's cost savings is complicated by the difficulty in classifying plans according to their cost-saving features. The extensive combination of features utilized by the various plans makes it difficult to control for the differences, making comparisons tricky. By designing benefit packages that appeal to low users, plans can successfully segment their market and avoid high users. Thus, cost differences across plans may be a phenomenon due in part to patient selection.

Empirical research on the effectiveness of managed care has examined several important issues: selection bias, utilization of services, quality of care, and ability to control costs (Glied, 1999). Hellinger (1995) examined the differences between the characteristics of managed care and traditional indemnity insurance enrollees.

Overall, the research suggests that managed care plans attract a healthier group of enrollees than indemnity plans do. However, the evidence is mixed. It is difficult to determine how health differences affect utilization and cost because of differences in group characteristics (Newhouse, 1996).

A number of studies have attempted to estimate the difference in medical care utilization between managed care and traditional indemnity insurance. Luft (1981) conducted one of the earliest studies on HMO utilization. Using data from 1959 through 1975, he concluded that managed care plans had 10 to 40 percent lower costs per enrollee than conventional health plans such as Blue Cross. Although HMO enrollees experienced as many ambulatory visits, they had 25 to 45 percent fewer hospital days per capita. The reason was not shorter hospital stays but fewer admissions.

The most extensive study of the cost-saving potential of health maintenance organizations was the RAND Health Insurance Experiment (see Manning et al., 1984). This study avoided selection bias by randomly assigning individuals to a staff-model HMO or to one of several indemnity plans. The results of this study confirmed the cost-savings potential of managed care. The HMO had per capita costs that were 28 percent lower than the indemnity plan without cost sharing. This difference was due largely to 40 percent fewer hospital admissions and shorter hospital stays.

Miller and Luft (1994, 1997) analyzed more recent literature comparing HMO and fee-for-service costs. Their findings suggest that HMOs provide care comparable to traditional fee-for-service care at costs that are 10 to 15 percent lower. Cost savings are due to shorter hospital stays, fewer tests, and the use of less costly medical procedures. HMOs are able to accomplish these savings in spite of higher rates of physician office visits and more comprehensive benefits packages than fee-for-service plans.

A few studies have attempted to explain the cost-saving features of the newer forms of managed care, especially the network-based PPOs and POS plans. The results of these studies are mixed. Using data from the Medical Outcomes Study of 20,000 adult patients, Greenfield and colleagues (1992) found no statistically significant difference in four treatment categories between three types of managed care organizations and two fee-for-service arrangements.[5] Murray and colleagues (1992) examined two small, private group practices that treated both HMO and fee-for-service patients diagnosed with hypertension and found that HMO patients had fewer laboratory tests and consequently lower spending. Smith (1997) found that preferred provider plans reduced costs and Hosek, Marquis, and Wells (1990) found that they increased costs.

Overall, the evidence suggests that managed care can reduce health care spending, even after controlling for enrollee characteristics and type of plan. In most cases, these cost savings have been accomplished primarily through the initial reduction in hospital use. A great deal of resource savings was possible at first by simply reducing the rate of hospitalization. As summarized in Glied (1999), the evidence is far from conclusive, and the long-run cost-saving potential of managed care is still open to debate.

EVIDENCE OF QUALITY DIFFERENCES BETWEEN MANAGED CARE AND FEE-FOR-SERVICE CARE

Another issue explored by the empirical literature is whether there are quality differences between managed care and traditional fee-for-service care. Building on their earlier research, Miller and Luft (1997) summarized the research on

POLICY ISSUE

Managed care has been shown to be cost saving. But is there a quality trade-off?

---

[5] The four treatment categories were the percent of enrollees hospitalized, the use of office visits, the number of prescription drugs utilized, and the number of tests per patient per year.

the relationship between the type of plan and quality of care. In their review of 15 studies comparing quality of care, they found equal numbers of statistically significant positive and negative effects of managed care on quality. Four studies found significantly better quality in managed care, and four found worse. The others found insignificant differences or were inconclusive.

Robinson (2000) reviewed 24 studies, mostly from 1988 to 1995. The overall patterns identified by these studies suggested lower levels of utilization for managed care plans. In most cases managed care had fewer hospitalizations, shorter hospital stays, and lower levels of discretionary services. Another important difference was the relative emphasis on preventive care as evidenced by more diagnostic screening and testing among managed care plans. Once again Robinson found little conclusive evidence that managed care quality was lower than that found in fee-for-service plans.

Even though managed care has not decreased the overall effectiveness of care, certain vulnerable subpopulations—including older patients, sicker patients, and patients with low incomes—may have less favorable outcomes under managed care (Ware et al., 1996). Robinson (2000) identified five studies that compared quality of care for Medicare enrollees under fee-for-service and managed care plans. He found some evidence that managed care fared worse than fee-for-service, but most of the studies were inconclusive. Hellinger (1998) reported that managed care enrollees are less satisfied with their health plans than fee-for-service enrollees. Their lower levels of satisfaction resulted from difficulties in accessing specialized care, leaving enrollees with the perception that the overall quality of care was somewhat lower.

The strongest disincentive for providing quality care is for the sickest and costliest patients. Plans that provide quality care for their sickest patients will attract the sickest patients. At average premiums, this strategy leads to losses. If premiums are increased to cover higher costs, the plans lose enrollment.

To summarize, the empirical research does not provide definitive evidence about the overall effect of managed care on quality of care.

MANAGED CARE AND ITS PUBLIC IMAGE

Accustomed to the lack of restrictions in fee-for-service medicine, the American consumer has found it difficult to adjust to the limitations of managed care delivery. Everyone has a favorite HMO story they like to tell. The anecdotes abound. In the movie *As Good as It Gets*, Helen Hunt treats the viewing audience to a diatribe against a fictitious HMO that has denied care to her asthmatic son. The fee-for-service physician who finally diagnoses and treats him is viewed sympathetically. In light of the lack of evidence suggesting poor quality of care, why does managed care have such a poor public image?

Miller and Luft (1997) offer one possible answer to this question. They note the inevitable time lag for published research to get into print. The result of the delay is that the most recent research findings are not published in a timely manner. As a result, available research results do not relate well to current market conditions.

A second possible explanation relates to the diversity of managed care arrangements. Few studies to date have taken into consideration the newer types of managed care plans and the preponderance of cost-cutting rules and financial incentives that have affected providers since the early 1990s. Anecdotal evidence abounds, but lack of empirical research makes generalizations difficult. Additionally, many of the newer managed care organizations are for-profit in nature and thus

The accounting firm PriceWaterhouseCoopers maintains an active consulting practice in the managed care industry. Access survey and research information through their Web site at

http://www.pwc.com

place a greater emphasis on cost-saving strategies, which eventually may affect managed care quality. To the extent that they exist, these differences will not show up in the research for several years.

Finally, the role of medical providers in influencing public perception about managed care should not be ignored. Managed care is unpopular among health care professionals. Their clinical autonomy is challenged and their incomes are lower as a result of certain managed care strategies. When physicians complain loudly about the restrictions of managed care, their patients are likely to pick up on the discontent and mimic the criticism. This combination has resulted in a powerful force that has found a sympathetic hearing among policymakers at all levels of government.

ISSUES IN MEDICAL CARE DELIVERY

The Managed Care "Blues"

For over 70 years, Blue Cross and Blue Shield were virtually synonymous with health insurance. A network of 42 independent, community-based plans nationwide, they have dominated the industry, covering 85 million people, or about 30 percent of the total U.S. population. Their nationwide dominance does not accurately reflect their importance. In many states, a single Blue Cross entity covers over half the population.

These nonprofit companies, once considered the insurer of last resort for many, are rapidly changing their operating practices and drawing sharp criticism from some circles. Over the first half of the 1990s, the market had witnessed the private, for-profit health insurers transforming themselves into managed care companies. While the "Blues" have not reacted as quickly as many of the commercial insurers — such as Prudential, CIGNA, and Aetna — many have adopted an aggressive strategy for setting up managed care networks.

Simply by virtue of their size, the Blues are the largest providers of managed care in the country. The various Blues plans own 84 HMOs, 72 PPOs, and 66 POS plans, with over 52 million enrollees, or over two-thirds of the total number of enrollees in managed care plans nationwide. The system is also the largest provider of managed care to Medicare and Medicaid, enrolling 2.7 million in the two programs combined.

The most controversial step by plan administrators was the approval in July 1994 of a change in organizational status. Traditionally nonprofit in nature, the plans can now become for-profit entities or establish for-profit subsidiaries, which will affect more than their tax-exempt status: It will allow the Blues greater access to the private capital market and increase their ability to expand, which is essential if they are to be competitive with the commercial carriers.

No one is quite sure what the new health care environment will look like. But one thing is certain: The Blues, once dominant players in the health insurance market, are not sitting around, waiting to be swallowed up by the system. They are merging, partnering, and integrating; in general, they are preparing for the new managed care environment of the twenty-first century.

Source: Steven Findlay, "The Remaking of the Blues; Blue Cross and Blue Shield Association; Company Profile," *Business and Health* 12(8), August 1994, 37ff.

The Future of Managed Care

In many ways the future of medical care financing and delivery and the future of managed care are intimately connected. Patient dissatisfaction with managed care has led Congress to consider legislation to protect patients' rights and increase patient choice. Regardless of future legislative measures, however, some form of managed care will likely remain an important feature in the landscape of the medical care marketplace.

The nature of health care delivery has changed. As it became more competitive, the shift to more restrictive managed care gained momentum. With that shift came increased utilization management, increased use of capitation, and an expanding role for general practitioners. Ironically, in seeking market alternatives, the United States has turned to a private version of the government-run systems that prevail in the rest of the world. Problems are inherent in any system that emphasizes cost containment over quality and access. All fixed-budget systems, whether government run or privately run, are learning this lesson and finding that rationing becomes a necessary part of any system that does not give both patient and provider incentives to control costs.

Whether the new forms of managed care that have emerged in the market actually lower costs system wide is a question that has yet to be answered. Plans that are more restrictive in terms of patient choice and physician practice seem to have more cost-saving potential than those that allow extensive out-of-plan options. To make managed care more attractive, many of the more restrictive plans have had to increase flexibility by including more patient options, which translates directly into higher costs.

Despite the public relations problems that managed care has suffered in the United States, policymakers in many European countries are seriously considering adopting elements of managed care for their systems. Automated record keeping systems, clinical guidelines, and the gatekeeper system are just a few of the features of U.S.-style managed care that are being adopted in other countries. In fact, countries such as Israel, the Philippines, and Switzerland already have well-established managed care sectors. Other nations, such as Germany, New Zealand, and the United Kingdom, are using features of managed care to control costs and improve the quality of care. Even though it may not yet be called a movement, managed care giants such as Cigna and Aetna have significant investments in the world health market (Gentry, 1999).

The retreat from managed care in the United States will likely improve access, but it will also remove many of the constraints on spending that existed. With the supply-side constraints relaxed, the consumer may be left as the last defense against excess spending. The consumer is uniquely equipped to take on the role of the cost-conscious decision maker, provided that the appropriate incentives are in place. An exclusively consumer-driven health care system is unlikely. Other stakeholders—payers, providers, politicians, and employers—will continue to influence decision making. It is difficult to predict what the future system will look like, but one thing is certain: if the trend of escalating costs continues, another consumer backlash will occur and with it an increased willingness to support more structure in the way we make medical care decisions.

As the focus of health care delivery has shifted, there have been casualties. Open-ended fee-for-service financed by traditional indemnity insurance is well down the road to extinction. The wealthy will always have access to fee-for-service care, but maintaining that option for all Americans will be difficult, if not impossible.

SUMMARY AND CONCLUSIONS

In this chapter we have examined how managed care emerged as the alternative payment and delivery mechanism to traditional fee-for-service indemnity insurance. What began as an experiment expanded in the 1990s, and now more than 90 percent of all Americans with insurance are covered under a managed care plan.

Legitimately viewed as an economic success, managed care, for all practical purposes, can be considered a sociopolitical failure. Promising comprehensive benefits at lower premiums, managed care delivered on the premium promise but at the expense of consumer choice. Lower costs were accomplished by limiting patients' choice of provider and providers' choice of treatment. Stakeholders learned valuable lessons from the experience of the past decade.

- *Patients* learned that a one-size-fits-all solution to medical care is too restrictive. As medical technology provides more treatment options, the definition of what constitutes medical care also expands. Rising expectations against a backdrop of access restrictions creates tension.
- *Providers* learned that risk sharing presents a challenge to their clinical autonomy and financial security. Forced into a double-agent role (as agent for both patient and plan), providers dislike the restrictions as much as patients do.

- *Payers* learned that cost control is unpopular. The backlash against managed care presented not only an image problem but was dangerous for corporate survival.
- *Employers* learned that there is no magic pill to solve the health care cost problem. Overly aggressive measures to control costs are not only unpopular among employees, but they can lead to litigation problems as plaintiffs search for deep pockets.
- *Politicians* learned that restrictions on access and limits to spending are unpopular and cost votes. They also learned that expansions of treatment options and increases in spending are popular and win votes.

It may be a bit too early to talk about the demise of managed care. But the dynamics of change are at work. Medical consumers like choice, and they are also concerned about cost. The desire for more patient autonomy is not likely to disappear soon, and cost concerns are always an issue, especially with premiums rising at annual rates exceeding 8 percent (except for one year, true every year since 1998). To control costs, patients must be involved in medical decision making. Without cost-conscious consumers and providers, the goal of controlling costs is unattainable.

PROFILE

William B. Schwartz

Trained as an internist, William B. Schwartz had invested a lifetime in academic medicine and became a respected biomedical researcher and national authority on kidney disease. So when this distinguished scholar announced his plans for a midcareer change from clinical medicine to health policy, it raised more than a few eyebrows. Many of his colleagues probably thought he was taking the midlife crisis thing a bit too far. They could understand gold chains and a red sports car, but giving up a medical career to study economics seemed a bit extreme.

Schwartz's medical career reads like a Who's Who in academic medicine. He graduated from Duke medical school in 1945. Five years later, he settled at Tufts University, where he became head of the Nephrology Division at the New England Medical Center. In 1971 he was appointed chair of the Department of Medicine and Physician-in-Chief at the medical center. That same year, he spent the first of several summers working with health economists Charles Phelps and Joseph Newhouse at the RAND Corporation. Under their tutelage, Schwartz was introduced to the economic concepts of scarcity and opportunity cost, and his professional career as a health policy analyst began to bud.

continued

Because his administrative and clinical duties at Tufts required most of his energies, he had little time left to devote to his research interests. Lack of research opportunities and a newly acquired interest in health care policy analysis provided enough incentive to convince Schwartz to resign as department chair and pursue an alternative career path.

Since shifting to health policy, his research interests have focused on applying economics to problems in medical care delivery. His first article on health policy was published in *Science* in 1972. Since that time, Schwartz has devoted his efforts to explaining the role of market forces and competition in promoting efficiency in medical care delivery.

One of his most widely read works was coauthored in 1984 with Brookings economist Henry J. Aaron. Entitled *The Painful Prescription: Rationing Health Care*, the publication examines nonprice rationing of hospital services in the United Kingdom. His book is not a criticism of the National Health Service, but an honest attempt to understand resource allocation within that system and learn from the British experience. The consummate iconoclast, Schwartz has also challenged the conventional wisdom on physician supply in the United States. Instead of forecasting a surplus of 150,000 physicians by the year 2000, he made a solid case for a balance between supply and demand.

Currently the Vannevar Bush University Professor at Tufts University, Schwartz has distinguished himself as a clinician and health policy analyst. Most scholars work a lifetime to make a contribution in a single preferred field of study. William Schwartz has had the good fortune of contributing in two areas, and his accomplishments stand as an inspiration to clinicians and economists everywhere.

Source: John K. Iglehart, "From Research to Rationing: A Conversation with William B. Schwartz," *Health Affairs* 8(3), Fall 1989, 60–75; and William B. Schwartz, Frank A. Sloan, and David N. Mendelson, "Why There Will Be Little or No Physician Surplus Between Now and the Year 2000," *New England Journal of Medicine* 318(14), April 1988, 892–897.

QUESTIONS AND PROBLEMS

1. Define each of the following terms used regularly by the major third-party payers, and explain how they are supposed to affect providers' incentives, fees, and overall utilization:
   a. fee-for-service
   b. assignment
   c. capitation

2. "As the health care delivery system becomes increasingly cost conscious, physicians are no longer able to serve as advocates for their patients' medical needs." In light of this concern, discuss the changing role of the physician in the managed care environment.

3. What are the distinguishing characteristics of a health maintenance organization? How do HMOs differ from other insurers operating in the health insurance industry?

4. What are the primary cost-saving features of managed care?

5. How will the expansion of managed care produce competitive effects throughout the health care system?

6. In theory, how is managed care expected to affect patient and provider incentives, and hence, the cost and use of medical care? What is the evidence?

7. In a series of articles in the February 10, 1993, issue of the *Journal of the American Medical Association*, researchers were said to have estimated that 2.4 percent of all bypass surgeries

are inappropriate, and 7 percent are clearly unnecessary—roughly one-fourth as much as previously estimated. Similar results were found for coronary angioplasty and coronary angiography. Some analysts are using these results to claim the problem is now underuse instead of overuse. How do you define terms such as "inappropriate" and "unnecessary"? What are the lessons to be learned about the use of outcomes research?

REFERENCES

Laurence C. Baker and Ciaran S. Phibbs, "Managed Care, Technology Adoption, and Health Care: The Adoption of Neonatal Intensive Care," *Working Paper No. 7883*, Cambridge, MA: National Bureau of Economic Research, September 2000.

David M. Cutler and Louise Sheiner, "Managed Care and the Growth in Medical Expenditures," in A. M. Garber, ed., *Frontiers of Health Policy Research*, Volume 1, Cambridge, MA: MIT Press, 1998.

E. S. Friedman, "Capitation, Integration, and Managed Care: Lessons from Early Experiments," *Journal of the American Medical Association* 275(12), 1996, 957–962.

Carol Gentry, "A Surprisingly Popular U.S. Export: Managed Care," *Wall Street Journal*, December 20, 1999, B1, B4.

Sherry Glied, "Managed Care," *NBER Working Paper Series No. 7205*, Cambridge, MA: National Bureau of Economic Research, July 1999.

Sheldon Greenfield et al., "Variations in Resource Utilization among Medical Specialties and Systems of Care," *Journal of the American Medical Association* 267(12), March 25, 1992, 1624–1630.

Lynn R. Gruber, Maureen Shadle, and Cynthia L. Polich, "From Movement to Industry: The Growth of HMOs," *Health Affairs* 7(3), Summer 1988, 197–208.

Fred J. Hellinger, "The Effect of Managed Care on Quality: A Review of Recent Evidence," *Archives of Internal Medicine* 158, April 27, 1998, 833–841.

_____, "Selection Bias in HMOs and PPOs: A Review of the Evidence," *Inquiry* 32, Summer 1995, 135–143.

S. D. Hosek, M. S. Marquis, and K. B. Wells, *Health Care Utilization in Employer Plans with Preferred Provider Organizations*, RAND Corporation, February 1990.

John K. Iglehart, "The American Health Care System: Managed Care," *New England Journal of Medicine* 327(10), September 3, 1992, 724–747.

Kaiser Family Foundation and Health Research and Educational Trust, "Survey of Employer Health Benefits: 2007," September 11, 2007, available at http://www.kff.org/insurance/7672/upload/7693.pdf/ [Accessed December 26, 2007].

Peter R. Kongstvedt, *Essentials of Managed Health Care*, Gaithersburg, MD: Aspen Publishers, 1997.

Harold S. Luft, *Health Maintenance Organizations: Dimensions of Performance*, New York: Wiley, 1981.

Willard Manning, Arleen Leibowitz, George Goldberg, William Rogers, and Joseph Newhouse, "A Controlled Trial of the Effect of a Prepaid Group Practice on Use of Services," *New England Journal of Medicine* 310(23), June 7, 1984, 1505–1510.

Mercer Human Resource Consulting, "U.S., Employers' Health Benefit Cost Continues to Rise at Twice Inflation Rates, Mercer Survey Finds," November 19, 2007, available at http://www.mercer.com/referencecontent.jhtml?idContent=1287790 [Accessed December 26, 2007].

Robert H. Miller and Harold S. Luft, "Does Managed Care Lead to Better or Worse Quality of Care?" *Health Affairs* 16(5), September/October 1997, 7–25.

_____, "Managed Care Plan Performance Since 1980: A Literature Analysis," *Journal of the American Medical Association* 271(19), May 18, 1994, 1512–1519.

J. Murray, Sheldon Greenfield, S. Kaplan, and E. Yano, "Ambulatory Testing for Capitation and Fee-for-Service Patients in the Same Practice Setting: Relationship to Outcome," *Medical Care* 30(2), March 1992, 252–261.

Joseph Newhouse, "Reimbursing Health Plans and Health Providers: Selection versus Efficiency in Production," *Journal of Economic Literature* 34(3), September 1996, 1236–1263.

Ray Robinson, "Managed Care in the United States" A Dilemma for Evidence-Based Policy?" *Health Economics* 9(1), January 2000, 1–7.

D. G. Smith, "The Effects of Preferred Provider Organizations on Health Care Use and Cost," *Inquiry* 34, Winter 1997, 278–287.

J. E. Ware, M. S. Bayliss, W. H. Rogers, M. Kosinski, et al., "Differences in Four-Year Health Outcomes for Elderly and Poor, Chronically Ill Patients Treated in HMO and Fee-for-Service Systems: Results from the Medial Outcomes Study," *Journal of the American Medical Association* 13, 1996, 1039–1047.

8

The Physicians' Services Market

Physicians occupy the central role in the provision of medical services. Even though physicians receive less than one-fourth of total medical spending, they determine how much money is spent on medical care. Physicians are responsible for admitting patients to the hospital, recommending treatment, writing prescriptions, and scheduling and performing surgeries. In addition to the details of patient care, physicians also control other important aspects of the decision-making process in medical care delivery, including the acquisition of medical equipment in hospitals, the direction of biomedical research, and medical school curricula.

The past decade was an unsettling period for both active physicians and those hoping to someday practice the healing arts. Major changes in the market include a movement away from fee-for-service practice toward managed care and shifts from retrospective to prospective payment and back again. During this period, physicians experienced increased intrusion into medical practice from both public and private payers. We begin with a brief discussion of the theory of labor markets, and then we focus our analysis on the physicians' services market. The final two sections will explore briefly the markets for nursing services and dental services.

THE THEORY OF LABOR MARKETS

The standard economic theory of labor markets views individual marginal productivity as one of the main determinants of labor income. Because wages are determined by productivity, higher productivity is translated into greater demand for labor services, and in turn, higher wages.

Input Pricing

Broadly speaking, the theory of input pricing is no different from the theory of pricing goods and services presented in Chapter 2. Both are based on the interaction of demand and supply. However, several important differences arise. First, demand for an input is determined by its marginal contribution in the production process. The second important difference between input demand and product demand is related to the first: Inputs are not consumed directly; therefore, the quantity of the input demanded will depend on the amount of the final product desired for consumption. Thus, input demand is derived from the demand for the final product and affected by the prevailing conditions in the market for the final product.[1]

---

[1] When examining the demand for physicians' services, keep in mind that the final product is a desired level of health.

The economic model of input pricing is based on a firm's decisions concerning the input combination used to produce a given level of output; or in the case of physicians' services, an individual's decisions concerning the combination of medical services used to produce a given level of health. Once the firm (individual) decides on a level of production (health), the level of input demand is simultaneously determined. The process involves determining the optimal, or least-cost combination of inputs required to produce the profit-maximizing (utility-maximizing) level of output (health). Generalizing from the discussion in Appendix 3B, the least cost combination of inputs in the production process $Q = Q (X, Y, \ldots, Z)$ may be written as the following equilibrium condition:

$$\frac{MP_X}{P_X} = \frac{MP_Y}{P_Y} = \ldots = \frac{MP_Z}{P_Z}$$

where MP_i is the marginal product of the ith input ($i = X, Y, \ldots, Z$) and P_i is its price.

It can also be shown that the reciprocal of each of the ratios is equal to the marginal cost of production (MC), or

$$\frac{P_X}{MP_X} = \frac{P_Y}{MP_Y} = \ldots = \frac{P_Z}{MP_Z} = MC$$

To prove this equality, consider that the use of one more unit of input X, holding the other inputs constant, will increase output by MP_X units. Thus, using an additional $1/MP_X$ units of input X will increase output by one unit. If one unit of input X costs P_X, then $1/MP_X$ units of X costs P_X/MP_X, which is the cost of producing an additional unit of output, or marginal cost.

If firms are maximizing profit, they are producing an output level at which marginal revenue (MR) equals marginal cost. Thus, it follows that

$$\frac{P_X}{MP_X} = \frac{P_Y}{MP_Y} = \ldots = \frac{P_Z}{MP_Z} = MR$$

By rearranging terms and writing a separate equation for each input, it follows that

$$P_X = MP_X \cdot MR$$
$$P_Y = MP_Y \cdot MR$$
$$.$$
$$.$$
$$.$$
$$P_Z = MP_Z \cdot MR$$

Interpreting these results, we see that in a world where buyers are profit (utility) maximizers, inputs used in a production process are paid an amount—in this case P_X, P_Y, and P_Z—equal to each input's marginal product multiplied by the marginal revenue generated by the production and sale of an additional unit of the final product. This result serves as the underlying principle for deriving the demand curve for an input.

Demand for Inputs

In order to derive the demand curve for an input, we must first determine the maximum price buyers are willing to pay to obtain the desired amount of the input. The maximum price that buyers are willing to pay is determined by the incremental value placed on an additional unit of the input in the production process. As already demonstrated, price is determined by the value of the input's marginal productivity ($MP_i \cdot MR$), or what is called **marginal revenue product (MRP)**.

Figure 8.1 represents the marginal revenue product for any given input. It is downward sloping for the same reason that the marginal product curve is downward sloping: the law of diminishing returns. If the input is labor, the market wage rate determines the number of workers hired. At wage rate W_0, L_0 workers will be hired. If the wage rate falls to W_1, more workers will be hired (L_1). Thus the marginal revenue product curve is the input demand curve, reflecting the two important concepts that determine input demand: the marginal productivity of the input and the level of product demand.

Generally speaking, more productive inputs command higher prices in the market, as do inputs that are used in the production of highly valued commodities. It is no wonder that most medical inputs carry such high price tags. They are very effective in improving health status, something consumers value highly.

marginal revenue product
The change in total revenue resulting from the sale of the output produced by an additional unit of a resource.

Human Capital Investment

One of the most popular ways for an individual to improve his or her marginal productivity is to attend school. Presumably school attendance enables a person to learn a set of skills that enhances productivity. Schooling affects income in two important ways: First, while a person is attending school, income is lower due to forgone earnings. The time spent in school could have been used in gainful employment. In other words, the opportunity cost of attending school is the income that could have been earned if the individual had chosen to work. Second, after completing school, the individual's income will be higher. Individuals who attend school make more money than those who do not. The time spent in school valued by the opportunity cost of the income forgone is called *human capital investment*.

Investment in Medical Education Medical education is a time-consuming process—four years of undergraduate study followed by four years of medical

Figure 8.1: Marginal Revenue Product

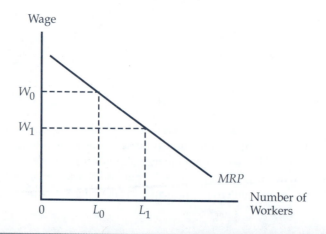

school. And that is only the beginning. After eight years of formal education, the medical school graduate must complete a clinical residency program that lasts a minimum of three years before beginning a medical practice. Forgone income is obviously a major expense of attending medical school. Even though tuition and fees make up less than five percent of overall medical school revenues, the median educational debt of the graduate of a public university was $120,000 in 2006. The graduate of a private medical school had a median debt of $160,000 (*AAMC Data Book*, 2006).

No one undertakes such a course of action without at least considering the payoff. The potential earnings must be enough to overcome the huge cost of the investment. As is the case with many investments, the costs are borne early in a person's life, and the returns are realized later on. Is attending medical school a good economic investment? To answer this question we must compare the value of forgone earnings early in a person's life with the value of the extra earnings later in life. One major complication comes into play: Most individuals exhibit a positive rate of time preference, meaning that one dollar invested today has a higher value than one dollar earned tomorrow.

The Rate of Return to Investment   To determine whether medical school attendance is a good economic investment, we can calculate the **rate of return** on that investment. Recall from our discussion on present-value discounting from Chapter 4, the net present value of a human capital investment can be calculated by comparing the present value of the costs with the present value of the benefits over the lifetime of the investor.

rate of return
The amount earned on an investment translated into an annual interest rate.

The present value of a net-benefits stream over time (NB) is defined by the difference between the annual benefits (B_t) and the annual costs (C_t) of the investment.

$$NB = \sum_{t=1}^{n} \frac{B_t - C_t}{(1 + r)^t}$$

The costs of pursuing a medical degree tend to be front-loaded and take the form of forgone income, tuition, and fees. The benefits tend to be realized later and come in the form of increased earnings. The value of the investment depends on the discount rate: the higher the discount rate, the smaller the present value of the net benefit stream. The rate of return on an investment is the discount rate that results in a net-benefit stream summing to zero.

BACK-OF-THE-ENVELOPE

Estimating Rates of Return for Schooling

For the past three decades, economists have used an approach popularized by Jacob Mincer (1974) to estimate rates of return for education. The returns for schooling can be calculated by comparing the age-earnings profiles of individuals with different levels of schooling. In the following diagram, Y_0 represents the earnings profile of an individual with no schooling, and Y_1 represents that of someone with one year of schooling.

Ignoring the direct costs of training, which are usually small relative to forgone income, an additional year of schooling will cost the individual Y_0 income for one year. In return the individual will receive an increment $Y_1 - Y_0$ for the remainder of his or her work life.

continued

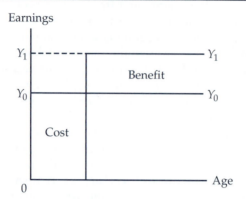

The rate of return for the additional year of schooling can be estimated as follows:

$$r_1 = \frac{Y_1 - Y_0}{Y_0}$$

Solving for Y_1, we get

$$Y_1 = Y_0(1 + r_1)$$

Similarly, the return to the second year of schooling, r_2, would be

$$r_2 = \frac{Y_2 - Y_1}{Y_1}$$

Likewise,

$$Y_2 = Y_1(1 + r_2)$$

Substituting from above,

$$Y_2 = Y_0(1 + r_1)(1 + r_2)$$

After s years of schooling,

$$Y_s = Y_0(1 + r_1)(1 + r_2)\cdots(1 + r_s)$$

If the returns to schooling are small (i.e., less than 100%) and similar in size, then:

$$Y_s = Y_0 e^{rs}$$

The estimated rate of return is calculated by taking the natural logarithm (*ln*) of both sides of the equation, resulting in:

$$lnY_s = lnY_0 + rs$$

Empirical tests are conducted by gathering data on earnings and schooling for a cross section of individuals. Regressing the logarithm of income on the number of years of schooling results in a coefficient estimate for the schooling variable, r, that is interpreted as the estimated rate of return for additional schooling.

Key Concept 2
Opportunity Cost

Source: Jacob Mincer, *Schooling, Experience, and Earnings*, (New York: National Bureau of Economic Research, 1974).

How does the income physicians receive compare to that of other professionals? Higher rates of return for a medical education will encourage more students to pursue medicine as a career. Is the investment a good one from the individual's perspective? Even with the high salaries of physicians, the forgone income during the long investment period may discourage many from pursuing medicine and instead attend business or law school. Should society encourage more students to pursue medicine as a career? Greater subsidies in the form of grants to medical schools and loan forgiveness programs lower the cost of attending medical school and increase the rate of return on the investment.

What is the rate of return for a medical education? Weeks and colleagues (1994) compared the rate of return on the investment made by the typical physician, both primary care and specialist, with those of college graduates entering business, law, and dentistry. Estimated returns were adjusted for the amount of time required to train for the chosen profession and the average number of hours worked.

Empirical results indicated that the annual rate of return on the educational investment made by primary care physicians was 15.9 percent. Dentists and medical specialists fared substantially better, enjoying a 20.7 and 20.9 percent return respectively. However, attorneys and those entering business fared much better with 25.4 and 29.0 percent rates of return. Even though these are crude estimates for the respective rates of return, it is clear that despite their high incomes, individuals who choose medical careers receive lower economic returns on their educational investments than many other professionals. The lower returns are due to much higher training costs, 7 to 12 years of forgone income, and the resulting shorter payoff periods.

The perception that high physicians' salaries are a contributing factor in the high cost of medical care is widely shared by the public and policy makers. To better address this issue, we need to strive for a better understanding of the market for physicians' services.

THE MARKET FOR PHYSICIANS' SERVICES

The changing demographics of the population have played an important role in determining demand and supply in the physicians' services market. The population in the United States was 203 million in 1970 and increased to 296 million by 2005, or approximately 46 percent. At the same time, the number of active physicians increased two and one-half times, from 310,929 to 801,742. The result, clearly shown in Table 8.1, was a 75 percent increase in the ratio of physicians per 100,000 population from 153 to 270, indicating a greater relative supply of physicians today than 35 years ago.

In 2007 the United States had 126 medical schools with an enrollment of 70,225 students and 20 schools of osteopathic medicine with an enrollment of 11,857. These medical schools graduated 15,925 (plus 2,756 D.O.s), a number expected to remain stable for the foreseeable future. Approximately one-fourth of the physicians currently practicing in the United States graduated from foreign medical schools. Reliance on graduates of foreign medical schools has increased dramatically over the past 30 years, from less than 15 percent of the total number of practicing physicians in the mid-1960s to approximately 25 percent today. By the mid-1990s, international medical graduates (IMGs) filled about 20 percent of all residency positions. Much of the attraction of the U.S. medical market may be attributable to higher relative salaries and fewer practice restrictions than in other countries.

POLICY ISSUE

International medical graduates make up 25 percent of the physician workforce in the U.S.

Table 8.1: Active Physicians in the United States

Year	Active Physicians	Rate per 100,000 Residents	Primary Care Physicians	Primary Care as a Percent of Active
1960	247,257	138	125,359	50.7
1970	310,929	153	134,354	43.2
1980	435,545	192	170,705	39.2
1990	559,988	225	213,514	38.1
1995	646,022	244	241,329	37.4
2000	737,504	262	274,653	37.2
2005	801,742	270	300,022	37.4

Source: *Health, United States, 2007 with Chartbook on Trends in the Health of Americans*, Hyattsville, MD: National Center for Health Statistics, Table 108, 2007.

ISSUES IN MEDICAL CARE DELIVERY

Defending the Borders from Foreign Competition

The 1996 election focused the legislative and media spotlight on the intense nationalistic tendencies of the American electorate at the time. Proposition 187 in California was the first political move to tap into this anti-immigrant sentiment. The aborted presidential bid by Republican Pat Buchannan and the strong populist rhetoric of on-again, off-again presidential candidate Ross Perot fed on this anti-NAFTA, anti-foreigner, anti–free-trade mindset. But it is a long way from campaign rhetoric to actual practice — or is it?

The 104th Congress considered legislation that would have enacted some of the most restrictive policies regarding both legal and illegal immigration in recent history. Sponsored by retiring Republican Senator Alan Simpson, the bill was intended to do three things:

- Limit the flow of immigrants into the United States by increasing border enforcement.

- Install a verification system that would make it feasible to require employers to check the legal status of all foreign workers.

- Require employers to pay a fee for every foreigner hired equal to the greater of 10 percent of the first-year salary or $10,000.

Even though the legislation did not pass, its potential impact on U.S. industry — and especially on those who recruit specially trained technical and professional workers in the global marketplace — highlights the predicament of many employers in areas of labor shortage. Falling into this category, the medical care industry would be seriously affected by similar legislation should it ever become law. Nationwide, international medical graduates (IMGs) occupy almost one-fourth of all residency positions. Many rural and inner-city areas, facing severe physician shortages, have relied heavily on foreign-trained physicians to staff their facilities. More than half of the hospital residents in New York City alone are IMGs. Similarly, medical facilities in remote areas of North Dakota and inner-city New Jersey recruit graduates of foreign medical schools to staff their operations.

continued

> Foreign-trained physicians have been more inclined to accept positions in unpopular places. Many from India and even Canada can have fewer restrictions placed on them and earn more, even in rural and inner-city settings.
>
> Hospitals under pressure to cut costs could see personnel costs escalate significantly if such restrictive legislation ever passes. In New York City, some estimate that costs could rise by $60 million annually by restricting the pool of foreign-trained physicians. For patients in underserved areas, this could mean longer waits to see a physician and, in some cases, fewer specialty services available.
>
> **Source**: Almar Larour, "How Curbing Immigration Could Hurt Health Care in Inner Cities, Rural Areas," *Wall Street Journal*, March 5, 1996, B1, B6

Key Concept 6
Supply and Demand

Another important aspect of physician supply has been the number of U.S. citizens attending foreign medical schools. As the ratio of applicants per opening in U.S. medical schools rose to 2.8 in the mid-1970s, many Americans were attracted to the option of studying in foreign countries. Some schools in Mexico and the Caribbean began accepting large numbers of American citizens, causing concern about the future quality of medical school graduates to fill residency positions in academic health centers.

Anyone trained in a foreign medical school and seeking admission to a residency-training program in the United States must pass an examination and be certified by the Educational Commission for Foreign Medical Graduates. The number of U.S. citizens receiving certification increased steadily until 1984, when a more rigorous exam was administered. The number certified for residency programs has fallen dramatically, from over 1,500 per year in the mid-1980s to less than 500 in recent years.

Given the long training period for physicians, one would expect the supply of physicians to be fairly inelastic in the short run. The slow supply response means that changes in physicians' incomes do not translate into immediate adjustments in the number of physicians practicing medicine. U.S. immigration laws, however, currently place relatively few restrictions on the entry of foreign-trained physicians, especially during times of perceived shortages. This allows physician supply to remain fairly responsive to market conditions. The importance of foreign-trained physicians in staffing many rural and inner-city facilities highlights the potential impact of changes in U.S. immigration policy on physician supply.

Increases in relative supply do not tell the entire story. Policy makers have voiced concern over certain aspects of the supply side of the market, including the distribution of physicians across specialty areas and regions of the country, the relative salaries of physicians, the pricing of their services, and the organizational structure of physicians' practices.

POLICY ISSUE

Many rural and inner-city hospitals rely on foreign-trained physicians to staff their facilities.

Key Concept 6
Supply and Demand

Specialty Distribution

Many policy analysts and health maintenance organizations have established a goal to increase the number of physicians in the primary care specialties to 50 percent of the physician workforce. In the rest of the developed world, this percentage is not unusual. In fact, primary care physicians make up 50 to 70 percent of the total number of active physicians in most developed countries (Schroeder and Sandy, 1993). In the United States, however, only about one-third of all active physicians are in primary care.[2]

POLICY ISSUE

Only one-third of the active physicians in the U.S. are involved in primary care compared with 50 to 70 percent in most developed countries.

---

[2] For purposes of this discussion, *primary care* is defined as family practice, general internists, and pediatricians.

POLICY ISSUE

Should the U.S. rely on
market forces to adjust the
specialty mix, or should
government adjust resi-
dency financing to bring
about the desired mix?

POLICY ISSUE

Access to medical care
in many rural and inner-
city areas is inadequate
because of relatively fewer
physicians and facilities.

The percentage of generalists has been on a downward trend since 1970, when the figure was over 40 percent. Referring again to Table 8.1, between 1970 and 2004, the number of primary care physicians increased from 134,354 to 296,495, or 120 percent. Over the same time period, the number of specialists increased from 176,575 to 495,659, or 180 percent. While the number of active physicians per 100,000 people grew 76 percent over this 35-year period, the rate of growth differed significantly by specialty. Primary care physicians increased from 66 per 100,000 people to 101, or 53 percent. Specialists increased from 87 per 100,000 to 169, or 94 percent.

At least a dozen large, national organizations, including the Accreditation Council for Graduate Medical Education (ACGME), the American Medical Association (AMA), the National Governors Association, and the Robert Wood Johnson Foundation have voiced concern over the falling percentage of generalists and advocated a reversal of the trend. With only 15 percent of recent medical graduates pursuing a generalist career, the prospects for reaching the goal of 50 percent generalists appears bleak at best (Levinsky, 1993).

The appropriate percentage of primary care physicians is not easy to determine. Policy concerns are based on the projected number of patients compared to the number of physicians required to provide for their primary care needs. Several studies have examined this physicians' services market and identified a mismatch between supply and demand. Analyzing the results of five different projection methods, Politzer and colleagues (1996) predict a substantial shortage of primary care physicians and a surplus of specialists by the year 2020. Other studies have reached similar conclusions, pointing to some challenging policy issues. Since specialists use more expensive technology, the obvious concern is that more specialists will lead to higher spending. With government at all levels playing such a large role in financing medical education, what role if any should it play in determining specialty mix?[3] Or should we simply rely on market forces to drive down fees in the surplus specialty market and raise them in the shortage primary care market?

Geographic Distribution

Even as the concern for the falling percentage of generalists grows, so does the concern for the declining number of physicians willing to practice in rural and inner-city areas. The problem of providing medical care in many rural areas has reached near critical stages. Overall, almost 30 percent of the U.S. population lives in market areas with fewer than 180,000 inhabitants, where the physician–population ratios are substantially lower. The majority of the population in 19 states lives in these small market areas, and over 20 percent of the population in 42 states lives in such areas (Kronick et al., 1993).

The nation's inner cities face the same challenge in attracting and keeping qualified physicians. With large minority and indigent populations, inner cities depend heavily on hospital emergency rooms and public clinics, staffed by international medical graduates, for a substantial portion of their medical care.

Pennsylvania provides a good example of the problem of attracting physicians to rural areas. According to the most recent census, Pennsylvania has the largest rural population in the country; *rural* is defined as an area with fewer than 2,500 population. The three counties surrounding the state's two major urban centers, Pittsburgh and Philadelphia, comprise approximately 25 percent of the state's population and over one-half of its physicians (Rabinowitz, 1993). The remaining 64 counties, with over 75 percent of the state's population, are severely underserved.

Nationwide, individuals living in the smaller market areas have fewer physicians per 100,000 than those living in more populated markets. The physician–population ratio

---

[3] By the time a physician finishes residency, he or she will have received an average federal subsidy of $70,000.

in the 700 counties with fewer than 10,000 inhabitants was one-third that of the rest of the country. Nurse practitioners and physicians' assistants are filling some of these gaps. A number of physicians operate satellite offices in rural areas, some at permanent sites and others using mobile units. Providing medical care to these low-density, remote areas will be a continuing challenge for the medical care delivery system.

ISSUES IN MEDICAL CARE DELIVERY

An Endangered Species: The Male Gynecologist

Obstetrics was once a field dominated by women. At one time, the local midwife delivered most of the babies. Modern medicine has changed that relationship in most urban areas. Over the course of the twentieth century, childbirth became an integral part of a medical practice, and midwifery lost much of its clientele.

Obstetricians deliver most of the babies born in the United States today. Obstetrics and gynecology (OB/GYN) has become a popular specialty, primarily because it is one of only a few that combines primary care with surgery. But women today are deserting their male gynecologists in increasing numbers and turning to female OB/GYNs. Just as men prefer a same-sex physician almost two to one, an increasing number of women are beginning to voice a similar preference. As recently as 1980, women filled less than 30 percent of the residency positions in obstetrics and gynecology. Today, that number has doubled to more than 60 percent.

The increase in supply of female OB/GYNs may be in part a response to the rapidly expanding demand for their services, especially among health maintenance organizations and previously all-male OB/GYN practices. This shift in preferences has several major implications, all indicative of a shortage of female OB/GYNs in the market:

- Initial salaries for women within the specialty are $20,000 a year more than for men.

- While the median salary for female physicians is about 70 percent of the male median, female OB/GYNs enjoy pay parity with their male counterparts.

- Patients have shown a willingness to wait for appointments with their female OB/GYNs who are booked months in advance.

For women this preference shift may not be solely an issue of seeing a same-sex physician. There seems to be a significant difference in practice styles between the sexes. Male gynecologists are more likely to perform hysterectomies, and patients of female gynecologists are more likely to be current on their Pap tests and mammograms. Whether female gynecologists are more sensitive to their patients' needs, or whether the practice styles of more recent graduates — male and female — are simply different, is an unanswered question.

For whatever reason, many newly trained female gynecologists are opening all-female practices and marketing them as such. This trend has opened up a completely different set of questions dealing with reverse discrimination. Can an obstetrical practice seeking to fill a vacancy on its staff advertise for females only? When patients are voicing a preference for female physicians, is it legal for employers to discriminate against male applicants? Under what circumstances is gender a legitimate qualification? When it comes to performing

continued

a gynecological exam, is patient preference an appropriate concern? It is only a matter of time, given our litigious society, before this issue will be addressed by our judicial system. How will the courts respond? Is the desire for a same-sex provider for a gynecological exam different from wanting a same-sex stock-broker or sales clerk in a shoe store? Reason is not always a good indicator. No matter how the courts respond, it is unlikely that the male gynecologist will vanish anytime soon. Over 70 percent of the practicing OB/GYNs are still male, so even if the trend toward female residencies continues unabated, it will take several decades before we see a female-dominated specialty.

Source: Andrea Gerlin, "The Male Gynecologist: Soon to Be Extinct?" *Wall Street Journal*, February 7, 1996, B1, B5.

Physician Compensation

To a large degree, the strength of the U.S. health care system may be attributed to the dominance of specialty care. The increasing number of specialists has been accompanied by a more frequent use of the latest diagnostic, therapeutic, and surgical procedures. This approach has contributed to improving the quality of care, but it has also consumed large quantities of resources and has served as a primary cost driver (Schroeder and Sandy, 1993).

Many critics of the U.S. system have focused on physicians' incomes as the primary cause of high and rising health care spending, even though physicians' compensation consumes only 20 to 25 percent of total spending. Based on Medical Group Management Association (MGMA) surveys, median compensation for all primary care physicians in 2006 was $171,519. The median for all specialists was

Table 8.2: Median Compensation, Selected Specialties 2002–2006

	2002	2003	2004	2005	2006
All primary care:	$153,231	$156,902	$161,816	$168,111	$171,519
Family Practice (without OB)	150,267	152,478	156,011	160,729	164,021
Internal Medicine	155,530	159,978	168,551	176,124	181,187
All specialists:	274,639	296,464	297,000	316,620	322,256
Anesthesiology	306,964	323,491	325,999	359,699	365,409
Invasive Cardiology	385,000	410,272	427,815	463,801	457,563
Dermatology	269,238	285,692	308,855	334,277	348,706
Emergency Medicine	211,709	215,859	221,679	243,449	250,030
Gastroenterology	321,023	351,614	368,733	384,015	406,345
Obstetrics/ Gynecology	233,061	237,191	247,348	256,485	271,425
Orthopedic Surgery	362,181	397,059	396,650	428,119	446,517
Psychiatry	163,144	162,572	182,799	189,409	192,609
Diagnostic Radiology	376,035	403,779	406,585	426,346	446,517
General Surgery	255,438	264,375	382,504	300,800	306,115

Source: *Physician Compensation and Production Survey*, 2006, Englewood, CO: Medical Group Management Association, 2006.

almost two times that amount, or \$322,256. The 1997 MGMA survey placed the primary care median at \$135,791 and the specialty median at \$220,476.

Over the decade spanning 1997 to 2006, primary care incomes rose 26 percent (or 2.4 percent per year) while specialty incomes rose 46 percent (or 3.9 percent per year). There is a substantial variation in the median incomes across specialties. At the lower end of the spectrum, family practice physicians without an OB practice earn \$164,021, compared to those in internal medicine, who earn \$181,187. Specialists' salaries range from psychiatry at \$192,609 to invasive cardiology, gastroenterology, orthopedic surgery, and diagnostic radiology, all greater than \$400,000.

BACK-OF-THE-ENVELOPE

Is There an Optimal Physician–Population Ratio?

How many physicians do we need? In theory, an optimal physician–population ratio can be determined. In practice, however, determining that ratio is not so easy. Even though other inputs in the medical care process must be considered, most medical services require at least one physician input. Some inputs complement physicians; others are substitutes. The list of other labor inputs includes nurses, physicians' assistants, receptionists, bookkeepers, lawyers, medical technicians, and therapists. Nonlabor inputs include the office and its equipment, computers, supplies, electricity, and, of course, medical malpractice insurance. Medical care can be provided using different combinations of physicians' services and these other inputs. The optimal combination depends on the relative price of the inputs and the preferences of the decision makers responsible for combining the inputs and making the medical care available.

Using the production isoquants developed in the appendix to Chapter 3, we can show how prices and preferences affect the optimal number of physicians used in the production of medical care. The isoquant mapping in the following diagram depicts the preferences of a managed care organization with a greater willingness to substitute other inputs for physicians' services. Increases in the price of physicians' services relative to the prices of the other inputs creates an incentive to use fewer physicians' services. The isocost curve rotates inward due to the increase in price, and the equilibrium number of physicians used falls from S_1 to S_0.

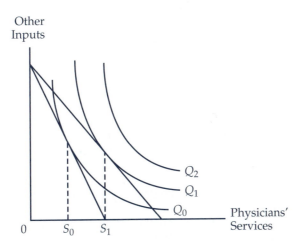

continued

staff-model HMO
An HMO in which physicians are employees of the HMO. Their incomes are usually paid in the form of a fixed salary, but may include supplemental payments based on some measure of performance.

Decision makers with a strong preference for using physicians in the production process will have steeper isoquants. Other things equal, any given increase in the price of physicians will have much less of an impact on the use of physicians' services than indicated in the diagram. The following diagram depicts the preference mapping of a physicians' group practice. Using the same starting point, S_1, defined as the equilibrium quantity of physicians' services, the same increase in the price of physicians' services (as shown in the previous diagram) has less of an impact on the use of physicians' services, lowering utilization to S_0'. The obvious implication deals with the use of physicians in the tightly controlled managed care environment. A good example is the **staff-model HMO**, in which substitution for high-cost physicians' services is more widely practiced, resulting in a flatter isoquant mapping (as shown in the first diagram) and a demand for physicians' services that is relatively price elastic. A difference in staffing patterns between the staff-model HMO and traditional fee-for-service physicians' practice (as shown in the second diagram) supports this view. Based on a nationwide survey of HMOs, Dial and colleagues (1995) estimated that the staff-model HMO uses about 140 physicians per 100,000 enrollees with 40 percent of those being involved in primary care. HMOs are also more likely to utilize nonphysician providers, advanced practice nurses (APNs) and physician assistants (PAs) to supplement their clinical staffing needs. The median number of APNs per 100,000 of the responding HMOs was 19.7. Overall, the median number of PAs was 8.1.

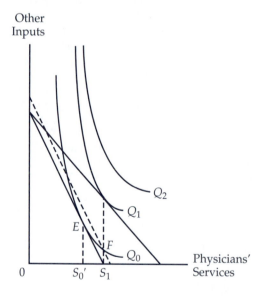

In contrast, the overall physician–population ratio stood at 230 per 100,000 in 1992 with only about one-third of those practicing primary care. Additionally, Kronick and colleagues (1993) reported that the ratio of physicians to population is anywhere from 10 to 200 percent higher in the fee-for-service sector when compared with the classic HMO, depending on specialty examined.

Restrictions on the minimum number of physicians used to produce a given level of care generally lead to higher costs. Suppose S_1 physicians'

continued

services are required by law to provide Q_0 medical care. Precluded from using the least-cost combination of inputs at point E, providers must use a minimum of S_1 at point F, resulting in equilibrium on a higher isocost curve.

Sources: Thomas H. Dial et al., "Clinical Staffing in Staff- and Group-Model HMOs," *Health Affairs* 14(2), Summer 1995, 169–180; and Richard Kronick et al., "The Marketplace in Health Care Reform—The Demographic Limitations of Managed Competition," *New England Journal of Medicine* 328(2), January 14, 1993, 148–152.

Pricing of Physicians' Services

Prior to widespread health insurance coverage, most patients made direct payment for physicians' services out-of-pocket. Physicians, on the other hand, practiced a form of Ramsey (1927) pricing, charging patients different prices based on their relative demand elasticities. As insurance became more popular, payers' concern over rapidly increasing medical spending resulted in a pricing model that limited physicians' fees to usual, customary, and reasonable (UCR) levels. Under the UCR standards, physicians could charge the minimum of usual charge, defined as the median charged during the past year, and the customary charge, defined by some percentile of the fees charged by other physicians in the area; and physicians were allowed reasonable increases from year to year. It is easy to understand the inflationary nature of UCR (Frech and Ginsburg, 1975). There is no reason for a physician's usual price to be below the customary price charged by other physicians in the area. If it were, the price received would be below prevailing prices in the area. Thus, physicians had an incentive to make sure that their usual fee was not the minimum in the formula.

As prices for physicians' services continued to escalate, payers looked for other ways to control spending. Since 1992 Medicare has paid physicians according to a fee schedule based on a relative value scale (RVS) that translates costs into payments. Under RVS, physicians' fees were divided into three cost components: work effort, practice expense, and malpractice expense. The RVS provides an index of resources used to produce medical services and procedures across all specialty areas. RVS actually translates into a dollar fee schedule by multiplying the relative values of over 7,000 procedure codes by a monetary conversion factor. The government influence is so prominent that many private insurers base their payment schedules on Medicare's relative values, typically using a percentage of the Medicare fee. Thus any change in the Medicare payment cascades through the entire system.

Since 2000, the consumer price index (CPI), not including medical care, rose 2.19 percent per year, and the medical services component of the CPI rose 4.71 percent per year. Using the latter measure, many observers argue that medical inflation is the primary reason that medical spending is a growing problem, increasing twice as fast as everything else. As discussed in the appendix to Chapter 1, several problems are inherent in using the CPI as a measure of inflation. These same problems may be applied to the use of the medical services CPI as a measure of inflation in the medical services market.

The desire to control medical spending has resulted in a moderation in the escalation of Medicare fees for many procedures. Table 8.3 provides Medicare pricing information on ten common procedures using Current Procedure Terminology (CPT) codes as identifiers. This listing, while not randomly chosen, is representative of recent experience with Medicare pricing. The prices of procedures such as total hip replacement, the insertion of a coronary stent, and a complete electrocardiogram have fallen. Prices of other procedures have risen at rates comparable with the CPI,

Table 8.3: Changes in Medicare Fees for Selected Physicians' Services Select Years

CPT Code	Description	2000	2005	2007	Annual Percent Change from 2000
27130	Total hip replacement	$ 1,423	$ 1,292	$ 1,361	−0.63
33533	Single CABG	1,853	1,794	1,909	+0.43
43239	Upper GI endoscopy	223	300	325	+5.53
67210	Treatment of retinal lesion	599	560	581	−0.48
92980	Insertion of coronary stent	979	772	796	−2.97
93000	Electrocardiogram	26	24	25	−0.71
99203	Office visit, new patient	83	90	92	+1.48
99213	Office visit, established patient	44	49	59	+4.28
99223	Initial hospital care	147	151	174	+2.43
99292	Additional 30 minutes of critical care	90	108	114	+3.43

Source: Centers for Medicare and Medicaid Services, Physician Fee Schedule Search, http://www.cms.hhs.gov/pfslookup/. Accessed November 1, 2007.

including coronary artery bypass graft (CABG) surgery, new patient office visits, and initial hospital care. Only a few have seen price increases that come close to the growth in the medical services component of the CPI. Explaining the reason for the overall increase in medical care spending in the United States is not as simple as saying, "It's the prices." More likely the increase in the overall utilization of services also plays a big role—more people are using more services.

Organization of Physicians' Practices

Research indicates that there are modest economies of scale in the provision of physicians' services (Reinhardt, 1972; Escarce and Pauly, 1998). As the relative number of physicians in solo practice has declined, the percentage of physicians in single specialty and multispecialty group practices of four or more has increased. Organizing into group practices not only lowers the overhead cost for each physician, it increases the range of services offered within the practice. The extra services may include a pharmacy, a clinical laboratory, radiology and ultrasound equipment, and even CT scanning and MRI facilities. The shift to group practice has enhanced the full-service capabilities of physicians' practices and has contributed to the shift in services from the hospital to the ambulatory setting.

The potential benefits of taking advantage of economies of scale in a medical practice are clearly shown in Figure 8.2. LAC depicts the long-run average cost of a typical medical practice. The small-group practice is able to carry a patient load equal to Q_S. At this service level, SAC_S represents the short-run average cost of the practice and AC_S, the actual average cost per patient. Larger practices can combine activities and spread administrative overhead over a larger number of patients. The larger practice is able to move down the LAC, utilizing a larger physical plant (larger offices, more equipment, an on-site laboratory, etc.). The short-run average cost of the larger operation is depicted by SAC_L and represents, in this case, the optimal plant size. Average cost per patient is lower at AC_L.

Figure 8.2: Economies of Scale in a Medical Practice

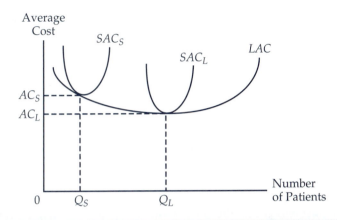

Patients will benefit from the lower operating costs when there is competition in the market. Competition forces providers to charge prices reflecting these lower costs. If, however, these consolidations lead to the concentration of market power, providers will be able to act more like monopolists, restrict the availability of services, and charge higher prices. Evidence provided by Noether (1986) indicates that the physician services market has become more competitive since 1965, resulting in an increased supply of physicians and subsequent downward pressure on their incomes.

Geographic Variations in Practice Patterns Regional variations in the incidence of surgery and other inpatient procedures are well documented (Phelps, 1992). Small-area variations (SAVs) refer to the wide dispersion in per capita utilization rates for many common medical procedures found among otherwise similar health care markets across the country. These cross-regional differences do not seem to be the product of demographic differences in education, income, and insurance coverage or the underlying pattern of diseases. Physicians faced with symptoms and syndromes are expected to make decisions on the appropriateness of care with the scientific accuracy of *Star Trek*'s Doctor McCoy. Patients do not always come to their physicians with readily identifiable diseases. Even if they did, the outcome of a particular treatment is not always predictable.

McPherson and colleagues (1982) compared the utilization rates for several common surgical procedures within New England and observed wide variations, even after adjusting for differences in the age and gender composition of the population. Procedures showing the most variation included hysterectomy, prostatectomy, and tonsillectomy. Additionally, they found significant differences in utilization rates when comparing New England with Norway and England.

Wennberg (1984) speculated that the observed variations in practice patterns across regions could be explained by the degree of scientific uncertainty associated with diagnosis and treatment. A lack of consensus on the efficacy of a medical procedure will lead individual physicians and groups of physicians to follow clinical rules of thumb to determine who needs surgery. Consistent application of these rules leads to the "surgical signature" phenomenon—rates of surgery in a region that are consistent over time and differ dramatically from those observed in otherwise similar regions.

A second reason for differences in the rates of surgery may be patient preferences for specific treatments. However, when patients are uninformed, they tend to delegate the decision-making responsibility to the physician, which leads to decisions that closely mirror the preferences of the provider.

Key Concept 7
Competition

POLICY ISSUE

Variations in practice patterns across geographic regions result in patients with similar health conditions being treated differently.

The important public policy issue deals with the costs and consequences of these variations. Do regional variations mean that some physicians overtreat and others undertreat? Do different treatment patterns indicate inappropriate and unnecessary care? From the individual's perspective, appropriate care is a level of care that the fully informed patient would demand upon comparing the marginal benefit of the care being considered with the out-of-pocket marginal cost of the care. Therein lies the problem. From society's perspective, the level of care demanded by the individual patient may be an inefficient use of scarce resources, since the fully insured patient bears only a small fraction of the total cost.

Key Concept 3
Marginal Analysis

Eddy (1990) explored the role of patient preferences in explaining the variations in treatment across regions. Figure 8.3 provides a framework for examining the role of patient preferences in determining the level of care provided in treating certain medical conditions. In the diagram, D_1 and S_1 represent the demand and supply conditions in Region 1, and P_1 and Q_1 represent the equilibrium price and quantity. Suppose there is a second region with the same physician supply, but where consumers have a different demand for the same medical procedure, represented by D_2. The different level of demand may be due to differences in income, insurance coverage, or other demographics, or it may be due to different health preferences or attitudes toward risk, pain, and discomfort. Information about these different demand preferences is communicated to providers specializing in this procedure. They, in turn, increase the quantity supplied to Q_2, receiving higher prices for their services, P_2. Assuming easy mobility between the two regions, there is an incentive for physicians to relocate to Region 2. Under these circumstances, utilization rates are even higher than Q_2.

Key Concept 6
Supply and Demand

Weinstein and colleagues (2004) examined utilization patterns for major orthopedic procedures including total hip replacement, total knee replacement, and back surgery. Rates of surgery differed more than five times between the high-rate regions and the low-rate regions, and the interquartile ratio—surgery rates for regions ranked in the 75th quartile relative to those ranked in the 25th quartile—was 1.31 for knee replacement and 1.45 for hip replacement. They also observed differences in overall medical spending across local communities. Per capita Medicare spending (adjusted for differences in age, gender, and race) was 1.65 times greater in Miami than in Ft. Myers, Florida ($10,113 versus $6,136).

Improving the scientific basis for clinical decisions through outcomes research should serve to reduce the variations over time. But old habits are difficult to change, and there is no reason to indicate that changing medical practice patterns will be easy. With few exceptions, medical services are highly localized in their

Figure 8.3: Small-Area Variations

delivery. As a result, the usual market forces that serve to eliminate inefficiencies in manufacturing, for example, are not as active in medical care markets.

Whether any gains are to be made by a more standardized approach to treatment remains to be seen. In a sense, patient welfare may actually be enhanced by the variations because of the treatment alternatives available across regions. It will be the goal of medical outcomes research to determine whether the gains in the efficacy and efficiency of medical care delivery outweigh the losses to patients by limiting the choice of treatment that will likely follow from the standardization of services.

MODELS OF PHYSICIAN BEHAVIOR

To adequately model physician behavior, we must take into consideration the characteristics of the market for physicians' services. Many urban markets have a substantial number of physicians practicing in the same specialty area; however, a large percentage of Americans live in geographic areas that are considered underserved. In his reexamination of the economics of health care, Rice (1998) points out that this market is also characterized by widespread uncertainty on the part of both the patient and the practitioner. A lack of readily available information makes it difficult for patients to make informed choices. Third-party insurance coverage makes moral hazard a dominant feature of both sides of the market. Barriers to entry in the form of strict licensing and a professional code of conduct that discourages direct-to-consumer advertising make it difficult for patients to price shop. These *imperfections*, as economists call them, seem to point to a market where providers have a certain degree of market power.

The Physician as Monopolistic Competitor

The physicians' services market shares many of the characteristics of the standard model of monopolistic competition with many sellers, each providing a slightly different product or service. Physicians strive to differentiate their practices by various means—location, hospital affiliations, and quality of care are but a few differences. At the same time, patients have little information to judge physicians and rely mainly on the recommendations of friends and family. As a result, physicians are imperfect substitutes for one another.

The major implication of market power is downward-sloping demand curves. Physicians with market power are not price takers, instead they vary the prices they charge, and patients respond to those price variations. In other words, demand is less than perfectly elastic.

The large percentage of patients with health insurance complicates the development of the model to explain physician pricing. Ignoring for the moment the impact of health insurance on the demand for physicians' services, Figure 8.4 depicts the pricing strategy of a physician with a degree of market power.[4] If the physician is a profit-maximizer, the optimal strategy will be to provide services as long as marginal revenue is greater than marginal cost. Profit is maximized where $MR = MC$ with the physician providing Q^* services and charging the maximum price that patients will pay to get those services, or P^*.

The availability of health insurance affects patients' responsiveness to changes in price. Less concerned about the prices they are charged, patients with insurance have demand curves that are more price inelastic. Inelastic demand, however, does not change the basic implications of the standard model. It merely provides the

---

[4] Refer to Figure 5.3 and the related discussion on the impact of insurance on the demand for medical care.

Figure 8.4: Pricing and Output Decision of Physician in Monopolistic Competition

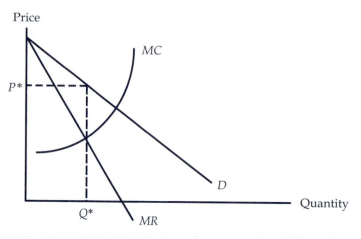

physician with the opportunity to charge patients different prices for the same services based on the extent of their insurance coverage. Patients with more elastic demand are charged lower prices, and patients with more inelastic demand are charged higher prices.

BACK-OF-THE-ENVELOPE

Price Discrimination in Medical Care

Key Concept 5
Markets and Pricing

When suppliers have market power, they are faced with downward-sloping demand curves. The price searcher will frequently discover that in searching for the profit-maximizing price, the opportunity arises to charge customers different prices for the same product. In order to be a successful price discriminator, two important conditions must be met:

- Customers must be classified according to willingness to pay, and providers must have some way to distinguish which customers are willing to pay higher prices. Conceptually, the provider attempts to determine each group's price elasticity of demand for the product.

arbitrage
The practice of simultaneously buying a commodity at one price and selling it at a higher price.

- **Arbitrage** must be difficult. Those customers who are able to buy at the low price must have no easy way to resell the product to those charged the higher price.

continued

Medical care delivery provides a classic case in which conditions exist that allow providers to practice **price discrimination.** Patients approach providers with certain identifiable characteristics that help determine their willingness to pay, most notably, whether they have insurance. As with any service, it is difficult for a low-pay patient to resell a medical procedure to a high-pay patient.

The preceding diagram provides a graphical depiction of how a supplier with market power becomes a price discriminator. Suppose that the medical provider identifies two distinct groups of patients — one with insurance and one without. Those patients with insurance (Group 1) are less price-sensitive than those paying out-of-pocket (Group 2) and thus have a steeper demand curve. To simplify the analysis, assume that marginal cost (MC) is constant and equal to average cost (AC). The profit-maximizing level of output for each group is determined by equating marginal revenue (MR) with marginal cost. For Group 1, $MR_1 = MC$ at Q_1. For Group 2, $MR_2 = MC$ at Q_2. At these respective output levels, the provider charges the highest price that the groups are willing to pay, P_1 for Group 1 and P_2 for Group 2.

Clearly, Group 2 pays a lower price for the same medical care: $P_2 < P_1$. Why? Without insurance, their demand is more elastic. Recognizing this, providers charge them less for the same services. Does this really happen in medical care delivery? Four decades ago, Kessel (1958) showed how the model of price discrimination applied to medical care. One of the more interesting conclusions of Kessel's research was the implication that the growing popularity of prepaid medical plans will reduce the ability of providers to practice price discrimination. More competition will mean less price discrimination.

Source: Reuben A. Kessel, "Price Discrimination in Medicine," *The Journal of Law and Economics* 1, 1958, 20–53.

price discrimination
The practice of selling the same good or service to two different consumers for different prices. The price differential is not based on differences in cost.

Key Concept 7
Competition

The Physician as Imperfect Agent

Another key assumption when using standard economic theory to model physicians' behavior is that supply and demand are independently determined. As we discussed in Chapter 5, the relationship between the patient and the physician can be described using a principal–agent model. The patient/principal seeks out the physician/agent for advice on a medical problem. The perfect agent will recommend only the treatment that a fully informed patient would demand. The problem arises because the physician not only serves as an adviser to the patient but is also the provider of the recommended services. This dual role as adviser and provider creates a potential conflict of interest between what is best for the patient in terms of clinical efficacy and what is best for the physician in terms of financial reward. By law the physician must act in the best interests of the patient. Due to the uncertainty of diagnosis and the question of best treatment alternative, the best interests of the patient are not always clear.

Physicians acting as imperfect agents will recommend unnecessary procedures, especially if they pose little clinical risk to the patient and the patient is fully insured. When prices fall, physicians may see their incomes fall due to inelastic demand for their services. To compensate for falling incomes, physicians may practice demand inducement, using their role as advisers to enhance their personal incomes. Reinhardt (1999) presents a model of physician behavior that incorporates the potential for demand inducement as one of the factors that affects a physician's

POLICY ISSUE

The physician's dual role as agent and provider creates a potential conflict of interest. The choice is whether to serve the patient's medical interest or the physician's own financial interest.

well-being or utility. In this model, a physician's utility depends on three factors: income, hours worked, and the extent of demand inducement. Income and leisure time increase a physician's utility. The practice of demand inducement reduces utility, presumably because of guilt feelings due to a professional code of ethics, or the stigma associated with the behavior should it become public knowledge. Physicians are faced with a trade-off among income, leisure, and conscience. Depending on individual circumstances, the trade-off can affect the quality of care provided to patients.

CONTROLLING PHYSICIAN BEHAVIOR

Patients delegate medical decisions to their physicians because physicians have better information about the causes and consequences of medical conditions. However, physicians' motives are unobserved and may not correspond perfectly with those of the patient and the payer. The problem with the arrangement is that there are two incentive regimes at work that generally interfere with one another. One is the financial arrangement between the payer and the provider, designed to control for moral hazard. The other is the moral obligation between patient and provider, designed to guarantee the provision of all medically necessary care. Both payer and patient compete for the providers' loyalty to advance their competing goals.

In search of ways to influence provider behavior, health plans have designed incentive regimes to influence the way physicians practice medicine. These regimes include capitation, withholdings and bonuses, diagnosis-related groups, clinical rules, and utilization reviews. To encourage cost-conscious practice patterns, some health plans pay primary care physicians on a capitation basis and make them responsible for referring patients to approved specialists. Under capitation, physicians are responsible for the management of care within a fixed budget. In other words, they accept some of the financial risk in making clinical decisions. When the managed care plan establishes a risk-sharing plan, using withholdings and bonuses, the end result curtails the independence of participating physicians. Management tends to focus on costs, and with few exceptions, the trade-off is between controlling costs and improving the quality of care.

Do Physicians Respond to Incentives?

Efforts to control costs have led many health plans to adjust the way physicians are paid. One popular approach establishes reduced fee-for-service rates for all covered procedures. When physicians are paid in this manner, many increase the dollar volume of services by changing the way they bill (e.g., **unbundling** of services and/or upcoding) and by providing more services (Lee, Bumbach, and Jameson, 1990; Wedig, Mitchell, and Cromwell, 1989; Holahan, Dor, and Zuckerman, 1990). Canada has learned that controlling physician fees does not lower expenditures on physicians' services. Fee schedules lead to changed patterns of medical care delivery, including an increased number of follow-up visits (Lomas et al., 1989; Hughes, 1991).

When financial incentives exert pressures, no matter how subtle, clinical decisions may be influenced (Hillman, 1990). Managed care places the physician's clinical judgment on a collision course with his or her pecuniary interests. Theoretically, physicians well schooled in economic principles will consider the costs to society when making clinical decisions. But in practice, the payment scheme used by many managed care plans induces physicians to take into consideration the impact of their clinical decisions on their own income. Since physicians

The American Medical Association, with over 300,000 members, is dedicated to promoting the art and science of medicine and the betterment of public health. Its Web site provides links to continuing education opportunities for physicians and offers access to the many journals published by the association. The address is

http://www.ama-assn.org

unbundling
Separating a number of related procedures and treating them as individual services for payment purposes.

share financial risk with managed care plans, they share the same incentives with insurance companies to avoid sick patients (Stone, 1997).

Strong financial incentives essentially turn a physician into an insurance company, usually without the patient base to adequately spread actuarial risk. In a fixed-budget environment, the care that a physician withholds is closely correlated with the income that he or she earns. Placing physicians at financial risk mixes two types of risk: probability risk and efficiency risk. Probability risk measures the likelihood that patients will utilize medical care based on the characteristics of the patient pool, including age, sex and health status. Efficiency risk measures how effectively the physician treats the patient. Although physicians control their own efficiency risk, they have no control over probability risk. It is appropriate to hold physicians responsible for efficiency risk; it is inappropriate to hold them responsible for probability risk.

If compensation is adjusted for population characteristics, at least part of the probability risk is transferred back to the insurer. But most plans adjust for only two variables, age and sex, even though these account for less than 20 percent of the annual costs of medical care among patients (Goldfield et al., 1996).

Managed care attempts to shape physician behavior through either clinical rules or financial incentives. **Clinical rules** establish guidelines that encourage physicians to adopt a particular practice style. The effectiveness of clinical rules depends on the ability of managed care plans to educate physicians about the appropriate practice style, to use peer pressure to ensure compliance, and to select the physicians who may participate in the provision of care. In contrast, financial incentives leave the treatment choice to the physician. But financial incentives create a conflict of interest by compromising the physician's fiduciary responsibility or exercise of independent clinical judgment. Both approaches share the goal of encouraging less expensive care.

Less expensive care, however, does not necessarily mean poor-quality care. Hellinger (1998) cites evidence that the cost-cutting measures practiced by managed care may adversely affect the health of certain vulnerable subpopulations, including older and sicker patients, and that managed care enrollees may suffer because of problems accessing certain specialized services. In fact, the strongest disincentive for quality care is for the sickest and most expensive patients. Physicians who provide quality care for their sickest patients will find their practices attracting the sickest patients. Because most capitation rates are adjusted only for age and gender, not health status, this strategy results in lost income for the provider. The alternative strategy is to offer a level of care that encourages sick patients to change providers. This strategy, sometimes called "patient dumping," does not have to be overt. It may be accomplished in more subtle ways, including delays in scheduling appointments for certain types of procedures, refusal to refer sick patients to specialists, and failure to meet patient expectations on treatments prescribed and provided.

In other research, Hellinger (1996) examines the impact of financial incentives on physician behavior, specifically capitation and the use of withholdings and bonuses, and concludes that financial incentives are a key element in explaining lower levels of spending and utilization in managed care plans. It is important to recognize that all of the studies comparing utilization rates in managed care with those in fee-for-service care are unable to differentiate between the impacts of financial incentives and those of clinical rules. To the extent that plans with strong financial incentives also include stringent clinical rules, it is difficult to separate the impact of the two. However, it is possible to conclude that plans with strong

POLICY ISSUE

Risk-sharing contracts, which subject physicians to financial incentives to limit health care spending, may adversely affect quality of care.

clinical rule
is a specific practice required of all participating physicians, such as a policy to refer patients only to a specific panel of specialists.

financial incentives and strong clinical rules have lower utilization rates compared to plans that do not.

Empirical Evidence on the Impact of Financial Incentives   The empirical literature examining the impact of financial incentives on physician behavior may be divided into three categories: randomized trials, same-disease studies, and same-physician studies. The largest and most widely cited randomized trial is the RAND Health Insurance Experiment (Manning et al., 1984). Results of this study concluded that participants in a group-model HMO had fewer inpatient hospital days and lower overall medical expenditures than did participants in a traditional fee-for-service plan. Martin and collegues (1989) examined the impact of a **gatekeeper** operating under a risk-sharing contract and concluded that physicians at risk for budget deficits had lower spending per enrollee, attributable to lower specialist referral costs.

A limited number of same-disease studies have examined the treatment decisions of physicians facing different financial incentives. These studies looked at the treatment and diagnostic services provided to patients with a variety of health conditions, including heart disease, colorectal cancer, childbirth, and acute myocardial infarction. These studies concluded that patients treated by HMO physicians received fewer procedures, diagnostic tests, and treatments than patients who used physicians paid under traditional indemnity insurance arrangements. Epstein, Begg, and McNeil (1986) studied the practices of 27 physicians certified in internal medicine, 10 with fee-for-service practices, and 17 in prepaid group practices. They concluded that patients treated in fee-for-service practices received 50 percent more electrocardiograms than patients treated in prepaid practices.

Finally, the same-physician studies avoid some of the potential biases inherent in other approaches. Because practice styles may differ substantially among physicians, by contrasting an individual physician's practices with fee-for-service patients and managed care patients, same-physician studies control for many of the sources of variation that incorrectly affect results. Using this approach, Welch, Pauly, and Hillman (1990) and Murray and colleagues (1992) conclude that physicians used more services in treating patients enrolled in fee-for-service plans than patients enrolled in prepaid plans.

Not all studies conclude that financial incentives systematically affect physician behavior. Cangialose and colleagues (1997) and Conrad and colleagues (1998) are two of the most often cited studies that reach the opposite conclusion. However, these studies have methodological problems that bring their results into question. Cangialose and colleagues (1997) published in a managed care industry journal, bringing into question the objectivity of the peer-review process. Conrad and colleagues (1998) chose health plans in which 96 percent of the enrollees were being treated by primary care physicians who shared in the financial risk of treatment. In their own words, this choice "eliminated the influence of health plan payment in this sample" (p. 857).

All of the studies on incentives are subject to certain biases. It may be that patients self-select physicians who practice the style of medicine they prefer. Healthy patients may cluster in prepaid practices. But virtually every study that adjusted for the available information on differences in type of enrollee, physician, and plan concluded that physicians facing financial incentives provided fewer services, diagnostic tests, and procedures than did physicians who were not faced with them. The robustness of these findings suggests that when faced with financial incentives, specifically capitation and the use of withholds and bonuses, physicians

gatekeeper
A primary care physician who directs health care delivery and determines whether patients are allowed access to specialty care.

The Agency for Health Care Policy and Research (AHCPR), established in 1989 as a part of the Department of Health and Human Services, is the lead agency supporting research designed to improve the quality of health care, reduce its cost, and broaden access to essential services. Part of the agency's mission is to support outcomes research with the goal of developing practice guidelines. Check it out at

http://www.ahcpr.gov

alter their practice style to provide fewer services, diagnostic tests, and procedures. This practice may not affect the health status of healthy patients; however, certain vulnerable patients—those who are sick or suffer from chronic conditions—may receive lower quality care.

Most physicians practice in a setting where a variety of insurance arrangements exist simultaneously, variations of both managed care and fee for service. Theory suggests that managed care patients will receive less intensive care than fee-for-service patients. However, a physician may find it difficult to modify his or her practice style based on the type of plan that covers the patient. Empirical findings by Glied and Zivin (2002) indicate that financial incentives in fact do affect treatment intensity among patients according to method of payment. Additionally, and more importantly, variations in treatment intensity depend on the relative mix of managed care and fee-for-service patients in the physician's practice. Physicians with a large percentage of their patients covered by HMOs change their practice styles across the board, treating all patients with the lower, managed care intensity.

THE MARKET FOR NURSING SERVICES

Nursing services may be provided by a number of different occupational groups. The two that have specific educational and licensing requirements are registered nurses (RNs) and licensed practical nurses (LPNs). Registered nurses make up the largest component of the nursing workforce. To qualify for the basic RN license, one of three educational programs must be completed—a two-year associate degree, a three-year hospital diploma, or a four-year baccalaureate degree. None of the attempts to raise the minimum educational requirement for the RN license to a baccalaureate degree have gone very far. Licensed practical nurses generally have only 12 to 14 months of training and earn about two-thirds of the $36,000 average annual income of a registered nurse.

ISSUES IN MEDICAL CARE DELIVERY

Do We Really Want Low-Cost Primary Care?

The shortage of primary care physicians and the increased popularity of managed care, with its emphasis on cutting costs, has provided momentum to those who advocate greater autonomy for nurses in treating patients. By allowing advanced-practice nurses to take over some of the more routine duties now reserved for physicians, the United States could save billions of dollars in medical care costs annually. Advanced-practice nurses comprise nurse practitioners, nurse anesthetists, and nurse midwives; they usually have two years of clinical training beyond the four-year baccalaureate degree. As such, even without experience, they have more training than first-year residents who provide a great deal of the primary care in the nation's teaching hospitals.

Legislation dating back to the 1930s restricts nurses in two important ways. First, nurse practitioners do not have prescriptive authority in many states, which means they are unable to write prescriptions unless they are in a collaborative practice with a licensed physician. Second, not all payment sources, including many private insurance companies and the government, recognize nurse practitioners as qualified providers and thus will not directly reimburse them for their services.

continued

Key Concept 1

Scarcity and Choice

Still, more than 100,000 advanced-practice nurses nationwide offer physical exams, immunizations, preventive screening, and treatment for minor illnesses such as ear infection, sore throat, and the flu. Many see nurse practitioners, who offer their services at a 30 to 70 percent cost-saving compared to general practitioners, as a way to lower costs and improve access to primary care in many underserved areas. Critics, however, feel that lowering the barriers to nurse practitioners will only drive more physicians from general practice into the higher-paying specialties and, in the long run, will do little to lower costs and improve access.

How many of the restrictions on nursing are based on concerns over quality of care, and how many are merely a cultural artifact of an era when female nurses assisted male physicians? One thing is certain: As concern over cost cutting grows, the barriers to an expanded role for nurses will gradually disappear. It is simply a matter of time until economics once again promotes a more effective use of scarce resources.

Source: Adrienne Perry, "Nurse Practitioners Fight Job Restrictions," *Wall Street Journal*, September 3, 1993, B1, B8.

As indicated in Table 8.4, registered nurses held over 2.3 million jobs in 2005, an increase of almost 12 percent over the decade. Approximately 70 percent of those jobs were in hospitals, and one-fourth were part time. In 1995 there were 1,516 programs nationwide training registered nurses. First-year nursing enrollment numbered over 120,000 with over 97,000 graduating that same year. Since 1995 the annual number of graduates has fallen by over one-third.

Efforts to curb the growth of health care costs are likely to have significant effects on the market for nursing services. By redesigning the medical workplace, hospitals will be able to use more nursing aides to provide much of the low-skill, routine care. Using lower-paid aides can save as much as $25,000 for each job converted from a registered nurse to an aide. In addition, demand will increase for advanced-practice nurses to help providers cut costs for routine primary and preventive care.

Table 8.4: Registered Nurses (RNs) in the United States

	Active RNs (thousands)	RNs per 100,000 Population	Nursing Programs	First-Year Enrollment	Nursing Graduates
1950	na	na	1,170	na	25,790
1960	na	na	1,137	na	30,113
1970	750	368	1,340	na	43,103
1980	1,273	560	1,385	105,952	75,523
1985	1,538	641	1,473	118,224	82,075
1990	1,790	714	1,470	108,580	66,088
1995	2,116	798	1,516	127,184	97,052
2000	2,190	778	na	na	68,709*
2005	2,368	798	na	na	na

* 1999

Source: *Statistical Abstracts of the United States 1999,* Table No. 196; U.S. Department of Health and Human Services, *Health, United States, 2007 with Chartbook on Trends in the Health of Americans*, Table 109, 2007.

BACK-OF-THE-ENVELOPE

Monopsony Power in the Market for Registered Nurses

Chronic shortages have often plagued the labor market for nurses. Public policy has traditionally focused on the supply side of the market, offering recommendations to increase the number of nursing graduates. Economists examine the problem from a different perspective. Chronic and persistent shortages may be an indicator of monopsony power. In competitive markets, a shortage results when wages are set below their equilibrium level. Employers compete to attract and retain workers by bidding up the wage until demand and supply are back in balance.

The market for registered nurses may not work this way. Several aspects of the market contribute to the development of monopsony power among employers. The hospital industry is the largest employer of nursing services. Over 70 percent of all nurses in the United States are employed in this setting. This institutional feature establishes a single-buyer model in the local labor market for nursing services with the hospital as the dominant purchaser. Mobile workers can overcome local market monopsony. If enough nurses were willing to move to other communities where wages are higher, or if they transferred their skills and experience to other types of work within the local labor market, competition would raise local wages.

Historically, these normal checks and balances on monopsony power are relatively inoperative in the nursing market. Nursing skills are very job-specific and do not readily transfer to other occupations. The wholesale exodus of nurses leaving the profession for jobs in some other industry poses little threat to the local hospital employer. Additionally, geographic mobility among nurses is also low. Most nurses are married females and often earn less than their spouses. As the secondary income earner within the family, the typical nurse is restricted to the geographic location chosen by the higher-paid spouse.

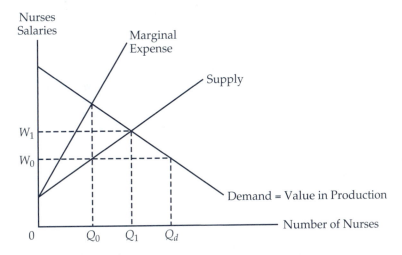

What do these factors mean for nurses in general? Using the diagram, we can see that the monopsonistic employer equates the workers' value in production with their marginal expense, and therefore only Q_0 are hired. To hire that number, the monopsonist pays a wage equal to W_0, substantially less than the competitive wage of W_1 determined by the intersection of supply

continued

Key Concept 6
Supply and Demand

Key Concept 7
Competition

and demand. With wages below the competitive equilibrium, a shortage $(Q_d - Q_0)$ exists. Normally, competitive pressures bid wages back up to W_1, but in this case — without competitive pressures — wages remain at W_0, and the shortage persists. Nursing unions and the increased mobility of professional women over the past decade have served to improve salaries and muffle the cry of shortages in the profession. In fact, by demanding the competitive wage W_1, the union actually increases the quantity of nurses demanded to Q_1.

Source: Lavonne A. Booten and Julia I. Lane, "Hospital Market Structure and the Return to Nursing Education," *Journal of Human Resources* 20(2), 1985, 184–196. Julia Lane and Stephan Gohmann, "Shortage or Surplus: Economic and Noneconomic Approaches to the Analysis of Nursing Labor Markets," *Southern Economic Journal* 61(3), January 1995, 644–653.

THE MARKET FOR DENTAL SERVICES

Nursing World is the official Web site of the American Nurses Association. In addition to legislative updates on issues affecting the profession, regular news releases, and job search information, the site provides access to the *Online Journal of Issues in Nursing* published at Kent State University. The address is

http://www.nursingworld.org/

Most of the 168,000 dentists actively practicing in the United States are general practitioners. The remainder practice as specialists. Orthodontists, which make up the largest group of specialists, straighten teeth. The next largest group is oral and maxillofacial surgeons, who specialize in surgery of the mouth and jaw. Other specialties include pediatric dentistry, periodontics, prosthodontics, endodontics, dental public health, and oral pathology.[5]

More than 90 percent of dentists practice privately as "solo practitioners." They own their own businesses and employ a small staff of assistants to complement their work effort. Some dentists practice in partnership with others, and a small percentage are employed as associates in a larger group practice.

As summarized in Table 8.5, there are 55 dental schools enrolling over 4,300 new students each year in four-year programs. Most dental schools require a minimum of two years of predental education at an accredited undergraduate

Table 8.5: Dentists in the United States

	Active Dentists (thousands)	Dentists per 100,000 Population	Dental Schools	First-Year Enrollment	Dental Graduates
1970	96.0	47	53	—	3,749
1980	121.9	54	60	6,132	5,256
1985	133.5	57	60	5,047	5,353
1990	147.5	59	58	3,979	4,233
1995	153.3	61	54	4,121	3,908
2000	168.0	61	55	4,314	4,171
2003	—	—	56	4,448	4,443
2004	—	—	56	4,618	4,350
2005	—	—	56	4,612	—

Source: *Statistical Abstracts of the United States 1999*, U.S. Department of Health and Human Services, *Health, United States, 2006 with Chartbook on Trends in the Health of Americans*, 2006.

---

[5] Dentists in these areas specialize in the practice of children's dentistry, the treatment of diseases of the gums and supporting bone structure, making dentures and artificial teeth, root canal therapy, epidemiology, and the study of diseases of the mouth.

institution. Most dental students, however, have at least a four-year baccalaureate degree in one of the physical sciences. The course work in dental school is similar to the medical school curriculum. The first two years are spent learning the basic sciences through classroom instruction and laboratory training. The final two years are spent in clinical work, treating patients under the supervision of licensed dental professors.

The net median income for dentists in private practice was $130,000 per year in 1995. For those in specialty practice, the median was $196,000, and for generalists it stood at $125,000. First-year dental school enrollment was 6,132 in the 1980 through 1981 academic year. By 2004, the size of the first-year class had fallen to 4,618. The job outlook for the dental profession looks relatively good. Demand for dental services will grow as the baby-boom generation ages. On average, this group has retained more of its teeth than previous generations and has more disposable income. Thus, the demand for preventive care will remain solid.

http://

ADAONLINE is the official Web site of the American Dental Association, providing access to educational opportunities, current research, and other clinical issues of interest to dentists. The ADA Newstand features news releases and links to other Web sites. The address is

http://www.ada.org

ISSUES IN MEDICAL CARE DELIVERY

The Demand for Dental Care

Dental care, hospital care, physicians' services, pharmaceuticals — all are medical care, so they must be the same. Right? If all these medical services are the same, why are they treated so differently in most health insurance plans? Out-of-pocket payments for medical care averaged roughly 20 percent of total spending in 1995. That percentage differs significantly when viewed by category of spending. It stands at 3 percent of hospital spending, 18 percent of physicians' services, 48 percent of dental services, and 60 percent of pharmaceuticals. Why do these percentages vary so dramatically?

The demand for dental care is associated with the same variables that affect the demand for other types of medical care — prices, income, tastes and preferences, and health status. But there are elements of dental care that are different from other types of medical care. A large portion of dental services is preventive in nature; some might even be considered elective. Since teeth may be thought of as a durable good, much of the normal demand for dental care is for maintenance or repair. Roughly 85 percent of the services performed are comprised of fillings, extractions, cleanings, and examinations. Much of the rest is performed for cosmetic reasons. We want good teeth so we can chew our food without pain and look good at the same time.

Insurance coverage for dental services has been slow in developing because of the individual's ability to postpone care, plus the fact that it is sometimes difficult to delineate the difference between maintenance and repair on the one hand and pure cosmetics on the other. Because of these characteristics, even partial insurance coverage results in a substantial increase in demand for services. The insured population spends roughly 1.8 times more on dental services than the population at large.

In terms of economics, the demand for dental care is more price elastic than the demand for other forms of medical care. Elasticity estimates vary by type of service and demographics. It is estimated that white females have the price elasticities of demand that range from −0.5 to −0.7. In general, demand of white males and children is more elastic than that of females. This means that adults with free dental care will spend twice

continued

Key Concept 6
Supply and Demand

as much as adults with no insurance, and fully insured children will spend three times as much as children with no insurance.

Any improvement in dental insurance coverage must be carefully coordinated with policies to increase the supply of dentists. Improved insurance coverage will mean increased demand for dental care. Increased demand coupled with an inelastic supply of dentists will mean increased prices, increased queues, and higher quasi-rents for dentists. Markets will ration scarce resources, and that rationing will take the form of higher prices or longer waiting times for office visits.

Source: Willard G. Manning and Charles E. Phelps, "The Demand for Dental Care," *The Bell Journal of Economics* 10, Autumn 1979, 503–525.

SUMMARY AND CONCLUSIONS

In this chapter we have examined the market for health care professionals, focusing on the market for physicians. Policy makers speak with near unanimity in their claim that residency programs in the United States are turning out too few generalists and too many specialists. The imbalance, if one actually exists, may be corrected by imposing more regulations on the medical education establishment or by relying on market forces. Those who would rely on regulation do not believe that the current system will respond to market incentives and change the proportion of residents entering general practice. Advocates of the market approach argue that regulators do not have enough information to correctly predict the needs of the medical care delivery system, and probably would not get it right if they tried. They argue that the proper specialty mix and geographic distribution are better determined through market incentives. In any event, managed care is already bidding up the salaries of primary care physicians; a phenomenon that many believe is the beginning of the adjustment process.

Another important topic in this chapter is the changing incentive structure of the physicians' services market. In a fee-for-service environment, the most valuable patient in the physician's practice is the sickest patient. More office visits, more services, and more procedures all translate directly into more income for the physician. In a capitated environment, the most valuable patient is the healthiest patient. Sick patients consume costly medical resources without contributing any additional income. Healthy patients generate the same income and do not consume valuable resources.

PROFILE

Gary S. Becker

Considered an imaginative, original thinker by his supporters — and accused of intellectual imperialism by his detractors — Gary S. Becker, more than any other scholar, has inspired a revolution in economic thought that is extending the boundaries of economic inquiry and ultimately redefining what economists do. Beginning with his dissertation research published in 1957 under the title *The Economics of Discrimination*, Becker's theoretical work has opened to economists the fertile research fields of the other social sciences. An entire generation of economists challenged by his insights has used his theories as a springboard for their own policy-oriented research.

In addition to his early work on discrimination, Becker is responsible for path-breaking research on important social issues such as fertility and demographics, education, crime and punishment, and marriage and divorce — all aspects of human behavior once considered outside the scope of economics. He is best known for his contribution to a symposium Investment

continued

in Human Beings, published in a special issue of the *Journal of Political Economy* in 1962. This work, expanded into a book in 1964 entitled *Human Capital*, is recognized as a classic piece of research by economists and serves as the theoretical foundation for a field of study under that same title. Within this framework, individuals spend and invest in themselves and their children with the future in mind. Education and training, job search, migration, and medical care are all viewed as investments in human capital. The decision to spend is based on a comparison of the present value of the expected benefits with the present value of the costs.

But Becker's innovative thought did not end there. His later research into crime and punishment and the economics of the family has been equally revolutionary, affecting not only economics but also criminology and sociology. In 1992, he became the third straight University of Chicago economist to be awarded the Nobel Prize in Economic Science for extending "the domain of microeconomic analysis to a wide range of human behavior and interaction including nonmarket behavior."

Born in Pottstown, Pennsylvania, Becker graduated from Princeton in 1951. He completed his doctoral training at the University of Chicago in 1955 and was asked to remain there as a member of the faculty. Except for 12 years at Columbia University and the National Bureau of Economic Research, Becker has maintained his Chicago affiliation throughout his professional career. Probably more than any other proponent of the Chicago School of Economics, he has developed and applied the ideas of classic free-market economics in ways his predecessors never considered.*

Becker appeared on the academic scene in the 1960s, when neoclassical economics was under attack from all fronts. The resurgence of the Marxist critique of capitalism challenged the orthodoxy from the outside, and a subtle movement toward a less rigorous analysis (as exemplified by the work of John K. Galbraith) challenged it from within. But Becker's unrivaled imagination saved the discipline from irrelevancy. For that we are all deeply thankful.

Source: J. R. Shackleton, "Gary S. Becker: the Economist as Empire Builder," in J. R. Shackleton and G. Locksley, eds., *Twelve Contemporary Economists, Macmillan, 1981;* Jonathan Peterson, "Chicago's Lock on the Nobel: Economics Professor Is University's Third Winner in Three Years," *Los Angeles Times,* Home Edition, October 14, 1992, D1; and Peter Passell, "New Nobel Laureate Takes Economics Far Afield," *The New York Times,* Late Edition, October 14, 1992, D1.

---

*The Chicago School is more than a geographic location. It is a school of thought based on a methodology rooted in the microeconomic foundations of all of economics. Its theoretical basis is one of self-interested decision makers, market equilibrium, the universal application of the concept of capital, and a healthy skepticism for government-based solutions to economic problems.

QUESTIONS AND PROBLEMS

1. If surgeons really have the ability to increase the demand for surgeries, which kinds of surgeries will likely be most affected? Can you think of a way to determine which surgeries are unnecessary? Provide several examples from your own readings or experience.

2. If the theory of supplier-induced demand is valid, what are the implications for public policy?

3. How does the dual nature of the physician's role as both adviser and provider support the demand-inducement hypothesis? What institutional mechanisms support the possibility of demand inducement? How is this effect reinforced by health insurance? What are the natural limits to the alleged problem?

4. Why is the supply of physicians a major cause of concern? How would you expect the supply of physicians to affect physicians' incomes and the price and quantity of medical services provided? What is the actual evidence?

5. The American Medical Association (AMA) has been actively involved in shaping the regulation of nursing and other health care practitioners. What are the arguments for and against the AMA determining the scope of legitimate activities for other health care practitioners?

6. "High salaries are essential if we are to have the most capable students pursuing medical careers." Comment.

REFERENCES

AAMC Data Book: Statistical Information Related to Medical Education, Washington, DC: Association of American Medical Colleges, January 1997.

Charles B. Cangialose, S. J. Cary, L. H. Hoffman, and D. J. Ballard, "Impact of Managed Care Arrangements on Quality of Care: Theory and Evidence," *American Journal of Managed Care* 3(8), August 1997, 1153–1170.

Douglas A. Conrad et al., "Primary Care Physician Compensation Method in Medical Groups: Does It Influence the Use and Cost of Health Services for Enrollees in Managed Care Organizations?" *Journal of the American Medical Association* 278, March 18, 1998, 853–858.

David M. Eddy, "Clinical Decision Making: From Theory to Practice," *Journal of the American Medical Association* 263(3), January 19, 1990, 441–443.

A. M. Epstein, C. B. Begg, and B. J. McNeil, "The Use of Ambulatory Testing in Prepaid and Fee-For-Service Group Practices: Relation to Perceived Profitability," *The New England Journal of Medicine* 314, April 24, 1986, 1089–1094.

Jose J. Escarce and Mark V. Pauly, "Physician Opportunity Costs in Physician Practice Cost Functions," *Journal of Health Economics* 17(2), April 1998, 129–151.

H. E. Frech and Paul Ginsburg, "Imposed Health Insurance in Monopolistic Markets: A Theoretical Analysis," *Economic Inquiry*, 1975, 55–70.

Sherry Glied and Joshua Graff Zivin, "How Do Doctors Behave When Some (But Not All) of Their Patients Are in Managed Care?" *Journal of Health Economics* 21(2), March 2002, 337–353.

Neil A. Godbey, "How Capitation Turned Red Ink to Black at Harris Methodist Health System," *Managed Care* 6(8), August 1997, 88–114.

N. Goldfield et al., "Methods of Compensating Managed Care Physicians and Hospitals," in N. Goldfield and P. Boland, eds., *Physician Profiling and Risk Adjustment*, Gaithersburg, MD: Aspen Publishers, 1996.

Fred J. Hellinger, "The Effect of Managed Care on Quality: A Review of Recent Evidence," *Archives of Internal Medicine* 158, April 27, 1998, 833–841.

———, "The Impact of Financial Incentives on Physician Behavior in Managed Care Plans: A Review of the Evidence," *Medical Care Research and Review* 53, September 1996, 294–314.

A. L. Hillman, "Health Maintenance Organizations, Financial Incentives, and Physicians' Judgements," *Annals of Internal Medicine* 112(12), June 15, 1990, 891–893.

J. Holahan, A. Dor, and S. Zuckerman, "Understanding the Recent Growth in Medicare Physician Expenditures," *Journal of the American Medical Association* 263(12), March 23–30, 1990, 1658–1661.

J. S. Hughes, "How Well Has Canada Contained the Costs of Doctoring?" *Journal of the American Medical Association* 265(18), May 8, 1991, 2347–2351.

Peter R. Kongstvedt and Jean Stanford, "Managed Care Maturity: A New Multidimensional Model," *Future Health: New Dimensions in Strategic Thought*, Washington, DC: Ernst & Young, March 1997.

P. Lee, K. Grumbach, and W. Jameson, "Physician Payment in the 1990s: Factors That Will Shape the Future," *Annual Review of Public Health* 11, 1990, 297–318.

Norman G. Levinsky, "Recruiting for Primary Care," *New England Journal of Medicine* 328(9), March 4, 1993, 656–660.

J. Lomas, C. Fooks, T. Rice, and R. Labelle, "Paying Physicians in Canada: Minding Our P's and Q's," *Health Affairs* 8(1), Spring 1989, 80–102.

W. F. Manning, A. Leibowitz, G. A. Goldberg, W. H. Rogers, and J. P. Rogers, "A Controlled Trial of the Effects of a Prepaid Group Practice on Use of Services," *New England Journal of Medicine* 310(23), June 7, 1984, 1505–1510.

D. P. Martin, P. Diehr, K. F. Price, and W. C. Richardson, "Effect of a Gatekeeper Plan on Health Services Use and Charges: A Randomized Trial," *American Journal of Public Health* 79(12), December 1989, 1628–1632.

Klim McPherson, John E. Wennberg, Ole B. Hovind, and Peter Gifford, "Small-Area Variations in the Use of Common Surgical Procedures: An International Comparison of New England, England, and Norway," *New England Journal of Medicine* 307(21), November 18, 1982, 1310–1313.

J. P. Murray, S. Greenfield, S. H. Kaplan, and E. M. Yano, "Ambulatory Testing for Capitation and Fee-For-Service Patients in the Same-Practice Setting: Relationships to Outcomes," *Medical Care* 30(3), March 1992, 252–261.

Monica Noether, "The Growing Supply of Physicians: Has the Market Become More Competitive?" *Journal of Labor Economics* 4(4), October 1986, 503–537.

Charles E. Phelps, "Diffusion of Information in Medical Care," *Journal of Economic Perspectives* 6(3), Summer 1992, 23–42.

Robert M. Politzer, Sandra R. Gamliel, James M. Cultice, Carol M. Bazell, Marc L. Rivo, and Fitzhugh Mullan, "Matching Physician Supply and Requirements: Testing Policy Recommendations," *Inquiry* 33(2), Summer 1996, 181–194.

Howard K. Rabinowitz, "Recruitment, Retention, and Follow-Up of Graduates of a Program to Increase the Number of Family Physicians in Rural and Underserved Areas," *New England Journal of Medicine* 328(13), April 1, 1993, 934–939.

Frank P. Ramsey, "A Contribution to the Theory of Taxation," *Economic Journal* 37(145), 1927, 47–61.

Uwe E. Reinhardt, "A Production Function for Physician Services," *Review of Economics and Statistics* 54(—), February 1972, 55–66.

———, "The Economist's Model of Physician Behavior," *Journal of the American Medical Association* 281(5), February 3, 1999, 462–465.

D. K. Remler et al., "What Do Managed Care Plans Do to Affect Care? Results from a Survey of Physicians," *Inquiry* 34, 1997, 196–204.

Thomas Rice, *The Economics of Health Reconsidered*, Chicago, IL: Health Administration Press, 1998.

James F. Rodgers and Sara L. Thran, "Trends in the Physician Services Market," in Martin L. Gonzalez, ed., *Socioeconomic Characteristics of Medical Practice 1994*, Center for Health Policy Research, American Medical Association, 1994, 17–23.

Steven A. Schroeder and Lewis G. Sandy, "Specialty Distribution of U.S. Physicians—The Invisible Driver of Health Care Costs," *New England Journal of Medicine* 328(13), April 1, 1993, 961–963.

D. A. Stone, "The Doctor as Businessman: The Changing Politics of a Cultural Icon," *Journal of Health Politics, Policy and Law* 22(2), April 1997, 533–556.

G. Wedig, J. B. Mitchell, and J. Cromwell, "Can Price Controls Induce Optimal Physician Behavior?" *Journal of Health Politics, Policy and Law* 14(3), Fall 1989, 601–620.

William B. Weeks, Amy E. Wallace, Myron M. Wallace, and H. Gilbert Welch, "A Comparison of the Educational Costs and Incomes of Physicians and Other Professionals," *New England Journal of Medicine* 330(18), May 5, 1994, 1280–1286.

James N. Weinstein, Kristen K. Bronner, Tamara Shawver Morgan, and John E. Wennberg, "Trends and Geographic Variations in Major Surgery for Degenerative Diseases of the Hip, Knee, and Spine," *Health Affairs – Web Exclusive*, October 7, 2004, VAR-81–89.

W. P. Welch, Mark V. Pauly, and Alan L. Hillman, "Toward New Topologies for HMOs," *Milbank Quarterly* 68(2), 1990, 221–230.

John E. Wennberg, "Dealing with Medical Practice Variations: A Proposal for Action," *Health Affairs* 3(2), Summer 1984, 6–32.

The Hospital Services Market

Flexner Report
A 1910 report published as part of a critical review of medical education in the United States. The response of the medical establishment led to significant changes in the accreditation procedures of medical schools and an improvement in the quality of medical care.

The publication of the **Flexner Report** in 1910 served as a catalyst for general reform in medical care delivery. Nowhere are the effects more noticeable than in the hospital services industry. Hospitals, once notorious places more likely to spread diseases than cure them, have since been transformed into the focal point of the medical care delivery system.

This chapter examines the market for hospital services. The first two sections provide a brief history of hospitals and an examination of the institutional setting in the United States. Following this is a discussion of the role of the private, not-for-profit hospital as the dominant organization in the industry. The chapter also examines several popular theories of hospital behavior, and finally, recent developments in the industry, in particular the trend toward multihospital systems.

A BRIEF HISTORY OF AMERICAN HOSPITALS[1]

Three important factors served to transform hospitals into the modern medical institutions they have become: the germ theory of disease, advances in medical technology, and increased urbanization. These changes have been accompanied by a dramatic change in patient expectations. No longer do patients seek a caring environment exclusively; they have come to expect a cure.

The development of the germ theory of disease, first articulated by Louis Pasteur in 1870, revolutionized the treatment of patients. Diseases were seen as having specific causes rather than merely being effects of disequilibria or the result of moral turpitude. The search for causal factors required more elaborate testing and diagnostic services. Centralized medical care, bringing the patient to the practitioner, became a necessity.

New hospital technology, especially advances in surgical and diagnostic imaging, provided physicians with the tools that would revolutionize medical intervention. Anesthesia was first used in surgery in 1846. But it was not until the adoption of antiseptic procedures, beginning in 1867, that the high rates of death from infection following surgery began to fall. The introduction of X-ray technology in the late 1800s, and more recently the development of more advanced imaging tools—such as computed tomography (CT) scans and magnetic resonance imaging (MRI)—have vastly improved the ability to diagnose injury and illness.

A third factor, urbanization, also played an important role in the centralization of medical facilities. Migration to the urban centers meant more one-person

http://

The American Hospital Association (AHA) is the national organization that represents and serves all types of hospitals, health care networks, and their patients and communities. Visit their Web site at

http://www.aha.org

[1] A more complete development of the history of the modern hospital can be found in Stevens (1989).

households and fewer extended-family living arrangements. People could no longer count on treatment at home. Home was an apartment building or boarding house and likely inappropriate for convalescence. Without family nearby, patients had no one to serve as caregiver anyway.

When hospitals were financed through taxation and philanthropy, patient fees were only of minor importance. As middle-class use of hospital services increased, changes in financing were inevitable. By 1900, patient fees comprised over one-third of hospital income.

What has come to be regarded as the modern hospital began to emerge in the twentieth century. Early in the century, the distinguished Flexner Report (1910) served as a pointed condemnation of medical education. In its wake, bogus medical schools were closed, standards became more stringent, and the goal of "scientific medicine" was formulated, leading to medical schools affiliating with hospitals and ultimately creating the teaching hospital.

The reforms continued throughout the 1920s, aimed at driving incompetent physicians out of the profession. Physician licensing became more structured, and hospital admission privileges were restricted to members of certain medical societies. The decade also saw the role of nurses change dramatically. Prior to the 1928 reforms in nursing education, poorly trained volunteers or nurses in training did most of the in-hospital nursing. Trained nurses established community practices that directly competed with hospitals. After the reforms, nurses were no longer competitors with the hospitals.

The reliance on patient fees caused severe financial problems for hospitals during the Great Depression. The introduction of private health insurance during the decade of the 1930s would later transform medical care financing. Developed by Baylor University Hospital in Dallas, Texas, and modeled after a prepaid hospital plan for Dallas schoolteachers, the American Hospital Association (AHA) established the first Blue Cross plan—and soon had a virtual monopoly in hospital insurance. The decade also saw a revolution in the pharmaceutical industry. The most important advance was the development of sulfa drugs and penicillin. For the first time, physicians had the power to cure diseases that resulted from infection.

Wartime demands resulted in a sharp increase in the number of physicians and nurses in the 1940s. World War II provided a unique opportunity to improve skills and also to develop new techniques. The federal government became actively involved in providing hospital care. The passage of the Hill–Burton Act of 1946 dedicated the government to replacing an aging hospital infrastructure that had deteriorated during the Depression and war. With priority given to hospital construction in rural and poor parts of the country, Hill–Burton served to create a climate in the hospital sector that made uncompensated care an expected element of the overall health care financing mechanism.

Precluded from offering higher wages because of rigid price controls, companies were forced to compete for workers by offering better benefits packages that included group health insurance. A ruling by the National Labor Relations Board in 1948 made health insurance a permanent feature in labor negotiations by ruling that it was subject to **collective bargaining**. Tax-deductible for the employer and tax-exempt for the employee, group health plans now cover over one-half of all workers with private health insurance.

Vaccines discovered in the 1950s against polio and rubella marked the true beginning of high-technology medicine. These developments, combined with the widespread use of antibiotics, helped change the image of medicine. Physicians were no longer practitioners with limited knowledge able only to ease suffering. We now expect to leave the doctor's office cured. The anticipated number of

collective bargaining
The negotiation process whereby representatives of employers and employees agree upon the terms of a labor contract, including wages and benefits.

doctor and hospital visits during a person's lifetime increased significantly, along with the concern over how to pay for them. The result was an increased demand for private health insurance.

In 1964, Congress passed legislation creating Medicare and Medicaid, making the federal government a major purchaser of health care services. No longer did providers have to worry about whether the elderly and the indigent would have money to pay their bills; provider earnings rose rapidly. Today, over half of provider income originates from government sources.

The decade also witnessed the beginnings of the investor-owned, for-profit hospital system. Prior to the 1960s, for-profit hospitals were small, rare, and established to benefit clearly defined patient groups. Until the creation of Medicare and Medicaid, the general population with large numbers of elderly and uninsured was not a dependable source of revenue. Thus, Medicare and Medicaid, serving as a stable funding source, actually facilitated the development of the for-profit hospital sector.

The 1970s witnessed the expansion of hospitals and clinics, medical school admissions, foreign educated doctors, open-heart surgery, organ transplantation, and the use of technology. The total number of surgeries increased from 14.8 million in 1972 to 24.6 million in 1997. Much of the increase may have been essential. Nevertheless, it was an ominous sign when the procedures most lucrative to physicians under the payment system in place escalated at the fastest rate.

The intensity of medical interventions also increased dramatically. Intensive care units (ICUs) became widely used. Trauma centers were established in most areas. Although the trauma center is one of those expenses that may be worth the cost, the ICU in contrast has created a painful dilemma. Originally designed for temporary use following shock or surgery, its function has been extended to the terminally ill and the declining elderly—patients with little likelihood of recovery.

All the developments of the decade shared one thing in common: They were all expensive. Health care expenditures increased at an average annual rate of 13 percent during the 1970s. By the end of the decade, Medicare expenditures were growing at an annual rate of over 20 percent. Concerned by the spending growth, state rate-setting legislation and certificate-of-need (CON) laws were used more frequently. CON laws required governmental approval for capital expansion projects in hospitals, including increases in bed capacity and acquisition of new medical equipment. The avoidance of costly duplication of services and the reduction of excess capacity were used to justify such restrictions. In practice, CON laws served to reduce competition and actually limited the entry of HMOs and nursing homes into some markets (Mayo and McFarland, 1989).

By 1982, health care expenditures exceeded 10 percent of gross domestic product (GDP) for the first time. To slow the rate of growth in federal expenditures, Medicare initiated a new hospital reimbursement scheme based on the principal diagnosis rather than services performed. Implemented in 1983, diagnosis-related groups (DRGs) have had profound effects on the hospital industry, moving a large percentage of the financing from retrospective to prospective payment.

Managed care was the dominant factor affecting medical care delivery during the decade of the 1990s. Hospitals are no longer the revenue generators they once were; instead, they have become cost centers. **Horizontal integration**, characterized by hospital mergers and consolidations, transformed an industry that was once highly fragmented with many stand-alone facilities into one in which multihospital systems are common. A system characterized by underutilization and overstaffing now experiences a move toward integrated systems and a wave

**horizontal
integration**
The merger of two or more firms that produce the same good or service.

of not-for-profit to for-profit conversions. With administrators downsizing in the name of efficiency, many are concerned about the quality of care and the provision of indigent care.

The new millennium has witnessed expansions in government involvement in health care with Congress enacting an outpatient prescription drug benefit for Medicare recipients and attempting to provide coverage to virtually all uninsured children through the State Children's Health Insurance Plan. Physicians, searching for ways to boost their income, have been more active investors in physician-owned facilities, including specialty hospitals and ambulatory surgery centers. In fact, the practice has so alarmed legislators that at present, a moratorium has temporarily halted all such ventures. The presidential elections of 2008 may prove to be a watershed event in the push for major reform in the U.S. health care system.

THE U.S. INSTITUTIONAL SETTING

Hospitals are by far the most important institutional setting for the provision of medical services. In 2006, hospital expenditures totaled more than $648 billion, approximately one-third of national health care spending and almost 5 percent of GDP. In addition to high overall spending, the hospital is also the most expensive setting on a per-unit basis.

ISSUES IN MEDICAL CARE DELIVERY

Federal Hospital Subsidies: Expansion in the Face of Surplus

Increasingly, hospitals are coming under pressure to expand outpatient capabilities. The general trend in the inpatient market is a downward one — admissions are down, and the average length of stay continues to fall. At the same time, the demand for outpatient procedures and places to perform them surges ahead. In 1980, less than one out of every six surgical procedures was done on an outpatient basis. Two decades later, over 60 percent were performed in an outpatient setting, and the number continues to grow.

In the face of these trends, and with a general surplus of beds, hospitals in New York State continued to expand. The hospital pricing structure in the state created perverse economic incentives, making it profitable for hospitals to expand in spite of the surplus. The state's system of price controls enabled hospitals to base their prices on a combination of the interest paid on long-term debt and depreciation on their physical plant. Repayments on long-term debt generally included interest plus a small principal reduction, making it profitable for hospitals to borrow to expand.

How does this situation result in a surplus? Using the graph above, we see that charging prices above the market equilibrium price (P_1) results in quantity supplied (Q_S) exceeding quantity demanded (Q_D). Some estimate that New York State has 40 percent more beds than patients.

For at least the first 15 years or so of a loan repayment, the depreciation expense tends to exceed the principal payments, and the hospital is able to generate solid cash flows. As the hospital's physical plant ages, depreciation expense falls, so the regulated prices also fall. At about the same time, the principal repayment on the loan begins to climb. The only way out of the dilemma is to expand again, whether or not the market requires additional facilities.

continued

Key Concept 6
Supply and Demand

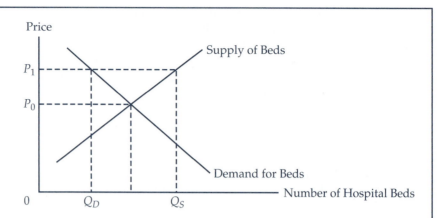

Normally, the credit market regulates this tendency by making capital costly, if it is available at all. Relative to the national average, New York hospitals suffered from poor profit margins. As a result, many were cash poor. More than one-fifth had such bad credit ratings that they were unable to raise money in the private capital markets.

Everyone needs a champion, and New York hospitals found one in the Hospital Mortgage Insurance Program. Created in 1968, the program was originally intended to provide federal insurance on small loans (up to $5 million) to hospitals otherwise shut out of private capital markets. Since its inception, 300 hospitals in 40 states have used the guaranty program. The vast majority of the outstanding loans are to 64 of New York's 221 hospitals. In contrast, only two California hospitals have federal loan guarantees, which represent a fraction of the New York total, and hospitals in 32 other states have none.

All good things must come to an end. The system of price controls was lifted on January 1, 1997. Harsh by some accounts and not subject to political manipulation, a market-driven transition to a deregulated system has not been easy. Staggered by a net loss of nearly $25 million, St. Luke's–Roosevelt Hospital in Manhattan merged with Beth Israel. Flushing Hospital in Queens filed for bankruptcy protection from its creditors. Even the elite New York Presbyterian Hospital did what was once considered unthinkable — it merged with for-profit Columbia.

Not all hospitals were losing money. In fact, 1997 was marked by an overall state hospital surplus of $739 million. But without the $1.3 billion in state subsidies for physician training and the provision of indigent care, the picture would not be as bright. Deregulation has cut deeply into hospital operating budgets, and life without subsidies began in 2001. Whether the system adjusts to market competition or collapses under its own bureaucratic weight will soon become clearer.

Source: Lucette Lagnado, "Hospitals' Building Sprees Subsidized by Government," *Wall Street Journal*, November 22, 1996, A1; Lucette Lagnado, "New York Study Could Stoke Hospital Debate," *Wall Street Journal*, January 25, 1999, B1, B4.

Key Concept 7
Competition

Hospital Classification

Hospitals are classified according to the length of stay, the major type of service delivered, and the type of ownership. Hospitals with an average length of stay of less than 30 days are classified as short-term hospitals. Long-term hospitals are those with an average length of stay of over 30 days.

Community Hospitals   Community hospitals are the most common hospital classified by types of services offered. Under the current classification scheme adopted in 1972, a *community hospital* is defined as a short-stay hospital, providing not only general services, but also specialty care, including obstetrics and gynecology; eye, ear, nose, and throat; and rehabilitation and orthopedic services. Other hospitals are classified according to specialized services offered. These include hospitals that provide psychiatric services and hospitals that treat individuals with tuberculosis and other respiratory diseases.

Community hospitals are also classified according to control or ownership. The most prominent form of ownership is the private not-for-profit hospital, which represented 59.9 percent of all hospitals in 2005. This figure understates somewhat the importance of this organizational form, which tends to be larger on average than the other hospital types, controlling 69.9 percent of all beds. For-profit hospitals represent 17.6 percent of all community hospitals and 14.1 percent of all beds. The remaining 22.5 percent of community hospitals and 15.9 percent of beds are government owned, usually by the states. Community hospital figures do not include 243 federal hospitals with over 51,000 beds.

Over 88 percent of all nonfederal hospitals are classified as community hospitals. Selected measures for the community hospital are shown in Table 9.1. The number of community hospitals in existence peaked in the early 1980s. Since that time, the decline has been about 1 percent per year, until 2005 when the number stood at 4,936. Most of the decline has come from the small and rural hospitals, many of which had been government owned. The number of beds experienced a similar downward trend. In fact, until the mid-1980s, the number of beds was declining faster than the number of hospitals. The number of beds per 1,000 population stood at 4.38 in 1980. The steady decline since then left the United States with 2.71 beds per 1,000 in 2005.

Despite the number of hospitals declining, the number of beds falling, and physicians admitting fewer patients, the average occupancy rates have also fallen dramatically. In 1980 on average over three-fourths of all beds were occupied. That fraction had fallen to barely two-thirds by 1990 and further decreased to 63.9 percent by 2000. Since 2000 the percentage of beds occupied has risen back to 1990 levels.

The other major trends evident from the table have been driven by the goal of controlling costs. Between 1980 and 2005, the cost per hospital day increased from $245 to $1,522. This increase translates into an annual compound rate of 7.58 percent, more than two times the 3.51 percent annual increase in consumer prices. Cost per stay increased from $1,851 to $8,535, or an annual compound rate of 6.30 percent. To counter the rising costs, the focus has been on controlling inpatient hospital stays, the most expensive episode of care usually encountered. With admissions down, outpatient visits have increased substantially, from 202.3 million in 1980 to 584.4 million in 2005. Almost 90 percent of all hospitals have outpatient departments that perform 63.3 percent of all surgical operations. As a result, the average length of stay for inpatient services has fallen from 7.6 days to 5.6 days over the same period.

Physician-Owned Specialty Hospitals   Even as the number of hospitals has decreased, the number of physician-owned ambulatory surgery centers (ASCs), diagnostic testing facilities, and specialty hospitals has increased dramatically. In 2000 physicians had ownership interest in 3,028 ambulatory surgery centers, 1,784 diagnostic testing facilities, and 56 specialty hospitals (Iglehart, 2005). By 2003 the number of ASCs had increased 23 percent to 3,735; the number of diagnostic testing facilities had increased 35 percent to 2,403; and the number of specialty hospitals had doubled to 113 with an additional 26 facilities under construction.

The AHA news is a weekly online publication of the American Hospital Association. Access this site at

http://www.ahanews.com/ ahanews_app/index.jsp

Table 9.1: Selected Characteristics of Non-Federal, Short-Stay Community Hospitals, Selected Years

Measure	1970	1980	1990	1995	2000	2003	2004	2005
Number of hospitals	5,859	5,904	5,420	5,194	4,915	4,895	4,919	4,936
Beds (thousands)	848.2	992.0	929.4	872.7	823.6	813.3	808.1	802.3
Beds per 1,000 population	4.17	4.38	3.73	3.32	2.93	2.80	2.75	2.71
Admissions (thousands)	29,252	36,143	31,181	30,945	33,089	34,783	35,086	35,239
Admissions per 1,000 population	144.0	159.6	125.4	117.9	117.6	119.6	119.5	118.9
Resident U.S. population	203.2	226.5	248.7	262.5	281.4	290.8	293.7	296.4
Average length of stay (days)	7.7	7.6	7.2	6.5	5.8	5.7	5.6	5.6
Occupancy rate	78.0	75.4	66.8	62.8	63.9	66.2	67.0	67.3
Outpatient visits (millions)	133.5	202.3	301.3	414.3	521.4	563.2	571.6	584.4
Outpatient visits per admission	4.6	5.6	9.7	13.4	158	16.2	16.3	16.6
Outpatient surgeries as a percent of total	—	16.3	50.5	58.1	62.7	63.3	63.3	63.3
Cost per day ($)	74	245	687	968	1,149	1,379	1,450	1,522
Cost per stay ($)	605	1,851	4,947	6,216	6,649	7,796	8,166	8,535

Source: *Statistical Abstracts of the United States*, various years; and National Center for Health Statistics, *Health, United States, 2007: With Chartbook on Trends in the Health of Americans*, 2007.

The Government Accountability Office (GAO) defines a *specialty hospital* as one in which more than two-thirds of its Medicare patients were treated in no more than two DRG categories or were classified in one of the surgical DRGs. Five types of specialty hospitals were identified: cardiac, orthopedic, surgical, women's, and other; and not surprisingly, these areas are among the most profitable for hospitals in general.

Physician ownership has increased competition in the hospital industry, encouraging improvements in efficiency and productivity and potentially lowering costs to everyone involved. The bigger issue, however, may be the impact of these facilities on the ability of hospitals to provide free care for the indigent and uninsured, an expense estimated at over $23 billion in 2001, or about 6 percent of total hospital revenue (Hadley and Holahan, 2003). Many are for-profit and do not have a legal requirement to provide charity care. By taking only fully insured patients—a practice called *cream skimming*—they reduce the operating base of not-for-profit hospitals and make cost shifting more difficult.

About two-thirds of the specialty hospitals are located in seven states, including Arizona, California, Kansas, Louisiana, Oklahoma, South Dakota, and Texas—states that do not require certificate-of-need permission to open new facilities.

POLICY ISSUE

Compared with not-for-profit hospitals, for-profit clinics operate under a different set of requirements with respect to the provision of free care.

Most are located in urban areas, are organized as for-profit entities, lack emergency departments, and do not accept Medicaid patients or the uninsured. Specialty hospitals tend to have higher financial margins than general hospitals due primarily to greater efficiencies and higher productivity.

In general, for patients covered by Medicare and Medicaid, federal law does not permit referrals to free-standing facilities by the physician–owners of those facilities. One exception to this prohibition is called the *whole-hospital exception*, in which physicians are allowed to hold ownership interest in an entire hospital. Competing directly with hospitals, free-standing facilities may have a competitive advantage, but both rely on referrals from physicians. Concerned with the rapid growth of physician-owned specialty hospitals, in 2003 Congress enacted an 18-month moratorium on new facilities to allow the Centers for Medicare and Medicaid Services (CMS) to study the effects of these entities on general hospitals. With the moratorium lifted in August 2006, the future will likely see more physicians taking advantage of this investment opportunity.

The Department of Health and Human Services (HHS) developed a strategic plan to address physician investment, reimbursement, and patient referrals. The plan recommends changes in reimbursement for some of the more profitable services, including cardiac and other surgeries, to alter the incentive structure that encouraged the explosive growth in physician-owned facilities in the first place. Also implemented were guidelines that encouraged more transparency to the patient regarding physician ownership.

Teaching Hospitals About 20 percent of all hospitals in the United States have an affiliation with one or more of the nation's 125 medical schools and sponsor at least one residency training program. More than 400 hospitals are members of the Council of Teaching Hospitals of the Association of American Medical Colleges. To qualify for membership in this association, a hospital must participate in at least four approved residency programs. Nationwide, 80 of these teaching hospitals are university owned, and 70 are operated by the Department of Veterans Affairs (AAMC, 1999).

Most of the teaching hospitals are located in major metropolitan areas with populations in excess of 1 million. On average they have more beds, longer patient stays, and higher occupancy rates than their nonteaching counterparts, with predictable results—higher costs. Not only are teaching and research expensive, these facilities have a significant presence in the inner city and often find their emergency rooms and outpatient clinics filled with uninsured patients seeking free care.

Recognizing the legitimacy of these higher costs of education and research, the federal government provides subsidies, both direct and indirect, to supplement hospital revenues. Direct subsidies include stipends for residents, salaries for teaching physicians, grants for research, and overhead payments for administrative expenses. Indirect subsidies are provided in the form of higher reimbursement rates for Medicare patients. But with cutbacks in Medicare reimbursements, teaching hospitals are finding that they, too, must respond to the prospects of a more competitive marketplace.

Hospital Spending

The growth in the hospital sector can be seen more clearly upon examining the change in expenses (excluding new construction) for community hospitals and the total hospital sector. Hospital spending has increased from $9.2 billion in 1960 to over $648 billion in 2006. The average growth rates in spending were well over

POLICY ISSUE

The nation's teaching hospitals shoulder a disproportionate share of the burden of providing free care to the indigent and uninsured.

Key Concept 7
Competition

10 percent per year through much of the 1980s. Since then spending has abated somewhat, increasing about 6 percent per year since 1995.

The moderation in spending growth may be in part attributable to the introduction of prospective payment in 1983. Hospital spending had increased to almost 40 percent of total health care expenditures by 1985. Since that time, hospital spending has fallen to 30.8 percent of total health care expenditures.

Most hospital services are covered by third-party payers. Government sources pay 56.8 percent of all hospital spending, and Medicare and Medicaid provide about three-fourths of that amount. Private insurance pays about 35 percent, and patients pay 3.3 percent out-of-pocket. The remainder is paid from other private funds, primarily from charitable donations and miscellaneous hospital revenues (gift shops, parking, and cafeterias). The patient share of hospital spending, 3 cents out of every dollar, has fallen over the past half-century from almost 21 cents in 1960.

Key Concept 5
Markets and Pricing

With Medicare and Medicaid paying such a large percentage of the total hospital bill, government reimbursement rules play a big role in determining the financial stability of the hospital sector. Pressure from Congress to slow the rate of spending has contributed to a complicated system of subsidies and cross-subsidies among payers. Dobson, DaVanzo, and Sen (2006) reported that in the aggregate Medicare paid 95 percent of the actual costs incurred by hospitals in 2002, and Medicaid paid 92 percent. In addition to these underpayments, hospitals provided billions of dollars in uncompensated care to the uninsured. To make up the shortfall, patients covered by private insurance were charged 122 percent of actual costs incurred in treating them, a practice called *cost shifting*.

BACK-OF-THE-ENVELOPE

The Theory of Cost Shifting

Key Concept 6
Supply and Demand

How do hospitals provide free care to the uninsured? How can a hospital afford to provide care to Medicare patients at prices substantially below the price paid by those who have private insurance? The evidence seems to support the claim that hospitals merely shift the cost of care for the elderly and indigent to private pay patients (PPAC, 1995). In the early 1990s, Medicare payment rates fell 11 percent below the cost of treating patients, and private patients paid 29 percent more than cost. Are Medicare patients simply receiving a discount, or are private patients paying higher prices to subsidize care for the elderly?

We can gain insights into these issues using a simple model of hospital behavior. In the diagram, a hospital treating only private patients will have a demand curve of D_P and a marginal revenue curve of MR_P. Assuming profit (or surplus) maximization, the hospital will set MR_P equal to MC and provide Q_1 services at P_1.

A hospital that accepts Medicare patients is obliged to accept Medicare prospective payment for the services provided. Typically, this means a lower price, P_M, represented by the demand curve D_M and marginal revenue curve MR_M. The hospital is faced with a new demand curve equal to D_P down to point a, dropping down to D_M thereafter. More importantly, the new marginal revenue curve is MR_P to point b and then becomes MR_M. Profit is maximized where $MR = MC$, providing Q_T services. The hospital sees Q_2 private patients and charges them a higher price P_2 ($> P_1$). The ($Q_T - Q_2$) Medicare patients will be provided medical care at

continued

a price equal to P_M. (Note, at point *b* the hospital quits seeing private patients; beyond that point, the marginal revenue from Medicare patients, MR_M, is greater than that from private patients, MR_P.)

What happens when Medicare lowers the payment rates to hospitals, similar to what happened in the Balanced Budget Act of 1997? In the diagram above, the Medicare price falls to P'_M and the Medicare demand and marginal revenue curves fall accordingly. The hospital's marginal revenue curve changes to MR_P down to point *c* and MR_M thereafter. Now, more private patients are seen (Q_3) and the price they pay (P_3) is lower, but still greater than P_1. Likewise, fewer Medicare patients are served ($Q'_T - Q_3$).

This analysis seems to indicate that the government payment mechanism has a tremendous impact on the amount private patients pay for hospital services. In general, private sector prices are higher due to Medicare. However, when Medicare lowers the rates paid to hospitals for treating the elderly, there is downward pressure on prices paid by everyone else.

Several extensions could be added to the analysis. Suppose that the hospital had constant marginal cost and significant excess capacity. In that case, the hospital would treat each payer group as separate markets and merely practice classic price discrimination. Under those conditions, changes in the payment structure for Medicare would have no impact on prices paid by the private sector. A second issue that could be examined deals with how low the Medicare price can fall before the elderly find themselves priced out of the market. If payment rates are set below the intersection of MR_P and MC, the hospital will find it unprofitable to treat Medicare patients, period, and will likely do everything legally possible to discourage their admission.

Source: Prospective Payment Assessment Commission (PPAC), *Medicare and the American Health Care System*, Report to Congress, June 1995; and Michael A. Morrisey, *Cost Shifting in Health Care: Separating Evidence from Rhetoric*, Washington, DC: AEI Press, 1995.

Key Concept 3
Marginal Analysis

Structure of the Hospital Market

Economics predicts that competition in most markets improves economic welfare. This improvement in economic welfare comes about as a result of lower prices,

Key Concept 7
Competition

HCA owns and operates over 200 hospitals and 70 outpatient surgery centers in 24 states, England, and Switzerland. A for-profit corporation, HCA's strategy is to build comprehensive networks of medical servic-es in local markets and to integrate various services to deliver patient care with maximum efficiency. Check it out at

http://www.hcahealthcare.
com/CPM/index.html

Key Concept 9
Market Failure

improved efficiency, and higher quality. But does this prediction hold true in the hospital sector? Before answering that question, maybe we should explore how competitive the hospital sector is in the first place.

Competition may be viewed from the perspective of how well a market fits the characteristics of the perfectly competitive model. Applying the discussion from Chapter 2, competition depends on the number of operating firms in the market, the nature of the product or services offered, the relative ease of entering the market with a competing firm, and the amount of information available to consumers.

Hospital markets may not fit the competitive model very well, because so many of the structural characteristics of perfect competition are violated. Local markets, where most hospital services are purchased, typically have a limited number of hospitals.[2] Services are not standardized across hospitals. In fact, hos-pitals expend a considerable amount of resources to differentiate themselves from their rivals. Relatively uninformed consumers who, for the most part, leave the decision making to their physicians characterize the decision-making process. Third-party insurance pays for most of the care, leaving patients insensitive to price differences.

No theoretical basis is available for determining the minimum number of hospitals needed to sustain a competitive environment. How many providers are needed to promote competition? In many metropolitan areas, numerous hospi-tals provide a complete range of medical services, conveniently located within a short distance of perhaps several hundred thousand residents. For example, the Dallas–Fort Worth metroplex, with a population of 4.86 million in 1998, had 70 hospitals, most located within a reasonable commute of one another. In fact, over 42 percent of the population of the United States lives in metropoli-tan areas with over 1.2 million inhabitants. Based on the number of hospitals per 1,000 inhabitants nationwide, a metropolitan area of this size would have approximately 23 hospitals. The other 58 percent of the population are dis-tributed according to the data presented in Table 9.2. More than 70 percent of the population in 1990 lived in markets with more than 180,000 inhabitants, a minimum size necessary to provide a full range of acute care hospital services to the surrounding community. This size area could likely support three to four community hospitals.

**Table 9.2: Population Distribution
United States, 1990**

Metropolitan Area Size	Percent of Population
Less than 180,000	29
180,000 to 360,000	8
360,000 to 1.2 million	21
Greater than 1.2 million	42

Source: Kronick et al. (1993).

---

[2] The markets for both primary and secondary care tend to be local in nature. The market for tertiary care, in contrast, is regional or even national in scope.

ISSUES IN MEDICAL CARE DELIVERY

Population Required to Support a Hospital

The gap in the availability of health care services between urban and rural areas has increased substantially with the recent changes in health care delivery, including improved transportation services, expanded use of outpatient services, and the increased use of medical technology. Access to health care services in a community is largely determined by the presence of a hospital. The empirical evidence seems to indicate that rural communities are underserved relative to their urban counterparts. Does it make more sense to bring medical services to rural communities, or is it more efficient to bring rural residents to urban centers, where medical services can be delivered more effectively?

Using 1996 cross-sectional data on hospital locations in Texas, Henderson and Taylor (2003) estimated the impact of patient demand and rural isolation on the availability of hospital services. Drawing from a large body of literature called *central place theory,* they estimated the minimum market size, or population threshold, needed to support any given number of hospitals. Their results suggest that the number of hospitals in a given geographic area depends on area demand patterns, usually measured by population size, population density, per capita income, and factors affecting transportation costs, measured by rural isolation.

The empirical results suggest that the typical community in Texas, one that is 47 miles from the nearest metropolitan area with a per capita income of $18,000, must have a population of 35,675 to support a single community hospital and a population of over 80,000 to support two. Results also identify a noticeable trade-off between per capita income and population. Communities with higher per capita income require fewer residents to support a hospital. As per capita income approaches $30,000, the number of residents required to support a hospital falls below 20,000.

Many of the services available in the hospital setting are considered *higher-ordered services,* those services that are expensive to offer and require specialized resources to provide. Theory predicts that higher-ordered services will cluster in geographic areas that can support them, driving down the average cost of providing the service. As a result, the number of people required to support a hospital actually declines as a community becomes more urbanized due to these so-called agglomeration economies.

Source: James W. Henderson and Beck A. Taylor, "Rural Isolation and the Availability of Hospital Services," *Journal of Rural Studies* 19, 2003, 363–372.

The fact that physicians make most of the important decisions regarding hospital care may be a problem if demand inducement can be shown to be extensive. As you may recall, most of the research has shown that physicians tend to be responsible agents for their patients. Even though patients pay only a small percentage of their hospital bills and may be unconcerned about prices, the third-party payers are concerned and expend a great deal of time and resources to cut costs.

Is the hospital market competitive? Several attempts have been made to examine the issue empirically. Held and Pauly (1983) found little evidence of price competition among hospitals. They do seem to compete, but competition is based on quality of care and other amenities, not price. Robinson and colleagues (1988)

Key Concept 5
Markets and Pricing

could find competition only on certain nonprice aspects of the hospital stay, in particular, longer stays in regions where there are more hospitals. Following this line of reasoning, research seems to indicate that as competition increases in the hospital sector, costs tend to increase (Luft et al., 1986; and Robinson and Luft, 1987).

Feldman and Dowd (1986) approached the question from a different perspective. They suggested that the answer to the question could be determined by estimating the price elasticity of demand for individual hospitals. Price elasticities close to infinity, or at least those significantly greater than one, would provide evidence for competitive markets. Using data from the early 1980s, they concluded that certain patient groups, especially Medicare patients, had no price sensitivity at all. Thus, hospital markets did not seem to be competitive.

Although early empirical evidence does not seem to support the hypothesis that hospital markets are competitive, the research was conducted prior to the recent expansion of managed care as a way of organizing and financing medical care delivery. As you may recall from Chapter 7, these changes have had a significant impact on the nature of competition in medical care delivery. The use of DRGs began to put pressure on hospitals in the mid-1980s to limit the use of nonprice competitive strategies that had been so prevalent. The expanded use of prospective payment in managed care has resulted in more price competition. The relationship between payer and provider is changing dramatically, characterized by aggressive negotiation over prices. Some hospital markets may be more competitive than others, but all are experiencing increased competition.

POLICY ISSUE

Will more competition in the hospital sector improve economic welfare?

Key Concept 8
Efficiency

Back to the original question, will increased competition in the hospital sector improve economic welfare? The answer to this question is rife with policy implications, particularly with respect to mergers, acquisitions, and collaborative decisions regarding services offered. There are two views on this issue. The first argues that increased competition leads to a "medical arms race" and the provision of services of questionable medical necessity. Two factors play an important role in this race: First, patients pay only a small percentage of their hospital costs; second, the prices paid for services are highly regulated with over half of hospital services paid by Medicare and Medicaid. Because patient demand is price inelastic, hospitals do not practice price competition. Rather they compete for patients by providing more services and higher quality services than patients would demand under more normal conditions. Excessive quality is inefficient and does not unequivocally improve economic welfare. The alternative view argues that increased competition in the hospital sector yields the same benefits to economic welfare that it does in any other market; namely, lower prices, increased efficiency, and improved quality.

Early empirical research by Feldstein (1971) and Robinson and Luft (1985) provided support for the existence of a medical arms race in the hospital sector. Later research by Pauly (1987) and Dranove and colleagues (1992) supported the alternative view that competition in the hospital sector actually improved economic welfare by lowering prices and costs. This ambiguity has been cleared up to some extent by more recent empirical evidence. Dranove and White (1994) identified a trend beginning in the mid-1980s in which increasing competition in the U.S. hospital sector lowered both price and cost. More recently, Gaynor and Haas-Wilson (1999) and Keeler, Melnick, and Zwanziger (1999) confirmed these results. Together, their research documented the price-reducing effects of competition in both the for-profit and not-for-profit sectors. Kessler and McClellan (2000), correcting for certain empirical shortcomings of the previous research, found that increased competition in the hospital sector did increase prices and costs in the

1980s, lending support to the medical arms race explanation. At the same time, this quality-based competition resulted in improvements in medical outcomes for some patients, leaving unanswered the question of whether competition improved economic welfare. They went on, however, to find that competition in the 1990s not only increased quality in the hospital sector but also lowered costs, unequivocally improving economic welfare. Testing the hypothesis that more efficient firms grow faster, Frech and Mobley (2000) confirmed that concentration in the hospital industry, via merger and consolidation, has improved efficiency in that industry.

The best evidence available at this time leads us to conclude that competition in the hospital sector during the 1980s did result in a medical arms race that improved the quality of care for some patients, but also drove up costs substantially. Furthermore, as competition continued to escalate in the 1990s, quality continued to improve and costs began to fall in spite of increased concentration, supporting the predictions of traditional economic analysis.

ISSUES IN MEDICAL CARE DELIVERY

For-Profit or Not-for-Profit: That's a Good Question

The practice of converting not-for-profit hospitals to investor-owned, for-profit hospitals has received a great deal of attention recently. State attorneys general have the oversight responsibilities in these cases, because such cases involve the disbursement of charitable assets. Over half the states and the U.S. Congress are considering legislation to regulate the conversion process. Public distrust for these for-profit conversions is evidenced by a Kaiser Family Foundation survey conducted in March 1997. By a margin of 42 percent to 20 percent, Americans responded that such conversions are bad for health care.

Between 1994 and 1996, over 100 not-for-profit community hospitals were taken over by for-profit hospital chains with Columbia/HCA leading the way with over 50 acquisitions. Along with these conversions has come the largest transfer of charitable assets in U.S. history — over $9 billion. The sale of Presbyterian/St. Luke's (P/SL) in Denver provides a good example of the magnitude of these conversions. When P/SL was sold in 1995, Colorado Trust was created with assets of $310 million, making it the largest single trust in Colorado. The purchase of Rose Medical Center by Columbia endowed the Rose Community Foundation with more than $175 million. The planned conversion of Blue Cross and Blue Shield into a for-profit entity may spin off over $300 million into a charitable foundation. Staggering as they may be, these numbers pale in comparison to the conversion of California Blue Cross, which created two new trusts with $3.2 billion in assets.

Critics have a number of legitimate concerns in the wake of these conversions.

• Are the charitable assets properly valued, or are they being sold too cheaply?

• Will the transaction be subject to independent review?

• Is the community at risk of losing valuable health care services?

• Will the new entity continue to provide uncompensated care?

continued

- Will the proceeds of the sale be used for appropriate charitable purposes? According to federal tax law, when a not-for-profit hospital is sold to a for-profit concern, the proceeds must be put into a charitable trust and used to promote the original, not-for-profit mission.

- Will members of the not-for-profit board of directors or the for-profit purchaser benefit unfairly from the sale?

- Will the trust be independent of the hospital?

- Will hospital board members control the newly created charitable trust?

Proponents argue that these conversions are introducing an element of competition into markets characterized by complacency and inefficiency. Regardless of how you feel personally about these conversions, expect more as not-for-profit hospitals find that they must become part of larger, integrated systems to ensure their own survival as competition heats up for managed care contracts.

Source: John Leifer, "Inside the Predator: Former Columbia Executive Tells How to Avoid Becoming the Giant's Next Victim," *Modern Healthcare*, April 14, 1997, 46; Tamar Lewin and Martin Gottlieb, "Health Care Dividend—A Special Report; In Hospital Sales, an Overlooked Side Effect," *The New York Times*, April 27, 1997, Section 1, page 1; and Stuart Steers, "Roll On, Columbia; The Nation's Largest For-Profit Hospital Chain is Out to Flatten its Denver Competition," *Denver Westword*, April 24, 1997.

Pricing Hospital Services

By the time Blue Cross and Blue Shield became household names in the health insurance industry in the 1950s, hospitals were paid on a per diem basis, an amount determined by the average cost of a hospital day plus a small increment. Medicare and Medicaid adopted cost-plus pricing from their inception in 1965, solidifying this approach as the standard method of payment for hospital services for the next two decades. But by 1983, the government abandoned the cost-plus pricing model in favor of a fixed payment per case determined by the principal diagnosis at the time of admission. Procedures are bundled into approximately 600 DRGs and given a relative weight determined by resource use. The price of a DRG is the product of the relative weight and a monetary conversion factor. The monetary conversion factor is set nationally, updated annually, and adjusted for geographic location and other factors that affect the cost of providing care. Private insurance went an entirely different direction, paying negotiated prices based on discounts from billed charges. These two approaches exist simultaneously, relying each in part on the billed charges established by the individual hospital.

After an initial period of overly generous payment rates, hospitals saw Medicare margins drop from an average of 13 percent in 1985 to −2.4 percent by 1991, as Medicare lowered payment rates (Tompkins, Altman, and Eilat, 2006). To compensate for this significant shortfall, hospitals began increasing the prices paid by privately insured patients faster than costs, a practice commonly known as *cost shifting*. By the early 1990s, while Medicare and Medicaid were both paying approximately 90 percent of hospital costs, private payers were being charged 130 percent of costs.

With the growth of managed care and the bargaining power it represented, hospital pricing moved from charged-based rates to negotiated rates determined by contract. The result was a shrinking percentage of patients paying billed charges and a growing gap between billed charges and the prices paid by most payers. The shrinking pool of self-paying patients is still an important revenue source, so hospitals continue to raise charged-based rates. The American Hospital Association (2005) estimated that in 2004, gross patient revenues at U.S. community hospitals based on billed charges were 260 percent higher than net patient revenues based on actual receipts.

Hospitals keep track of the prices they charge for procedures through a file system referred to as the *chargemaster*. While the form and content of the charge-master may vary from hospital to hospital, the goal of a successful pricing policy is to cover resource costs and generate a positive margin to guarantee flexibility for future operations. But when billed charges have little in common with the actual prices paid for services, prices cease to serve as market signals to guide optimal resource allocation. Differential pricing, instead of being based on Ramsey principles, charges those payers with the most purchasing power the lowest prices and forces the self-payers, including the uninsured, to pay the inflated prices stipulated by the chargemaster.

In 2000 Congress mandated an ambulatory payment classification (APC) scheme in which outpatient services are categorized into 600 distinct groupings that represent clinically similar procedures. Thus, prices for outpatient services are determined by multiplying the relative weight of the APC (determined by resource use) by a monetary conversion factor.

As originally envisioned, the hospital pricing mechanism was an elaborate system designed to subsidize the cost of medical care provided to the indigent poor by charging privately insured patients more than the cost of their care. This cost shifting is nothing short of a *de facto* tax on those with private insurance. With private payers aggressively challenging the status quo, those with substantial market shares wield enough market power to effectively turn hospitals into classic price takers for covered patients (Tompkins, Altman, and Eilat, 2006). Those patients without a powerful payer backing them in the market are forced to pay significantly higher prices for services. If hospitals are to continue to provide free care to a significant portion of its customers, hospitals must have the ability to practice price discrimination; otherwise the system as we have come to know it will have to change.

THE ROLE OF THE NOT-FOR-PROFIT ORGANIZATION IN THE HOSPITAL INDUSTRY

Using the neoclassical model with profit-maximizing decision makers may seem inappropriate in an industry dominated by not-for-profit institutions. Physicians receive their training in not-for-profit medical schools. A large percentage of all hospitals are not-for-profit in nature, and for many years, the regional not-for-profit carriers, Blue Cross and Blue Shield, dominated the health insurance industry.

At the beginning of the twentieth century, most hospitals were organized as not-for-profit institutions. Their main responsibility was the provision of free care for the poor and indigent. Hospitals were notorious institutions—avoided at all costs by any self-respecting person. Medical reform during the interwar period enhanced the quality and respectability of the industry. Paying customers provided the incentive for the development of the proprietary, for-profit institution. The financial challenges of the Great Depression, and government policy favoring the not-for-profit structure, led to the dominance of the private, not-for-profit hospital after the Second World War. With their tax-exempt status, not-for-profit hospitals were able to accept tax-deductible, charitable contributions. Many also received construction subsidies from the federal government under the Hill–Burton Act. Some state legislatures even made the for-profit form illegal altogether. As a result, by 2000,

The Shriners Hospitals for Crippled Children provides pediatric care to needy children at no charge. The organization operates 19 orthopedic units and three burn institutes. In addition, three of the hospitals specialize in treating spinal cord injuries. A guide to the Shriners Hospitals can be found at

http://www.shrinershq.org/

over three-fourths of all community hospitals were either government owned or not-for-profit. Data presented in Table 9.3 show that the percentage of for-profit hospitals has been increasing steadily since 1980, when it stood at 12.5 percent of the total, until 2005, when it stood at 17.6 percent. For-profit hospitals have increased their share of the total beds to 14.1 percent, at the expense of a shrinking share for government-owned hospitals.

The Not-for-Profit Organizational Form

Substantial differences can be seen in the institutional constraints facing for-profit and not-for-profit hospitals. For all practical purposes, the differences can be summarized as differences in the right to transfer assets. A not-for-profit hospital does not have shareholders in the typical sense of the term. Thus, equity capital does not come from the sale of stock but from donations. Without shares of stock, there are no dividends to be paid. Surplus funds are restricted and may not be used to provide *ex post* incentives to managers. In other words, hospital administrators may not receive dividends or other distributions of residual earnings at the end of the accounting period. Finally, in the event of liquidation or sale of assets, no individual owner receives the proceeds.

Only recently have economists begun to examine the incentive structure facing not-for-profit managers. Influential research by Alchian and Demsetz (1972) contrasted the incentives facing for-profit and the not-for-profit managers. Pauly

POLICY ISSUE

Is the provision of services through not-for-profit hospitals desired over provision through for-profits?

Table 9.3: Number of Community Hospitals and Beds By Ownership Type, Selected Years

Year	Number of Hospitals	For Profit No.	For Profit %	Nongovernment Not-for-Profit No.	Nongovernment Not-for-Profit %	Government No.	Government %
1975	5,875	775	13.2	3,339	56.8	1,761	30.0
1980	5,830	730	12.5	3,322	57.0	1,778	30.5
1985	5,732	805	14.0	3,349	58.5	1,578	27.5
1990	5,384	749	13.9	3,191	59.3	1,444	26.8
1995	5,194	752	14.5	3,092	59.5	1,350	26.0
2000	4,915	749	15.2	3,003	61.1	1,163	23.7
2003	4,893	790	16.1	2,984	61.0	1,121	22.9
2004	4,919	835	17.0	2,967	60.3	1,117	22.7
2005	4,936	868	17.6	2,958	59.9	1,110	22.5

Year	Number of Beds (thousands)	For Profit No.	For Profit %	Nongovernment Not-for-Profit No.	Nongovernment Not-for-Profit %	Government No.	Government %
1975	941.8	73.5	7.8	658.2	69.9	210.2	22.3
1980	988.4	87.0	8.8	692.5	70.0	208.9	21.2
1985	1,000.7	103.9	10.4	707.5	70.7	189.3	18.9
1990	927.4	101.4	11.0	656.8	70.8	169.2	18.2
1995	872.7	105.7	12.1	609.7	69.9	157.3	18.0
2000	823.6	109.9	13.3	583.0	70.8	130.7	15.9
2003	813.3	109.7	13.5	574.6	70.7	129.0	15.9
2004	808.1	112.7	13.9	567.9	70.3	127.6	15.8
2005	802.3	113.5	14.1	561.1	69.9	127.7	15.9

Source: *Health, United States, 2007: With Chartbook on the Health of Americans*, 2007.

(1987) extended the thinking by noting that all successful enterprises generate surplus income. Not-for-profit managers, unable to extract the surplus for themselves in the form of profit sharing, will extract it in some nonpecuniary form.

Key Concept 4
Self-Interest

Nature of Competition in the Not-for-Profit Sector

The popularity of the not-for-profit organizational form in the hospital industry may seem a bit odd given the dominance of the for-profit organizational form in the rest of the U.S. economy. Sloan (1988) addressed the conventional wisdom regarding the prevalence of not-for-profit hospitals. The first argument was based on asymmetric information in the hospital market. Because patients have a difficult time evaluating the quality of medical care, they prefer to purchase their medical care from providers who do not suffer from the profit motive. If this is true, however, there is no good explanation why virtually every other provider—physicians, optometrists, pharmacists, and dentists—works in the for-profit sector.

Key Concept 7
Competition

A second argument is based on the notion that profit-maximizing hospitals will not undertake any activity in which the marginal revenue is less than the marginal cost. Activities such as biomedical research, medical education, and public health measures would not be provided at optimal levels. In addition, patients without insurance or other means of paying would be less likely to receive care. This line of reasoning, while relevant for teaching hospitals and large public hospitals, cannot explain why the rest of the not-for-profit sector engages in little research, undertakes few public health activities, and provides no more uncompensated care than hospitals in the for-profit sector (Sloan et al., 1986).

Based on arguments by Pauly and Redisch (1973) and Shalit (1977), hospitals are not-for-profit because this form of organization provides the most benefits for physicians. Patients do not purchase hospital services directly. Their physician–agents do it for them. Rather than competing for patients, hospitals actually compete for physicians who admit the patients.[3] Physicians interested in maximizing their own productivity will have more control over decisions relating to input mix in the absence of the profit motive.

Key Concept 4
Self-Interest

Many argue that even with the preponderance of not-for-profits in the industry, the profit-maximizing objective is a reasonable operating assumption. Operating margins (operating revenues less operating expenses) are positive for most hospitals, even the not-for-profit ones. This operating surplus has many uses. It can be used to increase the incomes of staff physicians or other personnel, or it can be used to promote desired activities, such as teaching and research. To the extent that hospitals are run to further the interests of physicians, financial and otherwise, the use of the profit-maximizing model may be reasonable.

Thus, decision making in a not-for-profit hospital could resemble decision making in a for-profit hospital (Danzon, 1982). Newhouse (1970) has noted that in an environment of free entry and free exit, all hospitals—for-profit or not-for-profit—are required to produce efficiently in order to survive. The empirical evidence is far from unanimous on the issue. Zelder (1999) reviewed 24 studies comparing for-profit and not-for-profit performance in the hospital sector. Half of the studies found no significant differences in operating behavior between the two organizational forms. The other 12 studies were split on the issue, with 7 favoring the for-profit form and 5 favoring the not-for-profit form.

---

[3] **Competition for physician referrals is more important than ever for hospital survival, particularly as system consolidations and for-profit conversions create integrated networks of medical care services.**

Pauly (1987) best summarized these results when he observed that holding size, quality, and teaching status remaining constant, there is little difference in the provision of hospital care attributable to ownership status. The one exception is the operating performance of public, not-for-profit hospitals. Zelder (1999) reviewed 15 studies comparing public and private hospital performance and found compelling evidence that private hospitals are more efficient than public hospitals.

Key Concept 8
Efficiency

ISSUES IN MEDICAL CARE DELIVERY

Report on the Top 100 U.S. Hospitals

"Looking good! How do I look? Do these pants make me look fat? That's the look I'm after." It's human nature to seek approval from others — whether it's how we look, how we behave, or, in the case of a hospital, how we are satisfying our patients. For the past several years, two prominent health care consulting firms, HCIA and William M. Mercer, have collaborated to compile an annual report card of the top 100 hospitals in the United States. The stated purpose of the report card is to recognize hospitals that "provide high-quality care, operate efficiently, and produce superior financial results" (Top 100). Although the report card is not intended as a tool for hospital choice decisions, recognition as one of America's top 100 hospitals is a public relations bonanza.

Ratings tend to encourage certain types of behavior. What does the Top 100 report card actually measure? The stated measures include financial management, operations, and clinical performance. Chen and colleagues (1999) used hospital ratings to examine whether a Top 100 rating makes any difference in the quality of care and patient outcomes. Using the diagnosis of acute myocardial infarction (AMI), their research compared the Top 100 with nonrated hospitals in three areas: clinical outcomes, quality of care, and resource use.

Even though the top 100 hospitals had higher AMI volumes than nonrated hospitals, no difference was found in risk-adjusted mortality rates or readmission rates. If the quality of care is the same, what is the difference? The real difference between rated and nonrated hospitals is in the areas of resource use and financial performance. The average AMI stay in a Top 100 hospital is 10 to 15 percent shorter, and the cost of that stay is 5 to 13 percent lower. What does the report card actually measure? Rather than measuring clinical superiority, the report card as it is currently constructed seems to be measuring operating efficiency.

Source: *Top 100 Hospitals: Benchmarks for Success,* Baltimore, MD: HCIA, and New York: William M. Mercer, 1997; and Jersey Chen, Martha J. Radford, Yun Wang, Thomas A. Marciniak, and Harlan M. Krumholz, "Performance of the '100 Top Hospitals': What Does the Report Card Report?" *Health Affairs* 18(4), July/August 1999, 53–68.

ALTERNATIVE MODELS OF HOSPITAL BEHAVIOR

Accepted alternatives to the profit-maximizing model share a common approach: utility maximization. In practice, profit maximization is simply a special case of utility maximization. The only practical difference between the two models is the way residual earnings are distributed. Because utility is unobservable, the challenge is to specify a model with an objective function that is observable.

Key Concept 4
Self-Interest

Utility-Maximizing Models

According to these models, decision makers in a not-for-profit environment maximize utility subject to a break-even constraint. The objective of the decision makers may be their own utility. In this case, they will operate the hospital to maximize their own pecuniary and nonpecuniary benefits. Pecuniary benefits include salary and fringe benefits. Nonpecuniary benefits include the prestige and authority that go along with the position. Empirical research has explored many possible elements in the utility function for hospital administrators. The most popular elements include output and quality or some combination of the two.

The utility-maximizing approach assumes that the hospital decision maker's objective is to be in charge of the largest or the highest-quality hospital possible given the resources available. Studies by Newhouse (1970), Sloan (1980), and Danzon (1982) use this approach to modeling the behavior of not-for-profit hospital managers. Quality is typically measured by the level of technology, the type of facility and services, the quality of the staff, and the number of specialists. Running a hospital that ranks high in these quality measures provides a great deal of prestige to the manager. Recruiting quality staff is easier, as is generating charitable donations for further enhancements to quality.

In practice, the assumption of quality maximization is merely a variant of profit-maximizing (and cost-minimizing) behavior to support other objectives. Short-run profit-maximizing behavior may be pursued in order to invest profit in quality. Adding quality in most cases serves to increase costs and shift demand. Quality enhancements are not free, and consumers have a demand for quality. Figure 9.1 provides an illustration of the hypothesized relationship between quality enhancements and the average cost and demand curves.

Suppose a not-for-profit hospital has average costs and demand depicted by AC_1 and D_1. The not-for-profit assumption implies that the hospital will operate where price and average cost are equal, indicating an output of Q_1 and price of P_1. An increase in quality moves the average costs up to AC_2. If the enhancement also increases demand, the demand curve shifts to D_2, and output and price increase to Q_2 and P_2. At some point, however, further increases in quality will only increase costs (to AC_3) without changing demand. At this point, patients are unwilling to pay for quality improvements, and hospital charges fall short of average costs. In other words, over-investing in certain quality improvements begins to produce a

Figure 9.1: The Impact of Quality Improvements on Average Cost and Demand

Key Concept 2
Opportunity Cost

higher-quality product than consumers are willing to buy. These models explain certain behavior, such as the investment in technology to increase prestige, but they shed little light on the important role that physicians play in the hospital setting.

Physician-Control Models

If physicians are the relevant decision makers, they have a stake in what combination of inputs is used. Staff physicians may have a financial stake in maintaining an efficient operation. In contrast, private practice physicians with hospital-admitting privileges may be more concerned about their own productivity than hospital efficiency. Excess hospital capacity enables physicians to maximize their own incomes. Because the prices of other inputs are effectively zero to nonstaff physicians, they have little concern for the productivity or the actual prices of these inputs. Thus, any increase in demand is met by increases in hospital capacity rather than increases in physician staff. The excess capacity enables physicians to maximize the use of their own time.[4]

Key Concept 8
Efficiency

Physician control leads to technical inefficiency in production. When the physician faces a zero price for other inputs, too many other inputs are used relative to physician inputs. This suggests that physicians are interested in the hospital investing in additional services to increase hospital capacity, such as interns and residents who provide services for which the physician can charge, additional operating rooms and obstetric facilities, and any other investment that will serve to economize on their own time.

The physician wants the hospital to price complementary services to increase demand for physicians' services. They also want the hospital to provide outpatient services and preventive care. The former reduces the risk of treating nonpaying patients. The latter is time intensive for the physician and is to be avoided.

Certain services provided by physicians and hospitals are somewhat substitutable for one another. As the number of physicians increases, more services will be provided in physicians' offices than in hospitals. If payments for medical care are based on total price, the lower the hospital charges, the greater the residual for the physician.

Payment for hospital services is separated from payment for physician services, making the physician neither financially responsible to the hospital nor accountable to the patient for the cost of the hospital portion of the care. Any attempt to control costs without the cooperation of physicians has little chance of success.

THE TREND TOWARD MULTIHOSPITAL SYSTEMS

One of the most important trends in the hospital market during the past two decades has been the increase in multihospital systems (see Ermann and Gabel, 1984; and Morrisey and Alexander, 1987). In 1975, one out of every four hospitals in the United States was part of a multihospital system.[5] Merger activity increased dramatically in the late 1980s; over 1,300 separate hospital acquisitions took place between 1989 and 1993 (Danzon, 1994). By 1993, one out of every two hospitals was part of a multihospital system. Today, there are over 450 multihospital systems, covering over 90 percent of all hospitals in the country (*Official National Hospital Blue Book*, 2000). Except for a few large systems—such as Hospital Corporation of

---

[4] This phenomenon is unique to the American hospital system. In most countries, a fairly distinct line of demarcation is drawn between hospital physicians and private-practice physicians. Mobility between the two categories is controlled, and there are few opportunities to practice in both simultaneously.

[5] A multihospital system is defined as two or more hospitals that are owned, managed, or leased by a single entity.

America (HCA), a nationwide chain of 169 hospitals and 115 outpatient surgery centers in 20 states and England—most consolidations in the industry have been among hospitals at the local level (Dranove et al., 1996).

The Theory of Consolidation

Mergers, acquisitions, and other forms of consolidation occur in the hospital industry for the same reasons they occur in any other industry. Horizontal integration allows businesses to take advantage of economies of scale, reduce administrative costs, and improve customer access to information.[6]

Firms are said to experience economies of scale when long-run average costs fall as the size of the operation expands. The notion of scale economies can be seen more clearly in Figure 9.2. The figure depicts short-run average costs of producing a product with five different size plants, shown as AC_1 through AC_5. The average cost of production (LAC) falls as the scale or size of the operation increases up to a point. In this case, AC_3 represents the most efficient plant size, the one in which economies of scale are exhausted and average cost minimized. Beyond that point, average costs increase as plant size increases, and the firm experiences diseconomies of scale.

If economies of scale are to result in improved efficiency, a number of technical advantages must be realized because of increased size. These advantages may include the ability to secure discounts through bulk purchasing and the ability to take advantage of specialization and division of labor, especially in the use of highly skilled personnel. Because case mix differs so dramatically from hospital to hospital, the relationship between cost and output is difficult to measure. Larger hospitals tend to treat more seriously ill patients and thus have higher average costs (Cowing, Holtman, and Powers, 1983; Vitaliano, 1987).

The relationship between cost and size may resemble more closely the average cost curves in Figure 9.3. Hospital A is on a higher long-run average cost curve (LAC_2) than Hospitals B and C because it provides more complicated services and treats sicker patients. Merely looking at the level of average cost would indicate that Hospital C is more efficient than Hospital A, which would be incorrect. With Hospital B yet to fully capture all its economies, and Hospital C experiencing

Key Concept 8
Efficiency

Figure 9.2: The Long-Run Average Cost Curve

---

[6] **Horizontal integration occurs when two or more firms that make the same product or provide the same service combine.**

Figure 9.3: Differences in Long-Run Average Costs Based on Services Offered

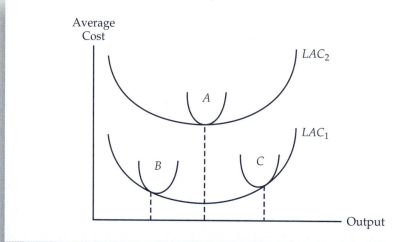

diseconomies of scale, Hospital A is more efficient relative to its service mix than either of the other two hospitals.

The Empirical Evidence on Consolidation

Most of the empirical research on the growth of hospital systems and efficiency is based on data from a time when cost-plus reimbursement was the standard practice. Under such conditions, hospitals had little incentive to lower costs (Renn et al., 1985; Santerre and Bennett, 1992).

As hospital reimbursement shifted from retrospective to prospective payment beginning in the mid-1980s, the efficiencies of the multihospital system have become more evident. Research by Dranove, Shandley, and Simon (1992) suggests that there may be substantial unexploited opportunities for economies of scale in the hospital industry, especially in smaller markets. Although antitrust policy has shown a tendency to reject the efficiency argument, these potential economies may serve as a justification for future hospital mergers.

Dranove and Shanley (1995) focus on the marketing strategy used by hospital chains to promote brand-name identity. This strategy, similar to the one used by international franchises in the fast-food industry, has as its goal creating a perception of standardized quality in the minds of potential customers. Danzon (1994) argues that chains have a comparative advantage in providing information on product quality that customers value in their decision-making process. Given the uncertainties of the hospital market, customers seek out inexpensive information on quality and service. Identification with an established chain of respected hospitals improves customer access to information, in turn increasing demand and allowing higher margins over cost.

Mobley (1997) examines the differences in merger activities between for-profit and not-for-profit hospitals. Her findings indicate that for-profits and not-for-profits seem to have different motives for consolidating. For-profits apparently seek lucrative niche markets sheltered from competition. In contrast, the not-for-profit acquisitions are more focused on markets in which managed care penetration is higher. By consolidating in markets with high managed care penetration, hospitals are better positioned to bargain with managed care plans. Also, hospitals can take advantage of the economies of scale without having to expand any one facility beyond its maximum level of efficiency. By satisfying the demand of the managed care plans for a full range of services, they are better able to compete in these market areas.

Consolidation activity presents an interesting challenge to antitrust policy. If consolidation leads to efficiency gains, then patients could benefit from higher-quality care at lower prices. With the volume of consolidation activity that has taken place in the past decade, it is surprising how little consensus exists on the extent of scale economies in this industry.

SUMMARY AND CONCLUSIONS

Hospital care tends to be the most expensive aspect of medical care delivery. Dominated by the private not-for-profit hospital, the hospital industry is responsible for approximately one-third of all medical care spending. Of interest for policy purposes has been the recent increase in consolidations and mergers, particularly the high-profile, not-for-profit to for-profit conversions. Lessons to be learned from this chapter include:

- Efficiency is not rewarded in a cost-plus environment. Thus, finding little difference in efficiency between for-profit hospitals and not-for-profit hospitals is not surprising, or at least it should not be. With the increasing popularity of managed care and prospective payment, only recently have hospitals been given an incentive to be efficient.
- The economic models predict that competition on the payment side will eventually eliminate the inefficiencies in the market. Inefficient hospitals become prime targets for acquisition by multihospital chains.
- As the inefficiencies are eliminated, so too is the ability to subsidize medical education and charity care for the uninsured. With increased pressure on hospitals to provide care to nonpaying patients, hospitals in turn will increase pressure on public policy makers to improve the social safety net for the more vulnerable population groups, including pregnant women, children, and the poor in general.
- Increased hospital competition in the 1980s promoted quality enhancement, not cost efficiency, which led to a medical arms race. Further competition in the 1990s continued to see quality improvements and, at the same time, increased cost efficiencies.

The changes that began in the 1980s pushed hospitals to become competitive and profit oriented. This corporate mentality has led to extensive local marketing, leveraging with debt, multihospital chains, and administrators earning salaries rivaling those of corporate executives. Will the industry become money oriented and self-serving, or will the changes lead to an industry that is technologically innovative and caring?

PROFILE

Frank A. Sloan

After receiving an undergraduate degree from Oberlin College and a Ph.D. from Harvard, Frank Sloan spent the first three years of his professional career as a research economist with the RAND Corporation. While at RAND, he explored the implications and extensions of his dissertation research on the supply of physicians. An academic appointment at the University of Florida brought him back to the East Coast. After five years at Florida, he moved to Vanderbilt University in Nashville, Tennessee, where he spent the next 17 years as chair of the department and Centennial Professor of Economics. Three decades after first leaving his home state, Sloan returned to North Carolina in 1993 to become a member of the faculty at Duke University near his hometown of Greensboro. In addition to his appointment as the Alexander McMahon Professor of Health Policy and Management, he is also Professor of Economics and Senior Research Fellow at the Center for Demographic Studies.

continued

With over 200 publications in some of the profession's most prestigious journals, including the *American Economic Review*, *Journal of Health Economics*, *Journal of the American Medical Association*, and *New England Journal of Medicine*, Sloan shows few signs of slowing down. If anything the pace of his scholarly activities has actually increased in the past few years. He is adding to the list of publications at a rate of five to six new journal articles per year, and the flow of new ideas shows no signs of diminishing anytime soon. Sloan typically has 10 to 15 articles under consideration for publication at any given time.

Sloan's early work focused on physicians and their workshops — the nation's hospitals. His article in the 1983 *Journal of the American Medical Association,* "More Doctors: What Will They Cost?" challenged the conventional wisdom that increasing the supply of physicians would lower the cost of medical care. The paradox was striking. Although economic theory suggests that more supply lowers costs, the physicians' service market did not seem to follow the same discipline as other markets.

In the mid-1980s, Sloan's research interests began to shift. With separate articles on medical malpractice and medical care for the elderly, both published in 1985, a gradual change in research emphasis began. Today his scholarship interests lean heavily toward issues of tort liability and elder care.

Sloan's research exhibits a practical side as well. Over the years, he has shown that economics is relevant to real-world problems by lending his expertise as a private consultant to dozens of public and private organizations, including individual hospitals and hospital associations, pharmaceutical associations, physicians' associations, and federal agencies. He also provides litigation support for a number of law firms across the country, using his expertise as a forensic economist to testify in lawsuits requiring estimates of economic damages.

Over the years, Sloan has been the principal investigator on over 40 research grants, generating millions of dollars for his affiliated institutions. He is a member of the Institute of Medicine, National Academy of Science. Equally productive in his many roles — teacher, writer, reviewer, consultant — his influence within health care circles knows no boundaries. He is currently studying long-term care issues in Germany and is working with the World Bank on a study of the health care system of Sri Lanka.

Source: Frank A. Sloan *curriculum vitae* and Duke University Web site.

QUESTIONS AND PROBLEMS

1. What are the major criticisms of the for-profit hospital?

2. In theory, describe the different operating characteristics of the for-profit and the not-for-profit hospital.

3. The critical issue in the debate over the merits of the for-profit hospital structure is whether the profit motive has a negative impact on quality of care and access for the poor and uninsured. Is there a significant difference in quality and access between for-profit and not-for-profit hospitals? What is the empirical evidence? (Clearly distinguish between private not-for-profit hospitals and public hospitals.)

4. Does the not-for-profit structure in a hospital eliminate for-profit behavior? Explain.

5. What is cost-plus pricing? How does cost-plus pricing affect supplier behavior?

6. What is a horizontal merger? A vertical merger? Provide examples of each in the current hospital marketplace.

REFERENCES

AAMC Council of Teaching Hospitals: Geographic Listing, Washington, DC: Association of American Medical Colleges, 1999.

American Hospital Association, *Hospital Statistics 2005*, Chicago: AHA, October 2005.

Armen A. Alchian and Harold Demzetz, "Production, Information Costs, and Economic Organization," *American Economic Review* 62(5), December 1972, 777–795.

Thomas G. Cowing, Alphonse G. Holtmann, and Susan Powers, "Hospital Cost Analysis: A Survey and Evaluation of Recent Studies," in Richard M. Scheffler and Louis R. Rossiter, eds., *Advances in Health Economics and Health Services Research*, Vol. 4, Greenwich, CT: JAI Press, 1983, 257–303.

Patricia Danzon, "Hospital 'Profits': The Effects of Reimbursement Policies," *Journal of Health Economics* 1(1), May 1982, 29–52.

———, "Merger Mania," *Health Systems Review* 27(6), 1994, 18–28.

Allen Dobson, Joan DaVanzo, and Namrata Sen, "The Cost-Shift Payment 'Hydraulic': Foundation, History, and Implications," *Health Affairs* 25(1), January/February 2006, 22–33.

David Dranove, Amy Durkac, and Mark Shanley, "Are Multihospital Systems More Efficient?" *Health Affairs* 15(1), Spring 1996, 100–104.

David Dranove and Mark Shanley, "Cost Reductions or Reputation Enhancement as Motives for Mergers: The Logic of Multihospital Systems," *Strategic Management Journal* 16(1), January 1995, 55–74.

David Dranove, Mark Shanley, and Carol Simon, "Is Hospital Competition Wasteful?" *RAND Journal of Economics* 23(2), Summer 1992, 247–262.

David Dranove and William D. White, "Recent Theory and Evidence on Competition in Hospital Markets," *Journal of Economics and Management Strategy* 3(1), Spring 1994, 169–209.

Dan Ermann and Jon Gabel, "Multihospital Systems: Issues and Empirical Findings," *Health Affairs* 3(1), Spring 1984, 50–64.

Roger Feldman and Bryan Dowd, "Is There a Competitive Market for Hospital Services?" *Journal of Health Economics* 5(3), September 1986, 277–292.

Martin S. Feldstein, "Hospital Price Inflation: A Study of Nonprofit Price Dynamics," *American Economic Review* 61(5), December 1971, 853–872.

Abraham Flexner, *Medical Education in the United States and Canada*, Bulletin No. 4, The Carnegie Foundation for the Advancement of Teaching, Boston: D. B. Updike, 1910.

H. W. Frech III and Lee R. Mobley, "Efficiency, Growth, and Concentration: An Empirical Analysis of Hospital Markets," *Economic Inquiry* 38(3), July 2000, 369–384.

Martin Gaynor and Deborah Haas-Wilson, "Change, Consolidation, and Competition in Health Care Markets," *Journal of Economic Perspectives* 13(1), Winter 1999, 141–164.

Jack Hadley and John Holahan, "How Much Medical Care Do the Uninsured Use, and Who Pays for It?" *Health Affairs* – Web Exclusive, February 12, 2003, W3–66–81.

Philip Held and Mark Pauly, "Competition and Efficiency in the End Stage Renal Disease Program," *Journal of Health Economics* 2(2), August 1983, 95–118.

John K. Iglehart, "The Emergence of Physician-Owned Specialty Hospitals," *New England Journal of Medicine* 352(1), January 6, 2005, 78–84.

Emmett B. Keeler, Glenn Melnick, and Jack Zwanziger, "The Changing Effects of Competition on Non-Profit and for-Profit Hospital Pricing Behavior," *Journal of Health Economics* 18(1), January 1999, 69–86.

Daniel P. Kessler and Mark B. McClellan, "Is Hospital Competition Socially Wasteful?" *Quarterly Journal of Economics* 115(2), May 2000, 577–615.

Richard Kronick, David C. Goodman, John Wennberg, and Edward Wagner, "The Marketplace in Health Care Reform: The Demographic Limitations of Managed Competition," *The New England Journal of Medicine* 328(2), January 14, 1993, 148–152.

Lucette Lagnado, "One Critical Appendectomy Later, Young Woman Has a $19,000 Debt," *Wall Street Journal*, March 17, 2003, A1.

Harold S. Luft, James C. Robinson, Deborah Garnick, Susan C. Maerki, and Stephen J. McPhee, "The Role of Specialized Clinical Services in Competition among Hospitals," *Inquiry* 23(1), Spring 1986, 83–94.

John W. Mayo and Deborah A. McFarland, "Regulation, Market Structure, and Hospital Costs," *Southern Economic Journal* 55(3), January 1989, 559–569.

Lee R. Mobley, "Multihospital Chain Acquisitions and Competition in Local Healthcare Markets," *Review of Industrial Organization* 12(2), April 1997, 185–202.

Michael A. Morrisey, *Cost Shifting in Health Care: Separating Evidence from Rhetoric* Washington, DC: AEI Press, 1995.

——— and Jeffrey A. Alexander, "Hospital Participation in Multihospital Systems," in Richard M. Scheffler and Louis R. Rossiter, eds., *Advances in Health Economics and Health Services Research*, Vol. 7, Greenwich, CT: JAI Press, 1987, 59–82.

Joseph Newhouse, "Toward a Theory of Nonprofit Institutions: An Economic Model of a Hospital," *American Economic Review* 60(1), March 1970, 66–74.

Official National Hospital Blue Book, Atlanta, Georgia: Billian Publishing, Inc./Trans World Publishing, 2000.

Mark V. Pauly, "Nonprofit Firms in Medical Markets," *American Economic Review Proceedings* 77(2), May 1987, 257–262.

———— and Michael Redisch, "The Not-for-Profit Hospital as a Physicians' Cooperative," *American Economic Review* 63(1), March 1973, 87–99.

Steven C. Renn, Carl J. Schramm, J. Michael Watt, and Robert A. Derzon, "The Effects of Ownership and System Affiliation on the Economic Performance of Hospitals," *Inquiry* 22(3), Fall 1985, 219–236.

James C. Robinson and Harold S. Luft, "Competition and the Cost of Hospital Care, 1972 to 1982," *Journal of the American Medical Association* 257(23), June 19, 1987, 3241–3245.

————, "The Impact of Hospital Market Structure on Patient Volume, Average Length of Stay, and the Cost of Care," *Journal of Health Economics* 4(4), December 1985, 333–356.

————, Stephen J. McPhee, and Sandra S. Hunt, "Hospital Competition and Surgical Length of Stay," *Journal of the American Medical Association* 259(5), February 5, 1988, 696–700.

Rexford E. Santerre and Dana C. Bennett, "Hospital Market Structure and Cost Performance: A Case Study," *Eastern Economic Journal* 18(2), Spring 1992, 209–219.

Sol S. Shalit, " A Doctor-Hospital Cartel Theory," *Journal of Business* 50(1), January 1977, 1–20.

Frank A. Sloan, "Property Rights in the Hospital Industry," in *Health Care in America: The Political Economy of Hospitals and Health Insurance*, H. E. Frech III, ed., San Francisco: Pacific Research Institute for Public Policy, 1988, 103–141.

————, "The Internal Organization of Hospitals: A Descriptive Study," *Health Services Research* 15(3), Fall 1980, 203–230.

————, Joseph Valvona, and Ross Mullner, "Identifying the Issues: Statistical Profile," in Frank A. Sloan, James F. Blumstein, and James M. Perrin, eds., *Uncompensated Hospital Care: Rights and Responsibilities*, Baltimore, MD: Johns Hopkins University Press, 1986, 16–53.

Rosemary Stevens, *In Sickness and in Wealth: American Hospitals in the Twentieth Century*, New York: Basic Books, 1989.

Christopher P. Tompkins, Stuart H. Altman, and Efrat Eilat, "The Precarious Pricing System for Hospital Services," *Health Affairs* 25(1), January/February 2006, 45–56.

Donald F. Vitaliano, "On the Estimation of Hospital Cost Functions," *Journal of Health Economics* 6(4), December 1987, 305–318.

Marvin Zelder, "How Private Hospital Competition Can Improve Canadian Health Care," Online Public Policy Source Paper No. 35, Vancouver, B.C.: The Fraser Institute, 1999.

CHAPTER 10

The Market for Pharmaceuticals

Economists began studying the pharmaceutical industry in response to questions that arose from the 1959 Congressional investigations of the Kefauver committee. The main issues that concerned the committee dealt with pricing, profitability, competition, product safety, and outlays for research and development. Over four decades have passed since the Kefauver investigation, but the issues remain the same. Fueled by concern over the high out-of-pocket spending by the elderly and rising government outlays through Medicare and Medicaid, many reformers today are targeting the pharmaceutical industry for more stringent drug-price regulation in an effort to curb overall health care spending.

For all the attention that the industry receives in the medical care reform debate, it is actually relatively small, only 10.3 percent of total health expenditures (in 2006). Americans spend twice as much on computers and three times as much on automobiles as they do on prescription drugs. That figure is less than every European country except Sweden and Norway and far less than the Japanese, who spend 40 percent more per capita on drugs than Americans. The low percentage spent on pharmaceuticals in the United States is somewhat deceiving, because working-aged adults with low hospitalization rates spend 20 to 25 percent of their individual health care dollars on pharmaceuticals. The Centers for Medicare and Medicaid Services (CMS) project national pharmaceutical spending to remain at around 11 percent of total health care spending through 2015. Even as pharmaceutical spending growth moderates in the future, it remains the fastest growing major component in the health care system. The effects of the expansion of the Medicare outpatient prescription drug program will be offset by increased generic competition as important blockbuster drugs lose their patent protection over the next decade and increased cost sharing as private insurance copays rise.

In this chapter we will examine the market for pharmaceuticals. We will look at the structure of the industry, discussing the research and development (R&D) process, the role of patents, and issues relating to pricing in the global market.

The Structure of the Industry

Traditionally, the United States has relied on private sector initiative and market mechanisms to influence the direction of research and development in the overall economy. The pharmaceutical industry provides an interesting case study in which government, private philanthropy, and academia have become intimately involved in the process of new product development. In most cases, the U.S. government sponsors very little **applied research**, the purpose of

applied research
Research whose purpose is typically the commercialization of a product.

which is usually commercialization of a product. Through a network of nationally owned laboratories, such as the National Institutes of Health (NIH), and through grants to universities, government and private philanthropy have taken a direct role in funding **basic research**, the purpose of which is to advance fundamental knowledge.

basic research
Research whose purpose is to advance fundamental knowledge.

National Institutes of Health—one of the world's foremost biomedical research centers, and the Federal focal point for biomedical research in the U.S.

http://www.nih.gov

Basic research is essential. Denison (1985) argued that it is the primary source of the innovative technologies responsible for a substantial portion of economic growth. The U.S. leadership position in pharmaceuticals is due, at least in part, to a commitment to basic research, but ultimately the success of the pharmaceutical industry depends on its ability to discover, develop, and market new drugs.

The Role of Research in the Age of Technology

The pharmaceutical industry relies heavily on research and development to discover new chemical compounds that save lives and improve the quality of life. Innovative research and the discovery of new compounds are becoming increasingly important in a world where government price controls are responsible for falling prices in many markets. R&D spending was $55.2 billion in 2006. Approximately 80 percent of the world's total R&D spending in pharmaceuticals is concentrated in the United States, where firms either innovate or they do not survive.

Pharmaceutical Research and Manufacturers of America (PhRMA) provides facts and figures on pharmaceutical research and drugs in development.

http://www.phrma.org

U.S. supremacy in the development of new drugs is clear. Data from the Pharmaceutical Manufacturers Association reported by Weidenbaum (1993b) show that over 60 percent of the 1,265 new drugs introduced into the U.S. market between 1940 and 1990 were developed by U.S. firms. Switzerland was second with 89 new drug introductions, followed by the United Kingdom, Germany, and France. Furthermore, 45 percent of the 152 drugs introduced worldwide between 1975 and 1994 were developed in the United States. The United Kingdom was the country of origin in 14 percent of the cases, Switzerland in 9 percent, and Japan and Germany in 7 percent each (PhRMA, 2000). This trend is likely to continue. In 2005, there were over 2,700 compounds in development in the United States—twice the number in the entire European Union, and five times the number in Japan. Europe's once thriving pharmaceutical industry is migrating to the United States. Since 1995, Pharmacia (Sweden), Novartis (Switzerland), Avantis (France/Germany), and GlaxoSmithKline (United Kingdom) have moved some aspect of their operations to the United States.

return on sales
A financial measure of a firm's ability to generate after-tax profit out of its total sales. Calculated by dividing after-tax profit by total sales.

The introduction of new drugs has been shown to be a major determinant in profitability (Baily, 1972). The longer a drug is on the market, the lower its **return on sales**. Firms earn normal profits on older drugs and higher profits on newer drugs. The importance of discovering new chemical compounds leads pharmaceutical firms to spend a large percentage of their sales on research and development. Branded pharmaceutical companies spend an average of 13 percent on R&D, but biotech firms spend an average of 25 percent, a figure that is much higher than other technology-based industries. In comparison, the aerospace and defense industry spends 3.9 percent and the telecommunications industry spends 6.4 percent. The U.S. industry average, excluding drugs and medicine, is only 4.1 percent. In 1997, nine of the top twenty U.S. corporations ranked according to R&D spending were pharmaceutical companies.

The U.S. Food and Drug Administration (FDA) approved 108 new medicines in 2006, including 18 new drugs—called new *molecular entities* (*NMEs*)—11 new biologics, and 79 additional new medicines. These 29 NMEs and biologics target 15 different diseases affecting millions of people worldwide. They include new treatments for diabetes, age-related causes of blindness, chronic angina, HIV, hepatitis B, stomach ulcers, influenza, and HPV. The FDA has approved over 500 new drugs for use in the United States since 1980. Of that number, only about 20 have been withdrawn for safety reasons.[1]

Prior to the mid-1970s, pharmaceutical research was mainly conducted on the basis of trial and error. Natural compounds were extracted from dirt samples or plants and then injected into animals to see what would happen. As many as 60,000 compounds might be tried in order to develop a drug with annual sales of $100 million. Not until the late 1970s did scientists begin to understand the role of receptors in the body that block or trigger biochemical responses. It then became possible to fashion molecules to fit those receptors. One of the first chemical compounds to be developed this way was Tagamet, developed by SmithKline. This ulcer medication works by blocking a histamine receptor in the intestines that triggers the secretion of acid. It has proven far more effective than ordinary antacids, virtually eliminating the need for ulcer surgery.

In 1986, less than 10 years after its introduction, Tagamet became the first billion-dollar-a-year drug in worldwide sales. By 1992 four drugs had reached this blockbuster status. In 1998 there were 29 and in 2000 there were 55. In 2005 the top selling drugs worldwide were two cholesterol-lowering drugs: Pfizer's Lipitor, with sales of $8.4 billion, and Merck's Zocor, with sales of $4.4 billion. Nexium, a heartburn medication produced by AstraZenica, had sales of $4.4 billion. Plavix, a treatment for heart disease, is produced jointly by Bristol-Myers Squibb and Sanofi-Aventis; it had sales of $3.5 billion. In fact, every one of the top 20 drugs in worldwide sales generated over $2 billion in revenues.

ISSUES IN MEDICAL CARE DELIVERY

Orphan Drugs

Given the expense of developing new drugs, pharmaceutical firms seek to protect their intellectual property rights through the use of **patent** law. Patents provide exclusive rights to the production of a product for a specified time period, usually 20 years. The long developmental period for the typical drug — 12 to 15 years — means that the market benefit of the patent is usually only around 5 to 8 years.

The one important exception to this rule emerges when firms pursue "orphan drug" status for drugs used to treat rare diseases (defined by the FDA as those affecting less than 200,000 U.S. patients). Congress passed the Orphan Drug Act in 1983 to encourage the development of drugs that have limited commercial value. The status carries with it the exclusive marketing rights to the drug. As amended in 1984, the act makes it easier for firms to get orphan status for drugs that have market potential. For example, the drug Taxol (made from the bark of the Pacific yew tree) was approved for the treatment of ovarian cancer in 1992. With only 30,000 women affected by the cancer, orphan drug status seemed to make sense. Even before Taxol was designated an orphan drug, however, it was clear that its full market potential extended well beyond the treatment of ovarian cancer. The American Cancer Society has speculated that Taxol's commercial potential extends to other

continued

patent
An exclusive right to supply a good for a specific time period, usually 20 years. It serves as a barrier to entry, virtually eliminating all competition for the life of the patent.

---

[1] Of these withdrawals, Merck's blockbuster Vioxx was the most recent casualty, withdrawn because of complications associated with its use. The FDA estimates that Vioxx may have been responsible for upwards of 27,000 deaths in the United States between 1999 and 2003. By 2005 there were over 4,000 lawsuits against Merck in the United States and the United Kingdom.

cancers — including malignant melanoma, breast cancer, and lung cancer — with over 300,000 potential beneficiaries. Today Taxol's annual sales revenue exceeds $1 billion.

Firms that receive orphan drug status for compounds that would have been developed without it stand to receive substantial economic rents, payments in excess of the minimum necessary to guarantee production. Granted, some drugs would never be developed without the provision of this status. But two of the top-selling biotech drugs — Epogen and Protropin — are orphan drugs. Epogen's sales of approximately $3 billion in 2005 make it the most successful biotech drug on the market.

Source: Suzanne Tregarthen, "Pharmaceutical Firms Seek Monopoly Protection from the U.S. Government," *The Margin*, Fall 1992, 50–51; *CMS Health Care Industry Market Update: Pharmaceuticals*, January 10, 2003, available at http://www.cms.hhs.gov/marketupdate.

ISSUES IN MEDICAL CARE DELIVERY

Biotechnology: What Is a Fair Price?

The images that we have of gene splicing are, for the most part, the products of Hollywood movie magic. Cloning dinosaurs from DNA fragments in prehistoric mosquitoes makes good science fiction, but a more realistic assessment of the current state of biotech research reveals the potential for far more important commercial applications.

Biotechnology is an attempt to understand the basic function of the human body and disease. As an industry, biotechnology is relatively new. In the early 1970s, scientists developed the capability of identifying specific genes and harnessing them to make the specific proteins the body uses to protect itself against disease. A 1980 Supreme Court ruling paved the way for the creation of biotechnology as an industry. The court ruled that scientists could patent the new life forms developed when genes were spliced into other organisms or cells.

Today over 1,300 biotech firms exist, employing over 100,000 people nationwide. The industry has yet to turn a profit, but investors are pouring billions in equity capital every year into the search for the cures for such diseases as cancer, AIDS, and heart disease. The price of success is high. Amgen sells a year's supply of EPO, a protein that counters anemia, for $4,000 to $6,000. The price of the human growth hormone sold by Genentech can run as high as $18,000 per year.

No single product epitomizes the drug-pricing dilemma better than Ceredase, produced by Genzyme Corporation as a treatment for Gaucher's disease. Gaucher's disease is a rare genetic disorder in which the body fails to produce an essential enzyme to break down fat deposits in cells. If left untreated, body functions degenerate, vital organs enlarge, and joints deteriorate. Ceredase provides the enzyme, reversing any damage, but at an average cost of $150,000 per year — as high as $300,000 per year early in the treatment of the disease. Ceredase is expensive to produce. Extracted from human placentas, it takes 20,000 placentas, or about 27 tons of afterbirth, to produce a year's supply for one person. About 1,100 patients are currently being treated for the disorder, requiring 30,000 tons of placentas annually.

Given the high cost of production, Genzyme reached a break-even point on the drug in 1994, recovering its development costs. By the time

continued

the patent expired in 2002, the company was earning a 25 percent after-tax return on its investment. Is a 25 percent return too high, or is it needed to attract investors? Critics contend that the federal government's National Institutes of Health performed much of the scientific research, and that Genzyme had what amounted to "a sure thing." In 1994, Genzyme developed a genetically engineered version of the drug, Cerezyme, which targeted the disease process itself. Both Ceredase and Cerezyme were developed as orphan drugs and are therefore very expensive.

Biotechnology as an industry is barely 20 years old. As new genetic discoveries are made, their economic implications are not always obvious. Discovery through basic research is one thing. Commercial application is a separate and oftentimes more complex issue. What is a fair price? Ask the sufferers of Gaucher's disease who are spared the costly surgeries to repair damage to vital organs and joints.

Sources: Elyse Tanouye, "What's Fair?" *Wall Street Journal*, May 20, 1994, R11; Michael Waldholz, "An Industry in Adolescence," *Wall Street Journal*, May 20, 1994, R4; and Genzyme's Web site at http://www.genzyme.com/.

Key Concept 5
Markets and Pricing

The R&D Process The profit potential for successful new drugs is exceptionally good. This is due, at least in part, to the patent protection that grants monopoly rights to the firm that discovers an NCE. This high-profit potential is offset to a large degree by the low probability that a chemical compound will find its way onto the shelves of the local pharmacy. The odds of getting a new drug approved by the Food and Drug Administration (FDA) are extremely low. For every 5,000 compounds evaluated, 250 proceed to the preclinical testing phase, five enter human trials, and only one is approved for use. The odds of making a profit on an approved drug are even lower—only 30 percent generate enough sales to cover average R&D expenditures.

The R&D process for a typical drug approval takes about 12 to 15 years, approximately two times the 6.5 years it took in 1964. Testing progresses sequentially, and the drug's status is reviewed periodically to determine whether the process will continue. Table 10.1 summarizes the steps in the pharmaceutical R&D process.

The preclinical phase of the R&D process includes a significant amount of discovery research undertaken to develop new concepts in treating diseases. This phase includes the synthesis and extraction of a new chemical compound to determine whether it brings about the desired change in a biological system. After the new compound is synthesized, it is screened for pharmacological activity and toxicity in the laboratory. For every 5,000 compounds synthesized, approximately 5 percent, or 250, are later tested in animals (Weidenbaum, 1993b). When a promising compound is identified, firms file an Investigational New Drug (IND) application with the FDA. After 30 days, the firm is allowed to begin three phases of clinical testing on humans.

The FDA approves approximately 2 percent, only five of the 250 compounds tested in animals, for the three phases of human testing. Phase I testing is performed on a small number of healthy volunteers, usually 20 to 100, to determine the drug's safety profile: toxicity to humans, absorption and distribution rates, safe dosage levels, metabolic effects, and other information needed to establish human tolerance to the compound. Phase II evaluation is the first of two controlled clinical trials conducted on a small number (between 100 and 500) of volunteer patients the drug is intended to benefit. Efficacy and safety are the primary issues examined during this phase. The final development phase involves large-scale testing in hospital and outpatient settings and usually involves 1,000 to 5,000 patients. By using

Activities of the U.S. Food and Drug Administration may be found at their Web site.

http://www.fda.gov

Table 10.1:   Steps in the Pharmaceutical R&D Process

Testing Phase	Mean Phase Length (Years)	2005 Spending (billions)
Discovery – Preclinical Testing	6.5	$10.3
Clinical Trials		
Phase I	1.5	2.3
Phase II	2.0	4.7
Phase III	3.5	10.2
FDA Review	1.5	2.8
Post-marketing Testing – Phase IV*	—	5.3
Other	—	4.4
Total Testing	15.0	39.9

Source: Pharmaceutical Research and Manufacturers of America, *New Drug Approvals in 2006*, March 2007.

* Additional testing required by the FDA.

a large number of patients, Phase III testing gathers essential effectiveness and safety information by approximating the actual manner of usage in the event that marketing approval is eventually granted by the FDA.

Throughout the clinical testing period, additional long-term toxicology experiments on animals are performed. The purpose of these experiments is to determine the teratologic and carcinogenic effects of the compounds. At the same time, formulation work and process development are conducted to determine if the compound can be manufactured in quantities that are sufficient to satisfy potential demand for the drug. If the firm is satisfied with the evidence compiled from the clinical studies, it will submit a New Drug Application (NDA) to the FDA. The NDA typically runs over 100,000 pages and contains all the scientific information gathered during the clinical trials. By law the FDA is allowed six months to review each NDA. In practice the process takes one and one-half years. The FDA ultimately approves for human use only one out of five compounds that reach the clinical trial stage.

Once approved the new medication becomes available for use. Even as marketing efforts begin, the pharmaceutical companies continue the testing process. Reports to the FDA track adverse health events, including deaths. In some cases the FDA will require additional study to evaluate the long-term effects of the drug, often referred to as Phase IV of the trial process.

The entire process is long and expensive. DiMasi and colleagues (2003) studied 538 investigational drugs first tested on humans between 1983 and 1994, out of which only 15 percent had been approved for marketing. They estimated the average out-of-pocket cost for a new approved drug was $403 million, and the fully capitalized cost was $802 million (in 2000). With costs growing at a compound rate of 7.4 percent, drug research initiated in 2001 would cost $970 million in out-of-pocket spending and $1.9 billion in fully capitalized costs over the average 12-year period prior to FDA approval.

Policy toward Innovation   Encouraging innovation has long been an interest of government. Statutes traced back to seventeenth century England rewarded innovation by granting special monopoly rights to the inventor. The U.S. patent system emerged as colonists in the New World recognized that rewarding individual innovators would benefit society as a whole. Patent policy was eventually codified in the U.S. Constitution. Article I, Section 8 grants Congress the authority "to promote the progress of science and useful arts, by securing for limited times to authors and inventors the exclusive right to their respective writings and discoveries." Policy change often outpaces implementation: It was not until 1836 that the U.S. Patent Office was actually authorized to determine if proposed inventions qualified for patent protection.

Regulation of pharmaceutical drugs became the responsibility of the Food and Drug Administration (FDA) in the early twentieth century. Initially, concern focused primarily on drug safety. Then, with the passage of the Kefauver-Harris Drug Amendments in 1962, the scope of regulation expanded to include not only safety but also effectiveness. Adopted in the wake of the thalidomide tranquilizer disaster in Europe, where over 12,000 babies were born with severe birth defects, the Kefauver amendments required drug makers to prove the effectiveness of a drug in treating a specific disease or medical condition. In addition, the FDA was given strict control over investigational drug studies, Phase II and Phase III of human trials. DiMasi and colleagues (2003) estimated that these last two phases of human trials are responsible for approximately three-fourths of the $467 million capital-ized clinical costs for a new drug approval. This single aspect of drug regulation is responsible for approximately half of the cost of developing a new drug entity.

The most significant change in patent law, and its profound impact on the phar-maceutical industry, came in 1984 with the passage of the Drug Price Competition and Patent Term Restoration Act. The Hatch–Waxman Act extended the effective life of a drug patent up to five years and, at the same time, made it easier for generic drugs to enter the market. The patent-life extension was intended to restore part of the patent life lost to the expanded regulatory process; it is equal to the sum of the FDA review time for the new drug application and half the time consumed by the clinical trials. Prior to the Hatch–Waxman Act, generic drug companies were required to submit their own safety and efficacy evidence to support their new drug application. As a result of the new law, if the generic company could demonstrate bioequivalence to the existing branded drug, it might rely on the original safety and efficacy evidence provided by the branded drug. This Abbreviated New Drug Application (ANDA) is a low-cost option compared to the earlier requirement, cutting at least two years off the application process and saving millions of dollars (Grabowski and Vernon, 1986). Since passage of the Act, the generic share of the unit volume increased from 19 percent to over 50 percent. Now, within months of patent expiration, a branded drug's market share falls substantially.

International property rights were further strengthened as part of the Uruguay Round in the General Agreement on Tariffs and Trade (GATT) negotiations in 1993. Patent infringement by developing countries had become a serious issue in trade negotiations. The Uruguay Round produced an agreement on Trade-Related Aspects of Intellectual Property (TRIPs) that brought about major changes in the patent policies of other countries. For U.S. domestic policy, the most important change was increasing the patent term, from 17 years from the date of grant to 20 years from the date of application. Other important changes included providing patent holders the right to prohibit the importation of products that infringe on a valid patent and a limit on the use of compulsory licensing policies that force patent holders to relinquish property rights on certain essential drugs (Jaffe, 2000; Barton, 2004).

Patents The goal of the patent system is to insure adequate rewards for research and development consistent with the dissemination of the patented product and information related to it. The economic rationale for patents is based on the understanding that the primary product of R&D, scientific knowledge, has many of the attributes of a public good (Levin, 1986). Though patents create monopoly price distortions, this defect was overshadowed in the early years of the American republic by the advantage that the nation did not need to rely on its tax system for revenues: the inventor or author generated his own reward through selling his invention.

Spence (1984) identified three issues that lead to market failure associated with large investments in research and development. First, the value of research and development is determined by what buyers are willing to pay for the product of R&D, and total revenues understate social benefits, both in the aggregate and at the margin. Thus there is no *a priori* reason to think that unaided market outcomes will be optimal in any sense. Second, because R&D is often associated with significant fixed costs (certainly true in the case of pharmaceuticals), imperfect competition and its consequences are likely to characterize the industry. Third, substantial investment in R&D frequently is associated with an appropriability problem, thereby reducing the firm's incentive to conduct R&D.[2] As many have noted, solving the R&D incentive problem by creating a monopoly problem merely trades one inefficiency for another.

With modern economics we can better describe the flaws of the patent system:

- Patents do not transfer to the holder the social surplus that the invention generates. The failure to account for full consumer surplus may mean that the incentive to invent is inefficiently low.

- The well-known experiences of Louis Daguerre (Daguerreotype) and Eli Whitney (cotton gin) whose inventions were quickly stolen, or effectively expropriated, by the public show that the patent is often little defense against inventions being purloined by others (Kremer, 1998). Once a product has been manufactured, pharmaceutical knowledge is often easily reverse engineered.

- The patent system fails to account for beneficial externalities that result from the patent. Daguerre's photographic process had a tremendous impact on spurring the widespread development of photography, a positive externality never captured by the inventor. In the case of new drugs, knowledge spillovers resulting in imperfect appropriability diminish incentives for R&D. The marginal cost of the understanding required to produce a pharmaceutical drug is often close to zero, comprising only the cost of transmitting the scientific knowledge.

- Finally, by their nature, patents create monopoly rents. These distort research incentives and encourage inefficient efforts by other firms to create copycat inventions that undercut the patent holder in pursuit of the monopoly rents.

The point that patents respond in part to the appropriability problem but provide imperfect protection bears repeating. In its capacity as a barrier to entry, a patent increases the cost of supplying a perfect substitute, but it does not preclude the development of similar drugs designed to treat the same medical condition (Waterson, 1990). In 2000 there were six different proton pump inhibitors and six histamine H2 receptor antagonists under patent for the treatment of ulcers. Seven patented drugs were available for the treatment of high cholesterol, five patented antidepressants were available, and there were 27 different patented drugs for the treatment of hypertension (MedAdNews, 2000). Taking into consideration the eventuality of in-class competition, the first mover can expect only a temporary advantage until follower drugs in the class are approved. For most classes of drugs, competitors are able to develop imitations or close substitutes in a short period of time. The process of filing for and

---

[2] Because many inventions are easily reverse engineered, they are relatively simple to duplicate, allowing rivals to appropriate, or rather expropriate, financial returns normally considered the property of the original inventor.

receiving a patent sometimes discloses enough scientific knowledge to encourage further innovation, when combined with the prospect of market rents. Even presuming that markets are monopolistically competitive, patents create allocation problems, provide the innovator with market power, and cause pricing distortions.

A natural response to this dilemma is to ask whether we can improve social outcomes by adjusting the patent rules to create a system that provides the optimal balance between the short-run efficiency of marginal cost pricing and the long-run incentives to innovate. Unfortunately, it is unlikely that the patent system, as it is traditionally envisioned, can be fine-tuned to improve social welfare (Scotchmer, 1991). The number of instruments available to policy makers limits the scope of patent law to achieve the desired objectives. In addition to the length of the patent life (20 years for pharmaceuticals), policy is constrained by the breadth of protection, which connects to the likelihood that second-generation technology will infringe on the patent. Whether the patent is awarded to the first to invent, as is the case with the US/Canada priority rule, or to the first to apply, which is the case in the rest of the world, it remains a restricted instrument.

The Impact of Patents on Drug Prices

The special treatment of intellectual property through the patent system distorts drug prices, limits treatment options for individuals who do not have the means to pay, and causes American consumers to pay too much for their prescription medications. Lower prices on certain branded drugs purchased in Canada have many arguing for a public policy response targeting high U.S. prices.

The awarding of a patent provides the innovator with monopoly power—the ability to limit availability of the product and set prices above the marginal cost of production. A pharmaceutical patent holder facing a downward-sloping demand curve for its prescription drug, D_1, will set output at Q_1 and charge a price P_1. A competitive market that prices the drug at marginal cost, C_1 (equal to average variable cost, AVC, when MC is constant), improves welfare; output is higher, at Q_2, and the producer earns only normal profits.

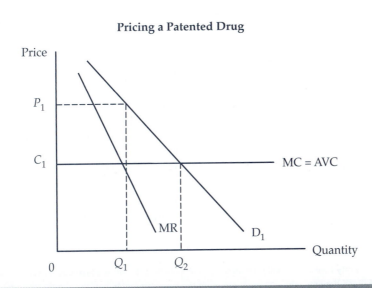

Pricing a Patented Drug

The Impact of Insurance on Drug Prices   Creating a prescription drug insurance plan with a copayment provision invites the monopolist's response, which is to raise the drug price in proportion to the inverse of the copay. A 50 percent copay, for example, would imply that the monopolist would double prices from their initial level; the monopolist could adjust the resulting price-quantity point on the effective demand curve by moving from the initial quantity only if profits are thereby raised (Grinols and Henderson, 2007). In the figure below, consumer demand without insurance is D_1 with its associated equilibrium price and quantity of P_1 and Q_1. With a 50 percent copay—insurance pays half of the cost—demand rises to D_2, and prices virtually double, to P_2.[3]

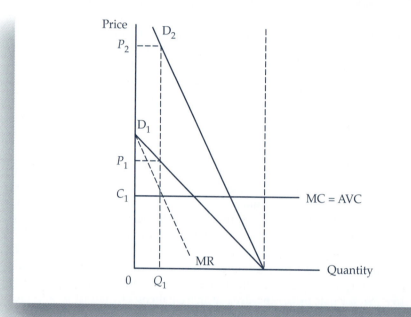

The monopoly response is important, because the percentage of prescription drug expenditures paid out-of-pocket by U.S. consumers has fallen, from 60 percent in 1990 to 30 percent today. Absent other market changes, this fact would predict an approximate increase in drug prices of 100 percent. From 1990 to 2005, the pharmaceutical component of the Medical CPI actually increased 92 percent. Consumer advocates express concern that the prices of drugs, especially those consumed by the elderly, have surged since the Medicare drug program was first introduced in mid-2001 (Martinez, 2004). However, the industry's actions should elicit little surprise. They are the natural result of an inefficient and outmoded means of encouraging research and development.

Large sunk costs, high fixed costs, low variable costs, segmentable markets, and strong patent protection for drug discoveries characterize the pharmaceutical industry. Market power restricts competition and guarantees to patent holders a monopoly position for the effective life of the patent, currently about 8 to 10 years after introducing the drug on the market. Pharmaceutical companies maintain that they must be allowed to charge high prices to support continued innovation and an uninterrupted flow of new products. Because of the high cost of developing a drug, patent protection does not guarantee that a drug will be economically successful.

---

[3] A slight quantity adjustment will take place to maximize profits, and the final equilibrium price will be somewhat lower than P_2.

It is reported that the likelihood of recovering research expenditures on a marketable drug is less than one in three [Grabowski, Vernon, and DiMasi, 2002].

Those who believe that the problems associated with rewarding innovation are solved with our current patent system are mistaken. Patents create monopolies, and monopolists effectively exercise market power, restricting output below its social optimum and charging high prices. Patents may not be the best way to reward successful innovation while spreading their benefits as quickly and widely as possible. The profit earned by the monopolist may not accurately reflect the optimal reward to ensure the optimal future R&D effort.

Take, for example, the question of calculating a reward. In principle, as much of the benefits of a new invention should accrue to the inventor to ensure optimal effort toward possible future inventions.[4] In a static setting, this involves, among other things, knowing the consumer surplus associated with an invention. If patent rights are granted, consumer surplus information is not provided by the monopoly profits of the seller, and such information is not provided by other immediate price and quantity observations if the patent is not granted.

Pharmaceutical Pricing Issues

The cost of producing a modern pharmaceutical drug is high, primarily because of the high expenditures on research and development (DiMasi, Hansen, and Grabowski, 2003). The relevant question may be, are they worth the high cost? If drug therapy reduces the need for more expensive treatments such as surgery, hospitalization, and long-term care, then it may be worth the price. The estimates in Table 10.2 show that for three disease categories—ulcers, heart disease, and gallstones—the cost of drug treatment ranges from less than one percent to 8.3 percent of the cost of surgery. More recent estimates by Lichtenberg (2002) indicate that the extra spending on more recently introduced drugs reduces all types of nondrug medical spending by almost $7 for every additional $1 spent on the drug, 62 percent of which is due to a reduction in inpatient hospital expense.

Key Concept 2
Opportunity Cost

More recently Zhang and Soumerai (2007) argue that Lichtenberg's estimates may be overstated. Using plausible alternative assumptions, newer drugs may decrease overall spending by only $1.31 for every additional dollar spent on newer drugs.[5]

Table 10.2: The Cost of Drug Therapy vs. Surgery Three Disease Categories

Disease Category	Cost of Surgery	Cost of Drug Therapy	Drug Therapy as Percent of Surgery
Ulcers	$28,900	$ 900	3.1
Heart Disease	43,370	300	0.7
Gallstones	12,000	1,000	8.3

Source: Murray Weidenbaum, "Are Drug Prices Too High?" *The Public Interest* 112, Summer 1993.

[4] It is sometimes asserted that, for this to happen, all of the future social value of an invention should go to the inventor, but this is not true if full inventive effort is reached short of this amount. Could it be that Paul McCartney might still have devoted all of his efforts to creating new songs for less than he actually earned for his work?

[5] Correcting for drug pricing alone, Zhang and Soumerai (2007) estimate an overall savings of $2.54 for every additional dollar spent on newer drugs.

POLICY ISSUE

Do pharmaceutical companies make too much money? Should government control drug prices?

The discovery of medicines to cure or significantly alter the progression of chronic and degenerative diseases represents the single best prescription for increasing profitability in the industry. Increased competition and government oversight have resulted in an environment where innovation is the key to survival. Finding a drug that deals effectively with diseases such as cancer, Alzheimer's disease, arthritis, and AIDS will not only save money, it will ensure healthy profit margins for successful innovators.

Protection of intellectual property through the patent system establishes a mechanism to keep prices significantly above the marginal cost of manufacturing. Predictably, covering the fixed costs of research and development requires high prices during the patent period. Once a patent expires, generic competitors emerge to offer chemically equivalent drugs at much lower prices. The prices that really matter for most consumers are the prices they actually pay at the pharmacy. Health plans including Medicare and Medicaid use benchmark prices based on average wholesale prices (AWP) to determine how much pharmacies are paying for drugs. Many plans use pharmacy benefit managers (PBMs) to administer their plans, and PBMs often use the AWP of a drug—adjusted by an estimated mark-up of up to 20 percent—to determine how much they will pay pharmacies.

As wholesalers became more efficient, they began selling drugs to pharmacies at much lower markups, as low as 2 to 3 percent; but a 20 percent markup was still commonly used as the wholesaler's drug acquisition cost. A shift to a 25 percent markup in 2002 brought the entire pricing system under attack (Martinez, 2006). Litigation settled in 2006 revealed that the survey used to determine the AWP of all drugs sold in the United States was based on information provided by a single national wholesaler and did not gather actual pricing data. In addition to a price rollback, as part of the settlement in the lawsuit, publication of the AWP will stop in 2008. PBMs and other payers have until that time to come up with another way to determine how much they will pay pharmacies for prescription drugs.

ISSUES IN MEDICAL CARE DELIVERY

Gene-Based Research

Almost all of the new chemical entities discovered to date act on proteins, the chemicals that do the work in all living cells. But advances in basic research have pharmaceutical companies changing their focus to the development of drugs that act directly on human genes, not just the chemicals they produce.

A $3 billion international research effort called the Human Genome Project was undertaken to decode the estimated 100,000 genes that make up the human structure. As scientists discovered new genes, they were able to identify the molecular causes of certain inherited disorders and discern how genes trigger common illnesses. In 1980, only 40 genes were known. In 2000, the project was declared complete. Recent discoveries include genes linked to lung cancer, osteoporosis, and Alzheimer's disease.

The basic notion behind gene research is that a defective gene — one that fails to produce a protein when it should, or one that produces a protein when it should not — is the cause of all illness. With the proper understanding of the genetic code, scientists hope to switch on genes to produce therapeutic proteins (gene therapy) and switch off genes so that they stop making harmful proteins (gene blocking).

continued

> Despite the fact that over 1,500 disease-related genes have been isolated, there is no conclusive scientific evidence that gene therapy works. Still the pharmaceutical industry is risking large sums of money, betting that it will pay off in the future. While the cost-savings potential is enormous, we may be years away from a developed technology. The near-term market potential is highly speculative at this time; industry analysts estimate that sales could be upwards of tens of billions of dollars within the next two decades. Each gene produces its own protein, and each new protein is a potential new drug.
>
> **Sources:** Clive Cookson, "Poised for the Big Switch-Off," *Financial Times*, April 22, 1993; and Laura Johannes, "Detailed Map of Genome is Now Ready," *Wall Street Journal*, December 22, 1995, B1, B11.

Advertising and Promotion

Pharmaceutical companies have quickly learned the power of marketing. The industry spent $29.9 billion on marketing in 2005, including $18.4 billion in free samples (Donohue, Cevasco, and Rosenthal, 2007). For all the money spent on research and development, many pharmaceutical firms, especially those that specialize in copycat drugs, spend twice as much on administration and marketing than they do on R&D. It is not uncommon for new drugs to sell at wholesale prices that are three to six times higher than their costs of production. These unusually high gross profit margins allow the drug companies to funnel large sums of money into advertising and promotion. Most of the sales efforts are directed at providers—sending pharmaceutical representatives to see physicians, providing free samples, sponsoring seminars, and funding research—to educate them about the benefits of drugs.

Although most pharmaceutical advertising is directed at physicians, the fastest growing segment is advertising directed at the end consumers. This so-called "direct to consumer" (DTC) advertising had reached $985 million in 1996 and rose to $4.65 billion in 2005, approximately 14 percent of the industry's promotion and advertising expense. This activity, essentially illegal prior to 1996, has been sparked by a new FDA policy that allows television advertising to provide information on the benefits of specific drugs by name without also listing all of the side effects and warnings that normally accompany print ads. Wording is still under consideration for the so-called "major statement" of risks similar to the disclosures used in ads for over-the-counter drugs. Television commercials are required to list a toll-free telephone number or Web-page address for viewers to contact to get the full disclosure information. Print advertising is unaffected by the new policy.

The policy is extremely controversial. Pharmaceutical companies have always advertised in medical journals, read primarily by an audience that can understand the details of the disclosure statements. Some critics fear that the new advertising directed at consumers will simply motivate and not educate. The ads can urge consumers to read the fine print of the disclosure statements, call the toll-free number, access the Web site, or consult with a physician. Almost half of all physicians report an increase in specific drug requests, but less than 10 percent of patients ask for a specific drug. DTC provides vital information. Most physicians believe that DTC advertising informs and educates patients, and the vast majority of patients say ads increase awareness of new drugs and improve communication with physicians about health issues (Moser, 2002).

The DTC strategy has proved to be very effective. According to IMS Health (Jenkins, 2000), the $1.8 billion spent on DTC advertising in 1999 generated an

POLICY ISSUE

Is it good policy to allow direct-to-consumer advertising for prescription drugs?

extra $9 billion in sales. That may seem like a lot of advertising relative to sales, but remember these are marginal dollars. The advertising is aimed at unsatisfied demand from patients who otherwise would go undiagnosed and untreated. These revenues would not exist without the advertising. Since marginal production costs are a fraction of the selling price, the difference is all profit. Attracting the marginal patient makes economic sense. More sales will spread the overhead costs of R&D over more users, allowing the pharmaceutical companies to sell at lower prices.

Key Concept 3
Marginal Analysis

The next time you are watching television and one of these commercials comes on, instead of reaching for the remote, watch and learn. Notice the products that are being promoted. The pharmaceutical companies are not solely promoting the so-called lifestyle drugs in this manner (Viagra and Rogaine). They are promoting drugs for allergies, arthritis, depression, high cholesterol, asthma, insomnia, heartburn, depression, and many more conditions that go largely untreated. The five most heavily advertised drugs in 2005 were Lunesta ($227.9 million), Nexium ($205.9 million), Vytorin ($163.2 million), Crestor $159.8 million), and Plavix (152.5 million).[6]

BACK-OF-THE-ENVELOPE

Pharmaceutical Advertising: Informing or Merely Promoting?

What is the purpose of pharmaceutical advertising? Does it serve any useful purpose other than promoting a product? One argument subscribes to the notion that advertising provides patients, or their physician–agents, with information on the usefulness of the product. Whether the function is to provide information or merely to promote a consumer item, the economic impact is the same. Either way, it is clear that advertising is meant to change customer perception of the product and shift demand. The diagram shows that advertising expenditures shift the demand curve to the right, from D_0 to D_1. As a result, the quantity demanded increases from Q_0 to Q_1.

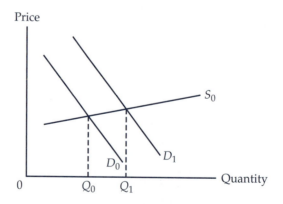

Key Concept 6
Supply and Demand

Whether advertising provides information or merely promotes the product, the intended result is more sales and higher prices.

Source: Mark A. Hurwitz and Richard E. Caves, "Persuasion or Information? Promotion and the Shares of Brand Name and Generic Pharmaceuticals," *Journal of Law and Economics* 31(2), October 1988, 299–320.

---

[6] These drugs treat insomnia, heartburn, high cholesterol (2), and blood clotting, respectively.

The Role of Government

The FDA has been criticized for being too cautious in the regulatory process and thus causing substantial delays in the approval of new drugs. Grabowski and Vernon (1983) examined the trade-off from a statistical perspective. They explained FDA behavior as an attempt to minimize **Type I error**, mistakenly allowing a harmful drug onto the market before it has been fully tested and determined to be safe. The success in keeping the drug thalidomide out of the U.S. market in the 1960s is an excellent example of the benefits of minimizing Type I error.[7] The market functions to minimize **Type II error**, delaying a beneficial drug from reaching the market until its safety and efficacy is fully understood. The cost of delaying a potentially beneficial drug from reaching the market is more difficult to determine. DiMasi and colleagues (1991) estimated that a one-year reduction in Phase I testing would save $13.5 million in R&D expenditures. That cost does not even begin to take into consideration the vast numbers of people who die prematurely because of FDA delays. Kazman (1990) estimated that 10,000 Americans died prematurely between 1967 and 1976 because of the FDA delay in approving beta blockers for reducing the risk of heart attacks.

POLICY ISSUE

Is the FDA drug-approval process too long and costly?

Type I error
Rejecting a hypothesis that is actually true.

Type II error
Accepting a hypothesis that is actually false.

BACK-OF-THE-ENVELOPE

Generic Competition and Brand-Name Pricing

How does competition from a generic substitute affect the pricing of a name-brand drug? Many generics are based on the same chemical compound as their name-brand equivalents and therefore may be considered close substitutes. In theory the impact on pricing should work something like this: The brand-name drug sells for a high price, P_M in the left-hand side of the diagram below. The generic substitute with its lower development costs is priced much lower, at P_G.

Based on the theory, we expect the introduction of low-price substitutes to cause the level of demand for the brand-name drug to fall, which is depicted by a leftward shift in the brand-name demand curve from D_0 to D_1, resulting in a lowering of its price to P'_M. Empirical research by Grabowski and Vernon (1992) supports this prediction—the more substitutes available, the lower the name-brand price.

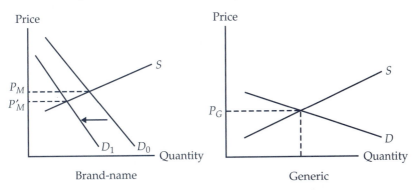

Source: Henry Grabowski and John Vernon, "Brand Loyalty, Entry, and Price Competition in Pharmaceuticals after the 1984 Drug Act," *Journal of Law and Economics* 35(2), October 1992, 331–350.

---

[7] This tranquilizer, used widely in Europe to combat the symptoms of nausea in pregnant women, was responsible for thousands of serious birth defects (children born without arms and legs).

Future Directions for the Industry

The pharmaceutical industry has been widely criticized for high markups, high profit margins, and high and rising prices on its most popular products. Consumer advocates and certain members of Congress have long called for aggressive public policy to control the industry's ability to raise prices, thus limiting profitability.[8] According to a U.S. Government Accountability Office (GAO) report (1992), price controls on prescription drugs have resulted in substantially lower prices in Canada than in the United States. On average, the differential was reported to be 25 percent at the wholesale level. Price controls have had a choking effect on pharmaceutical research in Canada. Since price controls on prescription drugs were adopted in 1969, virtually no new pharmaceutical products have been developed in that country. In general, countries with the most stringent controls on pharmaceutical prices, for example, France and Austria, also do the least amount of research. Another GAO study (1994) compared prices of 77 leading branded pharmaceuticals in the United States and abroad and concluded that U.S. prices were substantially higher than those found in the United Kingdom and other European countries.

Price controls take on different forms across the world. The United Kingdom places profit limits on pharmaceutical companies, Germany uses reference pricing (where prices are set for entire therapeutic categories of drugs equal to the cheapest one in the category), and Canada negotiates price ceilings. Whether prices fall below market levels is difficult to determine. Danzon and Furukawa (2003) estimate that disparities between U.S. prices and those of western Europe are roughly in line with differences in per capita GDP and, in turn, with the predictions of a Ramsey (1927) pricing scheme.

Danzon (1994) probes the validity of the apparent price differentials by examining the methodology on which it is based. She concludes that GAO results are biased toward finding higher prices in the U.S. market. First, GAO research was based on an unrepresentative sample of drugs marketed in the United States. Only one of many possible dosage forms, strengths, and package sizes was included in the pricing survey. Second, it ignored the importance of generics, which accounted for 47 percent of the dispensed prescriptions in the U.S. market in 2001, up from 18.6 percent at the end of 1984 (CMS, 2003). Generic competition in the United States has increased significantly in the last decade. Today, a generic competitor will receive approximately half of the new prescription volume in less than two months after its introduction. Generics were quick to enter the market when the two leading ulcer medications lost their patent protection. Tagamet's patent expired in 1994 and Zantac, the best-selling drug worldwide in 1993 with sales of $3.5 billion, began feeling generic competition in 1996 because of patent expiration.[9] Four of the five best-selling drugs in the world have already lost their patent protection. Branded drugs with combined 2001 sales of more than $30 billion lost their patent protection by 2004. Such industry giants as Merck's Vasotec and Pepcid and Lilly's Prozac are included on the list. Finally, the GAO study also ignored the practices of discounting and rebating, which are especially common in managed care, Medicaid, and other government programs.

Eli Lilly is developing a major advertising campaign to promote its antidepressant Prozac. The campaign, appearing in over 20 U.S. magazines, will remind consumers of the benefits of the drug. The Lilly Web site provides more information.

http://www.lilly.com/

---

[8] Investment in the pharmaceutical industry can be characterized as high risk. Rewards for success must be in line with risk, or shareholders will take their liquid capital elsewhere. In 2005, when operating margins in the pharmaceutical industry averaged around 21 percent, the average margin for publicly traded newspapers was 19.2 percent—more than double those of oil and gas producers.

[9] Smith-Kline Beecham launched an aggressive counterattack on generics by releasing an over-the-counter version of its ulcer-treatment drug Tagamet before the expiration date of its patent.

Taking these issues into consideration, Danzon's 1996 study of drug prices in nine countries reached far different conclusions. When unit prices (price per dose) were compared, Canada, Germany, Switzerland, and Sweden all had higher prices than the United States. Prices in the United Kingdom were 24 percent lower than in the United States—not 60 percent the GAO study had reported—and prices in France were even lower.

Opponents of price controls, sometimes referred to as **spending caps** in policy discussions, claim that they have been uniformly disastrous, resulting in market distortions, shortages, poor quality, and black markets. In the case of the pharmaceutical industry, it is argued that price controls will limit innovation, lower quality and availability, and result in reduced well-being for Americans. Price controls still receive widespread popular support. Proponents focus on the monopoly rents and the high markups, and they have a legitimate case. Who is right? Who is to blame? It is important to study the evidence, understand its implications, and make informed judgments.

spending cap
A limit on total spending for a given time period.

Key Concept 6
Supply and Demand

BACK-OF-THE-ENVELOPE

The Economics of Regulating Drug Prices

Advances in pharmaceuticals normally receive patent protection for a period of 20 years. The patent serves as an effective barrier to entry that insulates the firm from competitive pressures and grants monopoly power in the area of pricing practices. It does not mean that the pharmaceutical company can set any price it desires; price changes are still limited by demand. A profit-maximizing pricing strategy may include establishing different prices in different markets (classic price discrimination), selling at prices many multiples of the actual cost of production (price is greater than marginal cost), and enjoying monopoly profits for the life of the patent.

Two additional features may help define the economics of drug pricing: the extremely high fixed costs of research and development and the extraordinarily long product development phase that extends through much of the patent protection period. The results may be shown in the accompanying diagram. The demand for a drug protected by a patent can be depicted by a relatively inelastic demand curve (D). Marginal revenue (MR), marginal cost (MC), average variable cost (AVC), and average total cost (ATC) are defined in the usual manner.

The monopolist first determines the level of output that will maximize profitability (at point E, where $MR = MC$). In this case, the profit-maximizing quantity is Q_M. At this level of output, the pharmaceutical company will charge the maximum price that prospective customers are willing to pay (P_M in this example). The firm will earn monopoly profits, revenues in excess of fully allocated costs, including the opportunity costs of invested capital; this is depicted by the rectangular area $P_M A B C_0$.

From society's perspective, this pricing strategy results in a deadweight economic loss represented by the triangle ACE. This loss is caused by the voluntary quantity restrictions practiced by the supplier to ensure the profit-maximizing price P_M.

The government response to this situation is often price regulation. A price fixed at the competitive price (P_C) would satisfy the efficiency criterion ($P = MC$) but would result in a loss to the firm, because the price

Key Concept 5
Markets and Pricing

continued

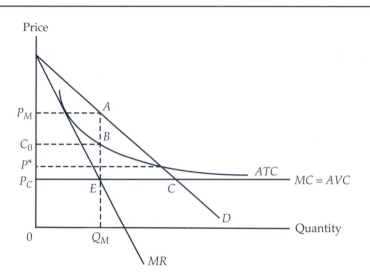

would be less than the average total cost of production. This dilemma could be solved in one of two ways: set the price at P_C and subsidize the firm by the amount of the loss, or set the price at P^* (where $P = ATC$ and the firm earns a normal profit) and sacrifice some efficiency.

Although this regulating strategy may seem simple in theory, it is actually quite complex in practice. Because the demand and cost curves are not known with certainty, regulators must rely on accounting data to make their "fair" pricing determination. Two issues dominate regulatory deliberations: defining the fair rate of return and determining what to include in average cost of production. The issues are complex, and the stakes are high. Before venturing too far down the slippery slope of price regulation, it is important that we fully understand the implications of such policy changes.

ISSUES IN MEDICAL CARE DELIVERY

Herbal Cures: Complementary Medicine or Quackery?

Stop aging now. Miracle cure for your heart. The natural way.
How can you be certain whether the so-called "alternative medicines" have the curative power their proponents claim, or whether the results represent merely a placebo effect? One thing is certain, a lot of Americans use herbal cures. One-third of the adult population, or approximately 60 million people, say they frequently use herbal remedies. Eisenberg and colleagues (1997) estimated that Americans spent approximately $13.7 billion in 1990 on unconventional treatments, including herbal medicine.

Alternative therapies have not made their way into mainstream medicine in the United States. Pharmaceutical companies spend a lot of money promoting their patented "magic bullets" and have no vested interest in encouraging consumers to use natural substances instead. Most research on alternative treatments has been conducted in Europe and published in English-speaking journals such as *Lancet* and the *British Medical Journal*.

continued

In fact, most of the natural remedies available in the United States are produced in foreign countries, primarily Japan and Germany, and packaged for U.S. consumption.

The herbal remedies that Americans buy in health foods stores are widely used abroad to treat such common problems as depression, anxiety, migraine headaches, enlarged prostate, and dementia. Proponents of the herbal alternatives will recognize St. John's wort, valerian, feverfew, saw palmetto, and ginkgo as natural treatments for the listed ailments. Herbal remedies account for almost one-third of all over-the-counter medications sold in Germany, and over 80 percent of all German physicians prescribe them. With thousands of Americans harmed or killed each year from adverse drug reactions, it makes sense to study the effectiveness of these natural remedies.

Source: David M. Eisenberg, Ronald C. Kessler, Cindy Foster, Frances E. Norlock, David R. Calkins, and Thomas L. Delbanco, "Unconventional Medicine in the United States: Prevalence, Costs, and Patterns of Use," *New England Journal of Medicine* 328(4), January 28, 1997, 247–252.

International Issues

Supporting pharmaceutical R&D requires incentives that reach beyond the borders of a single country. A global challenge requires a global strategy. The fact that pharmaceutical R&D spending is a global joint cost that benefits consumers around the world creates a cost-allocation problem. The cost of R&D is a quasi-fixed cost, no matter how many consumers or how many countries receive access to the drug. In most countries, drug spending is reimbursed through government-run programs at regulated prices. Regulators tend to focus on country-specific costs in setting prices. But cost structure provides little insight in determining how much of the R&D spending is attributable to any one specific country. The challenge is determining how much each country should contribute to the innovator for use of the patented drug.

The most direct way to cover global joint costs is to allow the patent holder to charge different prices in different countries. Equitable cost sharing across countries should be aimed at estimating the value of the drug to residents of each country. The appropriate price paid by each country then would replicate a Ramsey pricing strategy with each country paying a different price based on its price elasticity of demand (Ramsey, 1927). Paying a price equal to the marginal cost of producing the drug but not including a fair share of R&D expense results in free riding.

At stake is the ability to equitably support pharmaceutical R&D worldwide. Countries that try to acquire drugs through reimportation are merely trying to circumvent their obligation to share in the cost of developing innovative drugs that provide value to their residents.

Key Concept 3
Marginal Analysis

SUMMARY AND CONCLUSIONS

Analysts agree that one of the primary reasons for high health care spending is the third-party payment system. Individuals, both patients and providers, fail to practice economizing behavior because there is very little direct benefit to the individual who economizes. The availability of insurance, public or private, and the social mandate of providing free care to those who cannot afford to purchase it themselves result in patients demanding, and physicians supplying, a level of care that, at the margin, provides little benefit for the resources expended.

Over the past 50 years, insurance coverage has expanded to a larger segment of the population, providing a growing array of medical benefits. Better access to health insurance has also created a powerful incentive for industry to develop new, and often more expensive, technologies to deal with the maladies of modern society.

Medical research has accomplished countless miracles over the years, especially in the lifetimes of most of those who are reading this book. The most important pharmaceutical innovations include developments in the areas of the treatment of heart disease (including ACE inhibitors to control high blood pressure, blood thinning agents to control clotting, and statins to treat high cholesterol) and inhaled steroids to treat asthma (Fuchs and Sox, 2001).

Is technological change worth the cost? Cutler and McClellan (2001) try to answer this question by examining five conditions: heart attacks, low–birth-weight infants, depression, cataracts, and breast cancer. For each condition except breast cancer, the net benefits of the new treatment have been significantly positive due to substantial improvements in outcomes at reasonable costs.

It is important that we understand the close causality between the availability of medical technology and the ability to pay for it. In our desire to control expenditures, it is essential that we preserve the financial incentives that foster and promote scientific inquiry at its basic level. We must also reward the applied research that creates marketable products that enhance the quality of medical care for millions.

Using history as a guide, we might conclude that rapid technological change in medical care will lead to increased spending. If biotechnology provides for the effective treatment of genetic diseases, however, we could see a shift from cost-increasing technology to cost-saving technology. It is not just wishful thinking to expect advances in cell biology in the next few decades to lead to cures for certain types of cancers and heart disease. It is equally important that the price mechanism not put these products out of the reach of those who stand to benefit from the discoveries.

PROFILE

Patricia M. Danzon

If the makeup of a Ph.D. dissertation committee can be used as an indicator of future success, then Patricia Danzon's climb to the pinnacle of her profession comes as no surprise. In addition to her supervising professor, Nobel Prize winner George Stigler, the other members of her committee included future Nobel laureates in economics Ronald Coase and Gary Becker.

Soon after she was born, Danzon's father moved the family from England to Pretoria, South Africa, where they lived until she was a teenager. Returning to England, Danzon graduated from Oxford University in 1968 with a B.A. in politics, philosophy, and economics. She decided to attend graduate school in the United States and applied to the six best graduate programs in economics. Only one, the University of Chicago, accepted her, and they even provided a full fellowship to cover the cost of her studies.

Danzon received her Ph.D. in 1973 and began working for the RAND Corporation. She was able to turn her dissertation on exploring eminent domain into her first publication in the prestigious *Journal of Political Economy*. Her work with RAND initially dealt primarily with military manpower issues. Even though the issue was of growing importance with the end of the Vietnam War and emergence of the all-volunteer army in the United States, Danzon was soon ready to tackle another challenge. At about this time, the first malpractice insurance crisis was gripping the medical community. Joseph Newhouse, then head of the health group at RAND, came to her suggesting that someone really ought to look into the problem from an economic perspective. Danzon saw this as an opportunity to combine several fields of study: health economics, insurance, law, and economics. She had to overcome one minor problem — her background was in law and economics, and she knew little about the other two. Undaunted by the limitation, she became self-taught in both health economics and insurance.

continued

Danzon was assigned as the staff person on professional liability at the California Commission on Tort Reform. There she teamed up with Dennis Smallwood to publish empirical research on the property/casualty industry in the 1980 *Bell Journal of Economics*, the first of over 40 books, journal articles, and book chapters on insurance and medical liability. Her work has been published in the most highly regarded journals in economics and health care, including the *American Economic Review*, the *Journal of Health Economics*, and *Health Affairs*. She may be best known for her book *Medical Malpractice: Theory, Evidence, and Public Policy* (Harvard University Press, 1985).

Danzon left RAND in 1980. After relatively short stays at Stanford's Hoover Institute and Duke University, she moved to the University of Pennsylvania in 1985, where she is the Celia Z. Moh Professor and Professor of Health Care Systems and Insurance and Risk Management at The Wharton School.

Over the past two decades, Danzon has emerged as an international expert on medical malpractice, but the exclusive focus on one issue left her desiring a little variety in her scholarly pursuits. So in 1991, funded by a grant from the University Research Council, Danzon ventured into a new field of study: the pharmaceutical industry. She has turned her interest in health care and pharmaceutical pricing into consultancies with the World Bank, the Asian Development Bank, and the United States Agency for International Development, examining drug pricing in Europe and New Zealand.

Danzon has maintained a practical focus in her scholarly pursuits. The testing of economic theory with empirical evidence is a way of thinking she acquired during her graduate studies under Stigler and developed in the years since. Everyone interested in the study of health care, insurance, and legal liability is richer for her efforts.

Source: *Curriculum vitae* and personal correspondence.

QUESTIONS AND PROBLEMS

1. Pharmaceutical spending is less than 8 percent of total health care spending in the United States. Why do you suppose the industry is the target of such severe criticism?

2. What are some of the important economic issues that help us understand availability and pricing in the pharmaceutical industry?

3. A person learns from a genetic test that she has a predisposition for a certain disease, say, Alzheimer's disease. Who should have access to that genetic information? Medical practitioners? Insurance companies? The individual? Would you want to know? Why?

REFERENCES

Martin N. Baily, "Research and Development Costs and Returns: The U.S. Pharmaceutical Industry," *Journal of Political Economy* 80(1), January/February 1972, 70–85.

John H. Barton, "TRIPS and the Global Pharmaceutical Market," *Health Affairs* 23(3), 2004, 146–154.

Centers for Medicare and Medicaid Services (CMS), Health Care Industry Market Update: Pharmaceuticals, January 10, 2003. Available at: http://www.cms.hhs.gov/marketupdate.

David M. Cutler and Mark McClellan, "Is Technological Change in Medicine Worth It?" *Health Affairs* 20(5), September/October 2001, 11–29.

Patricia M. Danzon, "Drug Price Controls, Wrong Prescription," *Wall Street Journal*, February 4, 1994, A10.

————, "International Drug Price Comparisons: Uses and Abuses," in Richard B. Helms, ed., *Competition Strategies in the Pharmaceutical Industry*, Washington, DC: The AEI Press, 1996.

———— and Michael F. Fukukawa, "Prices and the Availability of Pharmaceuticals: Evidence from Nine Countries," *Health Affairs* web exclusive, October 29, 2003, w3 521–536.

Joseph A. DiMasi, Ronald W. Hansen, and Henry G. Grabowski, "The Price of Innovation: New Estimates of Drug Development Costs," *Journal of Health Economics* 22, 2003, 151–185.

————, and Louis Lasagna, "Cost of Innovation in the Pharmaceutical Industry," *Journal of Health Economics* 10(2), July 1991, 107–142.

Julie M. Donohue, Marisa Cevasco, and Meredith B. Rosenthal, "A Decade of Direct-to-Consumer Advertising of Prescription Drugs," *New England Journal of Medicine* 357(7), August 16, 2007, 673–681.

Roger W. Evans, "Health Care Technology and the Inevitability of Resource Allocation and Rationing Decisions, Part I," *Journal of the American Medical Association* 249(15), April 15, 1983, 2047–2053.

Victor R. Fuchs and Harold C. Sox, Jr., "Physicians' Views of the Relative Importance of Thirty Medical Innovations," *Health Affairs* 20(5), September/October 2001, 30–42.

Henry G. Grabowski and John Vernon, "A New Look at the Returns and Risks to Pharmaceutical R&D," *Management Science* 36(7), July 1990, 804–821.

————, "Brand Loyalty, Entry, and Price Competition in Pharmaceuticals after the 1984 Drug Act," *Journal of Law and Economics* 35(2), October 1992, 331–350.

————, "Longer Patents for Lower Imitation Barriers: The 1984 Drug Act," *The American Economic Review Papers and Proceedings* 76(2), 1986, 195–198.

————, *The Regulation of Pharmaceuticals: Balancing the Benefits and Risks*, Washington, DC: American Enterprise Institute, 1983.

Earl L. Grinols and James W. Henderson, "Replace Pharmaceutical Patents Now," *Pharmacoeconomics* 25(5), 2007, 355–363.

Mark A. Hurwitz and Richard E. Caves, "Persuasion or Information? Promotion and the Shares of Brand Name and Generic Pharmaceuticals," *Journal of Law and Economics* 31(2), October 1988, 299–320.

Adam B. Jaffe, "The U.S. Patent System in Transition: Policy Innovation and the Innovation Process," *Research Policy* (29), 2000, 531–557.

Holman W. Jenkins, Jr., "Lazy Insurers Hitch a Ride on the Drug Wars," *Wall Street Journal*, August 9, 2000, A23.

Kenneth Kaitin, N. Mattison, F. K. Northington, and Louis Lasagna, "The Drug Lag: An Update of New Drug Introductions in the United States and in the United Kingdom, 1977 through 1987," *Clinical Pharmacology and Therapeutics*, August 1989, 121–138.

Sam Kazman, "Deadly Overcaution: FDA's Drug Approval Process," *Journal of Regulation and Social Costs*, September 1990.

Michael Kremer, "Patent Buyouts: A Mechanism for Encouraging Innovation," *Quarterly Journal of Economics* 113(4), November 1998, 1137–1167.

Keith B. Leffler, "Persuasion or Information? The Economics of Prescription Drug Advertising," *Journal of Law and Economics* 24(1), April 1981, 45–74.

Richard C. Levin, "A New Look at the Patent System," *American Economic Review Papers and Proceedings* 76(2), 1986, 199–202.

Frank R. Lichtenberg, "Benefits and Costs of Newer Drugs: An Update," *NBER Working Paper No. 8996*, Cambridge, MA: National Bureau of Economic Research, 2002.

Barbara Martinez, "Drug-Price Surge May Erode Savings from Medicard Card," *Wall Street Journal*, March 24, 2004, B1.

Joe Moser, "Direct-to-Consumer Advertising: Helpful of Costly? A Fact Sheet," Galen Institute, September 12, 2002. Available at http://www.galen.org/news/091202.html.

Joseph P. Newhouse, "Medical Care Costs: How Much Welfare Loss?" *Journal of Economic Perspectives* 6(3), Summer 1992, 3–21.

Pharmaceutical Research and Manufacturers of America, *Pharmaceutical Industry Profile 2007* Washington, DC: PhRMA, March 2007.

Frank Ramsey, "A Contribution to the Theory of Taxation," *Economic Journal* 37, 1927, 47–61.

Anne A. Scitovsky, "Changes in the Costs of Treatment of Selected Illnesses, 1971–1981," *Medical Care* 23(12), December 1985, 1345–1357.

Suzanne Scotchmer, "Standing on the Shoulders of Giants: Cumulative Research and the Patent Law," *Journal of Economic Perspectives* 5(1), 1991, 29–41.

Michael Spence, "Cost Reduction, Competition, and Industry Performance." Econometrica, 52(1), 1984, 101–121.

"The Top 500 Drugs by Class of Drugs," *MedAdNews* 19(5), 2000, 77–82.

U.S. Government Accountability Office (GAO), *Prescription Drugs: Companies Typically Charge More in the United States Than in Canada*, Washington, DC: USGAO, 1992.

————, *Prescription Drugs: Improvements Needed in FDA's Oversight of Direct-to-Consumer Advertising,*" GAO-07–54, Washington, DC: USGAO, November 2006.

————, *Prescription Drugs: Spending Controls in Four European Countries*, Washington, DC: USGAO, 1994.

Michael Waterson, "The Economics of Product Patents," *American Economic Review* 80(4), 1990, 860–869.

Lewis Thomas, *The Lives of a Cell*, New York: Bantam Books, 1975.

Murray Weidenbaum, "Are Drug Prices Too High?" *The Public Interest* 112, Summer 1993a, 84–89.

————, *Restraining Medicine Prices: Controls vs. Competition*, St. Louis, MO: Washington University Center for the Study of American Business, Policy Study No. 116, April 1993b.

Burton A. Weisbrod, "The Health Care Quadrilemma: An Essay on Technological Change, Insurance, Quality of Care, and Cost Containment," *Journal of Economic Literature* 29(2), June 1991, 523–552.

L. John Wilkerson and Robert Easton, ". . . But Don't Kill the Golden Goose," *The New York Times*, March 7, 1993, F13.

Yuting Zhang and Stephen B. Soumerai, "Do Newer Prescription Drugs Pay for Themselves? A Reassessment of the Evidence," *Health Affairs* 26(3), May/June 2007, 880–886.

Confounding Factors

Americans spend more on medical care than any other people in the world, whether measured in total dollars spent, per capita outlays, or as a share of total economic output. For all of our spending, it is not clear that we are any healthier than our foreign counterparts. In fact, critics of the system cite a never-ending litany of statistics, primarily on life expectancy and infant mortality, to bolster their argument that the U.S. health care delivery system is seriously flawed and in immediate need of radical overhaul. Is the U.S. medical care sector woefully negligent in providing the necessary care to improve health outcomes, or does something else explain high spending and outcomes that do not meet our high expectations? Is it appropriate to blame our medical care delivery system for the poor relative outcomes we observe?

In this chapter, we will examine several confounding factors that contribute to high health care spending in the United States: lifestyle considerations, population aging, the high cost of medical malpractice, and the use of expensive medical technology. The goal of this chapter is to develop an understanding of how these problems contribute to medical care spending and the health outcomes that we observe. These problems are not unique to the United States, but if we are to understand the challenges facing American health care, we must understand these issues and the confounding role they play in the delivery of medical care.

LIFESTYLE CONSIDERATIONS

The health problems associated with American lifestyles presents a serious challenge for the U.S. medical sector. The cost to society can be measured in terms of the obvious health problems, such as heart disease, stroke, cancer, and other chronic conditions, but also in terms of the lost productivity due to disability and premature death. Discussions of relative performance of medical care delivery systems tend to focus on measures of health outcomes, when in truth, health outcomes may be more dependent on factors other than medical care that include lifestyle considerations. A number of social problems and lifestyle considerations will be discussed in this section: HIV/AIDS, teenage pregnancies, alcohol and tobacco use, food consumption, and the prevalence of obesity and diabetes.

AIDS in America

More than 42 million people alive today worldwide have been infected with the human immunodeficiency virus (HIV) that causes acquired immunodeficiency syndrome (AIDS). More than 16 million have already died as a result of complications from the disease. The consequences of the disease have both social and economic components. AIDS has left in its wake over 11 million orphaned

The Centers for Disease Control provides health information and links to publications and statistics on disease prevention and control. Links are also available to Mortality and Morbidity Weekly Report and the journal *Emerging Infectious Diseases.*

http://www.cdc.com

children who have lost both parents to the disease. In many parts of the world, gaps are being created in the workforce due to prime-age workers being lost during their most productive years. Life expectancy after contracting AIDS is relatively short in developing countries, primarily due to the lack of funds allocated to caring for those affected. Daniel Tarantola of the Harvard School of Public Health reports that an African AIDS patient can expect to receive $400 in medical treatment during a single year. In contrast, an AIDS patient in the United States receives around $20,000 in AIDS-related medical care annually. More than 95 percent of all people with AIDS live or lived in the developing world, but only 6 percent of the money spent on treating the disease is spent in these countries (Chase, 1992).[1]

AIDS results when the human immune system is so weakened by HIV that the body can no longer fight off serious infections. From 1981, when AIDS was first discovered in clinical studies, until 2005, approximately 988,376 cases were reported in the United States. The fatality rate for those infected is quite high, over 55 percent for adults and children. About 45,000 new cases are diagnosed annually in the United States.[2] At the end of 2005, an estimated 437,982 Americans were living with AIDS, and another 250,000 were living with HIV (CDC, 2006b). Fortunately, the disease has not spread much beyond the traditional risk groups, which includes homosexual and bisexual males, IV-drug users, and those who have sexual contact with them. These groups account for approximately 80 percent of all infections. Heterosexual contact cases of AIDS have not grown as rapidly as initially predicted. About 165,000 cases can be traced to heterosexual contact, or about 17.2 percent of the total cases diagnosed, and most had sexual partners who were members of the high-risk groups.

The Centers for Disease Control (CDC) estimated that over half of all new HIV infections occur in the drug-injecting population. Changing the behavior of IV-drug users represents the biggest challenge in the battle to control the spread of this disease. Unsafe practices, such as sharing needles and promiscuous sex (homosexual, heterosexual, and bisexual), are the leading cause of infection.

Risk to the Population Even though the extent of AIDS in the United States is nowhere near that experienced in the less developed world, the same cannot be said when comparing the U.S. experience with other advanced countries. As shown in Table 11.1, cumulative AIDS cases per 100,000 are roughly 140 times greater in the United States than in Japan, almost 10 times greater than in the United Kingdom, and three times greater than in France. The cumulative rate in the United States is five and one-half times the average rate of the six-country comparison group. The 45,000 new cases in the United States annually translate into almost 15 per 100,000 population, substantially higher than any of the other six countries and seven times the average. Even though the death rate from AIDS is relatively high in the United States, the mortality ratio compares favorably with that of Germany, Switzerland, and the United Kingdom and is much better than that of Canada and France.

Medical Care Issues Bozzette and colleagues (2001) estimated that the annual cost of care for treating HIV-infected patients was $18,300 in 1998, down from $20,300 in 1996. Examining the cost effectiveness of a highly active antiretroviral treatment

---

[1] Part of the problem is the high cost of drug treatment. Responding to this issue, the U.S. government pledged to triple spending on combating AIDS in some of the world's poorest countries to $15 billion from 2003 to 2008.

[2] To put these statistics into perspective, according to the American Cancer Society (http://www.cancer.org/docroot/home/index.asp), 180,500 new breast cancer diagnoses and over 40,000 breast cancer deaths were expected in 2007. For prostate cancer, the numbers were 218,890 new cases and 27,050 deaths. In 2003, over 840,000 Americans died of cardiovascular diseases (including stroke) and 556,900 died of cancer (including breast and prostate cancer).

Table 11.1: Acquired Immune Deficiency Syndrome

	Cumulative Cases/100,000 (As of 2001)	New Cases/100,000 (2000)	Death Rate/100,000 (2002)	Mortality Ratio (Death Rate/New Cases) %
Canada	61.7	2.1	1.0	47.6
France	90.8	3.1	1.4	45.2
Germany	24.9	1.8	0.5	27.8
Japan	2.0	0.3	0.0	—
Switzerland	99.7	3.6	1.1	30.6
United Kingdom	31.1	1.3	0.3	23.1
United States	282.7	14.9	4.2	28.2

Source: UNAIDS/WHO Global HIV/AIDS Online Database.

(HAART), Freedberg and colleagues (2001) estimated that the lifetime treatment cost with the current three-drug therapy was $77,300.[3] These estimates are highly dependent on when the treatment begins. The higher the initial values of the CD4 cell count, the higher the lifetime cost of treatment because of higher life expectancies. Patients who start therapy with CD4 cell counts below 50/mm^2 can expect to live an additional 2.84 years. Those who begin treatment with cell counts above 500/mm^2 have a life expectancy of 9.13 years. Thus, earlier treatment can result in the lifetime cost of treatment approaching $100,000, consistent with Hellinger's (1993) earlier estimate of $102,000.

Although the majority of all AIDS care is financed by government sources, two-thirds from Medicare and Medicaid, the overall impact on the economy is relatively small. Total government spending on AIDS care and treatment approached $14.7 billion in 2002, more than double the level of spending in 1995 (Summers et al., 2003). Spending on AIDS treatment is less than 1 percent of total health care spending, but its impact falls disproportionately on public hospitals, especially large teaching hospitals in urban areas.

ISSUES IN MEDICAL CARE DELIVERY

Is Addiction Rational?

When does a habit become an addiction? If you enjoy something and practice it regularly, are you addicted? People get addicted to all sorts of things: cigarettes, alcohol, drugs, work, food, sex, music videos, and computer games. Like many other interesting questions concerning human behavior, economists have discovered that the theory of rational choice can tell us a great deal about addictive behavior and the optimal public policy to deal with it.

continued

---

[3] The standard treatment uses a class of drugs called "protease inhibitors," which deprive the AIDS virus of a critical enzyme it needs for reproduction. When combined with older drugs, such as AZT and 3TC, this three-drug cocktail suppresses the AIDS virus. Current scientific wisdom suggests that the drug regime begin early, even before AIDS symptoms develop.

A paper by Becker and Murphy (1988) influenced the early economic literature on addiction. They show that consumers of addictive goods are rational, meaning that they consistently maximize utility over time, and that the potential for addiction increases if past consumption increases current consumption. Their model is also able to explain the observed instability of consumption that manifests itself in "cold turkey" withdrawal and binge consumption. They also show that people who discount the future more heavily are more likely to become addicts.

This model relies on the premise that individuals recognize the total cost of their addictive behavior, both in terms of the current monetary price of the addictive good and the cost in terms of the future. Within this framework, forward-looking behavior has one problem: It requires individual behavior that is time consistent — in other words, future behavior is consistent with current desires regarding future behavior. Using the case of cigarette consumption, Gruber and Koszegi (2001) established that forward-looking behavior is not consistent over time. Incorporating time inconsistency into a model with forward-looking behavior, they show that the optimal government policy should take into consideration not only the externalities imposed on others, but also the "internalities" imposed on the addict.

As interest in regulating addictive behavior grows, we have seen increased taxation, increased regulation of public consumption, and a rash of litigation against the tobacco industry. Using standard values for average age and life expectancy, Gruber and Koszegi estimate that an extra year at the end of a worker's life is worth almost $100,000. Since the typical smoker dies 6.1 years prematurely, the cost of smoking a pack of cigarettes in terms of life-years lost is $30.45. Thus, the internal costs are over 10 times the external costs. Policy conclusions based on the research are a significant departure from those based on the earlier model. Even if the government only considers a small portion of the internal costs in establishing tax policy, a strong case could be made for a substantial increase in the current average excise tax of 65 cents per pack. Even if the external costs are also considered — secondhand smoke estimated at 19 to 70 cents per pack and the long-run costs of low birth weight due to maternal smoking estimated at 42 to 70 cents per pack — the internal costs still dwarf the calculation. This line of research has important implications for other forms of addictive behavior, in particular illegal drugs.

Source: Gary S. Becker and Kevin M. Murphy, "A Theory of Rational Addiction," *Journal of Political Economy* 96(4), August 1988, 675–700; and Jonathan Gruber and Botond Koszegi, "Is Addiction 'Rational'? Theory and Evidence," *Quarterly Journal of Economics* 116(4), November 2001, 1261–1303.

Tobacco Use

CDC estimates show that between 1997 and 2001, the health-related economic costs associated with tobacco use averaged $75 billion in direct medical costs per year and over $90 billion in lost productivity. Approximately 14 percent of all Medicaid expenditures were related to tobacco use (CDC, 2005). Even though the economic cost has been staggering, any dollar amount reported pales in comparison to the toll in human suffering. It is estimated that over 440,000 deaths are attributable to tobacco use annually. When added to the 100,000 who die as a result of alcohol abuse, the total comes to a half million premature deaths each year from these two substances alone. Peto and colleagues (1992) have estimated that over one-fifth of the population of the developed world, over 250 million people, will die prematurely of tobacco-related diseases. In every country listed in Table 11.2, the percentage of males who smoke daily exceeds that of females.

Table 11.2: Lifestyle Issues

	Tobacco (% age group who smoke daily, males)[1]	Tobacco (% age group who smoke daily, females)[1]	Alcohol (liters per capita)[2] 2003	Fat Consumed per Day (Grams per capita)[2] 2003	Calories Consumed per Day (per capita)[2] 2003	Obesity (% population BMI > 30)[1,4] 2005	Diabetes (% population with diagnosis)[1]
Canada	19.4[3,13]	16.2[3,13]	7.9	148.4	3,605	23.5	4.9[3,13]
France	28.2[3,14]	21.7[3,14]	14.0	168.3	3,623	7.2	1.4[8,9]
Germany	29.8[4,14]	19.1[4,14]	10.2	141.9	3,484	20.7	3.9[6,13]
Japan	45.9[7,11]	9.9[7,11]	7.6	86.2	2,768	1.6	2.2[8,10]
Switzerland	26.5[4,12]	23.1[4,12]	10.8	157.8	3,545	15.6	3.8[4,12]
United Kingdom	27.0[5,12]	25.0[5,12]	11.2	134.7	3,450	22.9	3.9[5,13]
United States	25.7[6,13]	20.8[6,13]	8.4	155.3	3,754	39.2	6.8[7,13]

Source:

[1] WHO Global InfoBase Online at http://www.who.int/ncd_surveillance/infobase/web/InfoBaseCommon
[2] *OECD Health Data 2006.*
[3] **Age 12 and over.**
[4] **Age 15 and over.**
[5] **Age 16 and over.**
[6] **Age 18 and over.**
[7] **Age 20 and over.**
[8] **Age 30 and over.**
[9] **1989.**
[10] **2000.**
[11] **2001.**
[12] **2002.**
[13] **2003.**
[14] **2005.**

The difference is more dramatic in Japan, where 46 percent of males over the age of 20 smoke daily, compared to only 10 percent of females.

ISSUES IN MEDICAL CARE DELIVERY

Are Cigarette and Alcohol Consumption Sensitive to Price Increases?

Conventional wisdom would have us believe that individuals who smoke and drink will do so at any price. Several economic researchers have offered evidence that may force us to rethink this common belief (Becker, Grossman, and Murphy, 1993; Chaloupka, 1991; Chaloupka et al., 1993). Taking into consideration the powerful reinforcing properties of addictive substances (increases in past consumption increase the marginal benefit of current consumption), this research finds evidence of rational addiction. In other words, consumers of addictive substances take into account the long-term harmful effects of their behavior when deciding how much of an addictive substance to consume.

As is the case with all goods, addictive and nonaddictive, long-run price elasticities are larger in absolute value than short-run elasticities. Consumers, when given enough time, have the ability to adjust to price changes by shifting to substitutes. The lesson from these studies is that in the long run, addictive behavior is price sensitive; that is, raising cigarette and alcohol prices will reduce consumption over time.

Source: Gary S. Becker, Michael Grossman, and K. M. Murphy, "An Empirical Analysis of Cigarette Addiction," *NBER Working Paper No. 3322*, April 1990, revised March 1993; Frank J. Chaloupka, "Rational Addictive Behavior and Cigarette Smoking," *Journal of Political Economy* 99(4), August 1991, 722–742; and Frank J. Chaloupka, Michael Grossman, Gary S. Becker, and K. M. Murphy, "Alcohol Addiction: An Econometric Analysis," paper presented at the annual meeting of the American Economic Association, January 1993.

Key Concept 6
Supply and Demand

One of the reasons that women live longer in most societies is that they do not smoke with the same regularity as men. However, the gap between male and female smoking rates has narrowed substantially over the past four decades. As a consequence, more than 500,000 women are dying worldwide every year of smoking-related illnesses. By the time today's young female population reaches middle age, more than one million females will be dying annually in the developed world alone.

BACK-OF-THE-ENVELOPE

Alcohol Consumption and Traffic Deaths: The Case for Higher Excise Taxes

Motor vehicle accidents are the leading cause of death for people under age 35. In over half of all fatal crashes, alcohol is a factor. A major dilemma for policy makers is how to reduce the number of alcohol-related traffic fatalities. In 1984 Congress passed the Federal Uniform Drinking Age Act, raising the legal drinking age to 21. States were forced to conform or risk losing federal highway funding.

continued

Another suggested strategy to reduce alcohol-related traffic fatalities is to raise the price of alcoholic beverages through an excise tax. Substantial evidence exists relating higher alcoholic beverage prices — and state excise tax rates on alcohol — to a lower incidence of youth alcohol consumption and, subsequently, to fewer deaths as a result of motor vehicle accidents (Chaloupka, Saffer, and Laizuthai; 1993). But raising excise taxes on alcohol to reduce consumption is a forgotten strategy. In 1991, the federal excise tax on beer and wine was raised for the first time since 1951, and the federal excise tax on distilled spirits was raised for only the second time over that same 40-year period. How would an increase in excise taxes affect alcohol consumption?

In the diagrams, the alcohol-dependent demand curve is drawn much steeper than that of the occasional drinker, indicating a more inelastic demand. An increase in the excise tax will shift the supply curve leftward (remember, the vertical distance between S_1 and S_2 represents the amount of the excise tax increase). In both cases, the resulting price increase causes the quantity demanded to decrease. But in the case of the occasional drinker, quantity demanded falls considerably more than it does for the alcohol dependent.

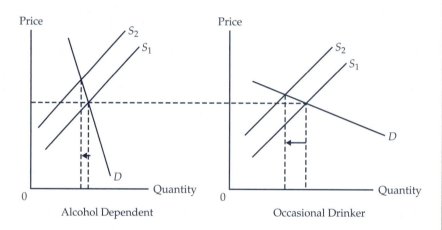

Alcohol Dependent   Occasional Drinker

Due partly to lagging federal excise taxes, the real prices of alcoholic beverages have actually fallen in recent years. Between 1975 and 1990, the real price of beer fell 20 percent, the real price of wine 28 percent, and the real price of distilled spirits 32 percent. If real alcohol prices had actually remained constant, youth alcohol consumption would have been lower, along with fewer traffic fatalities. Chaloupka, Grossman, and Saffer (1993) estimate that if the federal excise tax on beer had been indexed to the rate of inflation since 1951 that approximately 5,000 fewer traffic fatalities would have occurred annually. In addition, a uniform minimum drinking age of 21 would have saved more than 650 lives per year prior to the Federal Uniform Drinking Age Act of 1984. This and other research (Manning et al., 1989) suggest that excise taxes on alcoholic beverages are probably below optimal levels.

Sources: F. J. Chaloupka, H. Saffer, and A. Laizuthai, "Alcohol Price Policy and Youths: A Summary of Economic Research," *Journal of Research on Adolescence*, forthcoming; F. J. Chaloupka, Michael Grossman, and H. Saffer, "Alcohol Control Policies and Motor Vehicle Fatalities," *Journal of Legal Studies*, forthcoming; and Willard G. Manning, Emmett B. Keeler, Joseph P. Newhouse, Elizabeth M. Sloss, and Jeffrey Wasserman, "The Taxes of Sin: Do Smokers and Drinkers Pay Their Way?" *Journal of the American Medical Association 261*, March 17, 1989, 1604–1609.

Alcohol Use

Almost half of all Americans over the age of 12 report they currently use alcohol. Even so, compared to consumers in the rest of the developed world, Americans are relatively moderate drinkers, with an annual consumption of 8.4 liters per capita. The prevalence of drinking, however, increases dramatically with age until early adulthood (ages 21 to 25) and then gradually declines. The cost of alcohol abuse in the United States was estimated at approximately $276 billion in 1995, the latest year sufficient data was available (NIH, 1998). Over two-thirds of the costs are caused by the lost productivity due to alcohol-related illnesses and premature death. In over 2 million alcohol-related automobile accidents, almost 17,000 die and over 500,000 are injured (NHTSA, 2005). Additionally, alcohol plays a role in a significant proportion of all violent crime: assault, rape, murder, suicide, domestic violence, and child abuse.

Alcohol use is a double-edged sword. For some people, even moderate alcohol consumption carries with it severe health risks. However, there is substantial medical evidence that moderate consumption can actually be beneficial, the so-called "French Paradox."[4] The medical evidence suggests that moderate daily consumption, one drink for women and two for men, offers some protection against heart disease and stroke (Abramson et al., 2001, and Reynolds et al., 2003). Specifically, it raises HDL (the good cholesterol), lowers blood pressure, inhibits the formation of blood clots, and prevents arterial damage caused by LDL (the bad cholesterol).

BACK-OF-THE-ENVELOPE

The Question of Drug Legalization

Many proponents of drug legalization use economics to make their case. They argue that banned drugs are just that: banned. With no distinction among illegal substances, young people may get the impression that one is no worse than the other — PCP, crack cocaine, heroin, marijuana — they're all the same, aren't they? Consumers have no assurance regarding the quality of the drugs they buy, and the government can generate no tax revenue from the sale and purchase of the banned substances. Public costs are high with a large percentage of the costs of police, courts, and prisons directly or indirectly attributable to the war on drugs. Despite all the spending to stop drug trafficking, only 10 to 15 percent of all drugs entering the country are seized. Proponents of legalization suggest that we control the sale of drugs, tax the profits, supervise production, and at the same time discourage their use.

Citing the fact that increased spending for interdiction has little effect on the amount of drugs reaching the market, legalization proponents argue that the demand for drugs is likely to be inelastic. As depicted in the graph, when demand is relatively inelastic, increasing the cost to suppliers, and thus shifting the supply curve to the left, has little effect on the equilibrium quantity (reducing quantity from Q_0 to Q_1). The only thing the interdiction strategy accomplishes is to raise the price of drugs and increase the incentives for suppliers. In addition, those who use drugs are forced into lives of crime to support their expensive habit.

continued

Key Concept 5
Markets and Pricing

---

[4] The *French Paradox* refers to the observation that the French have less heart disease than Americans despite a high-fat diet. Red wine and olive oil are thought to be at least partially responsible.

Opponents of legalization argue that prohibition may create crime by classifying certain activities as criminal, but it is not victimless crime. People under the influence of drugs are more likely to injure others, and the medical complications of drug use impose indirect costs on everybody. In any event, hard-core drug users were committing crimes long before they were using drugs. It is these hard-core users whose demand is price inelastic. For the millions who do not use drugs, demand is quite elastic. Any relaxation in standards will cause a substantial increase in use. The legal sanctions and the social stigma are enough to dissuade the curious. So the demand curve for these potential users is much flatter than the one shown above. Legalization will not only increase quantity demanded for this group, but will actually shift the demand curve to the right, further increasing consumption.

Organizations such as NORML (National Organization to Reform Marijuana Laws) argue that legalization of pot makes sense. They claim that it is nonaddictive, widely used, and no worse than alcohol. It is already the largest cash crop in the state of California. On the other hand, opponents ask the question: Do we need another social problem along the lines of tobacco and alcohol to add to the pathologies we already suffer? If we legalize, where do we draw the line? Do we stop at marijuana? Should PCP, crack, and LSD be added to the list? How soon before proponents begin calling on governing bodies in sports to sanction the use of anabolic steroids? Should we try to legislate the moral behavior of society? Or should we follow the libertarian (some would say, libertine) principles and tolerate such behavior? Expect disagreement when you bring up this topic at your next social gathering.

Source: James W. Henderson, "Economic Impact of Cocaine and Crack Abuse: Private and Social Issues," in Glen E. Lich, ed., *Doing Drugs and Dropping Out: Assessing the Costs to Society of Substance Abuse and Dropping Out of School.* A Report prepared for the Subcommittee on Economic Growth, Trade, and Taxes of the Joint Economic Committee, Congress of the United States, Washington, D.C.: U.S. Government Printing Office, August 1991.

Key Concept 6
Supply and Demand

Obesity and Its Consequences

Over the course of the past 25 years, there has been an alarming increase in obesity in the United States. In the late 1970s, according to government survey data, fifteen percent of the adult population was obese. By 1994 the rate of obesity had increased to 23 percent. Recent evidence from the World Health Organization indicated that the United States is the world leader in obesity with 39 percent of Americans falling into that category. Obesity is technically defined as a person with a body mass index (BMI) greater than 30.[5] Even though obesity is a problem affecting the entire developed world, no other country has the problem to the extent found in the United States. In 2005, an estimated 23 percent of Britons were considered obese, 7 percent of the French, and only 2 percent of the Japanese.

An estimated 300,000 Americans die annually from health problems related to obesity and a sedentary lifestyle (Mokdad et al., 2001). These deaths are caused by coronary artery disease, stroke, high blood pressure, cancer, and diabetes. Almost 7 percent of Americans over the age of 30 are diagnosed with diabetes, substantially higher than any other developed country. Wolf and Colditz (1998) estimated that the direct costs of obesity amounted to $99.2 billion in 1995, or approximately 10 percent of total U.S. health care spending.

Research by Cutler, Glaeser, and Shapiro (2003) explains the increase as a result of higher calorie consumption. Women today consume 9 percent more than they did 20 years ago, and men consume 13 percent more. The reason for these increases: Food is cheaper, not only in terms of the hours required to earn the money to buy it, but in terms of the time it takes to cook it. Remember, because demand curves slope downward, when something is cheaper, consumers demand more. Americans consume an average of 3,754 calories per day, more than any country in the comparison group.

Not only is calorie consumption increasing, much of what we buy to eat is processed before we get it, either in a restaurant or packaged and purchased in a grocery store. With more women working, less time is spent in food preparation. According to time-use surveys, married women who work outside the home spent an average of 41 minutes a day in food chores in 1995, compared to 85 minutes a day 30 years earlier. For those women without jobs outside the home, the average was 69 minutes in 1995 compared to 138 minutes in 1965. The same trends were also true for single individuals (Wessel, 2003). Consumers usually view decreases in price as a good thing. In the case of food, however, people may lack the self-control to limit their consumption to levels that are healthy.

Infant Health

Critics of U.S. medical care often cite high infant mortality rates as evidence of a breakdown in the current delivery system. One can make a very compelling argument linking poverty and poor access to care with high mortality rates. In 2004 the United States had the highest infant mortality rate among the seven advanced countries in Table 11.3. At 6.9 deaths per 1,000 live births, the U.S. rate was twice that of Japan. The focus on the overall infant mortality rate masks the differences in rates between blacks and whites in the United States. The rate for blacks was 13.5 compared with 5.7 for whites.

Much of the evidence examining the cause of high infant mortality point to the high risk associated with low birth weight. Data indicate that the U.S. infant mortality rate for very low–birth-weight babies (those born weighing less than 1,500 grams) was 252.8, over 90 times the rate of 2.7 for infants born weighing more than 2,500 grams. Even though these very low–birth-weight babies make up only about 1.4 percent of all births, they account for over 50 percent of all infant deaths (MacDorman and Atkinson, 1999). The United States has the second highest rate

Calculate your body mass index. Go to the Centers for Disease Control web site to learn more:

http://www.cdc.gov/nccdphp/dnpa/bmi/

Key Concept 6
Supply and Demand

Key Concept 3
Opportunity Cost

---

[5] $BMI = \dfrac{Weight \ (in \ kilograms)}{Height \ (in \ meters)^2}$. **Optimal BMI is between 20 and 25. A person with a BMI between 25 and 30 is considered overweight.**

Table 11.3: Infant Health

	Infant Mortality Rate[1] (2004)	Perinatal Mortality Rate[2] (2001)	Low Birth Weight Births[3] (2004)
Canada	5.3[4]	6.3	5.8[4]
France	3.9	6.9	6.8
Germany	4.1	5.9	6.9
Japan	2.8	3.6	9.4
Switzerland	4.2	8.0	6.3
United Kingdom	5.1	6.7	7.6[4]
United States	6.9[4]	6.9	8.1

Source: *OECD Health Data 2006.*

[1] Per 1,000 live births.
[2] Per 1,000 live births plus late fetal deaths.
[3] Percentage of live births.
[4] 2003.

of low–birth-weight infants with 8.1 percent of all infants born weighing less than 2,500 grams, which is considered a normal birth weight). Only Japan fares worse than the United States.[6]

POLICY ISSUE

Better access to prenatal care will improve birth outcomes. Is free care the answer?

Limited access to prenatal care due to limited finances, while often cited as a factor in low birth weights, may not be the primary cause of infant death. In other research, Murray and Bernfield (1988) studied over 31,000 births in California's Kaiser-Permanente hospitals, where prenatal care and delivery were available on a prepaid basis. Adjusting for the mothers' age, education, and other characteristics related to risk, black mothers were more likely to forgo prenatal care completely, to begin prenatal care later than their white counterparts, and to have fewer prenatal physician visits when they do take advantage of their medical benefits. Black mothers in the study had twice the rate of low–birth-weight babies than whites.

Low birth weights lead to longer hospital stays, driving up the cost of newborn care. Normal-sized infants, those weighing more than 2,500 grams, can expect to stay in the hospital around three days. Smaller infants, those weighing between 1,500 and 2,500 grams, have average stays of 24 days. Those born weighing less than 1,500 grams have average stays of 57 days, and those weighing less than 1,000 grams, 89 days (McCormick, 1985). Low birth weight is a costly proposition; it is expensive and deadly.

Are the high infant-mortality statistics presenting an accurate picture of the U.S. health care delivery system? Comparing perinatal mortality statistics avoids the differences in definition of a live birth and may provide a more accurate comparison of differences in infant mortality. The use of 2001 perinatal mortality statistics presents a slightly different picture. The U.S. rate is no longer the highest; more importantly, the gap with comparison countries narrows significantly.

In fact, earlier studies indicate that birth-weight–specific perinatal mortality rates are actually higher in Japan than in the United States (Eberstadt, 1991; Hoffman, Bergsjol, and Denman, 1990). Kramer and colleagues (2005) examined differences in birth-weight–specific infant mortality rates in Canada and the United

---

[6] The incidence of low–birth-weight babies continues to increase in the United States. In 2000, 7.5 percent of all infants born weighed less than 2,500 grams: by race, the figure was 6.6 percent of white infants, 6.4 percent of Hispanic infants, and 13.0 percent of all black infants.

States and concluded that babies weighing less than 2,500 grams at birth had a better chance of survival in the United States despite the higher overall infant mortality rates. These findings suggest that the relatively poor infant mortality ranking of the United States is largely due to the higher proportion of very low–birth-weight infants. These facts suggest that medical care for infants in the United States may be relatively better than the infant mortality statistics would suggest.

Part of these differences in birth weights may be due to biological factors and the heterogeneous nature of the U.S. population. The median birth weight for white babies is higher than for black babies born in the United States. Even after adjusting for differences in mothers' ages, education, and income, the proportion of low–birth-weight babies is still twice as high for blacks as for whites, suggesting that at least part of the birth weight differential between blacks and whites may be due to physiological and behavioral differences among ethnic groups. In addition, the birth weight differential stays the same at all levels of prenatal care availability and use (Henderson, 1994).

An alternative explanation for the high incidence of low birth weight is the high rate of teen pregnancy in the United States, a sociological factor strongly correlated with low birth weight and infant mortality. Teen pregnancy and illegitimacy may actually serve as proxy variables for maternal behavior and attitude about the pregnancy.[7] Teen mothers are less likely to receive timely prenatal care and are more likely to smoke cigarettes, leading to inadequate weight gain, lower birth weights, and a higher incidence of preterm births (Ventura et al., 2000). The relationship between infant mortality rates and illegitimacy is striking. Eberstadt (1991) reports that unmarried college graduates, both black and white, have higher infant mortality rates than married women regardless of their educational attainment.

Table 11.4 compares the teen pregnancy rates in seven developed countries in 2004. The United States had a higher rate of teenage pregnancy than any of the others listed. At 41.2 per 1,000 females and 10.3 percent of all live births, the U.S. rate is about 50 percent higher than the U.K. rate and seven times the Japanese rate.

Table 11.4: Teen Pregnancy

2004	Births to Women 10–19 years old (% total births)	Births to Women 15–19 years old (per 1,000 population)
Canada	4.5*	14.4*
France	2.0	8.0*
Germany	3.6	10.9
Japan	1.7	5.6
Switzerland	1.5	5.1
United Kingdom	7.1	26.7
United States	10.3	41.2

Source: *United Nations Demographic Yearbook 2004. Accessed at* http://unstats.un.org/unsd/demographic/products/dyb/DYB2004/Table10.pdf

* 2003

---

[7] Research has shown that "mistimed or unwanted" babies were more likely to be born at low birth weights than those who were planned or "wanted" (Pamuk and Mosher, 1988).

In 2004, 35.8 percent of all U.S. births were to unmarried mothers, 25.4 percent of all white births, 46.4 percent of all Hispanic births, and 69.4 percent of all African-American births (CDC, 2006a). In contrast, less than 1 percent of all Japanese mothers are teenagers or unmarried, due to the social stigma of such behavior. Interestingly, the same social customs and low infant mortality rates can be found among Japanese-American women (Wegman, 1993).

A bit of encouraging news about teenage and unmarried births in the United States is that the rates are falling in almost all categories. The black and Hispanic rates have fallen to 63.1 per 1,000 teenage females and 82.6 per 1,000, but are still two to three times the white rate of 26.7. The rate of teenage births has dropped 24 percent from its 1994 peak, and the overall increase in the percentage of births to unmarried women is due entirely to the increased rate among women over the age of 20.

External Causes of Death

External causes of death, including homicide, suicide, and accidents of all types, are the most prevalent reason for death among 20- to 44-year-olds. While high in most developed countries, there are still significant differences in death rates due to external causes. In terms of deaths per 100,000 population, the United States has the highest death rate for non–disease-related factors, including motor vehicle accidents and homicides. The U.S. rate for all external causes, 51.8 per 100,000, is 35 percent higher than the group average.

This excess mortality from all external causes has a significant impact on the life expectancy of Americans. Lemaire (2005) estimates that in 2000, the U.S. life expectancy of 76.9 years would have been 1.2 years higher without these external causes. That same year, the population-weighted average life expectancy of the 33 richest counties in the world was 79.2 years. Thus, over half of the gap in life expectancy between the United States and the other developed countries of the world is due to external causes of death, primarily motor vehicle accidents and homicide.

Table 11.5: External Causes of Death
Deaths Per 100,000 Population

2002	Suicide	Accidental Falls	Motor Vehicle Accidents	Homicide	All External Causes
Canada	10.6	4.1	9.3	1.5	37.7
France	15.1	5.4	12.0	0.8	52.8
Germany	10.8	5.0	8.6	0.7	32.9
Japan	18.7	3.0	7.7	0.5	43.2
Switzerland	16.3	8.0	6.7	0.9	39.5
United Kingdom	6.3	3.4	5.7	0.9	27.1
United States	10.2	4.1	15.9	6.2	51.8

Source: *OECD Health Data 2006.*

POPULATION AGING

Economic theory often cites changing demographics as a major factor in determining the demand for goods and services. The popular notion that demand changes as an individual, family, or nation grows in size and matures is familiar to most students of economic theory. In fact, partly because of his pioneering research in life-cycle changes in savings, investment, and consumption, Franco Modigliani was awarded the Nobel Prize for Economic Science in 1985. When exploring the causes of high and rising medical care spending, the aging population makes everyone's top ten list.

In this section we will examine the changing demographics of the population and its impact on overall medical care spending. As Americans live longer, the changing age and gender structure will have a significant effect on medical care demand in the coming century. Elder care is often the focus of cost-control discussions, but just how big of a factor is it?

The Aging Population

Since 1950 the percentage of the U.S. population over the age of 65 has increased from 8.1 percent to 12.4 percent. Due primarily to low fertility rates, the percentage of the population less than 5 years of age has fallen from 10.8 percent to just under 8 percent. The baby-boom generation (those born between 1946 and 1964) may get a lot of attention regarding their demand for goods and services, but to date, they have had only a modest effect on demand for medical care services, largely fertility related. As this cohort begins to retire in 2010, the percentage of the population over the age of 65 will increase substantially, along with their medical costs. The percentage of the population over the age of 65 will begin to rise from 13 percent in 2010 to over 20 percent in 2030. By that time almost 70 million Americans will be over age 65. The major concern for policy makers is that this rapidly growing, aged population will not be matched by a growing working-age population, jeopardizing the solvency of the entire federal old-age entitlement apparatus, particularly Social Security and Medicare.

Up until now, the age and sex composition of the population has contributed little to the growth in health expenditures in the United States. Studies examining the causes of the rise in medical care spending attribute less than 10 percent to the change in the age and sex composition of the population. Such factors as intensity of care and medical care price inflation have been much more important (Aaron, 1991; Gordon, 1992).

To date population aging has been much more of an issue in Europe than in North America. In most European countries, higher life expectancies and lower

Key Concept 6
Supply and Demand

POLICY ISSUE

How will federal entitlement programs remain solvent as the percentage of the population over age 65 continues to expand?

http://

The American Association of Retired Persons (AARP) issues papers, press releases, and other information relevant to the interests of older adults.

http://www.aarp.org/

Table 11.6: Population Aging

	Percent of Population over Age 65 (2004)	Male Life Expectancy at Birth (2003)	Female Life Expectancy at Birth (2003)	Male Life Expectancy at Age 65 (2003)	Female Life Expectancy at Age 65 (2003)
Canada	13.0	77.4	82.4	17.4	20.8
France	16.3	75.9	82.9	17.1*	21.4*
Germany	19.3	75.7	81.4	16.1	19.6
Japan	19.5	78.4	85.3	18.0	23.0
Switzerland	16.4	78.0	83.1	17.5	21.0
United Kingdom	16.0	76.2	80.7	16.1*	19.1*
United States	12.4	74.8	80.1	16.8	19.8

Source: *OECD Health Data 2006.*

* 2002.

fertility rates have resulted in 16 to 19 percent of their populations falling in the over-age-65 category. The United States and Canada are about 20 years behind Europe and Japan in feeling the impact of an aging population.

Life Expectancy

The Administration on Aging provides access to statistical information on older persons, including profiles, projections, and trends. This site provides an excellent resource for topics on aging.

http://www.aoa.dhhs.gov

Often cited as evidence of the superiority of government-run health care systems over market-oriented systems, life expectancy is the most commonly used measure of health outcomes. In the entire developed world, life expectancies have risen dramatically during the last century. The average American female was expected to live 48.3 years at birth in 1900, and the average male 46.3 years. For most of the century, life expectancies have risen steadily; by 2003 they reached 74.8 years for men and 80.1 years for women. Improvements in the rest of the developed world have been even more dramatic. Life expectancy in Europe and Japan averages 2.1 years higher for men and 2.4 years higher for women.

The elimination of premature death—particularly infant mortality, maternal death, and death from acute illnesses—is a primary reason for this improvement. Improved living conditions, including clean water, sanitation, and other public health measures have also made significant contributions to longevity.

Mortality rates for the elderly are declining faster than any other age group. There is no overwhelming consensus on the reasons for this improvement. Some medical experts tend to think that the elderly are living longer because of healthier lifestyles, led by improved dietary habits, less smoking, and better exercise. Those more technologically inclined attribute the improved longevity to better medical care, especially better control of hypertension, and to special coronary care units and open-heart surgery. In practice, the likely explanation includes elements of both perspectives.

More relevant to the issue of medical care spending is the number of years a person is expected to live after they reach a certain age. In 2003, an American male reaching age 65 could expect to live on average 16.8 more years, a female 19.8 more years. The U.S. relative ranking improves slightly when this measure of life expectancy is used.

Americans reaching their eightieth birthday can expect to live longer than their counterparts in many other developed nations, including France, Germany, Italy, Sweden, Switzerland, and the United Kingdom. Using data from 2003, American men lived 8 years on average after their eightieth birthday, and American women lived 9.6 years (OECD, 2006). An 80-year-old man would be expected to live 7.8 years more in France, 7.2 in Germany, 7.6 in Italy, 7.2 in Sweden, 7.5 in Switzerland, and 7.1 in England. An 80-year-old woman would be expected to live 8.5 more years in Germany, 9.1 in Sweden, 9.3 in Switzerland, and 8.6 in the United Kingdom.

The U.S. Census Bureau is the official collector of demographic data on the people and economy of the United States. The site provides access to the official statistics primarily through its links to "Subjects A-Z."

http://www.census.gov

A number of individuals in their sixties and seventies are frail and impaired, but most are healthy, active, and relatively well-off. It is the rapid growth in the population over age 85 that presents a challenge to policy makers concerned with the rise in medical care spending. Individuals in the ninth and tenth decades of life begin to show their age. They are more prone to chronic conditions that lead to disability and the need for long-term care: Alzheimer's disease and other forms of dementia, Parkinson's disease, hypertension, diabetes, osteoarthritis, hip fractures, and peripheral vascular diseases. Today, an estimated 72,000 Americans are over 100 years old—the fastest growing age cohort in the country. By 2010, centenarians will number 129,000 and by 2050, one million (U.S. Census, 2002).

The increasing number of the oldest old raises certain bioethical issues. There is already talk of rationing medical care to the oldest old (Callahan, 1987). Assisted suicide, euthanasia, and denial of treatment are all cutting-edge ethical issues. These issues are not unique to the United States. Throughout history every culture and every society has had to deal with how to allocate scarce resources. Whenever resources were marginalized, the elderly were the first to see their shares limited. The old Eskimo accepted his fate and willingly stepped onto the ice floe, never to be seen again.

Medical Care Costs for the Elderly

The elderly make up only 12 percent of the population, yet they consume over one-third of all medical resources. Over half of lifetime medical costs are incurred after age 65. A look at Table 11.7 shows that per capita spending on the elderly was $11,089 in 1999, about four times the $2,793 spent on the average nonelderly person, and seven times the $1,646 spent on each young person (those less than 19 years of age). These relative spending levels across age groups have changed little from the late 1970s (Waldo et al., 1989). Even within the elderly population, the oldest old spend considerably more on medical care than the younger cohorts. In 1999, overall spending by those over 85 years of age was some 2.5 times that of the 65- to 74-year-old group.

What is true for overall spending is also true for individual spending categories. Hospital care and physicians' services follow a pattern similar to overall spending. Per capita nursing home spending is more heavily weighted toward the oldest old. Those over the age of 85 spend $7,819 per capita on nursing home care, or 13 times more than the 65- to 74-year-old age cohort.

The use of most medical procedures increases as we age. Table 11.8 provides details of medical care utilization by age group for 2000. A greater proportion of the older cohorts are admitted to hospitals. Hospital admissions result in more days of hospital care and longer hospital stays for older individuals. As we get older, we have more emergency department visits, more hospital outpatient visits, spend more time in the hospital, and visit our physicians more often.

POLICY ISSUE

The high cost of care associated with aging has more to do with the incidence of chronic illnesses than the cost of dying.

Table 11.7: Personal Medical Care Expenditures By Age and Type of Service, 1999

Age Group	Personal Medical Care	Hospital Care	Physicians' Services	Prescription Drugs	Nursing Home Services	Other
All ages	$ 3,834	$ 1,416	$ 975	$ 376	$ 323	$ 744
Under 65	2,793	1,027	815	301	69	581
Less than 19	1,646	601	551	112	13	367
19 to 44	2,706	1,023	780	264	70	568
45 to 54	3,713	1,213	1,051	509	111	829
55 to 64	5,590	2,177	1,482	771	191	970
65 and over	11,089	4,132	2,092	900	2,087	1,879
65 to 74	8,167	3,298	2,006	895	611	1,358
75 to 84	12,244	4,786	2,263	922	2,221	2,052
85 and over	20,001	5,791	1,977	858	7,819	3,556

Source: Sean P. Keehan, Helen C. Lazenby, Mark A. Zezza, and Aaron C. Catlin, "Age Estimates in the National Health Accounts," *Health Care Financing Review*/Web Exclusive 1(1), December 2, 2004.

Table 11.8:   Utilization of Medical Care Resources Annually by Age Group, 2004

Age Group	Emergency Department Visits per 100 Population	Outpatient Visits per 100 Population	Days of Hospital Care per 100 Population	Physician Office Visits per 100 Population
Less than 18	37	30	19.3	235
18 to 44	42	25	33.5	219
45 to 54	32	29	49.1	327
55 to 64	29	36	73.5	446
65 to 74	34	39	140.5	623
Over 75	58	36	271.5	734
All persons	38	30	56.9	316

Source: National Center for Health Statistics, *Health, United States, 2006.*

ISSUES IN MEDICAL CARE DELIVERY

Have We Discovered the Mythical Fountain of Youth?

The quest for immortality is fueled by our inherent fear of the unknown. Early explorers of the New World led by Ponce de Leon searched for the Fountain of Youth. Even the fictional archeological explorer Indiana Jones survived his last crusade to see the restoration of life to those who drank from the Holy Grail used by Jesus to celebrate the Last Supper. Current exploration, somewhat more scientifically based, has taken the form of medical research into the gene that controls the aging process and the fierce debate that it fosters.

The current medical approach to the study of mortality is based on a model of disease. From this viewpoint, death results from disease. Except for trauma and violence, without disease there is no death. Actuarial data from the Social Security Administration predict that life expectancies will continue to climb throughout the next century. According to these estimates, white females born in 2080 can expect to live over 90 years.

Fries (1980) advocates a different viewpoint. From his perspective, the human life span is genetically determined. Organs that have substantial reserves to restore health after an illness at age 30 have very limited capacity at older ages. Thus, the elderly die, not from disease as much as from the body's inability to restore health after an illness. Fries's perspective suggests a maximum life expectancy of 85 years.

Proponents of the theory of ever-increasing life expectancies must face the prospect that living longer does not necessarily mean living better. Aging still has its consequences. Currently, those consequences involve living a longer proportion of our lives affected by chronic disease. Unless we find a way to treat or minimize the effects of these chronic diseases, we will be faced with an increasing number of frail elderly in need of partial or total assistance for longer periods of time.

Proponents of a limited life expectancy see things differently. As life expectancies reach their upper limits, the period of diminished activity

continued

> due to chronic illnesses diminishes, along with the need for costly medical care. Depending on which viewpoint is correct, the implications for future resource needs will be quite different.
>
> **Source:** James F. Fries, "Aging, Natural Death, and the Compression of Morbidity," *New England Journal of Medicine* 303(3), July 17, 1980, 130–135; Edward L. Schneider and Jacob A. Brody, "Aging, Natural Death, and the Compression of Morbidity: Another View," *New England Journal of Medicine* 309(14), October 6, 1983, 854–856.

The Challenge of Treating Chronic Diseases

The conventional wisdom attributes much of the medical cost explosion to the high cost of treating the elderly, particularly during the last year of life. Dying is expensive, and the United States devotes about $100 billion per year to medical care treatment during the last six months of life. The real issue is not the cost of dying but the multiplicity of illnesses that affect us as we age and the increased use of services to treat those illnesses. Chronic problems strike with increased frequency and severity as we age.

Medical progress has resulted in improved longevity and a change in the focus of medical research. The acute medical problems experienced at earlier ages no longer occupy our attention. Influenza, small pox, diphtheria, and polio, once feared, are no longer major concerns. Developments in medicine have exchanged these acute problems for chronic ones. Individuals once struck down by an acute illness early in life are surviving to experience chronic problems later in life. The trade-off is a low-cost, early death with a more expensive, later death.

As Americans live longer, the focus of attention shifts from responding to acute illnesses to treating chronic conditions such as hypertension, diabetes, heart disease, depression, and arthritis. In fact, these five chronic conditions were among the 15 most expensive conditions treated in 1997 (Cohen and Krauss, 2003). The combined cost of treating these five conditions was $141.4 billion, or 12.9 percent of total health care spending.

Hwang and colleagues (2001) estimated that over 125 million Americans suffer from one or more chronic conditions, a disability, or a functional limitation. About 10.7 million of these have functional limitations, in combination with one or more chronic conditions or a disability, and need assistance to perform certain activities of daily living (ADL).[8] The cost of treating these individuals consumes approximately 75 percent of total health care spending. Health insurance generally provides better coverage for the treatment of acute care episodes than for ongoing care for a chronic illness. As a result, services designed to slow the progression of chronic illnesses may not be covered or may have only limited coverage. And those needing assistance with ADL will find that most insurance plans do not pay for these services at all.

The Cost of Long-Term Care

The issue of long-term care is a growing concern in modern industrial societies. As societies develop and mature, they have more elderly and fewer children to provide elder care. The only option available for many families is institutional care, sending the aging parent to a nursing home.

---

[8] *Activities of daily living* are defined as the activities of basic self-care, including feeding, washing, and toileting.

Those reaching the age of 85 today can expect to live longer, but their remaining years will be increasingly dominated by chronic health problems. As we age, episodes of illness increase in frequency and severity, along with the need for medical care for longer periods of time. The two major problems facing this age group are the various forms of dementia, including Alzheimer's disease, and hip fractures. The incidence of dementia doubles every five years after age 65. The median prevalence is 2.8 percent for those ages 65 to 74, increasing to 9 percent for those ages 74 to 84, and 28 percent for those over age 85 (Schneider and Guralnik, 1990).

Many view long-term care as the ticking medical care time bomb, especially as the baby-boom generation begins to enter the oldest-old age category beginning in 2020. In 2000 over $100 billion was spent on nursing home care for the elderly—almost 7 percent of total health care spending. By 2040, we can expect to spend three to five times that amount in real terms. Federal and state governments are the largest payers for long-term care, financing over 50 percent of the total spending primarily through Medicaid.

In 1999, more than 1.47 million elderly residents lived in nursing homes across America, 50 percent of whom were over age 85. The probability of residing in a nursing home increases with age. One percent of the population between the ages of 65 and 74 lives in nursing homes. That figure increases to 4.7 percent of those between 75 and 84 and almost 18.3 percent of those over the age of 85. By 2040, the nursing home population may reach as high as 5.9 million, with at least 2 million of those over the age of 85. Over the next five decades, the 85-plus nursing home population will be almost twice as large as the total number of elderly currently residing in nursing homes (Fried et al., 2003).

Comments on Aging

In part, our attitude toward death drives us to aggressively treat terminally ill patients, fueling the debate. Survey results by the Robert Wood Johnson Foundation show that Americans are not nearly so willing to accept this aspect of life as are citizens of other countries. When asked what they would do if told by their personal physician that they had an incurable and fatal disease, 90 percent of Americans over age 65 said they would seek a second opinion. One-third of Britons and one-half of Australians responded similarly ("The Immortal American," 1995).

As a result, Americans receive four times the number of bypass operations of the Japanese, Germans, and Britons. We have higher rates of use of all the major high-tech treatment and diagnostic services, including chemotherapy, kidney dialysis, and advanced imaging. The higher usage rates are due in part to the fact that the United States has very few supply restrictions, unlike the crude **triage** system used in Britain or the regionalized services in Canada.

For most middle-aged baby boomers, the prospect of living longer and healthier is appealing. (Bypass surgery may not lengthen my life, but if it enables me to enjoy tennis in my retirement years, who is to say it is not worth it?) The policy issue is clear and will continue to grow in critical importance: Who should bear the costs of our desire for longer, happier lives?

Researchers at the Cleveland Federal Reserve Bank provide a unique look at how the burden of paying for government spending on goods and services is distributed among current and future generations (Auerbach, Gokhale, and Kotlikoff, 1995). Using the 1993 benefit and tax structure, the typical 65-year-old American male could expect to receive transfers from Social Security, Medicare, and Medicaid, net of any taxes paid, in excess of $100,000 over his remaining lifetime. That same year, the typical 65-year-old female could expect net transfers of almost $140,000 before her death. In fact, males over the age of 55 and females over the age of 50 could expect

http://

The Intrauniversity Consortium for Political and Social Research (ICPSR) provides access to the world's largest archive of computerized social science data. The National Archive of Computerized Data on Aging (NACDA) preserves the largest library of electronic data on aging in the United States.

http://www.icpsr.umich.edu

triage
A military screening technique adopted for use in a crowded emergency room to determine the order in which patients are treated. In battlefield hospitals, three categories of patients are identified: those who will survive without care, those who will survive if they receive care, and those who will not survive regardless of the amount of care they receive.

a positive net transfer over the remaining years of their lives. In contrast, younger Americans could expect a net tax payment. For example, a 25-year-old male had a prospective net tax burden (taxes over transfers) of $200,000 over his expected lifetime. Nowhere is fairness such an issue as when dealing with this generational imbalance.

The apparent relationship between health care spending and the proximity to death is due primarily to the relationship between age and mortality. The end-of-life medical episode tends to be expensive. As we live longer, it is increasingly likely that this event will take place after age 65. Is it cost effective to provide certain services to individuals once they reach a particular age—for example, kidney dialysis, organ transplantation, or joint replacement after age 65? The United States is still a long way from establishing a formal rationing scheme for medical care based on age. If cost-effective care were the sole criterion for access to the medical care system, we would end up with a society where euthanasia at retirement was the norm. What are the chances that we will one day initiate the end-of-life episode shown in the 1960s movie *Logan's Run*? In the futuristic society depicted, when people reached 30, they submitted to the Carousel for the final death spiral. Are the actions of Dr. Kevorkian the first step toward that future?

POLICY ISSUE

Should cost-effective care be the sole criterion for access to the medical care system?

http://

The National Institute on Aging (NIA), one of the National Institutes of Health, promotes healthy aging by conducting and supporting biomedical, social, and behavioral research and public education.

http://www.nih.gov/nia

ISSUES IN MEDICAL CARE DELIVERY

Life Is Short: Make It Count

As for the days of our life, they contain seventy years,
Or if due to strength, eighty years,
Yet their pride is but labor and sorrow;
For soon it is gone and we fly away.

Psalms 90:10

MEDICAL MALPRACTICE

Modern medicine is inherently a dangerous undertaking. A medical care system that takes the responsibility for more ambitious interventions in the case of increasingly sicker patients will see the incidence of *iatrogenic disease* or injury increase, in turn increasing the number of tort cases. Medicine is continuously developing new techniques and more sophisticated medical technology and placing them in the hands of imperfect human agents. It is no wonder errors result, leading to harm to patients. In this section, we will explore how medical malpractice affects the cost of medical care in the United States.

The Purpose and Function of Tort Law

The purpose of medical malpractice law is to force physicians to act as responsible agents for the patient and expose the patient only to that level of risk that a fully informed patient would be willing to accept. In this context, medical malpractice law serves three functions: compensation, deterrence, and retribution.

Tort law has evolved as a method of compensating individuals who are injured as a result of the negligent behavior of others. Compensatory damages are awarded to compensate the successful plaintiff for actual losses, both economic and noneconomic. Economic losses include lost income and any tangible expenses, including all medical and rehabilitation expenses. Noneconomic losses or general damages include pain and suffering, disfigurement, shock, and loss of association.

The tort system compensates injured parties through the use of private third-party liability insurance. This is a mechanism of spreading the risk of loss among policyholders through the payment of insurance premiums. In the case of medical care, the losses are actually spread among patients who pay higher prices for medical care services. Thus, the cost of risk avoidance falls primarily on patients as providers pass through the cost of medical malpractice insurance to their customers in the form of higher fees.

Another important function of tort law is to deter specific behavior that causes injuries. In fact, if the tort system is evaluated according to a standard of economic efficiency, then its justification is based solely on its ability to deter injurious behavior. Compensation and the spreading of risk can actually be accomplished at a lower cost and more equitably through a mechanism of first-party liability in which the patient buys health and disability insurance.

Key Concept 8
Economic Efficiency

Injuries are costly. Likewise, steps taken to avoid injuries are also costly. The goal is not the avoidance of all accidents, but that only the optimal number of accidents will take place. Suppose that a $20,000 injury can be avoided by either the medical provider, taking steps costing $1,000, or by the patient spending $10,000. In this case, it is in society's best interest for the provider to take the responsibility for accident prevention. Likewise, if prevention costs either provider or patient more than $20,000, then failure to take steps to prevent the injury should not be considered negligent behavior.[9]

Key Concept 3
Marginal Analysis

The rules of tort will deter negligent behavior if the responsibility for compensating the victims of injurious behavior rests squarely on those who can prevent the losses at the lowest cost. Holding the low-cost avoider responsible for the costs of the injury should guarantee that efficient precautions will be taken to prevent such accidents in the future.

A third function of the tort system is to exact retribution on those guilty of negligent behavior. Many legal scholars will argue that anyone responsible for an injury to another person should be punished for his or her actions. To the extent that the actions are intentional, only by assigning responsibility can we be sure that justice will be served.

The argument for punitive damages is based on the retribution function. Punitive damages serve the same purpose as criminal and civil penalties, such as jail sentences and fines, in the event that someone is guilty of particularly egregious or malicious behavior. In the case of large damage awards, punitive damages often make up a large percentage of the total compensation to the victim.[10]

International Differences

The legal system for dealing with medical malpractice claims is markedly different in the United States than in other developed countries. These differences are, at least in part, responsible for the differences in the liability costs imposed on medical practitioners. As a percentage of gross domestic product the United States spends two to three times more than the other advanced countries in the world to settle

---

[9] The legal standard of negligence has been laid down by Judge Learned Hand, 159 Federal Reporter 2d 169 (1947), where he defines *negligence* as the failure to take precautions (measures to avoid injury) if the cost of taking precautions is less than the expected cost of damages averted; or, as an economist would say, if the marginal costs are less than the marginal benefits. According to this principle, *negligence* is defined as failure to take adequate precautions in a situation where $C < pD$; where C is the cost of taking precautions, p is the probability that damages will occur without intervention, and D is the amount of the damages.

[10] Of course, if the defendant has insurance coverage that includes the payment of punitive damages, this function is not served efficiently.

tort disputes.[11] Even though the legal climate abroad is generally less favorable to potential plaintiffs, the upward trend in the frequency and severity of claims seems to be a worldwide phenomenon.

Data on malpractice claims in other countries are less comprehensive than data available in the United States. The information in Table 11.9 indicates that the number and severity of malpractice claims is much higher in the United States than in either Canada or the United Kingdom. The number of claims per physician is roughly eight times higher in the United States than in Canada. Claims frequency in the United Kingdom, measured in terms of the population, varied across regions from 21 to 70 percent of the U.S. frequency.

Several important differences contribute to the differences in the size and frequency of claims. These include differences in legal rules, social values, and the costs of filing litigation. The differences are difficult to measure empirically, but their influence on the incentive structure affects the costs and benefits of filing lawsuits.

In theory, there is little difference in the negligence rule of liability across countries. Regardless of country, plaintiffs must show that negligent care from a medical provider caused an injury. More specifically, it must be shown that a duty of care existed, that the defendant failed to conform to the required standard of care either by act or failure to act, that the plaintiff sustained damages, and that the breach of duty was the proximate cause of the injury.

Table 11.9: International Comparisons of Malpractice Awards Annual Claims Frequency and Severity, 2001

	United States	Australia	Canada	United Kingdom
Claims per 100 physicians	7.67	4.72	1.90	6.00
Claims per 100,000 population	18	12	4	12
Average claim awarded (PPP U.S. dollars)	$265,103	$97,014	$249,750[a]	$411,171

Source: Anderson, Hussey, Frogner, and Waters, 2005.

[a] Excluding a single large class-action suit. If included, the value would be $309,417.

Some evidence indicates that differences in the rate of surgical procedures have some bearing on the frequency of malpractice lawsuits. But differences in the rate of lawsuits cannot be fully explained by differences in the rate of adverse surgical outcomes. Major differences in rules governing compensation determine the expected payoff from a lawsuit. Differences in punitive damages, caps on payments for pain and suffering, contingency fees for attorneys, and the U.S. rule on costs provide a greater incentive to sue.

Punitive damages, often a substantial portion of large awards in the United States, are rare in other countries. Awards for pain and suffering are typically subject to judicial caps. The cap in Canada, set at $100,000 (Canadian) in 1978 and indexed to the rate of inflation, has reached around $200,000. The contingency-fee system, used extensively in the United States, is used infrequently in Canada

POLICY ISSUE

Why are claims frequency and severity so much higher in the United States than in other developed countries?

---

[11] Tillinghast-Towers Perrin's (2006) analysis tracks tort costs worldwide and has found that in 2003, the U.S. system cost 250 percent of the average in the industrialized world. Tort costs amounted to 0.69 percent of GDP in the United Kingdom, 0.74 percent in France, 0.75 percent in Switzerland, 0.80 percent in Japan, 1.14 percent in Germany, and 2.22 percent in the United States.

and is illegal in the United Kingdom. The English rule of costs, by which the loser pays court costs and all attorneys' fees, is the standard rule everywhere except the United States. The combined effect of these features lowers the expected return for a successful lawsuit and increases the expected cost of litigation for plaintiffs, which tends to discourage the initiation of lawsuits with little chance of success.

Key Concept 3
Marginal Analysis

Most countries have uniform rules that govern tort claims nationwide. In contrast, the U.S. system has fostered the development of a diverse standard of law in each of the 50 states. A judge alone, without the aid of a jury, decides almost all medical malpractice cases in Canada. Canadian judges tend to hand out more modest awards than American juries in similar situations.

The U.S. legal system does fulfill the three functions of tort law—compensation, deterrence, and retribution—but at a very high administrative cost, upwards of 50 to 60 percent of the total amount awarded. For all the fanfare medical malpractice receives, at the national level it is probably not a major cost driver for health care spending. Malpractice insurance premiums as a percentage of total spending have remained at roughly the same level for the past several decades.

Despite the high cost, the tort system may still be worth the trouble if it serves to deter injurious behavior, but the tort system can only do so much to punish and deter. State medical boards, traditionally hesitant to discipline incompetent behavior, must take the lead in addressing this issue by expanding the use of sanctions that include probation, suspension, and revocation of licenses. Until the public is certain that the medical profession is taking this issue seriously, we will continue to see juries used as inefficient instruments in addressing negligent behavior. No one has a bigger stake in the outcome of this debate than the patients who ultimately pay the bills. If meaningful reform is to happen, it will require our sincere efforts to ensure that the public interest is served instead of merely the special interest.

ISSUES IN MEDICAL CARE DELIVERY

Silicone Breast Implant Litigation: A Case of Rent-Seeking Behavior

Economic rent is best understood as a payment to a resource that exceeds its true opportunity cost. Ann O. Krueger (1974) introduced the concept as a way of explaining the use of scarce resources to secure monopoly profits. It can best be understood by use of the following diagram.

In a competitive environment, price, depicted by *PP*, reflects the underlying average cost of production. With demand *DD*, output would equal *Q*. Any distortion introduced into the market will raise price to *P'P'* and lower output to *Q'*. The dotted triangle depicts the social cost of the distortion measured by the lost consumer surplus. The shaded rectangle represents a transfer from consumers to producers, or economic rent.

The case of the silicone gel breast implant provides a classic case of rent-seeking behavior. From 1962 to 1992, somewhere between 1.0 and 2.2 million women received breast implants in the United States and Canada. A large percentage of these implants were provided for reconstructive surgery following mastectomy, but most were strictly for cosmetic augmentation.

In the early 1990s, a number of reports surfaced linking implants with a variety of illnesses, including lupus, scleroderma, joint swelling, and chronic fatigue. Public awareness was heightened with the December 10,

continued

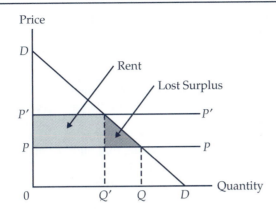

1990, broadcast of the CBS television show *Face-to-Face* entitled "Hazards of Silicone Breast Implants." The show presented a number of case reports claiming that implants were the cause of silicone poisoning in implant recipients. Those women whose implants were not yet leaking or ruptured were said to be carrying around "ticking time bombs."

Where are the rents? As you might guess, the publicity sparked a firestorm of litigation. In addition to over 45 class action lawsuits, more than 19,000 individual product liability lawsuits were filed nationwide, most claiming unspecified economic damages. In suits where damages are specified, they range from $100,000 to $140 million. Although a number of these lawsuits were settled separately, a settlement in a national class action lawsuit provided a $4.5 billion settlement to members of the class of plaintiffs. Individual awards ranged from $105,000 to $1.4 million, based on the severity of the injury and age of the recipient.

Rents represent surplus transferred from customers of implant manufacturers to successful plaintiffs, their attorneys, and all the expert witnesses providing litigation support services in these cases. These "expert" witnesses included toxicologists, pathologists, and economists who make up to $500 per hour; many have received over $250,000 for their testimony. Attorneys paid by the contingency-fee system receive up to 40 percent of the damage awards. According to *Forbes* magazine, one Houston firm had over 2,000 implant clients, and a partner in that firm reportedly made over $40 million in 1994 on implant litigation (Alster, 1999).

An interesting feature of this episode in tort history is how silicone implants were ever approved for human use in the first place. The product was never tested on human subjects. The product had already been in use for more than a decade when the FDA inherited jurisdiction with the passage of the Medical Devices Act in 1975. The product remained in use until 1992, pending the filing of safety data that were in fact never filed. The FDA, under intense pressure from the mounting case evidence concerning the product's safety, banned further use of the device in April 1992.

From a scientific viewpoint, case evidence is useful in formulating a theory but inadequate for testing a hypothesis. In other words, the 300 plus medical case studies in the English literature, while compelling emotionally, are merely descriptive and prove nothing. The scientific issue is causation. The only way to prove causation is to compile scientific evidence showing that implants contribute to the diseases in question — an issue that has so far been avoided by the courts.

Several basic research studies have shown how silicone gel may influence the immune system. Three notable attempts studied the impact

continued

of silicone implants on the immune system. The Nurses' Health Study (Sanchez-Guerrero et al., 1994) and the Women's Health Study (Hennekens et al., 1996) used self-reporting data to examine the relationship. To date the only major epidemiological study on the issue was done at the Mayo Clinic (Gabriel et al., 1994). Based on these studies, it is clear that there is little or no evidence of an "association between breast implants and connective-tissue disease" and no evidence of "large risks of connective-tissue diseases following breast implants."

These studies have their critics, and, admittedly, such studies cannot be considered definitive. The original claim, that silicone implants cause autoimmune diseases, has become that implants cause "atypical" disease. This claim presents a problem for science, because atypical disease cannot be defined. If it cannot be defined, it cannot be studied systematically. It therefore presents an even bigger problem for defendants in the courts, because the association between silicone implants and atypical disease cannot be disproved. To clear up the confusion, a federal judge appointed an independent panel of experts to examine the evidence and provide an opinion as to whether there is a connection between silicone implants and autoimmune diseases. Based on the panel's recommendation, the National Academy of Sciences' Institutes of Medicine declared in 1999 that implants — saline or silicone — do not cause disease. Still, concerns about the safety of implants and their related side effects abound. Recent studies indicate that most women will have at least one rupture within 11 to 15 years. Despite the warnings, at least 130,000 women have received implants annually since 1999.

And the saga is not over. In 2003 an FDA committee recommended that silicone implants be made available to women who want them. When rents are this large, participants manipulate evidence to ensure that they receive their fair share. Whether this rent-seeking behavior will leave women who desire reconstructive surgery with more or fewer options is yet to be determined.

Source: Ann O. Krueger, "The Political Economy of the Rent-Seeking Society," *American Economic Review* 64(3), June 1974, 291–303; Jorge Sanchez-Guerrero, Graham A. Colditz, Elizabeth W. Karlson et al., "Silicone Breast Implants and the Risk of Connective-Tissue Diseases and Symptoms," *The New England Journal of Medicine* 332(25), June 22, 1995, 1666–1670; Charles H. Hennekens, Nancy R. Cook, Patricia R. Hebert et al., "Self-Reported Breast Implants and Connective-Tissue Diseases in Female Health Professionals: A Retrospective Cohort Study," *Journal of the American Medical Association* 275(8), February 28, 1996, 616–621; and Sherine E. Gabriel, W. Michael O'Fallon, Leonard T. Kurland et al., "Risk of Connective-Tissue Diseases and Other Disorders After Breast Implantation," *The New England Journal of Medicine* 330(24), June 16, 1994, 1697–1702. Those interested in reading further on this topic may look at Marcia Angell, *Science on Trial: The Clash of Medical Evidence and the Law in the Breast Implant Case*, Norton, 1996; Norm Alster, "Getting the Middleman's Share," *Forbes* 154, July 4, 1999, 108–109.

MEDICAL TECHNOLOGY

Consensus research concludes that medical technology is responsible for much of the increase in medical care spending over the past several decades (Baker et al., 2003; Fuchs, 1996; Newhouse, 1992; Weisbrod, 1991). If medical spending is indeed determined to a great extent by the availability and use of medical technology, then differences in its availability and use may be a determinant of spending differences across countries. Limiting access to expensive technology and procedures is one strategy to control medical care spending.

In almost every category presented in Table 11.10, the United States ranks at or near the top. With more CT scanners than any country except Japan, the United States has almost two times the average of all countries in the European Union

Table 11.10: Medical Technology[1]

	CT Scanners (2004)	MRI (2004)	Radiation Therapy (2002)	Lithotripters (2004)	Liver Transplants (2002)	Percentage of Women Age 50–69 Receiving Annual Mammograms (2003)	Percentage of Women Age 20–69 Receiving Annual Cervical Cancer Screening (2003)
Canada	10.8	4.9	7.0[2]	0.5	10.0	70.6	74.9
France	7.5	3.2	6.0	0.6	4.6	72.8	74.9
Germany	15.4	6.6	4.6	3.5	—	—	55.9[3]
Japan	92.6[3]	35.3[3]	6.6	6.4[3]	—	2.6	23.7
Switzerland	17.9	14.3	10.6	4.7	—	27.0[3]	—
United Kingdom	7.0	5.0	3.9	—	4.6	75.3	69.7[4]
United States	32.2	26.6	4.0[3]	3.2[3]	18.5	60.8	82.6
EU average	17.5	8.0	5.4	2.1		75.1	62.9

Source: *OECD Health Data 2006.* (U.S. data for radiation therapy and lithotripters from *OECD Health Data 2005.*) Gottlieb (2008).

[1] Per 1,000,000 population.
[2] 2000.
[3] 2002.
[4] 2005.

(EU), three times the number found in Canada, and four times that in the United Kingdom. Much the same story can be told when analyzing the availability of magnetic resonance imaging (MRI) equipment. The U.S. rate is three times that of the EU, five times that of Canada and the United Kingdom, and eight times that of France.[12] The United States trails Europe in the availability of radiation therapy equipment, but has 50 percent more lithotripters than the EU average. The same story can be told regarding the rate of organ transplantation of all kinds and the number of patients being treated for end-stage renal failure.[13] Physicians in the United States performed 18.5 liver transplants per million, almost 4 times the rate in France and the United Kingdom and twice the rate in Canada (Gottlieb, 2008).

Only 60 percent of all American women between the ages of 50 and 69 receive annual mammography screening, less than the EU average of about 75 percent, but higher than the percentage of women screened in either Japan or Switzerland. In contrast, over 82 percent of American women are screened for cervical cancer, higher than in any other advanced country.[14]

Table 11.11 provides comparison statistics on hospitals across the developed world. Even though the United States lags behind most of the rest of the developed world in acute care bed availability, much of the difference can be explained by differences in hospital admission rates and average length of stay. Taking into consideration differences in average lengths of stay and inpatient utilization rates, the United States has substantially more excess bed capacity that the other countries.

Advances in medical technology lead to improved health outcomes. However, the more important question may be: Are the improvements in medical outcomes worth the increases in medical spending? Answering this question requires that we

Table 11.11: Hospital Statistics

2004	Acute Care Beds per 1,000 Population	Average Length of Stay (days)	Inpatient Utilization Rate (%)	Excess Bed Capacity per 1,000 Population[1]
Canada	2.9	7.3	90.0	0.29
France	3.8	5.5	74.9	0.95
Germany	6.4	8.7	75.5	1.57
Japan	8.4	20.2	79.3	1.74
Switzerland	3.8	8.8	86.3	0.52
United Kingdom	3.2	6.6	83.8	0.52
United States	2.8	5.6	66.9	0.93

Source: *OECD Health Data 2007*

[1] Equal to [1 − (inpatient utilization rate)] × [number of acute care beds per 1,000 population]

---

[12] The U.S. rate is an underestimate, because OECD counts the number of hospitals with at least one MRI scanner and not the total number of scanners (Steinbrook, 2006).

[13] For example, in 2006 there were 28,931 organ transplants of all kinds in the United States, or 96.8 per million Americans. That same year, there were 2,999 organ transplants in the United Kingdom, or 49.5 per million.

[14] O'Neill and O'Neill (2007) report that 54.2 percent of American men have had at least one PSA screening in their lifetimes, compared to 16.4 percent of Canadian men. For American men age 40 to 69 years, 29.0 percent have had at least one colonoscopy, compared to 4.6 percent of Canadian men. The same is true when comparing American women with Canadian women.

place a value on the improved outcomes, either in terms of increased life expectancy or improved quality of life. Cutler and McClellan (2001) by studying technological change in the treatment of five common conditions: heart attacks, low birth weight, depression, cataracts, and breast cancer. Their results clearly indicate that for the first four conditions, improved outcomes are well worth increased treatment costs.

SUMMARY AND CONCLUSIONS

In this chapter we discussed a number of confounding factors that affect the overall health of the population. Alcohol, tobacco, and drug use, and their associated health problems, increase the demand for medical care and are responsible for a large percentage of the overall health care spending in this country. The United States has a higher incidence of many of these confounding factors. For example, the rate of AIDS cases is three times higher in the United States than in Canada and six times higher than in Germany. In addition, the problem of drug-exposed infants is virtually nonexistent in Canada. Teen pregnancy, illegitimacy, domestic violence, the use and availability of handguns, STDs, and obesity are experienced at higher levels in the United States than in other developed countries around the world. The higher frequency of medical malpractice lawsuits and the higher availability and use of medical technology also play a role in higher overall health care spending.

How does public policy impact these problems? Government's role is not limited to legislative options. Subsidy and tax options can also serve to encourage healthy behavior and discourage unhealthy behavior. The challenges are enormous and suggest that economics can play a role in this sensitive area of public policy making.

PROFILE

Jonathan Gruber

If the number of publications is a measure of the influence of a scholar, Jonathan Gruber may be the most influential health economist of the past decade. Since he received his Ph.D. in 1992, Gruber has published 70 articles in refereed journals, 33 book chapters, 5 books and edited volumes, and numerous essays. In addition, he has 8 working papers in the National Bureau of Economic Research (NBER) working paper series. Accomplishing this body of work in a lifetime is no minor feat; accomplishing it at such a young age is remarkable.

Born in New Jersey, Gruber received his undergraduate degree in economics from the Massachusetts Institute of Technology (MIT) in 1987 then moved to Harvard University. Introduced to the power of policy-oriented economics at an early age, Gruber spent two summers at the Brookings Institution in Washington, DC. At Brookings he began applying his knowledge of economics to inform policy makers on issues of importance to ordinary Americans.

After graduating from Harvard, he returned to his undergraduate alma mater, a move that some view as dangerous for a scholarly career, especially for a first academic appointment. Whatever the possible pitfalls, Gruber's progression through the ranks was just short of amazing — a promotion to associate professor after three years and then to full professor two years later. In addition to his position at MIT, he is a research associate at the NBER and director of their program on children. He is currently coeditor of the *Journal of Public Economics* and associate editor of the *Journal of Health Economics*. He has also served as Deputy Assistant

continued

Secretary for Economic Policy at the U.S. Treasury Department during the Clinton administration and is currently a member of the Congressional Budget Office Long-Term Modeling Advisory Group.

Trained in public finance and labor economics, Gruber's early work reflected that perspective to examine the impact of health insurance mandates on labor markets. His research interests turned quickly to more standard health economics issues. With articles published in some of the most prestigious journals in economics, Gruber is not relying on past accomplishments to guide public policy. His future research will focus on some of the most important issues in health policy, including the impact of public insurance programs (Medicaid and SCHIP) on health outcomes, the impact of reimbursement rates on the quality of nursing home care, and how religion and religiosity affect well-being.

Gruber has always had a penchant for looking at a well-discussed problem from a different perspective. Until his work on unemployment insurance, the focus in the literature was primarily on the labor market distortions of the program. Instead, Gruber studied the issue from the workers' perspective, looking at the impact on family consumption, savings, and labor supply decisions. His research on smoking and other addictive behavior has introduced a more realistic assumption of human behavior into the model (see "Is Addiction Rational?" in Issues in Medical Care Delivery earlier in this chapter). As a result of this improvement, the normative implications for government policy options differ significantly from previous research.

Despite his scholarly success, Gruber's main avocation is his family. Whether it is spending time at the beach or just wrestling with his kids in the playroom, his goal is to strike a balance between a successful professional career and a fulfilling family life. Jonathan Gruber serves as an inspiration to any discouraged economists who think that what they do does not matter.

Source: *Curriculum Vitea* and personal correspondence.

QUESTIONS AND PROBLEMS

1. How important is the deterioration of the social system in contributing to the health care spending crisis, assuming one exists?

2. Is it important to characterize such social problems as alcoholism and drug abuse as diseases rather than behavior disorders? What are the implications of treating other social problems as diseases? What about anorexia? Obesity? Domestic violence? What are the implications for the medical care system of the proliferation of these new "diseases"?

3. What are the costs to society of cocaine use? Alcohol use? Tobacco use? Which of these presents the biggest problem? Explain.

4. "Drug use is a classic example of a victimless crime. Therefore it should not be prohibited." Comment.

5. As individuals grow older, how does their demand for medical care change? How does aging affect the provision of medical services?

6. How will an aging population influence health policy makers in the twenty-first century?

7. In 1993, the Census Bureau estimated that elderly men were nearly twice as likely to be married and living with their spouses as elderly women (75 percent versus 41 percent). What are the economic and medical care implications of this phenomenon?

8. Since the passage of Medicare in 1965, what has happened to overall medical spending for the elderly? Per capita spending? Out-of-pocket spending? How does this compare with health care spending by the nonelderly?

9. The high cost of dying has been identified by some policy makers as a primary reason for increased medical spending by the elderly. What is the evidence?

10. How serious is the issue of medical malpractice in the United States today?

11. What are the intended purposes of medical malpractice? Does the threat of a lawsuit accomplish these purposes?

12. "It is impossible to place a dollar value on life. In other words, life is priceless." How does this view create a dilemma for social decision making and effective resource allocation?

13. Environmentalists and economists often find themselves at odds with each other. The conflict between the romantics and the rationalists surfaced again in the debate over air-quality standards set under the Clean Air Act of 1990. Under the law, the Environmental Protection Agency (EPA) must establish standards that promote []public health. The EPA's cost-benefit analysis assigns a value for each life saved of $4.8 million. Is $4.8 million a reasonable value to place a life? What questions would economists consider relevant in determining the value of a life? How would environmentalists react to the questions economists ask?

14. The term *iatroepidemic* describes a practice introduced into medicine without sound scientific evidence to establish its efficacy. Such practices result in systematic harm to large numbers of patients. Blood letting during the fifteenth and sixteenth centuries, tonsillectomies in the 1950s, and the practice of psychosurgery have been identified as practices with little therapeutic value that actually harmed many patients. Can you think of other examples of iatroepidemics? When systematic medical error imposes costs on individuals, whom do we blame? Should individual physicians be liable for injuries under these situations?

REFERENCES

Henry J. Aaron, *Serious and Unstable Condition: Financing America's Health Care*, Washington, DC: The Brookings Institute, 1991.

Jerome L. Abramson et al., "Moderate Alcohol Consumption and the Risk of Heart Failure Among Older Persons," *Journal of the American Medical Association* 285(15), April 18, 2001, 1971–1977.

Gerald F. Anderson, Peter S. Hussey, Bianca K. Frogner, and Hugh R. Waters, "Health Spending in the United States and the Rest of the Industrialized World," *Health Affairs* 24(4), July/August 2005, 903–714.

Alan J. Auerbach, Jagadeesh Gokhale, and Laurence J. Kotlikoff, "Restoring Generational Balance in U.S. Fiscal Policy: What Will It Take?" *Economic Review* 31(1), Quarter 1 1995, 2–12.

Laurence Baker, Howard Birnbaum, Jeffrey Geppert, David Mishol, and Erik Moyneur, "The Relationship between Technology Availability and Health Care Spending," *Health Affairs—Web Exclusive*, November 5, 2003, W3–537–551.

Daniel Callahan, *Setting Limits: Medical Goals in an Aging Society*, New York: Simon and Schuster, 1987.

Centers for Disease Control and Prevention (CDC), "Births: Final Data for 2004," *National Vital Statistics Reports* 55(1), September 29, 2006a.

_____, *HIV/AIDS Surveillance Report: HIV Infection and AIDS in the United States and Dependent Areas, 2005*, Volume 17, 2006b. Accessed at http://www.cdc.gov/hiv/topics/surveillance/resources/reports.

_____, "Preventing Tobacco Use," *Preventing Chronic Diseases: Investing Wisely in Health*, August 2005. Accessed at http://www.cdc.gov/nccdphp/publications/factsheets/Prevention/pdf/tobacco.pdf.

Marilyn Chase, "Researcher Sees U.S. Cost of Treating AIDS Virus Rising Sharply by 1995," *Wall Street Journal*, July 23, 1992, B8.

Joel W. Cohen and Nancy A. Krauss, "Spending and Service Use Among People with the Fifteen Most Costly Medical Conditions, 1997," *Health Affairs* 22(2), March/April 2003, 129–138.

David M. Cutler, Edward L. Glaeser, and Jesse M. Shapiro, "Why Have Americans Become More Obese?" *NBER Working Paper No. 9446*, Cambridge, MA: National Bureau of Economic Research, January 2003.

Nicholas Eberstadt, "America's Infant-Mortality Puzzle," *The Public Interest* 105, Fall 1991, 30–47.

Victor Fuchs, "Economics, Values, and Health Care Reform," *American Economic Review* 86(1), 1996, 1–24.

John Steele Gordon, "How America's Health Care Fell Ill," *American Heritage*, May/June 1992, 49–65.

Scott Gottlieb, "Edwards and Organ Transplants," *Wall Street Journal*, January 11, 2008, A11.

Fred J. Hellinger, "The Lifetime Costs of Treating a Person with HIV," *Journal of the American Medical Association* 270(4), July 28, 1993, 474–478.

James W. Henderson, "The Cost Effectiveness of Prenatal Care," *Health Care Financing Review* 15(4), Summer 1994, 21–32.

H. J. Hoffman, P. Bergsjol, and D. W. Denman, "Trends in Birth-Weight Specific Perinatal Mortality Rates: 1970–1983," *Proceedings of the International Collaborative Effort on Perinatal and Infant Mortality 2*, Hyattsville, MD: National Center for Health Statistics, March 1990.

Wenke Hwang et al., "Out-of-Pocket Medical Spending for Care of Chronic Conditions," *Health Affairs* 20(6), November/December 2001, 267–278.

Michael Kramer, Fernando Barros, Kitaw Demissie et al., "Does Reducing Infant Mortality Depend on Preventing Low Birth Weight? An Analysis of Temporal Trends in the Americas," *Pediatric and Perinatal Epidemiology* 19(6), November 2005, 445–451.

Jean Lemaire, "The Cost of Firearm Deaths in the United States: Reduced Life Expectancies and Increased Insurance Costs," *Journal of Risk and Insurance* 72(3), 2005, 359–374.

Marian F. MacDorman and Jonnae O. Atkinson, "Infant Mortality Statistics from the 1997 Period Linked Birth/Infant Death Data Set," *National Vital Statistics Reports* 47(23), Hyattsville, MD: National Center for Health Statistics, 1999.

Marie C. McCormick, "The Contribution of Low Birth Weight to Infant Mortality and Childhood Morbidity," *New England Journal of Medicine* 312(2), January 1985, 82–90.

Ali H. Mokdad et al., "The Continuing Epidemics of Obesity and Diabetes in the United States," *Journal of the American Medical Association* 286(10), September 12, 2001, 1195–1200.

Jann L. Murray and Merton Bernfield, "The Differential Effect of Prenatal Care on the Incidence of Low Birth Weight Among Blacks and Whites in a Prepaid Health Care Plan," *New England Journal of Medicine* 319(21), November 24, 1988, 1385–1390.

National Highway Transportation and Safety Administration, *Traffic Safety Facts: 2005 Data*, National Center for Statistics and Analysis, DOT HS 810 616, accessed at http://www.nhtsa.gov.

Joseph P. Newhouse, "Medical Care Costs: How Much Welfare Loss?" *Journal of Economic Perspectives* 6(3), 1992, 3–21.

June E. O'Neill and Dave M. O'Neill, "Health Status, Health Care, and Inequality: Canada vs. the U.S." *NBER Working Paper No. 13429*, Cambridge, MA: National Bureau of Economic Research, September 2007.

E. R. Pamuk and W. D. Mosher, *Health Aspects of Pregnancy and Childbirth, United States, 1982*, Hyattsville, MD: National Center for Health Statistics, Series 23, No. 16, 1988, 52–53.

Richard Peto, Alan Lopez, Jillian Boreham, Michael Thun, and Clark Heath, Jr., "Mortality from Tobacco in Developed Countries: Indirect Estimation from National Vital Statistics," *The Lancet* 339(8804), May 1992, 1268–1278.

Kristi Reynolds, L. Brian Lewis, John David L. Nolen et al., "Alcohol Consumption and Risk of Stroke: A Meta-Analysis," Journal of the American Medical Association 289(5), February 5, 2003, 579–588.

Marc A. Rodwin, Hak J. Chang, and Jeffrey Clausen, "Malpractice Premiums and Physicians' Income: Perceptions of a Crisis Conflict with Empirical Evidence," *Health Affairs* 25(3), May/June 2006, 750–758.

Edward L. Schneider and Jack M. Guralnik, "The Aging of America: Impact on Health Care Costs," *Journal of the American Medical Association* 263(17), May 2, 1990, 2335–2340.

Todd Summers, Priya Alagiri, and Jennifer Cates, *Federal HIV/AIDS Spending: A Budget Chartbook, Fiscal Year 2002*, Fifth Edition, The Henry J. Kaiser Family Foundation, September 2003.

"The Immortal American," *Wall Street Journal*, May 31, 1995, A14.

Robert Steinbrook, "Private Health Care in Canada," *New England Journal of Medicine* 354(16), April 20, 2006, 1661–1664.

Tillinghast-Towers Perrin, "U.S. Tort Costs and Cross-Border Perspectives: 2005 Update," available at http://www.towersperrin.com/tillinghast, 2006.

U.S. Census Bureau, *National Population Projections: Summary Files*, available at http://www.census.gov/population/www/projections/natsum-T3.html, 2002.

Stephanie J. Ventura, Sally C. Curtin, and T. J. Mathews, "Variations in Teenage Birth Rates, 1991–98: National and State Trends," *National Vital Statistics Reports* 48(6), Hyattsville, MD: National Center for Health Statistics, 2000.

Daniel R. Waldo, Sally T. Sonnefeld, David R. McKusick, and Ross H. Arnett, III, "Health Expenditures by Age Group, 1977 and 1987," *Health Care Financing Review* 10(4), Summer 1989, 111–120.

Myron E. Wegman, "Annual Summary of Vital Statistics, 1992," *Pediatrics* 92(8), December 1993, 743–754.

Burton Weisbrod, "The Health Care Quadrilemma: An Essay of Technological Change, Insurance, Quality of Care, and Cost Containment," *Journal of Economic Literature* 29(2), 1991, 523–552.

David Wessel, "Americans are Getting Fatter, and Technology is to Blame," *Wall Street Journal*, February 13, 2003, A2.

Anne Wolf and Graham Colditz, "Current Estimates of the Economics of Obesity in the United States," *Obesity Research* 6(2), March 1998, 97–106.

CHAPTER 12

Policies that Enhance Access

The federal government's role in funding medical care in the United States continues to be defined and revised. To date the major responsibility has been focused on vulnerable population groups: the poor, the elderly, military veterans, the disabled, and those with certain chronic diseases. Total government spending on health care—including federal, state, and local spending—was approximately $970 billion in 2006, including over $725 billion spent on Medicare and Medicaid. When expenditures on public health, research, construction, and administration are included, government's share of total health care spending approaches 50 percent.

As Americans continue to debate the direction and shape of health care reform, the defining issue is the extent to which we are willing to embrace the principle of universal entitlement to medical care. The principle is already in place in the form of a legal framework that guarantees medical care to certain vulnerable segments of the population; namely, the elderly, those eligible for cash welfare assistance, children under age 18, and military veterans with service-related disabilities.

The development of government's role in the provision of medical care to these vulnerable populations is instructive when we examine public policy as it relates to health care reform. The government is instrumental in providing medical care to over 80 million people under the three major programs: Medicare, Medicaid, and Veterans' Affairs. Any major overhaul of the present medical care delivery system will have to carefully consider how these programs will be affected.

MEDICARE: MEDICAL CARE FOR THE ELDERLY

The elderly, defined as the adult population over the age of 65, are the fastest growing segment of the U.S. population. In 2004, they made up 12.4 percent of the total population but accounted for over one-third of total health care spending. Politically active, this group is comprised of over 35 million voters who are not afraid to let policy makers know how they feel about issues that affect their well-being.

Medicare was established in 1965 to guarantee elderly Americans access to quality health care regardless of their financial circumstances. When combined with Social Security, it represents the most important source of economic security for our nation's elderly. Serving 19.1 million in 1966, Medicare enrollment reached 43.2 million Americans in 2006; over 14 percent of the total population (see Table 12.1). This figure included 36.3 million senior citizens over age 65 and approximately 7 million permanently disabled, including over 300,000 suffering from end-stage kidney failure. Although 75 percent of the beneficiaries of Medicare are between the ages of 65 and 84, the disabled and those over 85 are the fastest growing segments. In 1966, the first complete year of the program, total Medicare

Table 12.1: Actual and Projected Medicare Spending Calendar Years 1966–2006 with Projections to 2016

Year	Total Number of Recipients (millions)	Total Spending (billions of current dollars)	Annual Rate of Change in Spending[1] (percent)
1966	19.1	$ 1.6	—
1970	20.4	7.5	45.6
1975	24.9	16.3	16.9
1980	28.4	36.8	17.7
1985	31.1	72.3	14.5
1990	34.3	111.0	9.0
1995	37.6	184.2	10.7
2000	39.7	221.8	3.8
2005	42.6	336.4	8.7
2006	43.4	408.4	21.4[2]
2007	44.1	431.5	5.7
Projections			
2008	44.9	468.1	8.4
2009	45.8	501.4	7.1
2010	46.7	533.0	6.3
2015	53.7	753.5	7.2
2016	55.3	811.6	7.7
2017	56.9	883.3	8.8

Source: 2007 Annual Reports of the Board of Trustees of the HI and SMI Trust Funds, Tables III.A.1 and III.A.3.

[1] Average annual change from the previous entry.
[2] Addition of Part D benefits responsible for larger than normal increase.

spending was $1.6 billion. Medicare spending reached $431.5 billion in 2007 and is expected to grow to $883.3 billion by 2017 (2008 Medicare Trustees Report).

Institutional Features

Administered by the Centers for Medicare and Medicaid Services (CMS), Medicare provides benefits through three major programs: Part A, Part B, and Part D. Part A is medical hospital insurance; Part B is supplemental medical insurance; and Part D is outpatient prescription drug insurance. Individuals who have paid into the social security system for 10 years, and/or their spouses, are automatically enrolled in Part A upon reaching their sixty-fifth birthday. Enrollment in both Part B and Part D is voluntary. Over 95 percent of all those who are eligible enroll in Part B. Approximately 90 percent of all seniors have prescription drug benefits, either through Part D or some other source.

The basic idea underlying Part A payments is simple. The patient pays a deductible equal to the cost of the first day in the hospital; Medicare pays for days 2 through 60 with no coinsurance requirement; days 61 through 90 are covered, but the patient must pay coinsurance equal to 25 percent of the deductible; and days 91 through 150 are covered if the lifetime reserve days are available, but the patient pays coinsurance equal to 50 percent of the deductible amount. After 150 days in the hospital, Medicare pays nothing. This limitation is easily the most serious flaw in the current system, because it provides enrollees with no protection against catastrophic losses.

Health Care Financing Administration, an agency of the Department of Health and Human Services, was created in 1977 to administer Medicare and Medicaid. This site links to both the Medicare and Medicaid home pages.

http://www.hcfa.gov:80

The 2007 figures translate as follows. The first 60 days of inpatient hospital care during each benefit period is provided to patients with the only out-of-pocket expense being a deductible payment equal to $992.[1] The patient is responsible for a copayment of $248 per day for the next 30 days. After 90 days in the hospital during each benefit period, the patient is responsible for all costs unless reserve days are available.[2]

Additional benefits include 100 days in a skilled-nursing facility during each benefit period. This benefit is provided as a supplement to hospital care and is only available after a minimum three-day hospitalization. The first 20 days are provided at no charge to the patient; days 21 through 100 require a daily copayment of $124 (one-eighth of the hospital deductible). Beyond 100 days, the patient is responsible for the entire bill. Inpatient psychiatric care is available for up to a 190-day lifetime maximum. Home health benefits include up to four days of care per week with no limit and up to three full weeks of care per illness. Individuals with life expectancies of less than six months are eligible for 210 days of hospice care.

Participation in Part B is voluntary and pays for physicians' services and outpatient hospital services, including emergency room services, diagnostic testing, laboratory services, outpatient physical therapy, speech-pathology services, and durable medical equipment. Of interest to most participants is what Medicare does not cover: Routine physical examinations, most preventive care, and custodial nursing home care are not included in the basic benefit package.[3]

After the patient pays a $131 annual deductible, Part B pays 80 percent of the prescribed fee set by Medicare. The majority of physicians who accept Medicare **assignment** accept Medicare's reimbursement as payment in full for the covered services. Approximately half of all practicing physicians accept Medicare assignment, and these **participating physicians** bill over 90 percent of Part B's covered charges (Gillis, Lee, and Willke, 1992).

assignment
A Medicare policy providing physicians with a guaranteed payment of 80% of the allowable fee. By accepting assignment, physicians agree to accept the allowable fee as full payment and forgo the practice of balance billing.

participating physician
A physician who agrees to accept Medicare assignment.

BACK-OF-THE-ENVELOPE

The Impact of Medicare Assignment on Medical Practice

Physicians who provide care to Medicare patients must decide whether or not to accept the Medicare allowable fee as payment in full for the services provided. In other words, physicians must decide whether to take "assignment" on their Medicare patients. Physicians who take assignment bill Medicare and receive 80 percent of the allowable fee directly from the federal government. Those who do not take assignment bill their patients directly, but no more than 15 percent over the allowable fee. Medicare will pay 80 percent of the allowable fee to the patient, who in turn is responsible for paying the physician. The excess charges over the allowable fee are referred to as **balance billing**. Physicians who take assignment are reasonably certain they will collect 80 percent of the allowable fee. Those who do not take assignment have no such assurances.

From the physician's perspective, the problem centers on the relationship between the fee usually charged for the service provided and the Medicare allowable fee, which is often much lower. The impact of

continued

balance billing
Billing a patient for the difference between the physician's usual charge for a service and the maximum charge allowed by the patient's health plan.

---

[1] A benefit period is defined as the time period that begins on the first day the patient is admitted into the hospital and extends to 30 days after that patient is discharged.

[2] Each enrollee is provided 60 lifetime reserve days with a daily copayment of $496. These are used to pay hospital expenses beyond the 90 days of coverage during each benefit period. Once a patient uses these reserve days, Part A benefits stop after 90 days in the hospital during a benefit period.

[3] This is true unless the participant is enrolled in an HMO; then these services may be covered.

assignment on the physicians' services market is addressed in the following diagram.

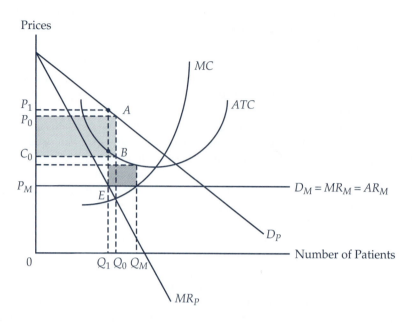

For those physicians who accept assignment, the market for a physician's services can be divided into two segments: private patients and Medicare. Private-patient demand is given by the downward-sloping demand curve labeled D_P. To maximize profits, the physician will set $MR_P = MC$ and provide Q_0 services at a price of P_0. Profits are depicted graphically as the shaded area bounded by the points $P_0 ABC_0$.

Physicians who accept Medicare assignment agree to a fixed price (P_M) for their Medicare patients. As a price taker, the demand curve for this segment of the market becomes $D_M = MR_M = AR_M$. Now the physician is faced with a more complicated decision. The new marginal revenue curve has a floor established at P_M. The combined marginal revenue curve is now MR_P to point E, where MR_P and MR_M intersect, and MR_M thereafter. The physician will see a total of Q_M patients (Q_1 private patients and $Q_M - Q_1$ Medicare patients). Private patients now pay a higher price for services, or P_1, which is sometimes called *cost shifting*.

Physicians complain that the Medicare allowable fee is below their average cost of providing medical services. In the diagram above, the shaded area between *ATC* and *PM* shows this loss. Although providing care to the Medicare segment of the market may not cover fully allocated costs, each one of those transactions is reimbursed at a rate that covers the physician's opportunity cost; all relevant costs as measured by *MC*. Whether the physician is better off or worse off (determined by the change in profit) depends on whether the extra profits from private patients offset the losses incurred in providing care to Medicare patients.

Key Concept 3
Marginal Analysis

Key Concept 5
Markets and Pricing

Key Concept 6
Supply and Demand

Participants receive medical coverage either through the traditional fee-for-service option or by joining privately administered Medicare Advantage (MA) plans. In addition to the standard benefits, many MA plans cover additional services including vision, dental, and many preventive services. In addition, many offer protection against catastrophic medical costs. In 2007, about 8.3 million seniors participated in MA plans, or about 20 percent of the eligible population.

Outpatient prescription drug coverage was added as Part D in 2006. By the middle of the year, an estimated 22.5 million seniors had enrolled in one of the 4,000 plans nationwide with 72 percent covered by the ten largest. Another 15.8 million had creditable drug coverage from some other source, such as an employer plan or the Veterans' Administration.

Enrollees pay monthly premiums that vary depending on the plan chosen. Premiums for the basic plan were $27.35 per month in 2006. An annual deductible of $265 with a coinsurance rate of 25 percent covered a basic formulary. This rate applied up to the point where the infamous donut hole is reached at the initial benefit limit of $2,400. The enrollee then pays 100 percent of the cost up to a catastrophic out-of-pocket limit of $3,850. At that point the coinsurance rate falls to 5 percent, or $2 for generic drugs and $5 for preferred drugs, whichever is lower. Program cost during the first year was $32 billion, with the cumulative estimated cost through 2015 of $797 billion.

Who Pays?

Medicare funding comes from four major sources: payroll taxes, income taxes, trust fund interest, and enrollee premiums. Almost 90 percent of the funding comes directly and indirectly from individuals who are less than 65 years old. The remainder comes in the form of enrollee premiums from those who are over 65. A payroll tax of 2.9 percent is levied on the gross income of all employees and is collected along with the Social Security tax. This tax is divided equally between employer and employee. Until 1994, tax law included a cap on the income that was subject to the Medicare tax—$51,300 in 1990, $135,000 in 1993. Legislation passed in 1993 removed the income ceiling, subjecting all payroll income to the 2.9 percent Medicare levy.

This 2.9 percent payroll tax on all workers in the U.S. labor force—over $181 billion in 2006—is dedicated entirely to the trust fund to pay Part A benefits. In recent years, program receipts have exceeded benefit payments, accumulating a surplus in the Medicare trust fund amounting to $305.4 billion in 2006.[4] A major problem resurfaced in 1997 when spending outlays exceeded receipts by approximately $250 per enrollee. Congress acted in 1997 with the Balanced Budget Act, significantly reducing hospital spending. Coupled with higher than expected economic growth, the shortfall has turned into a surplus that is expected to run until 2011. According to the 2007 trustees' report, the trust fund is expected to remain solvent until 2019.[5]

In 2007, Enrollees in Part B paid a monthly premium, usually deducted from the monthly Social Security check, equal to $93.50. Premiums finance approximately 25 percent of all Part B costs. General tax revenues and interest on the assets of the Medicare trust fund cover the remainder.

Who Benefits?

Medicare's allocation pattern closely fits the usual experience of underwriting medical care spending for large groups. Underwriters often refer to this pattern as the 80–20 rule: 80 percent of the spending benefits 20 percent of the covered

[4] Many argue that because the "trust fund" is invested in interest-bearing U.S. Treasury securities, it is not really a trust fund at all. To use the fund, the federal government must liquidate the securities by reissuing debt, raising additional tax revenues, or printing money.

[5] At this time there are no provisions to use general revenues to cover this deficit.

population. As illustrated in Table 12.2, about 31 million enrollees, or 77 percent of the eligible population, actually received paid benefits in 2001. Approximately 86 percent of the program's outlays of $197.5 billion purchased care for 19.9 percent of the population, whose per capita spending exceeded $5,000. Per capita spending for this high-cost group was $21,332. An additional 56.7 percent of the enrollees spent $27.88 billion, 14.1 percent of the total outlays, or $1,227 per capita. The other 23.4 percent received no paid benefits. Average spending per enrollee was $4,933; average spending for the 78.6 percent who actually received paid benefits was $6,437.

Medicare has proven to be a good financial investment for the individual enrollee. A couple retiring in 1994, who had been paying the average Medicare tax since 1966, would have paid $20,000 in payroll taxes into the program (including the employer's share). Lifetime benefits, discounted to 1994, exceed the amount paid in premiums and taxes by an average of $117,200, or six times the amount paid into the system. Because Part B premiums account for only 25 percent of the outlays for medical benefits, an **actuarially fair premium** would have to be four times greater than the current $93.50, or $374 per month, to cover 100 percent of Part B spending.[6]

Economic Consequences

Medicare's spending pattern highlights the fundamental flaw in Medicare coverage, the fact that it provides virtually no protection against low probability, catastrophic losses. For short hospital stays, Medicare pays virtually all the bill beyond the deductible. Longer hospital stays, in excess of 150 days, subject the individual to larger percentages of the total bill. This failure to cover very long but infrequent hospital stays is the result of the original "spell of illness" concept originally considered beneficial to participants. Under this concept, if a patient is discharged from the hospital and then readmitted within 30 days, the readmission is considered part of the same illness. As part of the same illness, the patient does not have to pay

actuarially fair premium
Insurance premium based on the actuarial probability that an event will occur.

POLICY ISSUE

Medicare coverage provides little protection against catastrophic illnesses.

Table 12.2: Medicare Payments Allocation, 2001

Payment Range	Number of Beneficiaries (millions)	Percent of Total	Spending (billions)	Percent of Total	Average per Enrollee
Over $25,000	2.12	5.3	$101.31	51.3	$47,732
$20,000 to $24,999	0.66	1.7	14.82	7.5	22,365
$10,000 to $19,999	2.33	5.8	33.35	16.9	14,313
$5,000 to $9,999	2.84	7.1	20.11	10.2	7,084
$2,000 to $4,999	5.01	12.5	16.06	8.1	3,205
$1,000 to $1,999	4.65	11.6	6.67	3.4	1,437
$500 to $999	4.54	11.3	3.30	1.7	728
Less than $500	8.53	21.3	1.85	0.9	217
Zero	9.36	23.4	0	0.0	0
Total	40.04	100.0	$197.50	100.0	$4,933

Source: *Health Care Financing Review: Medicare and Medicaid Statistical Supplement, 2003*, Table 16.

---

[6] Private insurance coverage for comparable benefits under Parts A and B would cost the average 65- to 74-year-old between $6,400 and $8,500 per year, or $500 to 700 per month.

the deductible again. The intent is to save the patient from the financial burden of paying the deductible over and over and to guarantee that elders will seek care when it is needed. The unintended consequence of this provision is to increase the chance that a long hospital stay will expose the individual to the financial risk of a catastrophic illness, in which the patient is responsible for the entire bill after the 60 lifetime reserve days are exhausted.

Key Concept 9
Market Failure

Overall, Medicare pays 87 percent of inpatient hospital charges and 67 percent of physician's services, but only 0.5 percent of long-term care. Because of gaps in coverage, an active supplementary insurance market has developed. In 1999, approximately 22.2 million elderly Americans had supplemental insurance benefits from Medicaid, private insurance companies, or their previous employers.[7] Many of the so-called Medigap policies have the same problem as Medicare itself: an upside-down structure. In other words, they cover the up-front costs—deductibles and copayments—and provide for some noncovered expenses, such as outpatient prescription drugs; but they do not provide protection against catastrophic financial risk. In addition, they are costly; annual premiums range from about $720 to as much as $5,000.

Key Concept 8
Efficiency

Federal laws passed in the 1980s to regulate this growing insurance market failed to address this flaw completely. Congress created minimum standards for all **Medigap insurance** policies, but rather than provide true catastrophic coverage for the extremely rare, long hospital stay, the government has forced the private insurance market to provide Medigap policies that offer first-dollar coverage. This practice is not only inefficient, but it encourages participants to overutilize medical resources and drives up the premium costs without providing genuine catastrophic insurance coverage. As a result, the typical senior pays approximately 31 percent of his or her own medical bills either out-of-pocket or through private insurance premiums (Vladeck and King, 1995; Dallek, 1996). In addition, Medicare does not cover most long-term care or mental illness treatment, and does not provide protection against catastrophic losses due to extended illnesses, which has resulted in mounting political pressure on policy makers to act.

Medigap insurance
A supplemental insurance policy sold to Medicare-eligible individuals to pay the deductibles and coinsurance that are not covered by Medicare. These policies must conform to one of ten standardized benefit plans established by the federal government.

BACK-OF-THE-ENVELOPE

Medical Inflation and Medicare

Many argue that medical care costs and spending were of little macroeconomic consequence until the mid 1960s, when the government stepped up its involvement with the creation of Medicare and Medicaid. The theoretical underpinnings of this argument are fairly straightforward. In general, insurance coverage increases the demand for medical care. The elderly are no different.

Key Concept 5
Markets and Pricing

In the diagram on the following page, D_0 and D_1 represent the elderly demand before and after the passage of Medicare. This rightward shift in demand will result in increased utilization (Q_0 to Q_1), which is desirable, and increased prices (P_0 to P_1), which are not. Physicians who were treating their nonelderly patients and charging them the same price will find that the opportunity cost of their time has increased due to the higher prices paid by the elderly. Greater opportunity costs are shown by a leftward

continued

[7] This number is down from 23.8 million covered by supplemental insurance in 1991. The decrease is offset by the increase in the number of elderly enrolled in Medicare managed care plans that all but eliminate the need for supplemental insurance.

shift in the physicians' supply curve in the right-hand side of the diagram, forcing prices paid by the nonelderly to rise accordingly. There are obviously other reasons for the rise in medical care spending, but as the diagram shows, Medicare's impact should not be ignored.

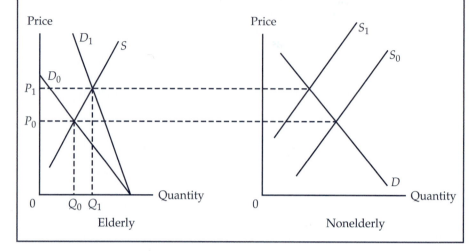

MEDICAID: MEDICAL CARE FOR THE POOR

Medicaid was passed in 1965 as part of the same legislative package with the federal Medicare program. The program served approximately 10 million low-income Americans in 1967, increasing to 45.8 million in 2001. Medicaid spending amounted to $1.66 billion in 1966 and grew to $303.9 billion in 2006 (see Table 12.3).

Table 12.3: Medicaid Spending Select Years, 1966–2006

Year	Total Enrollment Year End (millions)	Total Spending (billions of current dollars)[1]	Annual Rate of Change in Spending[2] (in percentages)
1966	10.0	$ 1.7	—
1970	—	4.9	30.3
1975	22.0	12.1	20.8
1980	21.6	24.0	13.8
1985	21.8	39.4	10.4
1990	25.3	69.8	11.8
1995	36.3	151.7	17.2
2000	34.5	195.5	5.2
2001	37.9	216.2	10.6
2002	41.1	246.6	13.9
2003	43.6	262.6	6.6
2004	44.6	281.8	7.3
2005	45.7	300.7	6.7
2006	45.2	303.9	1.1

Source: Medicaid Financial Management Reports available at http://www.cms.hhs.gov/ MedicaidBudget ExpendSystem/Downloads/2004to1997.pdf.

[1] Includes payments made to "disproportionate share hospitals"; does not include administration.
[2] Average annual change from the previous entry

ISSUES IN MEDICAL CARE DELIVERY

The Politics of Medicare

The 1965 legislation that created Medicare included aspects of the three major proposals that were popular at the time. Democrats favored a hospital trust fund that included mandatory participation and financing from a broad-based tax, which became Medicare Part A. Republicans wanted traditional indemnity insurance with voluntary participation, funded by a premium paid by all participants and subsidized out of general tax revenues, which became Medicare Part B. Finally, the medical community, led by the American Medical Association, wanted medical insurance for the indigent paid out of general tax revenues, which became Medicaid.

Since the creation of the program, numerous changes have expanded the system's coverage and method of paying providers. Medical benefits for the disabled were added in 1975, and the end-stage renal program was created in 1980. Prospective payment to hospitals was put in place in 1983, and a relative-value scale to pay physicians was started in 1994.

In addition to expanding benefits and controlling spending, Congress addressed the major weakness of the program in 1988, namely, its inability to provide catastrophic financial protection, by passing the Medicare Catastrophic Coverage Act. Instead of a crowning achievement, this act represents one of the most embarrassing moments in congressional history.

The intent of the legislation was to guard against the high cost of a prolonged or debilitating illness. The unique feature of the plan was that the entire cost of a social welfare program was borne by the intended beneficiaries. After considering its effect, the majority of the elderly population, or at least an extremely vocal minority, determined that the extra benefits provided by the program were not worth the added costs. Most Medicare beneficiaries already had supplemental coverage that they considered superior to the benefits provided by the new legislation. The failure of the act to provide additional benefits — especially long-term care benefits — led to its ultimate demise. Protests by the elderly — and reversals in positions by advocates of the elderly, including the American Association of Retired People — led to the act's repeal in November 1989.

More recent legislation has attempted to address the expected short-fall in the hospital trust fund. According to the 1996 trustees' report, the trust fund was expected to run out of assets by 2001 if no changes to the system were adopted. Acting on this report, Congress included Medicare reform in the 1998 federal budget. Originally, the proposed reform package was designed to reduce Medicare spending growth by over $270 billion by reducing the fees paid to providers, increasing premiums and copayments to recipients, and extending the eligibility age to 67. Opposition quickly mobilized and successfully defeated the proposal, reinforcing the perception that Medicare is politically untouchable.

Congress was able to address the short-term insolvency by cutting provider payments by $115 billion over the 1998 to 2002 time period, extending the trust fund's solvency until the year 2029 (at the time). Furthermore, the legislation encouraged enrollment in managed care plans and allowed the option of setting up medical savings accounts. But these changes were not enough to address the long-term structural deficiencies in the system that will become evident when the baby-boom

continued

> generation starts retiring in 2010. A bipartisan congressional commission will be formed in 1998 to study the problem and recommend alternative solutions for Congress to consider. The commission, headed by Democrat John Breaux, agreed on a reform package designed along the same lines as the Federal Employee Health Benefit Plan that featured a choice of plans for all enrollees, along with a prescription drug benefit. A threatened veto by President Clinton killed the bill in committee.
>
> Since then President George W. Bush has voiced support for this plan and delivered the promised outpatient prescription drug benefit in 2006. While everyone speaks of major reform, it has been largely elusive. The new president will likely commit to incorporate Medicare change into a comprehensive health care reform package in his first term in office.
>
> **Source:** Thomas Rice, Katherine Desmond, and Jon Gabel, "The Medicare Catastrophic Coverage Act: A Postmortem," *Health Affairs*, 9(3), Fall 1990, 75–87.

Institutional Features

Medicaid is a means-tested entitlement program, administered by the states and financed jointly with the federal government. The federal portion of Medicaid payments is based on each state's per capita income relative to national per capita income. The national average for the federal matching rate was 57 percent in 2006, ranging from 50 to 76.8 percent.[8] The states have some flexibility in designing their own programs as long as certain federal guidelines are met. These guidelines mandate that a basic medical benefits package must be provided to specific population groups, primarily low-income groups traditionally eligible for welfare. States also have some flexibility in determining the level of payment to providers. Beyond these requirements, states have the option of expanding benefits and covering additional groups. As a result, eligibility standards and benefits vary considerably, creating unequal coverage across the nation. Individuals who are eligible for benefits in one state would not be eligible, under similar circumstances, for benefits in another.

Mandated benefits cover a full range of services including both inpatient and outpatient hospital services, physicians' services, family planning services (not including abortion services), ambulatory care, diagnostic screenings, nursing home care, home health care, and nurse practitioners' services. Many states also include an optional benefits package covering outpatient prescription drugs, optometry and dental services, prosthetic devices, physical therapy, and intermediate care for the mentally retarded.

Eligibility The original legislation provided coverage for recipients of public assistance, primarily single-parent families and the aged, blind, and disabled. Since its original enactment, 20 major legislative actions have expanded benefits to additional groups and have covered additional services (Gruber, 2000b). These steps have resulted in the dramatic escalation in spending over the original projections. After moderating somewhat in the 1980s, spending increased over 25 percent per year in the early 1990s and has only recently settled down to single-digit annual increases.

---

[8] **The federal share, or federal medical assistance percentage (FMAP), is determined by the formula**
FMAP $= 1 - [(\text{State per capita income})^2/(\text{U.S. per capita income})^2] \times 0.45]$.

Since the mid-1980s, the program has been marked by nearly continuous expansion of eligibility. Legislation during the 1984 to 1987 period weakened the link between eligibility for cash welfare assistance and Medicaid eligibility. These changes in eligibility standards foreshadowed later changes that have all but severed that link. The first major change allowed states to cover children who met the financial standards but lived in two-parent households. By 1992, states were required to provide pregnancy-related benefits for pregnant women and children under age 6 who had family incomes that were less than 133 percent of the federal poverty level ($22,836 for a family of three in 2007).[9] Children aged 6 to 18 must also be covered if their family income is less than 100 percent of the poverty level ($17,170 for a family of three in 2007).

The second major change allowed states to extend coverage to the "medically needy" according to standards established by the state. Families who are not eligible for poverty-related coverage may be classified as "medically needy" if their income falls below an established level or if their medical expenses are very large. This category of coverage has become less important with the expansion of benefits to pregnant women and children. It remains, however, a significant source of benefits for the elderly and disabled.

Since 1987, most of the changes in the program have increased the income threshold for eligibility. Federal law requires that all infants living in households with incomes at 75 percent of the poverty level be covered. Some states raised age eligibility to age 7 or 8, and others raised the threshold to as high as 185 percent of the poverty income level.

In the summer of 1996, Congress enacted a sweeping welfare reform bill that included changes to Medicaid. The main feature of the legislation was a new program called **Temporary Aid to Needy Families (TANF)** replacing the old **Aid for Families with Dependent Children (AFDC)** program. Under TANF, each state receives a block grant—a fixed, lump-sum payment—to design its own welfare program. More importantly, cash assistance is no longer a guaranteed entitlement to everyone who meets a state's eligibility requirements.

The Medicaid program was left virtually intact by this legislation, but several features of the new law affected Medicaid eligibility. One of the main paths to Medicaid eligibility had been through AFDC. Now that AFDC had been replaced by TANF, eligibility for TANF did not guarantee Medicaid benefits. In other words, the link between cash welfare assistance and Medicaid coverage had been severed. Possibly the harshest aspect of the legislation dealt with the treatment of legal immigrants. Under current law, legal immigrants arriving after August 22, 1996, are not eligible for Medicaid benefits until they have resided in the U.S. for five years. Even with the passage of TANF, states continue to base eligibility on the income thresholds used to determine eligibility for cash welfare assistance.

State Children's Health Insurance Program

Passage of the Balanced Budget Act of 1997 created the **State Children's Health Insurance Program (SCHIP)** and provided nearly $40 billion in matching funds to states that provided health insurance to low-income children without insurance.[10] The amended Title XXI of the Social Security Act gave states the option of setting up separate insurance programs for children, expanding Medicaid to cover children,

Temporary Aid to Needy Families (TANF)
Temporary Aid to Needy Families replaced the old AFDC program in 1996 as the main cash assistance program for the poor.

Aid for Families with Dependent Children (AFDC)
Aid for Families with Dependent Children, created in 1935, was the primary cash assistance program for the poor and needy in the U.S. welfare system until 1996, when it was replaced by a block-grant program.

State Children's Health Insurance Program (CHIP)
A state administered program, similar to Medicaid, targeted to provide affordable health insurance to children from low-income families who are otherwise ineligible for Medicaid benefits.

---

[9] States are allowed to establish eligibility standards that extend benefits to families with incomes up to 185 percent of the poverty level.

[10] Children in families with incomes exceeding the Medicare threshold, but less than 200 percent of the federal poverty level, are eligible.

or a combination of the two. As of 2007, 18 states operated a separate program, 11 simply expanded Medicaid, and 21 used a combination of the two. In 2005, over 6 million low-income children were covered by SCHIP at a cost of over $7 billion. SCHIP programs must provide enrollees with the same benefits available under Medicaid. Patient out-of-pocket costs are allowed but are limited to 5 percent of family income.

Forty-one states cover children who live in families with incomes up to 200 percent of the federal poverty level. SCHIP is not set up as an entitlement program. Children who are eligible must still pay monthly premiums to participate. Census data estimate that over 9 million children remain uninsured with the majority eligible for either Medicaid or SCHIP but not enrolled.

Premium assistance programs and coverage waivers have also been passed in a number of states. States have used these waivers to cover other uninsured individuals in addition to eligible children, including parents of eligible children, childless adults, and pregnant women. Under these programs, states are allowed to subsidize employers who offer insurance to otherwise eligible participants and in some cases to purchase family coverage if it is proven to be cost effective.

Economic Consequences

Key Concept 6
Supply and Demand

Results of a study by the Kaiser Foundation (1995) conclude that most of the increase in Medicaid spending since 1988 has been due to three factors: 1) program expansions mandated by the federal government that have lead to dramatic increases in enrollment; 2) the overall increase in medical care costs; and 3) increases in reimbursement rates to hospitals and other providers.

Congress moved to expand Medicaid eligibility as part of the Deficit Reduction Act of 1984. In an attempt to reduce infant mortality and improve access to child health services, the act was the first in a series of seven legislative steps that extended eligibility to all pregnant women and children under the age of 19.

At the same time, Congress also required the states to add new services to the mandatory benefits package. States must cover the services of nurse practitioners, care provided in community and migrant health centers, and any service needed to treat a condition discovered during a diagnostic screening, even if the treatment is considered an optional benefit.

In addition, Congress acted to improve reimbursement levels for providers. The 1980 Boren amendment allowed states to deviate from Medicare's cost-reimbursement system for hospitals and nursing homes but also required that reimbursement levels be sufficient to allow for their efficient and economical operation. A decade later, hospitals and nursing homes began filing Boren lawsuits asking for federal review of the states' reimbursement systems, and within a year litigation was in progress in 29 states.

disproportionate share ("Dispro") payments
A payment adjustment under Medicare and Medicaid that pays hospitals that serve a large number of indigent patients.

In order to increase physician participation and advance the goal of increasing health services for children and pregnant women, legislation was passed to improve payments to pediatricians and obstetricians. Hospitals that serve a **disproportionate share** of Medicaid patients receive supplemental payments as part of the Disproportionate Share Hospital Program, in part to make up for low initial reimbursement rates. According to the Kaiser Foundation study, "Dispro" payments accounted for over 16 percent of the increase in Medicaid spending between 1987 and 1992.

Nationwide, approximately 60 percent of all Americans younger than age 65 living below the poverty level receive assistance through Medicaid. States set their own income threshold for eligibility, so the percentages vary considerably from state to state. In 2002, the average income for an eligible family of three was $6,158, ranging from a low of $3,048 in Alabama to $40,224 in Minnesota. The average eligibility threshold for pregnant women with children has been established by federal law at a minimum of 133 percent of the poverty level, or $26,267 in 2007 for a family of three, and it ranges up to 185 percent of the poverty level, or $36,537. Since the early origins of federal involvement in medical care for the needy, spending has been concentrated in the states with the largest populations. In FY 2004 when spending was $257.7 billion (excluding disproportionate share payments to hospitals), almost half of that total was spent in the seven states with populations over 10 million (see Table 12.4). Nationwide, the average payment per beneficiary was $4,685, compared to $4,550 for the seven most populous states and $4,816 for the remaining 43 states.

State differences in eligibility standards and average spending per beneficiary do not begin to tell the whole story of gaps in coverage across the country. Some Americans cannot qualify for Medicaid under any circumstances. Individuals with incomes over the eligibility standard, and those who do not fall within a certain category—blind, disabled, pregnant, or single-parent with dependent children—are, of course, ineligible. These requirements make it extremely difficult for males who are not blind or disabled and who are not living with children to establish eligibility for the program.

The Medicaid program was originally established to provide basic medical benefits, including hospital and physicians' services, for those who were receiving cash assistance through state welfare programs. Although medical payments for welfare recipients remain a key element of the program, nursing home care and home health care, primarily for the Medicare-eligible population, constitute over 70 percent of the total outlays. Table 12.5 summarizes program spending by eligibility category. Approximately 70 percent of the program spending in FY 2001 went to the elderly and disabled. Per capita payments to these two groups were $12,691 and $11,310. Children and adults received approximately 27 percent of the total program outlays. Per capita payments for these two groups were $1,454 and $2,067.

Table 12.4: Medicaid Payments, Fiscal Year 2004
           Seven Most Populous States

State	Total Payments (in billions)	Payment per Beneficiary	Number of Beneficiaries (in millions)
California	$ 27.4	$2,741	10.01
Florida	12.8	4,350	2.95
Illinois	10.8	5,318	2.03
New York	37.3	7,914	4.71
Ohio	11.4	5,999	1.90
Pennsylvania	10.1	5,495	1.83
Texas	13.2	3,671	3.60
Seven-state total	123.0	4,550	27.03
Rest of the U.S.	134.7	4,816	27.97
Total U.S.	257.7	4,685	55.00

Source: Medicaid Statistical Information System, *MSIS Tables, FY 2004.*

**Table 12.5: Medicaid Spending by Eligibility Category
Fiscal Year 2001**

Category	Payment per Capita	Number Eligible (in millions)	Percent of Total Eligible Population	Total Spending (in billions)	Percent of Total Spending
Aged	$12,691	3.8	8.3	$48.4	25.9
Disabled	11,310	7.1	15.5	80.4	43.0
Children	1,454	21.1	46.0	30.6	16.4
Adults	2,067	9.8	21.3	20.2	10.8
Other	1,825	4.0	8.8	7.3	3.9
Total	$4,084	45.8	100.0	$186.9	100.0

Source: *Health Care Financing Review: Medicare and Medicaid Statistical Supplement, 2003,* Table 94.

Almost half of the poverty-level population is ineligible for Medicaid benefits of any kind, and many of those who are eligible have a difficult time finding a physician who will treat them. Expansion of the program at the state level is unlikely, because Medicaid is viewed as the one item in state budgets that is out of control. Mandated expansion of the eligible population resulted in a doubling of spending between 1989 and 1992. Not only has the number of beneficiaries increased, but diseases associated with lower socioeconomic groups have escalated, especially medical problems related to smoking, drug use, obesity, and AIDS. In fact, Medicaid has become the primary insurance carrier for many AIDS patients with the program paying for over 40 percent of all AIDS-related medical costs.

States have a limited range of responses to rising costs. Program cutbacks jeopardize federal funding, and tax increases jeopardize political careers. To date, only Oregon has moved to ration care by prioritizing services and restricting access to services that are not cost effective (more will be said about the Oregon plan in Chapter 15). Most states are turning to managed care to reduce Medicaid spending. In fact, almost 60 percent of the Medicaid population—23 million individuals—were enrolled in managed care plans in 2002, making the Centers for Medicare and Medicaid Services, the agency that administers Medicare and Medicaid, the nation's largest purchaser of managed care.

Other Economic Issues

As with any other entitlement program, researchers are interested in its impact on the behavior and well-being of its participants. Research has examined the economic impact of the Medicaid program to determine its effect on health outcomes, enrollment in private insurance, labor supply, family structure, and savings.

POLICY ISSUE

To what extent does better access to medical care improve health outcomes?

Health Outcomes One of the stated goals of the Medicaid program is to improve the health of the eligible population. Although policy makers cannot legislate better health, they can improve access to providers in hopes that better access will result in better health outcomes. Expansions in eligibility since the mid-1980s have focused primarily on enrolling pregnant women and children. A number of studies have examined the connection between Medicaid eligibility and health outcomes for these two groups. Currie and Gruber (1996a) found evidence that Medicaid eligibility expansions among pregnant women improved prenatal care utilization and resulted in a reduction in the proportion of low–birth-weight deliveries and an improvement in birth outcomes. They estimate that a 10 percent increase in Medicaid eligibility leads to a 2.8 percent decrease in infant mortality rates for the affected population. Currie and Gruber (1996b) also found that expansions in eligibility for children increased hospitalizations but reduced avoidable hospitalizations. An increase in eligibility of only 10 percent resulted in a 3.4 percent decrease in child mortality rates, due to better access to primary and preventive care.

Dubay and colleagues (2000) found that Medicaid expansions increased medical care utilization by pregnant women. However, their research showed no significant impact on the incidence of low birth weight. They concluded that their results were due to the fact that expansions in the early 1990s included mainly pregnant women with higher family incomes. Better birth outcomes are normally associated with higher family incomes in the first place. The lesson may be that further expansions to women with higher incomes will have even smaller marginal effects on birth outcomes.

Many policy makers are convinced that there is a shortage of physicians willing to serve the Medicaid population due to low reimbursement rates. Research has shown that higher fees increase physician participation in the program (Sloan, Mitchell, and Cromwell, 1978; Hadley, 1979; Mitchell, 1991), especially among physicians specializing in obstetrics and gynecology (Mitchell and Schurman, 1984; Adams, 1994). This research, however, does not make the connection between higher physician participation rates and better health outcomes.

Enrollment in Private Insurance As the value of free, public insurance coverage increases, holders of costly, private insurance are likely to drop private coverage and enroll in Medicaid. Cutler and Gruber (1996) examine the economics of crowding out and conclude that hundreds of thousands of women have dropped private insurance as Medicaid expands eligibility. The decision to drop private insurance coverage is often encouraged by employers who decrease their own share of the private insurance premium, creating an incentive for employees to "voluntarily" drop private coverage.

Labor Supply For individuals on public welfare assistance, Medicaid eligibility is a valuable benefit. Many hesitate to accept jobs, fearing the loss of free, public health insurance. This so-called "welfare lock" has been documented by Yelowitz (1995) and Winkler (1991) and is especially profound in the case of women with small children. This literature is summarized in Gruber (2000a).

Family Structure Another important aspect of Medicaid eligibility is its impact on family structure—the marriage decision and the decision to have children. Yelowitz (1998) showed that the Medicaid program as traditionally structured created a bias favoring single-parent families. Women with children remained single to qualify for the program, because potential marriage partners may not have been able to provide health insurance for the family. Between 1987 and 1992, the fraction of women of childbearing age eligible for Medicaid doubled, and the fraction of children eligible increased by 50 percent (Cutler and Gruber, 1996). Medicaid's pregnancy coverage lowers the cost of childbearing, and its generous child coverage lowers the discounted present value of raising a child. These two factors resulted in a significant increase in fertility among eligible women (Joyce, Kaestner, and Kwan, 1998). In fact, Medicaid expansions were estimated to be responsible for up to a 10 percent increase in the birth rate for this group (Bitler and Zavodny, 2000).

Savings Finally, Gruber and Yelowitz (1999) discuss the channels whereby Medicaid expansions have an impact on individual savings decisions. By reducing the financial risk associated with an illness, the need for precautionary savings is diminished. Research by Kotlikoff (1988) provides the empirical evidence supporting this claim.

POLICY ISSUE

Does Medicare pay high enough fees to attract a sufficient number of physicians who are willing to treat eligible participants?

Key Concept 4
Self-Interest

Most public assistance programs include an asset test, whereby family wealth is a determining factor of eligibility. Hubbard, Skinner, and Zeldes (1995) show that the Medicaid asset test is empirically important. The wealth holdings of Medicaid families are 16.3 percent lower because of the asset test. Another potentially important concern for policy makers is the possibility that the elderly will transfer assets to their children to qualify for Medicaid financing for nursing home care. While the evidence is mixed, there is some empirical support that at least a portion of the elderly engage in this activity (Norton, 2000; Cutler and Sheiner, 1994).[11]

Critics of Medicaid contend that eligibility standards create incentives and disincentives that lead to serious socioeconomic disruptions. Family breakups are promoted by basing eligibility standards on marital status. A disincentive for work arises when eligibility is predicated on income. Dependence is encouraged because disability is used for categorical eligibility. Illegitimate births are encouraged by tying eligibility to pregnancy and the presence of children in single-parent families. Possibly the single greatest disruption is the minimum asset requirement for eligibility. This forces many elderly females into poverty in order to qualify for long-term care.

Those who defend the system contend that Medicaid provides coverage for millions of Americans who would otherwise have no health insurance. Those who are eligible for Medicaid are among the most vulnerable population subgroups in the country, including 21.1 million children, 8 million unwed mothers, almost 4 million seniors, and 7.1 million Americans who are either disabled or blind.

OTHER GOVERNMENT PROGRAMS

In addition to Medicare and Medicaid, the federal government administers several other major health care programs, serving approximately 30 million Americans and spending over $70 billion. Another 23 million military veterans who have private health insurance are eligible for benefits through the program administered by the Veterans' Administration.

Department of Defense

The U.S. Department of Defense (DOD) has established the military health system for military personnel and their dependents. Medical services are available for both active duty and retired members, including survivors of deceased personnel. The system is divided into two parts: direct care and Civilian Health and TriCare Standard, formerly called Civilian Health and Medical Program of the Uniformed Services (CHAMPUS). Uniformed Services Family Health Plan is an added option for military personnel and their dependents in seven geographic areas across the country.

The Armed Forces operate 70 hospitals and 400 clinics worldwide, staffed with over 150,000 medical personnel and spending over $45 billion annually. These facilities range from small clinics that provide limited services to large teaching hospitals. Most are located on military bases throughout the world. Most Americans have heard of Walter Reed Army Hospital and the Bethesda Naval Hospital in Washington, DC, in connection with the medical care of members of Congress and the President. In 2007, the direct-care military system provided medical care to over 9 million beneficiaries, including almost one million active duty personnel and their dependents, retirees and their dependents, and survivors of deceased military personnel.

---

[11] In Germany, the incomes of the children of elderly parents are counted when calculating the resource base for government-provided nursing home care.

DOD also administers TriCare, a health insurance plan originally created in 1966 as CHAMPUS to provide benefits similar to those available to civilian federal employees under the Federal Employees Health Benefit Plan (FEHBP). The benefits under TriCare are similar to any standard private insurance plan with deductibles and copayments. Hospital care must be provided at a military hospital if one is available. Otherwise, the plan is like any private insurance plan, and recipients are able to purchase care from private providers.

http://

The Century Foundation is a nonpartisan foundation involved in researching and writing about public policy issues. Visit this Web site to stay abreast of the policy implications of important legislation.

http://www.tcf.org

ISSUES IN MEDICAL CARE DELIVERY

Defining Service-Connected Disabilities in the VA

A 1993 ruling by the Secretary of Veterans' Affairs significantly expanded the definition of "service-connected" disabilities. During the Vietnam War, the U.S. military used the defoliant Agent Orange extensively. Now, decades later, a large number of veterans are claiming that exposure to this substance is responsible for various medical problems. Under this ruling, Vietnam veterans who suffer from certain types of respiratory problems are eligible for disability pensions and free medical care.

A similar scenario has emerged with Gulf War Syndrome, a mysterious medical problem afflicting about 100,000 veterans who fought in the Persian Gulf in 1990 and 1991. The most common complaints include chronic fatigue, headaches, skin rashes, muscle and joint pain, memory loss, sleep disorders, chronic diarrhea, and depression. At the request of Congress, an 18-member committee assembled by the Institutes of Medicine reviewed all the relevant research on the problem and issued its final report in late 1996 (Presidential Advisory Committee, 1996). Despite accusations of a cover-up of an incidental or accidental exposure to nerve agents, the committee found no scientific evidence to support a causal link between the symptoms and illnesses reported by Gulf War veterans and exposures while in the Gulf region to chemical or biological agents (Brown, 1996). Scientists from the Naval Research Center (2000) surveyed 1,500 veterans and catalogued their symptoms and illnesses. They found veterans who had symptoms and veterans who were sick. They identified over 40 different conditions responsible for nearly 500 different diagnoses, but they did not find evidence of Gulf War-related illness.

Despite the lack of evidence, many still consider Gulf War Syndrome a serious long-term problem. Researchers from the Southwestern Medical Center of the University of Texas have found evidence that veterans who suffer from the symptoms may be at risk of developing neurological diseases including Parkinson's disease. Still concerned about possible links, Congress has ordered a study to address a possible association between 33 specific chemical agents and the problems of Gulf War veterans (MIT, 2000). In April 2003, the DOD issued its final report on the subject, concluding that overexposure to certain pesticides may have contributed to the unexplained illnesses reported by some Gulf War veterans.

Source: David Brown, "Scientists Say Evidence Lacking to Tie 'Syndrome' to 1991 Gulf War," *The Washington Post*, October 10, 1996, A06; *Presidential Advisory Committee on the Gulf War Veteran's Illnesses: Final Report*, Washington, DC: U.S. Government Printing Office, December 1996; Naval Research Center, "Factor Analysis of Self-Reported Symptoms: Does It Identify a Gulf War Syndrome?" *American Journal of Epidemiology*, August 2000; and Medical Industry Today, "Study Finds Link Between Gulf War Syndrome, Parkinson's," MDI Online, http://www.medicaldata.com, September 21, 2000. Those interested in further information on the Gulf War Syndrome should visit GulfLINK at http://www.gulflink.osd.mil.

Veterans' Administration Medical Care Program   The Department of Veterans' Affairs (VA) provides medical care to military veterans who meet established active-duty service requirements.[12] In addition, veterans with service-connected disabilities, low incomes, or other special status (such as prisoner of war or World War I veteran) are also eligible for benefits. As of 2007, single veterans with incomes of less than $28,429 and no dependents were eligible for mandatory benefits. If married or single with one dependent, the income threshold rose to $34,117 and increased in increments of $1,909 for every dependent. This means test varied considerably, ranging as low as $21,750 in parts of Mississippi to as much as $63,350 in northern California. Veterans with incomes above these thresholds and those with non–service-connected disabilities are placed in the "discretionary care" category, for which medical care is provided if space and resources are available.

The VA operates one of the largest health care delivery systems in the world. Over 200,000 employees provide medical services to over 5 million American veterans and their families. In fiscal year 2003, the VA spent $25.9 billion on medical services. VA facilities are located in each of the 48 contiguous states, the District of Columbia, Puerto Rico, Guam, and other U.S. Territories. In 2007 the VA operated 157 hospitals, 860 community-based clinics, 137 nursing homes, 43 domiciliaries, and 73 comprehensive home care programs. Long-term care is also provided in thousands of community nursing homes nationwide on a contractual basis and in over 70 state-run nursing homes on a per diem basis.

Medical care is generally free. Veterans who are placed in the discretionary-care category are required to contribute toward the cost of their care. Veterans are subject to four basic charges. For hospital stays of less than 90 days, the required payment is equal to the Medicare hospital deductible plus $10 per day. For hospitalizations that extend beyond 90 days, there is an extra out-of-pocket charge equal to half of the Medicare hospital deductible plus $10 per day. Patients are charged $15 for outpatient primary care visits and $50 for specialty care visits. A $7 copay is required for outpatient prescription drugs, and charges for long-term care vary by type of service and ability to pay.

In addition to the 15,000 physicians employed by the VA, over 100,000 private-practice physicians treat veterans on a fee-for-service basis every year. In many ways, these facts understate the VA's involvement in the medical care delivery system in the United States. The link between the VA and private sector medicine is evident in medical education. VA facilities are affiliated with 107 medical schools and 55 dental schools, training over 81,000 health professionals annually. Because of this link, approximately half of all medical residents rotate through a VA medical facility every year.

The system is not without its critics. A U.S. Government Accounting Office study (1993) found extensive service delays that compromise the quality of care provided at even the best VA medical centers. More than 50 percent of the patients with routine medical care needs wait at least one hour to see a physician in the VA's emergency/screening clinics. One out of every eight patients suffering from an urgent medical problem had to wait at least one hour and some as much as three hours to see a physician. Those veterans requiring care at specialty clinics experienced long delays in scheduling appointments. The average waiting time for an appointment was 62 days, with over 60 percent waiting more than 30 days.

POLICY ISSUE

How far does the federal government's responsibility extend in providing medical care to military veterans?

---

[12] **The active-duty service requirements vary depending on when the person entered the military.**

Waits of over 120 days were not uncommon: one in ten experienced such lengthy delays.

The VA has experienced many significant accomplishments in its 65-year history. It has one of the best spinal-cord injury centers in the world and was instrumental in the development of the cardiac pacemaker and the CT scan. Researchers within the system are actively contributing to studies on aging, women's health, AIDS, post-traumatic stress disorder, and other mental health issues. Funded research in 2001 was approximately $351 million. Grants from the National Institutes of Health and support from pharmaceutical companies contributed another $500 million, funding over 10,000 research projects. The VA medical system is experiencing many of the problems of a fixed-budget medical care system. When government attempts to micromanage medical care delivery and provide "free" care to a well-organized constituency, shortages develop—as evidenced by the long waiting times—and the quality of specialized care deteriorates.

Key Concept 3
Marginal Analysis

Key Concept 7
Competition

SUMMARY AND CONCLUSIONS

The history of American health care cannot be understood without careful consideration of the government's expanding role in providing medical care. Medicare and Medicaid were created in 1965 to provide access to medical care for the elderly and indigent, two of the nation's most vulnerable population groups. The programs proved to be a mixed blessing. Both have been successful in fulfilling their stated missions, providing care to over 80 million of the nation's poor, elderly, and disabled. The success has come at a tremendous cost with the government spending over $970 billion on health care.[13]

Medicare and Medicaid reform will receive a great deal of attention in future congressional sessions. Still, the electorate applies substantial pressure to maintain a balanced federal budget, and the perception is that spending in these two programs must be controlled for that to happen.

The introduction of prospective payment to hospitals through the use of diagnosis-related groups and physician payment reform applying the relative-value scale represent major changes on the spending side.[14] About all that is left on the cost side of the ledger is the unpopular prospect of asking the elderly to accept a more moderate benefits package—something most policy makers are unwilling to do—or encourage seniors to enroll in health maintenance organizations, which is something that most seniors have

been unwilling to do. The alternatives on the revenue side are equally problematic. The general population could be asked to pay more in taxes, or the elderly could be asked to pay higher premiums and copays.

The Balanced Budget Act of 1997, along with a booming economy, pushed back the expected date of Medicare's insolvency to the year 2026. The spending restrictions imposed by Congress have improved the short-term outlook for the system and have changed the political debate considerably. In the short term, pressure to add an outpatient prescription drug benefit culminated with the passage of Part D in 2006.[15] Adding the prescription drug benefit and restoring some of the cuts in hospital reimbursement changed Medicare's insolvency date and brought into focus the underlying problem facing the system. Policy makers have still not addressed the long-term demographic problem facing the system—the aging baby-boom generation—and the fact that Medicare is still insulated from the market forces that serve as a moderating influence on the rest of the health care sector. Like the rest of the health care sector, Medicare suffers from the same structural deficiencies brought on by a third-party payment system that insulates its recipients from any incentives to economize. If the system is to be put on a sound financial basis, its structural deficiencies must be addressed (Gokhale, 1997).

---

[13] Considering only Medicare and Medicaid expenditures, every person in the United States pays an average of $2,450 in taxes to care for the poor and elderly.

[14] These two cost-cutting measures are discussed in the next chapter.

[15] In 2000, almost two-thirds of the elderly already had a prescription drug benefit through supplemental insurance or an HMO.

PROFILE

John K. Iglehart

When listing individuals who have had a profound influence on intellectual thought in the area of health policy, the name of John K. Iglehart makes everyone's top ten. Born in Milwaukee, Mr. Iglehart received his B.S. in journalism at the University of Wisconsin in 1961. After four years with the *Milwaukee Sentinel*, he spent six years with the Associated Press in Chicago and eventually was promoted to night city editor. In 1969, he took a position with the *National Journal* in Washington, DC, where he is still one of their contributing editors.

In addition to the numerous articles he has written in health and medical journals, Mr. Iglehart is the journalist in residence at the Harvard School of Public Health and national correspondent for the *New England Journal of Medicine*. In 1981, William B. Walsh, the founder of Project HOPE (Health Opportunities for People Everywhere), recruited him to guide the creation of a new health policy journal, *Health Affairs*. Under his direction, the journal's circulation has risen to over 10,000 — the largest for a journal of its type. Dedicated to the goal of Project HOPE, *Health Affairs* has become a highly respected journal among academicians, policy makers, and journalists. Faculty all over the country are using the journal as a textbook in their health economics and policy classes. Policy makers have come to rely on it as a source of background information on the complexities of health care delivery and finance. Journalists quote its pages regularly, using it as a source of breaking news in health policy research.

Iglehart is widely known for his research on the medical care delivery systems of Canada, Germany, and Japan. His recent series in the *New England Journal of Medicine* on "The American Health Care System," with subtitles ranging from "Private Insurance" to "Medicare" to "Managed Care," provides an excellent introduction into the diverse viewpoints, proposals, and perspectives on the problems faced by the U.S. medical care delivery system today.

Source: Project HOPE Web site (http://www.projhope.org/HA/aboutha.htm) and Who's Who in America.

QUESTIONS AND PROBLEMS

1. Comment on the following statement: "The proposal to increase Medicare cost sharing (increasing premiums, deductibles, and coinsurance) will deprive the elderly poor of needed medical services."

2. You have recently been hired as a research assistant to the Secretary of Health and Human Services. To keep the administration informed on health care issues, you have been asked to research options for changing the Medicare system. Current concerns stem from the fear that if Medicare remains an open-ended entitlement program, its share of the federal budget will continue to increase over time. Prepare a brief memo to the Secretary examining one or more of the following proposed changes. Use your best economic reasoning.

   a. A freeze in physicians' fees and a requirement of mandatory assignment.

   b. A plan to enroll everyone eligible for Medicare in managed care networks and pay a fixed, capitated amount per enrollee equal to the current per capita Medicare spending level.

   c. Allowing all Medicare recipients to buy high-deductible insurance policies and use the premium savings to set up medical savings accounts.

3. One of the major problems in dealing with any welfare program is the tension between individual and social responsibility—Medicare is no different. Should adult children be responsible for the medical expenses of their parents? Where does individual and familial responsibility end and social responsibility begin?

4. What is Medigap insurance? How does the existence of Medigap policies affect the cost of providing medical services to the elderly? Was Mark Pauly right in his observation that the provision of some insurance might be suboptimal? (See "The Economics of Moral Hazard: Comment," *American Economic Review* 58(2), June 1968, 531–538.)

5. Define the following terms and describe the effect of each on the provision of medical care for the elderly:
   a. mandatory assignment
   b. balance billing
   c. capitation
   d. free choice of provider

REFERENCES

E. Kathleen Adams, "The Effect of Increased Medicaid Fees on Physician Participation and Enrollee Service Utilization in Tennessee," *Inquiry* 31(2), Summer 1994, 173–189.

Marianne Bitler and Madeline Zavodny, "The Effect of Medicaid Eligibility Expansions on Births," Federal Reserve Bank of Atlanta, *Working Paper 2000–4*, March 2000.

Janet Currie and Jonathan Gruber, "Saving Babies: The Efficacy and Cost of Recent Changes in the Medicaid Eligibility of Pregnant Women," *Journal of Political Economy* 104(6), December 1996a, 1263–1296.

———, "Health Insurance Eligibility, Utilization of Medical Care, and Child Health," *Quarterly Journal of Economics* 111(2), May 1996b, 431–466.

David M. Cutler and Jonathan Gruber, "Does Public Insurance Crowd Out Private Insurance?" *Quarterly Journal of Economics* 111(2), May 1996, 391–430.

David M. Cutler and Louise Sheiner, "Policy Options for Long Term Care," in David Wise, ed., *Studies in the Economics of Aging*, Chicago: University of Chicago Press, 1994, 395–434.

Geraldine Dallek, "The Crushing Costs of Medicare Supplemental Policies," Washington: Families USA, No. 96–103, October 1996.

Lisa Dubay, Theodore Joyce, Robert Kaestner, and Genevieve Kenney, "Changes in Prenatal Care Timing and Low Birth Weight by Race and Socioeconomic Status: Implications for the Medicaid Expansions for Pregnant Women," *Health Services Research*, 2000.

Kurt D. Gillis, David W. Lee, and Richard J. Willke, "Physician-Based Measures of Medical Access," *Inquiry* 29(3), Fall 1992, 321–331.

Jagadeesh Gokhale, "Medicare: Usual and Customary Remedies Will No Longer Work," *Economic Commentary*, Federal Reserve Bank of Cleveland, April 1, 1997.

Jonathan Gruber, "Health Insurance and the Labor Market," in Joseph P. Newhouse and Anthony J. Culyer, eds., *Handbook of Health Economics*, Amsterdam: North Holland, 2000a.

———, "Medicaid," *National Bureau of Economic Research Working Paper 7829*, August 2000b.

——— and Aaron Yelowitz, "Public Health Insurance and Private Savings," *Journal of Political Economy* 107(6 Part 1), December 1999, 1249–1274.

Jack Hadley, "Physician Participation in Medicaid: Evidence from California," *Health Services Research* 14, 1979, 266–280.

Health Care Financing Administration, "National Health Expenditures Projections: 1998–2008," based on the 1999 Medicare Trustees' Reports, 1999.

Geoffrey R. Hileman et al., "Medicare+Choice Individual and Group Enrollment: 2001 and 2002," *Health Care Financing Review* 24(1), Fall 2002, 145–153.

Earl Dirk Hoffman, Barbara S. Klees, and Catherine A. Curtis, "Overview of the Medicare and Medicaid Programs," *Health Care Financing Review*, Medicare and Medicaid Supplement, 2003, 1–357.

R. Glenn Hubbard, Jonathan Skinner, and Stephen P. Zeldes, "Precautionary Saving and Social Insurance," *Journal of Political Economy* 103(2), April 1995, 360–399.

Theodore Joyce, Robert Kaestner, and Florence Kwan, "Is Medicaid Pronatalist: The Effect of Eligibility Expansion on Abortions and Births," *Family Planning Perspectives* 30(3), 1998, 108–113.

Kaiser Commission on the Future of Medicaid, *Medicaid and Federal, State, and Local Budgets*, Washington, DC: Kaiser Commission on the Future of Medicaid, May, 1995.

Laurence J. Kotlikoff, "Health Expenditures and Precautionary Saving," in Laurence J. Kotlikoff, ed., *What Determines Saving*? Cambridge: MIT Press, 1988, 141–162.

Janet B. Mitchell, "Physician Participation in Medicaid Revisited," *Medical Care* 29, 1991, 645–653.

——— and Rachel Schurman, "Access to Private Obstetrics/Gynecological Services Under Medicaid," *Medical Care* 22, 1984, 1026–1037.

Edward C. Norton, "Long Term Care," in Anthony Culyer and Joseph Newhouse, eds., *Handbook of Health Economics*, Amsterdam: North Holland, 2000.

Karen Pallarito, "Study Raises Concerns about Future of Medicare HMO Program," Reuters Medical News, June 27, 2000.

Frank Sloan, Janet Mitchell, and Jerry Cromwell, "Physician Participation in State Medicaid Programs," *Journal of Human Resources* 13(Supplement) 1978, 211–245.

U.S. General Accounting Office, "VA Health Care: Restructuring Ambulatory Care System Would Improve Services to Veterans," Report to the Chairman, Subcommittee on Oversight and Investigations, Committee on Veterans' Affairs, House of Representatives, October 1993.

Bruce C. Vladeck and Kathleen M. King, "Medicare at 30: Preparing for the Future," *Journal of the American Medical Association* 274(3), July 19, 1995, 259–262.

Anne E. Winkler, "The Incentive Effects of Medicaid on Women's Labor Supply," *Journal of Human Resources* 26(2), Spring 1991, 308–337.

Aaron Yelowitz, "The Medicaid Notch, Labor Supply, and Welfare Participation: Evidence from Eligibility Expansions," *Quarterly Journal of Economics* 110(4), November 1995, 909–939.

———, "Will Extending Medicaid to Two-Parent Families Encourage Marriage?" *Journal of Human Resources* 33(4), Fall 1998, 833–865.

A Note on "Projections"

One of the intriguing questions that puzzle those with inquiring minds is "Just where do they come up with these numbers anyway?" Anyone who forecasts for a living knows that change is the order of the day. Seldom do things stay the same. Underlying economic conditions change, and institutional characteristics change. About the only thing that stays the same is human nature, and that is sometimes the most unpredictable piece in the entire puzzle.

Forecasting, by its very nature, has an element of extrapolation associated with it. Examining trends and extending those trends into the future is a common technique used to project all sorts of economic variables. Currently, an estimated 4 million Americans are afflicted with Alzheimer's disease. With 1 percent of all 65-year-olds and 25 percent of all 85-year-olds diagnosed with the disease, as the number of elderly increase—especially those who reach their eighty-fifth birthday—the number of people with Alzheimer's disease will skyrocket. It is expected that 15 million people will have the disorder by 2050 if an effective form of prevention and treatment is not found. Extrapolation plays a key role in this kind of prediction. There is nothing inherently wrong with making these predictions as long as we understand the qualifying statement: "if an effective form of prevention and treatment is not found."

Predictions of health care spending absorbing 25 to 40 percent of GDP by the year 2030 are political fodder in policy making circles (Waldo et al., 1991). The spending scenarios necessary to bring about these results make little intuitive sense when examined closely. Centers for Medicare and Medicaid Services (CMS) projections shown in Table 12A.1 are based on actuarial models using trend analysis. According to CMS projections, personal health care spending will increase to approximately $4 trillion by 2016, representing 19.6 percent of GDP and $12,782 per capita. Actuarial projections reflect what would happen if nothing changed. The baseline projections assume a continuation

Table 12A.1: National Health Care Expenditures 2005 with Projections (2010, 2015, and 2016)

Category	2005	2010	2015	2016
Personal Health Care (billions)	$1,661.4	$2,312.9	$3,227.9	$3,449.4
National Health Expenditures (billions)	$1,987.7	$2,776.4	$3,874.6	$4,136.9
Per Capita Personal Spending	$5,598	$7,485	$10,049	$10,658
Per Capita National Spending	$6,697	$8,985	$12,062	$12,782
National Spending as a Percent of GDP	16.0	17.2	19.2	19.6

Source: Centers for Medicare and Medicaid Services, National Health Expenditure Data available at http://www.cms.hhs.gov/NationalHealthExpendData/.

of current policies and trends. In other words, current programs, regulations, and practices remain unchanged. In addition, economy-wide shocks, all technological innovation, and any reform of health care delivery and finance are ruled out.

In 1992, the Congressional Budget Office (CBO), known for its "fair" numbers, projected medical care spending at 18 percent of GDP by the year 2000 (Lemieux and Williams, 1992). The current conventional wisdom projects spending to reach 16 percent of GDP by the year 2010, a far cry from the 1992 CBO projections (Burner and Waldo, 1995).

Policy based on these projections would call for immediate action, but for medical care spending to reach, say, 25 percent of GDP, substantially more than 25 percent of the annual changes in GDP must be spent in the health care sector. Except for recessionary periods, the change in health care spending relative to the change in GDP rarely reaches 0.15, placing an upper bound on the ratio of health care spending to GDP at 15 percent. In fact, from 1984 to 1990, the change in health care spending represented 15.5 percent of the total change in GDP and was never greater than 17 percent.

The key phrase in the above scenario is "except for recessionary periods." Over the past 35 years, only twice has the change in medical care spending exceeded 17 percent of the GDP change. The 1981–1982 recession and the 1990–1991 recession saw this figure rise to over 30 percent.

It is easy to criticize those who make predictions for a living. Meteorologists have difficulty forecasting what the weather will be like tomorrow morning. The economist always seems to have an explanation for why those interest rate predictions were incorrect. And when is the last time Jean Dixon or even the Amazing Kreskin got it just right? Most projections are based on some variant of extrapolation, analyzing trends based on certain assumptions about the state of the world at some future date. The further that date is into the future, the more careful we need to be about relying too heavily on those predictions. Remember what they say: "The only two things certain in this world are death and taxes."

REFERENCES

Sally T. Burner and Daniel R. Waldo, "National Health Expenditure Projections, 1994–2005," *Health Care Financing Review* 16(4), Summer 1995, 221–242.

Jeffrey A. Lemieux and Christopher Williams, *Projections of National Health Expenditures*, Congress of the United States, Congressional Budget Office, October, 1992.

Daniel R. Waldo, Sally T. Sonnefeld, Jeffrey A. Lemieux, and David R. McKusick, "Health Spending Through 2000: Three Scenarios," *Health Affairs* 10(4), Winter 1991, 231–242.

Policies to Contain Costs

As the cost of medical care rises, policy makers throughout the world have had to face difficult decisions concerning quality, access, and spending. The problems of medical care delivery affect the quality of life of millions of people, particularly the poor and uninsured. Concern for this segment of the population has resulted in the provision of universal coverage in most developed countries around the world—with the notable exception of the United States. With access guaranteed, spending has become the primary issue directing public debate.

This chapter examines the options available to policy makers in their quest to control rising costs and spending growth. Fee schedules, **global budgets**, and resource rationing are the topics of the first section. Next, the U.S. experience with these options is explored in a discussion of the Medicare payment mechanism. Prospective payments to hospitals with diagnosis related groups (DRGs) and physicians' fee schedules using a relative value scale are examined here. Further analysis of cost-containment through managed care and other market alternatives concludes the discussion.

POLICY OPTIONS

Systems that guarantee free access to medical care must eventually confront the issue of escalating costs. The way most health care delivery systems are organized, relying on the third-party payment system, no natural mechanisms control cost and spending. That task is left to policy makers, who usually rely on a combination of three approaches to reign in spending growth: mandated fee schedules, global budgets, and resource rationing. Market economists classify all three under the same general heading of price controls and recognize the common element they share—interference with the market.

Policy makers soon realize that fee schedules by themselves cannot control spending. The two independent variables in the spending identity are price and quantity.[1] To control spending, one must control both price and quantity. Direct limits on the quantity of services available are too easily identified as *rationing*—the dreaded "R" word that all policy makers seek to avoid. Thus, the three cost-control measures go hand in hand. Once fee schedules are mandated, global budgeting soon follows. Inevitably, the unintended consequence of fee schedules and global budgeting is resource rationing. To paraphrase a wise saying: The road to rationing is paved with good intentions.

global budget
A limit on the amount of money available to a health care system during a specified time. All medically necessary care must be provided to all eligible patients within the limits placed on the provider by the fixed budget.

POLICY ISSUE

How can a health care system that relies on third-party insurance control spending?

Key Concept 5
Markets and Pricing

---

[1] In other words, $TE = P \times Q$, where *TE* is total expenditures, *P* is price, and *Q* is quantity.

BACK-OF-THE-ENVELOPE

Why a Price Ceiling May Not Lower Spending

It is easy to understand why the casual observer could expect price controls to slow spending growth. Using the following diagram, the demand for medical care is depicted by the downward-sloping demand curve, labeled D_0. For purposes of this discussion, assume that providers are accommodating to the wishes of the patient population and supply all the medical care desired at the prevailing price. If equilibrium is at point A, quantity Q_0 is demanded at price P_0. Total spending will be P_0 times Q_0, depicted by the area $0P_0AQ_0$. If a price ceiling is enacted at P_1, the new equilibrium will be at point B, and quantity will be Q_1. Since demand for medical care is relatively price inelastic, the new level of spending, $0P_1BQ_1$, is less than before. (If the demand were relatively elastic, the new level of spending would be greater.)

Key Concept 6

Supply and Demand

It would be great for policy makers if things worked out this way. Controlling the growth in medical care spending would be simple. Mandate lower prices in a market characterized by inelastic demand, and spending levels will fall. Several problems are inherent in this approach. Providers will only accommodate patient desires up to a point. Drive the price down below cost, and quantity supplied will go down. (That issue is discussed in the next Back-of-the-Envelope feature, "The Economics of Price Controls.") Even with accommodating providers, spending is likely to rise. The following diagram shows how.

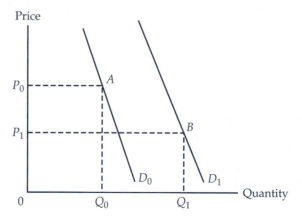

continued

Begin with the same demand curve D_0, price P_0, quantity Q_0, and spending $0P_0AQ_0$. A price ceiling at P_1 creates an incentive for providers to increase service intensity and maybe even influence demand (remember the concept of supplier-induced demand). Expanding the size of the eligible population, and incorporating advances in technology created for the uncontrolled segment of the market — which is three to four times larger than the controlled segment — work together to shift demand to the right, to D_1. The resulting level of spending, $0P_1BQ_1$, is actually higher than before the drop in price.

Mandated Fee Schedules

Almost every government-run system has resorted to some form of price setting in an attempt to control spending. Whether referred to as a *price freeze* or a *price ceiling*, the price schedules are commonly negotiated between the government and representatives of the medical community. They may be interim, voluntary, or mandatory. Sometimes the prices are loosely determined through a relative-value schema that attempts to place a value on services according to some comparative scale. More often than not, this scale measures the political influence of the various specialties and not relative resource use.

POLICY ISSUE

Are price ceilings and spending caps the way to control the problem of rising health care spending?

Providers can still maintain their profit margins by lowering their own expenses. If there is waste in the system, price controls serve as a stimulus toward more efficient resource use. Thus, price controls can provide some short-term relief from the spiral of medical spending, but over time, the short-term beneficial effects are exhausted. Providers often find that they can get around the controls, and the associated erosion in their incomes, by seeing more patients and treating them more intensively. Thus, physician-induced demand may actually shift the demand curve for services to the right, resulting in a higher level of spending and an increase in the physician's income. This shift means less time spent with each patient, so more patients can be seen, and more follow-up visits scheduled.

Key Concept 7
Competition
Key Concept 8
Efficiency

Another common practice used to avoid the heavy hand of price controls is the unbundling of services. *Unbundling* refers to the practice of breaking down a service into its various component parts. Instead of billing for the service, the provider bills for each part of the treatment. The practice defies logic, because the sum of the parts is greater than the whole. Standard care for treating a broken bone, when decomposed into its component parts with a separate bill for each, will cost more than the complete item. The amount that can be billed for an office visit, two X-rays, and a follow-up visit is often greater than the bill for the total package including the cast and its removal. A patient billed separately for the component parts of a wheelchair—wheels, armrests, cushions, and so on—will pay more than the cost of the complete item. A glucose monitoring kit will cost $12 at the local pharmacy, but as much as $250 when unbundled.

Controlled prices seldom result in the desired level of spending. In almost every situation in which price controls have been tried, the fee schedule is ultimately revised downward, either through some automatic mechanism or unilaterally by the government authority. A system of negotiated fee schedules eventually becomes one of regulated fee schedules with an elaborate government mechanism to ensure compliance.

Global Budgeting

Unable to control spending with fee schedules, and desiring to avoid the direct plunge into rationing, the next step has historically been to establish a global budget.

Global budgets are nothing more than spending caps.[2] These caps may be established either as targeted or mandatory budgets. In politics, targeted caps serve merely as "backstop" measures. In other words, they are really not binding in the sense that they would force rationing. In reality, however, the targets soon become mandatory budgets, and what was never intended becomes part of the apparatus of control.

Global budgets may be used in various ways. Canada and Germany set global budgets for hospitals, providing each institution with a set amount of money to be used to provide services to all comers. Should actual spending exceed budgeted spending, hospital providers are then faced with a dilemma. Providers handle this situation in a straightforward manner. Anything that can be delayed is delayed. Hospital wards are closed, operating rooms are unused, and personnel take unpaid vacations. All elective surgery is wait-listed until the next budget period. What resources remain available are used to treat only life-threatening conditions.

POLICY ISSUE

Will global budgeting for hospitals reduce spending in this sector?

Key Concept 6
Supply and Demand

BACK-OF-THE-ENVELOPE

The Economics of Price Controls

The impact of government-imposed price controls depends on the competitive nature of the market in which they exist. In a competitive market, a binding price ceiling — one where the legal price is below the equilibrium price — will cause a shortage.

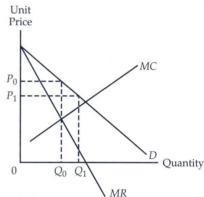

The left-hand side of the diagram depicts the demand curve (*D*) and supply curve (*S*) for a product sold in a competitive market. With no market interference, the equilibrium is established at the intersection of supply and demand, yielding the market-clearing price (P_0) and quantity (Q_0). If government uses its authority to set a binding price ceiling (P_1), producers will choose to produce at a lower level of output (Q_1). At the lower price, however, consumers will want more (Q_2). The resulting discrepancy between the quantity demanded and the quantity supplied $Q_2 - Q_1$ is the shortage.

Ironically, the unintended consequence of this action to lower the price of the product has actually raised its effective price to consumers. How? In their quest to secure desired quantities of the product at the

continued

[2] Global budgets were referred to as "prospective budgets" in the U.S. health care reform terminology.

lower price, consumers will compete in other ways. If price does not serve to ration the product, another mechanism will emerge. Consumers will get up early, stay up late, become friends with producers, resort to bribes, and buy in large quantities when the product is available, all of which adds to the nonpecuniary cost of the product. Added to these costs is the anxiety brought about by the increased uncertainty of not knowing whether you will ever have as much of the product as you want.

Referring back to the diagram, the nonpecuniary costs grow until their combined effects shift the consumers' demand curve down to D'. At the new equilibrium, consumers are paying less in money terms (P_1), but more when you combine both monetary costs and nonmonetary costs (P_2).

Price controls can be effective in a market controlled by a monopolist. The right-hand side of the diagram shows a monopolist, as sole seller, facing the market demand curve and producing where marginal revenue (MR) equals marginal cost (MC). The equilibrium price and quantity are established at P_0 and Q_0. In this case, the government can set a price below P_0 and actually increase the quantity produced. A price ceiling set at P_1 will change the effective shape of the demand and marginal revenue curves. They both become a horizontal line at the ceiling price. Thus, marginal revenue (now P_1) equals marginal cost at the quantity Q_1.

Do price controls produce shortages, black markets, and reduced quality? It depends on the nature of the market, whether it is competitive or a monopoly. How do price controls affect medical markets? It depends, once again, on which segment of the medical market you are considering. The market for patented drugs probably fits the classical case of monopoly better than any other aspect of the medical market. A suitably chosen price could improve the efficiency in this market, assuming that regulators are clever enough to choose the right price. Failure to choose the right price will, however, lead to reduced research and development, fewer discoveries, and the loss of consumer welfare (read that "lost lives"). The markets for physicians' and hospital services are much closer to the competitive model, and price controls are likely to have undesirable effects.

At least one former government policy analyst seems to agree that price controls could lead to restrictions on the rate of technological development and ultimately the rationing of health care (Wagner, 1993). As director of the Congressional Budget Office (CBO), Robert Reischauer testified before the House Ways and Means health subcommittee on the possible effects of price controls on medical care. Research by the CBO, which conducts financial analysis for the Congress, concluded that price controls could severely limit the quality and quantity of medical care in the United States. Reischauer went on to argue that the only way to control medical care spending is by imposing global health care budgets at the national level. Thus, Reischauer exhibits the irony of government policy makers — arguing for and against price controls at the same time.

Source: Lynn Wagner, "CBO Head Warns Price Controls Could Severely Limit Quality, Quantity of Medical Care in the U.S.," *Modern Healthcare* 23(3), March 8, 1993, 22.

---

[3] A system in which payment is based on capitation, including a significant portion of the managed care system in the United States, is a fixed-budget system.

Resource Rationing

Frustrated with their inability to control medical spending with price controls even in a fixed-budget system, policy makers are left with their last alternative—resource rationing.[3] Policy makers rarely use the term *rationing*. But for all its various names, its results are the same; rationing limits access to the high-cost hospital and specialty sector.

The first step toward resource rationing begins with improving access to primary and preventive care by encouraging, or possibly even mandating, more physicians to practice primary and family medicine.[4] As the system evolves, primary care physicians are cast in the role of gatekeeper. Patients must first go through them before they are admitted to a hospital or are allowed to see a specialist.

To ensure cost containment, access to high-cost medical technology must be restricted. Designating certain facilities as technology centers usually accomplishes this task. Rationing takes the form of increased cost of travel to distant facilities, especially for patients living in rural areas, and waiting lists.

In summary, price controls in medical care seem to benefit patients at the expense of providers, at least in the short term. Initially, this may seem desirable to many policy makers. The beneficial effects are immediate, but the harmful effects take longer to materialize and are difficult to understand. The lessons, however, are clear. After the initial cost efficiencies are realized, the lower prices associated with the fee schedules lead to fixed budgets and eventually limits on services. Targets become mandates and, sooner or later, nonprice rationing becomes prevalent, resulting in an inefficient distribution of services among patients. Quality of care does not improve with controls; in fact, it deteriorates. In the end, controls actually increase costs, because the distortions created by controls stifle the innovative activities that would lower costs. So the root cause of increased spending, limited cost-conscious behavior on the part of buyers or sellers, is never addressed.

POLICY ISSUE

Is resource rationing a feasible alternative to control medical spending when fee schedules and global budgets fail?

COST-CONTAINMENT STRATEGIES IN THE UNITED STATES

To date, providers in the United States have had limited experience with these popular rationing schemes.[5] Resource allocation is still primarily based on market mechanisms and not artificial controls. As medical prices continue to escalate, the pressure on policy makers to find a new approach has grown. Instead of developing policies that encourage market solutions, policy makers are more likely to propose government solutions that include price controls.

The U.S. government pays for almost half of all the medical care provided in this country; therefore, government solutions have focused on controlling federal outlays, especially for Medicare and Medicaid. The temptation facing policy makers is the simplistic appeal of price controls to limit expenditures, which is much like

http://

The Congressional Budget Office site has links to reports and studies published by the CBO in the last year, some online, and to other federal information sources.

http://www.cbo.gov/

---

[4] Establishing quotas for residency programs or paying all providers according to the same fee schedule creates strong incentives to specialize in primary care.

[5] The notable exception has been state certificate-of-need (CON) legislation. The objective of CON laws was to limit the proliferation of capital expansion in the hospital industry. Most analysts would conclude the laws have experienced mixed results across the country.

trying to limit the spread of the flu by passing a law against running a temperature greater than 98.6 degrees. You cannot legislate an illness out of existence. Likewise, you cannot legislate price increases out of existence. Price controls bring about unintended consequences that are potentially more difficult to deal with than the price increases they were designed to limit. Changes in Medicare reimbursement for hospitals and physicians over the past decade provide a good case study in the limitations of price controls in controlling medical spending.

Diagnosis Related Groups

Until 1983, Medicare reimbursed hospitals on a cost-plus basis for all inpatient services. The hospital provided services to an eligible recipient and billed Medicare for the cost of that care. Thus, payment was determined retrospectively, based on per-unit or per-service charges determined by what the hospital billed for the services provided. This payment mechanism, coupled with private, third-party financing, was largely responsible for the increased volume and intensity of services observed in the hospital sector, and to varying degrees, for the growing inefficiencies within the industry evidenced by overinvestment in capital equipment.

Key Concept 6
Efficiency

To counter the increased spending and growing inefficiencies, federal strategy focused its cost-containment efforts on devising a prospective payment mechanism for the hospital sector. Introduced in 1983, prospective payment took the form of flat-rate reimbursement for hospitals based on principal diagnosis of the patient plus a number of adjustments.[6] In principle, prospective payment will provide economic incentives to conserve scarce medical resources, which will in turn hold down the growth in expenditures.

Diagnosis related groups (DRGs) have actually redefined the unit of measure used in determining Medicare payments. No longer are charges determined on a per-item or a per-service basis. Now charges are determined in advance on a per-case basis. Payment is based on a point system and is determined by a reimbursement rate that is set for each case-weighted point. These relative weights are set nationally and adjusted for a rural or urban location, the number of residents and interns per bed for teaching facilities, and the number of low-income patients treated by the hospital. In 2000, the unadjusted reimbursement rate for hospitals in large urban areas was $3,951.03 per weighted point. Teaching hospitals received a percentage increment over that amount for every resident and intern. All hospitals receive a capital adjustment, and certain hospitals that provide a substantial amount of free care are provided with another adjustment.

Table 13.1 ranks the 25 most frequently used DRGs based on 2005 hospital discharge data for Medicare patients. Clearly, cases related to the heart, lung, and stomach dominate the list of hospital services provided to enrollees. Of all the 2005 Medicare hospital discharges, over 50 percent are represented in these 25 DRGs.

The Nature of DRGs It is instructive to examine the organization of the DRG classification scheme. Medicare initially set up 467 DRG categories based

---

[6] The legislative history of prospective payment can be dated September 1982, when the Tax Equity and Financial Responsibility Act became law. It required the Secretary of Health and Human Services to report back to Congress with a prospective payment system by the end of 1982. The DRG system was created as an amendment to the Social Security Act and passed on April 20, 1983.

**Table 13.1. Twenty-Five Most Frequent DRGs
All Medicare Discharges, 2005**

Rank	Code	Description
1	127	Heart failure and shock
2	089	Simple pneumonia and pleurisy, age >17 with CC[1]
3	209	Major joint and limb reattachment procedures of lower extremity
4	088	Chronic obstructive pulmonary disease
5	430	Psychoses
6	182	Esophagitis, gastroenteritis, and miscellaneous digestive disorders, age >17 with CC
7	416	Septicemia, age >17
8	462	Rehabilitation
9	014	Specific cerebrovascular disorders except transient ischemic attack
10	174	Gastrointestinal hemorrhage with CC
11	296	Nutritional and miscellaneous metabolic disorders, age >17 with CC
12	527	Perc cardiovascular procedure with coronary artery stent without AMI
13	143	Chest pain
14	320	Kidney and urinary tract infections, age >17 with CC
15	138	Cardiac arrhythmia and conduction disorders with CC
16	316	Renal failure
17	079	Respiratory infections and inflammations, age >17 with CC
18	121	Circulatory disorders with acute myocardial infarction and cardiovascular complications, discharged alive
19	148	Major small and large bowel procedures with CC
20	210	Hip and femur procedures except major joint, age >17 with CC
21	141	Syncope and collapse with CC
22	475	Respiratory system diagnosis with ventilator support
23	124	Circulatory disorders except acute myocardial infarction, with cardiac catheterization and complex diagnosis
24	277	Cellulitis, age >17 with CC
25	395	Red blood cell disorders, age >17

Source: CMS, Medicare Rankings for all Short-Stay Hospitals, 2005.

[1] **Complicating conditions**

on principal diagnosis, the age of the patient, the presence of comorbidity conditions, the use of surgical procedures, and the discharge status of the patient. There are currently over 500 DRGs and each assigned a relative weight to approximate the resource usage of the average case within that diagnosis category.

Figure 13.1 provides details on the classification system and relative-resource usage for a pregnant female who presents herself to the labor and delivery area of a hospital. Under these circumstances, the two possibilities are either the female is experiencing labor or she is not. A female in labor may or may not be experiencing complications and may end up delivering the baby in the normal manner (i.e., vaginal delivery) or may have a cesarean section. The normal delivery without complications or other procedures is DRG 373 with a resource-use weighting of

Figure 13.1: Diagnosis Related Groups for Labor and Delivery

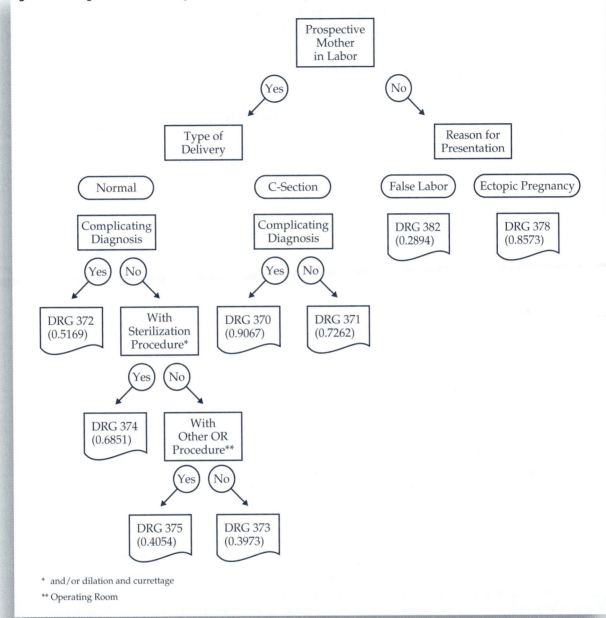

* and/or dilation and currettage

** Operating Room

0.3562. The cesarean delivery with complications is DRG 370 and has a resource-use weighting of 0.8956, implying a little over two-and-one-half times the resource use of a DRG 373 delivery.

These eight related DRGs have relative-resource weightings ranging from 0.2071 for false labor to 0.8956 for a cesarean delivery with complications. For a **monetary conversion factor** of $3,950 per weighting point, the hospital would be reimbursed $818 for the services provided a female experiencing false labor and $3,538 for a female with a complicating diagnosis receiving a cesarean section.[7]

monetary conversion factor
A monetary value used to translate relative value units into dollar amounts to determine a fee schedule.

BACK-OF-THE-ENVELOPE

Explaining the Surge in Outpatient Visits

From 1995 to 2004, hospital admissions rose 13 percent to 35 million, but outpatient visits increased 38 percent to 571 million. Outpatient surgeries now total almost two-thirds of all surgeries. Moderation in one segment of the market is being matched by unprecedented growth in the other. What's going on here? This shift may be understood, at least in part, by recognizing that the inpatient sector of the hospital market is regulated, but the outpatient sector is not. The impact is depicted in the diagram.

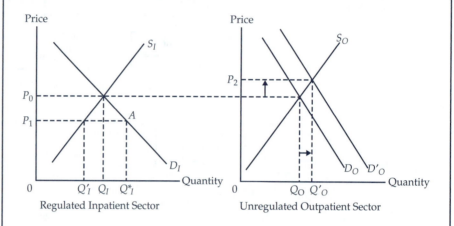

Equilibrium will take place in both sectors where their respective supply and demand curves intersect at price P_0. A price ceiling in the regulated inpatient sector changes the demand curve from D_I to P_1AD, and the equilibrium quantity supplied falls from Q_I to Q'_I. With more people desiring inpatient services, Q^*_I, and fewer services provided, Q'_I, patients are directed to the outpatient sector, and resources are transferred to meet the higher level of demand. The result is easy to predict — higher service volume, higher prices, and greater spending.

POLICY ISSUE

How does the change to prospective payment affect medical care delivery in the hospital sector?

Economic Impact of DRGs on Hospital Behavior The stated goals of introducing prospective payment for hospitals were to control the growth in hospital spending under Medicare and promote cost efficiencies in the provision of hospital services. Evidence indicates that prospective payment has succeeded in reducing Medicare hospital expenditures (Russell and Manning, 1989). Using 1990 prices, the savings from prospective payment amounted to approximately $18 billion from what had earlier been projected for that year. Much of the savings can be attributed to decreases in the number of hospital admissions and the average length of a hospital stay. Between 1982 and 1985, the average length of stay for a Medicare patient fell 15 percent. In fact, the number of admissions and the average length of stay fell

---

[7] There are further adjustments if the hospital is a teaching hospital, a rural hospital, or serves a disproportionate number of indigents.

across the board in response to these changes in reimbursement, an indication of system-wide inefficiencies.

In general, hospital reimbursement under Medicare is determined at the point of diagnosis.[8] If the cost of treatment is less than the DRG reimbursement rate, the hospital keeps the surplus.[9] If costs exceed reimbursement, the hospital absorbs the loss. In theory, hospitals that treat a large number of Medicare recipients in each diagnostic category should be able to cover costs with overall reimbursements. During the first few years after implementation of the program, hospitals experienced healthy operating margins on Medicare patients, ranging from 8 to 15 percent (Sheingold, 1989). These margins were due primarily to aggressive cost reductions and clever gaming of the DRG system.[10] In response, Congress legislated changes in reimbursement rates, and by the late 1980s, operating margins on Medicare patients were negative (Folland and Kleiman, 1990).

Evidence also indicates that the reduction in admissions was partially offset by an increase in outpatient services (Feinglass and Holloway, 1991). Thus, the principal question on whether Medicare prospective payment has reduced overall health care spending is somewhat ambiguous. In reality, whenever price controls are applied to one segment of the market, incentives encourage providers to transfer resources to the unregulated segment.

In 1997, the federal government faced what seemed at the time large and insurmountable budget deficits. Projections that year had the Medicare Hospital Insurance Trust Fund bankrupt by the year 2002 unless action was taken. Congress responded with the Balanced Budget Act of 1997 (BBA), which was supposed to reduce the growth of Medicare by $116 billion from 1998 to 2002. About half of these reductions were scheduled to come from reduced payments to hospitals. Subsequent projections estimate the five-year impact at over $200 billion, almost twice the intended result. The Lewin Group (1999) estimated that the BBA reductions would result in negative Medicare margins for the U.S. hospital industry, averaging a negative 4.4 percent by 2002. Forcing 70 percent of all hospitals to operate at negative margins was not the intention of Congress, so in 1999, the Balanced Budget Refinement Act was passed, restoring an estimated $16 billion of the original reductions. Without further relief, Lewin (1999) estimated that 60 percent of all hospitals would still have been losing money on Medicare patients at the end of 2004.

Key Concept 5
Markets and Pricing

POLICY ISSUE

How has the change to prospective payment affected the financial health of U.S. hospitals?

ISSUES IN MEDICAL CARE DELIVERY

The Rochester Model

Presidential candidate Bill Clinton's 1992 visit to Rochester, New York, served to focus national attention on the city's medical care delivery system. Based on that visit, many felt it likely that as president, Mr. Clinton would use Rochester as a model for reform nationwide.

continued

---

[8] Hospitals can petition for additional reimbursement in those cases where unusual circumstances drive the cost of treatment beyond expected levels.

[9] The correct term is *surplus* in a not-for-profit hospital. In a for-profit hospital, the same concept is called *profit*.

[10] In the late 1990s, Columbia/HCA was investigated for fraudulent practices in classifying patients and billing Medicare. In December 2000, they paid the U.S. government $850 million in criminal and civil penalties related to guilty pleas as the first stage in the settlement of the fraud actions against it.

Examination of the Rochester model provides insight into the importance of crafting local solutions to the health care delivery problem. During a period when only 85 percent of the U.S. population has some form of health insurance coverage, the Rochester plan provided insurance for over 93 percent of the residents of a six-county area.

Rochester's approach to medical care delivery has emerged over the past 40 years as a cooperative effort among medical care providers, local employers and their employees, and health insurance companies. A key reason for Rochester's success is the refusal of its seven area hospitals to participate in the so-called "medical arms race." Instead of competing for patients by investing in all the latest technologies, each hospital specializes in a different area — one offers neonatal intensive care, another cardiology, still another cancer therapy, thus avoiding costly duplication of services. Physicians have given up some of their freedom by accepting a negotiated fee schedule that pays them approximately two-thirds of the fees charged elsewhere. Large corporations have played an important role by participating in the community insurance pool and rejecting the popular trend toward self-insurance.

Health insurance costs for local employers were $2,730 per employee in 1992, about 70 percent of the national average of $3,968. The source of these savings is the subject of intense debate. Proponents of the plan focus on the regional cooperation that holds down medical inflation. Officials from the Rochester Area Blue Cross attribute the savings to the expanded use of electronic claims processing, the high productivity of insurance industry employees, and the relatively low spending on advertising.

Critics of the plan argue that the cost savings are due to the large percentage of the population enrolled in managed care plans — over 55 percent of the 1.1 million residents. In addition, they point out that while medical costs are lower, they are escalating at the same rate in Rochester as they are in the rest of the country. They point out that hospitals must secure the approval of the area Hospital Corporation before expanding facilities or adding services. As a result, there have been no new hospital beds added in the community since the 1960s. Average occupancy rates are almost 90 percent as compared with barely 60 percent nationwide, which frequently results in overcrowding, canceled surgeries, and regular closings of area emergency rooms because of the lack of available beds. The lesson to be learned from Rochester is simple. Whatever is decided nationally, it should not jeopardize a system created by a local community to solve community problems.

Sources: Sherry Jacobson, "Rochester's 'Model' Health Plan Suffers a Backlash from Clinton," *The Dallas Morning News*, June 12, 1994, 1A, 26A; and Milt Freudenheim, "Rochester: An American Success Story," in Erik Eckholm, *Solving America's Health Care Crisis* (New York: Times Books, 1993), 206–211.

Setting Physicians' Fees: Resource-Based Relative Value Scale (RBRVS)

Between 1975 and 1987, Medicare's spending per enrollee for physicians' services grew at a compound annual rate of 15 percent, or almost twice the compound rate of growth in per capita gross domestic product. Approximately half of this increase was due to an increase in prices, and the other half was due to an increase in volume. Budgetary constraints in an era of deficit awareness highlighted two main concerns: spending is not necessarily cost effective, and previous payment schedules have inequitable rates between procedural services (i.e., surgery and invasive testing) and evaluation and management (E/M) services (i.e., office visits and consultations).

An inequitable fee structure provides incentives to overperform certain services and underperform others. Medical school graduates can also be influenced by the distorted fee structure in their choice of specialty and the geographic location of their practice.

Key Concept 4
Self-Interest

Fee-For-Service Payment Under Medicare   Under Medicare, the payment structure for physicians was based on the principle of customary, prevailing, and reasonable charges. Medicare payments were limited to the minimum of the customary, prevailing, and reasonable charges for a particular physician practicing in a specific geographic area. The customary charge is defined as the median charge (50th percentile) of the physician's charges during the previous year. The prevailing charge is the charge at the 75th percentile of area physicians' charges for services during the previous year. The price the physician normally charged for the procedure was also factored into the process. If the actual charge was lower than the customary, prevailing, and reasonable charge, then it was the price allowed by Medicare.

Under the old fee-for-service system, physician payment had a built-in inflationary bias. Physicians had no incentive to compete on the basis of price. If a physician's actual charges were less than the customary charge in the area, the physician received the actual charge. The incentive was to raise fees to the customary charge. As fees escalated, physician and patient behavior was distorted. Physicians criticized the system as complex and unpredictable. Others argued that it was irrational, inequitable, and open to abuse.

Key Concept 5
Markets and Pricing

Establishing a Relative Value Scale   In 1986 Congress commissioned a study to determine the feasibility of developing a **resource-based relative value scale (RBRVS)** for physician payment. Hsiao and colleagues (1988) conducted a two-year study of physician compensation and developed resource-based relative values for physicians' services in 18 specialty areas.

A relative value scale is an index of the relative levels of resource use when physicians produce services or procedures. Although the relative value scale is denominated in nonmonetary units, the logical extension translates relative resource use into a fee schedule. To establish a fee schedule based on the RBRVS, relative values are multiplied by a monetary conversion factor (dollars per unit) to get dollar cost per service or procedure.

Relative value scales were first developed in the United States by individual state medical societies in response to the increased complexity of medical practice and the need to develop a means of determining the amount to charge for various services provided. In other countries, Japan for example, relative value scales are used in various forms to establish a technical basis for the established fee schedules. The relative value scale provides guidelines in establishing weights that reflect the time it takes to perform a procedure and its complexity. In theory, weighting should reflect changing technologies. As methods of treating various conditions change, so should the weighting.

Today, Medicare physician payment is based on the principle that differences in payments should reflect differences in work effort. Physicians incur three types of costs to produce medical services for their patients: 1) work effort measured by their own time, energy, and skill level; 2) the overhead cost of their practice; and

resource-based relative value scale (RBRVS)
A classification system for physicians' services, using a weighting scheme that reflects the relative value of the various services performed. Developed for Medicare by a group of Harvard researchers, the RBRVS considers time, skill, and overhead cost required for each service. When used in conjunction with a monetary conversion factor, medical fees are determined.

3) professional liability insurance premiums. The Medicare fee schedule calculates a total relative-value unit for each service based on these costs.

Determining a Payment Schedule from Relative Values A relative value scale does not automatically translate into a fee schedule. It is, however, simply a matter of applying a monetary conversion factor to the scale. Theoretically, once the conversion factor is set, the payment schedule is determined by applying it to the relative-value units. Under the old Medicare method of payment, physicians were paid more for performing invasive medical procedures than for general medical services. RBRVS has tried to address these discrepancies. As a result, certain specialties experienced substantial increases in revenues as a result of the change, including family practice, internal medicine, and allergy and immunology. Other specialties, including thoracic and cardiovascular surgery, ophthalmology, pathology, radiology, dermatology, and general surgery saw decreases in revenue.

A fee system based on the relative value scale is designed to reduce the disparities between procedures and services. Such a system focuses on the time and effort involved in providing the medical procedure or service, and it rewards physicians accordingly. Allowable fees for invasive procedures fell under this system, while those for the general services rose. It is not surprising that specialists whose practices were primarily in the former group were vehemently opposed to the new system. General practice physicians, whose practices fell predominantly in the latter group, strongly supported the changes.

When the Medicare fee schedule was first implemented in 1992, the monetary conversion factor was $31 per relative-value unit. A medical service with a relative weighting of 5 units would be paid $155 ($31 × 5). Congress has raised and lowered the conversion factor annually. In 2007, it stood at $35.99.

ISSUES IN MEDICAL CARE DELIVERY

Can Physicians Compete on Price?

Competitive markets depend on the free flow of information if they are to perform their assigned task of efficiently allocating goods and services. Lack of information on availability, quality, or price has been identified as a primary contributor to market failure in medical markets. Patients often find it difficult to acquire useful information on the pricing of physician services. Most have no idea what service or procedure to ask about, and those who do have limited success in finding valid comparisons across types of physicians.

The American Medical Association (AMA) has proposed a new approach to make comparisons among individual physicians easier and more meaningful — the advance disclosure of service rates. Here's how it would work: With the Medicare fee scale (resource-based relative value scale) every procedure has an established point value. If every physician posted a single number, a multiplier or "cost-conversion factor," patients could quickly compare fee schedules by comparing this single number. For example, if the standard office visit for an established patient had a point value of 0.78, a physician with a multiplier of $40 would charge $31.20 for that office visit, and the physician with a multiplier of $55 would charge $42.90 for the same office visit. Patients would have a way of comparing prices quickly simply by knowing each physician's multiplier.

continued

> Fee-for-service medicine is under attack from managed care. It may be that the only way to guarantee the long-term availability of fee-for-service for the middle class is to provide more information to patients so they can make more informed and thus better decisions on how to spend their medical dollars. Instead of complaining about the resource-based relative value scale, the AMA has found a way for physicians to use it. What remains to be seen is whether physicians can enter into an environment where they have to compete on the prices they charge.
>
> **Source:** George Anders, "AMA to Urge Doctors to Disclose Rates in Defending of Fee-for-Service Medicine," *Wall Street Journal*, May 5, 1994, B12.

Key Concept 7
Competition

The Economic Impact of a Fee Schedule for Physicians' Services In theory, a resource-based relative value scale approximates the relative fee schedule that would emerge in perfectly competitive equilibrium. Hence, the RBRVS could provide a fair and equitable approach to compensating physicians for the services they provide. By removing the distortions in current fee structure, the RBRVS would provide a neutral incentive structure for physicians in making medical decisions. By altering physician practice patterns, the rates of surgery, invasive diagnostic tests, and hospital use could be reduced significantly. Such an outcome would enhance the cost-effectiveness of medical care, leading to a reduction in the overall cost of health care.

Key Concept 8
Efficiency

In the long run, fee schedules based on the RBRVS would even change the supply of physicians according to specialty. Changes in the relative rewards across specialties would alter the specialty choices of medical school graduates. It might even alter the geographic distribution of physicians, thus affecting the accessibility, cost, and quality of care in currently underserved areas.

Key Concept 5
Markets and Pricing

Physician response is easy to predict. Those who have a solid patient base in the private sector will begin to refuse new Medicare patients. The elderly will find it increasingly difficult to secure the services of a primary care physician. In 2001, almost 30 percent of U.S. physicians were not accepting new Medicare patients (Trude and Ginsberg, 2002). Hospital emergency rooms will become the best alternative source of care for a great number of the elderly population. Shortages of health services for the elderly will begin to develop as resources are shifted into the unregulated, private sector. Physicians will encounter the same forces with private patients insured by HMOs and PPOs. In either case, the lesson is clear: If you do not ration via price, you will ration by queuing.

POLICY ISSUE

How do physicians respond when the government sets the prices they can charge for their services?

Managed Care Strategies

Medical care, whether in the United States or some other country, has traditionally been provided on a fee-for-service basis. Because of spiraling expenditures, fee-for-service medical plans began taking on cost-containment features during the 1980s. Frequently, these features include various aspects of the traditional managed care system: the use of a gatekeeper, required second surgical opinions, prior certification before hospital admissions, utilization reviews, and preadmission hospital testing. These cost-control measures approach the issue from different perspectives. But their common goal is to ensure the provision of medically necessary services in the appropriate setting at the appropriate levels and costs.

The results of these strategies are to restrict access to certain kinds of medical care (such as hospital and specialty care), to redirect medical care delivery to less expensive locations (such as outpatient and ambulatory settings), and to monitor

The Agency for Health Care Policy and Research was established in 1989 to support research designed to enhance the quality of medical care, reduce its cost, and improve access.

http://www.ahcpr.gov

the use of medical products, supplies, and services (such as prescription drugs and prosthetic devices). Not only has fee-for-service adopted many of the cost-savings features of managed care, managed care has increased its flexibility to better compete with fee-for-service. Instead of forcing recipients to use a closed panel of providers, more managed care systems offer open plans in which recipients are allowed to use providers outside the panel, subject to a deductible and higher coinsurance rates. Thus, managed care and fee-for-service systems are looking for the right mix of cost control and flexibility to compete in a changing medical care environment.

MARKET ALTERNATIVES

POLICY ISSUE

Can a market-based health care delivery system do a better job of controlling cost and spending?

Claiming government intervention as unnecessary and counterproductive, opponents of a government-run system argue that market alternatives are available. At least three are usually suggested: 1) capitation, 2) promotion of cost-reducing strategies in patient care systems and medical technology, and 3) increased competitiveness in health care delivery. Organizations are beginning to experiment with market forces and are finding that significant cost savings are possible.

The growth of managed care has increased the use of capitation across the system. Under capitation, providers receive a fixed payment in advance to provide medically necessary care for a well-defined patient population. This arrangement shifts some of the financial risk to providers and encourages the incorporation of cost-reducing strategies into the delivery system. The market is not a magic pill; there are always trade-offs to consider. The danger is that providers will attempt to cut costs that will lead to quality deterioration. Remember: There is no such thing as a free lunch.

Competitive bidding has also been a central factor in the market that has led to cost savings. Firms have pooled resources to increase their purchasing power when dealing with medical providers, especially HMOs. In turn, the HMOs have increased bargaining power with providers because of overcapacity in hospitals and various specialty sectors. This excess supply creates a buyers' market and gives the HMOs more leverage when negotiating contracts with medical providers. These savings can then be passed on to group health plans in the form of lower premiums.

These competitive forces provide the catalyst for all sorts of innovative behavior on the part of providers to lower cost and improve quality. Examples of this include the industry's move to total quality management (TQM). Originated by the Japanese, TQM is an industrial-management technique aimed at analyzing every step in the service delivery process. When applied to medical care delivery, it identifies which steps add to cost without improving health outcomes, allowing providers to eliminate those steps that are identified as ineffective.

BACK-OF-THE-ENVELOPE

The Elements of Cost Control in Medical Care

Controlling medical care spending begins by controlling medical care costs. Cost control depends on the ability to control the major elements of costs: resource prices, resource productivity, and utilization of services. The derivation of the cost-control identity can be shown as follows. In a standard two-input production process, output (Q) is a function of inputs A and B.

$$Q = Q(A, B) \qquad (1)$$

continued

Production of Q using the most efficient combination of A and B results in total cost (C) calculated as

$$C = P_A A + P_B B \tag{2}$$

where P_A is the price of input A, and P_B is the price of input B. Average cost (AC) is defined as total cost divided by output or

$$AC = C/Q. \tag{3}$$

Substituting (2) into (3), we get

$$AC = \frac{P_A A}{Q} + \frac{P_B B}{Q}$$

$$AC = P_A\left(\frac{A}{Q}\right) + P_B\left(\frac{B}{Q}\right) \tag{4}$$

Note that (3) implies $C = AC \times Q$. Thus, when (4) is restated, generalizing to n inputs, we find that

$$C = \left[P_A\left(\frac{A}{Q}\right) + P_B\left(\frac{B}{Q}\right) + \ldots + P_N\left(\frac{N}{Q}\right)\right]Q \tag{5}$$

From (5), the first element in the cost-control identity is the level of input prices, P_A through P_N. If you want to reduce costs, you must control input prices. The second element is input productivity, shown by the inverses of the technical efficiencies of the inputs, A/Q through N/Q. As input productivity increases, efficiency improves and costs fall. The final element is output, Q. Control the size of Q, limit utilization, and costs can be reduced.

The static world of cost identities may not provide much encouragement to would-be cost containers. Fuchs (1988), for one, argues against placing too much hope in our ability to moderate input prices, improve efficiency, or reduce utilization. Our ability to control cost may go back to equation (1), the production function for medical care itself. Cost-saving technological improvements and changes in the production mix from higher-priced to lower-priced inputs may provide some hope for continued moderation of medical costs.

Source: Victor R. Fuchs, "The Competition Revolution in Health Care," *Health Affairs* 7(3), Summer 1988, 5–24.

SUMMARY AND CONCLUSIONS

Health care systems around the world are struggling with the problem of increasing costs and growing expenditures. With the primary focus on the supply side of the exchange, government policy seems unable to stop the steady increase in spending. Two basic strategies have dominated policy around the world: either provide incentives for people to use less medical care, or increase regulation to control access and spending. Until recently, governments have chosen the regulatory option, relying primarily on fee schedules, global budgets, and resource rationing. The U.S. experience has been limited primarily to state CON laws and Medicare price controls, including DRGs for hospitals

and RBRVS for physicians. The success in slowing the growth in spending has been at least partially offset by a substantial increase in regulatory oversight. More recently the success of managed care in holding down the growth in spending makes the movement toward HMOs and PPOs more likely for enrollees in Medicare and Medicaid.

The growth in managed care presents the same concerns as the growth in any fixed-budget system—mandated fee schedules, global budgeting, and resource rationing. In fact, most managed care contracts with providers already incorporate the Medicare fee schedule into their reimbursement strategy. As a result, the hospital

DRG system and the relative value scale for physicians' services used by Medicare establishes a basis for virtually all provider payments in the private medical sector. The danger of managed care is its potential to transform the industry from its traditional medical mission to one more concerned with corporate issues, namely cost and returns. For better or for worse, profit incentives have invaded the not-for-profit sector. The positive changes associated with cost containment have resulted in an emphasis on the importance of lifestyle factors in determining health status, a concern for primary and preventive care, and a rethinking of the appropriateness, effectiveness, and efficiency of certain medical practices.

With the limited success of the supply-side measures, policy makers around the world are beginning to consider the role of the consumer in holding down spending. A more consumer-directed approach is being tried in many countries, including Switzerland and the United States. As consumers take more responsibility for their own care, the challenge becomes how to maintain access when financial considerations enter the decision. There is no single solution to the cost-control challenge.

PROFILE

Mark B. McClellan

It took Republican President George W. Bush almost two years to find a commissioner for the Food and Drug Administration (FDA) that the Democrats in Congress would accept. The long wait ended in November 2002, when Mark B. McClellan was confirmed unanimously by the U.S. Senate. After a brief stint as FDA Commissioner, McClellan is now Senior Fellow and Director of the Engelberg Center for Health Care Reform and holds the Leonard D. Schaeffer Chair in Health Policy Studies at the Brookings Institution.

McClellan has a unique pedigree, Ph.D. economist and board certified physician. He received his undergraduate education at the University of Texas at Austin and graduate degrees in public administration, medicine, and economics at Harvard and the Massachusetts Institute of Technology. He received his clinical training at Brigham and Women's Hospital in Boston and is board certified in internal medicine.

Upon finishing his residency, McClellan took a position as attending physician with Stanford Health Services and soon became the director of the Program on Health Outcomes Research at the Stanford Center for Health Policy. After a brief stint as Deputy Assistant Secretary for Economic Policy with the U.S. Department of Treasury, he was promoted to associate professor in the departments of economics and medicine at Stanford. He is associate editor of the *Journal of Health Economics* and visiting scholar with the American Enterprise Institute.

His publications include over 40 articles, books, and book chapters in some of the most prestigious journals in economics and health policy, including *American Economic Review, Journal of Health Economics, Health Affairs, RAND Journal of Economics,* and *Journal of Economic Perspectives.* In 1995, he received the Review of Economic Studies Award for his outstanding dissertation in economics, and in 1997, the International Health Economics Association awarded him with the Kenneth Arrow Award for Best Paper in Health Economics. He also received Griliches Award for Best Empirical Paper in both the *Quarterly Journal of Economics* and *Journal of Political Economy* in 1999. His current research includes working papers on quality of care, health outcomes, medical productivity, managed care report cards, and end-of-life care.

Before his appointment as FDA chief, he served on the President's Council of Economic Advisors, and at the same time was senior policy director for health care and related economic issues for the White House. McClellan is no stranger to politics. His mother, Carole Keeton Strayhorn, is the Comptroller of Public Accounts for the state of Texas. McClellan's

continued

brother, Scott, is the former White House press secretary for President George W. Bush.

McClellan's grandfather, former dean of the University of Texas Law School, once told him: "If you haven't made anybody mad, you haven't done anything." If his grandfather's words ring true, there must be some pretty mad folks around the country right now.

Source: Personal vitae and Department of Health and Human Services biography available at http://www.hhs.gov/about/bios/fda.html.

QUESTIONS AND PROBLEMS

1. Compared to fee-for-service payment, what are the advantages and disadvantages of payment based on diagnosis-related groups?

2. What was the motivation for changing the way physicians are compensated in the Medicare system? What are the implications for physicians' behavior as the resource-based relative value scale is fully implemented?

3. In his testimony before the House Ways and Means health subcommittee, Robert Reischauer stated that Congressional Budget Office research concluded that price controls could severely limit the quality and quantity of medical care in the United States. He also argued that the only way to control medical care spending is by imposing global health care budgets at the national level. Explain how price controls can be bad and global budgets good.

4. Advocates of a market orientation argue that exclusive reliance on the visible hand of government will never bring spending under control. The missing component has been the invisible hand of the market pricing mechanism. Patients spending their own money have an incentive to control spending. Comment.

5. In 1994, 565 economists sent President Bill Clinton a letter warning against the economic consequences of price controls that played such a prominent role in his health care reform plan. The price controls included mandated fee schedules for fee-for-service medical plans, prospective budgets for regional health alliances, increases in health insurance premiums tied to the cost of living, and price ceilings on prescription drugs. Discuss the economics of price controls. Under what circumstances do they accomplish their intended purpose? When do they fail?

REFERENCES

David M. Cutler, "Equality, Efficiency, and Market Fundamentals: The Dynamics of International Medical-Care Reform," *Journal of Economic Literature* 40(3), September 2002, 881–906.

Joe Feinglass and James J. Holloway, "The Initial Impact of the Medicare Prospective Payment System on U.S. Health Care: A Review of the Literature," *Medical Care Review* 48(1), Spring 1991, 91–115.

Sherman T. Folland and Robert Kleiman, "The Effects of Prospective Payment under DRGs on the Market Value of Hospitals," *Quarterly Review of Economics and Business* 30(2), Summer 1990, 50–68.

William C. Hsiao, et al., A National Study of Resource-Based Relative Value Scales for Physician Services: Final Report to the Health Care Financing Administration, publication 17-C-98795/1–03, Boston: Harvard University School of Public Health, 1988.

The Lewin Group, "The Balanced Budget Act and Hospitals: The Dollars and Cents of Medicare Payment Cuts," American Hospital Association, May 1999.

Louise B. Russell and Carrie Lynn Manning, "The Effect of Prospective Payment on Medicare Expenditures," *New England Journal of Medicine* 320(7), February 16, 1989, 439–444.

Steven H. Sheingold, "The First Three Years of PPS: Impact on Medicare Costs," *Health Affairs* 8(3), Fall 1989, 191–204.

Sally Trude and Paul B. Ginsburg, "Growing Physician Access Problems Complicate Medicare Payment Debate," Issue Brief No. 55, Washington, DC: Center for Studying Health System Change, September 2002.

Lynn Wagner, "CBO Head Warns Price Controls Could Severely Limit Quality, Quantity of Medical Care in the U.S.," *Modern Healthcare* 23(3), March 8, 1993, 22.

Medical Care Systems Worldwide

Anyone involved in the debate on health care reform in the United States will eventually get around to comparing the private insurance model used in the United States to the social insurance model used in most of the developed world. Comparisons across systems must be made carefully. As we learned in Chapter 11, differences in population demographics, per capita income, disease incidence, and institutional features often make direct comparisons difficult to interpret.

In the following sections, we will discuss the health care delivery systems in the six major countries whose health care systems are often compared to that of the U.S.—Canada, France, Germany, Japan, Switzerland, and the United Kingdom. No attempt is made to glamorize or debase any system of health care delivery. Every one of these countries, including the United States, no matter how its medical care delivery is organized and financed, is struggling with a common problem—controlling the growth in medical care spending. These problems will be carefully documented, not for the purpose of rating the delivery mechanisms of those countries, but to show that reform in the United States must take on a structure that is uniquely American, one that will work within the U.S. institutional framework.

ISSUES IN MEDICAL CARE DELIVERY

Who Has the Best Health Care System?

In 2000 the World Health Organization (WHO) released a report ranking the health care systems of the world's 191 countries. The first attempt of its kind, the report attracted a great deal of media attention and surprised many health experts in its findings. The WHO rankings were based on five composite indicators: 1) the overall level of health of the population, 2) health inequality within the population, 3) health system responsiveness, 4) the distribution of responsiveness to measure, and 5) how fairly the financial burden is shared across different socioeconomic groups.

The health of the population was measured in terms of disability-adjusted life expectancy and disparities in that measure across groups. Health system responsiveness measured how well patients are served and the degree of service disparity among different groups. This composite

continued

index was compiled from surveys administered to 1,791 public health experts in 35 selected countries. The fairness of the financial burden was recorded as an index based on survey data that measured the percentage of household income beyond subsistence spent on health care. A weighting scheme was used to develop an index of overall performance, giving a 25 percent weight to each of categories 1, 2, and 5, and a 12.5 percent weight each to categories 3 and 4.

WHO HEALTH CARE SYSTEM PERFORMANCE, 1997

| | HEALTH RESPONSIVENESS | | | | Goal Attain-ment | Overall Perfor-mance |
	Level	Distri-bution	Level	Distri-bution	Financial Fairness		
Canada	12	18	T7	T3	T17	7	30
France	3	12	T16	T3	T26	6	1
Germany	22	20	5	T3	T6	14	25
Japan	1	3	6	T3	T8	1	10
United Kingdom	14	2	T26	T3	T8	9	18
United States	24	32	1	T3	T54	15	37

Note: *Tn* indicates a tie for *n*th place.

Overall, the French health care system was rated number one. The only other country examined in this chapter that made the top 10 was Japan, finishing at number ten. The top spots were filled by countries that usually do not come to mind in discussions of the world's best health care systems: Italy, Spain, Oman, and Austria. The next large, developed country on the list was the United Kingdom at number 18; Germany finished twenty-fifth, Canada thirtieth, and the United States thirty-seventh.

Needless to say, the results were met with heavy criticism, mostly from those countries whose rankings did not meet expectations. Blendon, Kim, and Benson (2001) point out one methodological flaw in the WHO approach, namely that the rankings show little correlation between overall performance and the results of patient satisfaction surveys conducted in the countries. Italy, Portugal, and Greece ranked second, twelfth, and fourteenth respectively in the WHO study but consistently scored quite low on patient satisfaction surveys. And countries such as the Netherlands, Finland, and Denmark—ranked seventeenth, thirty-first, and thirty-fourth—rated high in patient satisfaction.

Despite its flaws, and despite the criticism, the WHO report was an attempt to do a thankless but necessary task: develop a method to compare health care systems.

Sources: Robert J. Blendon, Minah Kim, and John M. Benson, "The Public Versus the World Health Organization on Health System Performance," *Health Affairs* 20(3), May/June 2001, 10–20; World Health Organization, "Health Systems: Improving Performance," The World Health Report 2000, Geneva: WHO, 2000.

INTERNATIONAL COMPARISONS

Table 14.1 provides a listing of several key statistics on population, economics, and health for the United States and the six countries discussed in this chapter: Canada, France, Germany, Japan, Switzerland, and the United Kingdom. In 2005, national populations ranged from 7.4 million in Switzerland to 296.4 million in the United States. The U.S. population is approximately 40 times the population of Switzerland, five times that of both France and the United Kingdom, three times that of Germany, and twice Japan's. The United States has the largest economy as measured by gross domestic product (GDP), more than twice the size of the second largest, Japan. The widely used measure for relative standards of living, per capita GDP adjusted for purchasing power parity, is 16.3 percent higher in the United States than in Switzerland, 22.8 percent higher than in Canada, and almost 40 percent higher than in France, Germany, and Japan.

Health care spending, whether measured in U.S. per capita dollars or as a percentage of GDP, is significantly higher in the United States than in any other country. Switzerland, Canada, and France are ranked second, third, and fourth according to the two measures. Per capita spending in Japan is barely one-third that of the United States. Physicians per 1,000 population range from a low in Japan of 2.0 to a high in Switzerland of 3.8. The United States is ranked at the bottom of the list in terms of acute care hospital beds per 1,000, at 2.7 beds, and average length of hospital stay, at 5.6 days. Japan tops the list in both categories, with 8.2 beds per 1,000 and an average hospital stay of 19.8 days.[1]

Expenditures Across OECD Countries

Medical care spending in the United States is the highest in the world, both in per capita terms and as a percentage of GDP. Although health care spending as a percentage of GDP—the health-to-GDP ratio—is the most widely used performance measure for the health care sector, it is important to remember that there are actually two components to this ratio. Comparisons at a given point in time tend to focus on the ratio alone. If countries are compared over time, however, it is important to examine both the change in health spending and the change in GDP. In other words, both the numerator and the denominator of the ratio are important.

Table 14.2 presents a comparison of the growth rates for health care sector components for the past 25 years: the decades of the 1980s and 1990s and the half-decade from 2000 through 2005. Annual growth rates in health care spending were considerably higher in the 1980s than in the 1990s. The average growth rate in nominal health care spending was 7.73 percent, ranging from 4.19 percent in Germany to 9.78 percent in the United States. Nominal spending growth slowed to an average of 5.16 percent in the 1990s, ranging from 3.82 percent in France to 6.80 percent in the United Kingdom. Growth rates since 2000 have turned upwards in four of the seven countries—Canada, France, the United Kingdom, and the United States—averaging 7.44 percent. A portion of the increased spending is

Key Concept 2
Opportunity Cost

Organization for Economic Cooperation and Development provides information on economic issues, activities, and events for all member countries.

http://www.oecd.org

The World Bank reports regularly on health and health care issues worldwide. Their publications, including an annual world development report, provides data on economic, demographics, and infrastructure. The data are particularly useful in studying less developed countries.

http://worldbank.org

---

[1] Several cultural reasons explain why the Japanese average length of stay is so long—the sick are more pampered, more conditions are considered illnesses, and the Japanese place an emphasis on bed rest as a cure for most illnesses. For example, in contrast to the situation in the United States, where Congress must legislate a mandatory two-day hospital stay after childbirth, the length of stay following childbirth in Japan approaches two weeks. In addition, long-term care for the elderly is provided primarily in the hospital setting, substantially increasing length-of-stay calculations.

Table 14.1 Key Statistics

2005	Canada	France	Germany	Japan	Switzerland	United Kingdom	United States
Population (millions)	32.3	60.9	82.5	127.8	7.4	60.2	296.4
GDP (per capita)[1]	34,057	30,350	30,776	30,777	35,956	32,896	41,827
Health Expenditures							
Health care spending (per capita)	3,326	3,374	3,287	2,358[4]	4,177	2,724	6,401
Health care spending (percent of GDP)	9.8	11.1	10.7	8.0[4]	11.6	8.3	15.3
Medical Services							
Number of physicians (per 1,000)	2.2	3.4	3.4	2.0[4]	3.8	2.4	2.4
Acute care beds (per 1,000)	2.9[4]	3.7	6.4	8.2	3.6	3.1	2.7
Average length of stayacute care (days)	7.3[4]	5.4	8.6	19.8	8.5	6.1	5.6
Medical Technology[2]							
CT Scanners	11.2	9.8	15.4	92.6[5]	18.2	7.5	32.2[4]
MRI Units[3]	5.5	4.7	7.1	40.1	14.4	5.4	26.6[4]
Lithotripters	0.5	0.8	3.7	7.1	4.7	—	3.2[5]
Patients Undergoing Dialysis	6.1	—	7.7	20.2	—	3.5[3]	11.4[4]

Source: *OECD Health Data 2007*, OECD, Paris, 2007.

[1] In U.S. purchasing power parity (PPP) dollars—the exchange rate at which different currencies buy the same bundle of goods.
[2] Per 1 million population.
[3] Counts the number of hospitals with scanners, not the total number of scanners.
[4] 2004.
[5] 2002.

Table 14.2   Annual Compound Growth in Health Sector Components 1980 through 2005, in percentages

Decade of the 1980s	Canada	France	Germany	Japan	Switzerland	United Kingdom	United States
Nominal health care spending	9.64	9.64	4.19	4.73	7.17	8.91	9.78
Nominal per capita health care spending	8.47	9.06	4.11	4.19	6.59	8.78	8.90
Real health care spending[1]	4.68	3.59	1.63	2.94	2.99	3.13	5.69
Real per capita health care spending[1]	3.57	2.72	1.54	2.42	2.47	2.97	4.84
Decade of the 1990s							
Nominal health care spending	3.89	3.82	6.87	3.83	5.13	6.80	5.76
Nominal per capita health care spending	2.89	3.48	4.12	3.57	4.38	6.58	4.59
Real health care spending[1]	2.55	2.31	4.95	3.52	3.07	3.82	3.76
Real per capita health care spending[1]	1.57	1.97	2.24	3.26	2.43	3.61	2.61
2000–2005							
Nominal health care spending	7.12	6.67	2.42	0.89[2]	4.07	7.95	8.03
Nominal per capita health care spending	6.05	5.96	2.34	0.74[2]	3.35	7.46	6.98
Real health care spending[1]	4.67	4.67	1.38	2.28[2]	3.27	5.18	5.46
Real per capita health care spending[1]	3.62	3.98	1.31	2.12[2]	2.56	4.70	4.43

Source: *OECD Health Data 2007,* Paris: OECD.

[1] Spending adjusted by the GDP price deflator.
[2] 2000 through 2004.

Note: Measurements based on changes denominated in national currencies.

due to increased population, as evidenced by slightly lower per capita growth rates over the three periods.

Deflating health care expenditures by the GDP deflator adjusts nominal spending into real terms, providing a measure of the opportunity cost of resources absorbed by the health care sector. The United States and the United Kingdom consistently rank at the top of the list for all the sample periods, implying that Americans and Brits have been giving up substantially more non–health-related spending to accommodate their health sectors.[2]

---

[2] Note that during the 2000 through 2004 time period, Japan's real spending was actually higher than nominal spending. This phenomenon is due to a period of deflation in the Japanese economy, where overall prices have actually declined.

ISSUES IN MEDICAL CARE DELIVERY

Medical Care Spending and International Competitiveness

General Motors spends $4.8 billion for worker health insurance, the equivalent of $1,200 for every car produced, or roughly the total public and private health budget for all 40 million South Africans. Is medical care spending making American business less competitive in the global marketplace? This popular notion has a great deal of intuitive appeal, especially when members of the business community make the arguments.

The microeconomic argument examines the issue from the perspective of an individual firm. This argument assumes that the relevant price of labor is the cash wage paid to workers, and it treats fringe benefits as an add-on cost. Under this scenario, the firm has only two options when faced with increasing fringe costs: shift the costs forward to the firm's customers by raising product prices, or shift the costs backward to the firm's owners by reducing the firm's profits. The first option makes the firm's products less competitive in the marketplace; the second makes the firm's stock less attractive in the equity capital market.

The macroeconomic argument examines the issue from the perspective of the entire economy. Much of our medical care spending represents pure consumption. By devoting a large fraction of gross domestic product to medical care, less is available for savings and capital formation. In addition, spending less on medical care would allow resources to be shifted to more productive activities that would enhance economic efficiency and international competitiveness.

Overall, the argument that high medical care costs reduce competitiveness does not stand up under careful scrutiny. In particular, the microeconomic argument ignores a third option available to firms faced with rising fringe costs, namely, to shift the costs of increased fringe benefits to the workers who receive them. This option may be accomplished by merely paying the workers lower cash wages. To understand this perspective, realize that the relevant market-clearing wage is not solely the cash wage but the value of the total compensation package, including cash wages, health benefits, retirement benefits, the firm's share of social security taxes, and other payroll taxes. It makes little sense to single out any one component of the total compensation package and blame it for the lack of competitiveness in the global marketplace. Instead, it is important to realize that workers who receive fewer fringe benefits will merely demand higher cash wages.

On the other hand, the macroeconomic argument is based on the assumption that consumer spending in every other economic sector is "more productive" than spending on medical care. Because of the dominance of third-party payment in the medical care sector, a large percentage of medical care spending may be wasteful. Patients who do not pay the true incremental costs of the procedures they receive demand services that provide little benefit. Suggesting that spending in one sector is more productive than spending in any other, however, begs an important consideration: Who decides what type of spending is more productive? Would we be better off if half of the lawyers left their chosen profession and got "more productive" jobs in other sectors? Why not get half of all college professors engaged in scholarly research to spend their time in activities that are "more productive," for example, undergraduate teaching?

continued

Key Concept 8
Efficiency

POLICY ISSUE

Does the high cost of health insurance handicap U.S. business in the global market?

Key Concept 5
Markets and Pricing

Key Concept 2
Opportunity Cost

> The business sector's motivation to control medical care spending goes beyond the global competitiveness argument. Every dollar spent on medical care affects at least one of the firm's stakeholders: customers pay higher prices, workers accept lower cash wages, and/or owners receive reduced profits. It is important to use resources wisely, not just in the medical care sector but also throughout the economy.
>
> **Source:** Uwe E. Reinhardt, "Health Care Spending and American Competitiveness," *Health Affairs* 8(4), Winter 1989, 5–21.

International Comparison of Medical Outcomes

Many argue that high spending in the United States might be tolerable if the resulting health outcomes were better. Table 14.3 provides data on life expectancy at birth and infant mortality rates. When these two measures are used to assess health outcomes, the United States ranks at the bottom within the developed world. The U.S. infant mortality rate of 6.9 per 1,000 live births is over two times the rate in Japan and 20 to 50 percent higher than the other comparison countries. Some of the factors that complicate the comparison of infant mortality rates have already been discussed in Chapter 11, most notably the higher incidence of low–birth-weight babies born in the United States.[3]

Instead of comparing life expectancy at birth, if life expectancy at age 80 is used, the rankings change substantially. Rankings for both male and female life expectancies improve, and the United States now ranks third and fourth, respectively. There are several explanations for this improvement as the individual ages. A large part of the difference in life expectancy at birth is due to differences

POLICY ISSUE

Is the United States getting its money's worth in terms of health outcomes for the money spent on health care?

Table 14.3 Health Outcomes

| Country | Life Expectancy at Birth[1] | | Life Expectancy at Age 80[1] | | Infant Mortality Rate[2] | Perinatal Mortality Rate |
	Males (2003)	Females (2003)	Males (2003)	Females (2003)	(2004)	(2001)
Canada	77.4	82.4	8.0	9.9	5.3[3]	6.3
France	75.9	82.9	7.8[4]	9.7[4]	3.9	6.9
Germany	75.7	81.4	7.2	8.5	4.1	5.9
Japan	78.4	85.3	8.3	11.0	2.8	3.6
Switzerland	78.0	83.1	7.5	9.3	4.2	8.0
United Kingdom	76.2	80.7	7.1[4]	8.6[4]	5.1	6.7
United States	74.8	80.1	8.0	9.6	6.9[3]	6.9

Source: *OECD Health Data 2007*, Paris: Organization for Economic Cooperation and Development, 2007.

[1] In years.
[2] Perinatal deaths per 1,000 live births.
[3] 2003.
[4] 2002.

---

[3] Low-birth-weight babies as a percentage of all births range from 5.8 percent in Canada to 8.1 percent in Japan. The percentage is 7.6 in the United States.

in mortality factors at younger ages that have nothing to do with medical care delivery, such as the incidence of drug abuse, homicide, AIDS, and auto fatalities. The incidences of these factors tend to converge at older ages, and the differences in life expectancies may depict differences in the efficacy of health care delivery more accurately. The same is true when perinatal mortality rates are used instead of infant mortality rates.

A third way to compare systems examines differences in the effectiveness of treating various diseases. The World Health Organization (WHO) has published statistics on cancer incidence, mortality, and prevalence worldwide (Ferlay et al., 2001). Table 14.4 provides interesting insight into the effectiveness of treating cancer in the countries of interest. The mortality ratios listed in the table measure the estimated number of deaths that would occur as a result of the cancer relative to the number of estimated new cancer diagnoses. In other words, the mortality ratio is helpful in estimating the proportion of patients who will die from cancer in a given country. The calculation is actually the ratio of mortality to incidence.

Examining mortality ratios is a much better way of comparing the efficacy of the detection and treatment of a disease. A low mortality ratio indicates better survival possibilities for those who have the disease. High mortality rates may simply be due to high incidence, so they are not an indictment against a health care delivery system. Use of mortality rates alone tends to mask this important distinction.

Careful examination of the table shows that the United States has the lowest mortality ratio for colon/rectal, breast, and prostate cancer and is below the average for all developed countries in every case. In the summary measure for all sites except skin cancer, the United States does substantially better than the rest of the developed world. Only in the case of cervical cancer does the U.S. performance fall below any of the listed countries. The important question that needs to be addressed is whether differences in mortality among countries is related more to the incidence of disease or to differences in the quality of medical care available. Mortality ratios may not provide the definitive answer to this question; at the same time, mortality rates and incidence rates are not always good measures of the effectiveness of a health care system in treating various diseases.

http://

The World Health Organization promotes health worldwide. Their Web site provides important links for those interested in public health issues.

http://www.who.int

Table 14.4 Mortality Ratios for Cancer Selected Countries

| Country | Type of Cancer | | | | |
	Colon/Rectal*	Breast	Cervical	Prostate	All Sites Except Skin*
Canada	38.2	25.0	32.5	21.2	47.8
France	44.6	23.4	31.6	30.7	56.1
Germany	43.7	27.1	35.2	26.1	50.9
Japan	35.1	25.4	23.3	45.2	59.0
Switzerland	35.8	24.2	20.5	27.9	45.5
United Kingdom	44.6	27.9	37.3	34.3	56.7
United States	34.1	18.8	29.9	12.7	37.5
All Developed Countries	44.3	26.7	38.8	24.0	54.0

Source: J. Ferlay et al., *GLOBOCAN 2002: Cancer Incidence, Mortality, and Prevalence Worldwide*, Version 1.0, IARC Cancer Base No. 5, Lyon: IARC Press, 2001.

* Male only

Canadian National Health Insurance: Medicare

Canada is divided into ten provinces and two territories. Its total population is just over 32 million, and most live within 100 miles of the U.S. border. These demographics create quite a challenge for health care delivery in the rest of the country, where low population densities, long-distance travel requirements, and provider shortages are the norm. Only two provinces have populations exceeding one million, and only four metropolitan areas have sufficient population to support integrated delivery systems. Canadian policy makers have responded to these challenges by creating a **national health insurance** system that has demonstrated an ability to deliver high-quality medical care to the entire population at slightly over half of the per capita cost of U.S. health care.

The 1984 Canada Health Act defines the health care delivery system as it currently operates. Provisions of the act require that each provincial health plan be publicly administered, portable across provinces, accessible, and that each provide comprehensive first-dollar coverage of all medically necessary services. With minor exceptions, health coverage is available to all residents with no out-of-pocket charges. Most physicians are paid on a fee-for-service basis and enjoy a great deal of practice autonomy.[4]

The Canadian health care system began to take on its current form when the province of Saskatchewan set up a hospitalization plan immediately after the Second World War. In 1944, provincial voters elected a socialist-leaning government, the Cooperative Commonwealth Federation, or CCF (now called the New Democratic Party). The province was plagued by the kind of medical problems that one might expect in a predominantly rural, low-income population—shortages of both hospital beds and medical practitioners. By 1947, two years after coming into power, the CCF delivered on its campaign promise to provide a system of socialized medicine and enacted the Saskatchewan Hospital Services Plan. The main feature of this plan was the creation of a regional system of hospitals: local hospitals for primary care, district hospitals for more complex cases, and base hospitals for the most difficult cases.

British Columbia, Saskatchewan's western neighbor, enacted its own hospital insurance plan in 1949, providing momentum for the creation of a national hospital insurance system. In 1956, the federal parliament enacted the Hospital and Diagnostic Services Act, laying the groundwork for a nationwide system of hospital insurance. By 1961, all ten provinces and the two territories had hospital insurance plans of their own with the federal government paying half of the costs.

Within a year, Saskatchewan moved to provide for the funding of physicians' services. The Saskatchewan Medical Care Insurance Act of 1962 was passed; its main provision was a binding fee schedule for physicians' services. As a result, physicians in the province orchestrated the first-ever physicians' strike in all of North America to protest the fixed-fee schedule. To settle the dispute, the provincial government allowed the practice of "extra billing," which allowed physicians to charge fees in excess of those scheduled. Within two years, the average incomes of physicians in Saskatchewan moved from last among the provinces to first, fueling the engine of reform.

The other provinces began to fall in line, but this time national legislation was enacted in half the time—four years instead of nine. By 1971, Canada had its national health insurance plan, providing coverage for both hospitalization and physicians' services. To receive matching funds from the federal government, each provincial plan had to meet certain national standards. This included universal eligibility,

---

national health insurance
A government-run health insurance system covering the entire population for a well-defined medical benefits package. Usually administered by a government or quasi-government agency and financed through some form of taxation.

The Canadian Health Network provides links to over 30 health sites with information on Canadian medical care.

http://www.hc-sc.gc.ca/notice-avis

Key Concept 4
Self-Interest

---

[4] About 90 percent of all primary care is provided by fee-for-service general practitioners (GPs). The rest is provided by salaried GPs working in local community health centers.

BACK-OF-THE-ENVELOPE

Negotiating Fee Schedules: Bilateral Monopoly in Canada

In practice, each province in Canada offers a separate health care system. While the federal government helps finance these systems through an income tax, most of the money is raised at the provincial level either through general tax revenues, payroll taxes, or premiums. Each provincial health ministry tightly controls hospital spending through global budgets. Hospitals are given a fixed operating budget at the beginning of each fiscal year. Spending on physicians' services is controlled in a number of different ways across the country. The basic tool for controlling spending on physicians' services is a mandatory fee schedule negotiated between the provincial health ministry, representing the patients, and the provincial medical society, representing the physicians. This is a classic case of bilateral monopoly. Here is how it works.

Key Concept 3
Marginal Analysis

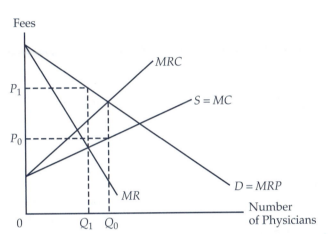

In the diagram, the demand curve for physicians' services is the marginal revenue product curve (*MRP*). This is the demand curve facing the medical association representing all the physicians in the province. The medical association functions in much the same way as a union and behaves like a labor monopolist. The marginal revenue curve (*MR*) is derived from the demand curve. The supply curve *S* represents the opportunity cost, or marginal cost (*MC*), of making an additional physician member available to the market. If the medical association behaves like a profit (or economic rent) maximizer, it sets $MR = MC$ and offers Q_1 physicians at a fee schedule equivalent to P_1.

The health ministry, acting as a monopsonist, maximizes profit where $MRP = MRC$. From its perspective, the optimal equilibrium will have Q_0 physicians available at a fee schedule equal to P_0. The final equilibrium will find fees somewhere between P_0 and P_1 and the number of physicians between Q_0 and Q_1.

In this situation, negotiations will likely begin with the medical association offering to make Q_1 physicians available and the health ministry refusing to pay fees higher than P_0. If the health ministry wants more physicians, then higher fees must be paid. The trade-off will be made, and a bargain will eventually be reached. In the Canadian case, it is likely that the medical association is in a weaker position. If the demand curve in the above figure is more inelastic and the supply curve more elastic, then Q_0 is less than Q_1. The health ministry wants fewer physicians in practice than the medical association is willing to provide. No longer is a bargaining trade-off possible.

continued

In this case the provincial health ministries set utilization targets to control overall spending. If these targets are exceeded in one year, the next year's fees are lowered accordingly, or physicians are forced to work for reduced fees until budgets are met, or income ceilings are established for individual physicians. The latter approach is taken in Quebec. Once physicians bill up to their quarterly limit, their fees are reduced by 75 percent for the remainder of the quarter. Many physicians who regularly reach their limit take time off at the end of each quarter. Many lease their office to colleagues in exchange for a percentage of those fees (Wolfe and Moran, 1993).

single-payer system

Usually associated with Canada, a system of financing medical care in which payment comes from a single source, typically the government. The single payer has considerable influence over virtually every aspect of health care financing and delivery.

Many of the provincial health ministries in Canada have their own Web sites. The British Columbia Ministry of Health has its own Web address.

http://www.gov.bc.ca/hlth

The Ontario Ministry of Health also has its own Web site.

http://www.health.gov.on.ca/

coverage of all medically necessary services (inpatient, outpatient, and physician), public administration, portability between provinces, and no financial barriers to service—which meant no hospital user charges and no extra billing by physicians.

The 50–50 cost-sharing arrangement was abandoned by the federal government in 1977 and replaced with a per capita grant to the provinces. The result has been steady erosion in the percentage of the costs covered by the federal government. The federal share has fallen from 30 percent in 1980 to 21.5 percent in 1996 (Naylor, 1999). With federal and provincial deficits considerably higher than U.S. per capita levels, the shifting financial burden has created a strong incentive to reduce spending and shift some of the expense onto the private sector. The public sector financed 75 percent of total health care spending in 1986. By 1996 that figure had dropped to 70 percent. The private sector covers 12.3 percent of hospital spending and 64.8 percent of pharmaceutical drug spending.

Many feel that it is inaccurate to characterize the Canadian system as a **"single-payer" system,** because there is considerable variation among the provincial plans. In spite of the differences, it is fair to say that each provincial plan is a public sector monopsony, serving as a single buyer of medical services within the province and holding medical care prices below market rates.

Theoretically, physician fee schedules are determined through bilateral negotiations at the provincial level between the Ministry of Health and the medical association. Practically, several provinces have reduced unilaterally the "binding" fee schedules. Five provinces, with 80 percent of the population, have mechanisms to control service volume by placing a limit on the quarterly gross billings allowed for the individual practitioner. Billings above the limit are reimbursed at one-fourth the prescribed fee schedule (Evans et al., 1989).[5] Several provinces have initiated an across-the-board, 25 percent reduction in fees for new physicians practicing in urban areas, for the purpose of reducing crowding in urban areas and scarcity in rural areas. To confront the fee problem head-on, the Ministry of Health for British Columbia has begun setting fee schedules unilaterally. By U.S. standards, physicians' incomes are on average low. In 2002 the income of primary care physicians ranged from $81,017 to $117,191; for hospital-based physicians, the range was $117,197 to $154,315 (NERA, 2004). The average physicians' income is about six times the average Canadian worker but less than two-thirds that of the typical U.S. physician.

If cost control is defined in terms of health care spending as a share of economic output, Canada has done far better in controlling health care costs than the United States. In 1970, Canada's health care spending as a share of GDP was 7.2 percent, compared to the U.S. figure of 7.4 percent. Over the next two decades, the increase

---

[5] Quebec has the strictest limitations with the billing threshold at $180,000 (U.S.).

in the health care spending-to-GDP ratio was significantly lower in Canada than in the United States. In 1987, the health care sector represented 8.6 percent of GDP in Canada and 11.2 percent of GDP in the United States. Critics of the Canadian system argue that this is a statistical phenomenon due not to more effective cost control but to faster economic growth. Between 1967 and 1987, real economic output in Canada increased 74 percent, while U.S. real output increased only 38 percent.

If cost control is measured in terms of growth in real per capita expenditures, the picture looks somewhat different. From 1967 through 1987, real per capita health care spending grew faster in Canada than in the United States. During those years, Canada's compound annual growth rate in real health care spending was 4.58 percent, compared to the 4.38 percent experienced in the United States. Between 1981 and 2000, real per capita spending in Canada (adjusted by the medical expenditures price deflator) grew at a rate of 2.12 percent per year, compared to 1.78 percent per year in the United States.

The key element in the Canadian strategy to control overall spending is the regionalization of high-tech services. Government regulators make resource-allocation decisions. This control extends to capital investment in hospitals, the specialty mix of medical practitioners, the location of recent medical graduates, and the diffusion of high-tech diagnostic and surgical equipment. In 2005 there were 178 magnetic resonance imagers in all of Canada, one for every 182,000 citizens. Contrast that to over 7,800 in the United States, one for every 37,500 Americans. There were 16 lithotripters in Canada in 2005 compared to 950 in the United States. That same year, there were 360 CT scanners in Canada, one for every 89,000 citizens. The United States had over 9,500 CT scanners, one for every 31,000 Americans. A study by Harriman, McArthur, and Zelder (1999) compared the availability of medical technology in community hospitals in British Columbia with those in Washington and Oregon. They found Canadian deficits in several areas, including angioplasty, cardiac catheterization, and intensive care.

It can be argued that U.S. hospitals have excess capacity in these technology areas while, at the same time, Canada experiences a shortage. Waiting lists for certain surgical and diagnostic procedures are common in Canada. In 2007 Canadians were waiting for 827,429 surgical procedures, an increase of 7.4 percent over 2006. Assuming one person per procedure, then 2.54 percent of the population is on a waiting list. Nationwide, the median wait from referral by a GP to treatment was 18.3 weeks, up from 17.8 weeks in 2006. Median waits ranged from 15.0 weeks in British Columbia to 27.2 weeks in Saskatchewan. Median waiting times are longest for orthopedic surgery (38.1 weeks), plastic surgery (34.8 weeks), and neurosurgery (27.2 weeks). General surgery, cardiovascular surgery, and oncological services have the shortest waits, ranging from 4.3 to 9.5 weeks. Comparisons between reasonable and actual waiting times were made for all 10 provinces and 13 specialties. The median waiting time was longer than Canadian physicians consider clinically reasonable in over 76 percent of the comparisons (Esmail and Walker, 2007).[6]

Key Concept 6
Supply and Demand

The problem does not end there. When care requires diagnostic imaging, waiting times are even longer. In 2007 patients had to wait 4.8 weeks for a CT scan, 10.1 weeks for an MRI, and 3.9 weeks for an ultrasound. Treatment delays are causing problems for certain vulnerable segments of the Canadian population, particularly the elderly who cannot get reasonable access to the medical care they demand, including hip and knee replacement (median wait of 25.4 weeks), cataract surgery (11.2 weeks), and nonemergent cardiac bypass surgery (5.4 weeks). Thus Canadians are sacrificing access to modern medical technology for first-dollar coverage for primary care.

---

[6] A clinically reasonable wait as defined by Canadian physicians is one-third to one-half longer than is considered reasonable by American physicians.

Another cost-control measure is global budgeting. Hospitals are provided with annual budgets to cover their operating expenses. They are expected to serve every patient within the level of funding provided by this budget. The resource allocation decision falls squarely on hospital administrators across the country, who must decide service availability given funding levels.

Several lessons can be learned from the Canadian experience. When government provides a product "free" to consumers, inevitably, demand escalates and spending increases. Products provided at zero price are treated as if they have zero resource cost. Resource allocation decisions become more inefficient over time, and government is forced either to raise more revenue or curb services. A number of the provincial health plans are moving to reduce spending by dropping services from the approved list of the "medically necessary." These include certain infertility treatments, routine newborn circumcisions, and tattoo removal, to name a few. A number of provinces have discontinued or changed the eligibility requirements for their dental plans for children (Leatt and Williams, 1997).

A second lesson is that everything has a cost. When care requires major diagnostic or surgical procedures, the "free" system must find some other mechanism to allocate scarce resources. The Canadian system delegates this authority to the government. Resource allocation is practiced not through the price mechanism but by setting limits on the investment in medical technology. Proponents will argue that using waiting lists as a rationing measure is reasonable and fair. Opponents find the lists unacceptable and an unwelcome encroachment on individual decision making in the medical sector.

Proponents of the single-payer alternative must deal with the fact that Canadians face waiting lists for some medical services, especially for high-tech specialty care. To avoid delays in treatment, many Canadians travel south for more advanced treatment. The head of health insurance for the Ontario Ministry of Health views the availability of medical care in the United States as a safety valve for Canadians (Berss, 1993). Blendon and colleagues (1993) reported that nearly one-third of all Canadian physicians have referred patients to treatment facilities outside the country in the past five years. The comparable figure for German physicians was 19 percent, and for U.S. physicians, 7 percent.

These cross-border transactions reached record levels in the early 1990s. Until 1991 Canadians were reimbursed for 100 percent of all emergency care received abroad and 75 percent of the cost of all elective surgery. These generous benefits were lowered to a flat per diem of $400 (Canadian) for emergency services and $200 for elective surgery. Since the change, the number of Canadians seeking care in the United States has sharply declined. A rise has occurred in major orthopedic procedures, experimental cancer treatments, and TMJ treatments. Most of these procedures are covered by private travel health insurance purchased by more than 10 percent of the population (Katz et al., 1998).

The system faces two significant challenges. The first is how to finance catastrophic drug coverage. Prescription drug coverage was not part of the original program, requiring most individuals in the private market to purchase supplemental insurance, primarily through employers; and until recently, private health insurance for covered services was illegal. The second challenge is how to respond to the Canadian Supreme Court ruling that this provision is unconstitutional. The ruling became effective in June 2006 and states that unless the provincial plan meets patient needs without undue waits, the government can no longer ban private insurance (Steinbrook, 2006). While this ruling technically affects only the province of Quebec, a similar lawsuit is currently challenging the ban in Ontario. It seems that it is only a matter of time before this patient backlash affects all provinces and leads to a growing private insurance sector and possibly a two-tiered system with shorter waiting times, increased demand for services, and more spending.

Key Concept 2
Opportunity Cost

Key Concept 1
Scarcity and Choice

POLICY ISSUE

What are the economic and political consequences of changing the U.S. health care delivery system to a Canadian-style single-payer system?

BACK-OF-THE-ENVELOPE

The Economics of a Safety Valve

The purpose of a safety valve is to relieve pressure. How is the notion of a safety valve relevant in analyzing medical care markets? Consider two medical care markets separated in some manner: the primary market and the safety valve. Supply is restricted through limits on the number of operating rooms, imaging devices, and other procedures requiring sophisticated medical technology. To keep prices and spending down, the governing authorities place a price ceiling in the primary market as shown in the left-hand side of the diagram.

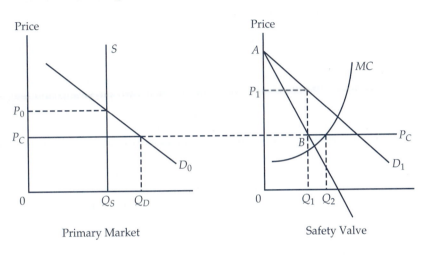

Primary Market   Safety Valve

The vertical supply curve S fixes the quantity supplied at Q_S. Instead of allowing the market price P_0 to prevail, government sets a price ceiling at P_C and creates a shortage of $Q_D - Q_S$. The excess demand causes problems with waiting lists and angry patients. Given a certain degree of geographic mobility, patients in the primary market can travel to the unrestricted market, the safety valve, and receive treatment.

Suppose the payer in the primary market agrees to finance the care received in the safety valve at the controlled price P_C. Providers in the unrestricted market face a marginal revenue curve with a downward-sloping segment, AB, and a horizontal segment, BP_0. Marginal cost crosses this combined marginal revenue curve at Q_2 output. If capacity in the unrestricted market is less than Q_1, all of the available capacity will be devoted to consumers in that market, because they willingly pay P_1. If providers in the unrestricted market have capacity beyond Q_1, those consumers shut out of the primary market can get care through the safety valve at price P_C. Providers in the unrestricted market practice price discrimination, charging P_1 to the original customers and P_C to the overflow from the primary market.

Information about the Pasteur Institute's contributions, conferences, and publications—much of it in English—may be found at their Web site.

http://www.pasteur.fr/english.html

laissez faire
A French term meaning literally "allow [them] to do." It depicts a situation in which individuals and firms are allowed to pursue their own self-interests without government restraint.

Key Concept 9
Market Failure

sickness fund
A quasi-governmental group that serves as an insurance company by collecting premiums and paying providers within the national health care system of France and Germany.

FRANCE: EQUALITY, LIBERTY, FRATERNITY[7]

Even though France is often depicted as the birthplace of European democracy, the nation actually adopted a highly centralized system of government during the reign of Napoleon Bonaparte. Since that time, the French have tried to maintain a delicate balance between individual freedom and collective action. Economic and social policy is based, in varying degrees, on three principles that the French hold dear: a national spirit of egalitarianism, a respect for individual freedom, and a commitment to minimal state intervention. In other words, the French attempt to strike a balance between solidarity, choice, and competition.

The potential for conflict among these principles is easy to recognize, and nowhere is it more evident than in the nation's complex system of medical care delivery. The national spirit of egalitarianism is manifested in the preamble to the French Constitution: "The nation guarantees to all protection of health." The social security system serves not only to provide health insurance for everyone, but also serves as a mechanism to redistribute income and provide social solidarity. Respect for individual freedom is evident in the provision for patient choice and physician autonomy. Patients are free to choose their own physicians and may see a specialist without referral.

As economic theory would suggest, unconstrained pursuit of these two principles has led to escalating costs. Again, patients who are provided with care at zero price use it as if it had zero resource cost. Providers who are free to treat with little consideration for cost effectiveness tend to overprescribe. In 1960, the government intervened with regulatory reform, maintaining the principles of liberty and solidarity but compromising the principle of **laissez faire.** In its place, state control over prices and budgets was substituted in an effort to moderate spending.

As in many other European countries, national health insurance in France grew out of a nineteenth-century system that provided certain industrial workers and miners with insurance through mutual aid societies, or **sickness funds.** Legislation passed in 1928 made membership compulsory for many low-wage occupations, but coverage was still far from universal. It was not until after World War II, when the economic and social infrastructure was being rebuilt, that everyone was brought into the system. The national health insurance system is administered through 16 regional and 133 local funds, each with a self-managing board. Seventeen other funds cover specific occupational groups, including agricultural workers, public employees, independent professionals, and full-time students. Deficits are also a common problem, and the system has consistently run a deficit since its inception in the 1950s. For example, the general health insurance fund that covers 80 percent of the population ran a deficit of €8 billion (approximately $9 billion) in 2005, creating strong dissatisfaction among patients and providers.[8]

Health policy makers have found it difficult to satisfy the goal of universal access and control cost at the same time. Financing is primarily from social insurance but with a significant private, complementary insurance component. The system was originally financed almost exclusively on a payroll tax. As of early 1994, the payroll

---

[7] This section is based on Henderson (1993).

[8] Substantial financial reform is expected in the near future with a transfer of some types of care to complementary insurance, including dental, optical, drugs, and hearing aids. Alternatively, some have suggested that national health insurance cover only a basic level of benefits with reimbursement based on strict guidelines, leaving complementary insurance to cover additional care, depending on the preferences and willingness to pay of the individual (LePen, 2003).

tax had increased to 18.95 percent with employers paying two-thirds of the tax directly.[9] As of 2001, salary-based contributions accounted for only 60 percent of the total public financing with the remainder coming from a special income tax. Employers now pay 12.8 percent of an employee's salary into the health insurance fund, and employees pay 0.75 percent. In addition, a tax on income and capital averages approximately 7.5 percent on income for those individuals who pay income tax. This reduced reliance on payroll taxes has taken some of the pressure off employers but has not decreased the overall cost of coverage, which now totals over 21 percent of the income of the typical worker.

All employees are covered by French social security legislation and must contribute to the national social security system. The system is divided into four branches: life and health insurance, occupational disability insurance, old-age pension, and family leave.

In addition to the premiums, patients must pay a substantial copayment for both ambulatory and hospital care. The typical arrangement is for the patient to pay the entire medical fee when services are received. After paying the physician, the patient may then apply for a reimbursement of 75 to 80 percent of the prescribed fee. Low-income individuals who earn less than €6,600 annually are not expected to pay in advance. Hospital patients must pay 20 percent for hospital services plus a daily room charge of €10 (approximately $15) subject to a 30-day maximum. The hospital then bills the appropriate national health insurance fund for the balance. Patient copays for laboratory tests and dental care are 30 percent. Patients must pay 35 to 65 percent of the cost of covered prescription drugs and 100 percent for noncovered prescription drugs.[10] The patient is responsible for any extra billing. To avoid copays at the point of service and balance billings, the French have shown a preference for paying for complementary insurance. The role of private, complementary insurance has expanded over the past 40 years, enabling the French to avoid most of the negative consequences associated with health care rationing. This coverage is available from mutual societies, not-for-profit insurance companies, and commercial, for-profit insurance companies. In 2001, approximately 87 percent of the population purchased complementary coverage, up from 31 percent in 1960. Private insurance premiums vary depending on labor force status but average 2.5 percent of income (Pomey and Poullier, 1997).

As of 2006 there were approximately 207,000 physicians in active practice nationwide, 340 per 100,000 population.[11] About one-third of all physicians are in exclusively private practice, and another one-third are fully salaried. The remainder have a mixed practice—they hold a salaried position with either a large public hospital or a municipality health center and, at the same time, have a part-time private practice. About half of the physicians are considered general practitioners (GPs). The other half are specialists, most with mixed practices.

Approximately 75 percent of medical practitioners are considered first-tier: 83 percent of all GPs and 62 percent of all specialists. First-tier physicians contract with the national health insurance agencies and are reimbursed on a fee-for-service

---

[9] This is somewhat high, even by European standards. German employers pay half of the health care premiums of their workers, which ranged from 10 to 16 percent of total payroll, with an average of 14.3 percent. U.S. employers contributed 5.3 percent of payroll toward health insurance premiums in 2005. For the 56 percent of businesses that offered health insurance, premiums accounted for 10.3 percent of payroll.

[10] Certain vital drugs required for individuals with serious or debilitating conditions are reimbursed 100 percent.

[11] Lack of an official census of physicians makes the actual figure somewhat of a guess.

basis according to a nationally negotiated fee schedule. The fee schedule combines a relative value scale that assigns points to the various services and procedures with a monetary conversion factor.[12]

Before 1980, physicians considered prestigious by a commission of their peers were allowed to charge fees that exceeded the legal ceiling. In 1980, pressure from physicians' organizations forced the government to allow any physician to apply for this second-tier status that carried with it the ability to balance bill at rates up to 50 percent over the approved fee schedule. By 1990, concern over high out-of-pocket costs for physicians' services led the government to suspend new entry into the second tier, effectively closing that means of resource allocation.[13] About 25 percent of all physicians are now second tier.

Even with the pricing flexibility enjoyed by some physicians, fee schedules have had a significant effect on physicians' incomes. In 2002, physician incomes ranged from $57,300 for primary care physicians to $116,000 for hospital physicians (Barham and Bremley-Harker, 2004). French physicians average less than one-third to one-half of what the typical American physician earned that same year. Not only are French physicians' salaries low by U.S. standards, their relative position within the country has eroded over the course of the past two decades. In 1970, the average physician's salary was three times that of the average French wage and salary worker. By 1997, it was barely twice that.

Key Concept 2
Opportunity Cost

Most medical students study at one of 29 university-affiliated hospital centers located primarily in the regional capitals. Although first year admission at the 41 medical schools is open to all comers, entry into the second year is controlled by a quota—less than 4,000 annually (down from 8,588 in 1972). The stated goal of 250 physicians per 100,000 population has been exceeded somewhat, and the geographic distribution of physicians is uneven with shortages in the north and in rural areas. No policy has been enacted to limit physician autonomy.[14]

Hospital care is provided at one of three types of institutions: public hospitals, private nonprofit hospitals, and private for-profit clinics. In 1998, public sector hospitals contained 72 percent of the total beds, private nonprofits had 6 percent, and private for-profit clinics had 22 percent (Green and Irvine, 2001). The most prestigious functions are performed in the public institutions: teaching, basic research, and high-tech diagnostic and surgical procedures. Public hospitals account for 75 percent of the hospital expenses but less than 60 percent of the short-stay hospital days.

Reform in 1983 changed the nature of the hospital reimbursement mechanism. Public hospitals, and the majority of the private nonprofit hospitals, are covered by prospective global budgeting with salaried physicians. Patients cannot choose their physicians in a public hospital unless they have first seen a specialist during that physician's part-time private practice. Private for-profit clinics receive the national per diem payment, and physicians treating patients in those clinics receive

---

[12] The French relative value scale assigns values for each service and procedure, much like the Medicare RBRVS, but the relative weightings for procedures are not technical (i.e., they are not based on time, intensity, complexity, or training requirements as in the United States). They are based more on the political influence of the various specialties and consumer preferences. The crude nature of the RVS has created price distortions in the fee schedule that encourage inefficient medical practices (Rodwin, 1981).

[13] With about 25 percent of all physicians allowed to balance bill, private spending for physicians' services was 23.5 percent in 2001, covered by complementary insurance and out-of-pocket spending.

[14] Policy makers continue to explore new ways to limit spending. Ministry of Health officials have considered the extension of utilization controls and prospective budgeting to individual physicians as a means of controlling expenditures on physicians' services (U.S. Government Accounting Office, November 1991).

the standard fee. Physicians in exclusively private practice cannot treat patients in public hospitals.[15]

Public hospitals are required by law to keep occupancy rates below 95 percent of capacity. In addition, they must remain open 24 hours a day, and they must maintain a fully equipped emergency room.[16] Private clinics usually focus on more profitable services, elective surgeries and maternity, and avoid the high-cost procedures. Not surprisingly, the average costs of public hospitals tend to be higher than private clinics. Over the years, clinics have been successful in maintaining profitability by unbundling their services and thus removing certain procedures from the standard per diem rates.

The introduction of advanced technology has caused policy makers some problems in controlling health care spending. In addition to the extra investment, modern medical equipment requires more technical expertise for those who operate the equipment. This requirement translates into advanced training for physicians, nurses, and technicians and greater rates of remuneration for this new expertise.

From 1980 to 1990, France experienced the largest increase in the volume and intensity of services among countries discussed in this chapter. This has increased the pressure to control the nominal increase in per capita health care spending. Recent increases in copays are an attempt to dampen consumer demand and slow the rate of growth in spending.

Key Concept 9
Market Failure

Economic theory clearly indicates that strict budget controls will lead to lower investment in high-cost technology. Budget considerations require regulation of investment in medical equipment. The more stringent the controls, the harder it will be for hospitals to adequately maintain their facilities and invest in quality-enhancing medical equipment. Theoretically, equipment standards are set to meet physician recommendations, but in actual practice, investment in medical equipment is a fiscal decision made with the approval of the Ministry of Health. The evidence suggests that since the introduction of global budgeting in 1984, innovation has been adversely affected, and quality of care has suffered. The National Health Authority has created a mechanism to judge the effectiveness of medical procedures and technology, using the concept of medical service rendered (MSR). If MSR is determined to be insufficient, the product or procedure is no longer eligible for reimbursement, effectively removing it from use.

POLICY ISSUE

Is it possible to establish a tightly controlled national health care budget without creating shortages of medical technology?

The introduction and diffusion of new technology, especially when it requires costly equipment, has been much slower in France than in the United States. A look at Table 14.1 provides a summary of the adoption levels for four costly diagnostic and treatment services. The French have less than one lithotripter for every million residents; the United States has one for every 312,500 residents. The French have one MRI for every 212,700 residents, compared to one per 37,600 in the U.S.; and there is one CT scanner for every 102,000, compared to one per 31,000 in the U.S.

Imposition of a single public insurance plan does not guarantee equal health outcomes. Occupational and geographic disparities in life expectancy exist despite universal access. Male life expectancy at age 35 varies by as much as seven years between professional workers and laborers. Life expectancy at birth in Midi-Pyrénées in the south is over four years greater than in Nord-Pas-de-Calais in the north.

---

[15] A limited number can admit patients for outpatient services.

[16] In order to promote uniform quality across the hospital system, air conditioning is not allowed. This restriction played a role in the high death toll, estimated at 15,000, resulting from the record heat wave experienced in central Europe in the summer of 2003.

Access to resources differs by region. Ile-de-France has 423 physicians per 100,000 compared to 249 in Picardie (Petkantchin, 2007).

The national health insurance system in France covers virtually 100 percent of the country's population. In their quest for social solidarity and equality, however, the French have given up a lot. Practitioners have suffered erosion in their real incomes relative to the rest of the population. The system imposes global budgets on public hospitals, limits the availability of medical technology, and requires high out-of-pocket spending in the name of cost control. Physician autonomy remains intact, at least in the private sector. Public support remains high, due at least in part to the system's ability to avoid the wait-list problems experienced in Canada and the United Kingdom. The French system is at a crossroads. Fundamental change is needed because of chronic operating deficits. But the change needed is a change in philosophy, something the French people are not prepared for (LePen, 2003).

GERMANY: SICKNESS FUNDS[17]

After World War II, Germany was divided into two separate entities by the Allies. The German Democratic Republic (East Germany) was under the influence of the former Soviet Union and adopted the Socialist form of government. The Federal Republic of Germany (West Germany) maintained its connections with the West and continued to utilize the prewar economic system, including the health care delivery system. East and West Germany were unified by treaty in 1990, and since that time, East Germany has been subjected to most West German laws, including legislation relating to the medical insurance system. With a combined population of 82.4 million, Germany is divided into 16 provinces or Laenders, each with a great deal of independence in determining matters related to health and education.

The overall provision of health insurance, from organization to financing, is a provincial responsibility. Administrative control was the responsibility of approximately 282 sickness funds in 2004, financed by the social insurance scheme established by federal law (Tamm, Tauchmann, Wasem, and Gress, 2006).[18]

Germany's health care system has its origins in the "mutual aid societies" created in the early nineteenth century. The German system of social benefits is based on the concept of social insurance as embodied in three founding principles: social solidarity, subsidiarity, and corporatism. The principle of social solidarity means that government is obligated to provide access to a wide range of social benefits to all citizens, including medical care, old-age pensions, unemployment insurance, disability payments, maternity benefits, and other forms of social welfare, and that everybody contributes according to their ability to pay. Subsidiarity refers to a decentralized system in which policy is implemented by the smallest possible administrative unit. Corporatism is manifested in the governing boards of sickness funds, which have widespread participation from business, medical providers, and insurers.

By the time Otto von Bismarck became Germany's first chancellor in 1871, hundreds of sickness insurance funds were already in operation. Bismarck, a member of the Prussian aristocracy, saw the working class movement represented by socialist-oriented political parties as a threat. This concern led him to advocate

---

[17] Thanks to Klaus Geldsetzer for his insightful comments on this section. Of course, any remaining errors and omissions are my responsibility.

[18] Legislation passed in 1993 and 1997 encouraged competition among sickness funds and led to a decrease in their number from over 1,300 in 1993. The number is expected to fall even further as a result of mergers and acquisitions.

the expansion of the existing sickness benefit societies to cover workers in all low-wage occupations. In 1883, the Sickness Insurance Act was passed, representing the first social insurance program organized on a national level.

In the past 130 years, the system has grown to the point that virtually all of the population is provided access to medical care. All individuals are required by law to have health insurance. Those earning less than €47,250 (in 2006, about $56,000) must join one of the sickness funds for their health care coverage. Those earning more than the threshold may choose private health insurance instead.[19] Approximately 74 percent of the population is compelled to join a sickness fund. Another 14 percent are members voluntarily, even though their income exceeds the statutory cutoff. The remaining 10 percent, about 8 million, have comprehensive private insurance.

By 2001, approximately one of every ten Germans covered by sickness fund insurance also purchased private supplementary insurance to cover copayments and other amenities, including overseas treatment, greater privacy during treatment, and private-room supplements. Private insurance may be tailored to meet the needs of individual patients; individuals may choose policies that offer full coverage with no deductibles or coinsurance requirements, or they may instead choose policies with those features (Green and Irvine, 2001).

Individual health insurance premiums for workers enrolled in sickness funds are calculated on the basis of income and not age or the number of dependents. Premiums are collected through a payroll deduction that varies from 10.2 to 15.7 percent of a worker's gross salary.[20] The average contribution was 14.3 percent in 2003. An additional contribution for long-term care insurance of 1.7 percent of income (1.95 percent for childless couples) has been required since 1996, bringing the average contribution for health insurance plus long-term care insurance to over 16 percent of payroll.[21] The average payroll tax has risen sharply over the past 40 years. It was 6 percent in 1950 and rose to 8.4 percent by 1960, 11.4 percent by 1980, and 13.2 percent in 1995. Employers pay half of the tax directly for their workers. The Federal Labor Administration or local welfare agencies pay the premiums of those who are unemployed.[22] Retirees pay a percentage of their pensions equal to the average contribution paid by workers. Private insurance premiums vary, depending on the type of policy chosen, and they average 20 percent less than the average payroll tax. Private benefits are better, and per capita administrative costs are half those of the public system (Prewo, 1993).

Membership in a sickness fund entitles a person to a comprehensive package of medical and dental benefits. Germans can expect to receive high-quality care that includes hospital care, ambulatory care, prescription drugs, dental care, disability income benefits, and even visits to health spas. The system is weak in several areas. In particular, public health services and psychiatric services are minimal.

The German health care system was experiencing the same problems as the rest of the developed world in controlling health care costs during the decades

---

[19] Regardless of salary, government employees and the self-employed can choose private insurance.

[20] Premiums are capped by the income threshold. Workers earning more than €47,250 and choosing a public sickness fund pay a premium equal to 14 percent of the first €47,250, or €6,615. This premium also covers nonworking family members.

[21] The long-term care fund has consistently run deficits since 1999. Unless benefits are reduced or the contribution rate increased, the program is unsustainable. Younger Germans are already paying an extra 0.7 percent of income into the fund, and it has been estimated that it will take an additional 3.2 to 5.9 percent of payroll income to make the fund solvent again (Arntz et al., 2006).

[22] Low-income individuals are also exempted from paying into the health insurance fund. The income limit for free care is approximately €500 per month in the East and €600 per month in the West.

of the 1960s and 1970s. Economic recession in the mid-1970s forced government policy makers to address the issue of the growth in medical expenditures. In 1977, the first of over 40 health care acts was passed to control rising health care spending and avoid the financial collapse of the system. The stated goal was to limit the growth of health care expenditures to the growth of wages and salaries while maintaining open access to the system.

Health care spending grew more rapidly than GDP, and government initiated five major reforms during the 1990s to slow spending growth. The 2004 reform added copayments for physicians' visits and increased them for prescription drugs.

Copayments are still low by U.S. standards. The first office visit to a physician during a calendar quarter has a patient copay of €10 (approximately $15) with an annual cap on out-of-pocket spending of 2 percent of income. There are no copays for preventive care visits, including physicals, dental exams, and cancer screenings. Fees for prescription drugs are 10 percent of the drug's price and range from €9 to €13 based on package size. Hospital charges are about €10 per day for the first 28 days, and inpatient preventive and rehabilitative care is also €10 per day. Copays for dental services are another matter, and many procedures have copays as high as 50 to 100 percent of the cost. Children and low-income individuals are exempt from most copays, and the chronically ill have an annual cap of 1 percent of income.

The results have been dramatic. Nominal per capita spending had increased at an annual rate of 12.2 percent during the 1970s. After initiation of the cost-control measures, the annual rate of growth in spending fell to 4.5 percent from 1980 to 1998. This record is second only to Japan among the major developed countries in the Organization of Economic Cooperation and Development (OECD).

Germany's success in controlling costs can be attributed to the institutional framework of the system itself. Physicians are divided into two categories: ambulatory care physicians and hospital physicians. Ambulatory care physicians are paid on a fee-for-service basis and, for the most part, are prohibited from treating patients in a hospital setting. Hospital physicians are paid a salary and are not allowed to treat patients on an outpatient basis. The fees that physicians are allowed to charge are determined through negotiations between the sickness funds and regional physicians' organizations.

Hospitals are paid under a dual financing scheme with operating expenses covered by the sickness funds and capital investments covered by the state. Diagnosis related groups (DRGs) have been introduced into the hospital sector. With over 2,000 hospitals subject to the growing list of DRGs, the health authorities hope to reduce the average length of stay, now among the highest in Europe, by 30 percent.[23]

More than 100,000 students attend one of the 29 medical schools run by the state. After completing the six-year curriculum, physicians must first practice in a hospital setting for six years before they are allowed to enter private practice. Approximately 9,500 graduate each year and enter hospital practice.

By linking medical expenditures to the income of sickness fund members, the success of the policy depends upon the continued growth in wages and salaries and the success of the negotiations between sickness funds and medical practitioners. The cost-containment measures have resulted in a dramatic decrease in the relative salaries of primary care physicians, falling from 5.1 times the average for wage and salary workers in 1975 to 2.7 times that average in 1990. By U.S. standards, physicians' salaries are relatively low. In 2003, the average primary care physician

Key Concept 2
Opportunity Cost

---

[23] By 2004, the new compulsory system contains over 600 DRGs.

earned $71,443; hospital-based physicians earned between $35,465 and $56,455 (Barham and Bramley-Harker, 2004).

In 2002, there were over 2,000 general hospitals with 600,000 beds (54 percent publicly owned, 38 percent private not-for-profit, and 8 percent private for-profit). An additional 190,000 beds were available in 1,400 preventive care and rehabilitation facilities. Hospitals also have less high-technology diagnostic, therapeutic, and surgical equipment than is available in the typical urban hospital in the United States. Germany has one-fourth fewer MRI units per million compared to the United States and half the number of CT scanners per million. The one area in which Germany has more technology is lithotripters: 3.7 per million compared to 3.2 in the United States.

Although the negotiated fee schedule controls the unit price of medical care, it does nothing to limit the volume of services provided. Individual physicians can increase their income by treating more patients, but if every physician tries this strategy, global budget limits reduce unit fees proportionately. Thus, physicians who treat sickness fund patients never know in advance exactly how much they will be paid for a certain procedure. Physicians who treat privately insured patients are allowed to charge fees that are up to 3.5 times higher than fees charged to sickness fund patients. As a result, privately insured patients tend to get better service.

The German system suffers from several problems that bring into question its ability to contain costs over the long term. Real spending rose almost 50 percent between 1990 and 1996. Possibly the biggest problem with the system, shared with all systems discussed in this chapter, is its reliance on third-party payment, which provides virtually no role for the cost-conscious consumer. Patients have little incentive to limit their demand, and medical providers have little incentive to limit their supply. The only competition is among medical practitioners to attract more patient volume. The ability of the system to control costs depends primarily on the relative bargaining power between sickness funds and medical providers. Because expenditures are determined by negotiations between these two groups, the recent success in controlling costs is the result of legislative reform that has shifted the relative bargaining strength to the sickness funds. Continued success depends on the willingness of physicians' organizations to accept the burden of the responsibility in controlling costs, which translates into falling relative incomes.

Key Concept 7
Competition

Recent reform has introduced a warning system, a budget-capping mechanism that directly challenges the independence of physicians. Those physicians whose per patient spending exceeds the average are subject to a medical practice review. Physicians who exceed the average spending by 5 to 15 percent must submit a letter of explanation. Those who exceed their budgets by 15 to 25 percent must convince a panel of physicians and sickness fund representatives that the spending was justified based on medical factors. Physicians exceeding their budgets by more than 25 percent are subject to fines in the form of reduced fees. About 7 percent of German physicians receive notice of overspending each year, and about half of those have their fees reduced. These fines amount to 100 percent of the amount in excess of 1.25 times their budgets.

The incentive structure created by the budget-capping mechanism has changed the way physicians relate to their patients. Anecdotal evidence indicates that physicians treat less-demanding patients less aggressively, which is cheaper, and that they use more expensive therapies and procedures that are not part of their budgets when less expensive means are available that are part of their budgets. Recent studies also indicate that private patients are up to four times more likely to receive the newest drugs than sickness fund patients (Green and Irvine, 2001).

Another problem with the system is its tendency to use resources inefficiently. Incentives promote the provision of invasive acute care procedures and discourage the provision of personal services. Based on the latest available OECD figures, Germans see their doctors more often, are provided more prescription drugs, have a higher hospital admission rate, and stay in the hospital longer than citizens of the major developed countries in the OECD. The average length of stay in the hospital was 50 percent higher in Germany than in the United States in 2005 (8.6 days compared to 5.6 days). Significant excess capacity in the number of hospital beds relative to the population exists in Germany, where there are 6.4 beds per 1,000 population, compared to 2.7 in the United States. Even with strict cost-containment measures for prescription drugs, average drug prices are higher in Germany than in any other member country of the European Community.

Key Concept 5
Markets and Pricing

What lessons can be learned from the German system of medical care delivery? First and foremost, a system that provides comprehensive coverage and mandates universal participation is expensive. Germans paid an average of 15.9 percent of their gross income in premiums in 2003, and over 11 percent of total medical expenditures are unreimbursed out-of-pocket charges. Secondly, cost control in a government-run system is usually accomplished through a system of global budgets and caps on expenditures for physicians' services. Germany has managed to keep spending within targeted amounts by establishing an explicit trade-off between volume and price. In other words, when utilization is higher than anticipated, fees are lowered proportionately. Thirdly, spending caps instituted in 1985 as a temporary cost-containment measure have become permanent. Legislation adopted in 1993 and 1997, designed to increase competition among sickness funds, lowered pharmaceutical prices and physicians' fees, increased required copayments, and placed more regulations on hospital billing practices—all to reach desired spending targets. Even with all these changes, support for the system remains high, in part because wealthy Germans have a private insurance safety valve and with it the ability to buy more physician time and better services.

POLICY ISSUE

How important is the private insurance safety valve in maintaining public support for a government-run health care system?

JAPAN: THE COMPANY IS PEOPLE

One of the most notable accomplishments of Japanese postwar development has been the exceptionally good record of health and longevity of the population. Life expectancy at birth for both males and females ranks at the top of the industrialized countries (in 2003, 78.4 years for males and 85.3 years for females). Likewise, infant mortality rates are among the lowest of the countries charted by the OECD (2.8 in 2004). Undoubtedly, the medical care system has contributed to this record, but the extent of the contribution is hard to define.[24]

The Japanese enjoy an environment that is relatively free of crime, pollution, and other social problems such as divorce, teen pregnancy, obesity, drug use, and HIV. When compared to the United States, the Japanese have a much lower incidence of alcohol consumption, AIDS, drug abuse, teen pregnancy, and motor vehicle accidents.[25] The Japanese diet is relatively low in fat, resulting, at least partially, in an extremely low rate of cardiovascular disease (Murdo, 1993). Some

---

[24] If the health of a population is measured by disease incidence, then it is not nearly as evident whether the Japanese are healthier. Self-reported health status in surveys of Japanese citizens is among the lowest among OECD countries with less than half reporting their perceived health as good. That same figure is over 90 percent in the United States (OECD Health Data, 2003).

[25] One major exception is the high percentage of the adult male population that uses tobacco products.

Japanese health experts have stated that by comparison, the delivery of medical care in Japan is like treating only the middle class in California (Sterngold, 1992).

Japan is a country of 127.8 million living on four major islands and 3,900 smaller islands. With most of the land mass—about the size of California—covered by mountains, the vast majority of the population is crowded into the urban areas. The population density is over 12 times that of the United States, making it the third most densely populated nation in the world, behind only Bangladesh and South Korea. Japan is divided into 47 prefectures with jurisdictional authority similar to that of states in the United States.

ISSUES IN MEDICAL CARE DELIVERY

In Search of the Perfect Bellybutton

Japanese women are increasingly taking action to correct one of those tiny flaws of nature—the misshapen bellybutton. Japanese culture is bellybutton conscious. Japanese mothers save remnants of their baby's umbilical cords in a wooden box, much like American mothers save a lock of their newborn's hair. In Japan, a naval bent out of shape means much the same as a nose bent out of shape in America. And in Japan "your mother has an outie" is a slang expression that would translate in America as "yeah, right, give me a break."

Bare midriffs and body ornamentation require the fashion-conscious Japanese twenty-something woman to have the perfect bellybutton. And if nature did not provide one, then cosmetic surgery will. Plastic surgeons all across the country are charging up to $2,000 for a procedure that can turn an unattractive outie into a perfectly symmetrical fashion statement. Because it is not considered health care, the procedure is not covered by national health insurance.

Source: Norihiko Shirouzu, "Reconstruction Boom in Tokyo: Perfecting Imperfect Bellybuttons," *Wall Street Journal*, October 5, 1995, B1.

The medical care delivery system in Japan has evolved from the modernization efforts initiated during the Meiji Restoration dating from 1868. In the place of the primitive structure of the feudal system, the institutions and practices of the developed world were adopted. Because Germany had what was considered the most advanced medical care system at that time, it was used as the model. The formation of "mutual aid associations" in the early 1900s served as the foundation for the medical care system. And like Germany, the development of these associations among workers in Japan had as much to do with controlling a disruptive socialist movement as with promoting social welfare. The promotion and improvement of public health is a national responsibility according to the constitution. Even so, universal coverage was not fully realized until 1961.

The Universal Health Insurance system is regulated by the Ministry of Health and Welfare. The entire population is organized into small, independently administered health insurance societies that serve as intermediaries for its members. Individuals and their dependents are assigned to one of these organizations according to profession, trade, or employer.

Prior to the Second World War, two national health insurance laws were enacted that serve as the basis for the modern-day system. The first act in 1922 created the Employee Health Insurance System (EHI) that now covers 64 percent of the population. Health coverage is provided by more than 5,000 independent plans that provide government-managed health insurance for firms with 5 to 300 employees, society managed health insurance for firms with more than 300 employees, seaman's insurance, public employees' insurance, and insurance for private school employees.

The second health insurance act passed in 1938 created the Citizens' Health Insurance System (CHI). The self-employed and pensioners, comprising 36 percent of the population, are covered under this plan. Since 1947, over 60 laws have been passed to further define the principles and policies of the national health care system. Because each plan was developed separately, they lack uniformity in terms of costs and cost-sharing arrangements.

Premiums are based on earnings, not health status or age. Employers are required by law to pay at least half of the monthly premium directly, which varies from 6.0 to 9.6 percent of monthly income, up to a maximum of $430 per household per month.[26] With few exceptions, each insurance plan sets its own premiums, which may vary as much as 200 percent from plan to plan. Copayments in all plans were raised from 10 percent to 20 percent in 1997. Dependent copays are even higher for some types of services. CHI copays are a uniform 30 percent, except for retirees, who pay 20 percent.

Out-of-pocket expenditures are capped for each plan. EHI maximums are 63,000 yen per month (about $530) for most members. Certain low-wage recipients have a 30,000-yen maximum per person (about $260) per month. In 1983, the Health and Medical Services System for the Elderly was established. One of the expressed goals of the plan was to reduce the incidence of moral hazard by providing a modest cost-sharing arrangement. Individuals over age 70 and all those bedridden over age 65 must pay a modest user charge of 700 yen (about $6) for every day in the hospital and 1,000 yen (about $9) per month for outpatient care. All out-of-pocket copays amount to 12 percent of total health care spending.

For 8 percent of GDP, the Japanese receive a comprehensive package of benefits for virtually every legal resident. Medical procedures that are not associated with the onset of a disease are not included in the basic insurance package. Virtually all preventive care, physical examinations, and procedures related to normal pregnancies are not covered by national health insurance. In fact, out-of-pocket spending for these services is not even counted as part of national health expenditures.[27]

Physicians fall into two categories: clinic-based and hospital-based. Clinic-based physicians operate out of more than 85,850 privately owned facilities. Over 22,000 of these clinics are actually short-term hospitals with less than 20 beds each. Statutory regulations requiring that patients be moved to hospitals after 48 hours are largely ignored and not enforced.

Medical services are provided on a fee-for-service basis using a fixed price, "point-fee" system. This negotiated schedule provides uniform pricing regardless of specialty of physician and service setting, and thus it offers few financial incentives to improve quality. Clinic-based physicians receive payments directly. Hospital-based physicians receive a salary, and hospitals receive payments for services performed there.

---

[26] The employer share ranges from 50 percent to 80 percent and averages 56 percent. The average payroll tax is 8.5 percent of income.

[27] National expenditure data also exclude expenses for physical exams, vaccinations, prescription eyeglasses, prosthetic devices, and treatment by alternative providers such as acupuncturists. Items such as spending on public health and medical research are not classified as medical expenditures.

The number of clinic-based physicians has been falling for the past 30 years, and thus their political influence is waning. In 1960, they comprised 45 percent of the total number of physicians. By 1988, this percentage had fallen to 30. There are several reasons for this decline. Land prices in urban areas have priced most newcomers out of the market, and the demand for high-tech diagnostic equipment has allowed the large hospitals to siphon off much of this market share. The slowly increasing average age of clinic-based physicians has been a factor, and a growing use of outpatient facilities has increased the use of large hospitals over clinics.

In 1994, physicians earned on average $53,000 (adjusted for purchasing power parity), approximately two times the income of the average wage and salary worker in Japan and only one-third that of U.S. physicians (Nakahara, 1997). Clinic-based physicians earn on average about twice the income of hospital-based physicians. Physicians working in the nation's 9,286 hospitals are paid the same regardless of specialty. There are two things that keep hospitals adequately staffed: the prestige of a hospital appointment and the "expressions of gratitude" paid by patients to secure the services of a specialist. It is not uncommon for patients to provide gifts ranging from $1,000 to $3,000 to obtain the services of a prominent specialist. These hidden charges, which some would call bribes, are not documented and go largely untaxed.[28]

The typical Japanese citizen has an extreme aversion to invasive treatment. They prefer medication and bed rest to surgery. Thus, surgical rates are among the lowest in the world, one-third the U.S. rates, and prescription drug use among the highest, over one-fourth of health care spending in 1997. In fact, the single most lucrative aspect of the clinic-based practice is the sale of prescription medicine. Not only are surgical rates low, but also organ transplantation is almost nonexistent. The Japanese failure to recognize death as the cessation of brain wave activity makes it extremely difficult to find suitable organ donors, placing an effective ban on transplants.

The point-fee system introduces a bias in the medical care delivery system, one that favors primary care. All physicians, regardless of specialty, practice like GPs: they focus on diagnostic and pharmaceutical services at the expense of technical and specialty care. Thus, no formal system of referral to specialists has emerged. Financial incentives encourage physicians to be protective of their patient volume, and expensive treatment areas tend to be ignored. Cancer treatment, neonatal pediatrics, and emergency/trauma medicine are specialties found only in the large public hospitals, where there is little incentive to provide high-quality service.

Direct comparison between health care spending in Japan and the United States is difficult for reasons already mentioned. Maternity expenses, the direct cost of medical education and research, grants to public hospitals, and public health promotions—all are included in the United States figure but ignored by the Japanese. Including these alone would increase Japanese spending by 1.5 percent of GDP. In addition, private room charges add about $100 per day to a hospital stay that already averages 20 days.[29]

Japanese physicians tend to overdiagnose and overmedicate, and patient volume tends to be high. It is not unusual for clinic-based physicians to see 30 to 35 patients

POLICY ISSUE

What role does culture play in the development of a national health care delivery system?

Key Concept 2
Opportunity Cost

---

[28] Interestingly enough, over half of the income of physicians is tax-free in the first place. Until recently, 72 percent of a physician's income was free from income taxes. Changes in the tax code have reduced the preferential status, so that only 52 to 72 percent escape taxation.

[29] This figure includes both chronic and acute care hospital stays. It does not include stays in TB hospitals that average 207 days or stays in psychiatric hospitals that average 536 days.

an hour. Specialists tend to spend more time with each patient. By U.S. standards, the total time spent with patients is still low. Ophthalmologists see 15 patients an hour, and OB/GYNs see 15 to 20. Appointments are almost nonexistent. Patients are seen on a first-come-first-served basis. Long waits are common, with queues for ambulatory visits and waiting lists for hospitalization.

Capital funding for hospital infrastructure must come from fee revenues. The Medical Care Law, amended in 1985 to "control the excessive increase in hospital beds," restricted the establishment of private hospitals. The law placed a ceiling on the number of hospital beds per region and has made it virtually impossible to build new hospitals in urban areas (Yoshikawa, Shirouzu, and Holt, 1991). Even prestigious hospitals in urban areas, including Tokyo, are marked by poor infrastructure, small rooms, and few support staff.

BACK-OF-THE-ENVELOPE

Promoting Equality

The rationale behind the public provision of medical care is easy to explain. Market failure results in a level of care that is less than optimal. Two approaches have been used with varying degrees of success to promote a more equal sharing of scarce medical care resources: subsidize and ration. Subsidies for the poor increase the amount of care they receive, and rationing reduces the amount of care provided to everyone else. Both policies promote a more equal distribution of medical care consumption. Why would a group of high-income consumers agree to limit their own access to care in the name of promoting equality? Lindsay (1969) provided a theoretical justification for the simultaneous use of rationing and subsidies to promote equality in medical care consumption.

In the diagram, D_1 and D_2 represent the respective demand curves for two different segments of the population. Group 1 has less income and a lower level of demand. Assuming a perfectly elastic supply, S, they will consume Q_1 units of medical care. Those with higher incomes have a higher level of demand, D_2, and will consume Q_2 units of medical care. Countries such as Great Britain and Canada have chosen to address the inequality $Q_2 - Q_1$ by providing universal coverage through taxation and subsidy and by placing limits on the availability of certain procedures.

The cost of these policies is shown in the right-hand side of the diagram. The cost of producing equality via rationing is the consumer surplus forgone by the higher income group. The vertical distance between D_2 and S represents the forgone consumer surplus. Thus, the marginal cost of promoting equality through rationing, MC_R, has a slope equal to the absolute value of the slope of D_2. Every unit of care given up by Group 2 creates a unit of equality at a marginal cost equal to the forgone consumer surplus of Group 2.

To induce the poor to consume more than Q_1 requires a subsidy. This subsidy can never be greater than P_1, the cost of care, but must be at least equal to the difference between the value of care as perceived by members of the group, represented by D_1, and the price of care, P_1. The slope of MC_S will be less than the slope of MC_R, because D_1 is more elastic than D_2. The marginal cost of promoting equality through a subsidy rises to point A and then becomes the horizontal line at P_1.

continued

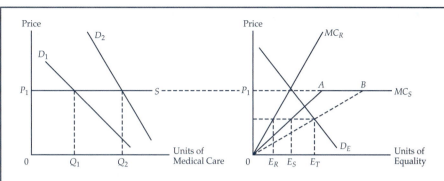

Using a combination of rationing and subsidies, more equality may be purchased at a lower overall cost. The combined marginal cost curve, $0B$, is the horizontal sum of MC_R and $0A$. Assuming D_E is the demand for equality in this case, a level of equality equal to E_T may be purchased using this combined strategy, E_R due to rationing and E_S due to the subsidy. Purchasing E_T equality using rationing or subsidies alone would require significantly higher spending. Countries that have a well-specified demand for equality can achieve desired levels at a lower overall cost by using a combination of subsidies for the poor and limited availability of certain procedures to everyone.

Source: Cotton M. Lindsay, "Medical Care and the Economics of Sharing," *Economica*, November 1969, 351–362.

The Japanese system of health care delivery is reflective of the basic approach business firms have toward their employees: "The company is people." Coverage is compulsory, and participation is mandatory. The success of the system lies in its ability to control costs and to provide universal access. Criticism may be targeted at the issue of quality, which is to be expected. Service distortions almost always accompany fixed fee schedules. In this regard, Japan is not immune. But with its emphasis on equality and community, the health care system has served the Japanese well.

SWITZERLAND: INDIVIDUAL RESPONSIBILITY IN A FEDERALIST FRAMEWORK[30]

Switzerland is divided into 26 political entities, called *cantons* and *demi-cantons*, which are sovereign in all matters not directly granted to the federal government by the constitution. Most of Switzerland's 7.3 million citizens live in the Swiss Plateau, the narrow region between the two mountain ranges that dominate the landscape, the Jura in the north and the Alps in the south. From its inception in 1911, the Swiss health insurance model has avoided the link between health insurance coverage and employment and has relied instead on personal responsibility.

The Swiss spend a lot on medical care. Second only to the United States, health care spending amounted to 11.6 percent of GDP and \$4,177 per capita in 2005. The generous supply of medical resources provides unprecedented access to medical services. Whether measured in terms of physicians per 1,000, acute care bed density, or access to medical technology, resource supply is among the highest in Europe.

---

[30] **This section draws heavily from Grinols and Henderson (2008).**

Characteristics of the Swiss System   Permanent residents of Switzerland are subject to an individual mandate to purchase compulsory health insurance. Refusal to do so results in forcible assignment to a health insurance plan. Compulsory insurance covers a generous package of medical benefits, including inpatient and outpatient hospital care, unlimited hospital stays, and complementary and alternative medicine. Despite the generosity of the basic package, between 25 and 40 percent of the Swiss pay risk-rated premiums to purchase a supplementary policy. The most popular supplementary policies ensure free choice of physician and private hospital rooms. Others cover medical services for those traveling abroad, dental services, and prescription drugs that are not covered under compulsory insurance. As the basic benefits package has expanded, the popularity of supplementary policies has fallen.

Compulsory insurance is provided by 93 sickness funds operating on a not-for-profit basis. Insurance funds have established a centralized risk-adjustment mechanism, called *Foundation 18*, which subsidizes funds that suffer disproportionately from adverse selection. The subsidies are based on a fund's deviation from average cost across 30 age-sex categories.

The public–private mix with respect to Swiss health care expenditures is unique among European nations. The proportion of expenditures from private sources, at 42.1 percent, is the highest in Europe—two to three times that of other countries in the region. The breakdown in spending is similar to that in the United States. The major differences occur in spending on physician services and nursing home care.

Physician fees are based on a uniform nationwide relative value scale (RVS). Negotiations between physician groups and health insurance associations within each canton determine the monetary conversion factor applied to the RVS. Physicians are paid on a fee-for-service basis and are not allowed to charge more than the negotiated fee. In over one-half of the cantons, physicians have freedom of prescription. These dispensing physicians are able to supplement their incomes by approximately one-third.

Cantons finance approximately 80 percent of all hospital investment and half of all hospital operating expenses directly through taxation. Based on European standards, the Swiss hospital system has a well-developed hospital infrastructure.

Financing   Individuals pay community-rated premiums within a canton. Approximately one-third of all individuals receive means-tested subsidies when premiums exceed 8 to 10 percent of their total income. In 2001, almost 20 percent of enrollee premiums were financed through these government subsidies.

Policies feature six different deductibles, ranging from 300 SwF ($240 US) for the standard policy, or for *franchise ordinare* (FO), up to 1,500 SwF ($1,205 US). Policies also include coinsurance provisions of 10 percent for spending over the deductible, with an annual cap on out-of-pocket spending of 700 SwF ($562 US). As the deductible increases, consumers receive premium discounts off the standard FO policy. Premium discounts range from 8 percent for the 400SwF ($322 US) deductible up to 40 percent for the 1,500 SwF ($1,205 US) deductible. The average premium for the standard FO policy in 2003 was $2,388. Children under age 18 and students under age 25 paid lower premiums. Premiums can vary as much as 50 percent between cantons. Though the standard FO plan is the most popular, the majority of the population has chosen either the higher deductibles or one of the managed care plans offered (Herzlinger and Parsa-Parsi, 2004).

Two types of managed care plans are available to Swiss consumers: one is a plan similar to the staff-model health maintenance organization; the other is a plan based on a GP network. The second type of plan utilizes a GP-gatekeeper model in a risk-sharing arrangement between physicians and insurers. Surpluses and deficits are shared equally with an annual cap on losses absorbed by physicians of 10,000 SwF ($8,040 US).

The Role of Markets   Three markets exist in Swiss health care: physicians compete for patients; insurers compete for customers; and, as a result of selective contracting, insurers compete for primary care physicians. In spite of the competitive rhetoric in the Revised Health Insurance Law, the reality of competition has fallen short of the promise. Physicians have virtually no latitude in the fees they charge or the services they provide. Competition among insurers is almost nonexistent. The generous nature of the compulsory benefits package allows little competition based on benefits offered. In fact, the appeal of supplementary insurance has been shrinking because of the expansion of the basic benefits package.

Competition among insurers is based on premiums charged and not benefits offered. The only exception to this rule is the ability to offer managed care plans that restrict access to certain providers. Since all policies are individually purchased, enrollees are aware of the full cost of their insurance.

There is some empirical evidence that high-deductible plans enroll a disproportionate number of healthy individuals. In 1999, high-deductible plans transferred an average of $510 per enrollee to low-deductible plans, which in turn received an average of $174 per enrollee.

Lessons from Switzerland

Deriving lessons for health care delivery and finance from other countries is always a risky proposition. There is a danger in thinking that all the elements of a system can be imported from a foreign counterpart. Regardless, there are lessons that can be learned from Switzerland.

- If universal coverage is the goal, mandatory participation must be considered.

- Universal access to high-quality medical care is possible without strict reliance on a single-payer system or a pure public sector approach.

- Price-conscious behavior can be encouraged as long as a certain degree of consumer choice and individual responsibility remain in the system.

- The link between insurance coverage and employment diminishes personal responsibility. When this link is broken, price transparency will provide the incentive required for responsible consumers to emerge.

- People who cannot afford to purchase health insurance on their own can still have access to essential services within a system of subsidized premiums. These tax-financed, means-tested subsidies promote the efficient delivery of health care services.

- Health status and spending are closely linked to income, education, and race.

- Enrollees in high-deductible plans use substantially fewer medical resources. In 1999, spending was 60 percent lower per capita in the 1,500 SwF deductible plan (including risk adjustment) than in the basic FO plan.

- Controls over benefits and premiums mitigate competitive incentives.

The Swiss system is a desirable alternative to the government-run insurance plans of most of the rest of Europe. It covers virtually all residents with a comprehensive benefits package financed primarily by payments from individuals and their private insurers. Those who want additional coverage are allowed to spend their own money to buy supplementary policies. All Swiss residents except the most destitute and incapable are expected to contribute something toward the purchase of their insurance, usually 8 to 10 percent of their income. Those who cannot afford to purchase a policy receive subsidies. With its heavy reliance on private payers, the Swiss system is worth careful consideration as a model for U.S. reform.

UNITED KINGDOM: NATIONAL HEALTH SERVICE[31]

The British National Health Service (NHS) stands as a symbol of social equality and collective compassion. Under the Health Authorities Act of 1995, the 110 District Health Authorities and the 90 Family Health Service Organizations were merged and replaced by approximately 100 Unitary Health Authorities. Each serves the medical needs of about 500,000 people. With an overall budget of approximately £50 billion in 2000, and nearly one million employees, the NHS is the largest single employer in Europe.

The origins of the national health care system can be traced back to the early nineteenth century. As was the case throughout much of Europe, labor unions and other fraternal associations provided health insurance to their members. Employers encouraged their workers to join these mutual aid societies to reduce public demand for charity care.

In 1911, under the leadership of Prime Minister Lloyd George, the British Parliament passed the first National Health Insurance Act, strengthening the voluntary insurance program and providing a funding mechanism for indigent care. Although membership in a mutual aid society was not mandatory, most workers joined. Health benefits included prescription drugs and the services of a GP. Specialty care and hospitalization were not covered under the law but were provided through local government support and charity care.

The Second World War brought profound changes in the political and social attitudes toward health care in Britain. Before the end of the war, Winston Churchill appointed Sir William Beveridge to study the delivery of health care and make recommendations for change. The Beveridge Report of 1942 outlined a comprehensive national health insurance plan that would extend coverage to everyone regardless of income level. The National Health Service Act was implemented in 1948. Its passage meant that the entire population was covered under one plan that provided a comprehensive package of benefits, paid out of general tax revenues and free to patients at the point of use.

The single-payer concept and limited supervision of providers kept the administrative costs of the system low, but from the beginning, the NHS was underfunded and dominated by the medical community. Budgetary constraints, especially during years of slow economic growth, politicized health care delivery and led to a series of crises, about one every three years, between government policy makers and medical practitioners.

The NHS inherited a geographic distribution of resources that favored the four metropolitan areas in and around London. One of the stated goals of the newly formed system was to eliminate the inequalities that existed. Targets were established to increase the availability of facilities in underserved regions and

The U.K. Department of Health, with links to the NHS Executive home page, provides information via the World Wide Web.

http://www.dh.gov.uk

---

[31] **Unless otherwise stated, institutional facts and figures are from "A Guide of the National Health Service," published by the NHS Executive, March 1995.**

restrict the expansion of facilities in overserved regions. To accomplish this goal, it was necessary to implement "standstill budgets" in certain parts of the country, particularly the London area. Thus the goal of equity required policy makers to cut services in certain designated areas. The Black Report, released in 1980, found little evidence of change in resource availability. Even today, the per capita hospital spending among the health authorities differs as much as 40 percent. The number of private hospital beds in the Northeast Thames region is 8 times greater than in the Northern region. The rate of kidney dialysis and transplant procedures performed is almost 30 percent higher in metro London than in Yorkshire and 75 percent higher than in the Western Midlands.

Every citizen is registered with a GP and receives all primary and preventive care in this setting. There are about 35,000 GPs in 9,000 practices, handling over 90 percent of all patients. The GP serves as a family doctor for the patient and gatekeeper to the system of specialists, or "consultants," and hospitals. Any patient that requires extensive testing or specialized treatment is referred to a consultant, that is a specialist, or is admitted directly into a hospital. Urgent cases are to be treated within a month, but those classified as nonurgent may have to wait up to a year.[32] Since internal market reforms were initiated in 1992, the number of patients waiting over 18 months for admission to NHS hospitals has fallen to nearly zero.

Largely because of the waiting lists for "elective" surgery, those who can afford private supplementary health insurance have purchased it. Over the past decade, the proportion of the population with private coverage has fallen to 11.5 percent due to increases in private premiums. Private insurance coverage is concentrated among those in the professional and managerial occupations, high-income earners, and those living in London and the southeast. Over two-thirds of those with private insurance have risk-rated group policies provided through their employers. Premiums must be paid out of pretax income, and any benefit is subject to an income tax and a 5 percent premium tax. To a great extent, patients with private insurance still use the NHS for emergency and chronic care. The private system deals largely with quality-of-life issues such as hernia repair, gall-bladder disease, and hip replacements. About 20 percent of all nonemergency surgeries are paid for privately. Thus, the private system serves as a safety valve for wait-listed patients, much the same way as the U.S. system serves as a safety valve for wait-listed Canadians. Critics of the private system argue that it has two main flaws: it takes the pressure off the national system, slowing improvements; and it creates a two-tiered system, undermining the perception of equality.

In the reformed NHS, general practitioners are independent contractors. They receive over half of their incomes from capitation payments and the rest from various incentives and allowances. For example, GPs receive additional pay for settling in underserved areas and bonuses for meeting immunization, screening, and vaccination targets. In 1992 the mean net earnings of British physicians was $120,000. In comparison, senior lawyers in private practice earned 2.5 times that amount. The pay scale for hospital-based physicians ranged from $63,500 to $81,900 in 1996 with 20 percent receiving bonuses beginning at $15,000 (Hatcher, 1997).

The NHS inherited nearly 3,000 hospitals at its inception. Today, fewer than half of them still exist. The number of hospital beds has also declined markedly, from 480,000 in 1948 to less than 136,000 in 1999. The most recent OECD figures

> **POLICY ISSUE**
>
> Are Americans willing to accept waiting lists for specialty care and certain surgical procedures as the price of universal coverage?

---

[32] According to Enthoven (1991, p. 64), patients in the queue system are told, "The doctor agrees you should have an operation; go home and we will call you to come into the hospital a week in advance in the next year or two."

place hospital occupancy rates at over 80 percent for all hospitals, including acute-care beds (OECD, 2000). In early 2000, it was announced that the number of Britons waiting for hospital admission had reached 1.04 million, about two percent of the population. With less than 6 million hospital admissions in 1999, this meant that for every six admissions, one person waited for hospitalization. Much as the 40 million uninsured Americans symbolize the shortcomings of the U.S. system, the waiting list of over one million symbolizes the shortcomings of the British system.

Standard practice in Britain has been to place anyone requiring an "elective" procedure on a waiting list. Procedures such as cataract surgery, hip replacement, coronary artery bypass, and breast reconstruction following a mastectomy are defined as elective procedures. In other words, if it is not life threatening, it can wait. A good indicator of the realities of the waiting list in Britain can be found in the national standards from the Patient's Charter. First published in 1991, the charter guarantees the provision of inpatient hospital treatment within 18 months of referral, establishes a standard wait of 12 months for coronary artery bypass surgery, and provides a 26-week standard wait to see a hospital consultant after referral from a general practitioner. Patients are now able to log onto the NHS Web site and see the expected length of time they will have to wait for medical treatment in the hospital of their choosing.

The paternalistic tradition of the NHS is evident in this method of resource allocation. It is a system that is largely invisible and uniquely British. Not only are patients in the United Kingdom among the least informed in the developed world, the culture tends to leave medical decisions to the individual physician and seldom questions the medical authorities. Physicians are considered the sole authority on determining patient needs and have no real pressure to respond to patient desires, so rationing may be disguised as a clinical decision.

British attitudes about waiting have changed since the end of World War II. As opportunities for productive enterprise have increased, acceptance for this method of rationing has decreased. As waiting lists grew, the problems were magnified and criticism abounded. Decision making was becoming more politicized, and overcentralization had led to managerial inefficiencies. The lack of economic incentives had completely stifled innovation. In response, the Thatcher government proposed major reforms that were implemented in 1991. *Working for Patients* (1989), a position paper on reform of the NHS, was an attempt to introduce competition and market incentives into the NHS in hopes of making it "more responsive to the needs of the patient."

Prior to the reform measures, each district was provided a fixed budget with no incentive for good performance. Greater efficiency and shorter waiting lists meant more referrals from other districts without an offsetting transfer of resources. Increased productivity added to workloads rather than revenues. Under the reformed system, resources followed patients. Theoretically, each local health authority had the responsibility of buying medical care for the community it served. Although each could contract with any provider throughout the nation, in practice, most contracting was still local.

The Thatcher reforms of 1993 created an internal market and GP fundholders, adding choice and competition to a system in which little of either existed. But competition failed to bring about the desired results. Money did not follow patients due to weak incentives, particularly in the hospital sector. Without the ability to keep surpluses, hospital administrators sought bigger budgets. Since it was politically impossible to close a failed hospital, there was little incentive to provide services efficiently.

To be providers of health services, health organizations became NHS trusts, independent organizations competing for patients. At the same time, many GPs became fundholders with their own budgets. By 1995 all health care was being provided through NHS trusts, a significant cultural shift even for the British. GPs who did not become fundholders had their budgets centrally controlled by the NHS. Patients who received treatment from fundholders often received better treatment, a source of complaints among the rest of the patient population. A two-tiered system was quickly developing.

A new government came into power with a pledge to get rid of the internal market. As a result, the NHS was reorganized in 1997 for the fifth time in 25 years. The Blair reforms, based on a "third way" of running the NHS, changed GP fundholding by placing 30,000 GPs in one of 500 primary care trusts (PCTs). Each PCT is a fully capitated budgetholder responsible for providing primary care, community health services, and virtually all other medical services for a geographically defined population of 50,000 to 250,000. The emphasis is no longer on a market model based on choice and competition but on a government-run system based on collaboration and cooperation. Secondary care is provided through approximately 200 NHS hospital trusts, 400 small-scale community hospitals, and specialized tertiary care hospitals. In addition, PCTs are able to contract with approximately 230 private hospitals, most in one of five for-profit chains.

A major aspect of the new NHS is a 10-year plan promising more hospitals, more physicians, cleaner facilities, increased standards, and shorter waiting times. Recognizing that the biggest problem facing the NHS has always been underfunding, the NHS budget was scheduled to increase by half in nominal terms and over one-third in real terms between March 2000 and the end of 2005. Such an increase called for an average annual growth rate in NHS spending of 6.3 percent. For that goal to be met, it will be necessary to reduce the maximum wait for an outpatient appointment to 3 months, and the maximum wait for an inpatient admission, to 6 months.

The lessons are clear. When health care is free, people treat it as if the resources used to provide it are free. If scarce health care resources are not rationed on the basis of relative prices, some other means must be used. Often, the alternative is limited availability of technology and waiting lists.

POLICY ISSUE

What is the appropriate role of cost effectiveness analysis in determining the availability of medical treatment?

The most recent reforms have also created the National Institute for Health and Clinical Excellence (NICE), a special health authority accountable to the Secretary of State for Health. NICE was established to determine the availability of treatments, technology, and services based on cost-effectiveness analysis. Under NICE guidelines, some treatments may be available to segments of the population with certain indicators but unavailable to others. For example, expensive drug treatment for Alzheimer's patients may be available for those who score over a certain cutoff on cognitive tests but unavailable to those who score below the cutoff.

Health inequalities remain within the British system. Life expectancy is higher for professional and managerial groups than the unskilled. Limitations from long-standing illnesses are also substantially lower for those in the former group. Death rates from coronary heart disease are three times higher in blue-collar Manchester than white-collar Oxfordshire (*Independent Inquiry*, 1998).

The system continues to have many strong supporters. Proponents point to a strong primary care system provided to everyone without regard to ability to pay. High-cost procedures that benefit only the few are rationed to ensure that the majority of the population receives basic care at a low cost.

ISSUES IN MEDICAL CARE DELIVERY

Physician Supply under the National Health System

In labor markets where wages are determined by the market, employment levels are determined by the market-clearing wage in the short run and by expected lifetime earnings in the long run. This situation exists in the U.S. health care industry today and existed in Britain before 1948, the year the industry was nationalized.

Before National Health, British physicians were self-employed and earned over four times the income of manual workers. Today, they are employees of the government and earn barely two times that of manual workers. The resultant effect on physicians' supply has been remarkable. The aggregate physicians' supply curve fits that of the standard economic model—upward sloping. As the real wage spiraled downward, net emigration of trained British physicians increased, reaching 500 per year by the 1960s. The trend continued for the next decade, and by the early 1970s, one-third of all NHS hospital staff was trained overseas, primarily in former Commonwealth countries. Without this infusion of foreign-trained physicians, there would be a serious shortage of trained medical practitioners in the NHS.

The lessons are clear. The fees charged by physicians serve as market-clearing prices in the short run. Over time physician supply will adjust to those levels based on the expected lifetime earnings potential. When the government controls the price at comparatively low levels, physicians will seek better opportunities elsewhere. To fill the gaps left by the outflow of trained physicians, the system will attract alternatives to domestically trained physicians. The foreign-trained physicians who immigrate do so because they consider the employment opportunities offered in the controlled environment superior to those in their home countries.

Since 1991 almost one-fourth of all NHS consultants graduated from medical school outside the United Kingdom, and by 2002 over half of all new physicians were trained in countries outside the European Union; in 2003 the proportion was over two-thirds.

Source: Cotton M. Lindsay, *National Health Issues: The British Experience*, Nutley, NJ: Roche Laboratories, 1980.

ISSUES IN MEDICAL CARE DELIVERY

A Matter of Life and Death

Baby boomers and their parents will remember the 1950s game show *Queen for a Day*, in which three women would tell their hard-luck stories to a studio audience. The one who received the most audience support would be chosen "Queen for a Day" and would receive a new washing machine or refrigerator or suite of furniture. The tears would flow as the crown was put into place and the royal robes draped over the new queen's shoulders.

That was America in the 1950s. A similar game show made its way onto Dutch television in the 1990s, except this time, it was not a matter of a new washing machine or a remodeled kitchen, it was often a matter of a new kidney or a bone marrow transplant. In a series partially sponsored

continued

by the Ministry of Health, viewers in the Netherlands witnessed real-life dramas of patients competing for scarce medical resources. Originally produced to focus attention on resource allocation in a government-run health care system, the show, called *A Matter of Life and Death*, pitted two patients in need of life-saving procedures against one another. The one who received the support of the studio audience received the treatment. The loser died. Every system must make decisions on the allocation of scarce medical resources. The Dutch system has chosen a most unusual way to pick winners and losers.

Source: "You Bet Your Life," *Wall Street Journal*, October 29, 1993, A14.

SUMMARY AND CONCLUSIONS

As we have learned, private health insurance systems operate under three guiding principles: the insurance principle, whereby premiums are risk-rated; the equivalence principle, whereby the premium paid determines the level of coverage; and the principle of personal responsibility, whereby individuals are responsible for their own health and premiums reflect lifestyle choices. In contrast, social insurance systems operate under a different set of principles: the principle of self-administration, whereby payers and providers operate as independent entities with their rights and responsibilities determined by law; the principle of social partnership, with costs shared by members of society, typically employers and employees; and the principle of social solidarity, whereby premiums are determined by income.

As U.S. policy makers debate health care reform, it is important to recognize that no other country has actually solved the health care spending problem. No patented solutions have been offered, only alternative approaches to the same problem. Proponents of the social insurance model will argue that countries like Canada, Germany, and France have better systems that deliver high-quality medical care to everyone with no financial barriers. Even though these systems meet the goal of universal access, they are not able to solve the overall spending problem. In other words, no single health care system offers a complete model that is universally applicable. However, we can use their successes and failures as a guide for our own reform plans.

National health insurance does not guarantee public satisfaction with the system. Results of several recent surveys by Blendon and colleagues (1990) and Donelan and colleagues (1999) are reported in Table 14.5. More than half of the citizens in six of the seven countries with nationalized systems responded that they felt that their systems needed fundamental changes or should be completely rebuilt, and fewer than half were happy with the way their systems

Table 14.5 Public Opinion of Their Own Health Care Delivery System (in percentages)

Country	Minor Changes Needed	Fundamental Changes Needed	Completely Rebuild System
Australia[2]	19	49	30
Canada[2]	20	56	23
France[1]	41	42	10
Germany[1]	41	35	13
Japan[1]	29	47	6
New Zealand[2]	9	57	32
United Kingdom[2]	25	58	14
United States[2]	17	46	33

Source:

[1] Blendon et al. (1990).
[2] Donelon et al. (1999).

worked. Citizens in Germany showed the greatest level of satisfaction with their system with 41 percent responding that they felt the system worked pretty well; only 48 percent saw a need for fundamental or complete change. Discontent ran very high in both Australia and New Zealand with 79 and 89 percent desiring fundamental or complete change in their respective systems. Canadians viewed their health care system similarly to the way Americans viewed theirs. In fact, Canadians had the biggest negative swing in their views over the decade of the 1990s. In the 1990 survey, 56 percent of the respondents felt that only minor changes were needed in Canada's health care system, and only 38 percent felt that fundamental changes or a completely rebuilt system was needed. By the end of the decade, only 20 percent of Canadians felt that minor changes were needed, and 79 percent wanted fundamental or complete change.

One extremely interesting phenomenon emerges from this survey. Americans show a great deal of support for reforming the U.S. health care system: 89 percent see the need for fundamental changes or a complete restructuring of the system. At the same time, 83 percent of Americans are pleased with their own insurance coverage and the benefits provided (Jajich-Toth and Roper, 1990). Americans seem to be happy with the quality of the care they receive personally but are unhappy with the health care delivery system. More recent survey results by Blendon and colleagues (1995) show little change in consumer satisfaction since the earlier studies.

When health care is provided at zero cost, there is no incentive to limit demand. As cost pressure mounts, financing provisions change. The unintended consequences of trying to satisfy the competing goals of universal access and cost control can be seen in the emerging inequalities of a tiered system and the imposition of limits on access to costly technology. The lesson to be learned is that everything has a cost, and what is promoted as free is really not free.

A great deal of the public anxiety over the health care system has to do with cost, access, and gaps in coverage. Financial barriers to access can be eliminated, but that does not guarantee that social disparities will disappear. National health insurance has done little to eliminate the inequalities across social classes in countries that use the social insurance model. Per capita consumption varies as much as 50 percent across income levels and as much as 100 percent between occupational categories.

Proponents of the social insurance model argue that equal access will improve health outcomes, especially for the low-income, indigent population. Opponents point out that nationalized systems do not eliminate or even substantially reduce health differences among population subgroups. Infant mortality rates and life expectancies vary considerably across socioeconomic categories. For example, England's lowest socioeconomic group has infant mortality rates that are double those of the highest socioeconomic group, a difference that has persisted since the inception of the NHS.[33] It is no different in the United States, where infant mortality rates for African Americans are roughly three to four times those of the white population.

If economics has anything to contribute to the health care reform debate it is this: If you do not allocate resources through the pricing mechanism, you do it through waiting lists and/or by limiting the access to medical technology. Although the French and German health care systems have managed to avoid the queuing problem, other nationalized systems, including Canada and the United Kingdom, experience significant waits for certain procedures.

Policy makers have a growing awareness of their inability to control utilization and thus spending in the private sector, where providers are paid on a fee-for-service basis with no spending caps. But cost control cannot be accomplished unless price controls and fixed budgets apply across the entire system. This inability to control expenditures for physicians' services and private hospitals leads to the extension of budget controls in these two areas. The results of this decision are easy to predict—just look at the queuing and technology rationing that takes place in the countries that use price controls, utilization controls, and fixed budgets system wide. The national insurance systems examined in this chapter all work reasonably well. But each has its safety valve: Canada has the United States, Britain and Germany have their private insurance sectors, Japan has its system of "gifts of appreciation" to ensure quality care, and France has, for now, maintained its commitment to the principle of "liberty" in the private sector. What would happen if these safety valves did not exist?

Key Concept 2
Opportunity Cost

Key Concept 1
Scarcity and Choice

POLICY ISSUE

What is the best way to ensure access to high-quality medical care while controlling cost at the same time? Or is it even possible to think in those terms?

Key Concept 6
Supply and Demand

PROFILE

Anthony J. Culyer

Desiring to "bring intellectual cohesion to the field," Tony Culyer has spent his professional career applying economic theory to the study of social problems, particularly those associated with health care. Born in Croydon, England, Culyer spent his early years in London during the Blitz. Moving frequently as a youth, his family finally settled in Worcester when he was a teenager. He attended Exeter University and graduated with a major in economics in 1964. After spending a year at the University of California at Los

continued

---

[33] Even in Scandinavia with its relatively homogeneous population, age-standardized mortality rates vary significantly across occupational categories. Certain low-income occupations, such as restaurant workers, have mortality rates that are twice as high as some high-income occupations, such as school teachers.

Angeles as a graduate student and teaching assistant, he returned to Exeter as a tutor and lecturer. In 1969 he moved to the University of York, where he is now Director of Health Development and Professor and Head of the Department of Economics and Related Studies. Culyer is also vice chair of the newly formed National Institute for Clinical Excellence.

The year 1971 marked the beginning of a steady stream of contributions to the field of health economics. Nine journal articles that year, including "The Nature of the Commodity 'Health Care' and Its Efficient Location" published in *Oxford Economic Papers* and "Medical Care and the Economics of Giving" published in *Economica,* quickly established Culyer as a major figure in health economics, not only in England but worldwide. Since that time, we can credit him with over 225 published articles, books, and monographs in some of the leading medical and economics journals around the world. Since becoming involved in academic administration, Culyer's research output has slowed from its previous breakneck pace, but he remains productive.

In addition to a strong research agenda, Culyer has played an important public policy role, most recently in the redesign of the entire system of public funding of research and development in Britain's National Health System. As a consultant to the World Health Organization, the Office of Economic Cooperation and Development, and government agencies in Britain, Canada, and New Zealand, his influence in public policy making is evidenced worldwide. As a teacher and mentor, Culyer has played a significant role in shaping the way a generation of British economists thinks about designing health care systems. Recognized for his work in the field of health economics, Culyer was awarded an honorary doctorate from the Stockholm School of Economics in 1999. That same year Queen Elizabeth II, in appreciation for his outstanding contribution to education in the United Kingdom, appointed him Commander of the British Empire.

Culyer considers church music his "private passion." His interest in the organ dates back to his teenage years at the King's School in Worcester. In addition to his position as organist in the rural Anglican parish church he attends, Culyer also leads the choir and serves as the local chair of the Royal School of Church Music.

Keenly aware of the importance of sound analytical reasoning in the public policy arena, Culyer has spent his professional lifetime trying to expunge ad hoc reasoning and political ideology from social policy making. His heavy involvement in government planning has provided him with a sound understanding of social systems and human nature. Lasting change does not come from a top-down mechanism, but rather it is driven from the bottom up.

Source: Anthony John Culyer, *Curriculum Vitae* and personal correspondence.

QUESTIONS AND PROBLEMS

1. Suggest several reasons why health care spending is higher in the United States than in other countries.

2. "The fact that the United States spends more per capita on medical care than any other developed country is evidence of the failure of the U.S. system." Comment.

3. Some view health care systems of other developed countries as reasonable models for the reform of the U.S. health care system. Choose one of the systems discussed in this chapter and describe it in some detail. Provide reasons why you consider it workable or unworkable in the United States.

4. It takes a 13.4 percent payroll tax in Germany to finance a system that in 1993 consumed 10.6 percent of the nation's economic output. If the United States used this as a model, would you expect the average

payroll tax charged to American workers to be larger or smaller than in Germany? Explain.

5. Ronald Coase in his classic October 1960 article "The Problem of Social Cost" (*Journal of Law and Economics* 3[1], pp. 1–44) discussed collective ownership of resources. Collective ownership often means that no one takes care of resources, or at minimum that resources are not cared for as well as if they were privately owned. What are some of the problems with collective ownership in the health care industry? Can you think of some examples in which collective ownership works? In what situations does it not work?

6. The Medicare system in the United States approximates the workings of a single-payer system. Using that program as evidence, critics say that expanding that program to cover all Americans "would give us all the compassion of the Internal Revenue Service and the efficiency of the postal service at Pentagon prices" (Constance Horner, HHS official under Bush, quoted in Stout, 1992). Proponents of a single-payer system point to our northern neighbors, whose Canadian version of Medicare works reasonably well. Although the Canadian system is not perfect, most citizens are satisfied with their medical care, which is available regardless of social or economic status. What is the evidence?

7. In 1989 the Chrysler Corporation released figures showing that its employee health care costs were $5,970 per employee and $700 per vehicle produced. According to the report, its foreign competitors fared much better. Health care costs for automobile companies averaged $375 in France, $337 in Germany, and $246 in Japan, placing Chrysler at a competitive disadvantage. Is there anything wrong with this conclusion? What are the microeconomic arguments and the macroeconomic arguments as they relate to this issue?

REFERENCES

General

Henry J. Aaron, "Issues Every Plan to Reform Health Care Financing Must Confront," *Journal of Economic Perspectives* 8(3), Summer 1994, 31–43.

Leela Barham and Edward Bramley-Harker, "Comparing Physicians' Earnings: Current Knowledge and Challenges," London: NERA Economic Consulting, May 2004.

Robert J. Blendon and Humphrey Taylor, "Views on Health Care: Public Opinions in Three Nations," *Health Affairs* 8(1), Spring 1989, 149–157.

———, Robert Leitman, Ian Morrison, and Karen Donelan, "Satisfaction with Health Systems in Ten Nations," *Health Affairs* 9(2), Summer 1990, 185–192.

——— et al., "Physicians' Perspectives on Caring for Patients in the United States, Canada, and West Germany," *New England Journal of Medicine* 328(14), April 8, 1993, 1011–1016.

——— et al., "Who Has the Best Health Care System? A Second Look," *Health Affairs* 14(4), Winter 1995, 220–230.

Karen Donelon, Robert J. Blendon, Cathy Schoen, Karen Davis, and Katherine Binns, "The Cost of Health System Change: Public Discontent in Five Nations," *Health Affairs* 18(3), May/June 1999, 206–216.

J. Ferlay et al., *GLOBOCAN 2000: Cancer Incidence, Mortality, and Prevalence Worldwide*, Version 1.0, IARC Cancer Base No. 5, Lyon: IARC Press, 2001.

John C. Goodman and Gerald L. Musgrave, *Patient Power: Solving America's Health Care Crisis*, Washington, DC: Cato Institute, 1992.

David G. Green and Benedict Irvine, "Health Care in France and Germany: Lessons for the UK," London: Civitas, Institute for the Study of Civil Society, 2001.

Cindy Jajich-Toth and Burns W. Roper, "Americans' Views on Health Care: A Study in Contradictions," *Health Affairs* 9(4), Winter 1990, 149–157.

Organization for Economic Cooperation and Development, *OECD Health Data, 2003*. A Comparative Analysis of 30 Countries, Paris: OECD, 2003.

Milton I. Roemer, *National Health Systems of the World, Volume One*, New York: Oxford University Press, 1991.

George J. Schieber and Jean-Pierre Poullier, "International Health Care Expenditure Trends: 1987," *Health Affairs* 8(3), Fall 1989, 167–177.

———, "International Health Spending: Issues and Trends," *Health Affairs* 10(1), Spring 1991, 106–116.

———, "Health Care Systems in Twenty-four Countries," *Health Affairs* 10(3), Fall 1991, 22–38.

———, and Leslie M. Greenwald, "U.S. Health Expenditure Performance: An International Comparison and Data Update," *Health Care Financing Review* 13(4), Summer 1992, 1–15.

Hilary Stout, "Health Care Choices: A Bigger Federal Role or a Market Approach?" *Wall Street Journal*, January 15, 1992, A1.

U.S. General Accounting Office, *Canadian Health Insurance: Lessons for the United States*, Washington, DC: United States General Accounting Office, June 1991.

———, *Health Care Spending and Control: The Experience of France, Germany, and Japan*, Washington, DC: United States General Accounting Office, November 1991.

Patrice R. Wolfe and Donald W. Moran, "Global Budgeting in the OECD Countries," *Health Care Financing Review* 14(3), Spring 1993, 55–71.

World Health Organization, "Health Systems: Improving Performance," The World Health Report 2000, Geneva: WHO, 2000.

Canada

Marcia Berss, "'Our System Is Just Overwhelmed,'" *Forbes* 151(11), May 24, 1993, 40–41.

Nadeem Esmail and Michael Walker, "How Good Is Canadian Health Care?" *Fraser Forum*, Vancouver: The Fraser Institute, August 2002a.

———, "Waiting Your Turn: Hospital Waiting Lists in Canada, 17th edition" *Critical Issues Bulletin*, Vancouver: The Fraser Institute, September 2007.

Robert G. Evans et al., "Controlling Health Expenditures—The Canadian Reality," *New England Journal of Medicine* 320(9), March 2, 1989, 571–577.

Hugh Grant and Ronald Oertel, "The Supply and Migration of Canadian Physicians, 1970–1995: Why We Should Learn to Love an Immigrant Doctor," *Canadian Journal of Regional Science* 21(2), Spring/Summer 1997, 157–168.

David Harriman, William McArthur, and Martin Zelder, "The Availability of Medical Technology in Canada: An International Comparative Study," *Public Policy Sources* No. 28, Vancouver, B.C.: The Fraser Institute, 1999.

Steven J. Katz, Diana Verrilli, and Morris L. Barer, "Canadians' Use of U.S. Medical Services," *Health Affairs* 17(1), January/February 1998, 225–235.

Peggy Leatt and A. Paul Williams, "The Health System of Canada," in Marshall W. Raffel ed., *Health Care and Reform in Industrialized Countries*, University Park, PA: The Pennsylvania University Press, 1997, 1–28.

C. David Naylor, "Health Care in Canada: Incrementalism Under Fiscal Duress," *Health Affairs* 18(3), May/June 1999, 9–26.

Robert Steinbrook, "Private Health Care in Canada," *New England Journal of Medicine* 354(16), April 20, 2006, 1661–1664.

France

Jonathan E. Fielding and Pierre-Jean Lancry, "Lessons from France—'Vive la Difference': The French Health Care System and U.S. Health System Reform," *Journal of the American Medical Association* 270(6), August 11, 1993, 748–756.

James W. Henderson, "Equality, Liberty, Fraternity, and the Delivery of Health Care in France," *Journal of the Medical Association of Georgia* 82(12), December 1993, 657–660.

Jean-Francois Lacronique, "Health Services in France," in Marshall W. Raffel, ed., *Comparative Health Systems: Descriptive Analyses of Fourteen National Health Systems*, University Park: Pennsylvania State University, 1984, 258–285.

Claude LePen, "The French Health Care System: In Search of a New Model," Presentation at the European School of Health Economics, Health Economics of Pharmaceuticals and other Medical Interventions, Sophia Antipole, France, June 11, 2003.

Valentin Petkantchin, "Pernicious Myths about Public Health Insurance in France," Economic Note, Institut Economique Molinari, January 2007.

Marie-Pascal Pomey and Jean-Pierre Poullier, "France's Health Policy Conundrum," in Marshall W. Raffel ed., *Health Care and Reform in Industrialized Countries*, University Park, PA: The Pennsylvania University Press, 1997, 49–75.

Jean-Pierre Poullier and Simone Sandier, "France," *Journal of Health Politics, Policy, and Law* 25(5), October 2000, 899–905.

Victor G. Rodwin, "The Marriage of National Health Insurance and La Medecine Liberale in France: A Costly Union," *Milbank Memorial Fund Quarterly* 59(1), 1981, 16–43.

Germany

Melanie Arntz, et al., "The German Social Long-Term Care Insurance—Structure and Reform Options," Center for European Economic Research (ZEW), *Discussion Paper No. 06-074*, November 2006, available at ftp://ftp.zew.de/pub/zew-docs/dp/dp06074.pdf (accessed December 18, 2007).

Boris Augurzky, Thomas K. Bauer, and Sandra Schaffner, "Copayments in the German Health System: Does It Work?" Institute for the Study of Labor (IZA), *Discussion Paper No. 2290*, September 2006, available at http://ssrn.com/abstract=932025 (accessed December 18, 2007).

Lawrence D. Brown and Volker E. Amelung, "'Manacled Competition': Market Reforms in German Health Care," *Health Affairs* 18(3), May/June 1999, 76–91.

Wolfgang Greiner and J.-Matthias Graf v.d. Schulenburg, "The Health System of Germany," in Marshall W. Raffel ed., *Health Care and Reform in Industrialized Countries*, University Park, PA: The Pennsylvania University Press, 1997, 76–104.

Jeremy W. Hurst, "Reform of Health Care in Germany," *Health Care Financing Review* 12(3), Spring 1991, 73–86.

——— and Jean-Pierre Poullier, "Paths to Health Reform," *OECD Observer* 179, December 1992/January 1993, 4–7.

John K. Iglehart, "Germany's Health Care System," in two parts, *New England Journal of Medicine* 324 (7 and 24), February 14, 1991, 503–508; June 13, 1991, 1750–1756.

Martin Pfaff and Dietmar Wassener, "Germany," *Journal of Health Politics, Policy and Law* 25(5), October 2000, 907–914.

Wilfried Prewo, "Germany Is Not a Model," *Wall Street Journal*, February 1, 1993, A14.

Markus Schneider, "Health Care Cost Containment in the Federal Republic of Germany," *Health Care Financing Review* 12(3), Spring 1991, 87–101.

Marcus Tamm, Harald Tauchmann, Jürgen Wasem, and Stefan Gress, "Elasticities of Market Shares and Social Health Insurance Choice in Germany: A Dynamic Panel Data Approach," *Health Economics* 16(3), March 2007, 243–256.

Ranier Winkelmann, "Co-payments for Prescription Drugs and the Demand for Doctor Visits—Evidence from a Natural Experiment," *Health Economics* 13(11), November 2004, 1081–1089.

Japan

John K. Iglehart, "Japan's Medical Care System," in two parts, *New England Journal of Medicine* 319(12 and 17), September 22, 1988, 807–812; October 27, 1988, 1166–1172.

Naoki Ikegami, "Japanese Health Care: Low Cost Through Regulated Fees," *Health Affairs* 10(3), Fall 1991, 87–109.

———, "The Economics of Health Care in Japan," *Science* 258, October 23, 1992, 614–618.

——— and Creighton Campbell, "Health Care Reform in Japan: The Virtues of Muddling Through," *Health Affairs* 18(3), May/June 1999, 56–75.

Hyoung-Sun Jeong and Jeremy Hurst, "An Assessment of the Performance of the Japanese Health Care System," *Labour Market and Social Policy Occasional Papers No. 56*, Paris: Organisation for Economic Co-operation and Development, December 2001.

Pat Murdo, "The Health Care Debate: What America Is Considering, What Japan Has Done," *JEI Report*, No. 8A, Japan Economic Institute, March 5, 1993.

Toshitaka Nakahara, "The Health System of Japan," in Marshall W. Raffel ed., *Health Care and Reform in Industrialized Countries*, University Park, PA: The Pennsylvania University Press, 1997, 105–133.

James Sterngold, "Japan's Health Care: Cradle, Grave and No Frills," *The New York Times*, December 28, 1992, A1, A8.

Aki Yoshikawa, Norihiko Shirouzu, and Matthew Holt, "How Does Japan Do It? Doctors and Hospitals in a Universal Health Care System," *Stanford Law & Policy Review* 3, Fall 1991, 111–137.

Switzerland

Konstantin Beck, Stefan Spycher, Alberto Holly, and Lucien Gardiol, "Risk Adjustment in Switzerland," *Health Policy* 65, 2003, 63–74.

Earl L. Grinols and James W. Henderson, *Health Care for Us All: Getting More for Our Investment*, New York: Cambridge University Press, 2008.

Regina E. Herzlinger and Ramin Parsa-Parsi, "Consumer-Driven Health Care: Lessons from Switzerland," *Journal of the American Medical Association* 292(10), September 8, 2004, 1213–1220.

Peter Zweifel, "Managed Care in Germany and Switzerland," *Pharmacoeconomics* 14(Suppl 1), 1998, 1–8.

United Kingdom

Patricia Day and Rudolf Klein, "Britain's Health Care Experiment," *Health Affairs* 10(3), Fall 1991, 39–59.

Alain C. Enthoven, "Internal Market Reform of the British National Health Service," *Health Affairs* 10(3), Fall 1991, 60–70.

Max Gammon, "Among Britain's Ills, A Health Care Crisis," *Wall Street Journal*, September 8, 1993, A12.

Peter R. Hatcher, "The Health System of the United Kingdom," in Marshall W. Raffel ed., *Health Care and Reform in Industrialized Countries*, University Park, PA: The Pennsylvania University Press, 1997, 227–261.

Independent Inquiry into Inequalities in Health, London: Her Majesty's Stationery Office, 1998.

Rudolph Klein, "Big Bang Health Care Reform—Does It Work? The Case of Britain's 1991 National Health Services Reforms," *The Milbank Quarterly* 73(3), 1995, 299–337.

———, "Why Britain's Conservatives Support a Socialist Health Care System," *Health Affairs* 4(1), Spring 1985, 41–58.

———, "Why Britain Is Reorganizing Its National Health Service—Yet Again," *Health Affairs* 17(4) July/August 1998, 111–125.

Julian Le Grand, "Competition, Cooperation, or Control? Tales from the British National Health Service," *Health Affairs* 18(3), May/June 1999, 27–39.

David Mechanic, "The Americanization of the British National Health Service," *Health Affairs* 14(2), Summer 1995, 51–67.

Secretary of State for Health, *Working for Patients* (London: Her Majesty's Stationery Office, 1989).

Clive Smee, "United Kingdom," *Journal of Health Politics, Policy and Law* 25(5), October 2000, 945–951.

CHAPTER 15

Medical Care Reform in the United States

The new possibilities afforded by advances in medical science force us to deal with issues that previous generations never faced. As we live longer, the incidence of chronic conditions such as Alzheimer's disease, arthritis, dementia, and coronary artery disease increases dramatically. We can expect continued improvement of life-extending technologies, such as mechanical ventilation, artificial resuscitation, antibiotics, and artificial nutrition and hydration.

The result of using these technologies on ever-sicker groups of patients is higher spending and spiraling costs. Quality and access are important, but financial issues that include overall spending and affordability seem to be the overriding concern in the current environment. In this chapter, we will explore the nature of the medical care reform movement in the United States: the pressures behind the movement, the goals of reform, and the alternative strategies competing for acceptance.

THE PUSH FOR REFORM

The temptation exists to turn the reform debate into a struggle among competing ideologies. We must be careful that the political battle does not become more important than its practical results. The issue being decided boils down to trust. Do we give the federal government the authority to decide the future of medical care? Should it be left in the hands of state government? Do we mandate coverage? Can a market really work in medical care delivery? Which presents the bigger problem, market failure or government failure?

The debate over reform of the medical sector is not new. Every congressional session since 1916 has generated at least one piece of federal legislation proposing to modify the system in some way. The issues are still the same—quality, access, and affordability—but the debate has risen to a new intensity. Within the last two decades, the upward spending spiral, exacerbated by a growing number of uninsured, has created an atmosphere of inevitability of reform in the arena of public opinion.

Based on recent polls, approximately three-fourths of all Americans are personally satisfied with the medical care they receive, a pattern that has persisted over time (Blendon et al., 1992, 1995, 2006; Donelan et al., 1999; and Robinson, 2000). While only 22 percent think the system is in crisis, many are critical of it and want government to do something about rising costs, but only 39 percent think that the current system should be replaced by a government-run system. Almost six out of ten Americans think that overall health care spending is too low, but two-thirds think the typical American family pays too much for the health care they receive (Blendon et al., 2006). About half think the United States should consider a plan similar to the one adopted in Massachusetts in 2007, but only 53 percent would be willing to pay higher taxes to ensure that everyone could afford health insurance (NBC, 2007).

These results may seem contradictory to some, but in reality they are not. Respondents are expressing a desire for guaranteed access at lower cost. The policy dilemma is that these desires for guaranteed access and lower costs compete with each other and are not simultaneously achievable, so fully satisfying these competing desires is not entirely possible.

To understand the most recent push for reform, not just in the United States but worldwide, we must recognize the forces behind the reform movement (Musgrave, 1993). Some argue that concern for the poor and elderly has caused this most recent push for reform. Others focus on the millions of uninsured who have only limited access to the private medical care system. Admittedly, concern for these groups is a factor in the movement, but the real pressure for reform is coming from two main sources: the middle class and business. The middle class is demanding action because they are the group that feels the pressure. With limited resources, middle class workers see themselves as only a paycheck away from personal bankruptcy and charity care (see Himmelstein et al., 2005, and Dranove and Millenson, 2006). Until recent changes were made in the insurance laws, many felt unable to change jobs for fear of being without health insurance during the typical waiting period before insurance coverage begins. Even though insurance plans are required to accept individuals transferring from other plans regardless of insurability, many workers must pay insurance premiums from their previous employment until their waiting period expires. Most workers feel the pinch of rising insurance premiums in the form of larger and larger payroll deductions. For this group, government involvement is perceived as shifting the financial burden to wealthy taxpayers or business.

And as far as most businesses are concerned, health insurance benefits are perceived as a big problem. With annual premiums rising from year to year, employee health benefits are often greater than the firm's profit margins. Although medical benefits represent only a small portion of the total cost of employing the typical worker, they represent a growing wedge between total compensation and salary income. As wages lag benefits, workers are becoming increasingly dissatisfied with the size of their take-home pay. A strong and growing sentiment in the business community desires to get rid of this problem by turning it over to the federal government. This case is one in which many policy makers are more than happy to accept the responsibility. Why? Because along with the responsibility comes control. Medical spending has reached 16 percent of total U.S. economic output, more than twice the size of the military industrial complex. The political stakes are enormous.

THE MORAL ISSUES: IS MEDICAL CARE A "RIGHT"?[1]

POLICY ISSUE

Do Americans consider access to medical care a right of citizenship?

It is essential that the issue of access to medical care be examined within a specific moral framework that clearly distinguishes between individual rights and social responsibility. The right to medical care has never been explicitly stated in the United States. While the Declaration of Independence states a right to "life, liberty, and the pursuit of happiness," nowhere does it state that access to medical

---

[1] The material in this section draws heavily from Henderson (1991).

care is a necessary condition to those rights. If access to medical care is not a right, should it be? What is a right anyway?

A number of different ways can be used to define rights. Rights can be defined by a social contract. They may be stated explicitly as the right to health care in the French Constitution or implied as the right to an education in the United States. Legal rights may be defined by legislation. In the United States, a person reaching the age of 65 has the legal right to have Medicare pay his or her hospital bills. An alternative way to look at rights is through the notion of natural rights. The defining characteristic for a natural right is who provides it. If you buy something with your own money, you have a right to it. If that same thing is available to everyone through nature or is "God-given," it is a right. Things we receive through voluntary exchange or the generosity of others, we have a right to.[2] Taking something by force or theft, however, does not give you a right to it.

In what sense is medical care a right? Consensus will be difficult to reach. But it is clear that in the United States, we have created legal rights for the elderly and indigent based on the notion that we have a social responsibility to provide access to care for those who cannot afford to purchase their own. Do we have a natural right to medical care access? Most policy makers avoid this discussion publicly and instead debate "access" to the health care system. One group argues for "universal coverage" through a system that requires mandatory participation, and the other supports "universal access" in a voluntary system in which everyone can buy health insurance if they desire to do so. Parties on both sides, reluctant to address the rights issue, talk around each other about access.[3]

Common sense requires that we adopt a standard of medical care access that is politically acceptable, morally responsible, and economically affordable. To achieve these goals, we must come up with an acceptable definition of an appropriate level of medical care to determine the extent of our collective social responsibility of providing care to those who cannot afford to purchase it. The economist's concept of "appropriate" is determined by the familiar marginalist's rule of thumb: The optimal level of care is defined as that amount of care at which the benefit from the last unit received is just equal to its cost to society. Within this framework, the question of allocation is ultimately one of valuation of outcomes. What value do we place on life? What value do we place on reduced pain and suffering? How do these values change when we are the ones receiving medical care, or a relative, or a friend? How do these values change when the person receiving medical care is a total stranger?

Using the economic approach as a guide to public policy requires the placement of justifiable restrictions on the use of certain medical options to use resources wisely. The challenge is to apply those restrictions uniformly across society without bias. Even so, it is difficult to imagine a society in which the ability to pay becomes the primary determinant of life and death.

A national health care policy cannot provide every person with all the health care he or she may desire. Such an open-ended policy is not appropriate in an environment in which health care is not the only objective. A national policy must be able to establish reasonable priorities, and it must devise acceptable means to allocate resources sensibly.

POLICY ISSUE

Are Americans ready to apply the principles of cost-effectiveness analysis to determine the appropriate level of care?

Key Concept 3
Marginal Analysis

---

[2] If someone gives you something, you have a right to the gift but no rights to future gifts.

[3] Politicians are not the only group uncomfortable with a "rights" discussion. Many economists view the purview of economics predominantly in terms of positive analysis, designing an efficient system to accomplish a given goal. Goal determination is too close to normative analysis for comfort.

THE GOALS OF REFORM

Key Concept 1
Scarcity and Choice

The challenge facing decision makers has always been one of attempting to satisfy the unlimited demands placed on the finite resources available to society. When dealing specifically with health policy, we must first recognize that health is not the only goal of society and may not be the most important goal. Individuals validate this claim daily in deciding to supersize their noontime fast food meal, smoke cigarettes, inject drugs, operate a motor vehicle while under the influence of alcohol, and ride a motorcycle without wearing a helmet.

Medical care must be placed within the context of other goals considered important by society: national defense, education, economic competitiveness abroad, environmental protection, reduction in the incidence of poverty, and balancing the federal budget. To a large extent, these are competing goals. The single-minded pursuit of one goal can lead to ever-larger expenditures in that area. In establishing spending priorities, health and medical care have a considerable advantage over other goals. The needs of this sector can be readily dramatized by citing individual cases in which human welfare is involved and, consequently, spending priorities are easily shifted.

Three issues stand out as critical: who is covered, what is covered, and who pays. It is important to examine proposed reforms carefully, if not critically, and judge them by how they address these three criteria.

Who Is Covered?

Most participants in the reform debate will agree that one of the goals of the U.S. medical care system is universal coverage. Our concern over fairness has prompted a discussion over the transition from the current system to the new system, whatever its final form. It is easy to express support for universal coverage, but how do we get from where we are to where we want to be? Do we follow the familiar maxim, "Just do it," or do we follow a more prudent approach: "First, do no harm"?

Expanded access will require, at least initially, additional funding. Policy makers, by now sensitive to voter preferences, are wary of grandiose schemes that require substantial tax increases for their implementation—unless, of course, it means raising somebody else's taxes. Concern over the cost of any change may necessitate the phasing in of access over a number of years, but any significant delay in coverage could be quickly labeled unfair to certain groups: the poor, the disabled, people of color, women (especially pregnant women), and children. Even with these concerns, the rallying cry for policy makers lately has become one for incremental reform.

The task facing lawmakers is complicated by a general confusion over the wishes of the American public. Is the common perception of fairness based on the notion of equal access to the system, equal health outcomes, or something else? Does equality mandate that everyone be required to participate, or should participation be voluntary?

Improved access may be accomplished with a mandatory system that features central control of the third-party payment mechanism. An example would be the single-payer system in the Canadian mold: defining a universal benefits package and limiting the choices available to those who can afford to pay for additional care by making private insurance illegal.

Alternatively, expanding coverage to groups at the margin represents a different approach to improving access. For example, expanding Medicaid eligibility to cover everyone with income below the federal poverty level would enhance the well-being of this group and improve overall equity in the system. Providing coverage for immunizations and preventive care for all children and prenatal care for all pregnant women would not only satisfy some of the concerns of many reformers, but according to most estimates, it would save money in the long run. Private insurance reform could provide small business owners, their employees, and dependents access to group insurance at affordable rates.

The incremental approach presents an interesting dilemma. Subsidized care for the poor, high-risk pools for the uninsurable, prenatal benefits for pregnant mothers living in poverty, and relaxing mandated benefits for small business insurance lead to a system in which individuals have different levels of coverage based on their individual characteristics—health, income, employment status, and so on. In other words, reform geared to enhancing social welfare could easily lead to a medical care system that provides two-tiered, three-tiered, or *n*-tiered coverage. Are we willing to accept that outcome or, at minimum, formally admit that the system we have now is multitiered?

POLICY ISSUE

Are Americans interested in a health care system that promotes universal coverage or universal access?

POLICY ISSUE

Are Americans willing to formally accept a multitiered health care system with more comprehensive coverage available to those who can afford it?

Key Concept 1

Scarcity and Choice

What Is Covered?

The next step is to define the basic benefits package. Reformers who suggest a basic benefits package that is less generous than those available in most private insurance plans are accused of promoting the rationing of services. What some critics call "rationing," economists call the "explicit allocation of scarce resources." In this context, defining a basic package of medical benefits is nothing more than an exercise in establishing priorities, determining how much money is to be spent, and allocating the funds to provide the services according to the rank ordering.

The decision-making process may be straightforward, but it is by no means easy. Competing interests have different priorities. Opinions vary on how the rank ordering should be applied. Certain groups rely on medical guidelines, others consider cost-effectiveness the determining factor. One group focuses on providing all essential care, the other on providing only necessary care.[4]

Even though we have to live with the ethical consequences of the medical care system, we must also pay for it. When a part of the system is collectively financed, it may be appropriate to consider a basic benefits package that is less generous than the standard insurance plan, even though a multitiered medical care system may not satisfy everyone's notion of the social ideal. Such a system, while not equal according to some definitions, is welfare enhancing. Those individuals who become eligible for the collectively provided plan are better off.

ISSUES IN MEDICAL CARE DELIVERY

Rationing Is Already Here

The debate over rising costs in health care has fueled a growing concern that many treatment decisions are based on financial pressures, not clinical evidence. The Society for Critical Care Medicine distributed the *SSCM Healthcare Resource Utilization Opinion Poll* to more than 5,000 of its members in 2002. One of the 11 questions asked was: "Have you rationed any of the following medications or procedures in the last 12 months?" In addition to high-cost drugs such as Activated Protein C (a high-powered antibiotic distributed by Eli Lilly under the brand name Xigris) and Paclitaxel (Bristol-Meyers Squibb's cancer drug Taxol), the list included MRI scans, PET scans, and coronary angiograms. Maybe even more interesting than what the respondents said they were rationing was the fact that less than one-third said that they never rationed.

Even though U.S. spending on medical care exceeds that of any other country using virtually any metric imaginable, there is not enough money or resources to provide everybody with all the medical care they desire. In a world characterized by scarcity, how do we determine who gets care and who does not? If we are unwilling to let the market price ration scarce resources, we must come up with another mechanism. The dilemma we face today stems from our unwillingness to establish a formal rationing mechanism. Other countries, particularly in Europe, have established formal guidelines that determine who receives a particular medication or treatment and under what circumstances they receive it. A drug treatment

continued

---

[4] Readers interested in learning more about the different approaches to defining "basic" care are encouraged to familiarize themselves with the debate over the Oregon Health Plan. Two studies that provide particularly good insight into this controversy are Eddy (1991) and Hadorn (1991).

that is appropriate for a young and otherwise healthy patient may be considered inappropriate for an elderly patient with a history of heart disease or stroke. The younger patient would receive the treatment and probably recover, but the older patient would be provided an alternative treatment and possibly die.

Is it ethical to withhold treatment from critically ill patients? Clearly most medical providers consider it unethical to withhold treatment if the primary reason is financial. However, most providers do not consider it unethical when patients and treatments are prioritized according to clinical evidence. The problem most providers have with the current ad hoc system of rationing is that the decision is usually made under conditions of medical urgency. Providers desire formal guidelines based on clear medical evidence, and most have no problem with interjecting a little cost-effectiveness analysis into the mix. In fact, the bedside rationing that already takes place often takes costs and benefits into consideration. The problem with the current practice is that it is usually crafted in terms of the costs and benefits to the hospital and not the costs and benefits to the patient.

The U.S. health care system rations medical resources, a statement that is also true for every government-run system throughout the world. The difference is that most of our foreign neighbors are more open about the rationing mechanism they use, and as a result, rationing has been subjected to national debate. At some point, we are going to be forced to admit that rationing occurs in the United States. Only then will we be able to move beyond the arbitrary guidelines of demand management to establish national norms based on medical evidence.

Source: A four-part series entitled "Who Gets Health Care? Rationing in an Age of Rising Costs," published on the front page of the *Wall Street Journal* from September 12, 2003, through September 23, 2003. Geeta Anand, "The Big Secret in Health Care: Rationing Is Here," September 12, 2003; Laurie McGinley, "Health Club: Behind Medicare's Decisions, An Invisible Web of Gatekeepers," September 16, 2003; Antonio Regalado, "To Sell Pricey Drug, Eli Lilly Fuels a Debate over Rationing," September 18, 2003; and Bernard Wysocki, Jr., "At One Hospital, A Stark Solution for Allocating Care," September 23, 2003.

Who Pays and How Much?

In most cases, the efficient use of scarce resources requires cost-conscious consumers, or at least decision makers, who behave in a responsible manner. It means that individual consumers must pay for what they consume and must benefit from any economizing behavior that they practice. In this regard, medical care is often considered different. Most health care systems—whether in the United States, Canada, or Europe—are collectively funded through some combination of taxes and insurance premiums. Thus it is difficult to build into any system the individual discipline that is necessary to naturally ensure its efficient operation.

Key Concept 6
Supply and Demand

Key Concept 9
Market Failure

Every reform plan must eventually face the sobering issues of cost, affordability, and overall spending. Inevitably, expanding access and providing generous benefits will drive up costs and spending. How much are we willing to pay? Who is ultimately going to pay? Individuals spending their own money will answer these questions differently than those spending someone else's money. Normally, the burden of responsibility falls on the individual to provide for his or her own care, but under certain conditions, we deem it socially responsible to collectively provide for those who cannot provide for themselves.

Key Concept 4
Self-Interest

The issue boils down to the distribution of the burden of the collectively provided portion of the medical care package. Is medical care primarily an individual or a collective responsibility? Should it be paid for by individuals, by employers, by taxpayers, or by some combination of payers? How should the costs be distributed among the payer groups? The answers to these questions will not come easily, but they must be answered before any reform plan can be implemented.

INDIVIDUAL STATE INITIATIVES

As far as the national media are concerned, the reform debate is centered in Washington, DC; but anyone following the issue closely understands that the real battle for reform is being fought at the state level. The stakes are high for the states. Health care costs are expanding rapidly, accounting for over 25 percent of most state budgets. The federal legislative process works slowly, so state and local officials have no reason to sit around and wait for federal solutions. Many problems require federal involvement, mandating that employers provide their workers with health insurance, for example; but much can be done to improve medical care delivery without federal legislation. So while Congress debates the problem, legislators from Tallahassee to Olympia are passing legislation in their efforts to improve medical care delivery within their borders and provide incentives to control costs.

Universal Coverage in Hawaii

The state of Hawaii implemented a mandatory employer-based health insurance system almost 30 years ago. The principles behind the Prepaid Health Care Act of 1974 (PHCA) are simple. Employers are required to provide a generous benefit package for all employees who work over 20 hours per week, but dependent coverage is not mandated. The coverage, based on the 1974 law and subsequent amendments passed in 1976 and 1983, includes at least 120 days in the hospital annually and provisions for surgical, medical, and diagnostic procedures; outpatient services; emergency, maternity, and well-baby care; substance abuse and mental health programs; mammogram screening; and even in vitro fertilization. The employer must adopt one of two model plans or seek state approval of an alternative plan. One option is a standard fee-for-service insurance plan offered by the state's Blue Cross–Blue Shield organization. The other is a health maintenance organization plan offered by the Kaiser Foundation.

In 1991, the State Health Insurance Program (SHIP) extended coverage to those still uninsured under PHCA. Technically, these two laws extend insurance coverage to the entire state population.[5] Employers are required to provide insurance to all employees who work over 20 hours per week, so the outcome should come as no surprise: many Hawaiians hold several part-time jobs with different employers. Because they work less than the legislated 20-hour minimum per week in each job, over 11 percent of the state's nonelderly population is without insurance.

Employers are required to pay at least half of the premiums, and the employee may not pay more than 1.5 percent of gross income directly toward premiums. In addition, employers do not have the option of increasing deductibles or coinsurance, because this would result in coverage that falls below the minimum standards.

PHCA was successfully challenged in the courts as a violation of the Employee Retirement and Income Security Act of 1974 (ERISA), a decision upheld in 1981 by the U.S. Supreme Court.[6] The status of Hawaii's health care system was uncertain until 1983, when Ronald Reagan signed into law an ERISA exemption for PHCA,

---

[5] Prior to the legislation, 90 percent of all Hawaiian workers had employment-based health insurance. Thus the legislation added fewer than 50,000 individuals to the health insurance rolls.

[6] ERISA does not require that employers establish or maintain specific benefit plans; but if a plan exists, it must conform to the provisions of the law, including minimum funding requirements and eligibility. The law precludes states from mandating that employers provide health insurance benefits. States regularly seek ERISA exemptions, but few succeed.

as long as no substantive changes are made in the 1974 act. Without this ERISA exemption, other states that try to copy the Hawaii plan will find health care reform much more expensive.

A major complaint of the Hawaii plan is its inflexibility. Firms wishing to offer an optional insurance package are not allowed to offer alternative benefits. In practice, all mandatory benefits must be provided, so "optional" only means "additional." The Hawaiian economy is dominated by small business with over 99 percent of its employers having less than 100 employees. Due to a relatively tight labor market, many employers have found it necessary to hire seniors who would prefer to have long-term care coverage rather than infertility benefits, but getting affordable options approved by state regulators has been difficult.

Hawaii's situation may be unique among the other states in the country. Its geographic isolation makes mobility, both business and individual, difficult. Proximity to the Asian market makes it attractive to business despite high costs, including the high costs of mandated employee health insurance. Health care administrative costs are lower in Hawaii, because 80 percent of all citizens are covered by one of the two main plans—either the Blue Cross–Blue Shield plan or the Kaiser Foundation plan.

Critics of the Hawaiian system point out that total health care spending has grown faster in Hawaii than in the United States as a whole. In the 1980s, the increase in nominal spending was 191 percent in Hawaii versus 163 percent in the rest of the country. Additionally, per capita spending is higher in Hawaii than in the rest of the country due primarily to higher Medicaid spending. Despite these complaints, insurance premiums in Hawaii are among the lowest in the country. Annual cost increases among the predominantly community-rated policies have slowed to less than 10 percent.

Responding to the growing costs, the state legislature passed Health QUEST in 1994. The legislation extends managed care to all public insurance beneficiaries and effectively combines SCHIP and Medicaid recipients into one large purchasing pool.

ISSUES IN MEDICAL CARE DELIVERY

MinnesotaCare: The Incremental Approach to Reform

After years of study and numerous legislative setbacks, the Minnesota legislature passed a comprehensive medical care reform law in 1992. MinnesotaCare was a complex piece of legislation. It provides basic medical benefits for low-income families at subsidized rates and modifies insurance standards to lower the cost to small businesses. Begun as a modest plan to provide medical care to pregnant women and their young children, MinnesotaCare has evolved into a comprehensive system of state-wide health care delivery.

The die was cast in 1987, when the Minnesota legislature passed a modest health care reform bill that provided basic care for pregnant women and children under age eight. Two years after the bill was enacted, the legislature voted to extend the age of eligibility for children to 18. Soon the parents of those children were also covered, and middle-income residents earning up to $40,000 and those temporarily out of work were also included.

MinnesotaCare provided insurance to approximately 144,000 residents in 2002. A program that was projected to cost $1.3 million annually

continued

actually cost $390 million. Minnesota taxpayers finance 55 percent of the cost, primarily from a 2 percent provider tax and a 1 percent premium tax. The remainder of the financing comes from enrollee premiums, copayments, and federal funding. In addition, the young and healthy have seen their premiums rise by as much as 93 percent since 1992. Their premiums have increased $600 million to provide access to the previously uninsured.

Starting in 1996, the state health commissioner was given the power to use price controls to hold costs down, and doctors and hospitals were forbidden to let per patient revenues rise by more than 5.3 percent annually. Practitioners were strongly encouraged to follow medical practice guidelines in treating their patients. Such a plan was not feasible in 1987, when the legislative process began; but as lawmakers soon found, a carefully orchestrated series of incremental reforms can get you where you want to go if you are patient enough. Once on the path toward universal coverage, it is difficult politically to turn back.

Sources: Barbara P. Yawn, William E. Jacott, and Roy A. Yawn, "MinnesotaCare (HealthRight): Myths and Miracles," *Journal of the American Medical Association* 269(4), January 27, 1993, 511–515; and Brigid McMenamin, "In Bed with the Devil," *Forbes*, 156(6), September 12, 1994, 200–210.

The Oregon Health Plan

Key Concept 1
Scarcity and Choice

One of the most innovative approaches to health care reform attempted to date may be the Medicaid experiment in the state of Oregon. Controversial because of its deliberate rationing of services, surprisingly the Oregon Health Plan has relatively few opponents within the state. Its planners used input from every conceivable interest group—patients, providers, payers, suppliers—and provided numerous public forums for debate and discussion on the various aspects of the plan. After three years of work, and one unsuccessful attempt to get the necessary federal waivers, in March 1993 the state was given permission to put the plan into effect. Thus Oregon became the first state to extend state-funded benefits to a larger number of recipients by limiting the services available.

The original goal of the Oregon Health Plan was to provide health insurance coverage for all the state's citizens through either private health insurance or Medicaid. To maintain budgetary restraint, the plan set out to ration care by limiting the range of services covered under the basic benefits package. This aspect of the plan, placing limits on the types of treatment available to patients, is the most controversial. Here is a clear case of politics versus economics. What is amazing about this situation is that the state's policy makers have been able to make the economic reality of choice politically acceptable.

The reform process began with the Oregon Health Services Commission placing over 10,000 diagnoses and treatments into roughly 700 diagnosis/treatment regimens. Using input from 50 town hall meetings across the state—attended by over 1,000 citizens—the diagnosis/treatment categories were ranked according to community preferences, the effect of treatment on the patient's quality of life, and medical effectiveness. After the rank ordering was accomplished, the list was turned over to the actuaries from the Coopers & Lybrand accounting firm to determine the cost of providing care to the citizens of Oregon. Finally, the legislature determined how much money the state could afford to spend on the plan.

The legislature decided to provide a generous package of care equivalent to the typical group medical plan. Most preventive care—including physical exams, mammograms, Pap tests, eye exams, and fluoride treatments for children—was made part of the plan. Also included are dental care, noncosmetic surgical services, hospice care, prescription drugs, and psychiatric services. Specifically, it was determined that the first 585 services on the list would be funded. Services ranked below 585 would not be funded.[7] The Oregon legislature faced the reality of the economic trade-off and remained firm in their commitment. The result was a plan that clearly broadened the population that received health care at the expense of limiting the services covered. This sort of pragmatism is unusual given the political pressures on elected officials.

Key Concept 1
Scarcity and Choice

The first stage of the Oregon Health Plan extended Medicaid eligibility to all citizens at incomes below the federal poverty level. The second stage, slated to go into effect in 1995, would have required all employers to provide comparable benefits to all their employees, including dependent coverage. Enactment of the second stage required the action of the U.S. Congress, specifically a waiver of certain provisions of ERISA; but Congress did not provide the necessary waivers, so the only expansion in coverage was the addition of 126,000 to the Medicaid rolls.

Critics of the approach from across the ideological spectrum argue that the process was flawed from the beginning, claiming that the diagnosis/treatment rankings were based on political considerations, bowing to pressures from disease constituencies and other special interest groups, including the elderly and provider groups, instead of the stated criteria. Others argue that the plan's provisions determine who lives and who dies, who suffers and how much, valuing one person's life over another's in a somewhat arbitrary fashion. Early results were not encouraging. Medicaid spending rose faster under the new plan compared with previous coverage. To pay for the expanded coverage, the legislature had to levy a 2 percent tax on the gross receipts of health care providers, shifting the costs of the plan to private insurance consumers. Attempts at further reforms were soundly defeated in 2002, when the electorate voted 4 to 1 against a state-level single-payer plan.

Oregon may not serve as the prototypical state for national health care reform because of its homogeneous population, but the state has made a serious effort to expand services to a larger segment of the indigent population. Oregon has approached the problem by systematizing the process. Rather than the haphazard rationing scheme that we have accepted nationally, the state has embraced an open approach. How it survives the test of time will play an important role in determining the direction of national reform.

The Massachusetts Plan[8]

The Massachusetts legislature, overwhelmingly Democrat, joined forces with a moderate Republican governor to enact a comprehensive health insurance plan to increase coverage and improve quality of care while simultaneously creating a sustainable cost structure that rationalizes the financing of medical care. Relying on individual responsibility and social solidarity, the plan became operational in July 2007, providing a mechanism to achieve universal insurance coverage for all residents of the state.

---

[7] The plan covers diagnosis for all conditions, but not all treatment. In general, the conditions that are not covered include those for which treatment is considered 1) less effective than treatments ranked higher on the list; 2) ineffective, and the condition will run a natural course regardless; 3) cosmetic in nature; or 4) futile. A complete list of the treatments not covered can be found in Mahar (1993).

[8] This section relies heavily on Grinols and Henderson (2008).

Possibly the most controversial aspect of the Massachusetts Plan is the requirement that individuals purchase health insurance or face penalties. The individual mandate is a legitimate response to a real problem: the free rider and over $40 billion in uncompensated care required to cover the health care needs of the uninsured. During the first year of the program, penalties for noncompliance were relatively modest. Individuals who remained uninsured lost their state income tax deduction valued at approximately $180. Beginning in mid 2008, however, the penalty for noncompliance increased to half of the annual premium on a standard insurance policy, as much as $2,000 for an individual and as much as $5,500 for an entire family. Individuals can satisfy the mandate by purchasing any health plan approved by the state insurance commissioner, including catastrophic insurance sold in conjunction with a health savings account (HSA) and managed care plans.

For the program to work, insurance must be affordable, subsidized enough for low-income residents, and deregulated enough for those who make too much money to qualify for subsidies. Health insurance is fully subsidized for those households with incomes less than 100 percent of the federal poverty level (FPL). Households with incomes up to 300 percent of the FPL are subsidized on a sliding scale. Those households with incomes greater than 300 percent of the FPL—approximately $58,500 for a couple with two children—are expected to secure their insurance without government subsidy.

Proponents argue that the individual mandate backed by a reasonable subsidy program is the least obtrusive way to reach the goal of universal insurance coverage. Rather than subsidizing providers for the uncompensated care they offer, the state uses those resources to subsidize individuals to purchase their own insurance coverage. With a modified community-rating law already in place, the individual mandate serves to strengthen the state risk pool by requiring the young and healthy to participate by purchasing coverage. Critics counter that the free-rider problem is overstated, that the mandate takes us a step closer to a government-run health care system (Tanner, 2006), and that our main concern should be cost and quality, not access.

The new law also places a "fair share" contribution on employers who do not provide health insurance for their workers. This employer mandate requires firms with more than 10 employees to pay up to $295 into the state's uncompensated care pool (UCP) for each uninsured worker. The "play-or-pay" mandate is intended to replicate the premium tax that employers who arrange insurance for their workers pay into the UCP already.

Additionally, these same employers are subject to a "free-rider surcharge" if their employees use free care. The surcharge is imposed when a single employee receives free care more than three times in a year, or when a firm's employees as a group receive free care more than five times. The surcharge can be up to 100 percent of any spending that exceeds $50,000. Employers may avoid the surcharge by setting up a Section 125 plan, often referred to as a "cafeteria plan," so employees can pay their premium share with after-tax earnings.

Arguably, the most innovative aspect of the legislation is the creation of the Massachusetts Health Care Connector. The Connector is a central clearinghouse— a single market for individual and small-group insurance. Here private insurers compete for customers, offering a choice of plan designs.

The restructured health insurance market in Massachusetts has been described as similar to the CarMax auto market, in which many different types of automobiles are available from one giant dealership (Haislmaier, 2006). A more accurate analogy, however, is the Federal Employee Health Benefit Program, a working example of Enthoven's model of managed competition (2003).

Enthoven's main thesis is that health insurance markets require a large concentration of potential consumers to effectively facilitate exchange. By merging the individual and small-group markets, the Connector provides a mechanism that lowers transactions costs by establishing uniform rules of engagement and by managing the administrative function relating to marketing, enrollment, and payment. This allows insurance providers to focus their competitive efforts on improving the quality and efficiency of health care delivery. Risk pooling through the Connector is expected to provide more affordable choices to individuals, lowering their premiums by an expected 28 percent. Because health insurers are not able to adjust premiums on the basis of age, sex or other risk factors, actual competition will be limited.

Based on the premise that better insurance coverage will improve access to basic health care and in turn improve health, the plan seeks to cover an additional 550,000 residents, half of whom earn more than 300 percent of FPL.[9] The cost of providing uncompensated care to Massachusetts' uninsured was $1.3 billion in 2005, or $2,364 per uninsured individual. On average, each of the 4.82 million privately insured residents was required to pay an extra $270 in taxes and cost shifting to cover the state's uninsured. In a culture that does not encourage individual responsibility when it comes to the purchase of health care, Massachusetts legislators have crafted a plan that creates the expectation that everyone will have insurance coverage. If you can afford to purchase it yourself, you are expected to do so. If you are unable to afford coverage, you will be subsidized up to a point where you can.

Despite the excitement among proponents of the new law, successful implementation of the plan presents formidable challenges, foremost among which is enforcement. For the first time, the legislation established a requirement that individuals purchase a specific product as a prerequisite for living in the state. Individuals must verify coverage by reporting their health insurance status when they file their state income tax returns. This requirement is complicated by the temporary nature of being uninsured for many who find themselves without coverage. Tracking the insurance status of illegal immigrants is not as big a problem in Massachusetts as it would be in some states, although 7 percent of the uninsured are in the country illegally. The legislation may not be perfect, but it challenges for the first time the entitlement mentality of many who support government provision of free care regardless of personal financial circumstances.

Other State Reforms

Most other attempts to reform medical care delivery at the state level have not been as extensive as Hawaii, Oregon, and Massachusetts. Two-thirds of the states have enacted legislation to authorize small-business purchasing pools. These insurance pools provide small companies with leverage to negotiate more favorable premiums.

Several states—including Maryland, Montana, Vermont, and Washington—have taken steps to control expenditures on medical care by enacting limits on overall spending and limiting fees charged by practitioners. Legislation passed in

---

[9] The majority of individuals at this income level choose to be uninsured despite significant evidence that they can afford coverage. Terminology originating with Bundorf and Pauly (2006) refers to these individuals as "uninsured afforders."

Maryland requires all insurers to provide a standard benefits package with premiums based on community ratings for firms of 2 to 50 employees. A commission has also been established to develop and implement a uniform payment system for all providers.

Clearly states have taken the initiative to reform the medical care delivery system in this country. Many of the efforts are piecemeal in nature and focused primarily on improving access to the traditional health insurance system. Given the lack of a national consensus on the direction of reform, the states are beginning to view themselves as laboratories to test the various reform alternatives. For all practical purposes, this constitutes a series of real-world experiments to determine what works and what does not work. Insights can then be drawn on what should be incorporated into a national plan and what should be avoided.

HEALTH INSURANCE MANDATES

As concerns over access and quality continue to mount, both the federal and state governments have intervened to correct the perceived deficiencies in the health insurance market. Government policy makers have generally responded by introducing additional regulation. Since 1983, state governments alone have passed over 800 health insurance mandates, taking the forms of mandated benefits, providers, and processes, bringing the cumulative number of mandates to over 1,400. The federal government has passed a series of laws creating federal mandates that ensure portability of insurance, mental health parity, minimum hospital stays after childbirth, and minimum hospital stays following mastectomy surgery.

Mandates are legislative requirements that some health insurance purchasers be given access, for example, to certain services or service providers. Typical legislation requires that health insurers provide, or at least offer, certain benefits; and it covers procedures when provided by alternative providers or establishes processes that insurers must follow. Benefit mandates are requirements for specific treatments, services, or procedures that health insurance policies must cover. Examples of benefit mandates include alcohol and drug treatment, contraceptives, mammography screening, prostate cancer screening, and well-child care. Provider mandates require that insurance policies cover the services of specific providers, such as chiropractors, acupuncturists, nurse practitioners, and psychologists. Process mandates impose requirements on how health plans operate internally as they seek to balance treatment quality and cost containment. These requirements include **guaranteed issue**, guaranteed renewability, restrictions on the exclusions of preexisting conditions, and the imposition of community-rated premiums.

POLICY ISSUE

Do state-level mandates offer the most effective way to improve health insurance access?

guaranteed issue
A feature of an insurance policy that requires the insurer to accept all applicants and guarantee renewal as long as premiums are paid, regardless of the health status of the applicant.

ISSUES IN MEDICAL CARE DELIVERY

How to Get a Health Care Reform Bill through Congress

Passing a health care reform bill will be no easy accomplishment. In addition to satisfying all the special interest groups on the plan, 1990 legislation prohibits any entitlement or tax-law change from adding to the overall budget deficit. If health care reform is to become law, it must be paid for by specific taxes or identified budget savings.

Five congressional committees have jurisdiction over health care issues, three in the House of Representatives and two in the Senate.

continued

On the House side, the Ways and Means Committee is the most influential, having jurisdiction over all matters dealing with taxes and
appropriations. Other House committees with jurisdiction are Energy
and Commerce and Education and Labor. On the Senate side, the two
key committees are the Finance Committee and the Labor and Human
Resources Committee.

Any bill reported out of the three House committees must be sent
to the Rules Committee where the rules governing the floor debate
are determined. These rules include whether amendments will be considered, how much time will be allotted to debate, and how long each
speaker will be allowed to talk. If more than one bill is received, the
differences must be reconciled before a bill is submitted to the entire
House.

If two separate bills emerge on the Senate side, they both could be
sent to the floor for debate. Under no circumstances will more than one
bill emerge from either chamber of Congress. If bills pass both cham-
bers, the two versions must then go to a joint House/Senate Conference
Committee, whereupon a single bill will emerge. That bill must pass both
houses and be signed by the president before it becomes law.

The ideological differences between Democrats and Republicans have
been enormous in the health care reform debate. It was, however, the
division between moderate and liberal Democrats that kept them from
uniting behind a single health care reform bill in 1994. As the opposition
party, the Republicans were united in their dislike for certain provisions of
the Clinton plan, especially the employer mandate. In their new role as the
majority party, Republicans likewise were unable to build a consensus and
pass a substantive health care reform bill. As is the case with most important economic issues, politics plays a big role.

Source: Sherry Jacobson, "Road to Health Care Reform Gets Jammed," *Dallas Morning News*, April 11,
1994, 1A, 8A.

The Economics of Mandates

Mandates are not free. They impose significant economic and social costs on their
intended beneficiaries. The propensity of legislative policy makers to add more
mandates, especially process mandates, will have long-term consequences on the
ability of the health care system to provide access to quality care at affordable
prices.

From a public interest perspective, mandates are designed to correct deficiencies
in the health insurance market. Insurers and purchasers may unknowingly undervalue
the benefits of certain types of care, such as substance abuse treatment and mental
health treatment, resulting in a demand for treatment that is too low from a societal
perspective. Without mandates, adverse selection is a significant problem with
high-risk individuals choosing to enroll in plans offering more extensive coverage
and low-risk individuals choosing low-benefit plans.

Some policy makers view the addition of mandates as a way of improving
insurance coverage without the costs that usually accompany the improvements.
But mandates are not free. They impose economic and social costs on the same
people they intend to benefit. These costs can include higher premiums, lower
wages, higher unemployment, and an increase in the number of uninsured.

In general, research indicates that mandates increase the costs of health care systems (USGAO, 1996; USGAO, 1997a, 1997b; Sing et al., 1998; Mitchell, 1990; Longley, 1994; Gabel and Jensen, 1989; Jensen and Morrisey, 1999). The cost of mandates is often estimated by calculating the share of claims associated with the different categories of spending associated with those mandates, called the *current expenditures approach*. Using the current expenditures approach, mandated benefits are responsible for anywhere from 5 to 22 percent of total claims. Alternatively, estimates based on actuarial projections are used to estimate the increase in premiums due to specific mandates. Using the actuarial approach, the added costs of the various mental health mandates have been estimated to range from 2 percent to 21 percent. Process mandates have also been evaluated with the cost ranging up to 19 percent. Acs and colleagues (1992) estimated the impact of mandates on premium costs using a national cross section of firm-level data, and they found premiums to be anywhere from 4 to 13 percent higher as a direct result of state-level mandates.

A third approach, called the *hedonic pricing approach*, provides a way to estimate the marginal impact of different insurance options on the overall price of a standard policy sold in different geographic regions of the country. Researchers using the hedonic pricing approach—including Gabel and Jensen (1989); Jensen and Morrisey (1999); and Henderson, Seward, and Taylor (2008)—have found that while many mandated benefits raise premiums, some actually lower them. Mandates requiring plans to cover bone-mass measurement, drug abuse treatment, infertility services, and off-label drug use tend to raise premiums. But mandating that policies cover alcoholism treatment, contraceptives, diabetic supplies, emergency services, and treatment provided by nurse practitioners and psychiatric nurses actually lowers premiums.

The evidence from studies on the cost of mandates creates an interesting problem for policy makers. Mandates are popular among certain well-defined constituencies: providers of clinical services, patient advocacy groups, and other political interest groups. Faced with pressure from the various special interest groups and the uncertainty of the true cost of mandates, legislation passes easily. In 1998, almost 100 bills mandating new health care benefits passed state legislatures. Mandated benefits attempt to make marginal improvements in the insurance benefits of those with insurance, but often at a price.

The economics of mandates are clear. If firms already offer the mandated benefit, there is no tangible effect on the availability of insurance or premium costs. However, firms that do not voluntarily offer the mandated coverage are required to add it to their employees' benefit package, which increases the cost of health insurance for those firms. Advocates of additional mandates argue that the new coverage benefits recipients. But recipients end up paying for the new coverage. Evidence presented by Jensen and Morrisey (1999) indicates that workers pay for mandated benefits in three ways: lower wages, fewer benefits, and higher premiums. Given ERISA exemptions, larger firms avoid mandates by self-insuring. Because owners of small businesses do not have the option of self-insuring, they are disproportionately affected by mandates (Jensen, Cotter, and Morrisey, 1995). Additionally, one in four uninsured Americans is without health insurance because of mandates.

One reason that a large percentage of the working poor remain uninsured is that state mandates make private insurance unaffordable for many. This is especially true for small business owners, their employees, and their families, who represent the majority of the employed uninsured in this country.

BACK-OF-THE-ENVELOPE

The Economics of Employer Mandates

Proponents of a universal system recognize that mandatory participation must be part of the system. Mandatory participation may take the form of government provision or some type of mandate, employer or individual. As a tool of social policy, mandates occupy the middle ground between the status quo and government provision. Conservatives prefer mandates to government provision, and liberals prefer mandates to the status quo. The employer mandate has occupied the compromise position in U.S. public policy debates as far back as the Nixon administration.

The case for mandating the employer provision of benefits is clear. The argument goes something like this: As with all merit goods, individuals underestimate the value of health insurance by underestimating the probability of a catastrophic loss due to illness. Because of the difficulty in making these kinds of intertemporal calculations, participation in a health insurance program should be mandatory. In the case of medical care, society may value equal consumption more highly than in the case of other goods and thus may mandate that a certain level of benefits be available to everyone. Finally, the externalities associated with medical care may be considerable. Even though the prevention of the spread of contagious disease is one aspect of this argument, the inability to pay for medical care creates pressures on society to pay the bills. This unwillingness to deny medical care to those in need is evidenced by the fact that uninsured Americans receive free care that amounts to approximately half of the per capita medical care received by the privately insured (Hadley and Holahan, 2003).

Those who argue against the employer mandate point out that it helps only the 60 percent who have some labor force attachment. The mandate places a wedge between the marginal cost of hiring an additional worker and the wage that can be offered. In other words, as benefit costs increase, actual wages decrease. Unable to adjust the wages of workers earning close to the minimum wage, employers are forced to eliminate some jobs, thereby creating unemployment in some sectors. Low-wage industries such as retail, construction, restaurants, agriculture, and personal and household services would be affected more than the rest of the economy.

continued

Key Concept 6
Supply and Demand

Economists tend to view mandated benefits as a disguised tax. Even though the viewpoint is true to a certain extent, it is not quite that simple. In the diagram, consider the original equilibrium of D_0 and S_0 with employment of E_0. A mandatory benefit that costs x dollars per hour shifts the employer's demand for workers down by that amount. If the worker values the mandated benefit at x dollars per hour, then the supply curve shifts out by the same amount, wages fall by x dollars per hour, and employment remains at E_0. However, workers are notorious for underestimating the value of health insurance, so the supply curve shifts by less than x. Wages fall by some fraction of x per hour, but employment also falls from E_0 to E_1.

It is an issue without an easy policy stance. Because of the externalities associated with health insurance, and the tendency of workers to underestimate its value, some argue that it is appropriate for government to intervene and mandate coverage. Others focus on the potential job losses and the associated dislocations that they will cause. As the debate rages on, we are no closer to a solution to the problem of the uninsured. The lesson may be that there are no solutions, only competing alternatives with their own individual drawbacks. This is an issue that cannot be ignored. It will not go away on its own.

Source: Lawrence H. Summers, "Some Simple Economics of Mandated Benefits," *American Economic Review* 79, May 1989, 177–183; Carlos Bonilla, "The Price of a Health Care Mandate," *Wall Street Journal*, August 20, 1993; and Jack Hadley and John Holahan, "How Much Medical Care Do the Uninsured Use, and Who Pays for It?" *Health Affairs – Web Exclusive* (W3), February 12, 2003, 66–81.

The States' Approach to Mandates

The average number of mandates per state in 2002 was 24, ranging from 6 to 49. Mandated coverage for providers was the most common. Most states require that insurance pay for medical services when they are provided by psychologists, chiropractors, optometrists, dentists, podiatrists, and nurse midwives. In addition, some states require coverage for acupuncturists, oral surgeons, speech therapists, and naturopaths. Mandates requiring coverage for mammography screening, alcoholism treatment, off-label drug use, well-child care, and drug abuse treatment are also common. A few states require coverage for ambulance transportation, in vitro fertilization, long-term care, and prescription drugs. Many of the mandates are considered by some to be little more than income protection for certain provider groups.

Many larger firms avoid the mandates by self-insuring, paying for medical care costs as they arise. This tendency does not imply that all mandates should be eliminated. Many argue that the best approach would be for the federal government to preempt state mandates and set national standards. Such standards might include an annual catastrophic limit on the out-of-pocket spending for an individual family, continuity of coverage for job losers and changers, automatic newborn coverage, and a prohibition on waiting periods and on exclusions for preexisting conditions. Reducing the number of mandates seems to be an integral part of any plan serious about increasing the availability of health insurance to those who are currently uninsured. Many argue for a basic-benefits package free of most mandates to enable insurance firms to market plans to small businesses at significantly lower premiums.

Mandated benefits and a mandatory system are quite different concepts. There is nothing inconsistent about requiring everyone to have insurance coverage and, at the same time, reducing the number of mandated benefits. A system that provides for universal coverage will eliminate the need for insurance companies to individually rate employee groups according to risk categories. The common insurance practice

POLICY ISSUE

Is comprehensive reform possible in the United States, or must we settle for the incremental approach?

of experience rating, in which premiums are based on the actual claims made by the group, makes underwriting the risk of small groups problematic. With over half of all U.S. workers either employed in groups of less than 100 or self-employed, the ability of group insurance to spread risk is compromised. Thus, a system where everyone must have insurance coverage opens the possibility of community rating, where underwriting risk is spread over the entire population. With the exception of Hawaii, states cannot require employers to provide health insurance to their employees because federal law, specifically ERISA, preempts state law on all issues dealing with employee benefits.

The individual states have recognized the limitations they face in changing health care delivery within their borders. The more comprehensive proposals—the ambitious plans with far-reaching provisions mandating employer provision of insurance, capping health insurance premiums, and requiring plans to follow managed care guidelines—have all failed to pass. The reform plans that have passed may be viewed as sequential in nature; they do not try to fix everything at once. The more comprehensive plans tend to get carved up by the special interests. The only approach that seems to work is based on gradualism, an important lesson for would-be reformers.

BACK-OF-THE-ENVELOPE

Employment Response to Increases in Labor Costs

The question of how much mandated labor costs will reduce employment opportunities has raged in policy circles for decades. Every time the debate turns to whether the minimum wage should be raised, both sides cite evidence from their research on what to expect. The direction of the change is not open to serious dispute. Even the strongest supporters of increases in minimum wages agree that employment opportunities will be reduced. The major controversy is the size of the employment effect. The answer is simple: It all depends on the size of the price elasticity of demand for labor.

A mandated benefit will have much the same effect on demand for labor as an increase in the minimum wage. As part of the total compensation package, each adds to the cost of hiring a worker. The employment effects are shown in the following diagrams.

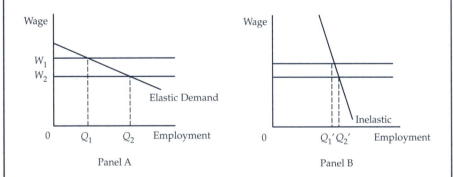

If demand is elastic, then increases in mandated benefits will cause a significant decline in employment, from Q_2 to Q_1 in Panel A. On the other hand, if demand is inelastic, as in Panel B, then the decline in employment opportunities will be minimal, Q_2' to Q_1' in this case.

Key Concept 5
Markets and Pricing

U.S. POLICY ALTERNATIVES

Most Americans favor legislation to provide health insurance to the uninsured, but little consensus has emerged on how to do it (Blendon et al., 2003). Americans are less supportive of major reform measures, such as the national single-payer system, and react more favorably to incremental changes that address the problem. The options most frequently favored are 1) expanding government programs such as Medicaid and SCHIP, 2) mandating insurance coverage secured through place of employment, and 3) expanding the use of market incentives to encourage and enable individuals to purchase insurance. These options will be examined in turn, followed by a discussion of **managed competition**, the compromise alternative that served as the basis of the Clinton health care reform plan in 1994.

Single-Payer National Health Insurance

The all-government, single-payer option attracts its support primarily from proponents of universal insurance coverage. Under this system, everyone would participate in a single health plan, administered and financed by the government or a quasi-governmental agency. A basic benefits package, defined to cover all medically necessary services, would be available to the entire population. Private insurance that duplicates covered services is viewed as a way for the wealthy to create for themselves a higher level of care. Strictly following the Canadian model requires the ban on certain types of private insurance to unite everyone into one equal plan. The elimination of financial barriers to the highest standards of care prohibits any form of deductible or copayment. In contrast, the Swedish model allows private insurance and requires a modest copayment from patients when they receive medical services.

Physicians would not bill patients directly. Instead, they would bill the single payer according to a fee schedule determined through negotiations between representatives of the medical profession and the single payer. Hospitals' reimbursement strategies would vary considerably. Paid either on a fee-for-service or per-diem basis, hospitals merely bill the appropriate government agency for reimbursement. If, however, hospitals are provided with global budgets, the traditional bill no longer exists; they become unnecessary, because hospitals receive a periodic appropriation. The single payer establishes global budgets annually. Hospitals are required to treat all patients who seek care. Spending is capped at the level established by the global operating budget. All capital acquisitions, including all diagnostic and high-tech surgical equipment, must be approved by the single payer and are typically paid out of a separate capital budget, controlling overall investment in medical technology.

The theoretical model that applies to the single-payer approach is referred to as *monopsony*. Under a monopsonistic health care system, the government is the only health care buyer. This is not socialized medicine in its pure form. Health care delivery is still based in the private sector, but it requires deep involvement by the government in setting global budgets for hospitals and nursing homes, establishing a ceiling on overall spending, and setting allowable fees for providers. Many proponents of this plan even recommend that growth in health care spending be limited to the growth in the economy, usually measured by the annual percentage change in gross domestic product.

The main advantage of a single-payer system is its administrative simplicity. Only one paper trail is created in a single-payer system—provider to payer. The U.S. system with its labyrinth of private insurance carriers is administratively complex, which is the reason for much of the "unnecessary" spending. Another important advantage is that everyone is covered regardless of employment status or financial circumstances. Furthermore, because it requires little or no out-of-pocket

managed competition
A health care reform plan first popularized by economist Alain Enthoven, whereby individuals are given a choice among competing health plans. A standard feature is the formation of health insurance alliances to increase the bargaining power of insurance purchasers.

The U.S. House of Representatives and the U.S. Senate have home pages that provide access to information about the legislative process, individual members, and the various committees. Links are also provided to review schedules of activities and access information available from Congress.

http://www.house.gov

http://www.senate.gov

spending, financing is not a barrier to access in any way. Proponents will argue that the single-payer system is the most equitable and efficient way to strike a balance between cost, access, and quality.

On the other hand, critics will argue that within the so-called strengths of the single-payer system lies its weaknesses. It may not be socialized medicine, but it increases government involvement in a system that already has too much. A single-payer system results in a higher tax burden. Higher taxes are netted out by the elimination of the private insurance premium, but as individuals lose the direct responsibility of paying insurance premiums, they also lose the motivation to do anything about rising expenditures. The benefits of wellness programs and aggressive action to reduce spending are spread over the entire population. Individual savings are insignificant in a system of community-rated insurance.

Key Concept 3
Marginal Analysis

The argument for a single-payer system usually focuses on the duplication of services caused by a system populated by multiple insurers. Eliminate the duplication and costs will naturally come down. If this is the solution, why not eliminate the duplication in other markets? Because duplication is beneficial. It ensures that if one source of supply is cut off, another will be there to take its place.

Employer-Based Health Insurance

More than 90 percent of the privately insured nonelderly population receives health insurance coverage through the workplace (EBRI, 2000). In keeping with this tradition, many reformers rely on a strategy that builds on the employer-based system. The popularity of employer-sponsored health insurance (ESI) is due to three important factors. First, administering insurance in a large group setting leads to economies of scale. Second, the workplace is an ideal setting to pool risk, because workers are on average healthier than nonworkers, and they form groups to work, not to buy health insurance. Finally, the U.S. tax code provides favorable tax treatment for health insurance benefits. This favorable treatment can be traced back to the wage-and-price controls in place during World War II. Considered different from all other forms of compensation, employers began providing health coverage as a substitute for increased pay. Not only were health benefits outside wage-and-price guidelines, but the Internal Revenue Service (IRS) also excluded them from taxable income, a benefit worth over $100 billion today. This IRS decision, subsequently upheld in a 1954 Supreme Court decision, has had a tremendous impact on the structure of the health insurance industry. Anyone doubting the power of tax incentives in shaping behavior need only study this example to gain an appreciation of their importance.

POLICY ISSUE

Should health insurance be tax exempt when provided as an employer-sponsored benefit?

http://

RAND is a nonprofit institution established to improve public policy through research and publications. Interdisciplinary in nature, the organization has a health sciences program that can be accessed at this address.

http://www.rand.org/

Employer-Mandated Insurance The concept of forcing employers to provide health care coverage for their workers originated from the belief that employers are better equipped to manage and finance health care delivery. The proponents of employer mandates have used this market-based principle to support their plan to provide universal insurance coverage to all working Americans and their dependents.

Employer mandates are commonly used across the world as a means of financing health care access. One way of implementing an employer mandate is through the so called **play-or-pay** approach. Under play-or-pay, employers would be required to purchase a basic health care package for their employees as defined by lawmakers. Employers would also have a second option. Instead of providing the basic benefits package, they could pay for a government-sponsored health plan through a new tax, most likely a payroll tax based on a certain percentage of total payroll.

Even strong proponents of play-or-pay recognize that the mechanism makes no provisions for the unemployed. And play-or-pay would likely increase considerably the number of unemployed. A study by the Joint Economic Committee

play-or-pay
A health care reform feature whereby employers "play" by providing health care coverage to their employees, or they pay a payroll tax to fund government-provided insurance.

of Congress estimated that play-or-pay with a 7 percent payroll tax option would increase unemployment by some 700,000 workers, over half from firms affected that employ fewer than 20 workers. In a study prepared for the Employment Policies Institute, June and David O'Neill estimate that such a mandate would lead to a loss of 3.1 million jobs (Bonilla, 1993). This mandated increase in labor costs would disproportionately impact seven low-wage industries, including restaurants, retail trade, construction, personal services, and agriculture.

Most firms in the United States already spend 10 to 12 percent of payroll on medical costs. If the tax rate for participation in the government-sponsored plan were set at a lower level, many firms would be motivated to move to the public system. The Congressional Budget Office estimated that half of the U.S. population would ultimately move to the government plan. With those numbers, we would soon have a system of health care delivery largely dominated by the federal government.

ISSUES IN MEDICAL CARE DELIVERY

Does Lack of Portability Result in Job-Lock?

Are employees who have health problems locked into their jobs because health insurance policies fail to provide benefits for preexisting conditions? A great deal of anecdotal evidence seems to support the link between job mobility and health insurance. In a CBS/New York Times poll, for example, 30 percent of the individuals questioned stated that they or a member of their household stayed in a job they wanted to leave primarily because of health insurance. Such polls, while informative, do not provide a sound empirical basis for the existence of insurance-related **job-lock**.

To answer the question of whether job-lock exists, it is important to understand what it is. *Job-lock* may be defined as a situation in which an employee decides to keep a job that he or she would rather leave for fear of losing health insurance coverage due to a preexisting medical problem. Job-lock is an important economy-wide concern if workers are precluded from moving to jobs where they are more productive. To the extent that this occurs, overall economic output is reduced.

Using data from the 1987 National Medical Expenditure Survey, Madrian (1994) was able to identify several tendencies. Individuals with high medical bills are less likely to leave a job that offers health insurance. The larger the family, the less likely a worker will leave a job that offers health insurance. Husbands with pregnant wives are less likely to leave a job that offers health insurance. In the study sample, job-lock reduced voluntary turnover of those employees with health insurance from 16 percent to 12 percent, a 25 percent reduction.

The 1985 Consolidated Omnibus Budget Reconciliation Act (COBRA) provided in principle some relief from job-lock by offering an option whereby workers who changed jobs could continue coverage for up to 18 months by paying 102 percent of the premium cost. In practice, employees found that a monthly premium of $400 to $500 was a significant impediment to mobility. The Health Insurance Portability and Accountability Act (HIPAA) passed by Congress in 1996 was intended to provide the legislative muscle to force insurance companies to expand portability and end the problem of job-lock.

Source: Brigitte C. Madrian, "Employment-Based Health Insurance and Job Mobility: Is There Evidence of Job-Lock?" *The Quarterly Journal of Economics*, 109(1), February 1994, 27–54.

job-lock
The inability of individual employees to change jobs because preexisting medical conditions make them or one of their dependents ineligible for health insurance benefits under a new plan.

Individual Mandates   Some notable health experts have suggested that the way to minimize the free-rider problem is to require individuals to provide their own insurance coverage (Reinhardt, 1992). Instead of an employer mandate, they prefer an **individual mandate**. This approach to mandated coverage is similar to the way automobile liability insurance is required for all registered vehicles.

By taking the employer out of the business of providing health benefits, individuals would be more aware of the actual costs of their health insurance (Pauly, 1994). Current arrangements perpetuate the myth that employers pay health insurance premiums. Business and labor have fostered this myth, creating the impression that employers are providing health benefits at no cost to the employee. Even the reference to a premium split between employer and employee is a veiled attempt to promote the idea that the employer pays. Business firms do not pay for health benefits. Treated as a cost of doing business, this expense is passed on to customers in the form of higher prices, absorbed by owners in the form of lower profits, or forced on employees in the form of lower wages and higher unemployment. In competitive industries where prices are market driven and profits modest, employers shift most of their health insurance costs onto workers. The shift is subtle and often unnoticed but real nevertheless. Actual wages are lower, and nonmedical benefits are less generous (Jensen and Morrisey, 1999).

Implementation of an individual mandate would require that employees who currently have health benefits receive the "employer-paid" portion of the premium as gross income. To purchase insurance coverage, the individual would then use these funds. An individual mandate would expose the myth of employer-paid insurance by making the employee more aware of the cost of medical coverage.

Market-Based Alternatives[10]

At the heart of the debate between advocates of market-based alternatives and those who would give the government a bigger role in the delivery and financing of medical care is a basic ideological struggle. Can the market for medical care work like the market for other commodities? Or is medical care different, an exception to the basic laws of economics and unsuited for market delivery? Will a medical care market work like one in automobiles or personal computers? Or should it be insulated from the market, as are defense and the interstate highway system?

Nearly every other developed country in the world has virtually given up on the market as a primary means of delivering health care. Only the United States, Switzerland, the Republic of South Africa, and, to a limited extent, the Netherlands rely on market mechanisms to any extent to address the important issues of cost and access.

Critics of market-based medical care argue from the unchallenged premise that private markets cannot be expected to address such a fundamentally important issue as the delivery of medical care. Highly respected health economist Uwe Reinhardt has noted that "no one can distribute Gucci loafers better than the market, but a pure market cannot distribute health care" (quoted in Stout, 1992).

This ideological debate allows no room for compromise. In many ways, the middle ground is the most difficult to defend. An example is the recent experience with President Clinton's 1994 health care reform proposal. Defenders of the market attacked the plan as a government takeover, and those who wanted a government-run system attacked it as a half-measure that did not fully address the real problems.

---

individual mandate
A legal requirement that individuals carry their own insurance protection.

The Congressional Budget Office (CBO) provides Congress with economic and budgetary information. The CBO develops forecasts and projections that serve as a baseline for measuring the effects of proposed changes in taxing and spending laws. Their site has links to reports, publications, and other information sources.

http://cbo.gov

The Cato Institute is a nonpartisan public policy research foundation with libertarian leanings. Their Web page spotlights research papers and books examining the role of government. The site provides numerous links to policy-related papers.

http://www.cato.org

POLICY ISSUE

Can market incentives be effectively used in the financing and provision of medical care in a way that also promotes fairness?

---

[10] Three market-oriented think tanks in Washington, DC best typify the market approach to the health care reform debate: the American Enterprise Institute, the Heritage Foundation, and the Cato Institute. The National Center for Policy Analysis, located in Dallas, is an active think tank located outside the Beltway.

POLICY ISSUE

Is meaningful health care reform possible given the ideological divide among the American electorate?

http://

The Heritage Foundation is a think tank whose mission is to formulate and promote conservative public policies based on the principles of free enterprise, limited government, individual freedom, traditional American values, and a strong national defense. The site includes a library, resource bank, and links to government and other public policy organizations.

http://www.heritage.org

Key Concept 3
Marginal Analysis

http://

The National Center for Policy Analysis attempts to develop and promote private alternatives to government regulation and control, solving problems by relying on the strengths of the competitive, entrepreneurial private sector. The site provides links to policy briefings, the organization's cybrary, and their publication *Executive Alert*.

http://www.ncpa.org

The Market Approach The failures of the current system are evident everywhere in limited access for the uninsured and high costs for everyone, but advocates of a market approach do not see these as market failures. In fact, the shortcomings are viewed as the government's failure to promote competitive markets as a means of addressing the problems of access and cost.

The market approach to health care reform is most commonly associated with the use of the tax code to make people more sensitive to the cost of medical care and health insurance reform to improve access for the uninsured and uninsurable. Tax credits or vouchers are suggested as one way to encourage low-income families to buy their own health insurance. This option would be limited to families with incomes less than some modest percentage of the poverty income level, usually 150 to 200 percent. At the heart of the debate is whether a credit or voucher for any amount less than the full insurance premium would be sufficient for a family with a $40,000 annual income to purchase its own insurance. Critics argue that this is nothing more than a symbolic gesture that would have little real impact on the number of uninsured. Proponents do not expect miracles from this proposal but do feel that a credit or voucher system would increase access for many low-income Americans. The goal of market proponents is to improve access, not by creating a vast system of government mandates, prospective budgets, price controls, and bureaucratic alliances, but by establishing a mechanism that provides incentives at the margin to encourage some to take responsibility for their own care.[11]

Many market advocates believe the major distortion in the health insurance market is the tax treatment of employer-sponsored health insurance. Because employer-sponsored health benefits are not treated as taxable income, employees have become desensitized to the actual cost of health insurance. Those reformers with the courage of their convictions have recommended a change in the tax exemption. A complete elimination of the tax exemption, or at least a limit on the current subsidy, would represent a big step in promoting cost-conscious behavior on the part of the consuming public. In addition, this change could result in as much as a $100 billion increase in income tax revenues that could be used to finance other parts of the reform plan, lower taxes, or reduce the federal budget deficit.

Proponents of the market approach see insurance reform as an essential element in improving access to the medical care system. A common complaint addressed by recent reform dealt with certain insurance practices that denied insurance coverage to certain vulnerable groups—job losers, job changers, and those with chronic medical conditions. HIPAA addressed the portability issue, effectively guaranteeing group-to-group portability for job changers who have at least 18 months of continuous coverage under their old plans. HIPAA also required that companies selling insurance in the small-group market (groups of less than 50 employees) guarantee issue of all insurance options regardless of the health status of individual members of the group. Finally, all coverage in the individual market must be guaranteed renewable. Despite these extensions, there is still limited access for the uninsured who have preexisting medical conditions, and insurance, for many, is still unaffordable. States still make their own decisions on regulating premiums.

Another problem that limits insurance availability is that individuals and small businesses are forced into small risk pools for underwriting purposes. Unable to spread risk over an appropriately large group, premiums are significantly higher because of the high costs of administering small risk pools, and they are subject to large increases in the event of a single catastrophic loss.

---

[11] Many market proponents seriously consider tax credits or vouchers as a possible replacement for Medicare and Medicaid.

A market solution to this problem must include measures to make it easier to form large risk pools. Concentrating purchasing power and spreading risk lowers costs. Specifically, antitrust laws that inhibit or prevent cooperative arrangements must be repealed or amended. Such changes would expedite the creation of health insurance purchasing cooperatives, or insurance markets similar to the Massachusetts Connector, to enhance access and lower the cost of insurance for individuals and small groups.

In another important cost-control measure, proponents of the market alternative recommend incentives for people to enroll in managed care plans. Over the past decade, the private sector has experienced an unprecedented growth in managed care enrollments. At the same time, public sector programs, especially Medicare, have not followed the same trends—less than 20 percent of Medicare enrollees who have a choice are in managed care plans.

The market alternative is built around the core idea that individual decisions are better than collective decisions. The market plan would provide more power to the individual, whereas the main alternatives would give more power to the government. The real debate is between those who believe that individuals can make their own decisions in matters involving medical care and those who think that medical care is too complex to rely on individual initiative.

Consumer-Directed Health Plans For many who believe that free enterprise works and that the market is the best way to organize the delivery of goods and services, medical care delivery presents a conundrum. Many are content to argue market failure and recommend reliance on a government-run plan, but government action has proven susceptible to many of the same failings of the market, plus others that are more difficult to correct. Most policy experts agree that the primary reason for the suboptimal results of the market in medical care delivery is the dominance of the third-party payment mechanism.

Defenders of the market believe that if the market is to work in medical care, individuals must have "skin in the game"—they must spend their own money when they receive care. Even though holders of a private insurance policy spend their own money on premiums—or their employer spends it for them—once paid, they represent a sunk cost and are irrelevant in the decision-making process. Faced with a low or zero marginal cost of care, individuals tend to overconsume; that is, they demand care that adds little to prospective outcomes. For the consumption decision to be optimal in the economic sense, individuals must take into consideration the alternative uses of the resources. If individuals are to economize on the use of resources, they must realize a direct benefit from their own economizing behavior.

For the market to work in medical care, consumers must spend their own money for routine (high frequency, low cost) medical services. In turn, to protect against catastrophic (low frequency, high cost) expenses, individuals would purchase a high-deductible insurance policy. Insurers use deductibles and coinsurance to get policyholders to spend their money more wisely, but often even small deductibles and low coinsurance rates create problems. For a single mother with three children, even a trip to the doctor to treat an earache can mean a financial hardship. Without money to pay the deductible, the earache often goes untreated, resulting in higher spending for an emergency room visit at a later date, and possibly long-term hearing loss for the child.

Quite possibly the most important advance in health insurance since the managed care movement in the 1990s was the introduction of consumer-directed health plans (CDHPs). A few small insurers began linking high-deductible coverage with health reimbursement accounts (HRAs) in the late 1990s. This arrangement

POLICY ISSUE

Do individual consumers have the ability to make their own decisions about matters concerning their own medical care?

Key Concept 4
Self-Interest

POLICY ISSUE

Is it possible to make medical consumers cost conscious and at the same time create a system that treats the sick and poor fairly?

Key Concept 3
Marginal Analysis

POLICY ISSUE

If you spend $2,500 on your annual health insurance premium but do not receive $2,500 worth of medical care, are you getting your money's worth?

allowed individuals and their employers to make tax-free contributions into accounts designated for out-of-pocket medical spending. The movement was slow to develop until Congress passed the Medicare Modernization Act in 2003, which allowed insurers to offer health savings accounts (HSAs) to those with high-deductible policies. The major difference between the two accounts is portability. Typically, in the HRA arrangement, ownership of the account rests with the employer. If the holder of an HRA leaves employment for any reason, the balance in the HRA stays with the employer. In contrast, the HSA is treated more like a 401(k) investment plan, in which ownership rests with the employee.

The basic idea behind the HSA is simple. Instead of buying a traditional indemnity insurance policy, individuals purchase a high-deductible policy, say $2,500, that would cover only medical expenses above that amount. Each year, approximately 90 percent of all claims and 70 percent of all medical spending are for amounts totaling less than $2,500. Annual deductibles in this range would result in significant savings on insurance premiums.[12]

The individual would have the health savings account to pay for the first $2,500 for an individual or $5,000 for a family. The catastrophic insurance policy would cover all expenses in excess of the deductible. If medical expenses were less than the deductible, the money would remain in the HSA. Accumulations in these accounts would be available to pay future health insurance premiums or other medical expenses, such as long-term care where current insurance coverage is especially weak. The important aspect of the plan is that the savings account belongs to the individual. It would grow through annual deposits and earn interest.

The major advantage of the health savings account is that it puts the individual in control of his or her own medical spending. Proponents of HSAs assert that the main reason medical markets fail is that there is no incentive to practice economizing behavior—either for the provider or the patient. With health savings accounts, patients are spending their own money, at least up to the deductible, so they have an incentive to economize. Rather than being indifferent to the prices they pay, consumers will benefit from shopping around. Such an environment is representative of consumer sovereignty in the real sense of the classical economic concept.

At a point, individual self-interest would take over. With patients benefiting from their own economizing behavior, savings balances would grow as spending moderated. Estimates of reduced spending are based primarily on the experience of individual employers. The movement to consumer-directed plans progressed slowly at first. The first HSAs became available in 2004, and by 2007, 5 percent of all workers covered by private insurance were covered under CDHPs.

Many do not believe that the HSA concept can work on a nationwide scale, dismissing the idea because it allows too much individual discretion in choosing medical care. Critics think that most people are incapable of making informed decisions about the quality and quantity of the health care they need. They argue that anything short of universally mandated free care does not provide the proper incentives for individuals to seek the correct mix of primary and preventive care. They fear that individuals with medical savings accounts would be tempted to save their money rather than spend it when they or their children are sick (U.S. House of Representatives, 1993).

POLICY ISSUE

Is it possible to change the way Americans view health insurance, or will they always treat it as prepaid medical care?

Key Concept 7
Competition

Key Concept 4
Self-Interest

---

[12] Golden Rule Insurance Company surveyed four insurance underwriters—Washington National, Pyramid Life, Time, and Union Bankers—in ten U.S. cities—Cincinnati, Dallas, Denver, Des Moines, Indianapolis, Omaha, Peoria, Portland, Richmond, and Scranton—on the price of a $2,500 deductible policy for a two-parent family with children. The survey results listed a median health insurance premium of $1,650. This amount represents a significant savings over the cost of a traditional indemnity insurance policy.

Many are hesitant to back the concept of the health savings account for fear that what may work for a small segment of the community may not work for the whole population. HSAs may work well for those who are healthy, but what about the small percentage of the population that gets sick? How would those unfortunate enough to have large medical bills be protected at a reasonable cost? Others worry that individual HSA holders would be no match for the more powerful provider networks.

Proponents argue that holders of CDHP plans will be smarter consumers of health care and will demand better price and quality information from providers. Additionally, early evidence does not support the claim that holders of high-deductible plans will underuse preventive services and drive up spending in the long run (Rowe, Brown-Stevenson, Downey, and Newhouse, 2008). Adverse risk selection can be handled by cross-subsidies across plans using the principles of risk sharing. Under any circumstance, greater cost sharing by policyholders is inevitable and, short of overt price controls, the CDHP model is better equipped to moderate spending than the alternatives.

Managed Competition

Can choice and competition, principles that have served so well in other sectors of the economy, be made to work in the medical care sector? To work, *choice* must mean more than whatever your employer chooses for you. Competition must be encouraged at the point at which the consumer purchase decision is made, and that is either at the time the type of health insurance coverage is determined or at the point of buying the care. The model of managed competition was first introduced by Alain Enthoven under the title "Consumer Choice Health Plan" (Enthoven, 1978). Revised and clarified extensively since its early beginnings, managed competition emerged as a central element of President Clinton's 1994 reform package.[13] Proponents of managed competition see it as a way to increase competition in the market for health insurance. In most employer-provided plans, the employee has little choice. As members of the same group, all employees get the plan provided by the employer—fee-for-service or managed care—and rarely have the option of choosing between the two.

ISSUES IN MEDICAL CARE DELIVERY

Managed Competition in Practice: The Federal Employees Health Benefit Plan

The Federal Employees Health Benefit Plan (FEHBP) was enacted in 1959 to cover all civilian employees of the federal government, including Congress, the executive branch, the judicial branch, civilian employees of the Pentagon, and federal retirees. Currently, FEHBP insures over 9 million civilians, one out of every 25 Americans, making it the largest employer-sponsored health insurance program in the country.

The distinguishing feature of the plan is that recipients are allowed to choose their own health benefits package from among nearly 400 private health insurance plans. Depending on geographic location, each individual

continued

Key Concept 7
Competition

---

[13] After details of Clinton's plan began to surface, Enthoven penned a harsh criticism of the president's version of "managed competition" (Enthoven, 1993).

Key Concept 3

Marginal Analysis

has at least 21, and in some cases as many as 37, plans from which to choose. The plans range from traditional Blue Cross–Blue Shield health insurance plans to one of over 300 managed care plans (HMOs). Premium costs vary depending on the type of coverage desired. Total annual premiums amount to over $12.6 billion in 1991 with the federal government paying around 72 percent of the average premium.

Each November brings with it an "open season" in which federal employees have several weeks to decide which type of coverage to choose for the upcoming year. Plans are marketed by health insurance companies, HMOs, local hospitals, and employee associations. Many consider the FEHBP a model for nationwide reform, but before nationwide implementation of this system is possible, fully informed consumers must be the norm, not the exception. Federal employees get plenty of information to assist them in making their decisions. Their options are clearly spelled out in advertising, association newsletters, and independently published consumer guides. When consumers perceive that they will benefit from additional information, they will demand information, and it will be provided.

In recent years, the growth rate in the average FEHBP premium has been significantly below rates experienced among private sector plans. After a 3 percent increase in premiums in 1994, they actually fell by 3.4 percent in 1995. Average premiums in 1996 increased 0.4 percent with one-fourth of the plans actually experiencing reductions in premiums. With all the plans available, two-thirds of the enrollees use one of six fee-for-service plans, and only three of the 400-plus HMOs have over 25,000 participants.

Given the number of choices available, enrollees tend to select health plans based on their own expected usage. In other words, enrollees self-select according to their likelihood of using medical care. To the extent that this market segmentation takes place, it actually defeats the purpose of insurance — the spreading of risk. Fine-tuning the system might include actually limiting the number of choices available to reduce this tendency. Though the system is by no means perfect, it works reasonably well for a large number of enrollees and is even considered by some analysts as a model for reform of the Medicare system.

Source: Robert E. Moffit, "FEHBP Controls Costs Again: More Lessons for Medicare Reformers," *The Heritage Foundation F.Y.I. No. 64*, September 25, 1995.

Under managed competition, employers would be required to make competing health plans available to all full-time employees. Employees, in turn, would choose among the competing plans, including fee-for-service arrangements, HMOs, preferred provider organizations, and point-of-service plans. Under most circumstances, employees would have a choice of a minimum of three plans. The employer would contribute a fixed sum toward the purchase of the health plan—the key element in managed competition.

Insurers would set premiums based on the basic benefit package specified by the legislation. The average premium of all eligible plans is called the *average employment-based plan cost*, referred to as *APC* in the following discussion. The employer would pay at least 80 percent of the APC regardless of the cost of the actual plan chosen, and the employee would pay the balance. The 80 percent employer share would be treated as a tax-free benefit. Any employer contribution in excess of 80 percent of APC would be considered taxable income. The employee share would be paid out of after-tax income.

For example, suppose three basic plans are available. Plan 1 costs $1,600, Plan 2 costs $2,000, and Plan 3 costs $2,400. The APC of these three plans is $2,000. The employer is required to pay 80 percent of the APC, or $1,600. Employees choosing Plan 1 would pay nothing extra. Those choosing Plan 3 would pay $800 extra. If the employer pays more than $1,600, the additional benefit is treated the same as ordinary income and taxed at the employee's highest marginal rate.

Proponents of managed competition see it as a way of making employees more price conscious and encouraging insurers to hold down costs to make plans more attractive. Policy makers who consider themselves moderates consider managed competition a workable middle ground between those advocating a government-run system and those wanting the market to play a bigger role. They see it solving the social problems of a growing class of uninsured and, at the same time, capturing many of the cost-saving benefits of competition.

Those opposed to managed competition feel that the emphasis is on management and not competition (Goodman, 1993). Government management requires that a standard benefit package be defined by law. The political battle becomes one of what is included in the basic plan and what is not. Special interest lobbies are bound to put pressure on lawmakers to include additional benefits in the basic plan.[14]

Managed competition places a strong emphasis on managed care as a way of controlling costs. Uniform billing procedures including standardized forms and electronic billing are suggested as ways of reducing administrative costs. The stipulation of guaranteed issue on the part of the insurer would be balanced by mandatory participation on the part of the public. Otherwise, the rational decision for the low-risk population—the healthy—would be to forgo insurance until they become sick.

For a market to work in medical care, cost-conscious behavior must become the rule rather than the exception. The two points of purchase in the medical marketplace are when the individual makes the decision about what type of medical plan to purchase and when the individual actually receives the service. Advocates of managed competition feel that, based on equity considerations, a system based on competition at the point of purchasing health insurance offers the best alternative for bringing competitive forces to bear in this market. Advocates of the CDHP approach disagree, viewing competition at the point of purchasing medical care as the appropriate choice.

MARKET RESPONSE TO UNCERTAINTY[15]

As was stated earlier, employer-sponsored insurance has been the dominant feature of the private sector health insurance market in the United States for the past 60 years. In all likelihood, most Americans will continue to receive health insurance coverage through their place of employment as long as public policy does not deviate substantially from the current state of affairs. This fact does not mitigate employer concerns over the ramifications of a changing public policy. Eliminating or even modifying the tax-exempt status of the health benefit would have a significant impact on the number of workers who are offered health insurance and the nature of the benefit package they would receive. Gruber (2001) estimated that each percentage-point increase in the after-tax price of health insurance decreased the

Project HOPE (Health Opportunities for People Everywhere) provides health education, health policy research, and humanitarian assistance in over 70 countries, including the United States. Community projects in Texas and West Virginia are featured on their Web site.

http://www.projhope.org

---

[14] Take for example the expanded benefits package suggested in the Clinton Health Care Plan that had some 40 pages of benefits and their explanations listed in Subtitle B of the proposed act.

[15] This section relies on a previously published paper by Henderson and Taylor (2002).

likelihood that workers would be offered insurance by 0.74 percentage points. Using this estimate, eliminating the tax exemption for ESI would lead to a 22-percentage point decrease in the probability of receiving health insurance for a person in the 30 percent marginal tax bracket.

Another concern for many employers who offer health benefits is the prospect that Congress will impose new federal oversight on health care delivery in the name of patients' rights. A Patients' Bill of Rights would likely impose hundreds of new federal regulations on private sector health plans, adding new rules and standards governing the delivery of care and increasing the employer's liability for decisions regarding the type of plan offered. Employers are concerned that if the new rules expand the patient's rights to sue health plans for denial of care, both plans and employers will be subject to litigation. This expanded threat of liability may cause employers to reexamine and modify their role in choosing health plans.

Many firms are not waiting around for the federal government to extend its oversight and are already making changes in the way the health care benefit is administered (Martin et al., 2002). Instead of following the current model for ESI, in which a single comprehensive plan is offered, many employers are adopting a consumer-driven model that gives employees more plan options that vary in terms of coverage and price, something that looks suspiciously like Enthoven's managed competition. Under these circumstances, it is the employee who chooses the plan. Consequently, the employer's responsibility becomes principally financial, providing an allowance or voucher to the employee for the express purpose of purchasing health insurance.

The movement to limit employer involvement and increase employee choice—it may be too early to call it a trend—has led to the introduction of the *defined-contribution plan*. Even though it is not a new concept in employee benefits, the defined contribution as applied to health insurance has not extended much beyond the administration of the FEHBP discussed earlier. A shift to the defined-contribution model will shift the primary responsibility of plan choice from the employer to the employee. Depending on how much responsibility they are willing to give up, employers can contract with a single insurance carrier or multiple carriers, who can offer a few options or a wide range of options. The choice depends on the size of the group and the ability of the underwriter to maintain the integrity of the individual risk pools.

The shift to the defined-contribution model raises a number of policy concerns, namely the tax-exempt status of the employer contribution and the segmentation of employee risk pools. Under current practices, the tax exemption for the employer contribution remains intact as long as it may be used solely for the purchase of health insurance. If all or part of the contribution may be used for anything else, the tax exemption may be questioned. Refundable tax credits may solve the dilemma by allowing the employee to decide how much of the voucher to spend on health insurance. The part spent on health insurance would be tax exempt, but the part spent on anything else would be taxable income.

As their popularity expands and plan options increase, defined contribution plans will contribute to the segmentation of risk pools. Employees with health problems will continue to purchase comprehensive plans with high premiums. Employees without health problems, unwilling to pay the high premiums, will choose catastrophic plans with high deductibles and lower premiums. The cost of comprehensive plans will increase as healthy employees leave them, and risk pooling will jeopardize the very existence of comprehensive plans. As premiums rise, individuals with chronic conditions may not be able to afford health insurance. Employers would then be faced with the prospects of having a segmented workforce, those who are healthy would have health coverage, and those with chronic health conditions would not have it.

The challenge for policy makers is obvious. Market solutions to problems are not always pleasant. It becomes the responsibility of government to shape public policy to make sure these types of market failures do not adversely affect those population groups who are most vulnerable, namely, the sick and poor.

ISSUES IN MEDICAL CARE DELIVERY

ClintonCare: Its Development and Downfall

Bill Clinton took the oath of office in January 1993 to become the forty-second president of the United States. With both houses of Congress controlled by the Democratic Party, most followers of politics expected that reform of the health care system, Clinton's top domestic priority, would soon become the law of the land. The Clinton team adopted the same "War Room" strategy that successfully catapulted Clinton into the presidency. Setting an ambitious 100-day deadline, Clinton and his advisers began the process of drafting what many considered to be the most important piece of social legislation since the New Deal.

The two most visible players on the Clinton team were his wife, Hillary Rodham Clinton, and long-time friend and fellow Rhodes scholar Ira Magaziner. As head of the health care reform task force, Ms. Clinton's primary responsibility was to sell the plan. Magaziner, Clinton's senior policy adviser and "health czar," supervised the day-to-day activities of the task force and became the primary drafter of the final plan presented to Congress in October 1993.

The development of the plan may be traced back to late 1991, when candidate Clinton made health care reform a major plank in his presidential platform. His early plan, "National Health Insurance Reform to Cut Costs and Cover Everybody," may be described as a government-run play-or-pay system. After Clinton received his party's nomination in August 1992, it became clear that the electorate supported a more market-oriented approach. In the final months of the presidential campaign, Clinton's approach shifted from play-or-pay to managed competition.

The idea for a health care task force emerged from the early policy discussions as a way to buy time, work out the details of the proposal, and build support for managed competition. After announcing the plan in his State of the Union address in February 1993, Clinton and his advisers went about the task of organizing the 511-member task force. Magaziner served as overseer of the operation, presiding over the major meetings, or "tollgates," as they are known in management theory. Some called it "policy-wonk heaven"; others said it was more like the Spanish Inquisition. These tollgate sessions lasted as long as 16 hours and served to inform Magaziner on the progress and direction of the committee meetings. Magaziner soon became the choke point in the flow of information. Little was committed to paper; everything was in his head. Although the task force missed the 100-day deadline, the plan was almost complete by June, except for one troubling detail — how to finance it.

The broader tasks of running the country began taking up precious administration time and using up political goodwill. The better part of Summer 1993 was spent in a particularly nasty budget battle that the president finally won by a 51 to 50 vote in the Senate with Vice President

continued

Al Gore casting the tie-breaking vote. Foreign policy issues, such as the military intervention in Somalia, also took up valuable time and energy.

Finally, on September 22, 1993, before a joint session of Congress, President Clinton announced his reform plan. Called by Ms. Clinton "the most anticipated document since Moses came down off Mount Sinai with the Ten Commandments," the legislative proposal filled 1,342 pages and was accompanied by an 800-page explanation and a paperback summary available in most local bookstores. The main principles of the plan as outlined in President Clinton's speech were easy to support — security, simplicity, savings, choice, quality, and responsibility. The ensuing debate focused on the details.

The plan was a remarkable document in scope and premise. It called for universal coverage as an entitlement, community rating of health insurance premiums, employer mandates, baseline (global) budgeting, uniform fee schedules, and the creation of 250 quasi-governmental agencies called **health alliances**. These health alliances would be under the supervision of a National Health Board created to issue regulations, establish requirements for state health plans, monitor compliance, and enforce budgets. The plan bowed to the interests of some groups and ignored those of others. The VA system would remain intact and even receive additional funding. The AMA wanted limits on awards for pain and suffering in medical malpractice cases, but the influence of the Trial Lawyers of America kept these limits out of the plan.

According to the president, everything in the plan was negotiable except universal coverage. In a classic good-cop-bad-cop routine, however, one administration spokesperson would talk about compromise, while another would criticize those who openly opposed aspects of the plan. Clinton found himself sidetracked again, spending the better part of the fall in the debate over the North American Free Trade Agreement (NAFTA). Instead of focusing on health care, Clinton had to fight a traditional ally, the AFL-CIO, over free trade. Ms. Clinton had early success on Capital Hill in committee hearings discussing the plan. Opponents were effectively muted in their criticism by her command over the details and her personal style.

Nevertheless, criticism came from all sides. Even members of the president's cabinet and key economic advisers had doubts about aspects of the plan, especially its financing assumptions. Opposition from several important special interest groups had to be addressed. The Health Insurance Association of America, fighting for its very existence, was quite vocal in opposing the plan. The association spent over $14 million on a series of "Harry and Louise" television advertisements featuring a young professional couple questioning various provisions in the plan and calling for "a better way" to fix health care. Small business — represented by the Chamber of Commerce, the National Association of Manufacturers, and the National Federation of Independent Business — was critical of the employer mandate.

At the same time, a number of alternative plans were being considered in Congress. Senator Paul Wellstone of Minnesota headed the single-payer group that occupied the left-of-center position. Representative Jim Cooper of Tennessee led the market-reform legislators with the main right-of-center alternative. As Congress debated through the summer of 1994, Republicans became convinced they could defeat the president and his bill. Public support for the president's version of health care reform had waned from 57 percent approval when it was first introduced to 37 percent. As the legislative session drew to a close in the early fall, it was difficult to find a member of Congress who would vote for any health care reform bill, even one they had personally sponsored.

continued

---

health alliances
Called by various names, including *health insurance purchasing cooperatives (HIPC)*, these provides a way for small employers to act collectively to purchase health insurance. Often geographically based and not-for-profit, the alliance contracts with insurers and/or providers for medical coverage for its members.

Legislation that looked so promising in 1993 failed miserably in 1994. What went wrong? Many different perspectives offer reasons for the plan's failure: The process was too secretive, the framers were politically naïve, they wasted too much time on details, and the plan was too complicated. Each of these perspectives may contain an element of the truth, but a separate line of reasoning may come closer to explaining the demise of the plan — trust. Whom do you trust to organize health care delivery? Americans in general are a bit cynical about government's ability to run anything efficiently.

In the end, the administration apparently failed to convince the public that health care was any different. The process seemed to breed suspicion rather than communicate ideas. By the fall of 1994, fewer than one in six Americans felt they clearly understood the plan, down from one in five just after its introduction. Proponents tried to sell the middle class on the basis of security — "health care that's always there." Opponents focused on cost, and in the end, Americans were not willing to pay the price for a program they did not understand fully.

Whitewater and other personal scandals touching the president himself eroded the trust factor with many Americans. In the end, the Democratic majority in Congress was never able to bring health care legislation to a vote. Mid-term elections in 1994 swept the Republican Party to its first majority in both houses of Congress in over 40 years and changed the dynamics of health care legislation for some time to come. It is true that these events took place in the past, but their importance remains. Those who ignore past events are doomed to repeat past mistakes.

Sources: Robert J. Blendon, Mollyann Brodie, and John Benson, "What Happened to Americans' Support for the Clinton Health Plan?" *Health Affairs* 14(1), Spring 1995, 24–26; Daniel Yankelovich, "The Debate that Wasn't: The Public and the Clinton Plan," *Health Affairs* 14(1), Spring 1995, 7–23; and Walter Zelman and Larry D. Brown, "Looking Back on Health Care Reform: 'No Easy Choices,' " *Health Affairs* 17(6), November/December 1998, 61–68.

POLICY ISSUE

Do Americans trust government enough to support the implementation of a government-run health care system?

SUMMARY AND CONCLUSIONS

A good starting point in establishing a health care policy is to set realistic goals and establish reasonable priorities. In other words, we are forced to make difficult choices. This is the purview of economics and one of the reasons that economics has been referred to as the "dismal science." In establishing a realistic medical care policy, we as a society recognize a moral responsibility to provide an adequate level of health care for those who, through no fault of their own, cannot afford it. And we as individual beneficiaries of the health care system must recognize a personal responsibility to share to the extent that we are able in providing the resources to make health care available to everyone.

Health care reform is a daunting challenge for U.S. policy makers. The public wants change, but there is little consensus on how to achieve it. Government action seems inevitable, but the extent of that action is likely to fall far short of what anyone could have imagined shortly after the Clinton Plan was first introduced in 1993. It does not mean, however, that we have lost the opportunity to improve the system. This historic "window" is not likely to close anytime soon; at least not as long as the public's desire for change remains strong.

But it is unlikely that any comprehensive plan for a government takeover of health care delivery will ever happen. Instead, we will probably witness a series of incremental steps to add coverage and access to groups at the margin. For example, in 1997 Congress enacted the State Children's Health Insurance Program (SCHIP), which provides matching funds to states that provide health insurance to low-income children without insurance. SCHIP represents the largest expansion of health insurance coverage for children since the enactment of Medicaid in 1965.

With so many Americans satisfied with their personal medical care arrangements, the call for reform seems motivated either out of concern for those without health insurance coverage or because of the perceived risk of joining the ranks of the uninsured. Proper diagnosis is essential if medical treatment is to be effective; likewise, it is imperative that system reform be based on a correct diagnosis of the problem. Many suggestions for reform focus on symptoms, but the real problem is that we spend other people's money. Reliance on the third-party payment mechanism desensitizes buyers to the true cost of the care they receive. The only way to ensure predictable access at reasonable prices is for individuals to exercise personal responsibility by spending their own money.

Differences in health care delivery systems worldwide reflect differences in the availability of resources and differences in the respective cultures. The attitude of the typical purchaser of medical care in the United States is to exhaust every possible course of treatment with little regard for cost. Everything must be done to cure any disease or illness. Cost is not a consideration when you are talking about a human life. In contrast, attitudes in other countries are very different. For example, British and Japanese societies are more ready to accept the inevitability of illness and are better prepared to deal with its consequences.

Instead of envying health care systems abroad, policy makers in the United States ought to envision reform that is compatible with the social and ideological characteristics that make America unique. Only then can we successfully implement a change that will work for all Americans. The real issue in the debate over medical care reform is political choice. The degree of government involvement is determined by political feasibility. The issue is whether the electorate desires a predominantly public or a private solution to health care delivery and financing. The inherent danger in our desire to reform the system is that we politicize an issue that should be apolitical. Our experience has taught us that whenever resource allocation is brought into the realm of political control, it becomes politicized, whether we like it or not.

PROFILE

Alain Enthoven

Without question, Alain Enthoven is a leading figure in the health care reform movement worldwide. His ideas have helped shape recent reforms in England and the Netherlands. It was also Enthoven who served as the intellectual backbone of the now-famous Jackson Hole Group, which has studied and discussed health care reform regularly since the mid-1970s. A respected Stanford economist, Enthoven is a strong proponent of managed competition, having developed the idea in collaboration with his long-time friend Dr. Paul Ellwood.

After completing his undergraduate work at Stanford, Enthoven won a Rhodes scholarship to study at Oxford. In 1956, he completed his Ph.D. in economics from MIT and went to work for the Rand Corporation in Santa Monica, California. His early work was on defense issues, and he soon became knowledgeable in the ways of the federal government. He became well known in government circles and went to work in the Pentagon in 1961. During his years in Washington, Enthoven became a director of Georgetown University. While on the board, he was chairman of the committee that built a major medical center at the school and created the university's group-practice HMO.

In 1973, Enthoven began consulting with the Kaiser-Permanente Group in California, where he developed most of his ideas for reforming medical care. That same year, Enthoven joined the Stanford faculty, where he is now the Marriner S. Eccles Professor of Public and Private Management, Emeritus, in the Graduate School of Business.

Conservative Democrats looking for an alternative to the Canadian-style single-payer approach have turned to Enthoven's plan of managed competition. Like many plans created by economists, when the politicians get through with them, they are barely recognizable. The major change that Enthoven found distasteful was the addition of budget caps, or price

continued

controls. Given his work developing the theory of managed competition, it is somewhat surprising that he was left off President Clinton's 1993 national task force on health care reform. Nevertheless, Enthoven is confident that policy makers will ultimately turn to managed competition as the only reform plan that can work within the American system.

Enthoven (1988) argued that "reform should start with cost-conscious choices made by the educated middle class. In this way, the organizational cultures of the health plans are created in an environment in which they serve intelligent, relatively informed people who have choices."

Sources: John Huber, "The Abandoned Father of Health-Care Reform," *The New York Times Magazine*, July 18, 1993, 24–26, 36–37; and Alain Enthoven, *Theory and Practice of Managed Competition in Health Care Finance*, Professor Dr. F. DeVries Lectures in Economics: Theory, Institutions, Policy, Volume 9, Amsterdam: North-Holland, 1988.

QUESTIONS AND PROBLEMS

1. What are the respective roles of the federal government and the state governments in providing health services?

2. Hundreds of state mandates nationwide require the provision of certain benefits or the coverage of certain providers for firms that make private health insurance available for their employees. Do these mandates address specific failures in the private insurance market, or do they reflect the political strength of certain provider groups, such as chiropractors and faith healers?

3. Describe a piece of health care legislation that is currently being discussed or one that has recently been passed into law either at the state or federal level. What problem is the legislation trying to address? How much is it expected to cost? How will the extra spending be financed? What are the major objections to the legislation?

4. The United States health care delivery system has been criticized for its structural defects: high costs, large numbers of uninsured, and a failure to promote high-quality health in the population. What possible approaches to health care reform do you think are morally acceptable, economically effective, and politically feasible?

Elaborate on the key features of your own national health care policy proposal.

5. Altman and Rodwin ("Halfway Competitive Markets and Ineffective Regulation," *Journal of Health Policy, Politics and Law* 13(2), Summer 1988, 323–339) argue that the medical care system in the United States exhibits neither effective competition nor effective government regulation. Would we be better off if we decisively adopted one approach or the other? Explain.

6. Is death an enemy that is to be fought off at all costs, or is it a condition of life that is to be accepted? How does the way we answer this question affect the kind of health care system we might embrace?

7. Should we shy away from specifying a collectively provided benefits package that is less generous than the standard package available to those who can afford to pay for it? Is that fair? Not everyone can afford to drive a Lexus either. Is that fair?

8. In what sense do Americans have a right to medical care? In what sense is access to medical care not a right? How have the reforms in Oregon and Hawaii helped define the nature of the right to medical care in this country?

REFERENCES

Gregory Acs, Colin Winterbottom, and Sheila Zedlewski, "Employers' Payroll and Insurance Costs: Implications for Play or Pay Employer Mandates," in *Health Benefits and the Workforce*, Washington, DC: U.S. Department of Labor, 1992.

Robert J. Blendon, Jennifer N. Edwards, and Andrew L. Hyams, "Making the Critical Choices," *Journal of the American Medical Association* 267(18), May 13, 1992, 2509–2520.

————, John M. Benson, and Catherine M. DesRoches, "Americans' Views of the Uninsured: An Era for Hybrid Proposals," *Health Affairs – Web Exclusive* (W3), August 27, 2003, 405–414.

————, et al., "Understanding the American Publics Health Priorities: A 2006 Perspective," *Health Affairs – Web Exclusive*, 17 October 2006, w508–w515.

————, et al., "Who Has the Best Health Care System? A Second Look," *Health Affairs* 14(4), Winter 1995, 220–230.

Carlos Bonilla, "The Price of a Health Care Mandate," *Wall Street Journal*, August 20, 1993, A10.

M. Kate Bundorf and Mark V. Pauly, "Is Health Insurance Affordable for the Uninsured?" *Journal of Health Economics* 25, 2006, 650–673.

Karen Donelon, Robert J. Blendon, Cathy Schoen, Karen Davis, and Katherine Binns, "The Cost of Health System Change: Public Discontent in Five Nations," *Health Affairs* 18(3), May/June 1999, 206–216.

David Dranove and Michael L. Millenson, "Medical Bankruptcy: Myth versus Fact," *Health Affairs* 25(2), March/April 2006, w89–w92.

David M. Eddy, "What Care Is 'Essential'? What Services Are 'Basic'?" *Journal of the American Medical Association* 265(6), February 13, 1991, 782, 786–788.

Employee Benefit Research Institute, "Sources of Health Insurance and Characteristics of the Uninsured: Analysis of the March 1999 Current Population Survey," Washington, DC: EBRI, 2000.

Alain C. Enthoven, "A Good Health Care Idea Gone Bad," *Wall Street Journal*, October 7, 1993, A18.

————, "Consumer Choice Health Plan," *New England Journal of Medicine* 298 (12 and 13), March 23 and March 30, 1978, 650–658 and 709–720.

————, Employment-Based Health Insurance Is Failing: Now What? *Health Affairs – Web exclusive (W3)*, May 28, 2003, 237–249.

————, *Theory and Practice of Managed Competition in Health Care Finance*, Professor Dr. F. DeVries Lectures in Economics: Theory, Institutions, Policy, Volume 9, Amsterdam: North-Holland, 1988.

Jon R. Gabel and Gail A. Jensen, "The Price of State Mandated Benefits," *Inquiry* 26, Winter 1989, 419–431.

John C. Goodman, "Managed Competition: Too Little Competition," *Wall Street Journal*, January 7, 1993, A14.

Earl L. Grinols and James W. Henderson, "Health Care for Us All: Getting More for Our Investment," New York: Cambridge University Press, 2008.

Jonathan Gruber, "The Impact of the Tax System on Health Insurance Coverage," *International Journal of Health Care Finance and Economics* 1(3/4) December 2001, 293–304.

David C. Hadorn, "Setting Health Care Priorities in Oregon: Cost-Effectiveness Meets the Rule of Reason," *Journal of the American Medical Association* 265(17), May 1, 1991, 2218–2225.

Edmund F. Haislmaier, "The Significance of Massachusetts Health Reform," *Web Memo #1035*, Washington, DC: The Heritage Foundation, April 11, 2006.

James W. Henderson, "Biblical Principles Applied to a National Health Policy," in Richard C. Chewning, ed., *Biblical Principles and Public Policy: The Practice*, Colorado Springs, CO: NavPress, 1991, 237–250.

David U. Himmelstein, Elizabeth Warren, Deborah Thorne, and Steffie Woolhandler, "Illness and Injury as Contributors to Bankruptcy," Health Affairs Web Exclusive W5, February 2, 2005, 63–73.

————, "The Politics of Health Care Reform," *Journal of the Medical Association of Georgia* 84(1), January 1995, 35–37.

————, J. Allen Seward, and Beck A. Taylor, "The Economic Costs of State Level Health Insurance Mandates," *Baylor University Economics Department Working Paper, 2008.*

———— and Beck A. Taylor, "Employer-Sponsored Health Insurance: Past, Present, and Future," *Journal of Forensic Economics* 15(2), 2002, 181–194.

Gail A. Jensen, Kevin D. Cotter, and Michael A. Morrisey, "State Insurance Regulation and Employers' Decisions to Self-Insure," *The Journal of Risk and Insurance* 62, June 1995, 185–213.

Gail A. Jensen and Michael A. Morrisey, *Mandated Benefit Laws and Employer-Sponsored Health Insurance*, Washington, DC: Health Insurance Association of America, 1999.

Dianne Longley, "Mandated Health Insurance Benefits: Report on Insurance Company Claims and Premium Costs 1992–1993," prepared for the Mandated Health Insurance Review Panel, Texas Department of Insurance. November 1994.

Maggie Mahar, "Memo to Hillary: Here's How to Cure What Ails Our Health-Care System," *Barron's*, March 1, 1993, 8–11 ff.

Katherine E. Martin et al., *Shifting Responsibilities: Models of Defined Contribution*, Washington, DC: Academy for Health Services Research and Health Policy, February 2002.

Olivia S. Mitchell, "The Effects of Mandating Benefits Packages," *Research in Labor Economics*, Volume 11, JAI Press Inc., 1990, 297–320.

Robert E. Moffit, "FEHBP Controls Costs Again: More Lessons for Medicare Reformers," *The Heritage Foundation F.Y.I.* No. 64, September 25, 1995.

Gerald L. Musgrave, "Emotions, Politics and Economics: An Introduction to Health Care," *Business Economics* 28, April 1993, 7–10.

NBC News/Wall Street Journal Poll available at http://www.pollingreport.com/health3.htm, January 17–20, 2007, accessed 21 February 2007.

Mark V. Pauly, "Making a Case for Employer-Enforced Individual Mandates," *Health Affairs* 13(2), Spring (II) 1994, 21–33.

Uwe Reinhardt, "You Pay When Business Bankrolls Health Care," *Wall Street Journal*, December 2, 1992, A10.

Ray Robinson, "Managed Care in the United States: A Dilemma for Evidence-Based Policy?" *Health Economics* 9(1), January 2000, 1–7.

John W. Rowe, Tina Brown-Stevenson, Roberta L. Downey, and Joseph P. Newhouse, "The Effect of Consumer-Directed Health Plans on the Use of Preventive and Chronic Illness Services," *Health Affairs* 27(1), January/February 2008, 113–120.

Merrile Sing, Steven Hill, Suzanne Smolkin, and Nancy Heiser, "The Cost and Effects of Parity for Mental Health and Substance Abuse Insurance Benefits," U.S. Department of Health and Human Services, Public Health Service, Substance Abuse and Mental Health Services Administration, Rockville, MD, 1998.

Hilary Stout, "Health Care Choices: A Bigger Federal Role of a Market Approach?" *Wall Street Journal*, January 15, 1992, A1.

Michael Tanner, "No Miracle in Massachusetts: Why Governor Romney's Health Care Reform Won't Work," *Briefing Papers No. 97*, Washington, DC: Cato Institute, June 6, 2006.

United States General Accounting Office, *Health Insurance Regulation: Varying State Requirements Affect Cost of Insurance*, Report to the Honorable James M. Jeffords, U.S. Senate, GAO/HEHS–96–161, Washington, DC, August 1996.

United States General Accounting Office, *Employment-Based Health Insurance: Costs Increase and Family Coverage Decreases*, Report to the Ranking Minority Member, Subcommittee on Children and Families, Committee on Labor and Human Resources, United States Senate, February 1997.

United States General Accounting Office, *Private Health Insurance: Continued Erosion of Coverage Linked to Cost Pressures*, Report to the Chairman, Committee on Labor and Human Resources, U.S. Senate, July 1997.

United States House of Representatives, *The President's Health Care Reform Proposal*, Hearings before the Committee on Ways and Means, House of Representatives, 103rd Congress, 1st Session, Washington, DC: U.S. Government Printing Office, 1993.

Barbara P. Yawn, William E. Jacott, and Roy A. Yawn, "MinnesotaCare (Health Right): Myths and Miracles," *Journal of the American Medical Association* 269(4), January 27, 1993, 511–515.

16

Lessons for Public Policy

Throughout the book we have attempted to use the ten key economic concepts as guiding principles to organize our approach to the study of health economics. Some of the lessons are obvious, some not quite so obvious. Because they are not all based on positive analysis, many of the following the propositions are likely to prompt some disagreement. By the very nature of public policy discussions, some are laced with normative implications. But now you are armed with many of the economic tools that will help you analyze the issues more carefully. Bracket numbers represent the chapters in which the principle is discussed more fully.

SCARCITY AND CHOICE

Economics recognizes the problem of limited resources and unlimited wants and desires. Without enough resources to satisfy all the desires of all the people, we are faced with the challenge of allocating those resources among competing objectives.

- We must face the fact that resources used in the delivery of medical care have alternative uses that are also beneficial. To strike a balance between scarce resources and unlimited wants involves making choices. We cannot have everything we want. In the world where most of us live, trade-offs are inevitable [2].

OPPORTUNITY COST

Everything and everyone has alternatives. Time and resources used to satisfy one set of desires cannot be used to satisfy another set. The cost of any decision or action is measured in terms of the value placed on the opportunity forgone.

- Medical care decisions involve costs as well as benefits. For many clinicians, allowing cost considerations into treatment decisions is morally repugnant. To counter this feeling, it is essential that practitioners have knowledge of the fundamentals of economics to provide a foundation for understanding the issues that affect medical care delivery and policy [2].

MARGINAL ANALYSIS

The economic way of thinking about the optimal resource allocation may be classified as marginal decision making. Choices are seldom made on an all-or-nothing basis—they are made "at the margin." Decision makers weigh the trade-offs considering the incremental benefits and incremental costs of decisions they are about to make. This principle manifests itself in medical markets in the following ways.

- When the marginal cost to the consumer is held at artificially low levels, resources are treated as if they have little or no value—a prescription for overconsumption [2].

- Balancing incremental benefits and incremental costs is essential for optimal resource allocation. Most choices in medical care involve determining the level of an activity, not its very existence. Decision making is seldom an all-or-nothing proposition. It usually involves a trade-off. If we are to spend a little more on one thing, we must spend a little less on something else [2].

- In an economy in which productivity is growing in most sectors and declining in none, consumers can have more of everything. True of many service industries, including education, the arts, and medical care, the benefits of economy-wide productivity gains may be transferred to enable consumers to consume more of these superior goods [3].

- The relevant issues deal with marginal changes in utilization and spending, not overall utilization and spending [5].

- Medical care spending is not the only way to improve the health status of an individual or population. Other factors, including lifestyle choices and genetics, play important roles [5].

- Risk-averse individuals will insure against low-probability, high-loss events, such as hospitalizations. Insurance covering routine care, such as primary and preventive care, physical examinations, and teeth cleaning, is not as common [6].

- People often engage in opportunistic behavior after they enter into an insurance contract because their behavior cannot be monitored. The fact that a person has insurance coverage increases expected medical care spending. Having insurance increases the likelihood of purchasing medical services and induces higher spending in the event of an illness. In other words, lowering the cost of medical care to the individual through the availability of insurance increases usage [6].

- The apparent relationship between health care spending and the proximity to death is due primarily to the relationship between age and mortality [11].

SELF-INTEREST

Economic decision makers are motivated to pursue their own self-interest. People respond to incentives and practice economizing behavior only when they individually benefit from such behavior. According to Adam Smith, this pursuit of self-interest leads each individual to a course of action that promotes the general welfare of everyone in society.

- Decision making is dominated by the pursuit of self-interest [1].

- Human behavior is responsive to incentives and constraints. If you want people to practice economizing behavior, they must benefit individually from their own economizing. People spending other people's money show little concern for how it is spent. People spending their own money tend to spend more wisely [2].

- When consumers perceive that acquiring and using information best serve their own interests, they demand that information [3].

- Decisions must be made by well-informed, cost-conscious consumers. Motivated by self-interest and adequately informed about treatment alternatives, cost-conscious consumers will economize because they will personally benefit from their own economizing behavior [3].

- The patient/buyer must be an active participant in the decision-making process if cost containment is to be achieved without artificial controls such as mandatory fee schedules, fixed budgets, and resource rationing [3].

- Patients and providers fail to practice economizing behavior because there is very little direct benefit to the individual who economizes [3].

- Good health is not always the primary goal in life for most people. Individual behavior proves this daily. Motorists fail to buckle their seat belts, cyclists refuse to wear helmets, millions engage in risky sexual practices, and others use drugs, smoke cigarettes, and consume unhealthy quantities of alcohol [5].

- If we ignore the demand side of the market, we may be forgoing one of the most powerful forces available for cost-control: individual self-interest [5].

- Economic incentives matter in determining the demand for medical care [5].

- The differences between the for-profit and not-for-profit organizational form may be classified as differences in property rights. The differences affect the incentive structure facing decision makers [9].

- When consumers perceive that they will benefit from additional information, they will demand information, and it will be provided [15].

▌MARKETS AND PRICING

The market has proven to be the most efficient way to allocate scarce resources. The market accomplishes its tasks through a system of prices, Adam Smith's "invisible hand." Resources can be allocated by the market because everyone and everything has a price. The price mechanism becomes a way to bring a firm's output decisions into balance with consumer desires—something that we refer to as *equilibrium*.

- Providing all necessary care for a fixed fee changes the nature of the physician–patient relationship [1].

- With Medicare and Medicaid paying such a large percentage of the total hospital bill, government reimbursement rules play a big role in determining the financial stability of the hospital sector [9].

- As the inefficiencies in the hospital system are eliminated, so too is the ability to subsidize charity care for the uninsured and medical education, increasing the pressure on public policy makers to improve the social safety net for the more vulnerable population groups, including pregnant women, children, and the poor [9].

SUPPLY AND DEMAND

Pricing and output decisions are based on the underlying forces of supply and demand. Goods and services are allocated among competing uses by equating the consumers' willingness to pay and the suppliers' willingness to provide—rationing via prices.

- The quantity of medical care demanded increases as the cost to the individual declines [1].

- When the price is held artificially below the equilibrium price, shortages will develop [2].

- The favorable tax treatment for employer-based health insurance distorts the composition of the typical employee compensation package [6].

- Information costs are a central factor in economic decision making [6].

- Managed care can control utilization when patient choice is restricted and physician practice is controlled [7].

- The problems inherent in any system emphasize cost containment over quality and access. Patient desires for expensive treatments will be sacrificed to the demand to control costs and spending [7].

- When the physician faces a zero price for other medical inputs, too many other inputs will be used relative to physician inputs, resulting in inefficiencies [9].

- When government attempts to micromanage medical care delivery and provide "free" care to a well-organized constituency, shortages develop in the form of long waits, and the quality of specialized care deteriorates [12].

- After the initial cost efficiencies are realized, the lower prices associated with the mandatory fee schedules lead to fixed budgets and eventually to limits on services [13].

COMPETITION

Competition forces resource owners to use their resources to promote the highest possible satisfaction of society: consumers, producers, and investors. If resource owners do this well, they are rewarded. If they are inept or inefficient, they are penalized. Competition takes production out of the hands of the less competent and puts it into the hands of the more efficient, constantly promoting more efficient methods of production.

- Competition among providers is essential for well-functioning markets. Competition guards against undue concentration because substitutes are readily available. Consumer demand becomes more sensitive to price changes [3].

- Competition forces providers to charge prices reflecting their costs. Consolidations leading to the concentration of market power will allow providers to act more like monopolists and price their services above costs [8].

- Competition on the demand side of the market serves to reduce inefficiencies. Inefficient hospitals become prime targets for acquisition by multihospital chains [9].

- The nature of competition in a market dominated by nonprofit providers does not promote cost efficiency but instead promotes quality enhancement. Providers have little incentive to increase productivity, consumers have no incentive to limit their demand, and providers have no incentive to limit their supply. This is a prescription for increased spending [9].

EFFICIENCY

Economic efficiency measures how well resources are being used to promote social welfare. Inefficient outcomes waste resources, but the efficient use of scarce resources enhances social welfare.

- Specialization leads to cost savings through a more efficient allocation of resources [7].

- Given the wide range of managed care arrangements, we must be cautious about forming conclusions about the overall effectiveness of the new forms of controlling costs [7].

- Efficiency is not rewarded in a cost-plus environment. Thus, finding little difference in efficiency between for-profit and not-for-profit hospitals is not surprising, or at least it should not be. With the increasing use of managed care and prospective payment, only recently have hospitals been given an incentive to be efficient [9].

MARKET FAILURE

Free markets sometimes fail to promote the efficient use of resources by either producing more or less than the optimal level of output. Sources of market failure include natural monopolies, externalities in production and consumption, and public goods. Other market imperfections, such as incomplete information and immobile resources, also contribute to this problem.

- Policy making based on sound economics is better than policy making in an economic vacuum [2].

- Various imperfections in medical markets make the dual task of delivering a product equitably and efficiently more difficult [3].

- Market power insulates a firm from the competitive forces that insure optimal resource allocation, resulting in a loss to society [3].

- The purpose of insurance is to share risk, not wealth. Policy makers, even those not interested in wealth redistribution, have used market failure to justify the provision of social insurance as a safety net [6].

- Because the private insurance market cannot provide adequate insurance for those with preexisting conditions, it becomes a collective responsibility if this group is to have access to medical care [6].

- Cream skimming is the result of regulation in the insurance industry, not competition [6].

- The market has found it increasingly difficult to subsidize care for the elderly, the indigent, and the uninsured, providing justification for collective action through government to ensure access for these groups [6].

- Hospital markets may not fit the competitive model very well, because so many of the structural characteristics of perfect competition are violated [9].

COMPARATIVE ADVANTAGE

Markets promote economic efficiency and ensure that all mutually beneficial transactions occur when individuals are free to engage in exchange based on opportunity cost. Every transaction that will benefit both a consumer and a provider takes place. The market system is grounded in the concept of consumer sovereignty: What is produced is determined by what people want and are able to buy. No one individual or group dictates what must be produced or purchased. No one limits the range of choice. Everyone specializes in the activity they do best—the one with the lowest opportunity cost.

- Transferring decision making from the private sector to the public sector substitutes bureaucratic discipline for economic discipline [3].

- Cost-conscious decisions are possible only if consumers who desire to enter the market have money to spend. Often phrased in terms of equity, the real issue is economic self-sufficiency. For medical care markets, this requires either universal insurance coverage or universal access to insurance. The choice depends on whether the majority of the populace is concerned with equal outcomes or equal opportunities. Satisfying this condition ensures that the system is morally acceptable to a majority of the people [3].

FINAL REFLECTIONS

By now you should be aware of the issues that can make the study of health economics both fascinating and frustrating. Those of you with little background in economics are likely fascinated with the wide range of issues for which economics has relevance. If you were expecting answers to many of the questions that confront policy makers, you are likely frustrated. Economics does not promise answers, only a systematic way to study the alternatives.

Whether this ends your formal training in health economics, or it is merely the first of many courses you will take, let this be the beginning of a lifetime of inquiry into health care issues using the tools of analysis introduced in this text. Remember, taking one course or reading one book cannot possibly teach you everything about health economics. Fortunately, the field is rich with opportunities for further research and study.

GLOSSARY

A

actuarially fair premium

Insurance premium based on the actuarial probability that an event will occur.

Aid for Families with Dependent Children (AFDC)

Aid for Families with Dependent Children, created in 1935, was the primary cash assistance program for the poor and needy in the U.S. welfare system until 1996, when it was replaced by a block-grant program.

allocative efficiency

The situation in which producers make the goods and services that consumers desire. For every item, the marginal cost of production is less than or equal to the marginal benefit received by consumers.

any willing provider

A situation in which a managed care organization allows any medical provider to become part of the network of providers for the covered group. Often, state law requires this practice.

applied research

Research whose purpose is typically the commercialization of a product.

arbitrage

The practice of simultaneously buying a commodity at one price and selling it at a higher price.

assignment

A Medicare policy providing physicians with a guaranteed payment of 80% of the allowable fee. By accepting assignment, physicians agree to accept the allowable fee as full payment and forgo the practice of balance billing.

asymmetric information

A situation in which information is unequally distributed between the individuals in a transaction. The person with more information will have an unfair advantage in determining the terms of any agreement.

B

balance billing

Billing a patient for the difference between the physician's usual charge for a service and the maximum charge allowed by the patient's health plan.

basic research

Research whose purpose is to advance fundamental knowledge.

bilateral monopoly

When there is monopoly on the seller's side of the market and monopsony on the buyer's side.

C

capitation

A payment method providing a fixed, per capita payment to providers for a specified medical benefits package. Providers are required

to treat a well-defined population for a fixed sum of money, paid in advance, without regard to the number or nature of the services provided to each person. This payment method is a characteristic of health maintenance organizations and many preferred provider organizations.

case management

A method of coordinating the provision of medical care for patients with specific high-cost diagnoses such as cancer and heart disease.

Centers for Disease Control (CDC)

Established in 1946, this agency of the U.S. Department of Health and Human Services is charged with promoting the public health of Americans around the world.

certificate of need

Regulations that attempt to avoid the costly duplication of services in the hospital industry. Providers are required to secure a certificate of need before undertaking a major expansion of facilities or services.

closed panel

A designated network of providers that serve the recipients of a health care plan. Patients are not allowed to choose a provider outside the network.

coinsurance

A standard feature of health insurance policies that requires the insured person to pay a certain percentage of a medical bill, usually 10 to 30 percent, per physician visit or hospital stay.

collective bargaining

The negotiation process whereby representatives of employers and employees agree upon the terms of a labor contract, including wages and benefits.

community rating

Basing health insurance premiums on the health care utilization experience of the entire population of a specific geographic area. Premiums are the same for all individuals regardless of age, gender, risk, or prior use of health care services.

copayment

A standard feature of many managed care plans that requires the insured person to pay a fixed sum for each office visit, hospital stay, or prescription drug.

cost containment

Strategies used to control the total spending on health care services.

cost-plus pricing

A pricing scheme in which a percentage profit is added to average cost.

cost shifting

The practice of charging higher prices to one group of patients, usually those with health insurance, in order to provide free care to the uninsured or discounted care to those served by Medicare and Medicaid.

cream skimming

A practice of pricing insurance policies so that healthy (low-risk) individuals will purchase coverage and those with a history of costly medical problems (high-risk) will not.

cross-price elasticity

The sensitivity of consumer demand for good A as the price of good B changes.

D

deductible

The amount of money that an insured person must pay before a health plan begins paying for all or part of the covered expenses.

defensive medicine

Medical services that have little or no medical benefit; their provision is simply to reduce the risk of being sued.

diagnosis-related group

A patient classification scheme based on certain demographic, diagnostic, and therapeutic characteristics developed by Medicare and used to compensate hospitals.

direct-contract–model HMO

A managed care organization that establishes contractual relationships with individual physicians to provide care for a specific group of patients.

disproportionate share ("Dispro") payments

A payment adjustment under Medicare and Medicaid that pays hospitals that serve a large number of indigent patients.

E

economic efficiency

Producing at a point at which average product is maximized and average variable cost is minimized.

economizing behavior

When individuals choose to limit their demand for goods and services voluntarily to save money.

Employee Retirement Income Security Act (ERISA)

Federal legislation passed in 1974 that sets minimum standards on employee benefit plans, such as pension, health insurance, and disability. The statute protects the interests of employees in matters concerning eligibility for benefits. The law also protects employers from certain state regulations. For example, states are not allowed to regulate self-insured plans and cannot mandate that employers provide health insurance to their employees.

employer mandate

A feature of certain health care reform proposals requiring employers to provide health insurance for their employees.

entitlement program

Government assistance programs where eligibility is determined by a specified criteria, such as age, health status, and level of income. These programs include Social Security, Medicare, Medicaid, TANF, and many more.

equilibrium

The market-clearing price at which every consumer wanting to purchase the good finds a willing seller.

expected value of an outcome

The weighted average of all possible outcomes, with the probabilities of those outcomes used as weights. In other words, $E(x) = x_i \times p_i$, where $E(x)$ is the expected value, x_i is the *ith* outcome, and p_i is its associated probability. The expected value is summed over all possible outcomes.

experience rating

Basing health insurance premiums on the utilization experience of a specific insured group. Premiums may vary by age, gender, or other risk factors, which are often taken into consideration when estimating the likely use of medical services.

externality

A cost or benefit that spills over to parties not directly involved in the actual transaction and is thus ignored by the buyer and seller.

F

fee-for-service

The traditional payment method for medical care in which a provider bills for each episode of care.

financial risk

The risk associated with contractual obligations that require fixed monetary outlays.

Flexner Report

A 1910 report published as part of a critical review of medical education in the United States. The response of the medical establishment led to significant changes in the accreditation procedures of medical schools and an improvement in the quality of medical care.

Food and Drug Administration (FDA)

A public health agency charged with protecting American consumers by enforcing federal public health laws. Food, medicine, medical devices, and cosmetics are under the jurisdiction of the FDA.

formulary

A list of approved pharmaceutical drugs that will be covered under a health plan. Other drugs are typically unavailable to members of the plan.

free rider

An individual who does not buy insurance, knowing that in the event of a serious illness, medical care will be provided free of charge.

G

gatekeeper

A primary care physician who directs health care delivery and determines whether patients are allowed access to specialty care.

global budget

A limit on the amount of money available to a health care system during a specified time. All medically necessary care must be provided to all eligible patients within the limits placed on the provider by the fixed budget.

gross domestic product (GDP)

The monetary value of the goods and services produced in a country during a given time period, usually a year.

group insurance

A plan whereby an entire group receives insurance under a single policy. The insurance is actually issued to the plan holder, usually an employer or association.

group-model HMO

A group of physicians—often a large, multispecialty group practice—that agrees to provide medical care to a defined patient group, usually the employees of the corporation, in return for a fixed per capita fee or for discounted fees. The physicians often provide medical care to several different groups concurrently.

guaranteed issue

A feature of an insurance policy that requires the insurer to accept all applicants and guarantee renewal as long as premiums are paid, regardless of the health status of the applicant.

H

health alliances

Called by various names, including *health insurance purchasing cooperatives (HIPC)*, these provides a way for small employers to act collectively to purchase health insurance. Often geographically based and not-for-profit, the alliance contracts with insurers and/or providers for medical coverage for its members.

health maintenance organization (HMO)

An insurer and provider of medical care.

horizontal integration

The merger of two or more firms that produce the same good or service.

I

iatrogenic disease

An injury or illness resulting from medical treatment.

income elasticity of demand

The sensitivity of demand to changes in consumer income, determined by the percentage change in quantity demanded relative to the percentage change in consumer income.

indemnity insurance

Insurance based on the principle that someone suffering an economic loss receives a payment approximately equal to the size of the loss. An insured person who suffers a loss merely makes a claim and receives compensation equal to the loss.

Independent Practice Association (IPA)

An organized group of health care providers that offers medical services to a specified group of enrollees of a health plan. Providers typically maintain their private practices and at the same time agree to the practice guidelines established by the health plan.

individual mandate

A legal requirement that individuals carry their own insurance protection.

in-kind transfer

Welfare subsidies provided in the form of vouchers for specific goods and services, such as food stamps and Medicaid.

J

job-lock

The inability of individual employees to change jobs because pre-existing medical conditions make them or one of their dependents ineligible for health insurance benefits under a new plan.

L

laissez faire

A French term meaning literally "allow [them] to do." It depicts a situation in which individuals and firms are allowed to pursue their own self-interests without government restraint.

luxury or superior good

Goods are considered superior if an increase in consumer income causes the percentage of the consumer's income spent on the good to increase and vice versa.

M

major medical

Health insurance to provide coverage for major illnesses requiring large financial outlays, characterized by payment for all expenses above a specified maximum out-of-pocket amount paid by the insured (often $1,000 to $5,000).

managed care

A medical care delivery system that integrates the financing and provision of health care into one organization.

marginal benefit

The change in total benefits resulting from a one-unit change in the level of output.

marginal cost

The change in total cost resulting from a one-unit change in the level of output.

marginal revenue product

The change in total revenue resulting from the sale of the output produced by an additional unit of a resource.

market failure

A situation in which a market fails to produce the socially optimal level of output.

Medicaid

Health insurance for the poor financed jointly by the federal government and the states.

medical savings account

A tax-exempt savings account used in conjunction with high-deductible health insurance. Individuals pay their own medical expenses using funds from the savings account up to the amount of the deductible. Once the deductible is met, the insurance policy pays all or most of the covered expenses.

Medicare

Health insurance for the elderly provided under an amendment to the Social Security Act, divided into two parts: mandatory hospital insurance and voluntary physicians insurance.

Medigap insurance

A supplemental insurance policy sold to Medicare-eligible individuals to pay the deductibles and coinsurance that are not covered by Medicare. These policies must conform to one of ten standardized benefit plans established by the federal government.

merit good

A good whose benefits are not fully appreciated by the average consumer and thus should be provided collectively.

microeconomics

The study of individual decision making, pricing behavior, and market organization.

monetary conversion factor

A monetary value used to translate relative value units into dollar amounts to determine a fee schedule.

moral hazard

Insurance coverage increases both the likelihood of making a claim and the actual size of the claim. Insurance reduces the net out-of-pocket price of medical services and thus increases the quantity demanded.

morbidity

The incidence and probability of illness or disability.

mortality

The probability of death at different ages, usually expressed as the number of deaths for a given population, either 1,000 or 100,000, or the expected number of years of life remaining at a given age.

N

national health insurance

A government-run health insurance system covering the entire population for a well-defined medical benefits package. Usually administered by a government or quasi-government agency and financed through some form of taxation.

natural monopoly

A firm becomes a natural monopoly based on its ability to provide a good or service at a lower cost than anyone else such as to satisfy consumer demand completely.

necessity

A good or service with an income elasticity between zero and one.

neoclassical economics

A branch of economic thought that uses microeconomic principles to defend the efficacy of perfectly competitive markets in resource allocation.

net loading costs

The difference between the actual premium and the minimum cost of the insurance based on actuarial principles.

no-fault

A method of compensating for injury where no attempt is made to determine fault. The magnitude of injury becomes the basis of the compensation and is the only issue in the legal proceedings.

nonexcludable goods

A good or service that is difficult to limit to a specific group of consumers. In other words, if the item is available to anyone, it becomes available to everyone.

nonrival goods

A good or service which does not, when consumed by one individual, limit the amount available to anyone else.

normative analysis

An economic statement based on opinion or ideology.

not-for-profit

A business classification that is exempt from paying most taxes. In return for this tax-exempt status, the firm is restricted in how any operating surplus may be distributed among its stakeholders.

O

opportunity cost

The cost of a decision based on the value of the foregone opportunity.

optimal output level

A market equilibrium in which the marginal benefit received from every unit of output is greater or equal to the marginal cost of producing each unit. The social optimum is that output level at which the marginal benefit of the last unit produced is equal to its marginal cost.

optimizing behavior, or optimization

A technique used to determine the best or most favorable outcome in a particular situation.

P

participating physician

A physician who agrees to accept Medicare assignment.

patent

An exclusive right to supply a good for a specific time period, usually 20 years. It serves as a barrier to entry, virtually eliminating all competition for the life of the patent.

physician-induced demand

A situation in which providers take advantage of uninformed consumers to purchase services that are largely unnecessary.

play-or-pay

A health care reform feature whereby employers "play" by providing health care coverage to their employees, or they pay a payroll tax to fund government-provided insurance.

point-of-service plan (POS)

A hybrid managed care plan that combines the features of a prepaid plan and a fee-for-service plan. Enrollees use network physicians with minimal out-of-pocket expenses and may choose to go out of the network by paying a higher coinsurance rate.

portability

A feature of an insurance policy that allows the individual to maintain coverage in the event of a job change.

positive analysis

A factually based statement whose validity can be tested empirically.

practice guideline

A specific statement about the appropriate course of treatment that should be taken for patients with given medical conditions.

preexisting condition

A medical condition caused by an injury or disease that existed prior to the application for health insurance. Policies often exclude preexisting conditions from individual coverage or, at minimum, include them only after a waiting period (usually 6 to 12 months).

preferred provider organization (PPO)

A group of medical providers that have contracted with an insurance company or employer to provide health care services to a well-defined group according to a well-defined fee schedule. By accepting discount fees, providers are included on the list of preferred providers.

premium

A periodic payment required to purchase an insurance policy.

prepaid group practice

An arrangement through which a group contracts with a number of providers who agree to provide medical services to members of the group for a fixed, capitated payment.

price discrimination

The practice of selling the same good or service to two different consumers for different prices. The price differential is not based on differences in cost.

primary and preventive care

Basic medical services that focus on prevention and treatment. Traditionally, primary care physicians have been family practitioners, gynecologists, and pediatricians.

principal–agent relationship

A relationship in which one person (the principal) gives another person (the agent) authority to make decisions on his or her behalf.

probability

The likelihood or chance that an event will occur. Probability is measured as a ratio that ranges in value from zero to one. A probability of one means that an event is certain to happen: it happens every time. A probability of 0.25 means that the event happens one-fourth of the time.

prospective payment

Payment determined prior to the provision of services. A feature of many managed care organizations that base payment on capitation.

public good

A good that is nonrival in distribution and nonexclusive in consumption.

public health

Collective action undertaken by government agencies to ensure the health of the community. These efforts include the prevention of disease, identification of health problems, and the assurance of sanitary conditions, especially in the areas of water treatment and waste disposal.

R

rate of return

The amount earned on an investment translated into an annual interest rate.

rational behavior

A key behavioral assumption in neoclassical economics that decision makers act in a purposeful manner. In other words, their actions are directed toward achieving an objective.

rational ignorance

A state in which consumers stop seeking information on a prospective purchase because the expected cost of the additional search exceeds the expected benefits.

reinsurance

Stop-loss insurance purchased by a health plan to protect itself against losses that exceed a specific dollar amount per claim, per individual, or per year.

relative-value scale

An index that assigns weights to various medical services used to determine the relative fees assigned to them.

resource-based relative value scale (RBRVS)

A classification system for physicians' services, using a weighting scheme that reflects the relative value of the various services performed. Developed for Medicare by a group of Harvard researchers, the RBRVS considers time, skill, and overhead cost required for each service. When used in conjunction with a monetary conversion factor, medical fees are determined.

retrospective payment

Payment determined after delivery of the good or service. Traditional fee-for-service medicine determines payment retrospectively.

return on sales

A financial measure of a firm's ability to generate after-tax profit out of its total sales. Calculated by dividing after-tax profit by total sales.

risk

A state in which multiple outcomes are possible, and the likelihood of each possible outcome is known or can be estimated.

S

scarcity

A situation that exists when the amount of a good or service demanded in the aggregate exceeds the amount available at a zero price.

self-insurance

A group practice of not buying health insurance, but setting aside funds in the amount of the combined premiums to cover any losses incurred by members of the group.

self-interest

A behavioral assumption of neoclassical economics that individuals are motivated to promote their own interests.

sickness fund

A quasi-governmental group that serves as an insurance company by collecting premiums and paying providers within the national health care system of France and Germany.

single-payer system

Usually associated with Canada, a system of financing medical care in which payment comes from a single source, typically the government. The single payer has considerable influence over virtually every aspect of health care financing and delivery.

social insurance

Serves as the basis of all government redistribution programs. An insurance plan supported by tax revenues and available to everyone regardless of age, health status, and ability to pay.

spending cap

A limit on total spending for a given time period.

staff-model HMO

An HMO in which physicians are employees of the HMO. Their incomes are usually paid in the form of a fixed salary, but may include supplemental payments based on some measure of performance.

State Children's Health Insurance Program (CHIP)

A state administered program, similar to Medicaid, targeted to provide affordable health insurance to children from low-income families who are otherwise ineligible for Medicaid benefits.

T

technical efficiency

Efficiency in production, or cost efficiency.

Temporary Aid to Needy Families (TANF)

Temporary Aid to Needy Families replaced the old AFDC program in 1996 as the main cash assistance program for the poor.

third-party payers

A health insurance arrangement where the individual, or an agent of the individual, pays a set premium to a third party (an insurance company, managed care organization, or the government) which in turn pays for health care services.

triage

A military screening technique adopted for use in a crowded emergency room to determine the order in which patients are treated. In battlefield hospitals, three categories of patients are identified: those who will survive without care, those who will survive if they receive care, and those who will not survive regardless of the amount of care they receive.

Type I error

Rejecting a hypothesis that is actually true.

Type II error

Accepting a hypothesis that is actually false.

U

unbundling

Separating a number of related procedures and treating them as individual services for payment purposes.

uncertainty

A state in which multiple outcomes are possible, but the likelihood of any one outcome is not known.

underwriting

The insurance practice of determining whether or not an application for insurance will be accepted. In the process, premiums are also determined. Factors considered may include age, gender, health status, and prior use of health care services.

universal access

A guarantee that all citizens who desire health insurance will have access to health insurance regardless of income or health status. Those who cannot afford insurance are usually subsidized, and participation is voluntary.

universal coverage

A guarantee that all citizens will have health insurance coverage regardless of income or health status. Coverage usually includes a well-defined benefits package and mandatory participation.

usual, customary, and reasonable charges (UCR)

A price ceiling set to limit fees to the minimum of the billed charge, the price customarily charged by the provider, and the prevailing charge in the geographic region.

utilization review

An evaluation of the appropriateness and efficiency of prescribed medical services and procedures, including hospital admissions, lengths of stay, and discharge procedures. A utilization review may be conducted concurrently or retrospectively.

W

workers' compensation

Insurance to protect employees against financial loss caused by work-related injury or illness.

INDEX